Drury's Guide to Best Plays

Fourth Edition

by

James M. Salem

The Scarecrow Press, Inc.
Metuchen, N.J., & London
1987

Library of Congress Cataloging-in-Publication Data

Drury, Francis K. W. (Francis Keese Wynkoop), 1878–1954.
 Drury's guide to best plays.

 Includes index.
 1. Drama––Bibliography. 2. Drama––Indexes.
3. Drama––Stories, plots, etc. I. Salem, James M.
II. Title. III. Title: Guide to best plays.
Z5781.D8 1987 [PN1655] 016.80882   87–380
ISBN 0–8108–1980–5

To Blanche Foot,

who took me to my first play

CONTENTS

The fourth edition of <u>Drury's Guide to Best Plays</u> includes information on approximately 1,500 selected, non-musical, full-length plays in English, covering all dramatic periods (Greece, Rome, Medieval, Renaissance, Restoration/Eighteenth Century, Victorian, Modern, Contemporary) and places (Europe, Asia, the Americas) from 400 B.C. to 1985.

Included are not only those plays considered best by traditional authorities (plays winning Pulitzers and other prizes, plays selected for inclusion in <u>The Best Plays of the Year</u> series), but also plays that were commercial successes, that are the most popular with amateur theater groups around the country, and that are produced most often by the several thousand high schools affiliated with the International Thespian Society.

When Francis K. W. Drury put together the original <u>Drury's Guide to Best Plays</u> in 1953, he wrote that he hoped the book would be of service to the groups for which it was intended: "Play-Givers, Play-Goers, Play-Readers, and the Librarians who serve them." Over the years I have kept this intention in mind, changing only slightly Mr. Drury's format to assist the Play-Giver.

In all cases where a play is available from one of the publishers handling amateur rights, I have provided the publisher's name and fee for producing the play. Where two amounts are indicated ($50-35) the first amount is for the first performance, the second for subsequent performances. It should be noted that fees cited are those current in the 1986 catalogs and are subject to change.

For plays which are not handled by a major play publisher I have retained Mr. Drury's original citations to drama collections and anthologies, adding new entries for titles which have dropped out of the play catalogs. These entries are not comprehensive, however, and the reader is advised to use the current <u>Ottemiller's Index to Plays in Collections</u> for the latest information.

WHAT THE FOURTH EDITION IS GOOD FOR

<u>Librarians</u>: Annotations/synopses, author-title connections, dates of

plays, names of main characters, reading editions, tracking down plays according to the following "subjects": Biographical, The Black Experience, Courtroom, Fantasy, Historical, Labor, Marriage, Mystery/Detective, Newspaper, Old-Fashioned Melodrama, Prison, Religious, School and College Life, Teenager, War, Western, and The Woman Experience.

Play-Readers and Goers: Miscellaneous information like the name of the crazy family in You Can't Take It with You, the title of Neil Simon's first hit play, what else the author of Equus has written, who wrote Dead End, what the new play Biloxi Blues is all about, the date of Tea and Sympathy, and what anthology includes Pirandello's Six Characters in Search of an Author.

Play-Givers: The essential information about old and new plays is here. The indexes can help track down a play about blacks, a play with a cast of 17, an all-female play, a new one with a courtroom setting, a comedy being played in high school theaters all over the country, a play requiring no scenery, one which won a Pulitzer, Drama Critics Circle, or Tony Award, the titles that the major play publishers consider their most popular with amateur groups, how much it costs to put on Greater Tuna, what the set requirements are for Agnes of God, and who has the acting editions.

ACKNOWLEDGMENTS

In preparing this edition I owe a debt of thanks to the following people: Mr. M. Abbott Van Nostrand of Samuel French, Inc.; Mr. F. Andrew Leslie of Dramatists Play Service, Inc.; Ms. Susan Sergel of The Dramatic Publishing Company; Mr. Ezra Goldstein, editor of Dramatics magazine; and Jennifer Salem, who wrote many of the high school theater annotations.

James M. Salem

Tuscaloosa, Alabama
August 1986

PLAYWRIGHTS AND THEIR PLAYS

ABBOT, Rick. Play On! (1980). Samuel French.
    In this comedy within a comedy, an amateur play company re-
hearses "Murder Most Foul," a badly written first play by local author Phyllis Montague, who keeps changing the lines, names, and
motivations as fast as the cast can learn the last changes. The dress
rehearsal of the play (act 2) is a disaster, and the opening night
(act 3) wonderfully funny (even reading the playscript can make you
laugh out loud), with Freudian slips, dropped lines, miscues, wrong
exits, misplaced props, late sound effects, and a couple of cast members with a couple of drinks under their belts struggling to reveal
the mystery and curse of the Delhi Diamond or the Ranchipur Ruby,
or the Darjeeling Diamond, or whatever Phyllis is calling it these
days.
    3 acts; 3 men, 7 women; 1 interior. Royalty: $50-25.

ABBOTT, George. Broadway. See entry under Dunning, Philip H.

_____ and Ann P. Bridges. Coquette (1927). BP 1927-28; Long-
    mans, Green & Co., 1928; French carried.
    Norma's father is a gentleman of the Old South and warns the
young man, Michael, away, as socially impossible. On his return he
is shot by her father, who pleads at the trial, defense of his daughter's honor. Since the little flirt is with child by Michael, she takes
her own life to avoid a medical examination and save her father.
    3 acts; 7 men, 4 women; 1 interior.

_____ and James Gleason. The Fall Guy (1925). BP 1924-25;
    French, 1928.
    Dannie Walsh, out of a job, is tricked into a rather dubious
one. But he helps capture and convict a "snow" peddler. His difficulties in keeping up the installment payments on his saxophone
provide much amusement.
    3 acts; 7 men, 2 women; 1 interior.

_____. Three Men on a Horse. See entry under Holm, John Cecil.

ABELL, Kjeld. Anna Sophie Hedvig (1939). Tr. by Larsen in Scan-
    dinavian Plays of the 20th Century, ser. 2, Princeton Univ. Pr.,
    1944 (SCA-2).
    Anna Sophie, a middle-aged provincial school-teacher, defends

1

her little school world against the appointment of evil-minded Fru
Møller, who is about to be made Director of her school. Her act of
defense is to kill Fru Møller. This is symbolic of protest and positive action against Nazi tyranny.
3 acts; 11 men, 10 women; 1 interior.

ABELMAN, Paul. Green Julia (1966). BP 1972-73; Dramatists Play
Service.
Jake and Bob are college roommates, sharing an untidy "dig"
in a university town in England. The most active communication between them is in the form of improvised gaming, in which they play
topdog-underdog parts where Jake is always "Carruthers" and Bob
is "Bradshaw." Jake is leaving school to work abroad, and most of
the time spent while he waits for his taxi is used in trying to "leave"
Bob his boozy mistress, "Green" Julia.
2 men; one interior. Royalty: $35-$25.

ACHARD, Marcel. Auprès de ma Blonde. See S.N. Behrman's I
Know My Love.

_____. A Shot in the Dark (1961). Adapted by Harry Kurnitz.
Samuel French.
A parlor maid who was found nude, unconscious, clutching a
gun, and lying beside her dead lover is brought before the magistrate on a murder charge. The judge is so impressed, though, with
her honest accounts of affairs with her lover (a chauffeur) and her
aristocratic employer that he decides she is not the guilty party.
The investigation is enlarged to include the employer and his wife
(carrying on an affair with her husband's best friend), and when
the judge does discover the murderer, the girl is so appreciative
that she offers herself as a present.
5 men, 3 women; 1 interior. Royalty: $50-25.

ADE, George. The County Chairman (1903). BP 1899-1909; COT;
French, 1924.
Local politics in a midwestern state in the 1880's, featuring
village types like Sassafras, who tells all the bigwigs that he's named
his son after them, and the love-starved Lorena, the village milliner.
The heat turns up when a young lawyer named Tillford Wheeler is
nominated for county prosecuting attorney against the incumbent,
Judge Elias Rigby. The campaign turns personal and jeopardizes the
romantic relationship between Wheeler, who wins the race, and Lucy,
the Judge's daughter.
4 acts; 17 men, 5 women, extras; 2 interiors, 2 exteriors;
costumes of 1880.

AESCHYLUS. Agamemnon (458 B.C.). Many translations, among
them: Smyth in Loeb Library, Blackie in Everyman's, Campbell
in World's Classics, & Buckley in Bohn's; other recommended
translations are: by Gilbert Murray, Oxford (also in CAR, TEN,
TRE-1, -2[v. 2]); TREA-1; by Morshead, Macmillan (also in

MAU); FIT; HAM; HARC-8; OAT.

Agamemnon returns in triumph from the victory of the Greeks at Troy, bringing with him Cassandra, a prophetess of woe, who is fated to be never believed. He is welcomed by his wife Clytemnestra, who leads him into the house but there kills him with the help of her paramour Aegisthus. She gives as her reason his immolation of their daughter Iphigenia.

1 continuous act; 4 men, 2 women, chorus of old men; 1 exterior (before palace of Argos).

_____. Prometheus Bound (ca 470 B.C.). Many translations, among them: Smyth in Loeb Library, Blackie in Everyman's, Campbell in World's Classics, & Buckley in Bohn's; other recommended translations are: by Gilbert Murray, Oxford; by Morshead, Macmillan, & CLF-1; GREN; HAM; SML; FIT; CLS; HARC v. 8.

For his presumption in bringing fire to men, Prometheus, the Titan incurs the wrath of Zeus and is chained to a mountain peak by Hephaestus. He is comforted by Io, beloved of Zeus but hated by Hera. Hermes brings him a message from Zeus, asking him to yield, but Prometheus defies the Olympian monarch, who then sends his thunderous lightning bolts whereby an earthquake causes the crag to sink with Prometheus to Hades.

1 continuous act; 6 men, 1 woman, chorus of sea nymphs; 1 exterior.

AESOP. See Paul Sills' Story Theatre.

AGEE, James. A Death in the Family. See Tad Mosel's All the Way Home.

AIDMAN, Charles. Spoon River Anthology (1966). Dramatic reading based on the poems of Edgar Lee Masters. Samuel French.

In a cemetery we are introduced to the ghosts of those who lived in Spoon River and to the secrets they carried to the grave. In the some sixty characterizations and vignettes there are young lovers, teachers, preachers, sordid stories, and humorous ones.

3 men, 2 women; bare stage; Royalty: $50-25.

AIKEN, George L. Uncle Tom's Cabin. See entry under Stowe, Harriet B.

AKINS, Zoë. Déclassée (1919). BP 1919-20; Boni & Liveright, 1923.

Lady Helen Haden insists that Edward Thayer, a guest at their fashionable London home, apologize to her husband, Sir Bruce, for cheating at cards. He refuses, and threatens to tell about their intimate relationship if she calls him a card cheater. In Act II, she has been divorced, has run out of money as a tourist in New York, and is spending her pearls (her last one she gives to a waiter of a hotel dining room). In Act III she has met Rudolph Solomon, a wealthy New Yorker, whose love for her has made him buy up all of the pearls she has spent in the city. He is going to present them

to her and ask her to marry him when Edward Thayer (now reformed) shows up. Solomon believes he should not stand in the way
of these two old lovers, but Lady Helen misunderstands, thinks she's
being jilted, and bolts from the apartment down into the street
where she is hit by a taxicab. She dies, dramatically, surrounded
by men who are in love with her.
3 acts; 7 men, 6 women; 3 interiors.

_____. The Old Maid. See entry under Wharton, Edith.

AKUTAGAWA. Rashomon. See entry under Kanin, Fay.

ALBEE, Edward. The Ballad of the Sad Café (1963). Adapted from
Carson McCullers' novel. Dramatists Play Service.
The play treats the love and violence of its three main characters: the huge, mannish woman who runs the Sad Cafe; her
moody, ex-convict husband; and her distant cousin, a hunch-backed
dwarf whose taunting brings on the violence between husband and
wife. The love relationships are mostly grotesque among the threesome. The husband is in love with the wife, the wife with the
dwarf, and the dwarf with the husband.
14 men, 6 women; unit set. Royalty: $55-30.

_____. A Delicate Balance (1966). BP 1966-67; Samuel French.
Into the loveless home of a man and wife comes their daughter, who has just left her fourth husband, and their two best
friends, who have just made a shocking discovery. Already in the
house is the wife's alcoholic sister. The visiting couple locks the
door and forces the group to face the reality of the same terror:
that they have lost love to the extent that they are at the delicate
balance between sanity and insanity.
2 men, 4 women; 1 interior. Royalty: $50-25.

_____. Everything in the Garden (1967). Based on the play by
Giles Cooper. Dramatists Play Service.
Jenny and Richard could be totally happy in their suburban
home if it were not for the money problem they always have. A
Mrs. Toothe shows Jenny how she can end their money troubles
forever and have the expensive greenhouse that the couple currently
cannot afford for their garden. Later, at a cocktail party Jenny
and Richard are throwing for their country club friends, Richard
realizes that Jenny is making the extra money with her body, that
in fact all the wives assembled at his house are, and that their husbands know it, and condone it, too.
5 men, 1 boy, 5 women; 1 interior. Royalty: $50-35.

_____. The Lady from Dubuque (1980). BP 1979-80; Dramatists
Play Service.
Sam and Jo are entertaining two other couples when Jo turns
cruel and vicious, ruining the evening because her terminal cancer
is causing such awful physical pain. No one is much comfort, not

even her husband. Only when a strange lady from Dubuque arrives with Oscar, her Negro companion, does Joe begin to get the help she needs. The woman says her name is Elizabeth and that she is Jo's mother. Sam knows better, but Jo is willing to be mothered and to die in peace.

    2 acts; 4 men, 4 women; 1 interior. Royalty: $50-35.

_____. Malcolm (1966). Based on the novel by James Purdy. Dramatists Play Service.

    A story about the destruction of a young adolescent boy named Malcolm, who is taken under the wing of an elderly astrologer named Cox. Cox sends Malcolm out on various visits ostensibly to integrate him with the world. He meets a former prostitute and her man (who claims to be 192 years old), a middle-aged couple in which the wife has four lovers, an author and painter couple who are hip, and a blonde pop singer who takes the boy on as a husband and kills him with alcohol and sex. All of these people know one another and meet to mourn at Malcolm's deathbed.

    16 men (doubling possible), 7 women; multiple simple sets. Royalty: $50-25

_____. Seascape (1975). BP 1974-75; Dramatists Play Service.

    Nancy and Charlie, a middle-aged married couple, are lounging on the beach, talking about their home and children and lives. Nancy wants to do something exciting; Charlie believes he deserves a rest. They are joined by a pair of humanoid lizards named Leslie and Sarah, who are at an advanced stage of evolution and have decided that maybe they should make the big break and begin to live on land. The lizards are frightened, though, about living out of the water and are curious about what it's like. Nancy and Charlie, bored by the kind of life that "living on land" entails, have the answers to the lizards' questions.

    2 men, 2 women; 1 exterior. Royalty: $50-35.

_____. Tiny Alice (1964). BP 1964-65; Dramatists Play Service.

    The play begins with a hostile conversation between a lawyer and a Roman Catholic Cardinal. The hatred between the two goes back to boyhood days. Eventually the lawyer offers the Cardinal a gift to the church of 100 million dollars a year for twenty years. The benefactress is Miss Alice, the richest woman in the world. When the Cardinal's secretary, Julian, goes to Miss Alice's castle to complete the details of the gift, she tries to make him her lover. As Norman Nadel observed, "The transmutation of his religious ecstacy into an orgasmic ecstacy is utterly candid, and terrifying."

    4 men, 1 woman; 2 interiors; 1 simple exterior. Royalty: $50-25.

_____. Who's Afraid of Virginia Woolf? (1962). BP 1962-63; Dramatists Play Service.

    George, a history professor at a small college, and Martha, his wife who is the daughter of the college president, invite Nick

and Honey, a new young instructor and his wife over for a nightcap.
The night and the drinks never end. Until the dawn the couples
tear at one another, singly and in pairs. Nick is revealed as a
scholar on the make--figuratively and literally. Honey is found to
be so violently afraid of childbirth that she has aborted her pregnan-
cies. And George and Martha, who play "games" with one another,
have a kind of outrageous bitterness toward one another that has its
roots in great personal sadness. A powerful psychological study
with the intensity of O'Neill's Long Day's Journey into Night.
2 men, 2 women; 1 interior. Royalty: $50.

_____. The Zoo Story (1960). Dramatists Play Service.
A young, neat, ordered, well-to-do, conventional man, reading in the sunlight in Central Park, is confronted by his opposite:
a young, unkempt, undisciplined bum. The bum is tortured and
anxious to communicate with the other man, who is fearful of him.
Finally the bum brings the conventional man down to his level.
2 men; simple set and props. Royalty: $25. (Presented
professionally with Beckett's Krapp's Last Tape.)

ALEICHEM, Sholom. Tevya and His Daughter. See entry under
Perl, Arnold.

ALENÇAR, José Marteniaño de. The Jesuit (1875). Tr. by de
Britto, in Poet Lore, v. 30, 1919.
The scene is laid in Rio de Janeiro in 1759. Dr. Samuel,
an Italian Jesuit, has a magnificent plan to populate and civilize
Brazil. He wants his adopted son, Estavao, to carry it on as a
Jesuit, but Estavao loves Constança and in the end marries her.
4 acts; 9 men, 2 women; 3 interiors, 1 exterior; costumes
of time and place.

ALEXANDER, Ronald. Time Out for Ginger (1953). Dramatists
Play Service.
High School Theater Classic, 1950-59; 1960-69. Ginger is
the tomboy daughter of a staid banker who has delivered a series
of lectures at her school on the need for self-fulfillment, and Ginger
decides that her own true fulfillment can best be realized by going
out for the football team. Any number of complications result: the
father's job is jeopardized because the bank president doesn't approve; Ginger's older sisters insist she has ruined their social life;
and worst of all, Ginger's boyfriend disapproves of her actions.
After many other mishaps the play ends on a happy note with the
entire family going to see one of the other sisters in the high school
play, Ginger escorted by her reconciled boyfriend.
5 men (2 are teenagers), 5 women (3 are teenagers); 1 interior. Royalty: $50-25.

ALFIERI, Vittorio. Saul (1782). Tr. by Lloyd in his Tragedies,
London, 1815, v. 3; Bohn, 1876, v. 2; tr. by Bowring in
CLF-2.

Before the battle at Gilboa, David comes to Jonathan and Michal his wife and is reconciled to Saul. But overnight Saul's mood changes and he wants to kill David and orders the death of Ahimelech, priest of Nob. Deserted and defeated in the battle, Saul falls on his sword.

5 acts; 5 men, 1 woman; extras; 1 exterior (camp); costumes of the period.

ALFRED, William. Hogan's Goat (1965). BP 1965-66; Samuel French.

The setting is turn-of-the-century Brooklyn. The mayor has been caught with his hand in the till, and Hogan runs against him as a reform candidate. The mayor learns, however, that Hogan is really married to two women, one of them dying of drunkeness and low living. Hogan not only loses the election, but causes the death of his wife. As he waits for the police to arrive he recognizes that he never really loved anyone but himself.

10 men, 5 women, 5 extras; composite interior-exterior convertible unit. Royalty: $50 25.

ALGREN, Nelson. The Man with the Golden Arm. See entry under Kirkland, Jack.

ALLEN, Jay. Forty Carats (1969). Adapted from the French of Barillet and Gredy. Samuel French.

A fortyish American divorcée traveling in Greece falls in love with a young man of 22. Back in New York after her trip, her life is complicated by her real estate business, her mother, her 17-year-old daughter, and a 45-year-old client who is courting her. A boy who comes to take her daughter out one night turns out to be the young man she had the affair with in Greece. The old attraction is as strong and mutual as ever, and she discovers that her middle-aged client is really interested in her daughter.

5 men, 6 women; 3 interiors. Royalty: $50-35.

_____. The Prime of Miss Jean Brodie (1968). Adapted from the novel by Muriel Spark. Samuel French.

Miss Brodie is a teacher in a girls' school in Edinburgh in the early 1930's. She is a formidable figure, and an interesting one, but she does not always practice what she preaches. Miss Brodie's girls write a letter in her name to her current lover (the music teacher, who has taken the place of her previous lover, the art teacher) which falls into the hands of the headmistress of the school. Miss Brodie saves herself from dismissal, but she is vulnerable to her students, who are growing too wise too fast.

4 men, 15 women; platform set. Royalty: $50-25.

ALLEN, Woody. Don't Drink the Water (1966). Samuel French.

An American tourist and his wife and daughter rush into the American Embassy in an Iron Curtain country. They are pursued by the secret police who insist they are spies who have photographed communist secrets. The embassy is not the best refuge, however, for the ambassador is absent and his son (who has been expelled from a dozen countries and all of Africa) is in charge. An escape plot is planned, and a romance is born.

    12 men, 4 women; 1 interior. Royalty: $50-25.

_____. The Floating Light Bulb (1981). BP 1980-81; Random House, 1981-82.

    Enid Pollack is doing her best at keeping the family together in the Canarsie section of Brooklyn in 1945, but she is getting no help at all from her husband, Max, who is into the loan sharks for big money he lost gambling and who will run off any day to Las Vegas with his young mistress. Paul, the sixteen-year-old son with the high I.Q., spends his time in his room practicing magic tricks (his best is the floating light bulb), which his mother out of desperation decides may be just the meal ticket the family will need to survive Max's imminent departure. She arranges an audition for Paul with Jerry Wexler, whom she takes to be a big-time talent agent. As it turns out he isn't big time, Paul will never make it in show business, and Enid and Jerry--lonely and vulnerable and attracted to one another as they are--will never be able to pursue their relationship. He is moving to Phoenix on account of his mother's asthma.

    2 acts; 4 men, 2 women; several interiors.

_____. Play It Again, Sam (1969). Samuel French.

    A homely man trying to make it in a world of beautiful people is rescued by his hero, Humphrey Bogart, who comes to him offering advice and urging him on. Bogart is so charming, in fact, that even the homely man's best friend's wife succumbs one night. A comedy in the Woody Allen manner.

    3 men, 8 women; 1 interior. Royalty: $50 35.

ALVAREZ, Quintero Serafín, and Joaquin Alvarez. Doña Clarines (1909). Tr. by Granville-Barker in their Four Comedies, French, 1932; CHA.

    The heroine, Doña Clarines, is a middle-aged lady who is reputed eccentric and even mad because of her absolute honesty of deed and speech. Marcela, her niece, fears to tell her of her love for Miguel because he is the son of the man who caused her aunt's hair to turn white and made a recluse of her when he left her years before. But she shows her generous spirit by bringing them together.

    2 acts; 4 men, 5 women; 1 interior.

_____. The Lady from Alfáqueque (1914). Tr. by Granville-Barker in their Four Comedies, French, 1932.

    Some small-town provincials come to Madrid where they mingle with their own kind of people and so remain provincials. Among them is a clever rascal who sponges on others, but his way of doing it is so perfect that no one can take offense.

    2 acts; 5 men, 6 women; 1 interior.

_____. Malvaloca (1912). Tr. by Fassett. Doubleday, 1916; DIE.

Salvador and his brother Leonardo are remolding a cracked bell in the cloister. Salvador has seduced Malvaloca, but she has come to love Leonardo. When the casting is finished, Leonardo tells her that he will seek to remold her life in the fire of his love.

3 acts; 7 men, 11 women; 2 interiors; 1 exterior.

_____. Papá Juan; or, The Centenarian (1909). Tr. by Walsh in Poet Lore, v. 29, 1918; tr. by Granville-Barker as A Hundred Years Old in their Four Plays, Lond., Sidgwick, 1927.

Papá Juan celebrates his 100th birthday, for which he gathers his descendants together. They represent great differences, from the combativeness of Doña Filamena to the waywardness of Gabriela. He insists on still running things, and unites his favorite great-granddaughter Currita and his free-thinking jolly grandson Trino, who as a gay blade has been rather scorned by the rest.

3 acts; 6 men, 6 women; 1 interior.

_____. The Woman's Town (1912). Tr. by Turrell in TUR; tr. by Granville-Barker as The Women Have Their Way in their Four Plays, Lond., Sidgwick, 1927.

A young lawyer from the city, Adolpho, comes to a small town, and without in the least intending it, finds that because of women's gossip, he has become engaged to a young girl whom he has had no thought of marrying. Though at first he demurs, he finally falls in love with her, thereby becoming a victim of feminine cleverness and match-making.

2 acts; 6 men, 8 women; 1 interior.

ANDERSON, Maxwell. Anne of the Thousand Days (1948). BP 1948-49; Dramatists Play Service.

Depicts episodes in the courtship and marriage of Henry VIII and Anne Boleyn. He is the rugged vital king; she the tempestuous lady who demands recognition as queen. A memory play in which the winds of passion blow on both.

11 men, 5 women, extras; 1 unit setting. Royalty: $50-25.

_____. The Bad Seed (1954). Adapted from William March's novel. BP 1954-55; Dramatists Play Service.

Little Rhoda Penwork is ostensibly a sweet, lovable, good natured child. Actually she is a diabolical beast. Her mother begins to suspect that something is awry when the boy who beat Rhoda for the penmanship award is mysteriously drowned. Then others are done away with and finally Mrs. Penwork herself. In the chilling last scene Rhoda has her arms around her distraught father, promising to take care of him.

7 men, 4 women, 1 small girl; 1 interior. Royalty: $50-35.

_____. Barefoot in Athens (1951). BP 1951-52; Dramatists Play Service.

Depicts Socrates at home, abroad, at his trial, and in his cell. Presents discussions with Pausanias concerning forms of government in Sparta and Athens. At his trial he insists on free inquiry and free discussion, but he is condemned on the charge of undermining the safety of the State. In his cell he is ready to drink the hemlock after his discussions with Pausanias, Crito, and Phaedo.

16 men, 2 women, extras; 2 interiors, 2 exteriors. Royalty: $50-25.

_____. Both Your Houses (1933). BP 1932-33; Samuel French.
A young, idealistic Congressman is able to pad the appropriations bill that is ridiculously dishonest and he expects it to be killed; but it is passed, and he is hailed as a political genius. One of the best propaganda plays, satirizing political corruption and grafting politicians.

13 men, 3 women; 2 interiors. Royalty: $25-20.

_____. Candle in the Wind (1941). BP 1941-42; Dramatists Play Service.
The curse of Hitlerism as experienced by an American actress living in occupied France. Madeline Guest arranges to meet the man she loves, Raoul St. Cloud, formerly a journalist with strong anti-Nazi convictions, and now a French officer on the run. He is captured in the gardens behind the palace at Versailles and taken to a concentration camp where "political criminals" are kept. Madeline tries time and again to see him there, to help him escape, but all she accomplishes is to lose a fortune in bribes that don't pay off. Finally German Lt. Schoen takes pity on her and arranges the escape. She meets Raoul at the same place, sends him off to a final destination in England where they will reunite, but she is herself captured by the evil camp commander, Col. Erfurt, who vows to make her talk. "I'd give my life gladly," she tells him, "to save one soldier to fight against you."

3 acts; 12 men, 6 women; 3 interiors, 1 exterior. Royalty: $35-25.

_____. Elizabeth the Queen (1930). BP 1930-31; Samuel French.
Presents the conflict between her love for Essex and her desire to rule alone. Essex, the popular general, sent by craft to Ireland, returns in power and considers his blood the equal of hers. The ambitious, cruel, and crafty queen has him arrested, expecting him to ask forgiveness and mercy. He will not plead and is condemned to die.

16 men, 7 women, extras; 4 interiors, 1 exterior. Royalty: $50-25.

_____. The Eve of St. Mark (1942). BP 1942-43; Dodd, Mead, 1942 for Anderson House; Dramatic Publishing Co., 1943.
Young Quizz West in the army goes with his outfit to an island in the Pacific, which is to be attacked in April 1942 on St. Mark's

Eve, the time when those who are about to die talk to their loved
ones. In a mystical scene, the young soldier talks with his girl at
home.
13 men, 8 women; 6 interiors, 2 exteriors.

_____. Gypsy (1928). BP 1928-29.
The trouble with David and Ellen Hastings' marriage is Ellen,
who behaves like a gypsy and blames her behavior on her mother,
Marilyn, who is just like her. Ellen has already left her husband
once to have an affair with Jerry, and though she has returned to
the stability David represents, she continues to seek the sexual
interest of other men. Since Ellen is a "modern" woman, she need
not explain herself to David, and he dare not exhibit aspects of
male ownership. This arrangement permits her to fall in love with
Cleve, and then Wells, a man she meets at the office. She can hurt
the men she loves by being truthful or by lying--she does both well,
and always to her advantage. By the end of the play she either
succumbs to the gas fumes she has filled her one-room apartment
with (most frequent ending in the Broadway run), or she answers
the phone and tells Wells, who is inviting her to an exciting overnight date, "Oh, Wells, darling, you saved my life, you really
did--" (author's original ending).
3 acts; 4 men, 3 women; 2 interiors.

_____. High Tor (1937). BP 1936-37; Dramatists Play Service.
The Hudson river headland, High Tor, owned by Van Dorn,
is threatened with removal for trap rock by unimaginative realtors.
He doesn't wish to sell. In a storm he is visited there by Henry
Hudson's ghostly crew and the maid Lise. Van realizes next morning he will be forced to sell.
3 acts; 14 men (& extras), 2 women; 1 exterior. Royalty:
$35-25.

_____. Joan of Lorraine (1946). BP 1946-47; Dramatists Play
Service.
Using the dramatic pattern of a stock company rehearsing a
play so that various aspects are brought out, Joan of Arc is shown
at home, en route to the Dauphin, at Orleans, at the coronation, at
the dedication of her armor, and finally at her trial and in her cell.
The actress who plays Joan learns the lessons Joan taught the world.
18 men, 5 women; bare stage. Royalty: $50-25.

_____. Key Largo (1939). BP 1939-40; Dramatists Play Service.
King McCloud, American volunteer for Loyalists in Spain,
leaves the battle ground in time to save his life; the other seven in
his company are killed. To expiate his desertion, he visits each
family to tell how their son died, coming finally to the d'Alcala
family on an island in the Florida Keys, where a gangster is terror-
izing the inhabitants. At first he plays deserter again, but finally

he understands that sacrifice is necessary to uphold truth. He kills the gangster and is himself killed.

      17 men, 7 women; 1 interior, 2 exteriors. Royalty: $35-25.

_____. Mary of Scotland (1933). BP 1933-34; Samuel French.

      Mary returns from France to be Queen of Scotland, wishing only to live, love, rule, and worship as she pleases. Three great forces are against her: Scottish oligarchy in her half-brother Murray; Scotch religious inflexibility in John Knox; and English jealousy in Queen Elizabeth. The star-crossed lady wins our sympathy in her 6-year, gallant, losing fight. She sees Elizabeth's hand in her betrayal to the English, but she claims victory over her as a woman, for she has lived and loved and born a child, while Elizabeth has only schemed and hated and has no heir.

      3 acts; 22 men, 5 women; 4 interiors, 1 exterior. Royalty: $35-25.

_____. Saturday's Children (1927). Longmans, 1927; GASE; TUCD; BP 1926-27.

      Intimate study of two middle-class Americans who try to prove that two can live as cheaply as one. When they quarrel over money and a job for her, she leaves. But they become reconciled, for their love is real and vital--more so than any materialistic considerations.

      3 men, 4 women; 3 interiors.

_____. The Star-Wagon (1937). BP 1937-1938; Dramatists Play Service.

      Stephen and Martha Minch have been married for 35 years, and Stephen's friend Hanus, who saved his life the day he proposed to Martha, has been "boarding" with the couple all this time. Hanus accompanies Stephen to the Arlington-Duffy tire factory every day, where Stephen earns $27.50 a week as an inventor. Hanus, he tells his wife, helps him "think of things." Martha has had enough of the whole deal. If he had married Hattie Arlington 35 years ago, and she had married someone else, they'd both be rich now, she believes. When Stephen is fired from his job for being late, he and Hanus experiment with the Star-Wagon they've been developing, and time-travel 35 years in the past, where Stephen makes sure that he marries Hattie and Martha has a chance at wealth and happiness. In Act III, the different reality as a result of changing history is so decadent and awful that Stephen and Hanus get out the Star-Wagon and change things the way they were at the beginning of Act I. Now, however, Mr. Duffy gives Stephen a raise to $200 a week, and offers to put Hanus on the payroll for $50 if he will come back to work.

      3 acts; 12 men, 6 women; 5 interiors, 1 exterior. Royalty: $35-25.

_____. Storm Operation (1943). BP 1943-44; Dramatists Play Service.

Written by the playwright about the invasion of North Africa in general (Anderson researched it there, with the permission of Gen. Dwight Eisenhower) and the cooperation among the Allied forces in particular. The military action is telescoped into the taking of a pass held by 200 Germans with a force of 30 American soldiers under the dual leadership of an American sergeant (Peter) and a British staff officer (Sutton). The two have already come into conflict over one another's ways and over the affections of an Australian nurse, Tommy, whom Peter has married in the field while under fire. Their cooperative effort leads to success in taking the pass and, by extension, to the Allied victory in Europe.

2 acts; 18 men, 3 women; 1 interior, 3 exteriors. Royalty: $35-25.

_____. Valley Forge (1934). Anderson House, 1935. French, 1937; in his Eleven Verse Plays, Harcourt, 1940; BP 1934-35.

A very human Washington is depicted in the dark winter of 1777/78 as he suffers with his men, rebels against the supercilious contempt of two fatuous Congressmen, and takes pride in the loyalty of his frontiersmen who will continue to fight for freedom.

3 acts; 32 men, 3 women, extras; 4 interiors.

_____. What Price Glory? with Laurence Stallings (1924). In his Three American Plays, Harcourt, 1926; CHA; GASE; TRE-1, 2, 3; TREA-3; BP 1924-25.

Captain Flagg and Sergeant Quirk, regular Army men, chafe under the hard unglamorous daily grind of war at the front. As rivals for the French girl Charmaine they come to hate each other, but respond immediately to the call of duty. The play is famous for its shocking language (at least to 1924 ears) and for its unromantic treatment of war.

26 men, 1 woman; 3 interiors.

_____. The Wingless Victory (1936). Dramatists Play Service.

Tragic story of the love of a Malay queen, Oparre, for the New England captain of the "Wingless Victory," Nathaniel McQueston. He marries her and brings her and their two children home with much wealth. His family and friends like his money but not his wife and children. McQueston tries to buy acceptance for his wife, but his brother blackmails him into sending her home. When she sees that her husband won't stand by her, she kills herself and her children.

8 men, 8 women; 2 interiors. Royalty: $35-25.

_____. Winterset (1935). BP 1935-36; Dramatists Play Service.

In the shadow of Brooklyn bridge, Mio seeks to clear his father's name. Here he meets and loves Miriamne, who however is loyal to her brother Garth, who could have testified for and cleared Mio's father's name. Over all hangs an atmosphere heavy with fate, introducing Trock, the leader of a murder gang, and Judge Gaunt, tortured in conscience as to the justice of his sentence. (A slightly fictionalized Sacco-Vanzetti case.)

16 men, 3 women, extras; 1 interior, 1 exterior. Royalty: $25.

ANDERSON, Robert. All Summer Long (1954). Adapted from Donald Wetzel's novel. Samuel French.

As the two boys (the oldest crippled from an accident) work together to make a retaining wall to save their home from the rising river, their father complains, criticizes, and accuses his sons of not having a sense of responsibility. The makeshift wall does not keep the water away, and the house crumbles. In addition, the daughter's vanity leads to her horrible death. Nothing can save this family, but during the summer the youngest came of age all by himself.

3 men, 2 women, 2 juveniles; composite interior-exterior. Royalty: $50-25.

_____. The Footsteps of Doves. See You Know I Can't Hear You....

_____. I Never Sang for My Father (1968). BP 1967-68; Dramatists Play Service.

Gene is a widower with an elderly mother he loves and an 80-year-old father he doesn't. Just as he is about to remarry and move to California his mother dies, and he is saddled with the father he has never been able to "sing for," to love and understand with the knowledge that the song will be accepted and appreciated. Gene's sister, who married a Jew and was driven away by the father years before, urges him not to throw his life away on a mean and ungenerous man.

7 men (several are bits), 4 women; area staging. Royalty: $50-35.

_____. I'll Be Home for Christmas. See You Know I Can't Hear You....

_____. I'm Herbert. See You Know I Can't Hear You....

_____. The Shock of Recognition. See You Know I Can't Hear You....

_____. Silent Night, Lonely Night (1959). Samuel French.

On Christmas Eve in a small New England town, two people meet at an inn: an unhappily married man and an unhappily married woman. They are alone except for a honeymooning couple. She worries over her woman-chasing husband while she awaits the release of her son from the nearby school infirmary. He worries over his wife, who has been in a mental institution since she learned, five years ago, that he was seeing another woman. In his wife's despair she let their child drown in a neighbor's pool. The two are lonely, and they give in to each other. The next day she takes a plane with her son to meet the repentant husband, and he learns that his wife is in one of her "good" periods.

2 men, 3 women, 1 child; 1 interior. Royalty: $50-25.

_____. Tea and Sympathy (1953). BP 1953-54; Samuel French.
The sympathy and understanding of the headmaster's wife enables a sensitive youth at a boarding school to regain his confidence
in this successful Broadway drama. The boy has become the object
of rumors because he played girls' parts in amateur theatricals and
because of his sensitivity. The headmaster joins in this persecution,
and even the boy's father fails to understand him. Determined to
prove his masculinity, the boy visits a local prostitute but is sickened at the sight of her. Now the rumor and hazing turns to out-
right ostracism, and the boy faces expulsion. The beautiful and understanding master's wife visits him in his room and offers him the
kindness and tenderness he needs to regain his confidence in his
masculinity.
9 men, 2 women; composite interior. Royalty: $50-25.

_____. You Know I Can't Hear You When the Water's Running
(1967). Four short comedies ("The Shock of Recognition,"
"The Footsteps of Doves," "I'll Be Home for Christmas," and
"I'm Herbert") under an omnibus title. BP 1966-67; Dramatists
Play Service.
In "The Shock of Recognition" a young dramatist and his producer are arguing about the opening of the dramatist's new play
(breakfasting in bed, a wife speaks to her husband who comes out
of the bathroom buck naked to say, "You know I can't hear you when
the water's running"). The conflict is one of taste. An out-of-work
actor enters the argument, gets into the spirit of the play, and even
strips to show how he would handle the role, playing opposite the
producer's secretary. (3 men, 1 woman; 1 interior.) In "Footsteps
of Doves" a couple who have been married for 25 years come to a
store to pick out a new bed (or beds). The salesman is not heterosexual enough to care what kind of bed/beds the couple should buy,
but a young blonde who enters the discussion opts for the big bed,
since she is all alone. (2 men, 2 women; 1 interior.) In "I'll Be
Home for Christmas" a couple discusses the sex education of their
almost-adult children, who are establishing their independence from
the family. (1 man, 2 women; 1 interior.) In "I'm Herbert" two
old people rock their chairs and talk about their lives. (1 man, 1
woman; 1 exterior.) The title You Know I Can't Hear You When the
Water's Running can be used only when all four plays (individual
royalty of $25 each) are presented.
Royalty: $50-35.

ANDERSON, Sherwood. Winesburg, Ohio. See entry under Sergel,
Christopher.

ANDREEV, Leonid N. Anathema (1909). Tr. by Bernstein. Macmillan, 1910.
The Devil, in this play called Anathema, requesting a glimpse
of heaven, is denied entrance. He returns to earth, determined to

get even with God. Working on David Leizer, a pious Jew, he
strips him of wealth and gloats as a mob stones him to death.
Anathema returns to the gates to point out God's failure, only to
be told that the patient David has been admitted to Christ-like
immortality and is even then seated at the right hand of the throne.
Anathema curses and returns to earth to begin another campaign.

Prolog & 7 scenes; 12 men, 6 women; 2 exteriors.

_____. The Black Maskers (1908). Tr. by Meader & Scott in
his Plays, Scribner, 1915.

The human soul in its castle (the body) is invaded by the
black maskers--doubt, despair, and madness, who represent the
hero's involuntary thoughts of evil. The soul of Duke Lorenzo
struggles, is overwhelmed, but dies unyielding; he is master of
his fate.

5 acts; 5 men, 1 woman, extras; 3 interiors.

_____. He Who Gets Slapped (1915). Tr. by Zilboorg. Dial
Pub. Co., 1921; Brentano, 1922; DIE; MOSH; TUCG; TUCM;
WATI; WATL-4; BP 1921-22. (Acting edition, Samuel French.)

To cover his personality, a lonely intellectual joins a circus
and becomes an absurd clown who amuses as a butt for blows, welcoming the slaps as preferable to suffering in the outside world.
He worships the lovely bareback rider, Consuelo. When he thinks
she is being sacrificed by her money-seeking guardian through marriage to a degenerate baron, he saves her from a living death by
poisoning her, and then himself.

4 acts; 20 men, 13 women; 1 interior; some circus costumes.
(French royalty: $35-25.)

_____. The Life of Man (1906). Tr. by Seltzer. Little, 1914
& 1920; DIK-2; MOSQ; tr. by Meader & Scott, Scribner, 1915;
SML; tr. by Hogarth, Lond., 1915.

Man is born in darkness; he lives and loves, but Inexorable
Fate (the Being in Grey) is ever by his side; till in darkness he
dies. Depicts the folly and futility of life, breathes despair and
bitterness.

Prolog & 5 scenes; 5 men, 3 women, extras; 5 interiors.

_____. The Sabine Women (1912). Tr. by Meader & Scott in
his Plays, ser. 1, Scribner, 1915; tr. by Seltzer as The Pretty
Sabine Women in Drama, #13, Feb., 1914.

A ludicrous skit on a bit of Roman history. The Romans
carry off the scratching, screaming, kicking women and are exhausted by the struggle; they beg a truce. The women are intrigued
by their new husbands but are disappointed that their old Sabine men
refuse to come and re-abduct them. The play is really a burlesque
satire on Russian politics of the time. The Romans represent daring
and force (the reactionary government of the Czar), the Sabines represent law, order, and reason (the Constitutional Democracy), the
women are the spoils of the stronger (their liberties are taken away).

3 acts; 7 men, 7 women, many extras; 2 exteriors; costumes of the period.

ANNUNZIO, Gabriele d'. The Daughter of Jorio (1904). Tr. by Porter in Poet Lore v. 18, 1907; Little, 1907; MOSQ.

A young shepherd, Aligi, wins the love of Mila, the daughter of the noted sorcerer, Jorio, and they live happily together in pastoral simplicity. Aligi's father, Lazaro, comes to their cave and attacks Mila; she calls for help; Aligi rushes in and strikes his father dead. When brought to trial for the patricide, Mila saves him by claiming she did it through some magic from her father Jorio. She is carried away to be burnt as a witch.

3 acts; 8 men, 11 women, extras; 1 interior, 2 exteriors; costumes of the period (16th century in Italy).

_____. Francesca da Rimini (1901). Tr. by Symons, Stokes, 1902; DIK-1; TUCG; TUCM; WATL-3.

Strongly characterizes each one in the eternal triangle, especially Francesca, who rather glories in her guilty intrigue since she believes she was trapped into marriage. D'Annunzio rather delights in depicting the more sensuous scenes and episodes; he writes in beautiful symbolic verse, ornate and colorful.

5 acts; 17 men, 8 women, extras; 2 interiors, 2 exteriors; costumes of the period (13th century in Italy).

_____. Gioconda (1898). Tr. by Simons, Heinemann, 1901; Russell, 1902; DID, SMI; abridged in Pierce & Matthews v. 2.

The sculptor Lucio finds his inspiration in his model Gioconda and not in his devoted wife Sylvia, who sacrifices her hands to save his masterpiece from breaking as it falls. He sacrifices her devotion; for art is a greater force than human passion.

4 acts; 3 men, 4 women, 1 girl; 3 interiors.

ANOUILH, Jean. Antigone (1944). Translated and adapted by Lewis Galantiere. BP 1945-46; Samuel French.

Based on the play of Sophocles, but developed in present-day situations, symbolic of the captive French nation nobly defiant of the Nazi's despotic tyrannical rule. Follows the plot of Sophocles: Antigone rebels at the edict and covers her brother's body with earth. Brought before the Regent Creon he orders her to be walled up alive. She hangs herself, his son stabs himself beside her, and Creon's wife also kills herself.

1 continuous act in 6 scenes; 8 men, 4 women, the chorus is represented by one man; 1 exterior. Royalty: $50-25.

_____. Becket (1959). Translated by Lucienne Hill. BP 1960-61; Samuel French.

Personal friendship and principle clash in this historical drama based on England's King Henry VIII's attempts to justify his divorce and remarriage. Since the church refused to allow it, Henry decided to make himself head of the church of England. Because he took this action he lost the friendship and support of his closest friend, Becket. Although he loved Becket, Henry felt he had no choice when faced with this affront to his authority; and through a suggestion, he brought about the death of his former friend.

15 men, 3 women; various interiors and exteriors. Royalty: $50-25.

_____. Dinner with the Family (1937). Translated by Edwin Owen Marsh. Samuel French.

A charming young man finds he can no longer stand his rich, hysterical wife and yearns for the simple joys of life with a quiet, unsophisticated young girl. The young man, Georges Delachume, not only has to endure his wife, Barbara, but also his parents and his best friend Jacques, all of whom live with him. Then Georges is swept off his feet by the sweet, uncomplicated Isabelle and describes for her the life he dreams of living. Isabelle, however, forces Georges into some panicky preparations when she insists on visiting this idyllic home. To preserve the illusion Georges hires a house and actors to pose as his family, but his dinner for Isabelle is suddenly interrupted by the appearance of his pistol-brandishing wife and the rest of his real "family." Isabelle proves that she is worthy of Georges' high estimation of her when she sticks by him as he frees himself from the entanglements of his Paris life.

6 men, 6 women; 2 interiors. Royalty: $35-25.

_____. The Fighting Cock (1959). Samuel French.

A strict, by-the-numbers general finds that his rigid devotion to moral absolutes is quite unworkable outside a military environment. Although he's now retired, he retains this attitude and tries to impose it on his countrymen. He launches a campaign to "rid the world of Maggots and teach the people honor." The general's posturings become more absurd as the play progresses. He fights a duel with a young man who jilts his daughter, and is humiliated. The final blow comes when Truth loses its appeal for him. He learns that his wife will always be true to him, out of truth itself rather than love. His new awareness leads him to admit, finally: "Ideals are all very well, but life does have to be lived."

9 men, 3 women, 2 children; 1 interior, 1 exterior. Royalty: $50-25.

_____. The Lark (1953). Adapted by Lillian Hellman. BP 1955-56; Dramatists Play Service.

The story of Joan of Arc, the country girl who heard voices which told her to lead the French armies against the invading British. In this version, an attempt has been made to divorce the drama from the limitations of time, sequence, and space. There is no scenery per se, merely platforms and lighting effects. Thus the story can move backward and forward in story line without interruption.

15 men, 5 women; movable platforms (no scenery). Royalty: $50-25.

_____. Mademoiselle Colombe (1950). Adapted by Louis Kron-
enberger. Samuel French.

A young man loses his sweetheart to the dazzling life of the
theater in this drama about the often capricious ways of romance.
A pretty girl delivering flowers to the home of a famous prima donna meets the opera heroine's son, and they immediately fall in love
and marry. Then the young man goes off to war and his mother
takes the girl to the theater, where she is enchanted by the glamour.
She forgets her husband and embraces the theater with all her love.
He returns to find her merrily pursuing her new career and their
romance ended.

10 men, 5 women; 4 interiors. Royalty: $50-25.

_____. Poor Bitos (1965). Translated by Lucienne Hill. BP
1964-65; Samuel French.

A seemingly innocent dinner party recreates the terrors of
the age of Robespierre. A group of French patricians have gathered
for a party in an old chateau, and among the guests is an intransi-
gent prosecutor named Bitos, whom the rest of the guests fear and
detest. To them he is the reincarnation of Robespierre and sets off
a chain of associations in their minds of the age of Revolution and
repression. Their mental images are recreated for the audience as
the guests change to coats of the Revolutionary period. Through
this shift in time the point becomes clear that the inflexible blindness of the dedicated often leads to more destruction than good.

10 men, 3 women; 1 interior. Royalty: $50-25.

_____. The Rehearsal (1950). English version by Pamela H.
Johnson and Kitty Black. Samuel French.

A count has decided to present a performance of Marivaux'
Double Inconstancy, and has cast himself, his wife, his mistress,
and his wife's lover in the principal roles. As they don their costumes the actors drift into the cynicism of the period. The count
falls in love with a young girl, the countess calls on a friend to
seduce the girl, the friend is reminded of his first love and invites
a duel and certain death. The rehearsal goes on.

5 men, 3 women; 1 interior, 1 inset. Royalty: $50-25.

_____. Ring Round the Moon (1948). Dramatists Play Service.

Twin brothers have very different temperaments: Hugo is a
cynical young man, heartless and aggressive; Frederick is sentimental, sensitive, and shy. Hugo introduces a ballet-dancer, Isabelle, at a houseparty to show that a child of the slums might be
the belle of the ball; also to break up Frederick's infatuation with
the heiress, Diana, who really craves the wilder Hugo.

6 men, 7 women, extras; 1 exterior. Royalty: $50-35.

_____. Romeo and Jeannette (1945). Translated by Miriam
John. Samuel French.

An upper class young man takes his mother to the lower class
family of his fiancée. The family is mostly degenerate, but the

young man falls in love with his fiancée's sister, Jeannette, a girl whose reputation is bad. The two run off to a cabin where Jeannette puts on a wedding dress and slashes her wrists to show her love for the youth. Just then word arrives that the abandoned sister has taken poison. Later, on the day that Jeannette is to wed her first lover, the two meet again and drown together embraced.

4 men, 3 women; 2 interiors. Royalty: $25-20.

_____. Thieves' Carnival (1938). Translated by Lucienne Hill. Samuel French.

An honest thief wants to continue thieving but is finally persuaded to give up his life of crime in this mystery farce. The setting is a palatial home where two attractive girls reside. Their happy life is soon rudely interrupted by the appearance of three thieves, and later, the most country of all country bumpkins. Then one of the girls falls in love with the youngest thief. Because he is so honest, however, he cannot accept her love. He refuses to let her marry a thief. But the girl soon outsmarts him and convinces him that he cannot be honest if he won't admit his love for her and give up his life of crime.

10 men, 3 women; 2 exteriors, 1 interior. Royalty: $50-25.

_____. Time Remembered (1939). Translated by Patricia Moyes. Samuel French.

A handsome prince aided by his aunt, the Duchess, struggles to keep the memory of his dead wife alive in this romantic comedy, but soon surrenders to the much stronger attraction of a living love. Amanda, a poor young milliner, has attracted the Duchess' interest because she so closely resembles the dear departed Leocadia. To make Amanda dependent on her, the Duchess causes Amanda's dismissal from her job and proposes that she try to impersonate Leocadia. As the Duchess is coaching Amanda, however, Prince Albert discovers them. But his initial anger soon turns to fascination when he realizes how closely Amanda resembles Leocadia. Amanda's attempts to impersonate the bizarre Leocadia only anger Albert, but the Duchess realizes that there is real love between the two and manages to persuade both to give their love a chance.

13 men, 2 women; 1 interior, 2 exteriors. Royalty: $50-25.

_____. Traveller Without Luggage (1936). Translated by John Whiting. Samuel French.

A psychiatrist's attempts to discover the identity of an amnesia victim lead to the former soldier's total disillusionment with his family in this drama. For eighteen years Gaston has had no memory of his life before the war. Then his doctor arranges for him to visit a family which is probably Gaston's. The mother is certain that Gaston is her son, and his sister-in-law, with whom he once had an affair, is equally convinced. Gaston, however, soon realizes that his brother was a cruel, vicious, and immoral individual and refuses to admit that this could be his family even though his identification seems more and more certain. Then another claimant appears, an orphan boy with no family and no past vices, adding a new complication to the already entangled situation. The intrigues and eventual resolution of these questions of identity result in an interesting drama.

8 men, 5 women; 2 interiors, 1 inset. Royalty: $50-25.

_____. The Waltz of the Toreadors (1951). Translated by Lucienne Hill. BP 1956-57; Samuel French.

The toreador in this farce is a general who considers himself quite a "toreador" with the ladies. Interspersed with the many comic scenes, however, are revealing moments in which the bitterness and disgust of the general toward his shallow conquests are shown.

4 men, 7 women; 1 interior. Royalty: $50-25.

ANSKY, S. The Dybbuk (1914). Tr. by Alsberg & Katzin, Boni, 1926; DIE; CEW; BP 1925-26.

The Dybbuk is believed to be an evil spirit which enters into a person. As a Russian Jew sect is worshipping in a synagogue, Sender, a wealthy merchant announces that he has found a bridgegroom for his daughter, Leah. When Channon, who had been betrothed to Leah at birth, drops dead, Sender is held responsible. The Dybbuk is exorcised, but Leah hears the call of the soul of Channon and joins him in death.

4 acts; 25 men, 7 women, extra children; 2 interiors, 1 exterior. Russian costumes.

ANSPACHER, Louis K. The Unchastened Woman (1915). Stokes, 1916; Harcourt, 1920; Dramatists Play Service, 1937 (in revised form); BAK, DIG; BP 1909-19.

Vigorously draws a memorable though unpleasant and unscrupulous heroine who seeks to ensnare a young architect but is outwitted by his loyal clearsighted wife. Exciting story with strongly contrasted groups, compelling attention to the vital social significance of such a person.

3 acts; 3 men, 5 women; 2 interiors.

ANTHONY, C. L. See entries under pseud. of Dodie Smith.

ANZENGRUBER, Ludwig. The Farmer Forsworn (1872). Tr. by Busse, FRA v. 16.

Matthias Ferner, a rather wicked farmer, swears that his brother left no will and thus deprives the daughter Veroni and the son Jacob of their inheritance. His son Frank has seen him burn the will; for 14 years this has been on their consciences. Frank returns to die and gives the family Bible to Veroni in which is an unopened letter proving the will. His father so worries that he shoots at Frank but fails to kill him.

3 acts; 11 men, 11 women, extras; 4 interiors, 2 exteriors; German costumes.

ARCHIBALD, William. The Innocents (1950). Adapted from Henry
James' story, "The Turn of the Screw." BP 1949-50; Samuel
French.
"The Innocents" begins when a young governess arrives at
an English estate to take charge of two inhibited, orphaned children.
A motherly cook completes the household, but the four are haunted
by fears and ghosts. Giant shadows and haunting faces terrify the
cook and the governess, but the two children, possessed by spirits,
welcome their presence with no fear. The two adults learn that the
visiting spirits are those of the former caretaker and maid who had
previously corrupted the souls of the young innocents. Finally, to
the governess' horror, the children and the spirits become insep-
arable. There is nothing anyone can do to reclaim the children.
1 man, 3 women, a boy and a girl aged 10 to 13; 1 interior.
Royalty: $50-25.

ARDREY, Robert. The Murderers. See Shadow of Heroes.

_____. Shadow of Heroes (Stone and Star) (1958). BP 1961-62;
in Ardrey's Plays of Three Decades, Atheneum, 1968.
A complex story told with the help of an author/narrator
about the Hungarian Revolution of 1956. The play begins with last
year of World War II and the work of Communist underground leader
Laszlo Rajk and his wife Julia, who are captured by the Nazis and
sent to Belsen Prison in Germany. After the war, as Minister of
the Interior, his popularity with the people causes his enemies in
the party to arrest him on charges of having "nationalist ideas."
Julia is arrested too, and their infant son is taken from her. In
prison, Rajk accepts a deal from his oldest friend and the godfather
to his child to confess to conspiring against the party in exchange
for a secret escape with his family to the Crimea. Instead, Rajk is
executed. A few years later, the new Krushchev Party Line makes
it necessary for the Hungarian Party to acknowledge that it has
"strayed from tenets of socialist legality," and Julia is brought into
public view for purposes of "rehabilitating" the reputation of her
husband. In a speech she is invited to give to the influential Peton
Club she blames the communist committee, collectively, of murdering
her husband, along with all decency, justice, and hope in Hungary.
At the next Peton Club meeting, 5,000 people try to enter the hall.
Four months later comes the Revolution. At the end, both the
Hungarian party and Julia are deceived by the Russians. The
people get tanks to quell their rioting, and Julia's "safe conduct"
sets her up for arrest and life in what the author believes to be a
Roumanian prison.
5 acts; large cast; bare stage with boxes.

_____. Stone and Star. See Shadow of Heroes.

_____. Thunder Rock (1939). Dramatists Play Service.
Charleston, a lighthouse keeper on Thunder Rock in Lake
Michigan, has fled the world as detestable, and is not persuaded by

4 acts; 10 men, 1 woman; 1 interior; costumes of the period.

AURTHUR, Robert Alan. A Very Special Baby (1957). BP 1956-57;
   Dramatists Play Service.
      Joey Casale, 34, has never really done anything with his life
except serve in World War II and Korea. He lives with his sister
Anna, unmarried and 46, in the Long Island family home of his
father, a self-made millionaire who stays mainly in Florida. Joey
has a shot at starting a partnership and business with his old army
sergeant (the only person who has never compared him to his older
brothers), but his father squelches the deal, ostensibly for Joey's
own good (he is a "very special baby" because his mother died in
childbirth and he has failed at everything he has attempted) but
really because he wants to run the lives of his last two children
for his own convenience. By the end of the play the father is estranged from all three of his sons, but Anna will give up what is
left of her life for him.
      2 acts; 5 men, 1 woman; unit set. Royalty: $35-25.

AUSTEN, Jane. Pride and Prejudice (1935). Dramatized version
   of the novel (1796) by Mrs. Helen B. Jerome. Doubleday, 1935;
   French, 1936; FOUP; THH; BP 1935-36. (Simplified version by
   Ann Coulter Martens, Dramatic Publishing Company.)
      Mrs. Bennet is determined to get her daughters married, for
to be a wife is to be a success. Elizabeth is not content with things
as they are; she actually refuses the pompous Rev. Mr. Collins. In
this her father backs her up. Darcy's pride is worn away and he is
acceptable to prejudiced Elizabeth after he proves himself a gentleman in bringing to a happy ending the elopement of Lydia, the dashing younger sister. Jane's beauty and sweetness overcome the resistance of Bingley's sister.
      10 men, 16 women; 3 interiors. Royalty: $35-25. (Martens
      version: 5 men, 11 women; 1 interior. Royalty: $35-25.)

AXELROD, George. Goodbye Charlie (1959). Samuel French.
      Charlie's contributions to the world were limited mostly to
his way with other men's wives. In fact, he died trying to escape
through a porthole of a cuckold's yacht. Now he has returned to
life reincarnated as a girl, and his big problem is to get rid of his
male attitudes, expressions, and gestures. Posing as his own wife,
Charlie meets many of his old mistresses and begins a collection (at
$5,000 apiece) for a memorial to himself. To complicate matters, his
old friend begins to feel romantically about the female Charley.
      4 men, 3 women; 1 interior. Royalty: $50-25.

_____. The Seven Year Itch (1952). Dramatists Play Service.
      A middle-aged man, whose wife is off to the country for the
summer, begins to believe that his life is passing him by. His nervous stomach has forced him to stop smoking and drinking, he has
never been unfaithful to his wife (though he's had plenty of opportunities), and he is lonesome. So he lights a cigarette, pours him-

self a scotch, and invites the girl upstairs down for a little hanky-
panky. Then his conscience gets to bothering him. He imagines
seducing the neighbor on the piano bench, his wife finding out about
it, shooting him through the heart, and refusing his dying wish for
a last cigarette.
      5 men, 1 boy, 5 women; 1 interior. Royalty: $50-35.

_____. Will Success Spoil Rock Hunter? (1955). Samuel French.
      An ineffectual young reporter comes to interview a motion
picture goddess. He meets a Hollywood agent who, for successive
ten percents of his soul, arranges for the goddess to fall in love
with him, writes him a successful screen play, and wins him an Oscar. In the last act, however, Rock Hunter manages to get free
from both Hollywood and the goddess.
      6 men, 2 women; 2 interiors. Royalty: $50-25.

AYCKBOURN, Alan. Bedroom Farce (1975). BP 1978-79. Samuel
      French.
      The action of the play takes place along a single time-line
set in the master bedrooms of three couples whose lives intersect
with those of Trevor and Susannah, a spacy, self-absorbed couple.
In one bedroom, Kate and Malcolm prepare for a party they are
giving (Malcolm will throw Trevor and Susannah out if they "start
in"). In another, Nick and Jan argue over her insistence on going
to the party alone (she is Trevor's ex-wife). In a third, Ernest
and Delia worry about the relationship between their son, Trevor,
and his new wife Susannah. By the time this Saturday night is
over, all three bedrooms will have served full-time dealing with
Trevor and Susannah's problems, but the couple themselves will be
in exactly the same circumstances as when the play started.
      2 acts; 4 men, 4 women; unit set. Royalty: $50-40.

_____. Living Together. See Norman Conquests.

_____. The Norman Conquests (1975). (An omnibus title
      for three interlocking plays: Living Together, Round
      and Round the Garden, and Table Manners.) BP 1975-76;
      Samuel French.
      Each play takes place on the same weekend, in three dif-
ferent parts of the same shabby Victorian house, peopled by the
same six characters. The plays are interlocking in the sense that
though they can be produced independently and in any order, they
play best by being produced simultaneously--taking turns with each
other. In Table Manners, for example, when Sarah learns that her
brother-in-law Norman is on the premises she rushes off the set.
In Round and Round the Garden she rushes on, to confront him.
The whole set deals effectively with a family of daughters and their
husbands/boyfriends, in which one blacksheep brother-in-law makes
everything of interest happen.
      3 men, 3 women; 2 interiors, 1 exterior. Royalty: $50-35
      each play.

_____. Round and Round the Garden. See Norman Conquests.

_____. Table Manners. See Norman Conquests.

BABE, Thomas. A Prayer for My Daughter (1977) BP 1977-78;
Samuel French.
On the graveyard shift of a downtown precinct squadroom,
plainclothes policemen Jack Delasante and Francis Kelly bring in two
homosexuals believed to have committed a gruesome murder. While
they are interrogating the suspects, Kelly's emotionally disturbed
daughter Margie calls her father and threatens to kill herself,
though this is not enough to unhook Kelly from the immediate task
at hand. The policemen take on the suspects one on one, in separate rooms. Jack takes Jimmy (the young one, a drug addict) and
shoots up some dilaudid in front of him. He will give Jimmy a fix,
too, if he will talk. Kelly takes the older prisoner, who calls
himself Sean, and intends to get a little drunk and beat him into
talking. In the course of the evening the identities of the cops and
suspects become confused and interrelated with bursts of brutality
and sexual involvement. At the end, Kelly's daughter has killed
herself and the wrong homosexual will be charged, and probably
convicted, of the murder.
2 acts; 4 men; 1 interior. Royalty: $50-35.

_____. Rebel Women (1976). BP 1975-76; Dramatists Play Ser-
fice.
The play gives personal dimension to the historical General
William Tecumseh Sherman, who commandeers the Georgia home of
three Southern ladies on his "march to the sea." Sherman is burned
out by the war--only his military pragmatism carries him from day
to day. The Southern ladies are also burned out, simultaneously
repelled and attracted to the Yankee general, but one of them is attracted enough to take Sherman to bed for the night.
9 men, 4 women (one black); 1 interior. Royalty: $50-25.

BACON, Frank. Lightnin'. See entry under Smith, Winchell.

BAGNOLD, Enid. The Chalk Garden (1954). BP 1955-56; Samuel
French.
An English woman lives with her granddaughter. Her life is
simple, centered around the child and her garden. She amuses herself by interviewing applicants for a companion to the child but never
hires one until one candidate shows up who is excellently qualified
and an excellent gardener to boot. Between the child, who is curious about the companion's background, and a famous jurist who
comes to dinner, it is revealed that the lady was a convicted murderer.
2 men, 7 women; 1 interior. Royalty: $50-25.

_____. The Chinese Prime Minister (1964). Samuel French.
An aging actress muses on the wisdom of age and the rever-

ence for age in the days of ancient China. At a party her husband appears, and it is revealed why he left her many years before. We also meet her two sons and their rowdy and unfaithful wives. But all three marriages are given a new breath of life.

   5 men, 3 women; 1 interior. Royalty: $50-25.

      . National Velvet (1946). Dramatists Play Service.

   A little girl who refuses to give up her dream of winning England's famous Grand National horse race makes this a warm and exciting play. The girl, Velvet Brown, wins an apparently useless horse in a lottery. Yet she is determined to enter him in the Grand National. Her mother shares her dreams since she too had tried the "impossible" and succeeded. She had swum the English Channel as a girl and knew that one should strive to achieve his goals even if they are seemingly out of reach. With the help of her mother and Mi Taylor, a friend, Velvet begins to transmute her dream to reality. How she accomplishes this and the obstacles she overcomes make this a very enjoyable play.

   3 girls, 1 woman, 1 boy, 6 men; many male parts which can be doubled; unit set. Royalty: $35-25.

BAHR, Hermann. The Concert (1909). Tr. by Morgan in DID.

   Gustav Hein is a piano-teacher maestro and virtuoso; he is also a philanderer, so that when he goes to give a "concert" it means a three-day meeting with a lady at his cottage. This time it will be with Delphina, wife of Frank Jura. Marie, Hein's wife, agrees to have a liaison with Jura and they follow him to the cottage. Here the shallowness of Delphina is revealed to him, and he is glad to give her up and return to Marie.

   3 acts; 3 men, 10 women; 2 interiors.

      . The Master (1903). Tr. by & adapted by Glazer. Nicholas Brown, 1918.

   A strong superman from his heights of Reason and Sanity tries to subdue every emotion and pours out contempt for mere mortals and their frailty. His forcefulness drives his all-too-human wife away from his inhumanity to a less complex union. He pays dearly for his faith.

   3 acts; 9 men, 3 women; 1 interior.

BAKER, Elizabeth. Chains (1909). Lond., Sidgwick, 1910; Boston, Luce, 1912; DIG; PLAP, v. 1.

   Intimate study of the humdrum, dull, numbing life of the middleclass of London. The clerk thinks of going to Australia but never does; the shop-girl thinks of marrying a middle-aged widower but doesn't. They are irresistibly bound by the chains of convention.

   4 acts; 7 men, 5 women; 2 interiors.

BALDERSTON, J. L. and J. C. Squire. Berkeley Square (1926). BP 1929-30; Samuel French.

Peter Standish of New York City inherits an ancestral mansion in London. On visiting it, he exchanges places with Peter Standish of 1784, but retains his 20th century viewpoint. He loves the art and architecture and the girl of the 18th century (Helen), but not the conditions of life at that time. When he returns to the 20th century he is disillusioned, and breaks his engagement to the modern rich girl.

   3 acts; 7 men, 8 women; 2 interiors. Royalty: $35-25.

_____. Dracula. See entry under Deane, Hamilton.

BALDWIN, James. The Amen Corner (1965). Samuel French.

   The Amen Corner is a store-front church in Harlem. The preacher, a woman, is torn by the crumbling of the church world she has created. Her son, the church organist, is determined to follow in the footsteps of his father, a jazz musician, who finally comes home to die.

   4 men, 10 women; composite interior. Royalty: $50-25.

_____. Blues for Mr. Charlie (1964). Samuel French.

   Described by the New York Times as having "Fires of fury in its belly, tears of anguish in its eyes and a roar of protest in its throat," this drama deals with the most disturbing theme of our time. A cynical, caustic Negro, a former junkie who has kicked the habit, returns from the North to his small southern hometown. With his often bitter temperament, he infuriates almost everyone he meets. In the eyes of an illiterate, poor white he goes too far, and the indignant Lyle kills him. Although at the trial the murderer is acquitted, the eulogy which has preceded it makes a violent, moving appeal for compassion for both white and black.

   16 men, 7 women; bare stage. Royalty: $50-25.

BARAKA, Imamu Amiri. See Jones, LeRoi.

BARILLET, Pierre and Jean P. Gredy. The Cactus Flower. See entry under Burrows, Abe.

_____. Forty Carats. See entry under Allen, Jay.

BARKER, James N. Superstition (1824). HAL; QUIK; QUIL.

   The love of Charles for Mary, the daughter of the Puritan clergyman, is opposed by her father because he believes that Charles' mother, Isabella, is a sorceress. Meantime the colony is saved from an Indian attack by an Unknown, who really is the father of Isabella and Charles' grandfather. Yet Charles is tried for sorcery and is executed; Mary dies. Impending doom hangs over the pair, though they struggle against evil fate wrought by prejudice and superstition.

   5 acts; 16 men, 4 women, extras (villagers & Indians); 2 interiors, 5 exteriors; costumes of the period.

BARRETT, William E. Lilies of the Field. See entry under Leslie, F. Andrew.

BARRIE, Sir James M.   The Admirable Crichton (1902).   Samuel French.
   Social positions are reversed in this fantasy as a group of highborn ladies and gentlemen are shipwrecked on a desert island. Crichton is the butler for the Earl of Loam and believes that in the natural order of things there must always be a master and a servant. Then a yachting cruise ends in disaster for the Earl, his three daughters, their guests, Crichton, and Tweeny, the ladies' maid. Through his resourcefulness Crichton gradually takes command of the party. In the process he wins the admiration of the women and decides to marry one of the Earl's daughters, Lady Mary. Then a liner appears and Crichton decides to signal to it, although he knows that in their rescue, all will revert to their former positions.
   13 men, 12 women; 2 interiors, 1 exterior.   Royalty: $35-25.

_____.   Alice Sit-By-The Fire (1905).   Samuel French.
   In whimsical fashion presents Alice, a popular vivacious mother, returning to her children from India, winning their love, and pretending with keen insight to give place to her growing, romantic daughter, Amy, who knows all about life from going to plays. Amy fears that a family friend is her mother's lover. Alice fears he is Amy's lover. He is neither, and the mistake is ironed out.
   3 men, 6 women; 2 interiors.   Royalty: $35-25.

_____.   The Boy David (1936).   BARR; French carried.
   A period in the boyhood of David is depicted in this play. Although he's the butt of his brothers' jokes, David is the son of Jesse whom Samuel anoints as the next king of Israel. Then David kills Goliath arousing the jealous wrath of King Saul. While upset by the King's anger, David finds comfort in his close friendship with Jonathan.
   14 men, 2 women, extras; 1 interior, 4 exteriors. Royalty: $35-25.

_____.   Dear Brutus (1917).   Samuel French.
   An amiable visualization of what might happen if restless mortals had the second chance, for which they crave, to reconstruct their lives. The members of a houseparty are sent into the magic woods on Midsummer Eve and find their chance, only to learn that it leaves them quite unchanged in spirit--"the fault, dear Brutus, is not in our stars, but in ourselves."
   3 acts; 4 men, 6 women; 1 interior, 1 exterior (the woods).
   Royalty: $35-25.

_____.   A Kiss for Cinderella (1916).   Samuel French.
   An undernourished little serving maid in her delirium dreams

of a prince and attends a ball as Cinderella, where she meets him
and populates her world as she would have it. On her return to
reality, she finds her prince in a friendly policeman.
    11 men, 10 women; 4 interiors. Royalty: $35-25.

_____. The Little Minister (1897). BP 1894-99; BARR.
    The Rev. Gavin Dishart, the "Little Minister," has straight-
ened out the whole Scottish village that he serves, when he inadver-
tently gets in the middle of a riot and meets Babbie, an enchanting
"gypsy girl" who is really the daughter of an English lord. In
spite of himself he falls in love with her, and when he tries to sacrifice himself for her, she is sure that she is in love with him. Her
father, thinking to make Rev. Dishart the common-law husband of
the gypsy girl, discovers that what he's really done is to promise his
daughter's hand in marriage. The villagers, initially disappointed to
learn that Gavin is subject to human emotions and temptations like
other people, are happy to be members of a church that the whole
area will envy.
    4 acts; 12 men, 4 women; 2 interiors, 2 exteriors.

_____. Mary Rose (1921). BP 1920-21; BARR.
    When Simon Blake asks Mr. and Mrs. Morland for daughter
Mary Rose's hand in marriage, they feel compelled to tell him that
Mary Rose is "different." When she was 12, it seems, she mysteriously disappeared from an island off the coast of Scotland. She ap-
poarod again 30 days later, not even acknowledging she had been
missing. Simon is not frightened off. Four years later she insists
on going to this same island again, and she disappears for 25 years.
When she returns, she has not aged at all in that time. She haunts
the house she lived in, always in search of her little boy Harry,
now a grown man. Harry returns to his boyhood home but can not
make his mother understand he is her son, though Mary Rose is
made free once more to listen to the island call her, and she walks
out the window into the empyrean.
    3 acts; 5 men, 3 women; 2 interiors, 1 exterior.

_____. Peter Pan; or, The Boy Who Would Not Grow Up (1904).
Samuel French.
    Care-free prankish Peter, the boy who would not grow up,
visits the Darling home and teaches Wendy, John and Michael to fly
as he does. They go with him to his fairy world in the Never-never
land, where they are attacked by Captain Hook and his pirates, whom
Peter subdues. Wendy promises to return each spring to do the annual cleaning of Peter's tree-top house.
    14 men, 4 women, 8 boys, extras; 2 interiors, 3 exteriors.
    Royalty: $50-35.

_____. Quality Street (1901). Samuel French.
    A delicate tale of two sisters who maintain a school to support
themselves till the men return from the wars. Then the men succumb
to the tantalizing Phoebe who dresses in lavender and swoons effec-

tively.
>6 men, 9 women, extras; 2 interiors. Royalty: $35-25.

_____. What Every Woman Knows (1908). Samuel French.
Contrasts and pits the wisdom of a woman against the una-
wareness of a man. After Maggie Wylie became the wife of stolid
John Shand, she kept herself in the background while supplying
clever ideas to her husband. When he has an affair with Lady Sybil,
Maggie gives her enough rope and wins John back. He still thinks
it is his own intelligence and ingenuity which gets him into Parliament.
>7 men, 4 women, extras; 4 interiors. Royalty: $35-25.

BARRINGTON, Eloise. Spring Dance. See entry under Barry,
>Philip.

BARRY, Philip. The Animal Kingdom (1932). BP 1931-2; Samuel
>French.
Tom has mistakenly married the wrong woman, for his wife
Cecilia acts more like a "kept woman," while Daisy, his former
sweetheart and mistress, is a truer spouse. He thinks marriage
should be a union of spiritual and intellectual equals rather than just
a physical relationship. He therefore casts off Cecilia and returns
to Daisy through whom he seeks to recover his soul.
>3 acts; 5 men, 4 women; 2 interiors. Royalty: $50-25.

_____. Cock Robin. See entry under Rice, Elmer.

_____. Foolish Notion (1944). BP 1944-45; Samuel French.
Jim Hapgood has been missing in action for almost five years,
and his wife, the actress Sophie Wing, plans to marry the actor
with whom she has been romantically linked by the press for a long
time: Gordon Roark. Just as the two are to take off on a South
American tour, a mysterious telegram and subsequent phone call reveal that Jim is not only still alive but on his way to the apartment.
Before he does arrive, Sophie, her father, her adopted daughter
Happy, and Gordon all get a chance to fantasize what this reunion
will be like, and all rehearse their parts. As it turns out, the script
is nothing like anyone imagined. Jim sets Sophie free to marry Gordon, and he remains to raise Happy with the assistance of a woman
he loved, and who loved him, even before the war--Florence Denny,
a former actress but now Happy's private companion and teacher.
>3 acts; 3 men, 5 women; 1 interior. Royalty: $50.

_____. Here Come the Clowns (1938). BP 1938-39; Samuel
>French.
The play deals with illusion and truth, and the search for
meaning in life. Clancy, an actor who has been absent for a year,
turns up at Ma Speedy's cafe, a hangout for theater people. Clancy
is looking for God, and Pabst, who calls himself an illusionist, proceeds to tell the people gathered there some truths about themselves.

Clancy, for example, discovers that when his wife left him she was pregnant with another man's child. One of the actors tries to shoot Pabst but kills Clancy instead.

10 men, 4 women; 1 interior. Royalty: $50.

_____. Holiday (1928). BP 1928-29; Samuel French.

Johnny Case doesn't want just to make money; life, he thinks, has something more worthwhile and he wants to enjoy it--more like a holiday. Such an attitude is denounced by his wealthy fiancée and cannot be conceived of by his prospective father-in-law. But Linda, the second daughter, realizes that he has something there and that the family may be wrong; she will marry him.

3 acts; 7 men, 5 women; 2 interiors. Royalty: $50-25.

_____. Hotel Universe (1930). Samuel French.

All the people at Ann Field's houseparty at her villa in Southern France feel thwarted, unhappy, and worried. They become introspective, debating what life is, what death is, where they are going and why--baffling problems that everyone faces. Ann's father helps each to go back in memory to some outstanding happenings in the past, some illusions still being cherished. These reminiscences serve to clear their minds and bring them back to normal.

2-hour play with no intermission indicated; 5 men, 4 women; 1 exterior throughout. Royalty: $50-25.

_____. In a Garden (1925). Samuel French.

Adrian Terry is a playwright who does not, his wife Lissa claims, make the proper distinction between art and real life. When Adrian discovers that his wife's old flame, Norrie Bliss, is coming to visit, he sets out to prove a thesis suggested for a new play: that every woman is at heart another man's mistress. Adrian knows that Norrie and Lissa once spent a romantic evening in a garden, and he sets out to prove that "romantic incidents don't bear repeating" by constructing a stage garden and leaving the two alone together. But everything backfires. Lissa discovers that Norrie, long ago, was following the plot of a novel he had read, and that Adrian was putting her through paces as if she were a stage character. She will neither go off with Norrie nor stay on with Adrian.

4 men, 2 women; 1 interior. Royalty: $35-25.

_____. John (1929). Samuel French, 1929.

Successfully depicts the heart and mind of John the Baptist through the more significant episodes of his life as he proclaims the arrival of the Messiah, who hovers in the background as a dominating influence.

5 acts; 16 men, 2 women; 3 interiors.

_____. The Joyous Season (1934). CATH; DAVI; French carried.

A youthful Mother Superior finds her faith and serenity enable her to bring peace to her family in this comedy. The Mother

Superior has inherited two houses, one in which her large family is
living. She must choose one for the convent and one for the family.
Because of her confidence and faith she solves the dilemma and
demonstrates to all involved that her choice was the right one.
    6 men, 6 women; 1 interior.

_____. Paris Bound (1927). BP 1927-28; Samuel French.
    Jim and Mary have married for love and have agreed not to
be jealous; but when Jim goes to Paris and the Riviera, where he
spends months with Miss Noel Farley, Mary thinks of divorce. But
Jim's father points out the difference between mere physical attraction and real love. Mary learns this when she is tempted to have an
affair with a young composer, so when Jim returns, happy to see
her and the children, she decides not to mention Noel.
    5 men, 5 women; 2 interiors. Royalty: $50.

_____. The Philadelphia Story (1939). BP 1938-39; Samuel
    French.
    A society gossip weekly sends Mike Connor to report on the
second marriage of Tracy Lord, a cold, unawakened, spoiled beauty,
with George Kittredge, a successful young snob. Tracy gets interested in Mike, and after a pre-wedding party, takes a dip au naturel
with him in the swimming pool. As he carries her back, they meet
George and her ex-husband Dexter. Next morning she breaks her
engagement with smug George. She will not marry Mike; she takes
Dexter back again to the satisfaction of all.
    9 men, 6 women; 1 interior. Royalty: $50-25.

_____. Second Threshold (1951). Revised version by Robert E.
    Sherwood. BP 1950-51; Dramatists Play Service.
    For Josiah Bolton, after a brilliant career in public service,
life has lost its savor; he has now no longer a wish to live; he feels
he stands on that second threshold which separates life from death.
His brilliant daughter, Miranda, is about to leave him for England
to marry a man twice her age. If she goes, it will break his last
tie. Dr. Toby Wells demonstrates by his love for Miranda the mistake both father and daughter are making; and when Miranda expresses her emotions of love and loyalty, Josiah discovers he does
not wish to die.
    2 acts; 4 men, 2 women; 1 interior. Royalty: $50-25.

_____. Spring Dance (1936). Adapted from an original play by
    Eleanor Gallen and Eloise Barrington. Samuel French.
    Alex Benson is a New England college girl who finds it very
difficult to attract men. She has set her heart on a Yale man, Sam
Thatcher, who is interested only in cameras and going to Russia.
However, Alex enlists the aid of her girl friends, and with this combination of feminine wiles arrayed against him, Sam has no chance.
The antics of the girls in making Sam jealous and in making Alex
the belle of the ball provide many amusing episodes in this comedy.
    6 men, 7 women; 2 interiors. Royalty: $25-20.

_____. Tomorrow and Tomorrow (1931). BP 1930-31; Samuel
French.

To a college town in the mid-West comes to lecture Dr. Nicholas Hay, distinguished and attractive psychologist. He falls in
love with Eve Redman, who has had no child by her staid reliable
husband. After Hay has left, she bears a boy, who some years
later meets with an accident. She sends for Dr. Hay, who cures
their son; but she will not go away with him, realizing what "tomorrow and tomorrow" would mean to her devoted husband. So she
stays rather than hurt him, accepting responsibility and becoming a
spiritually complete woman.

3 acts; 5 men, 6 women; 1 interior. Royalty: $50.

_____. Without Love (1942). Coward-McCann, 1943. French
carried.

Two people who have forsworn love rediscover it after they
have been married, in this deft and entertaining comedy. Jamie
Rowan is a rich young widow who has decided never to love again
because of the idealistic memory she holds of her deceased husband.
Patrick Jamieson, an Irish diplomat, shares Jamie's distaste for love
because the girl he loved suddenly married someone else. When
Patrick appears at Jamie's party to return one of her intoxicated
guests, Jamie is intrigued by him. He insults her guests and then
starts in on Jamie, and no one is supposed to insult wealthy, attractive widows. They soon decide to marry, but with the agreement that each is free to live his own life. Although they both resist it as much as possible, love finds its way. After much foigned
indifference, they surrender to their feelings.

7 men, 4 women; 1 interior.

_____. You and I (1923). BP 1922-23; Samuel French.

An artist father had to forego his desire for painting because
the heel of expediency rested on the neck of inclination; his son is
in a like situation in regard to architecture; both had to go into
business. The father paints a picture which his wife arranges shall
be sold at auction. Four thousand dollars is bid, but to his chagrin
he discovers that his old boss has bought it for advertising purposes.
He recognizes his own limitations, and sacrifices his pride for parental
duty.

4 men, 3 women; 2 interiors. Royalty: $35.

_____. The Youngest (1924). BP 1924-25; Samuel French.

Downtrodden youngest son Richard is inspired by Nancy, a
charming busybody, to revolt against his family's selfishness. The
revolt almost fails, but he learns he has a right to the family fortune. He asserts himself and turns on his oppressors in a comic
way.

4 men, 5 women; 1 interior, 1 exterior. Royalty: $35-25.

BAUM, Vicki. Grand Hotel (Menschen im Hotel, 1927). Tr. by
Creighton, Lond., Bles, 1930; Doubleday, 1931; CEW; BP

1930-31.

Depicts the episodic events during one day in the lives of several guests in such a hotel. An aging dancer, Grusinskaia, finds new life in her love for Baron von Gaigern; she leaves not knowing he has been killed. A stenographer, Flaemmchen, escapes from Preysing, a manufacturer, and goes with Kringslein, a clerk, who has heart trouble but is ready to spend his savings and enjoy life while he may.

18 scenes; 16 men, 5 women; 1 interior.

BEACH, Lewis. The Goose Hangs High (1923). BP 1923-24; Samuel French.

A play about the supposed irresponsibility of the younger generation--college-age children who come from a home in which the parents do without so that the "goose hangs high" for the kids. Bernard and Eunice Ingals have spoiled Hugh and the twins (Bradley and Lois) in precisely this fashion--everybody knows it but the parents and children. When Bernard gets pushed around by the politicians who control his job as City Assessor, he resigns, and all of the children's expensive plans must suffer. They come to see what sacrifices their parents have made for them, and fix everything on their own, even seeing that dad will have an opportunity to be in the nursery business for himself--something he has always wanted to do but felt it might jeopardize his financial responsibilities to the children.

3 acts; 7 men, 6 women; 1 interior. Royalty: $25.

BEAUMARCHAIS. The Barber of Seville (1775). Tr. by Myrick, Dent, & Dutton, 1905; MAU; tr. by Taylor, Baker, 1922; CLF-2; tr. by Robb, French, 1939.

The cunning scamp, Figaro the barber, a man of the people, helps to thwart the plans of Bartolo to marry his ward, Rosine, for she prefers Count Almavira. With Figaro's connivance the Count comes to the house, first as a soldier, then as a music teacher, to see Rosine. Bartolo is tricked into signing a marriage contract which he thinks is his own, but turns out to be her marriage to Almavira. His rage is allayed by the Count's dowry.

4 acts; 8 men, 2 women, extras; 1 interior, 1 exterior; costumes of the period.

_____. The Marriage of Figaro (1784). Tr. by T. Holcroft, Lond., 1785; tr. as "Follies of a Day" in Oxberry, v. 13; also in London Stage, v. 2, 1824.

Sequel to The Barber of Seville. Figaro wishes to marry Suzanne, both servants of Count and Countess Almavira. When the Count demands as reward that Suzanne become his mistress, they plan to deceive him by dressing Cherubin, a fellow servant, as Suzanne, but the Countess keeps the rendezvous. The Count then wishes Figaro to marry Marceline, but she turns out to be his mother. After a series of incidents of mistaken identity, Figaro and Suzanne are married and the Count and Countess are reconciled.

5 acts; 7 men, 3 women; interior and exterior scenes; costumes of the period.

BEAUMONT, Francis and John Fletcher. A King and No King (1611).
In their Works, various editions; in Mermaid ser., Scribner,
1887, v. 2; in Belles Lettres ser., Heath, 1910.
    Arbaces, King of Iberia, has not seen his sister Panthea for
years and now requires that Tigranes, conquered King of Armenia,
marry her. But when the three meet, an apparently incestuous passion for her is aroused in Arbaces, while Tigranes is in love with
an Armenian damsel, Spaconia. Gobrias, the ruling protector while
Arbaces has been at the wars, now reveals that Arbaces is really
his son, adopted by the former Queen; Panthea was born to her six
years later and is the rightful ruler of Iberia. Now, no longer king
nor brother, Arbaces and Panthea are married and so are Tigranes
and Spaconia.
    5 acts; 13 men, 3 women, extras; 5 interiors, 4 exteriors;
costumes of the Orient.

_____. The Knight of the Burning Pestle (1607). In various edi-
tions of their Works; BAS; BAT; HOW; NEI; OLH; OLI v. 2;
SCI; SPE; WHE.
    A burlesque parody of some plays of the period, ridiculing
the taste of the citizens. A grocer and his wife, in the audience,
insist on a play about a London merchant, instead of the romantic
play already prepared; they also nominate their apprentice to play
the lead. He, as Grocer Errant, undertakes adventurous errands,
with a burning pestle as his shield.
    5 acts; 19 men, 4 women, extras; many indoor and outdoor
scenes; costumes of the period.

_____. The Maid's Tragedy (1609). In various editions of their
Works; BAS; CLF v. 1; CLS; DUN; NEI; OLH; OLI v. 2; RUB;
SCI; SPE.
    The maid Aspatia is beloved by Amintor, a courtier; but he
is commanded by the King to marry Evadne, who has been the King's
mistress. He is smitten by Evadne's charm, but she remains true
to the King until her brother Melantius compels her to kill the King,
which she does. Meantime the rejected Aspatia, disguised as a boy,
claims to be brother to Aspatia and challenges Amintor to fight;
they fight and he mortally wounds her. Evadne now returns and
urges Amintor to accept her as his true wife; he refuses and she
kills herself. The dying Aspatia reveals herself to Amintor, who now
has no wish to live and kills himself.
    5 acts; 9 men, 5 women, extras; 8 interiors, 1 exterior;
costumes.

_____. Philaster; or, Love Lies Bleeding (1608), printed 1620.
In all editions of their Works; BAS; HARC v. 47; HOW; HUD;
LIE, MAT; NEI; OLH; OLI v. 2; PAR; SCH; SCI; SPE; TAU;
THA; WHE.

Prince Philaster, rightful heir to the throne of Sicily, loves and is beloved by Princess Arethusa of Spain. Euphrasia so worships Philaster that she disguises herself as a page Bellario to be with him, but she is given by him to wait on Arethusa. After much court intrigue Philaster and Arethusa are married. Later the King, on false testimony, orders them put to death, but an uprising of the people saves them.

5 acts; 7 men, 6 women, extras; 6 interiors, 4 exteriors; medieval costumes.

BECKETT, Samuel. Endgame (1957). Samuel French.

Hamm is blind, paralyzed, and tyrannical. He is served by Clov, his lame slave, and his parents Nagg and Nell, who live in garbage cans. Hamm unsuccessfully tries to find meaning in life while Nagg and Nell sentimentalize their memories and finally disintegrate.

3 men, 1 woman; bare stage. Royalty: $50-25.

_____. Happy Days (1961). Samuel French.

There are only two characters and two acts in this Beckett play, but there is an abundance of ideas and comments on life. In the first act Winnie is buried to her waist, yet she still has access to such personal paraphernalia as a toothbrush, mirror and pistol. In the second act she has sunk to her neck and has only her eyes and mind to work with. With only these things Winnie still has happy days.

1 man, 1 woman; 1 interior. Royalty: $50-25.

_____. Krapp's Last Tape (1958). Samuel French.

A vivid contrast between the vitality of a man's youth and the shabby decay of his old age is shown in this comedy. The playwright affectionately portrays an aging man living out his life in a lonely room. At the end of the year he takes a bottle of wine and a banana and turns on his tape recorder. The voice is his, from his more youthful days, and it recounts the hopes and glories of those times.

1 man. Royalty: $20-15.

_____. Waiting for Godot (1953). BP 1955-56; Dramatists Play Service.

Not so much a story as a comment on man's endurance in the face of little hope for the future. Two bums pass the time waiting for Godot, who will explain their insignificance or put an end to it. They bicker in the meantime, and depend upon one another. They observe a brutal man exploiting his slave, and the same man, now blind, being led by his slave--their relationship unchanged. Every day a child comes to put off Godot's arrival until the next day.

4 men, 1 boy; simple stylized exterior. Royalty: $50-35.

BECQUE, Henri. The Vultures (1882). Tr. by Tilden, Kennerley,

1913, later Little; MOSQ; WATL; tr. by Papot as The Crows in Drama, v. 2 #5, 1912; abridged in Pierce & Matthews, v. 2; TRE-3; TREA-2.

    The wealthy M. Vigneron dies suddenly. His widow and her three children are immediately beset by three of his quondam friends who turn from fawning to plotting how to fleece the family and pluck them bare. Her husband's unscrupulous associates are depicted with bitter irony and superior realism, especially Teissier, whom one of the daughters, Marie, is forced to marry in order to turn off the other vultures.

    4 acts; 11 men, 6 women; 2 interiors.

BEHAN, Brendan. Borstal Boy (1970). Adapted by Frank McMahon. Samuel French.

    A series of scenes dramatized from Brendan Behan's autobiography. At age 16 Behan is caught in England with a suitcase full of dynamite (he was going to blow up some English ships for the IRA). He is sent to a reformatory where he endures many hardships, and shipped back to Ireland where he shies away from revolutions forever after.

    19 men, 4 women, 20 extras; multiple setting. Royalty: $50-35.

_____. The Hostage (1958). BP 1960-61; Samuel French.

    In this comedy the author attempts only to entertain. Filled with a series of improbable episodes, the plot concerns an innocent British soldier who is captured and held as hostage in a bawdy Irish bar by the IRA. Although he is supposedly an enemy, the barmaid finds him attractive, and they have a romance going soon after he arrives. The British have captured an IRA youth and plan to execute him. If they carry out this intention the IRA has promised to kill the soldier. The barmaid hates the thought of losing her new love so soon after she's found him, so she tries to arrange his escape. But he's shot when he makes his attempt. Nothing is as it seems in this play, however. Right in the middle of his own requiem the soldier rises to sing a final rousing song.

    11 men, 7 women; composite interior, exterior. Royalty: $50-25.

_____. The Quare Fellow (1957). Samuel French.

    A grim indictment of capital punishment is given in this controversial drama. The scene is a jail where prisoners are awaiting the hanging of one of their fellows. One by one, through their bitter speeches they profane everything, revealing at the same time the failure of capital punishment.

    22 men; 1 interior, 1 exterior. Royalty: $35-25.

BEHRMAN, S. N. Amphitryon 38. See entry under Giraudoux, Jean.

_____. Biography (1932). BP 1932-33; Samuel French.

Unconventional liberal Marian is asked to paint the portrait
of her former lover, the stiff, cautious, ambitious statesman, Bunny
Nolan, and also to write her autobiography for the radical magazine
of which ardent Dick Kurt is editor. Nolan fears any disclosures
in the biography, and she is finally persuaded to burn the manuscript. Kurt raves, but she refuses him; she is left to pursue her
casual career, for she seems quite unsuited to marry him or anyone.
5 men, 3 women; 1 interior. Royalty: $35-25.

_____. Brief Moment (1931). Farrar, 1932; BP 1931-32.
After six months of marriage to Rodney, Abby is aping high
society and chasing celebrities. She cares little for Cass but encourages him. Rodney tells her to go to Cass, but she realizes she
loves Rodney and he agrees on a fresh start, as he really loves her.
3 acts; 6 men, 3 women; 1 interior.

_____. But for Whom Charlie (1964). Samuel French.
The owner of a foundation which gives grants to writers is a
book-wormish man who leaves the direction of affairs to an opportun-
istic man, formerly his college roommate. The two pressing problems of the foundation are an application by the drunken son of a
former Nobel Prize winner (and his daughter, who will go to any
lengths to help her brother) and Lilith, formerly the Nobel winner's
mistress, who magnetizes all of the men she meets, especially the
owner, the director, and the drunken son.
5 men, 5 women; composite interior. Royalty: $50-25.

_____. The Cold Wind and the Warm (1959). BP 1958-59; Random
House, 1959.
In this drama, a youth filled with idealistic visions finds
them destroyed one by one and soon looks for solace in death. The
boy's first jarring encounter with reality results from his devotion
to a self-centered neighborhood girl. After she spurns his devotion,
he finds the love he seeks from another girl, but soon realizes he is
not satisfied. One by one his visions evaporate, and in a dramatic
scene, he decides that only in death can he find the fulfillment he
seeks. His exaggeration of his situation and the final maturing
which results from it provide touching and often humorous episodes.
8 men, 4 women; unit composite set.

_____. The End of Summer (1936). BP 1935-36; Dramatists Play
Service.
Three generations react to present-day conditions and timely
problems. Grandma sees the old order ended; Leonie, her daughter,
finds her wealth cannot bring happiness; Paula, the granddaughter,
an energetic young woman, tries to adjust herself to the economic
inequalities, even to marrying a penniless writer. Dr. Rice, the
brilliant psychiatrist, makes love to both Leonie and Paula, and the
end of the summer comes for him as he is put out of the house.
7 men, 3 women; 1 interior. Royalty: $35-25.

_____. I Know My Love (1949). Based on Marcel Achard's Auprès de ma Blonde. BP 1949-50; Samuel French.
Thomas and Emily Chanler are celebrating their fiftieth wedding anniversary in 1939, surrounded by their children and grandchildren. Flashbacks show them becoming engaged in 1888, and then through various crises in their lives. Thomas, a penniless writer, marries a rich girl, Emily, despite her father's opposition. Tom sacrifices his craft of writing to become a business man, and in time assumes control of the family's textile mills. He expects his son to do the same. In 1920 he might have strayed, but his loyal wife holds him by her loving understanding.
3 acts; 11 men, 10 women; 1 interior. Royalty: $50.

_____. Jacobowsky and the Colonel. See entry under Werfel, Franz.

_____. Jane (1952). Based on a story by W. Somerset Maugham. BP 1951-52; Samuel French.
Jane is an unimpressive widow who marries an architect twenty years her junior. Her new husband transforms her into an attractive woman and a celebrity. When Jane tires of the social whirl, she gives her young husband his freedom and reforms a brash newspaper tycoon into a companion willing to live in peaceful tranquility.
5 men, 4 women; 1 interior. Royalty: $50-35.

_____. Lord Pengo (1962). Samuel French.
A fluent and persuasive art dealer gulls many uncultured American millionaires in this comedy, but also brings some of the world's greatest art treasures to America. As Lord Pengo repeatedly tells his potential customers, "No matter what you pay for a priceless picture, you are getting it cheap." As the nouveaux-riches of America flock to buy from his collection of Rembrandts, Van Dycks and Giorgiones, many betray their avaricious devotion to acquisition and the shallowness of their love for great art. Like the millionaire's passion for wealth, however, Pengo has made art his principal passion; and his family relations suffer from his neglect.
7 men, 4 women; 2 interiors. Royalty: $50-25.

_____. No Time for Comedy (1939). BP 1938-39; Samuel French.
Gaylord Easterbrook is a writer of comedy of manners plays which his wife, Linda, stars in. But he is dissatisfied with his life, especially since he is Jewish and World War II seems hardly the time to write such pleasant comedies. He comes under the influence of Amanda Smith, wife of a dull businessman and dabbler in the lives of artists, who encourages him to write serious tragedy. He does-- a terrible play about death and the Spanish Loyalists. Linda plays it cool, and Amanda gives up when she discovers that Gay will not elope with her.
4 men, 3 women; 2 interiors. Royalty: $35-25.

_____. Rain from Heaven (1934). Samuel French.

At a houseparty the English hostess serves as mediator among five diverse guests: a German-Jewish music critic, a Russian pianist, a Russian scholar, an American millionaire, and his younger brother, an aviator. They express their opinions on many social and political evils, such as Nazi inquisition and race prejudice, with recommended cures.

    3 acts; 6 men, 4 women; 1 interior. Royalty: $35-25.

_____. The Second Man (1927). Samuel French.

Novelist Storey Clark has a dual character: one is irresponsible, loving life and luxury; the other is calm, and observant, with witty counsels of common sense. The rich widow Mrs. Frayne wins him, over the young girl Monica, because she is aware of both sides of his nature.

    3 acts; 2 men, 2 women; 1 interior. Royalty: $50-25.

BELASCO, David and J. L. Long. The Darling of the Gods (1902). In his Six Plays, Little, Brown, 1928; BP 1899-1909.

Lovely Yo-San conceals the outlaw Kara, but the merciless war minister, Zakkuri, has means of torment and tricks her into revealing the hiding place of Kara's followers. Patriotism, heroism, and love are the fundamental themes.

    5 acts; 35 men, 11 women, many extras; 3 interiors, 6 exteriors; Japanese costumes.

_____. The Girl of the Golden West (1905). Samuel French, 1933; in his Six Plays, Little, Brown, 1928; MOSJ; MOSL.

A courageous, passionate heroine runs the Polka saloon and gambling parlor in the Western frontier. She is loved by all, but especially by Jack Rance, the sheriff. But she has met her man, Dick Johnson, a road-agent, who, pursued by the sheriff, and wounded, seeks shelter and is concealed in her loft. She and the sheriff play a game of poker for her or her lover, till a drop of blood from the loft reveals the wounded man. Touched by her great love, the miners let her and Johnson go to start a new life. Made into an opera by Puccini in 1910.

    4 acts; 21 men, 2 women; 3 interiors, 1 exterior; Western costumes. (S. French Royalty: $25-20.)

_____. The Heart of Maryland (1895). In his Heart of Maryland & other plays, Princeton Univ. pr., 1941 (Amer. Lost Plays, v. 18); BP 1899-1909.

Laid in the old Calvert home in Maryland during the American Civil war, the heroine keeps the big bell silent by clinging to its iron tongue so that her sweetheart, a Northern prisoner, may escape from the Confederate sentries.

    4 acts; 22 men, 1 boy, 4 women, extras; 3 interiors, 2 exteriors; costumes of 1860 and military.

_____. The Return of Peter Grimm (1911). In his Six Plays,

Little, Brown, 1928; French, 1933; BAK; MIL; MOSS-3; abridged in Pierce & Matthews v. 1.
    Grandfather Peter returns after death to visit his beloved
grandson. He is the means of uniting lovers and of saving the
family property from a scheming nephew.
    3 acts; 8 men, 3 women, 2 extras (men offstage); 1 interior.

_____ and R. W. Tully. The Rose of the Rancho (1906). French,
    1936.
    Lovely Juanita Castro, the rose of the rancho, attracts gov-
ernment agent Kearney when the United States takes over California
from Mexico and the land claims are being adjusted. The Castros,
along with other native landowners, refuse to register. Kearney
tells Juanita that land jumpers will take her home. She deceives
her family and her lover, Don Luis, when she gives Kearney the
papers for proper registration. When the land jumpers appear and
she sees Kearney with them, she is angry, but agrees to wait.
After a night of trouble, troops from Monterey arrive, the rancho
is given to its rightful owners, and the Rose finds happiness with
her Gringo.
    3 acts; 22 men, 9 women, extras; 1 interior, 2 exteriors;
American & Mexican costumes of 1850.

BENAVENTE y MARTÍNEZ, Jacinto. The Bonds of Interest (1907).
    Tr. by Underhill in Drama, v. 5, 1915; in his Plays, ser. 1,
    Scribner, 1917; DID; MOSQ.
    A deft and facile satire on the duality of human nature, con-
trasting the good and the bad, the generous and the sordid, when a
penniless adventurer, Leandro, is imposed on elegant society by
Crispin, who pretends to be his swaggering impudent servant.
Crispin plans to marry him to an heiress, but Leandro falls in love
with the fair Silvia--a happy union brought about by the material
bonds of interest.
    Prolog & 3 acts; 13 men, 6 women; 1 interior, 2 exteriors;
costumes of 17th century.

_____. The Governor's Wife (1901). Tr. by Underhill in Poet
    Lore, v. 29, 1918; in his Plays, ser. 2, Scribner, 1919.
    Josefina is a great influence and gets her husband, Governor
Don Santiago, to first forbid and then allow a theatrical production.
Shows how personalities underlie many actions.
    3 acts; 18 men, 10 women, extras; 2 interiors, 1 exterior.

_____. The Passion Flower (1908). Tr. by Underhill in his
    Plays, ser. 1, Scribner, 1917; TUCG; TUCM; WATL-3.
    A young girl, Acacia, thinks she hates her step-father, the
well-to-do farmer Estaban, who however has conceived a passion
for his step-daughter. He causes his servant to kill her betrothed,
Faustino, and later, when her hate has changed to love, they arrange
to elope. Her mother (his wife), Raimunda, blocks their path and
provokes Estaban to shoot her, believing that Acacia would never

care to marry the man who had killed her mother.
3 acts; 7 men, 8 women; 2 interiors.

BENELLI, Sem. The Jest (1909). Tr. & adapted by E. Sheldon,
French, 1939; BP 1919-20.
The mild-mannered artist Giannetto is in love with Ginevra,
the beautiful daughter of a fish monger. He is rather the butt for
cruel jests by his brothers Neri and Gabriello, so that, once escaping death, he plans a cunning revenge: he causes Neri to enter
Ginevra's house with intent to kill Gianetto, but he slays his brother
Gabriello by mistake. Then the madness attributed to Neri in jest
becomes madness in reality.
4 acts; 13 men, 5 women, extras; 3 interiors; costumes of
the period.

BENET, Stephen Vincent. "The Devil and Daniel Webster." See
Archibald MacLeish's Scratch.

BENNETT, Alan and Peter Cook, Jonathan Miller, and Dudley
Moore. Beyond the Fringe (Revue) (1963). Samuel French.
A series of funny sketches. One deals with a preacher who
gets carried away and strays so far from his text that he can't find
his way back. Another is a spoof on Shakespeare. Other scenes
find experts on nuclear war talking the subject to death; and two
philosophers arguing the importance of their profession to the real
world but using jargon that nobody can understand.
Flexible cast; various sets. Royalty: $50-25.

BENNETT, E. Arnold. The Great Adventure (1913). Lond.,
Methuen, 1913; Doran, 1913 & revised, 1927; carried by Baker;
COT.
Ilam Carve, famous artist, allows himself to be thought dead,
while his valet is buried with honors as himself at Westminster Ab-
bey. Unfortunately an art expert recognizes him and it may all be
disclosed, but Lord Alcar remedies the situation.
4 acts; 15 men, 3 women; 4 interiors.

_____. The Honeymoon (1911). Lond., Methuen, 1911; Doran,
1912.
An aviator feels the urge of his flying when he hears what
his competitor has done; but his bride claims an equal right to
charm as he to work. Shall business intrude on a honeymoon?
3 acts; 7 men, 2 women; 2 interiors, 1 exterior.

_____ and Edward Knoblock. Milestones (1912). Lond., Methuen,
& Doran, 1912; CEU; COD; DID; MAP; MOD; PEN; TUCJ.
Illustrates the march of ideas from one generation to another,
especially how the point of view grows more conservative as one
grows older.
3 acts; 9 men, 6 women; 1 interior, but with changes of
furniture; costumes change from 1860 to 1885 to 1912.

_____. What the Public Wants (1909). Lond., F. Palmer, 1910; Doran, 1911.

Sir Charles Morgan has made a success of publishing through papers which appeal to every sort, giving them what the public wants. Then he takes over a theatre, organizing it on a business basis and giving them Shakespeare. He asks the actress Emily to marry him, more as a business proposition, but she feels she can't because of their different points of view.

4 acts; 10 men, 6 women; 2 interiors.

BENRIMO, J. H. The Yellow Jacket. See entry under Hazelton, George C.

BENSON, Sally. Meet Me in St. Louis. See entry under Sergel, Christopher.

BENTHAM, Josephine, with Herschel Williams. Janie (1942). Samuel French.

The Colburn household is crowded with overnight guests, including Dick, Janie's boyfriend, and his mother, a Southern widow who is not about to let go of her son. When Janie, Dick and their friends have a party that gets out of hand while the old folks are having dinner at the country club, everything becomes complicated, partly as a result of Janie's seven year-old sister, who has an inventive mind and makes herself a terrible pain in the elbow.

13 men, 8 women; 1 interior. Royalty: $35-25.

BENTLEY, Eric, with Maja Bentley. The Caucasian Chalk Circle. See entry under Brecht, Bertolt.

_____. The Good Woman of Setzuan. See entry under Brecht, Bertolt.

_____. Mother Courage and Her Children. See entry under Brecht, Bertolt.

_____. The Private LIfe of the Master Race. See entry under Brecht, Bertolt.

_____. La Ronde. See entry under Schnitzler, Arthur.

BERG, Gertrude. Dear Me, the Sky Is Falling. See entry under Spigelgass, Leonard.

_____. Me and Molly (1948). BP 1947-48; Dramatists Play Service, 1948.

Depicts the trials and tribulations of a hardworking, honest, loyal, Jewish family in the Bronx. Jake asks Simon to be a partner in the dress-making business, but when Molly goes in for regularly-made half-sizes, Jake starts a successful business for himself. Uncle David provides a piano for Rosie, while Mollie and Jake plot

a romance between her piano-teacher and Mr. Mendel.
3 acts; 12 men, 9 women; 1 interior.

BERGSTRÖM, Hjalmar. Karen Borneman (1907). Tr. by Björkman
in his Two Plays, Kennerley, 1914.
A creature of passion, Karen has had two relations outside
marriage; one a novelist who died; the other a sculptor in Paris.
Back in Copenhagen she truly loves a doctor, but he withdraws
when the sculptor appears. Her father is shocked and embittered,
but she claims that the contemporary emancipated woman can have
affairs if she wants to; she is a modern adult and emotionally honest.
4 acts; 4 men, 6 women; 3 interiors.

_____. Lynggaard & Co. (1905). Tr. by Björkman in his Two
Plays, Kennerley, 1914.
Studies the social problem of labor and capital and presents,
without indicating a preference, the viewpoints of the impractical
socialist, the improvident philanthropist, the idle dilettante, and the
scheming efficient manager.
4 acts; 6 men, 3 women; 1 interior.

BERNARD, Jean-Jacques. Invitation to a Voyage (1924). Tr. by
Frith in his Five Plays, Lond., Cape, 1939; tr. by Boyd as
Invitation to Travel, in DIK-2; tr. by Katzin as Glamour in KAT.
Marie Louise, wife of Oliver Mailly, a country-bred heroine,
endows her husband's friend, Philippe, with glamor as he sails for
the Argentine on business, and morbidly dreams she is in love with
him. When he returns, she realizes how very business-like and
prosaic he really is; she is brought down to earth and back to her
husband.
3 acts; 3 men, 2 women, 1 boy; 1 interior.

_____. Martine (1922). Tr. by Katzin in Eight European Plays,
Brentano, 1927; tr. by Frith, Baker, 1932; also in his Five
Plays, Lond., Cape, 1939.
Martine is a peasant girl who romances about a city charmer,
Julien. Though married to Alfred, her heart still throbs for the
youth, casually met years before. Julien had abandoned her when
his cultured fiancée, Jeanne appeared, leaving the country lass to
her shattered dream.
5 scenes; 2 men, 3 women; 2 interiors, 1 exterior.

BERNEY, William. Dark of the Moon. See entry under Richardson,
Howard.

BERNSTEIN, Elsa Porges. Twilight (1894). Tr. by Grummann in
Poet Lore, v. 23, 1912; separately, Badger, 1912.
Delicate demure love of a highly educated woman, Sabine, an
eye doctor, for a happy old man, Henry Ritter. The raging jealousy
of his daughter, Isolde, who is going blind, requires their sacri-
fice--he to care for his daughter in her total blindness and she to

lose Carl who was too young to marry her. She goes on to Berlin to study.
>5 acts; 2 men, 4 women, 1 child; 1 interior.

BERNSTEIN, Henry. The Thief (1906). Tr. by Haughton, Doubleday, 1915; taken over by French; abridged in Pierce & Matthews,
v. 2.
>Because he has fallen in love with the wife of a guest, the son of the host in a chateau takes on himself the blame for the theft of certain funds which she has taken. When the husband discovers the truth, he forgives his wife; the son is sent away to recover from his infatuation. Cleverly throws the audience and reader off the track of the thief in Act I, thus increasing the surprise in Act II, which is rather unique in utilizing only two characters.
>3 acts; 5 men, 2 women; 3 interiors (can be played with only 2 interiors).

BERRIGAN, Daniel, with Saul Levitt. The Trial of the Catonsville
Nine (1971). BP 1970-71; Samuel French.
>An edited and condensed transcript of the Berrigan brothers and their seven confederates trial, where they were convicted of il-legally removing and burning Selective Service System records in protest against the Viet Nam War. Though the verdict is well known, the play is nevertheless compelling.
>9 men, 2 women; courtroom setting. Royalty: $50-35.

BESIER, Rudolf. The Barretts of Wimpole Street (1930). BP 1930
31; Dramatists Play Service.
>A sentimentally moving recital of the romance of Elizabeth Barrett and Robert Browning--the immortal lovers. The invalid Elizabeth is virtually a prisoner to her father, whose affection is tyrannical. Life for her is brightened by the liveliness of her sis-ters and brothers. Her interest in poetry leads to correspondence with Robert Browning, who at last comes to call on her and courts her against her father's wish. Forced to elope, they flee to Italy.
>3 acts; 12 men, 5 women (plus Flush, the dog); 1 interior; costumes of the period. Royalty: $50-25.

BETTI, Ugo. Corruption in the Palace of Justice (1949). Samuel
French.
>When one man gains justice someone else loses it in this melodrama about the universal corruption of man's mind and spirit. The suicide of a corruptor and a rumored bribery bring an investi-gation to discover which of the judges in the Palace of Justice is dishonest. As the investigation progresses, however, all are shown to be stained by some venality, illustrating that the reason of all men is corrupt.
>9 men, 2 women; 1 interior. Royalty: $35-25.

BEVAN, Donald and Edmund Trzcinski. Stalag 17 (1951). Dramatists

Play Service.
Some captured American airmen in a Nazi prison camp discuss with irrepressible humor the many subjects which interest them.
Since escape plots are revealed, they are sure that a German spy is
among them. Which one is it? They finally unmask the right one.
> 3 acts; 21 men, 0 women; 1 interior. Royalty: $50-25.

BIBLE. The Book of Job (ca 400 B.C.). Tr. in King James version in SML; tr. in American Revised version & adapted by
Kallen in TRE-1, -2 (v. 2).
Satan gets permission from God to try the faith of Job. He
causes him to suffer pain and the loss of family and goods. Job is
told by his comforting friends that he is being punished for sins committed. Job does not think so, though he has racking doubts as to
the nature of divine justice. His patience is rewarded by the Voice
of God cutting the tangled knot of human passion and doubt. After
this test, Job's family and goods are restored to him.
> Prolog, & 1 continuous act; 7 men, 0 women, chorus of
> men, prolog in Heaven, 1 exterior; oriental costumes.

BIDDLE, Cordelia Drexel. My Philadelphia Father. See Kyle
Crichton's The Happiest Millionaire.

BIGGERS, Earl Derr. Seven Keys to Baldpate. See entry under
Cohan, George M.

BILLETDOUX, François. Tchin-Tchin. See entry under Michaels,
Sidney.

BIRD, Robert M. The Broker of Bogota (1834). QUICK; QUIL.
A merchant of the middle-class, true to the standards and
pride of his own caste, resents the oppression of the ruling noblemen in South America, though his daughter is to be the wife of one
of them.
> 5 acts; 9 men, 2 women, extras; 3 interiors, 3 exteriors;
> costumes of the country and period.

_____. The Gladiator (1831). In Clement Foust's Life of Bird,
N.Y., 1919; HAL.
Spartacus leads the Roman gladiators in an insurrection after
he had been forced to fight his brother in the arena. Well represents the eternal struggle for freedom against tyranny, the rebellion
against a state of slavery.
> 5 acts; 12 men, 1 boy, 2 women, extras; 3 interiors, 7 ex-
> teriors; costumes of the period.

BIRO, Lajos. School for Slavery (1942). Tr. & ed. by Paxton in
his Plays, Lond., Faber, 1942.
A striking indictment of the German invasion of Poland,
1939-40, as the governor demonstrates the ruthlessness of the con-
querors. He takes over the house of the Pole, Dr. Jablonsky, and

forces him to take charge of the electric laboratory with another
Pole, Pawlik, and a wounded German, Richard, as his assistants.
He lets Richard keep Anna Jablonsky as his servant, and they fall
in love. Other Poles escape to an island in a marsh. Jablonsky
arranges to get the governor into his underground laboratory and
there practically tortures him till a fire and an explosion kill them
both.
> 4 acts; 9 men, 4 women, extras; 2 interiors, 1 exterior;
> some German military costumes.

BJÖRNSON, Björnstjerne. The Bankrupt (1874). Tr. by Sharp in
his Three Dramas, Dutton (Everyman's), 1914.
> A business man, Tjaelda has practiced dishonest dealings
in his commercial life where "white lies" are common. Through
his business failure he is regenerated and converted to integrity and
to the belief that the moral values must be the standards of action.
> 4 acts; 15 men, 3 women; 2 interiors, 1 exterior.

_____. Beyond Our Power (1883). Tr. by Björkman in his
Plays, Scribner, 1913; TUCG; abridged in Pierce & Matthews,
v. 2; tr. as Beyond Human Power by Hollander in DIC; tr. as
Pastor Sang by Wilson, Lond., Longmans, 1893.
> Pastor Sang, who has been able to work miracles through
prayer in such as believe, fails when he wills to do more than he
can perform; he is a man, not a superman. A careful study of the
various degrees of faith and doubt, and their effect on the will.
> 2 acts; 10 men, 4 women; 2 interiors.

_____. A Gauntlet (1883). Tr. by Braekstad, Lond., 1890; tr.
by Edwards, Longmans, 1894; BAT v. 17; tr. as A Glove by
Sogard in Poet Lore, v. 3, 1892; tr. by Björkman in his Plays,
Scribner, 1913; tr. by Sharp in his Three Dramas, Dutton,
1913.
> Svava Riis throws her glove into Alfred's face when she
learns of his unchastity. She claims a woman has a right to demand
of her fiance the same purity that he demands of her; there should
be no different standards of morality.
> 3 acts; 5 men, 4 women, extras (6 young girls); 1 interior.

_____. The Newly-Married Couple (1865). Tr. by Sharp in his
Three Dramas, Dutton (Everyman's), 1914.
> In this "lesson in marriage" a worthy young husband, Axel,
to preserve his self respect, takes his bride, Laura, to his own
house instead of going to live with her jealous protective parents.
Her parents are angry at first, and the young couple are estranged;
but later they are happily reconciled.
> 2 acts; 2 men, 3 women; 2 interiors (1 is possible).

_____. When the New Wine Blooms (1909). Tr. by Hollander in
Poet Lore, v. 22, 1911.
> Mrs. Arvik, in rather neglecting her husband, sets an

example to her daughters of lack of respect for their father. When
he turns for comfort to a young girl and is supposed to have eloped
with her, his wife learns a lesson of regard for him.
    3 acts; 4 men, 8 women; 1 exterior (a veranda).

BLACK, Kitty. The Rehearsal. See entry under Anouilh, Jean.

BOBRICK, Sam. Murder at the Howard Johnson's. See entry under
    Clark, Ron.

BOKER, George H. Francesca da Rimini (1855). In his Plays &
    Poems, Bost., 1856; in McDowell, T. ed. The Romantic Tri-
    umph, 1830-60, N.Y., 1933; HAL; MOSS-3; QUIK; QUIL.
    A sympathetic interpretation of Francesca, a woman much
alive and with great capacity for love, unintentionally deceived in
thinking Paolo, the younger brother, was her intended husband.
With a lofty conception of Lanciotto, a great soul imprisoned in a
misshapen body, depicts the pathos of the deformed husband. In
this play, Pepé, the jester, brings about the catastrophe.
    5 acts; 7 men, 2 women; 5 interiors, 4 exteriors; costumes
of 13th century Italy.

BOLITHO, William. Overture (1930). BP 1930-31; Simon &
    Schuster, 1931.
    The time is 1920, and the Municipal Council in a largish west
German industrial town has declared on orders from the central
government that workers, already burdened by post-war economic
conditions, must increase their workday to 12 hours and work for
one-half pay. The workers, led by upper-class Captain Karl Ritter
and a communist named Maxim, refuse to submit. The government
sends an old hard-line general to defeat a citizen's army and to declare martial law. The general insists that the leaders must die for
this revolt. The communist flees, and it is Ritter who pays with
his life for his ideals of liberty and justice.
    3 acts; 24 men, 3 women; 1 interior.

BOLOGNA, Joseph. Lovers and Other Strangers. See entry under
    Taylor, Renee.

BOLT, Robert. Flowering Cherry (1958). Samuel French.
    Cherry is an insignificant insurance clerk who, through his
many misfortunes, is sustained by the dream that someday he will
return to the land and plant an apple orchard. Now he has lost his
job, is drinking, and resorts to stealing money from his wife's
purse. At this point his family recognizes him as a complete failure.
To salvage some respect, he attempts to bend an iron bar in a show
of determination. The attempt causes a heart attack, from which he
dies.
    4 men, 3 women; 1 interior. Royalty: $35-25.

_____. A Man for All Seasons (1960). BP 1961-62; Samuel French.

This widely acclaimed tragedy portrays the conflict faced by Sir Thomas More when his friend, Henry VIII, wants to declare himself spiritual as well as secular master of England so he can marry Anne Boleyn. Henry is already married to Catherine of Aragon, and the Pope refuses to grant him a divorce. To by-pass this hindrance, the king contrives his Act of Supremacy which would give him authority to grant divorces. More, the Lord Chancellor, cannot agree to Henry's usurpation of spiritual authority and quietly follows his own conscience. Faced with Sir Thomas' lack of support, Henry accuses him of treason, but this still fails to make Sir Thomas compromise his convictions. This leads ultimately to his assassination, but his life remains a monument to a man unswervingly devoted to his integrity.

11 men, 3 women; Unit set. Royalty: $50-25.

_____. Vivat! Vivat Regina! (1971). BP 1971-72; Samuel French.
A modern version of the historical conflict between Mary Stuart and Queen Elizabeth for the British throne. The play covers the period from Mary's marriage to the French Dauphin to the edict calling for her execution, and the death scene itself.

27 men, 2 women, extras; area staging. Royalty: $50-35.

BOLTON, Guy. Adam and Eva (with George Middleton) (1919). BP 1919-20; Samuel French, 1924.
Unable to manage his extravagant selfish family, a wealthy business man goes on a long trip and leaves his young manager, Adam, in charge. Adam has his troubles, especially with Eva, the young daughter; but by deluding them into thinking their father's business is ruined, they pitch in to remedy the situation and meet the emergency. It does them all good and brings out the best in them.

3 acts; 6 men, 4 women; 1 interior, 1 exterior.

_____. Chicken Feed (Wages for Wives) (1923). French, 1924; BP 1923-24.
"Wages for wives"--should they have a proper share in the family income instead of "chicken feed" doled out by the husband? Organized by Nell Bailey, a group of women go on a strike to determine the rights of wives in the division of the family funds. A debatable family problem, during which a husband learns his lesson.

3 acts; 7 men, 4 women; 2 interiors (1 may be exterior).

BOND, Edward. Bingo (1976). Dramatic Publishing Company.
The last days of William Shakespeare's life, set in Warwickshire in 1615 and 1616. Shakespeare has land holdings in the Common Field at Welcombe near Stratford. The three big landowners want his help in enclosing these fields, though this will mean ruin for the smaller tenants with leases. The tenants take matters into their hands when they understand what is happening, and a man is shot and killed. Then a young girl is gibbeted for begging and setting fires. Meanwhile, Shakespeare's wife and daughter wait for

him to die so they can inherit his money. In the last scene
Shakespeare takes poison tablets, and while he dies his daughter
frantically searches for his latest will.
> 2 acts; 7 men, 5 women; 2 interiors, 3 simple exteriors.
> Royalty: $60-40.

_____. Spring Awakening. See entry under Wedekind, Frank.

BOOTHE, Clare (Mrs. H. R. Luce). Kiss the Boys Good-Bye
> (1938). BP 1938-39; Dramatists Play Service.

Parodies the attempt to find a Scarlet O'Hara for the movie
Gone with the Wind. A Southern belle, Cindy Lou, comes to a
houseparty in the North, hoping to get the role of Velvet in a movie,
based on a novel entitled "Kiss the boys good-bye." Though a lamb
among Northern wolves, waking up, she lets loose her full innate
talent and tells them a few things. Result: she may have what she
wants; and she is not slow in making her choice.
> 3 acts; 10 men, 3 women; 3 interiors. Royalty: $35-25.

_____. Margin for Error (1939). BP 1939-40; Dramatists Play
> Service.

The Nazi German consul to the U.S. is killed--stabbed,
poisoned, or even shot--while guarded by the Jewish policeman
(Finkelstein). Four suspects are in the room, any one of whom
might wish to kill him. Though the Nazis admitted to margin for
error, the consul was certainly dead; the question was who did it.
> 2 acts; 7 men, 2 women; 1 interior. Royalty: $35-25.

_____. The Women (1936). BP 1936-37; Dramatists Play Service.

A group of women play their respective roles in our modern
metropolitan world, entertainingly exposing some of the more common character weaknesses of the sex, especially the empty vicious
lives of the well-to-do idle rich. The plot revolves around Mary
Haines, who divorces her husband so that he may marry beautiful
but shallow Crystal, a shop girl. Two years later, when Mary
learns that Crystal is deceiving her ex-husband, Mary adopts Crystal's jungle technique and wins him back.
> 35 women; 11 simple interiors. Royalty: $35-30.

BORETZ, Allen. Room Service. See entry under Murray, John.

BOUCICAULT, Dion L. London Assurance (1841). Lond., Lacy,
> & N.Y., French, 186- ; Dramatic Pub. Co., 1877; Yale Univ.
> Dramatic Assn., 1910; Baker, 1911; BAT; MAT; MOSO.

Grace Harkaway is being forced by her father's will to marry
elderly Sir Harcourt Courtley or lose her inheritance. His son, under an assumed name, goes to the country estate with Dazzle and
London assurance, outfaces his father, wins Grace, and all is forgiven.
> 5 acts; 9 men, 3 women; 1 interior, 2 exteriors; costumes
> of the period.

tific writings surreptitiously.

27 men, 4 women, extras; cyclorama and platform set, 6 drops, set pieces. Royalty: $50-40.

_____. The Good Woman of Setzuan (1940). Translated by Eric Bentley. Samuel French.

The common human dilemma of kindness versus acquisitiveness is analyzed in this morality play. Three gods searching in a small village for one good woman find her in the prostitute Shen Te. With her reward of 1,000 pieces of money Shen Te buys a tobacco store and generously gives aid to the needy and parasitic alike. Because of her generosity and kindness her business begins to fail. Faced with this problem, Shen Te disguises herself as her cousin and no longer offers free room and board. Her business prospers, but the authorities are suspicious about the disappearance of Shen Te and arrest the "cousin" for kidnapping her. At the trial the gods appear and explain that while kindness pleases the gods, in the world only the mercenary prosper.

18 men, 11 women, extras; 4 interiors, 3 exteriors. Royalty: $50-40.

_____. Mother Courage and Her Children (1939). Translated by Eric Bentley. BP 1962-63; Samuel French.

The idea that war, like love, is perpetual is explored in this morality play. Set in early seventeenth century Sweden, the plot recounts the adventures of Mother Courage and her three children as they follow the holy war through Poland, Finland, Bavaria, and Italy. Although not very bright, Mother Courage's oldest son is an able soldier and greedy plunderer. Her second son is honest, but he soon dies, executed by a firing squad. Accompanied by her third child, a dumb daughter, Mother Courage follows the armies and her plundering soldier son. After a short-lived peace, the seemingly never-ending war resumes; and, in a final illustration of the futility of it all, the daughter, who has fallen in love and plans to get married, is shot instead.

18 men, 5 women, extras; 1 interior, 5 exteriors. Royalty: $50-40.

_____. The Private Life of the Master Race (1941). Translated by Eric Bentley. Samuel French.

Through a myriad of characters and scenes this melodrama presents a vivid picture of Hitler's war machine. The worker who only mumbles his "Heil Hitlers" is marked for life by the Gestapo. The unjustly accused Jew receives justice form a judge, and the judge is tortured for his actions. A mother and father live in terror because they believe their son has informed on them. Two bakers meet in prison and learn that one was imprisoned for putting bran in the bread, while the other was jailed because he didn't. Through these and other episodes this play follows Hitler's armies across Europe, providing a bitter and incisive commentary on Nazism.

Numerous characters and scenes. Royalty: $50-25.

BREIT, Harvey. The Disenchanted. See entry under Shulberg,
Budd.

BRIDGES, Ann P. Coquette. See entry under Abbott, George.

BRIDIE, James. The Anatomist (1930). Lond., Constable, 1931;
in his Anatomist & Other Plays, R. R. Smith, 1931; French
carried.
Wed to the science of anatomy, Robert Knox wishes corpses
for dissection; he uses them as furnished till he discovers that they
come not merely from body-snatching episodes but that murders are
being committed to provide the corpses. His assistant, Anderson,
is loyal to him till after the trial. The incidents are based on episodes in Scottish history.
3 acts; 7 men, 5 women, extras; 3 interiors; costumes of
1828.

_____. A Sleeping Clergyman (1933). Lond., Constable, 1934;
Dodd, 1934; in his A Sleeping Clergyman & Other Plays; Constable, 1934 & 1942.
Two doctors talk shop in a Glasgow club and point out how
unpredictable is heredity. They tell of Charles Cameron II, a famous physician, who was able to conquer a polio plague, for which
he was knighted. Yet he was descended from a debauched medical
student, whose daughter Wilhelmina also begat bastards. The doctors had the story of the three generations from the late Dr. Marshall.
2 acts; 13 men, 9 women; 8 interiors, 1 exterior.

_____. Susannah and the Elders (1937). In Susannah and the
Elders and Other Plays, Constable, 1940.
Two elderly judges are inflamed by the beauty of Susannah,
the wife of Joachim the Jew, and are jealous of young Dionysos the
Greek, who also desires the fair lady. The elders invite her to enjoy their garden with its swimming pool while they are away on the
king's business, but both return to spy on her. Daniel confutes
their testimony and proves them liars.
10 scenes in 3 acts; 15 men, 4 women, extras; 3 interiors,
2 exteriors; 2 street scenes; Babylonian costumes.

_____. Tobias and the Angel (1930). Samuel French.
Tobias, son of Tobit, is sent by his father to get some money
owed. Raphael, the archangel, accompanies him; he gets him to
bring in fish, whose liver and gall later exorcises the demon Asmo-
deus and later restores his father's sight. Raphael also helps him
to win Sara.
3 acts; 8 men, 8 women; 1 interior, 3 exteriors. Royalty:
$25-20.

BRIEUX, Eugène. Blanchette (1892). Tr. by Eisemann in his
Blanchette & The Escape, Luce, 1913.
Having qualified, Blanchette gets a certificate to teach in the
schools of France but finds no opening. She helps her father, an
innkeeper, and tries to get him to improve the place. She is driven
away by her father, but returns and accepts marriage with Auguste,
a peasant's son. The play is a criticism of social conditions which
will not give young girls an opportunity of earning a living by teaching.
3 acts; 8 men, 4 women; 1 interior.

_____. Damaged Goods (Les Avariés, 1902). Tr. by Pollock in
his Three Plays, Brentano, 1914; new tr. by Pollock, Lond.,
Cape, 1943.
Georges Dupont learns on the eve of his wedding that he has
syphilis. He gets six months' treatment from a quack; then marries Henriette. His child inherits the affliction; his wife wants to
divorce him, his father-in-law wants to shoot him. His physician
intervenes and pleads for tolerance, holding out hope if the treatment is continued. A thesis play attacking society's secrecy about
venereal diseases and pleading for compulsory premarital examination.
3 acts; 5 men, 6 women; 3 interiors.

_____. The Escape (1896). Tr. by Eisemann in his Blanchette
& The Escape, Luce, 1913.
Heredity is accepted as proved by Dr. Bertry. He proclaims
that Jean, his stepson, inherits melancholia and will kill himself because his father did, and that Lucienne, his brother's daughter, will
have loose morals because her mother was a courtesan; he therefore forbids their marriage. But Jean and Lucienne do marry; and
when the Doctor relaxes in his belief, they find their escape.
3 acts; 11 men, 5 women, extras; 2 interiors, 1 exterior.

_____. False Gods (1909). Tr. by Fagan, Brentano, 1916; TUCG.
Satni, a young priest in ancient Egypt, is convinced that the
gods of Egypt are false gods; he knows they are wood and stone.
But the High Priest appeals to his pity, because the people need
something to believe in; so he makes the stone figure of Isis bow
her head, though he knows he perpetuates a lie. Even his beloved
Yaouma is willing to sacrifice herself to the Nile.
5 acts; 13 men, 6 women, extras; 2 interiors, 1 exterior;
Egyptian costumes.

_____. The Red Robe (1900). Tr. by Reed in DIC; tr. by
Miall as The Letter of the Law in his The Woman on Her Own,
Lond., Jenkins, & Brentano, 1916; abridged in Pierce & Matthews, v. 2.
The lawyers Mouzon and Vagret falsely accuse an innocent
peasant, Etchepars, of murder so as to secure a conviction, thus
hoping to win popular approval and advance to the red robe of

magistrate, since promotion is based on the number of convictions.
4 acts; 15 men, 6 women; 3 interiors.

_____. The Three Daughters of M. Dupont (1897). Tr. by Han-
kin in his Three Plays, Lond., Cape, & Brentano, 1911.
    What shall a woman do? Attractive Julie claims for herself
an unhappy, loveless marriage is better than to remain unmarried,
than to seek the consolation of religion as Caroline did, or than to
live a life of license as Angèle does. Contains an amusing scene
marking the arrangements for the marriage settlement. A thesis
play demonstrating the evils of the French system of marriage.
    4 acts; 6 men, 8 women; 2 interiors.

BRINNIN, John M. Dylan. See entry under Michaels, Sidney.

BROADHURST, George H. What Happened to Jones (1897). Samuel
French.
    Jones is a travleing salesman, who sells hymnbooks when he
can and playing-cards when he can't. He escapes from a raided
prize fight to a professor's home, and disguises himself as a bishop
to put the police off the trail. An escaped lunatic further complicates matters. A celebrated and successful farce.
    3 acts; 7 men, 6 women; 1 interior. Royalty: $25-20.

BRONTË, Charlotte. Jane Eyre (1938). Dramatized from the novel
(1847) by Mrs. Helen B. Jerome, Samuel French; by Jane Kendall, Dramatic Publishing Company.
    Jane comes from a children's home as governess to Thorn-
field, Mr. Rochester's house. He is unhappy because of an insane
wife. He would like to marry Jane, but is prevented because of
his wife. Jane leaves for a time. Returning to Thornfield she finds
the lunatic wife has set fire to the house and perished in the flames.
Now Rochester is free to marry Jane.
    Jerome version: 10 men, 12 women; 2 interiors. Royalty:
    $25-20.
    Kendall version: 4 men, 9 women; 1 interior. Royalty:
    $35-25.

BRONTË, Emily. Wuthering Heights (1939). Dramatized from the
novel (1848) by Randolph Carter. Samuel French.
    Catherine, a willful tempestuous girl is willed Wuthering
Heights, a bleak house on the moors. Living with her besides the
servants is Heathcliff, a wild gypsy boy who has grown up with her
and loves her. He leaves after a quarrel. She marries Edgar Lin-
ton and goes to live there. Heathcliffe returns and goes to live in
the closed Wuthering Heights. He marries Edgar's sister, but more
to spite Catherine than because he loves Isabel. After another violent quarrel Catherine dies.
    3 acts; 3 men, 3 women; 2 interiors; costumes of early 19th
    century. Royalty: $35-25.

BROOKE, D. D. Rehearsal for Murder (1983). Based on the tele-
play by Richard Levinson and William Link. Dramatic Publishing
Company.
  In this play within a play, actress Monica Welles has fallen
from her apartment window, with a suicide note left in her typewriter.
She is said to have taken her own life because the opening night of
the play in which she starred, written by Alex Dennison, her fiancé,
flopped. Everyone believes this suicide story except Alex. A year
later he figures out who murdered Monica, calls together all of the
actors of his failed play, and has them act out scenes to his new
creation, the play explaining the circumstances of Monica's death.
  2 acts; 7-9 men, 6 women; 1 simple set. Royalty: $50-35.

BROWNE, Maurice. Wings Over Europe. See entry under Nichols,
Robert.

BROWNE, Porter E. The Bad Man (1920). French, 1926; BP 1920-
21.
  Scene is laid on the Mexican border in the time of Villa
(died 1923), where the Mexican bandit turns the tables on a group
of Americans. Satirically shows how the supposedly "bad man"
turns out better than some others.
  3 acts; 13 men, 2 women (or 12 men, 3 women; cook may be
either sex); 1 interior; some Mexican costumes.

BROWNING, Robert. A Blot in the 'Scutcheon (1843). In various
editions of his Poems and Plays; ASH; HARC; MOSO.
  The Earl of Mertoun wishes to marry Mildred at the adjoining
estate, but seduces her before asking permission of her brother, the
Earl of Tresham, whose boast is that no blot has ever stained their
'scutcheon. Thresham consents, but when he learns from her confession of her lover, he is beside himself with fury and shame. He
kills Mertoun and poisons himself. Mildred dies of a broken heart.
  3 acts; 4 men, 2 women, extras; 4 interiors, 1 exterior;
costumes of the 18th century.

BULLINS, Ed. The Taking of Miss Janie (1974). BP 1974-75;
Samuel French.
  The play begins with young and black Monty just having sexually "taken" a young blonde white girl named Janie, or "Miss Janie"
as he prefers to call her. She claims he raped her, but as the
flashbacks subsequently show, rape is much too strong a word. In
an extended party scene with each of the players doing monologues
and dialogues (wasps, Jews, Muslims, racists, musicians) white-
black relations are shown to be as simple, and as complex, as they
really are.
  5 men (3 black), 4 women (2 black); one abstract interior.
  Royalty: $50-35.

BURROWS, Abe. The Cactus Flower (1966). Based on a play by
Pierre Barillet and Jean P. Gredy. BP 1965-66; Samuel French.

To keep himself single, a bachelor dentist tells his girl friends that he has a wife and three children. It always works. But it backfires when he finds a girl he'd like to marry, for she demands to see the wife and children of the home she's been asked to wreck. The dentist is forced to find someone to play the part of his wife (he uses his nurse) and then to find a lover for the wife to soothe his girl friend's conscience. Complications follow.
7 men, 4 women; 4 sets. Royalty: $50-35.

BUTLER, Rachel Barton. Mama's Affair (1919). BP 1919-20; French, 1925.
Eve Orrin has spent practically her whole life caring for her mother, whose hypochondria controls not only her daughter but her best friend Mrs. Marchand and her son Henry as well. It is the wish of Mrs. Orrin and Mrs. Marchand that their children should wed soon. When the party of four arrives at a hotel in the Massachusetts Hills, the doctor Mrs. Orrin calls for is not willing to play along with her imagined illness. In fact, Dr. Jansen sees that Eve is the one who needs treatment, and by taking her on as a patient is able to keep the rest of them from her and to visibly cause her to "bloom." She falls in love with the doctor (she can't stand to think of marrying Henry) but will not agree to marry him until the doctor breaks down and confesses his real love for her.
3 acts; 3 men, 4 women; 4 interiors.

BYRNE, Dolly. Enter Madame. See entry under Varesi, Gilda.

CALDERON, George. The Fountain (1909). Lond., Gowans & Gray, 1911; French, 1911; in his Three Plays and a Pantomime, Lond., Richards, 1922.
Young Mrs. Wren doles out money to the poor in the slums, who are paying her a high rent from the houses she owns there. She is like a fountain which pours back into the basin the water pumped into the horn of plenty.
3 acts; 10 men, 7 women, extras; 1 interior.

CALDERON de la Barca, Pedro. Belshazzer's Feast (ca. 1625). Tr. by MacCarthy in BAT.
Belshazzer has apparently taken Vanity and Idolatry as his wives, but, as he boasts of his conquests at his feast, the hand of Death writes on the wall: Mene, Mene, Tekel, Upharsin. Daniel, who has been joined by Thought, is called in and interprets that Death has stepped in and claimed the king.
20 scenes; 5 men, 2 women, extras; 1 exterior (a garden).

_____. Life Is a Dream (1636). Tr. by MacCarthy, Lond., Paul, 1853; HARC-26; MAU; tr. by Fitz-Gerald as Such Stuff as Dreams Are Made Of, Macmillan, 1906.
Segismundo, son of Basilio, King of Poland, is kept from birth in solitary confinement in a mountain cave, but instructed by Clotaldo, because of predictions that he would be a monster and a

fatal enemy to his father and his country. Reaching the age of 21, he is brought in drugged sleep to the palace, and on awaking he is hailed as Prince. He shows violent wrath and his actions are so savage and arbitrary that he is returned to the cave. Here he comes to think that the day at court was all a dream, until Rosura, a Muscovite lady, brings help; they fight and defeat the king's men; he is really hailed as prince and king, with the expectation of marrying his cousin Estrella, who will be his queen.

    5 acts; 4 men, 3 women, extras; 3 interiors, 2 exteriors; costumes of the period and place (Warsaw).

_____. The Mayor of Zalamea (1651). Tr. by Fitzgerald in his Six Dramas, Lond., Chatto, 1903; also in his Eight Dramas, Macmillan, 1906.

    A farmer in Zalamea, Pedro Crespo, puts his daughter Isabel in the attic when a Captain is quartered in his house. By trickery the Captain abducts both Isabel and her father, and ravishes her. On his release, Crespo is advised by the citizens that he has been appointed Mayor; as such he imprisons the Captain. After King Phillip II has heard the complaints, he appoints Crespo as perpetual mayor of the city.

    3 acts; 8 men, 3 women, extras; 3 interiors, 9 exteriors; costumes of the period.

CALDWELL, Erskine. Tobacco Road (1933). Dramatized by Jack Kirkland. Samuel French.

    The scene is laid in the cotton region of Georgia on the exhausted farm of lazy degenerate Jeeter Lester, who, though impoverished and starving, clings to his land. His 16-year-old son, Dude, marries Sister Bessie, a lustful woman preacher, in order to drive her auto. The youngest daughter, Pearl, married in her teens to Lov, runs away from him and Ellie May with a hare-lip and animal instincts take her place. Prof. Quinn writes: "shows the depths of degradation to which drama may descend."

    3 acts; 6 men, 5 women; 1 exterior. Royalty: $50-25.

CALDWELL, Taylor. Dear and Glorious Physician. See entry under Fernand, Roland.

CAMUS, Albert. Caligula (1960). Translated and adapted by Justin O'Brien. BP 1959-60; Samuel French.

    Roman Emperor Caligula, experiencing the death of his sister-wife, decides he will have the impossible and seek unlimited freedom, dispensing with love, friendship, reason, logic, anything that other men hold in high esteem. He condemns the sons and fathers of patricians to death, puts their wives in brothels, kills men himself for ostensibly good reasons or for no reasons at all. Finally, he is overthrown by the leadership of Cherea, who doesn't care about preserving himself but who cares about preserving the meaning of life by which men live.

    2 acts; 18 men, 2 women; 1 exterior. Royalty: $50-25.

CANNAN, Denis. The Ik. See entry under Higgins, Colin.

CAPEK, Karel and Josef Capek. Adam the Creator (1927). Tr. by
    Round, Lond., Allen & Unwin, & R. R. Smith, 1929; MOSH.
    Adam destroys the world with his Cannon of Negation. Then
he tries to recreate it according to his plans. He tries five, and
finds the godhead is difficult and discouraging, for there are always
shortcomings. When done, the new earth is exactly like the old.
Adam favors the individual, his Alter Ego favors the masses; Oddly-
Come-Short represents the common man who would prevent Adam
from destroying the world, for, bad as things are, he prefers this
life to non-existence. The play attacks priestcraft, militarism, communism, capitalism, and skepticism.
    6 scenes & epilog; 21 men, 3 women, extras; 1 exterior with
    background changes; fanciful costumes.

_____. Insect Comedy. See The World We Live In.

_____. The Makropoulos Secret (1922). Adapted by Burrell.
    Luce, 1925.
    Elena Makropoulos, a Greek living in 1585, by a precious
formula is rejuvenated every 30 years. As a singer and idol of
men she lives 300 years, being at different times a German, a Russian, a Spaniard, a Scot, and a Czech. In her final incarnation,
as Emilia Marty, the secret is offered to several people; each declines, and one, Kristina, destroys it. Emilia now welcomes death.
Longevity is neither ideal nor desirable; eternal life would be terrible unless the key to eternal happiness were discovered.
    3 acts; 8 men, 4 women; 3 interiors.

_____. R.U.R. (Rossum's Universal Robots) (1922) English
    version by Paul Selver and Nigel Playfair. BP 1922-23; Samuel
    French.
    The robots are manufactured men turned out by the thousand
to perform the labor of the world; but they lack souls. They cannot
appreciate the higher things of life, and the real men do not know
how to, even with the leisure they have gained. Modern mechanistic
civilization is satirized in terms of a weird and fantastic melodrama,
which points out that human values are more important than the
machinery of civilization created by modern science.
    13 men, 4 women; 2 interiors (1 set possible). Royalty:
    $35-25.

_____ and Josef Capek. The World We Live In (The Insect Come-
    dy) (1921). Adapted by Owen Davis. Samuel French.
    Insects have affairs and problems strikingly like those of hu-
mans. The butterflies flutter and make violent love like philander-
ers, beetles hoard their wealth and live selfishly like avaricious mi-
sers, parasites greedily devour what others have worked to save,
red ants and yellow ants wage war to see which has the right of
way over two blades of grass comparable to the strifes of industry

and war. They struggle along with the same trivia of selfishness, self-importance, and futility as humans do.
21 men, 9 women, extras; 5 exteriors. Royalty: $35-25.

CAPEK, Josef. See entries under Capek, Karel.

CAPEK-CHOD, Karel M. The Solstice (1912). Tr. by Schonberger in Poet Lore, v. 35, 1924.
Hans Karvan returns home after several years of war service and exile, including five years in America, to find that Anna has married his cousin John; John has also taken over the business when he craftily showed that Hans had probably died. Julia, Anna's sister, is mistaken by Hans for Anna, as she so much resembles her. She has a five-year-old boy, Jackie, by a doctor who has died in an epidemic. John wants to get rid of Hans; Hans agrees to return to America, taking Julia and Jackie with him.
3 acts; 9 men, 3 women, 2 boys; 1 exterior; costumes of the period (1874).

CAPUS, Alfred. The Adventurer (1910). Tr. by Papot in Drama, v. 4, 1914.
Etienne Ranson, who went to Australia and Africa and made a fortune in 10 years, returns as a sort of prodigal now cleared of an accusation. He finds himself falling in love with Genevieve, who is engaged to André Vareze, who was his accuser. M. Gueroy at 60 and his son-in-law Jack have reached the end of their resources in maintaining a factory and ask Ranson to come in with his money. He refuses unless given sole authority. Gueroy refuses, but Jack agrees. Genevieve realizes Ranson's position and offers to become his wife, a situation which is confirmed when André backs out.
4 acts; 9 men, 7 women; 2 interiors, 1 exterior.

_____. Brignol and His Daughter (1894). Tr. by Clark. French, 1915.
A jolly impecunious optimist, Brignol, is always in debt and borrowing. He plans various marriages for his daughter, especially to recoup his finances. She straightens out his affairs when she marries the wealthy nephew of his chief creditor, with whom she luckily falls in love.
3 acts; 5 men, 4 women; 1 interior.

CAREY, Ernestine G. Cheaper by the Dozen. See entry under Sergel, Christopher.

CARISTI, Vincent. Tracers. See entry under DiFusco, John.

CARLETON, Margorie. Jane Eyre. See entry under Brontë, Charlotte.

CAROLE, Joseph and Alan Dinehart. Separate Rooms (1940). Samuel French.

The columnist Jim threatens to retaliate on Pam the actress for marrying his naive brother Don but failing to make him happy. He will blackmail her in his column into making her a good wife. His secretary pleads for a three months' armistice, after which he himself is lured into matrimony by his Girl Friday.
3 acts; 5 men, 3 women; 1 interior. Royalty: $35-25.

CARROLL, Lewis. Alice in Wonderland. See entry under Le Galliene, Eva.

CARROLL, Paul Vincent. Shadow and Substance (1934). BP 1937-38; Dramatists Play Service.
Contrasts three points of view in the Roman Catholic Church in Ireland: the scholarly, orthodox Canon, Thomas Skerritt, who is a bit cynical and worldly; the pugnacious, skeptical young schoolmaster, O'Flingsley; and the steadfast, unselfish Brigid, the maid in the Canon's household, who has a childlike acceptance of faith and who tries to reconcile these two and bring them together through her patron saint.
4 acts; 6 men, 4 women; 1 interior. Royalty: $35-25.

_____. The White Steed (1938). BP 1938-39; Samuel French.
Presents a clash between two Roman Catholic priests, one a skeptical humanist, Canon Matt Lavelle; the other a fanatic moralist, Father Shaughnessy. The latter wants to enforce right living through his Vigilance Committee. In the end the Canon must take hold of the situation.
3 acts; 8 men, 5 women; 3 interiors. Royalty: $25.

CARSON, Murray. Rosemary. See entry under Parker, Louis N.

CARTER, Randolph. A Texas Steer (1894). In the original version by C. H. Hoyt. French, 1940 in this modern version.
Hard-riding Texan cattle-king, Maverick Brander, is elected to Congress, to the embarrassment of the Washingtonians because of his crudeness. Two years later however they have been accepted socially; yet when three gun-toting Texans arrive, pandemonium breaks loose. Next morning, Maverick helps his daughter get the man she loves, rebels against his sycophants, and spirits away his three gun-shooting Texans.
3 acts; 13 men, 6 women; 1 interior, 1 exterior; some Texan costumes.

_____. Wuthering Heights. See entry under Brontë, Emily.

CARTER, Steve. Nevis Mountain Dew (1979). BP 1978-79; Dramatists Play Service.
Jared Philibert, a black man from Queens with a West Indian background, celebrates his 50th birthday in an iron lung, getting drunk on downhome rum and trying to hold together a family consisting of a wife, Billie, and two single sisters, Everelda and Zepora.

By the end of the play, he is able to persuade one of them or one of the invited guests (a couple of boyfriends and an uninterested party) to put him out of his misery. After he dies, only Everelda, the cruelest woman in the family ("Your drawers must have turned to ashes.") stays behind to reap the reward of the inherited property.

3 acts; 4 men, 3 women; unit set. Royalty: $50-35.

CASELLA, Alberto. <u>Death Takes a Holiday</u> (1929). American stage
    version by Walter Ferris. BP 1929-30; Samuel French.

    Wearied of defeat by Love, Death takes three days off to visit the world as a human, trying to discover the reason. As Prince Sirchi he visits an Italian family and falls in love with the daughter, Grazia. When he must leave, she begs to go with him; and Death takes her, for perfect love casts out fear.

3 acts; 7 men, 6 women; 1 interior. Royalty: $50-25.

CASPARY, Vera and George Sklar. <u>Laura</u> (1948). Based on Vera
    Caspary's novel. Dramatists Play Service.

    Mark McPherson, a Special Investigator, comes to Laura's apartment to try to solve her murder. He falls in love with the dead woman from her portrait, her letters, her personal effects, and the comments of the three men who loved her during her lifetime. But Laura turns up, alive, during a storm. Her girlfriend becomes the murder victim. All the evidence points to Laura's guilt. In spite of his love for her, Mark is about to pin the crime on Laura. But the real murderer returns and attempts to repeat the crime by killing the right girl. She is saved by Mark.

5 men, 3 women; 1 interior. Royalty: $50-35.

THE CHALK CIRCLE. (13th century). Tr. by Ethel Van der Veer
    in CLF-1; many parts in BAT-3.

    Hai'tang becomes the second wife of Ma. His first wife has a lover and plans to poison Ma and get the fortune through claiming his five-year-old son as hers. When Ma returns he is told by Mrs. Ma #1 that Hai'tang has a lover and has given her head-dress and ornaments to him. She bribes all witnesses with silver; Hai'tang is brought before the governor and supreme judge. He places the child in the chalk circle to let the two women lead him out. Mrs. Ma (wife #1) does it twice, but Hai'tang refuses to pull. The judge awards the child to Hai-tang.

Prolog & acts; 5 men, 5 women, extras; 4 interiors; Chinese costumes.

CHAMBERS, C. Haddon. <u>The Saving Grace</u> (1917). Brentano,
    1918; French carried.

    Buoyed through every crises by his sense of humor, Blinn Corbett regains his place in the army through his wife.

4 acts; 3 men, 4 women; 1 interior.

_____. <u>The Tyranny of Tears</u> (1899). Lond., Heinemann, &

Bost., Baker, 1902; abridged in Pierce & Matthews, v. 1.
   With sly humor and pleasing freshness relates how Clement
Parbury is ruled by a loving but tearful wife, Mabel. He is inclined to rebel at last, when his wife becomes jealous of his secretary, Hyacinth and desires her dismissal. The question is solved
when her brother returns and marries Hyacinth.
   4 acts; 4 men, 3 women; 1 interior, 1 exterior.

CHANDLER, Raymond. The Little Sister. See entry under Gordon,
   Stuart and Carolyn Purdy-Gordon.

CHAPIN, Harold. Art and Opportunity (1917). In his Comedies,
   Chatto, 1921; French, 1924.
   Presents the maneuvers of a fascinating widow, Pauline, dis-
playing her woman's art in using opportunity. She is pursued by
Lord Algernon, his father, and a duke, but she finally accepts the
secretary Henry Bently.
   3 acts; 5 men, 2 women; 2 interiors, 1 exterior (1 interior
   is possible).

_____. The New Morality (1920). French, 1924; MAP; in his
   Comedies, Chatto, 1921.
   From a houseboat on the Thames Mrs. Betty lets fly some
fierce public invectives at Mrs. Muriel on the next boat, caused by
her husband's trivial attentions. Muriel demands an apology which
Betty refuses to give. Betty's brother, a lawyer, advises about
libel and its consequences. Muriel's husband, after a few drinks,
boasts about the new morality of women, while Betty agrees to write
an apology.
   3 acts; 4 men, 3 women; 1 interior, 1 exterior.

CHAPMAN, Robert. Billy Budd. See entry under Coxe, Louis O.

CHASE, Mary Coyle. Bernardine (1951). BP 1952-53. Dramatists
   Play Service.
   Bernardine is a fantasy girl who loves to give boys what they
want, drives a 1952 Cadillac convertible, and hails from Sneaky
Falls, Idaho (on the banks of the Itching River), a little town where
all the mothers take orders from their teenage sons. She is dreamed
up, like the whole town of Sneaky Falls, by Arthur Beaumont (Beau),
the leader of a group of high school boys who hang out at a 3.2
beer joint called the Shamrock. They would be rough and tough,
but their hearts aren't really in it, and, in spite of their adolescent
sexual starvation, they are all like Wormy Weldy, who loses out to
adult experiences from being decent: "If you haven't got wolf's
teeth you never get them."
   3 acts; 13 men, 6 women; simple, stylized scenery. Royalty:
   $50-25.

_____. Harvey (1944). BP 1944-45; Dramatists Play Service.
   Pulitzer prize play 1945. An invisible white rabbit (Harvey)

always accompanies the amiable bibulous hero, Elwood. When he is sent to a sanitarium for observation, his sister gets the treatment by mistake.
 6 men, 6 women; 2 interiors. Royalty: $50–35.

_____. Mrs. McThing (1952). BP 1951–52; Dramatists Play Service.
 Rich Mrs. Larue and her small son Howay are hexed by the witch, Mrs. McThing, because her girl Mimi may not play in the guarded yard. Howay is replaced by a polite, obedient, but priggish Stick, while he hobnobs delightedly with gangsters. Likewise his mother is bewitched into a scrub-woman in the gangsters' lunch room. Finally the mother appreciates her son the way he is, and adopts Mimi in the bargain.
 8 men, 1 boy (doubles), 10 women; 2 interiors. Royalty: $50–25.

CHAUCER, Geoffrey. The Canterbury Pilgrims. See entry under MacKaye, Percy.

CHAVES, Richard. Tracers. See entry under DiFusco, John.

CHAYEFSKY, Paddy. Gideon (1961). BP 1961–62; Dramatists Play Service.
 It is 1100 B.C. in impoverished Palestine, where an army of Midianites is about to kill the Hebrews for their harvest. While the elders offer sacrifices to the god Baal, an Angel of the Lord appears to young Gideon (considered a "witless ass" by the elders) and complains about all of the binds he has got the Jews out of, and still they continue to worship false idols. Gideon is a hard one to convince, but The Angel of the Lord finally does, showing him how to defeat 120,000 Midianites with only 300 frightened men armed with oil lamps and horns (so it will be clear that Israel won by the hand of God alone). Gideon accomplishes this, but begins to like the acclaim of his people and increasingly ignores the Angel's directions because they seem to make mortal beings insignificant. Finally, Gideon explains the Midian victory as "the inevitable outgrowth of historico-economic, socio-psychological forces prevailing in these regions," and the Angel shakes His head in wonderment over man's belief in man.
 2 acts; 18 men, 1 boy, 6 women; unit set. Royalty: $50-25.

_____. Middle of the Night (1956). Samuel French.
 The question of the rights of an old man to claim the love of a young girl is treated in this drama. A 53-year-old widower meets an unhappy girl nearly 30 years his junior, the victim of a marriage with a fly-by-night musician. Although their families strenuously object, the decision ultimately is theirs as to whether to marry and bring the matter to a conclusion.
 3 men, 8 women; 1 interior. Royalty: $50–25.

_____. The Passion of Josef D. (1964). BP 1963-64; Samuel French.
    Lenin's intellectual Bolshevik zeal evolves to disillusionment in this historical drama about Stalin's fanatical dedication to canonizing Lenin. Stalin, a former seminarian, wants to make Lenin an object of veneration for Russian people, and in his single minded devotion to constructing the legend, reveals the inner soul of Lenin. The New York Daily News commented: "And here, too, is Lenin, surveying the years of the revolution, not with bitterness, but with the realization that (it) has done nothing to change mankind. The Soviets have done the same brutal things and give the same reasons that other governments have through history."
    20 men, 3 women; various sets. Royalty: $50-25.

_____. The Tenth Man (1959). BP 1959-60; Samuel French.
    An old meeting room used as a temple houses ten very interesting characters and the beginning of a romance. It is a winter day, and a group of Jewish men have gathered at their makeshift temple for prayer. Some are not so devout, however. One is an atheist who says he only comes to the temple to keep warm, and another is a young agnostic lawyer who can find no contentment in his cynicism and skepticism. Then the final worshippers arrive, an elderly man, and his attractive granddaughter, who is in a trance which some think is caused by a dybbuk, or evil spirit. At times she is irrational, then in the trance, and sometimes she is very lucid. During her saner moments she and the lawyer are strongly attracted to each other, and this developing love brings hope to the girl and a previously dormant capacity for love to the young agnostic.
    12 men, 1 woman; composite interior. Royalty: $50-25.

CHEKHOV, Anton P. The Cherry Orchard (1904). Tr. by Calderon in his Two Plays, Lond., Richards, 1912; same in DIC; in WATI & WATL-4; in HATS; tr. by West in his Plays, ser. 2, Scribner, & Lond., Duckworth, 1916; & in his Five Famous Plays, Scribner, 1939; tr. by Covan in MOS; tr. by Garnett, Lond., Chatto, 1923; same in his Plays, Modern Lib., 1930; & in TRE-1, 2, & 3; TREA-2; tr. by Butler, Lond., Deane, & Bost., Baker, 1934; tr. by Koteliansky in his Plays, Dutton (Everyman's) 1938); same, Penguin Bks, 1941; NOY; tr. by Young, French, 1947; in WOR. Acting edition: Samuel French.
    The aristocratic family, the Ranevskys, are forced to sell their estate because of indifference towards business and money matters. The family orchard is bought by Lopakhin, the son of a serf on their estate, and as they leave they hear the ring of the axes chopping down the cherry trees. Supplies one reason for the passing of the Old Russia before the New, depicting the triumph of industrial civilization over pastoral tradition. (From this play, in The Wisteria Trees, Joshua Logan fashioned an American equivalent of the same theme, laying the scene in the deep South).
    4 acts; 11 men, 4 women, extras; 3 interiors, 1 exterior (1

set is possible). (S. French Royalty: $35-25.)

_____. A Country Scandal (1881). Adapted by Alex Szogyi.
Samuel French.
Man's failures in times of crises are amusingly portrayed in
this comedy about a man who is irresistible to women. Women find
Misha almost unbearably attractive. His wife, a widow, and the
widow's daughter-in-law all pursue Misha, but this apparent good
fortune only makes trouble for him, as when the widow's son challenges Misha to a duel. Finally, succumbing to the pressures of
his scandalous life, Misha tries to commit suicide. But pointing up
the theme of the play, even this fails.
11 men, 5 women; 2 interiors, 2 exteriors. Royalty: $35-
25.

_____. The Good Doctor. See entry under Simon, Neil.

_____. The Sea Gull (1896). Tr. by Calderon in his Two Plays,
Lond., Richards, 1912; MOSQ; tr. by Fell in his Plays, ser. 1,
Scribner, 1912 & Lond., Duckworth, 1912; also in his Five Fa-
mous Plays, Scribner, 1939; tr. by Eisemann in Poet Lore, v.
24, 1913; tr. by West, Lond., Henderson, 1915; tr. by Garnett
in his Cherry Orchard, Lond., Chatto, 1923; & in his Plays,
Modern Lib., 1930; & in CEW; in CLS; tr. by Koteliansky in
his Plays & Stories, Dutton (Everyman's) 1938; & in his Three
Plays, Penguin Bks, 1941; tr. by Young, Scribner, 1939;
French, 1950; abridged in Pierce & Matthews, v. 2. Acting
edition: Samuel French.
Irina, an actress, is adored by Constantine, a sensitive poet,
but she turns from his symbolic plays to a better-known playwright,
Trigorin. After a time she finds herself deserted by him, turned
out by her father, and reduced to a third-rate company, but she
still refuses Constantine's attentions, feeling she is destined to fly
away alone like a wounded sea gull. Constantine is embittered by
his failure and dies a slave to love.
4 acts; 8 men, 5 women; 2 interiors, 2 exteriors. (S.
French Royalty: $35-25.

_____. The Three Sisters (1901). Tr. by West in his Plays,
ser. 2, Scribner, 1916 & his Five Famous Plays, Scribner,
1939; tr. by Covan, Brentano, 1922; tr. by Garnett in his
Cherry Orchard, Chatto, 1923; in his Plays, Modern Lib.,
1930; LEG; MOS; tr. by Young, French, 1941; BLO. Acting
edition: Samuel French.
The three sisters, Olga, Masha, and Irina, are stranded in
a small provincial town by their father's death, but are ever dreaming of returning to Moscow. Olga looks straight ahead, advancing
as a schoolteacher, but still weak. Masha looks down, for though
married to Kaligin, she falls in love with a visiting colonel. Irina
looks up, for she is still young and hopeful, though her lover is
killed in a duel. They lack the will to make their aspirations come

true.
> 4 acts; 9 men, 5 women; 2 interiors, 1 exterior; costumes
> of the period (1900). (S. French Royalty: $35-25.)

_____. Uncle Vanya (1899). Tr. by Fell in his Plays, ser. 1,
Scribner, 1912; & in his Five Famous Plays, Scribner, 1939; tr.
by Saphro in Poet Lore, v. 33, 1922; tr. by Garnett in his
Cherry Orchard, Lond., Chatto, 1923; MIL; MOS; WATI; WATL-
2. Acting edition: Samuel French.
> Uncle Vanya is disillusioned at 47. He and his relatives
have slaved to educate Alexander, who turns out rather shallow.
Vanya makes a futile attempt to kill his infuriating brother-in-law
Prof. Serebriakov who tries to sell the estate, to build up which
Uncle Vanya has given his life. Sofia begs him to stick at his job.
Life settles down to distressing mediocrity. For people without a
purpose life becomes sad and futile; depicts the corroding effect of
frustration.
> 4 acts; 5 men, 4 women; 3 interiors, 1 exterior. (S. French
> Royalty: $35-25.)

CHLUMBERG, Hans. The Miracle at Verdun (1930). Tr. by Leigh,
Brentano, 1931; tr. by Crankshaw, Lond., Gollancz, 1932; CHA;
FAMC.
> In 1934, Heydner, a German soldier, visits the French ceme-
tery at Verdun. He visions the dead soldiers arising to go to resume life. But in Paris, London, and Berlin they find the world
getting along very well without them. In fact the diplomats become
alarmed, fearing an international crisis. So they return to their
graves.
> 8 scenes; many characters & extras; many interior and ex-
> terior scenes; costumes.

CHODOROV, Edward. Decision (1944). BP 1943-44; French, 1946.
> A reactionary senator, who also owns the local newspaper,
dominates the city and stirs up racial feeling. A fearless high school
principal leads the better element in an effort to show the senator up.
He is arrested on a rape charge and hanged in the jail to make him
look guilty. The principal's soldier son on leave reacts to his
father's death to join the fight on the issues involved.
> 3 acts; 12 men, 5 women; 1 interior.

_____. Kind Lady (1935). Samuel French.
> Dramatized from a story by Hugh Walpole. Clever crooks
surround the dignified and aristocratic Mary Herries and gradually
alienate the kind lady from her relatives and friends. They almost
convince her that she herself is insane. With some skill she gets
word to her banker and help is on the way.
> 3 acts; 6 men, 8 women; 1 interior. Royalty: $35-25.

CHODOROV, Jerome, with Joseph Fields. Anniversary Waltz (1954).
Dramatists Play Service.

    Celebrating a 15th wedding anniversary with too much wine,
a husband makes the mistake of telling his wife's parents all that
went on between him and their daughter <u>before</u> the wedding ceremony. His in-laws are shocked and outraged, but his children are unimpressed. In fact, his 13-year-old daughter tells the whole world
about it on television. Tempers rise, and the husband leaves home.
He returns, but his irate wife leaves. Finally, they are brought
back together by news from another front: they are going to have
another baby.
    7 men, 5 women; 1 interior. Royalty: $50-25.

_____ with Joseph Fields. <u>Junior-Miss</u> (1941). BP 1941-42;
    Dramatists Play Service.
    Sub-deb Judy at 13 imitates her older sister Lois who is 16.
With her confidante, Fluffy, she plots to fix things up in general,
for father, mother, Uncle Willie, and all. This results in many
highly amusing situations.
    21 men (some have no lines), 3 women, 3 girls; 1 interior.
Royalty: $35-25.

_____. <u>My Sister Eileen</u>. See entry under Fields, Joseph.

_____. <u>The Ponder Heart</u>. See entry under Fields, Joseph.

CHRISTIE, Agatha. <u>The Hollow</u> (1952). Samuel French.
    The philandering of a wealthy society doctor leads to his mur-
der in this tension-filled mystery drama. Three women are in love
with Dr. John Cristow: a sculptress, Henrietta Angkatell, his
present mistress; film star Veronica Craye, his former mistress;
and Gerda, his wife. One weekend all four stay at a country home,
and Veronica persuades John to spend the night at her cottage.
Since John is not particularly secretive about his affairs, several
people know of his indiscretion. The next morning John refuses to
give up his wife, and Veronica threatens him. Within five minutes
John has been fatally shot. The suspects are many: Gerda, Henrietta, Veronica, and even the household servants who were not over-
ly fond of the doctor. The identity of the murderer remains unknown
as the suspense builds to the final scene.
    6 men, 6 women; 1 interior. Royalty: $50-25.

_____. <u>The Mousetrap</u> (1938). Samuel French.
    During a snow storm, a boarding house provides shelter for
a group of strangers, one of whom is killed. The newly married
couple who run the house, a spinster, an architect, a retired Army
major, a man whose car has overturned in a snowdrift, and a woman
jurist survive the murder. Then a policeman arrives on skis, and
the jurist is suddenly murdered. The policeman probes the background of everyone in the house, but it is discovered that the man
in the police uniform is the real culprit.
    5 men, 3 women; 1 interior. Royalty: $50-25.

_____. Spider's Web (1940). Samuel French.

A disorganized woman who is fascinated by the world of fancy she creates in the tales she tells to her daughter and her friends comes face to face with reality when a man is murdered in her living room. Clarissa, Henry's second wife, even spins wild yarns to the police as she tries to cover up for her daughter, Pippa, because she thinks Pippa committed the murder. To add to the complications, the victim is the man who was responsible for the failure of Henry's first marriage. Clarissa's main worry is in getting the case solved quickly, for Henry is expected shortly with a V.I.P., and a body lying in the living room might create a bad impression. Luckily for Clarissa the police are acute enough to unravel the truth from her wild stories, and after some hair-raising experiences, manage to un-mask the murderer. When Henry returns the house is quiet, but he is angry because no refreshments have been prepared for his guest. For once Clarissa tells him the truth to explain her lack of prepara-tion. Henry, of course, cannot accept such an obvious fabrication, but he loves her and with good-natured resignation forgives her.

8 men, 3 women; 1 interior. Royalty: $50-25.

_____. Ten Little Indians (1946). Samuel French.

Although "The Ten Little Indians" refers only to a static group of mantelpiece statuettes, these figures provide the background for some very lively action in this mystery comedy. Eight guests and two servants are assembled in a weird country house. At cock-tails a voice from an unseen speaker accuses all of murder. Sud-denly one Indian topples from the mantel and breaks, and immediate-ly thereafter one of the guests falls dead, choking from a poisoned drink. One by one the Indians fall and the guests die as the action moves toward the suspenseful climax.

8 men, 3 women; 1 interior. Royalty: $50-25.

_____ with Gerals Verner. Towards Zero (1957). Adapted from Miss Christie's novel. Dramatists Play Service.

Mystery, suspense, murder, and the twist at the end. Lady Tressilian's house guests are Kay and Nevile Strange; Nevile's first wife, Audrey; a man in love with Audrey; and Mary, the Lady's companion secretary. Near-by is Ted, a friend of Kay's. When Nevile tells Kay he wants to divorce her and remarry Audrey, his wife says she'll see them both dead before she permits it. The next morning Lady Tressilian is found murdered. At first it looks like Nevile is the culprit, then that someone is framing him, then that Audrey is the murderess. It takes the family lawyer and police to solve the crime.

7 men, 4 women; 1 interior. Royalty: $35-30.

_____. The Unexpected Guest (1960). Samuel French.

A stranger walks into a house to find a woman standing with a gun and her dead husband lying on the floor. The woman is dazed, though she admits the killing. The stranger is not convinced and decides to help her frame the murder on an intruder. The police, however, find clues implicating a man who died two years earlier. Then come the complications. Just as the murder seems solved there is an unexpected twist.

7 men, 3 women; 1 interior. Royalty: $50-25.

_____. Witness for the Prosecution (1954). BP 1954-55; Samuel French.

A young married man is accused of the murder of a rich older woman he has been seeing. At his trial, his wife gives such damaging testimony against him that it looks as if he will be convicted. Then a mysterious woman appears with letters which make the wife's testimony suspect, and the man is freed. The mystery woman turns out to be the wife herself, who felt this was the only way she could get her husband off. When he goes off with another woman (he was guilty of the murder all along), she kills him and prepares for her own trial.

17 men, 5 women, 8 extras; 2 interiors. Royalty: $50-25.

CHRISTOFER, Michael. The Shadow Box (1977). BP 1976-77; Samuel French.

In cottages on the grounds of a large hospital, three terminally ill patients face death as best they can, while friends and family try in feeble ways to help. Joe can't get his wife to talk about his illness, and can't get her to help him tell his teenage son. Brian, who is trying desperately to get in as much of life as he can before the end, can't keep his male lover and his former wife from ruining everything by quarreling with one another. And Felicity, an old woman in a wheelchair, seems to be kept alive by an elaborate lie her overworked and unappreciated daughter has concocted: letters from a favorite daughter who fled the family and died ages ago. The dying business gets messy, for the victims and for the survivors.

2 acts; 5 men, 4 women; 1 interior. Royalty: $50-35.

CHURCHILL, Caryl. Cloud 9 (1981). BP 1980-81; Samuel French.

This lampoon of human sexuality begins with a family living in a British colony in 1880's Africa. Clive, the father, is a woman-chaser. His wife, Betty, is played by a man--his son Edward by a woman. A white man plays the black servant and a rag doll plays the daughter. Everyone, it seems, is sexually interested in everyone. Act II takes place in 1980's London, where the main characters have aged only 25 years in the past 100, and where sexual confusion in a "liberated" society is only slightly different than in the earlier repressed one.

2 acts; 4 men, 3 women (with doubling); 2 exteriors. Royalty: $50-40.

CLARK, Brian. Whose Life Is It Anyway? (1978). BP 1978-79; Dramatic Publishing Company.

Ken Harrison lies in a hospital bed in England. An automobile accident has left him permanently paralyzed from the neck down, and while he still retains a sense of humor (gallows though it is) he has no interest in living the rest of his life with only his head. He comes into conflict with the professionalism of practically everyone on the hospital staff (they must dehumanize him in order to live their own lives) and with the entire medical establishment view of saving all lives even if it means chemically dulling the consciousness of the unwilling. Ken loses his first battle when he is injected with Valium against his will, but ultimately prevails when he forces a legal decision which will permit him to voluntarily check himself out of his intensive care room (he will die soon). Dr. Emerson, the patient's adversary throughout the play, offers at the end to assist Ken with his intentions: he will not, after all, have to move out of the hospital in order to die.

2 acts; 9 men, 5 women; area staging. Royalty: $60–40.

CLARK, Ron, with Sam Bobrick. Murder at the Howard Johnson's (1979). Samuel French.

In the first scene Arlene Miller waits in a motel room with her lover, Mitchell Lovell, a dentist. They plan to murder Arlene's dull and colorless husband Paul unless he consents to a divorce. He refuses and they proceed with their plan to drown him in the bathtub. They leave him for dead but he emerges, vowing to see a marriage counselor. In scene two, in a similar room in the motel six months later, Arlene has threatened to kill herself because Mitchell has been unfaithful to her. Paul comes to her rescue, and she persuades him to help her murder the dentist with a gun she bought at Sears (a Kenmore?). That plan is changed for one which looks like suicide, but that also fails. In the last scene, it is Paul and Mitchell who are luring Arlene to a similar room at the motel so that they can hang her for the havoc she has wrought on their lives and frame the murder on Malcolm Dewey, a millionaire she is involved with. They fail because the "bargain" rope they bought breaks, and because Arlene convinces them to plan to murder the millionaire.

2 acts; 2 men, 1 woman; 1 interior. Royalty: $50–40.

CLAUDEL, Paul. The Tidings Brought to Mary (1912). Tr. by Sill, Yale Univ. Pr., 1916; DIK-1; HAV; TUCG.

The good Violaine is made leprous through a lover's kiss. Exiled and suffering taunts and revilings, she yet restores to life her sister Mara's child, thus preaching that supreme faith and humility may work miracles.

Prolog & 4 acts; 5 men, 3 women, many extras; various exteriors; mediaeval costumes.

CLEMENTS, Colin C. See entry under Clements, Florence Ryerson.

CLEMENTS, Florence Ryerson and Colin C. Clements. Harriet (1943). BP 1942–43; Scribner, 1943; French, 1945.

Depicts very simply some episodes in the life of Harriet Beecher Stowe and how she came to write Uncle Tom's Cabin. She saw the evils of slavery when she started her married life in Cincinnati. When they transferred to Maine, circumstances brought about the writing of the book. Brings in all the Beechers, including Henry Ward Beecher. Reports her interview with Lincoln, from whom she learned a philosophy of hope and courage.

3 acts; 7 men, 10 women; 3 interiors (may be unit set or just curtains).

_____. Strange Bedfellows (1948). Samuel French.

A militant suffragette, Clarissa Blynn, marries Matthew Cromwell, the son of a conservative old-line senator and politician. Her invasion in the 1890's of the Nob Hill home in San Francisco is opposed by the fire-eating senator and his cronies, by the women of the household, and even by her husband. She fights for women's rights, and finally maneuvers first the women, then everybody else to her side of the political fence.

3 acts; 7 men, 11 women; 1 interior; costumes of 1896. Royalty: $50-25.

COBURN, D. L. The Gin Game (1978). BP 1977-78; Samuel French.

On the sun porch of the Bentley Nursing and Convalescent Home for the Aged, Weller Martin (mid 70's) offers to teach Fonsia Dorsey (late 60's) to play gin rummy. It is visitor's day, and neither is expecting visitors. He tells her about the marketing research business he was in. She tells him that her son lives far away and consequently can't visit. Meanwhile, she keeps going gin until he gets so angry that he overturns the cardtable in a rage. They try again the next evening, but when the old man finally wins a hand he accuses her of throwing the game. She wins some more hands and he stomps off, leaving her angry and frightened. The following Sunday afternoon they meet again, stripping away their own and one another's defenses and stories and pretentions (he has been cheated by his business partners, her son lives in the same town but hates her, they are both on welfare). He makes her angry enough to play a few more hands of gin again, but instead of connecting as people through the ritual of cards, her uncanny winning streak sends him into a threatening rage, destroying any kind of future interaction at cards or anything else at the Home.

2 acts; 1 man, 1 woman; 1 exterior. Royalty: $50-35.

COHAN, George M. Seven Keys to Baldpate (1913). Based on the novel by Earl Derr Biggers. BP 1909-1919; Samuel French.

On a bet that he can write a play in a week, an author goes to a supposedly deserted house on Baldpate mountain. But the place has become a rendezvous for thieves and others, whose comings and goings rather upset the author's writing schedule. He wins the bet.

3 acts; 9 men, 4 women; 1 interior. Royalty: $50-25.

COLETTE. Gigi. See entry under Loos, Anita.

COLMAN, George, Sr., and David Garrick. The Clandestine

<u>Marriage</u> (1766).   BAT; HAN; MCM; MOR; MOSE-2; INCH, v. 16;
OXB, v. 5.
    Fanny Sterling has been secretly married to penniless Love-
well against her father's wishes.   Meanwhile a couple of lords make
love to her, as they want to get some of the merchant's money.   The
final act is considered a masterpiece, when Lovewell is caught in his
wife's room.
    5 acts; 10 men, 6 women; 6 interiors, 2 exteriors; costumes
of the period.

COLTON, John R. with Clemence Randolph.   <u>Rain</u> (1922).   Adapted
    from a story by Somerset Maugham.   BP 1922-23; Smauel French.
    Sadie Thompson, a woman of the streets of San Francisco, is
detained with others for several days in Pago Pago on the island of
Tutuila, where the incessant rain oppresses them.   A zealous missionary believes he must save her soul, but in trying to do so, falls
a victim to her physical attractiveness.   Tortured by a sense of
guilt, he kills himself.   Instead of returning to San Francisco as
persuaded by him, Sadie feels free and leaves with the handsome
marine for Sydney for a fresh start.
    3 acts; 10 men, 5 women; 1 interior.   Royalty: $50-25.

_____.   <u>The Shanghai Gesture</u> (1926).   Boni, 1926.
    A Chinese princess was sold down the river to the junkmen
by a Britisher with whom she eloped.   Twenty years later, as Madame Goddam, she invites the same Britisher and his friends to
dinner, and before their eyes she sells a white girl to the junkmen;
then she informs him that she is his own daughter.   The girl has
become a dope fiend and degenerate; Mme. Goddam strangles her to
death.
    4 acts; 9 men, 8 women; 4 interiors; some Chinese cos-
tumes.

CONGREVE, William.   <u>Love for Love</u> (1695).   In Mermaid ser.,
    Scribner; in World's classics, Oxford; CAR; MIL; STM; TWE;
    BEL, v. 4; BRI, v. 2; DIB, v. 6; INCH, v. 13.
    Angelica, who has not acknowledged her love, believes that
Valentine is in love with her, though he pretends to be insane and
unable to sign over his inheritance to pay his debts.   She induces
her father to propose; she gets possession of the bond; but tears
it up when Valentine admits he is sane and ready to marry her.
Many characters are introduced, representing the affectations and
foibles of English society of that day, such as Tattle, Mrs. Frail,
Prue, and Ben Legend with his sea talk.
    5 acts; 11 men, 6 women, extras; 2 interiors; costumes of
the period.

_____.   <u>The Way of the World</u> (1700).   Acting edn, Baker, 1928;
    in his <u>Collected Works</u>; in Mermaid ser., Scribner; in World's
    classics, Oxford; ASH; BEL v. 2; GOSA; LIE; MAT; MCM; MOR;
    MOSE v. 1; NET; RUB; SMO; STM; TAU; TRE-1, & 2 (v. 2);

TREA-1; TUQ; TWE.

A philosophical gentleman, Mirabell, is in love with Millamant, but her aunt and guardian, Lady Wishfort, being angry at
Mirabell, threatens to deprive Millamant of her inheritance. Mirabell plots to have the stingy and tyrannical town coquette (Lady W.)
fall in love with Sir Rowland (really his servant in disguise); but he
also saves Lady Wishfort's fortune from the scheming Fainall. As
a comedy of manners, it is frequently revived.

5 acts; 6 men, 8 women; extras; 2 interiors, 1 exterior; costumes of the period.

CONKLE, E. P. Prologue to Glory (1938). BP 1937-38; Samuel
French.

Young Abe Lincoln at 22 is a rail-splitter who clerks in a
store at New Salem. He falls in love with Ann Rutledge and through
her influence becomes aware of his powers as he makes an election-
eering trip through Illinois.

8 scenes in 3 acts; 14 men, 7 women, extras; 1 interior,
5 exteriors. Royalty: $25-20.

_____. Two Hundred Were Chosen (1936). Samuel French, 1937.

To colonize Matanuska in Alaska, two hundred families were
located there in 1935 under the Army's direction. At first the living quarters were poor and fever broke out, but they are won over
to the government by Jim Conwell, a civil employee, and Jennie
Walters, a sane woman worker.

3 acts; 25 men, 7 women; 1 exterior (U.S. Govt. camp).

CONNELLY, Marc. Beggar on Horseback. See entry under Kaufman,
George S.

_____. Dulcy. See entry under Kaufman, George S.

_____. The Farmer Takes a Wife. See entry under Elser, Frank
B.

_____. The Green Pastures (1930). Based on Roark Bradford's
"Ol Man Adam and His Chillun." BP 1929-30; Dramatists Play
Service.

Pulitzer Prize play 1930. Effective expression of the Negro's
idea of creation, the flood, and the history of the world up to the
coming of Christ, adapted from material in "Ol' Man Adam an' His
Chillun" by Roark Bradford. The non-Biblical Hezdrel is a unique
conception, as well as the development of the idea of mercy and forgiveness through suffering.

18 scenes in 2 parts; 44 men, 10 women, children & extras;
5 interiors, 10 exteriors. Royalty: $35-25.

_____. Merton of the Movies. See entry under Kaufman, George
S.

_____. To the Ladies! See entry under Kaufman, George S.

_____. The Wisdom Tooth (1926). BP 1925-26; Samuel French.
    Bemis, an unsuccessful clerk of 30, has become a "yes-man"
and thinks of following each suggestion about his wisdom tooth. He
believes he is a failure and fears to ask for a raise which might
bring about his discharge. In his dreams he goes back to his grand-
parents and to his childhood successes. He awakens to make a
fresh start; he will go to his own dentist about his tooth. He is encouraged by Sally who now believes in him, which adds to his self-
respect.
    3 acts; 19 men, 10 women; 5 interiors. Royalty: $25-20.

CONNERS, Barry. Applesauce (1925). Samuel French.
    Small town folk show optimism and ability to tell others how
nice they are--it's applesauce. Hazel is really in love with Bill who
is hard up, but she has become engaged to Jenkins. But Bill
achieves success and also happiness as Hazel's future husband.
    3 acts; 4 men, 3 women; 2 interiors. Royalty: $25-20.

_____. The Patsy (1925). Samuel French.
    Blamed when anything goes wrong and playing second fiddle
to her older sister, Patricia is rescued from being the patsy by her
father, a traveling man who returns to find how things stand. She
wins the love of the man she wants--after studying a book on personality and being coached on how to do it.
    3 acts; 5 men, 4 women; 1 interior. Royalty: $25-20.

COPPEL, Alec. The Gazebo (1959). Based on a story by Alec and
    Myra Coppel. Dramatists Play Service.
    A television writer of mystery drama, a man always on the
lookout for "perfect crime" plots, has a wife who is being black-
mailed. Putting his story creation talents into direct action, he
murders the blackmailer and hides the body in a gazebo his wife is
having installed in the back yard. There are others, however, who
are interested in the gazebo. And soon the body gets stashed in the
middle of the living room. Things become further complicated when
the district attorney and detectives arrive and begin asking questions.
    9 men, 3 women; 1 interior. Royalty: $50-35.

COOK, Peter. Beyond the Fringe. See entry under Bennett, Alan.

COOPER, Giles. Everything in the Garden. See entry under Albee,
    Edward.

COOPER, Susan, with Hume Cronyn and Jonathan Holtzman. Fox-
    fire (1983). BP 1982-83; Samuel French.
    Most of the action in this play takes place on the front porch
of a farm called "Stony Lonesome," high in the Blue Ridge Mountain
territory of Rabun County, Georgia, and the home of 79-year-old

Annie Nations. The real estate people are trying to get her to sell out for an upscale housing development, and her son, Dillard, a folksinger playing the hillbilly role to the hilt, is trying to get her to move to Florida so he can watch out for her and she can help him with the children his wife has abandoned him with. What she would really rather do is to stay on the homestead and talk with Hector, her husband who has been dead for five years, whom she has "called back" from the grave where he is buried beneath the orchard. People know, but do not call her on the fiction that he is present-- which indeed he is on stage. Old Hector proves to be a strong, proud, and colorful man. When Annie reminds him that he is not really alive but buried in the orchard, he quips, "Was you brung me down." In addition, we see him interact with Dillard and other characters in various memory scenes and flashbacks until Annie decides to leave the family place and loses the ability to hear what the old man is saying.

  2 acts; 4 men, 2 women, 2 musicians; 1 exterior. Royalty: $60-40.

CORMACK, Bartlett. The Racket (1927). French, 1928; BP 1927- 28.

  A Chicago police captain, McQuigg, fights it out with the local gangster and powerful crook, Nick Scarsi. The play exposes with all the fervor of a muckraker the vice of linking city politics and crime.

  3 acts; 19 men, 1 woman, 2 interiors.

CORMAN, Eugene. The Two Orphans. See entry under d'Ennery, Adolphe P.

CORNEILLE, Pierre. The Cid (1636). Tr. by Landis & Henderson in Six Plays by Corneille and Racine, Modern Lib., 1931; tr. by Cooper in CLF-2; SMN; tr. by Lockert, Princeton Univ. Press, 1952.

  The conqueror of the Moors, declared the Cid (Comander-in- chief), is the lover of Chimène. He feels he must revenge an insult to his father and in the duel which follows he kills her father. She is torn between loyalty to her father and her love for Rodrigo. When he fights another duel with Don Sanche, who does so for Chimène, he will not injure the champion of Chimène; and she shows her love for him.

  5 acts; 7 men, 4 women, 1 page; 1 interior; costumes of the period.

_____. Cinna (1640). Tr. by Landis in Six Plays by Corneille and Racine, Modern Lib., 1931; KRE; tr. by Lockert, Princeton Univ. Press, 1952.

  Cinna, the grandson of Pompey, plots with Maximus to kill the Emperor Augustus if he may have Amelia as his reward. Augustus forgives them both and wins them to his side.

  5 acts; 6 men, 3 women; scenes in Rome; costumes of the period.

_____. Polyeucte (ca. 1641). Tr. by Nokes, Hachette, 1885; tr. by Constable in HARC v. 26; STA; tr. by Lockert, Princeton Univ. Press, 1952.

In Armenia, which the Romans had conquered in the days of the Emperor Decius (250 A.D.), Polyeucte, a Christian general, has married Pauline, the daughter of the Roman governor Felix. Polyeucte and Nearchus as Christians attack the idols of the Roman gods and are condemned to death. They go as willing martyrs. This so impresses Pauline that she becomes converted to Christianity and wins others to that belief.

5 acts; 7 men, 2 women, extras; scenes in the palace; costumes of the period.

CORWIN, Norman. The Rivalry (1960). Dramatists Play Service.

A dramatized presentation of the great debates between Lincoln and Stephen Douglas when they were campaigning for the Illinois Senatorship. These debates were held in seven Congressional districts during the campaign and attracted nationwide attention. The issues were not only partisan but also concerned basic questions of states rights vs. human rights. Douglas favored the right of separate states to make their own choice on the question of slavery. Although perhaps not quite the orator Douglas was, Lincoln's deep conviction that the nation could not endure half slave, half free added a tone of compelling sincerity to his arguments. In addition to the presentation of the political issues, this drama also shows the personal relationships and the changes of attitudes that developed during the debates.

2 men, 1 woman, 3 bit parts; no scenery; series of platforms. Royalty: $50-25.

COWARD, Noel. Blithe Spirit (1941). BP 1941-42; Samuel French.

Charles invites a medium to his home who summons back Elvira, his first wife of seven years ago. The wraith of Elvira torments him until Ruth, his second wife, is convinced that he is losing his mind. Elvira plots to get him to join her in the spirit world by a planned auto accident, which kills Ruth instead. Now he has two blithe spirits from whom to extricate himself.

3 acts; 2 men, 5 women; 1 interior. Royalty: $50-25.

_____. Come into the Garden Maud. See Noel Coward in Two Keys.

_____. Design for Living (1933). Doubleday, 1933; in his Play Parade, Doubleday, 1933; BP 1932-33; SIXH.

Three comrades in Paris, Gilda, Otto, and Leo, live a Bohemian life, taking outrageous liberties with established moral standards, until the two men leave on a freighter. An art connoisseur, Ernest, marries Gilda and they go to New York. The two wandering men reappear, cause Ernest to break with Gilda, and the three are left again to carry on their mad career.

3 acts; 7 men, 4 women; 3 interiors.

_____. Fallen Angels (1925). Samuel French.

A charming Frenchman asks to see two former mistresses together and provokes a chain of funny episodes in this sophisticated comedy. Julia and Jane are now both happily married, but Maurice's coming visit to London has them in a dither of excitement as they quarrel, make up, get high on champagne, and nervously await Maurice's arrival. He finally shows up, very late. Then the husbands return unexpectedly and the action becomes even more comic.
3 men, 3 women; 1 interior. Royalty: $50-25.

_____. Hay Fever (1925). Samuel French.

The Bliss family is ultra-Bohemian, headed by Judith, the mother and retired actress, who still plays many roles: neglected wife, sacrificing mother, sad but glamorous woman. Each of the family invites a guest for a week-end; it proves wild indeed, and all get mixed up in the free and easy life of the Bliss family. The guests stand it as long as they can and then escape back to London.
3 acts; 4 men, 5 women; 1 interior. Royalty: $50-25.

_____. I'll Leave It to You (1920). Samuel French.

A rather destitute widow with five grown-up children turns to her bachelor brother Daniel who has returned from South America, reputedly wealthy. Uncle Daniel says his doctor has given him only three years to live and that he will leave his money to the one who has made good. The rivalry spurs each to work and to win success; but his supposed riches are a myth. Nevertheless his plan has succeeded in rousing the family from its lethargy.
3 acts; 4 men, 6 women; 1 interior. Royalty: $35-25.

_____. Noel Coward in Two Keys (1966). BP 1973-74; Samuel French.

(Consists of two one-acts: "Come Into the Garden Maud" and "A Song at Twilight," which have the same set and the same number of actors.) In the first play, an awful American social-climbing wife is left by her husband--rich but uninterested in high society-- when he decides to go away with a woman who has real class. When he makes this decision, he and his wife are staying at a fashionable private suite in a luxurious Swiss hotel. In the second play, the occupants of the suite are another man and wife--a famous author and his wife of convenience. One of his former loves arrives, ostensibly asking for his permission to publish the letters he once wrote to her in her autobiography. He refuses, and then she reveals that she has another set of love letters--the ones he wrote to his homosexual lover. The writer's wife is able to take care of the whole matter.
2 men, 2 women; 1 interior. Royalty: $25-25 for the first play, $50-25 for the other.

_____. Nude with Violin (1956). Samuel French.

A great painter's death brings out a bizarre assortment of avaricious friends and relatives all eager for a share of his glory and his money. After they have all gathered, the painter's valet, Sebastian, startles the entire group with some jolting revelations about his former master. This leads to confession from other characters, like an eccentric Russian princess and an ex-show girl. When they are finished, reputations have been arranged and rearranged and Sebastian ends up with a sizable nest egg for his old age.

　　　　8 men, 6 women; 1 interior. Royalty: $50-25.

_____. "Peace in Our Time" (1947). Samuel French.
　　　　After the Nazis have conquered England and are in control, assorted people are depicted: the weak surrender to the enticements of the Nazis; the strong grow stubborn and rebellious. A resistance movement develops. With ironic justice, Americans and British Colonials storm onto England's shore to save the motherland and establish peace.

　　　　22 men, 13 women; 4 exteriors. Royalty: $50-25.

_____. Present Laughter (1946). Samuel French.
　　　　A popular actor, Garry Essendine, is called on by a stage-struck youngster, Daphne. While entertaining her, how is he to explain to his wife, his partners, his other admirers? He locks Daphne in a room and flees with his wife.

　　　　3 acts; 5 men, 6 women; 1 interior. Royalty: $50-25.

_____. Private Lives (1931). Samuel French.
　　　　Elyot Chase, arriving with his bride Sybil at a hotel on the Riviera, discovers his first wife Amanda (divorced five years before) as bride to Victor Prynne in the adjoining apartment and balcony. Elyot and Amanda suddenly realize they are still desperately in love with each other; so they run away to her flat in Paris. Here Victor and Sybil catch up with them, but they leave them for a second time.

　　　　3 acts; 2 men, 3 women; 2 interiors. Royalty: $50-25.

_____. Relative Values (1951). Samuel French.
　　　　Miranda, an American movie actress, is going to marry an English earl. But during a dinner party at the nobleman's home, a visitor arrives, Don--an actor and former flame of Miranda's. She tries to send Don away, but the Countess, who is not thrilled at the thought of Miranda as a daughter-in-law, encourages Don and invites him to stay over night. The engagement is broken soon after, when the maid shows up Miranda's pretenses by revealing that they are sisters. Don and Miranda go off together at the end.

　　　　5 men, 5 women; 1 interior. Royalty: $50-25.

_____. A Song at Twilight. See Noel Coward in Two Keys.

_____. This Happy Breed (1943). Samuel French.
　　　　Depicts incidents in the life of the Gibbons family (English middle class) over the 20-year period from 1919 to 1939. They are

ordinary folk, loyal to each other and their country, with common
devotion and a sense of responsibility for the happiness of others,
and showing England quiet and firm in its moments of crisis. Three
generations are presented: the querulous grandmother, Frank Gibbons and his wife Ethel; his sister Sylvia, a hypochondriac nuisance
till she becomes fairly happy and smug with her new-found religion;
and the three children, each with their problems, especially Queenie,
who runs away but settles down to marry Billy next door.
     6 men, 6 women; 1 interior. Royalty: $50-25.

_____. Waiting in the Wings (1960). Samuel French.
     Jealousies arise in a home for retired actresses in this
comedy, but the tragedy of one of their number brings them to their
senses. With the construction of a new solarium, their life becomes
so pleasant that one of the actresses even chooses to spend the rest
of her days there rather than join her son and his family in Canada.
     4 men, 14 women; 1 interior. Royalty: $50-25.

_____. The Young Idea (1923). Samuel French.
     After fourteen years George Brent's son and daughter come
to visit their father in England, having been brought up in Italy by
his divorced wife Jennifer. They force a break by their antics between their father (who is restive and unhappy) and his not too
happy second wife Cicely; they irritate her so much that she elopes
with a co-respondent. They also cause a break between their mother
and an American to whom she has become engaged. Then they bring
their father and mother together again in Italy.
     3 acts; 7 men, 7 women; 2 interiors. Royalty: $25.

COWEN, Lenore Coffee and William J. Cowen. Family Portrait
    (1939). BP 1938-39; Samuel French.
     Introduces the family and friends of Jesus during His last
three years. He is misunderstood--by His brothers in Nazareth
who blame him for leaving at the height of the building season;--by
the promoters in Capernaeum who wish to capitalize on His popularity;--by the fickle crowd in Jerusalem who sing hosannas on Palm
Sunday but turn against Him later in the week. All His family save
His mother have feelings of delusion, failure, and disgrace; but Mary
knows that some of His followers are continuing His work.
     3 acts; 12 men, 10 women; 1 interior, 3 exteriors; Biblical
costumes. Royalty: $35-25.

COWEN, William J. Family Portrait. See entry under Cowen,
    Lenore Coffee.

COXE, Louis O., with Robert Chapman. Billy Budd (1950). Based
    on Herman Melville's short story. BP 1950-51; Dramatists Play
    Service.
     Billy Budd, a young, handsome orphan, is impressed from a
British merchant ship to serve on the H.M.S. Indomitable. The time
is 1798, and England is at war with France. Billy is as innocent and

pure as John Claggart, the Master-at-Arms, is vicious and evil, and soon Claggart is working overtime to bring the young sailor to ruin. When this bit of evil proves difficult, Claggart accuses Billy of mutiny, lying to his face in front of Captain Starry Veere. Billy, who stammers when he's nervous, can't even speak to defend himself, and in his inarticulate rage strikes Claggart and kills him with a single blow. Though the Captain and the remaining officers know how innocent Billy is and how awful Claggart was, under the Mutiny Act even striking an officer calls for the death penalty. Stuck between their human instincts and the law, Veere persuades the drumhead court to sentence Billy to hang. On his way up the ropes, Billy calls out for his near-rebellious crewmembers to hear: "God Bless Captain Veere."

    3 acts; 22 men; 2 interiors, 1 exterior; costumes of the British Navy, 1798. Royalty: $50-25.

CRAVEN, Frank. The First Year (1920). BP 1920-21; Samuel French.
    One of the longest-running plays in the history of Broadway, this drama deals with the adjustments that Tommy and Grace have to make during their first year of marriage and the social and domestic difficulties that result from their move from a small town to a big city.
    5 men, 4 women; 2 interiors. Royalty: $25.

CREIGHTON, Anthony. Epitaph for George Dillon. See entry under Osborne, John.

CRICHTON, Kyle. The Happiest Millionaire (1957). Suggested by Cordelia Drexel Biddle and Kyle Crichton's My Philadelphia Father. Dramatists Play Service.
    Anthony J. Drexel Biddle is a Philadelphia millionaire described as having an enthusiasm for lunacy. Mr. Biddle collects alligators and prizefighters and rules his family by blustery gruffness. "You yelled, sir?" is the butler's standard response when Mr. Biddle summons. He also tries to rule his daughter, Cordelia, but when she falls in love with the multi-millionaire Southern boy, Angier Duke, he meets defeat. Mr. Biddle, an ardent amateur boxer, has no use for his prospective son-in-law because he knows nothing about boxing. Angier, however, turns to ju-jitsu and throws a professional boxer as well as Mr. Biddle to the floor. This wins Biddle's heart and he is resigned to losing his daughter.
    9 men, 6 women; 1 interior. Royalty: $50-25.

CRONYN, Hume. Foxfire. See entry under Cooper, Susan.

CROTHERS, Rachel. As Husbands Go (1931). BP 1930-31; Samuel French.
    Meeting two super-gigolos in Paris, two ladies from Dubuque rediscover romance; Lucile, married to a rather dullish business man, meets the Englishman, Ronald, who thinks mostly of himself;

Emmie, still an attractive widow, meets Hippolitus the Frenchman. Returning to crude America with these two friends, the ladies perceive the striking contrast between American and continental concepts of marriage. Lucile stays with her husband, but Emmie marries Hippolitus.
3 acts; 7 men, 5 women; 3 interiors. Royalty: $50-25.

_____. Expressing Willie (1924). Baker, 1925; in her Expressing Willie & other plays, Brentano, 1924; COT.
The son of a successful toothpaste manufacturer, Willie invites a group of faddists to a week-end party in the hope that they will help him to express himself. Despite this cult of self-expression, through his mother's shrewdness and a girl's unselfish love, Willie discovers Minnie and saves his money.
3 acts; 6 men, 5 women; 2 interiors.

_____. He and She (1911). Revised form 1920. Baker, 1933; QUIK; QUIL.
A story of woman's rights and responsibilities, centering about one who is artist, wife, and mother. Rivalry and professional jealousy are conflicting interests. Her design wins over her husband's, but she declines the commission.
3 acts; 3 men, 5 women; 2 interiors (1 interior possible).

_____. Let Us Be Gay (1929). BP 1928-29; Samuel French.
Although Bob declares their own love has been and is sincere and untouched, Kitty divorces him when she discovers he has been unfaithful. Three years later she is asked to rescue a girl from what is thought to be mistaken love for a certain man. To Kitty's surprise and chagrin he turns out to be her former husband, Bob. After some confusion, they become reconciled, a more tolerant pair.
3 acts; 7 men, 5 women; 2 interiors. Royalty: $50.

_____. A Little Journey (1918). French, 1923; in her Mary the Third, Brentano, 1923.
Through a railroad accident to a sleeping car bound from New York to the Pacific coast, a young woman, Julie, learns a lesson in human kindness and the joy of service; she also wins Jim as a husband.
3 acts; 8 men, 7 women; 1 interior, 1 exterior.

_____. Mary the Third (1923). Baker, 1925; in her Mary the Third and other plays, Brentano, 1923; DIG; TUCD; TUCJ; & TUCM: BP 1922-23.
Reveals the differences in points of view of three generations. Mary's grandmother mated by the lure of physical attraction; her mother married the most insistent of her lovers. Mary the Third intends to determine her marriage by considerations of economics and eugenics (even by trial). But she chooses her mate because she thinks he needs her; romantic love triumphs.

Prolog & 3 acts; 5 men, 5 women; 2 interiors.

_____. Nice People (1920). In her Expressing Willie & other
plays, Brentano, 1924; MOSJ; MOSL; QUI; BP 1920-21.
Presents an unflinching picture of the idle rich in their mad
search for pleasure, and of the flapper, her manners and morals
and lack of restraint. Teddy gets stranded with Scotty at the family's cottage in Westchester, into which Billy comes out of the storm.
Scandal seems about to land on Teddy, but a way out is shown by
the clean-cut Billy to the girl who is better than her background
though still of it.
3 acts; 6 men, 4 women; 2 interiors, 1 exterior.

_____. "Old Lady 31" (1916). French, 1923; in her Mary the
Third & other plays, Brentano, 1923.
Abe and Angie, an aged couple, must leave their little house;
she to go to the Old Ladies Home, he to the Poor Farm five miles
away. At the Home, Blossy proposes that she give up her big room
and let the couple stay. (Abe to be "Old Lady 31.") It works out
fairly well. He encourages Blossy to marry Sam Darby after thirty
years of courting. In the end, his 20-year-old stock pays off, and
they can go back to their old home.
Prolog & 3 acts; 4 men, 10 women; 1 interior, 2 exteriors.

_____. Susan and God (1937). BP 1937-38. Dramatists Play
Service.
A flighty social butterfly, Susan, returns from Europe, en-
thusiastic over a new religious cult, which she has taken up as a
sort of escape from an alcoholic husband. But Barrie, the husband,
is now contrite and wants to be included in this new way of salvation. So Susan must now put her religion into practice or admit
insincerity. She makes a home for her husband and her neglected
daughter, and in reclaiming her family she finds happiness and also
her God.
3 acts: 5 men, 6 women, 3 interiors. Royalty: $35-25.

_____. 39 East (1919). Baker, 1925; in her Expressing Willie
& other plays, Brentano, 1924.
In the boarding house at 39 East, romance comes to plucky
Penelope Penn who has come to New York to sing and dance but can
only get a job as a chorus girl. She is determined to stick it out.
Well-to-do Napoleon Gibbs stays on at the house just to be near her;
then he proposes to her and assures the landlady that Penelope is
really a good girl; so she takes her under her protection. The gos-
sipy boarders nearly wreck the romance.
3 acts; 6 men, 8 women; 2 interiors, 1 exterior.

_____. When Ladies Meet (1932). Samuel French.
A tolerant wife and a prospective mistress discuss an imaginary case of a philandering husband, without knowing their common
interest in the same man. Rogers loses them both when the wife

suspects and leaves him and the other no longer trusts him.
3 acts; 4 men, 3 women; 2 interiors. Royalty: $50-25.

CROUSE, Russel. Life with Father. See entry under Lindsay,
Howard.

_____. Life with Mother. See entry under Lindsay, Howard.

_____. Remains To Be Seen. See entry under Lindsay, Howard.

_____. State of the Union. See entry under Lindsay, Howard.

_____. Tall Story. See entry under Lindsay, Howard.

CROWLEY, Mart. The Boys in the Band (1968). Samuel French.
In this play a homosexual lifestyle is taken for granted.
Michael invites some of his gay friends over for a birthday party
in honor of one of them. (The present the birthday boy likes best,
by the way, is a male hustler, prepaid for the entire evening.)
The conflict comes by way of Michael's old college roommate, who
is straight, and who comes to the party uninvited and beats up the
most effeminate of the guests. Michael is sure that his old roommate is merely a homosexual who has never emerged from the
closet, so he devises a game which will let him "come out." The
game backfires, and Michael is left swimming in his own guilt.
9 men; 1 interior. Royalty: $50-35.

CUMBERLAND, Richard. The West Indian (1771). HAN; MCM;
MIL; MOR; collections: BEL v. 18; BRI v. 2; DIB v. 12; INCH
v. 18; OXB v. 1.
Brings Belcour from a plantation in the West Indies to London, where, as a child of nature, he has many adventures. The
other hero is an Irishman, Major O'Flaherty. Presents an attack
on dueling as a way of satisfying one's honor.
5 acts; 9 men, 6 women, extras; 6 interiors; costumes of
the period.

CUNNINGHAM, Derek. Bullshot Crummond. See entry under House,
Ron.

CUREL, François de. A False Saint (1892). Tr. by Clark, Doubleday, 1916.
Julie tried to kill a rival who had won her sweetheart, after
which she renounced the world and became a nun. Hearing that her
former lover was dead, she comes out of the cloister, wishing to
hear some message of tender sentiment from him. She meets Christine, the daughter of the woman she hated and the man she loved,
and the old resentment flares up; she becomes a spiteful vixen and
shows little that is saintly. But when she hears Christine repeat
her father's dying message of love, she encourages Christine to find
happiness in love. Julie returns to the convent content.

3 acts; 1 man, 5 women; 1 interior.

_____. The Fossils (1892). Tr. by Clark in Four Plays of the Free Theatre, Stewart & Kidd, 1914, Appleton, 1915; WATI-1.

An aristocratic Duke has retired with his wife, son, and daughter to a lonely castle in Northern France, where the family is in danger of becoming fossilized. The Duke has intrigues with Hélène the governess, but she falls in love with Robert, his son, by whom she has a child. Robert marries Hélène to give the boy the family name. Father and son quarrel over the boy's education; shall it be with the Duke or with Hélène? Certain to die soon of tuberculosis, Robert commits the care of his wife and son to his sister Claire and goes from Nice to the castle in the north where he dies. They give up happiness and honor to save the family name.

4 acts; 6 men, 4 women; 2 interiors.

DALE, Jim. Scapino. See entry under Dunlop, Frank.

DALY, Augustin. A Night Off (1885). Dick & Fitzgerald; French, c1897.

An old staid college professor wants to have his play produced. The tragedian-manager of a wandering theatrical company undertakes to put it on. The professor's wife objects and tries to prevent this. It is produced, but its run is "For one night only."

4 acts; 6 men, 5 women; 2 interiors.

DALZELL, William, with Anne Coulter Martens. Onions in the Stew (1956). Adapted from Betty MacDonald's novel. Dramatic Publishing Company.

High School Theater Classic, 1950-59, about a city family moving to a remove island home. Betty MacDonald has talked her husband and two attractive teen-age daughters into sinking every cent they have into this Puget Sound island home. They soon yearn for the city life they have left behind. The first day the tide comes in unexpectedly and washes half of their possessions out to sea. The girls are afraid they'll never have dates again because who wants to go out to an island to pick up a date? Betty is completely miserable at having brought this apparent disaster on them all. Yet, in the midst of the humorous difficulties, the family finds a special value in the life they are creating.

7 men, 11 women, extras optional; 1 interior. Royalty: $35-25.

DANE, Clemence. A Bill of Divorcement (1921). Lond., Heinemann, & Macmillan, 1921; French carried; COT; MAP, MOSO; BP 1921-22.

Under the terms of an English marriage law (assumed to be in effect), a husband or wife adjudged hopelessly insane may be divorced. On the eve of her remarriage, her divorced husband appears, cured after 18 years. Their daughter, learning of insanity in her father's family, true to the teachings of eugenics, gives up

her own idea of marriage and devotes herself to her father.
3 acts; 5 men, 4 women; 1 interior.

_____. Will Shakespeare (1921). Lond., Heinemann, & Macmillan, 1922.
Attempts to explain his literary power, his genius, and his rise to fame. Not founded on historical facts, for it depicts him as disillusioned with Anne Hathaway, as having ill-luck with Mary Fitton, the dark lady of the sonnets, and as the accidental slayer of Christopher Marlowe.
4 acts; 6 men, 5 women, 2 boys, many extras; 6 interiors; costumes of the period.

DAVIDSON, William. Brother Goose (1942). Dramatic Publishing Company.
High School Theater Classic, 1945-49. Jeff Adams is an architect and sole supporter of his orphaned brothers and sisters. He has been commissioned by Lenore Hudson to build her a new house on the neighborhood football lot. Lenore wants Jeff as a husband, but his brothers and sisters hate her for ruining their football field. Jeff discovers that he really doesn't want Lenore and her inherited million dollars. He's in love with Peggy, a poor girl who turns up one day at the Adams house selling hosiery but stays on to care for the children as a maid.
3 men, 9 women; 1 interior. Royalty: $35-25.

DAVIES, Hubert Henry. Cousin Kate (1903). Lond., Heinemann, & Boston, Baker, 1910; in his Plays, Chatto, 1921, v. 1.
Two days before her marriage with the artist Heath Desmond, Amy quarrels with him and he leaves. Returning, he encounters on the train her cousin Kate Curtis, who is unaware that he was Amy's fiancé. When Kate finds that out and they quarrel, she tries to reunite them, engaging in a delightful sparring love match with Heath. But Amy decides she is cut out more as a clergyman's wife than an artist's, so Kate can accept Heath.
3 acts; 3 men, 4 women, 2 interiors.

_____. The Mollusc (1907). Lond., Heinemann, 1907; Baker, 1914; in his Plays, Chatto, 1921, v. 2; DIG.
Skillfully details the process of energizing the invertebrate wife who spends all her ingenuity and even huge exertions to avoid being disturbed--mollusk-like, in order to stick instead of to move. She is reformed by her determined brother.
3 acts; 2 men, 2 women; 1 interior.

_____. A Single Man (1910). Baker, 1914; in his Plays, Chatto, 1921, v. 2.
Robin, a bachelor in his forties and a writer, sees how happy his younger brother is with his wife and thinks he might also marry. He looks around and picks Maggie Cottrell, age 17. His secretary for five years, Miss Heseltine, has been devoted to him,

but he has accepted her as part of his business. He becomes engaged to Maggie, but can't keep up with her youthful activities.
When Miss Heseltine brings back a typed article and is asked to
stay to supper, his eyes are opened to her good qualities. He
wants to break his engagement, but Maggie does it for him; and all
ends happily.
    4 acts; 3 men, 9 women; 2 interiors.

DAVIOT, Gordon. Richard of Bordeaux (1932). Gollancz, London,
    1933; Little, 1933; French, 1935; FAMD.
    Richard II, King of England, was born in Bordeaux, France,
and was far more French in his tastes and sympathies than an English hero. In his 19th year he rebelled against his guardian uncle,
John of Gaunt, dreaming of an England peaceful and rich and
wishing to avoid foreign wars, but he is beaten down by the nobles.
His gentle wife, Anne of Bohemia, and his best friend, Robert de
Vere, side with him, till both die. Then he overplays his luck, is
forced to abdicate, and dies in prison.
    12 scenes in 2 parts; 23 men, 6 women, extras; 10 interiors,
    1 exterior.

DAVIS, Bill C. Mass Appeal (1982). BP 1981-82; Dramatists Play
    Service.
    Mark Dolson, a young seminarian, shows up one day for the
dialogue sermon at Father Tim Farley's church, trying to engage the
middle-aged priest in debate. It is the first in a series of confrontations in which the older man is scolded for his heavy wine
habit and reminded of all of the compromises he has made with his
parishioners and the church hierarchy to remain popular and further
his career. In the meantime, Mark has defended two of his fellow
seminarians suspected of homosexuality too vigorously, and has admitted to Monsignor Burke (in spite of Father Farley's urging to lie)
that before he entered the seminary he had had sexual encounters
with both men and women. As a result, Mark is expelled, but Father
Tim finds the courage to defy the Monsignor, admit to his parishioners that he has lost Christ, and seek their help in fighting to
have Mark reinstated.
    2 acts; 2 men; unit set. Royalty: $50-40.

DAVIS, Hallie Flanagan, assisted by Sylvia Gassel and Day Tuttle.
    E=MC^2 (1947). Samuel French.
    Utilizing the "Living Newspaper" technique, this play shows
the past, present, and future of the atom bomb. Through dramatic
scenes, music and movies, it explains the nature of atomic power,
its potential for constructive use, and closes with a reminder of our
responsibility to use it wisely.
    6 men, 2 women, 20 or more extras. Various sets. Royalty:
    $25-20.

DAVIS, Ossie. Purlie Victorious (1961). Samuel French.
    Pokes fun at the popular clichés of the Old South and the

warm relationship between plantation owners and their slaves. The plot deals with Purlie Victorious's attempts to reacquire the local church and ring the freedom bell. Unfortunately, the plantation owner stands in the way of this plan, but by the end of the play he is defeated. As Purlie is about to beat the Southern colonel with the white man's own whip, the advice he is given is (as a sample of the play's dialogue): "You can't do wrong just because it's right."

    6 men, 3 women; exterior and 2 composites. Royalty: $50-25.

DAVIS, Owen. <u>The Detour</u> (1921). Samuel French.

    Sincerely and realistically depicts the revolt of a strong-willed woman against the narrowness of her life in New England, and her determination to secure a fuller life for her daughter. When these hopes come to nothing, she looks forward to her dreams being realized in her grandchild.

    5 men, 4 women; 1 interior, 1 exterior. Royalty: $25.

_____. <u>The Donovan Affair</u> (1926). Samuel French.

    Having boasted at a dinner party of the luminosity of his turquoise ring, Jack Donovan has the lights turned out so as to see it in the dark. When the lights come on, Donovan is sprawled on the table, dead, with the game knife in his ribs. Because of the ring's baleful influence, several present might have wished the ring done away with, as well as the owner.

    3 acts; 11 men, 6 women; 1 interior. Royalty: $25.

_____. <u>Ethan Frome</u> (1936). Adapted from Edith Wharton's novel. BP 1935-36; Dramatists Play Service.

    Ethan Frome is saddled with a mean and hypochondriachal wife, Zenobia, who makes his life miserable. Into the household comes a relative of Zenobia's, Mattie Silver, with whom Ethan falls in love. Instead of sending her away as Zenobia insists, Ethan takes Mattie on a romantic sled ride to their death. But death does not occur. Mattie is made an invalid by the accident and takes her turn at the Frome household--screaming at and complaining about her treatment at the hands of Ethan and Zenobia.

    7 men, 4 women, extras; interiors and exteriors. Royalty: $35-25.

_____. <u>The Haunted House</u> (1924). Samuel French.

    Jack and Emily arrive at Emily's father's cottage to spend their honeymoon. Queer sounds are heard in the house, and a murder is committed (Jack's ex-girlfriend). A neighbor, the local sheriff, and a New York detective try to solve the mystery. Several people are arrested, including the bride and her father. Finally everyone takes a truth potion to discover the real culprit.

    8 men, 3 women; 1 interior. Royalty: $25-20.

_____. <u>Icebound</u> (1923). BP 1922-23; Little Brown, 1923; CORF; DIG; HAL.

Pulitzer prize play 1923. The stern unemotional New England family of Jordans have greedy squabbles among themselves, nor do they welcome the return of Ben, the black sheep of the family. They are much put out to find the entire estate of Mother Jordan left to Cousin Jane, who has been caring for her. Jane gets Ben to stay and work on the farm; the drudge proves her mettle, rescues Ben from a life of crime, and makes a man of him. This is what Mother Jordan asked her to do; "to look after him till he is worthy of the money." When Jane announces she is ready to leave and will turn the farm over to Ben, he finds he loves her, and she marries him.

5 men, 6 women, 1 boy or girl; 1 interior.

_____. Mr. and Mrs. North (1941). Based on the stories by
    Frances and Richard Lockridge.
Pam and Gerald North live uneventful lives until a dead body falls out of their closet. Lt. Weigand investigates, hindered rather than helped by Pam, until she herself unmasks the murderer.

16 men, 4 women; 1 interior. Royalty: $35.

_____. The World We Live In. See entry under Capek, Karel.

DAY, Clarence. Life with Father. See entry under Lindsay,
    Howard.

_____. Life with Mother. See entry under Lindsay, Howard.

DAYTON, Katharine and G. S. Kaufman. First Lady (1935). BP
    1935-36; Dramatists Play Service.
Skillfully pictures the interrelation of social and political life in Washington. Irene has stolen Lucy's cook and the feud is on between these two Washington hostesses, each of whom thinks her husband should be in the White House.

3 acts; 14 men, 11 women, extras; 2 interiors. Royalty: $35-25.

DAZEY, Charles T. In Old Kentucky (1892). Fine Book Circle of
    Birmingham, Mich., 1937; released through Dramatists Play
    Service.
A mountain girl, Madge, helps her unfortunate sweetheart Frank out of financial difficulties by riding, disguised as a jockey, his famous horse, Queen Bess, in the Ashland Oaks to victory. This restores the family fortune, and of course they fall in love. The race is viewed through a knothole as Col. Doolittle woos and wins Aunt Lethe after twenty years of courtship. The underhanded villainies of Horace Holton are successfully foiled.

4 acts; 5 men, 3 women, extras; 2 interiors, 6 exteriors; costumes of 1870.

DEANE, Hamilton, with John L. Balderston. Dracula (1927). Based
    on Bram Stoker's novel. Samuel French.
Lucy Seward, daughter of a doctor in charge of an English

sanatorium, suffers from a mysterious illness. A specialist named Dr. Van Helsing believes that the girl has been attacked by a vampire--discovered to be Count Dracula, whose ghost is laid finally to rest in what is touted as a striking and novel manner.

6 men, 2 women; 3 interiors. Royalty: $50-35.

DEKKER, Thomas. Old Fortunatus; or, The Wishing Cap (1600). In his Works, 1873; in his Best Plays, Fisher Unwin; in Mermaid ser., Scribner; in Temple ser., Dutton; SCH.

Lady Fortune offers to the beggar Fortunatus on the brink of starvation his choice of wisdom, strength, long life, health, beauty, or riches. He chooses riches and receives a purse which never runs dry. So he starts on his travels with a wishing cap which will transport him anywhere. Just as life becomes enjoyable, he dies; and his son likewise dies miserably. The gift proves the ruin of both.

5 acts; 15 men, 7 women, extras; many scenes, simple or elaborate (out-of-doors production possible); costumes of the period.

_____. The Shoemakers' Holiday (1599). In his Works, 1873; In his Best Plays, Fisher Unwin; in Mermaid ser., Scribner; BAS, BLO; CLS; COF; DUN; HARC v. 47; HOW; MCI; NEI; PAR; RUB; SCI; SCW; SPE; TAU; WHE.

Rowland Lacy, a young nobleman in love with Rose Oateley, daughter of Sir Roger, disguises himself as a Dutch shoemaker, Hans, and works in a shop with Simon Eyre, having sent a friend to France in his place. He wins Rose. Through Hans, Eyre gets a fortune, becomes sheriff, and then Lord Mayor of London; as such he declares a shoemakers' holiday, feasting all apprentices.

5 acts; 17 men, 4 women, extras; 6 interiors, 8 exteriors; costumes of the period.

DE KRUIF, Paul. Yellow Jack. See entry under Howard, Sidney.

DELANEY, Shelagh. A Taste of Honey (1959). BP 1960-61; POP; SEVD.

When Jo, the illegitimate daughter of Helen, who is "little more than a whore," watches her mother go off again with a new man at Christmas time, she has a brief affair (her first) with a black sailor. Though he promises to marry her, all he leaves her with is an unwanted pregnancy. Geoffrey, a homosexual friend of Jo's, moves in to care for her and plan for the birth of the baby, but Helen returns to join up with her daughter again and kicks Geoffrey out. Then, when she hears that the expected baby had a black father, she goes out for a drink, leaving Jo alone, with labor pains, frightened, and calling Geoffrey's name.

2 acts; 3 men, 2 women; 1 interior.

DELL, Floyd, with Thomas Mitchell. Little Accident (1928). BP 1928-29.

Norman Overbeck has been on the rebound and is about to marry hometown girl Madge Ferris when a letter from a maternity ward in Chicago alerts him to the fact that Isabel Drury, a sophisticated art student he fell in love with in Boston, has had his baby and is putting it up for adoption. Though the whole thing was a "little accident," Norman can't permit his son be adopted no matter what the mother says, and he steals the baby from the hospital and hides away in Chicago. Soon the daughter of his landlady wants to marry him to protect the child, then Isabel wants the baby herself, and finally Madge, whom he left in the lurch at the wedding rehearsal, is willing to take the baby with the groom. As it turns out, Isabel will give up her bohemian notions to be a mother, and Norman will marry her—the only woman he ever really loved.

 3 acts; 7 men, 12 women; 3 interiors.

DEMILLE, H. C. The Lost Paradise. See entry under Fulda, Ludwig.

DeMILLE, William C. Strongheart (1905). French, 1909; abridged in Pierce & Matthews, v. 1.

 Strongheart, the son of an Indian chief, after studying at Carlisle, enters Columbia and stars as halfback. He is suspected of divulging the signals; and his love for the captain's sister is opposed by her family. Just as they decide to be married anyway, his tribe sends for him to become chief, succeeding his father. Torn between love and duty, he finally returns to his people.

 4 acts; 17 men, 5 women; 3 interiors.

DENKER, Henry. A Case of Libel (1963). Based on Louis Nizer's My Life in Court. Samuel French.

 A famous war correspondent sues a widely syndicated newspaper columnist for libel in this successful Broadway melodrama. The columnist, a dedicated defender of the extreme right, has made repeated unjust attacks on the columnist's patriotism and his personal life. The courtroom action centers around the prosecutor's attempts to expose the dangers of extremism and the defense attorney's spirited defense of justice and freedom of speech. The lively arguments and often heated cross-examinations keep a high interest level throughout the play.

 11 men, 3 women, 3 extras; 1 interior/inset. Royalty: $50-25.

_____. A Far Country (1961). BP 1960-61; Samuel French.

 The far country of the title has to do with the unconscious human mind, which 36-year-old Sigmund Freud is probing in 1893 against all established scientific and medical opposition. Even his mother is against the corner he is backing himself into as a Jew in gentile Vienna practicing "witchcraft." Freud is bound, however, to find a way to help Elizabeth von Ritter, who has lost the use of her legs after the death of first her father and then her sister. She does not want to be cured, Freud learns, because of her

feelings of guilt, but by the end of the play she is walking without the use of her crutches. The play is framed by a wheelchair-bound Freud in 1938, who is being ransomed for a quarter of a million schillings so that he can leave Nazi Vienna for England.
3 acts; 6 men, 6 women; 1 interior. Royalty: $50-25.

d'ENNERY, Adolphe P. and Eugène Cormon. The Two Orphans (1873). Adapted by N. H. Jackson. Dramatists Play Service, 1939; CERC.
Henriette and her blind sister Louise become separated as they arrive in Paris from the country. They are taken by abductors; blind Louise is made to beg, Henriette is made the plaything for dissolute nobility. Henriette is saved by Chevalier de Vaudrey who falls in love with her. The sisters search for each other and just miss; they are united in a melodramatic climax.
4 acts; 14 men, 10 women, extras; 4 interiors, 3 exteriors; costumes of the period (1785).

DENNIS, Patrick. Auntie Mame. See entry under Lawrence, Jerome.

DE SILVA, David. Fame. See entry under Sergel, Christopher.

DEVAL, Jacques. Tovarich (1933). Adapted by R. E. Sherwood. BP 1936-37; Samuel French.
Prince Mikail and Grand Duchess Tatiana, White Russians of the Czar's court, are impoverished in Paris, but take service as butler and maid in the home of Charles Dupont, a wealthy banker. The son and daughter of the house are glad to know them, but when their identity is revealed, they seem liable to lose their jobs. The Soviet Gorotchenko persuades Mikail to sign over the Czar's money for the glory and preservation of Russia; and Dupont asks them to stay on as servants. They do not try to return to the aristocracy but continue with the bourgeoisie with whom they happily mingle.
8 men, 7 women; 4 interiors. Royalty: $35-25.

DICKENS, Charles. The Life & Adventures of Nicholas Nickleby. See entry under Edgar, David.

DiFUSCO, John, with Vincent Caristi, Richard Chaves, Eric E. Emerson, Rick Gallavan, Merlin Marston, Harry Stephens, and Sheldon Lettich. Tracers (1985). BP 1984-85.
A work described as "personal improvisation, rap sessions, psycho-drama, physical work, trust and ensemble work," conceived through the improvisational process by Vietnam veterans and then "frozen" in script. The "tracers" of the title are the specific emotions and hangups of the individual vets after their years of training and then fighting in Vietnam. Episodes and incidents of warfare insanity and postwar trauma are played out with a pre-recorded rock score as background.
2 acts; 8 men; various interiors and exteriors.

DINEHART, Alan. Separate Rooms. See entry under Carole, Joseph.

DINELLI, Mel. The Man (1950). Dramatists Play Service.
Mrs. Gillis, a widow who has a rooming house, engages a handy man in Howard Wilton. She takes a motherly interest in him, and he wants to be loved and admired. He proves however to be a psychopathic criminal, and he has lapses, as when he prevents her from sending out any messages to her friends. She is imprisoned by a maniac in her home. The telephone man manages to get a call through to the police, but too late. (Play has an alternative ending, supplied on request.)
2 acts; 5 men, 2 women; 1 interior. Royalty: $50-25.

_____. The Spiral Staircase. See entry under Leslie, F. Andrew.

DODD, Lee Wilson. The Changelings (1923). Dutton, 1924; BP 1923-34.
Two couples, after a quarrel, decide to exchange partners. They are adult in their discussion of feminism and the new freedom, being an editor, a novelist, a publisher, and a college instructor. But they return to their former status.
3 acts & epilog; 6 men, 3 women; 2 interiors.

DONNAY, Maurice. Lovers (1895). Tr. by Clark in his Three Plays, Kennerley, later Little, 1915; also in MOSQ; tr. by Steeves in STE.
Two young people, Vetheuil and Claudine, are passionately devoted to each other, but circumstances prevent them from marrying. Their love buds, blossoms, but it also withers, since life has become as matter of fact as marriage. And so they part; he to marry an heiress, she to retire to the country with a Count, after he has been loosed from an uncongenial wife. The lovers do not allow defection to wreck their lives.
5 acts; 9 men, 6 women, 2 boys, 1 girl; 4 interiors, 1 exterior.

_____. The Other Danger (1902). Tr. by Charlotte T. David in Drama, v. 3, 1913; also in Three Modern Plays from the French, ed. by B. H. Clark, Holt, 1914.
An unhappily married mother, Claire Jadin, takes a lover, Freydières, but for her daughter Madeleine's sake she gives her to him for a husband, sacrificing her own love for him. Freydières finds in the daughter who resembles her mother his first and early love, so mother loses out to her daughter's youth. A thesis play demonstrating that happiness is short-lived, therefore seize it when it comes and accept with calmness its inevitable loss.
4 acts; 10 men, 8 women; 2 interiors, 1 exterior.

DOS PASSOS, John and Paul Shyre. U.S.A. (1960). Based on John

Dos Passos' trilogy. Samuel French.

A panorama of America from 1900 to the stock market crash of 1929. The story is of J. Ward Morehouse, who falls in love with a beautiful girl and works himself up to the top. Interwoven are the headlines and personalities of the period: Henry Ford, Valentino, Debs, the Wright Brothers, Isadora Duncan, the Suffragettes, etc.

3 men, 3 women; cyclorama and platform. Royalty: $50-25.

DRINKWATER, John. Abraham Lincoln (1918). BP 1919-20; Samuel French.

Pictures the beauty and power of Lincoln's soul and his stupendous coping with events as they occur, from accepting the nomination in Springfield, through the war years, pointing up Sumter, the emancipation proclamation, Lee's surrender, and the assassination.

Flexible cast of 30 to 50; 5 interiors. Royalty: $25-20.

_____. Bird in Hand (1927). Samuel French.

Joan, daughter of the proprietor of the Bird in Hand Inn, Thomas Greenleaf, falls in love with the Squire's son, Gerald. Thomas thinks that Gerald is only intending to seduce Joan; she thinks her father's fears ridiculous--she is a modern girl. One night Thomas drags Joan home and sits with three guests of the Inn to straighten matters out and help Thomas to reach a decision. Finally the Squire formally asks Joan to marry his Gerald.

3 acts; 6 men, 2 women; 2 interiors. Royalty: $25.

_____. A Man's House (1934). Lond., Sidgwick, & French, 1935.

Using a modern psychological approach, shows the subtle effect of the teachings of Jesus in a Jewish household in ancient Jerusalem, where youth is open-minded to new ideas but their elders have a well-ordered reactionary philosophy.

3 acts; 12 men, 2 women, extras; 1 interior, costumes of the period.

_____. Mary Stuart (1921). Samuel French.

The play opens with a prolog, that it is possible for some wives to love loyally and devotedly more than one man. The play then fades into Mary Stuart's affair with Riccio, who was killed by her husband Darnley, and points up her later interest in Bothwell. She was not fickle, but had ideals too high for one person to attain: she wanted strength, beauty, and passion--not to be found in one man.

6 men, 2 women; 2 interiors. Royalty: $25-20.

_____. Oliver Cromwell (1921). Lond., Sidgwick, & Houghton, 1921: French carried; in his Collected Plays, Sidgwick, 1925, v. 2; DIG.

Presents the impressive figure of Cromwell through his

military progress until he became Lord Protector of the Commonwealth; when offered the crown, he refused it. He was firm in his single purpose, being heart and soul for the Puritan cause.

    8 scenes; 18 men, 3 women; 7 interiors; costumes of the period (English, 17th century).

_____. Robert E. Lee (1923). Lond., Sidgwick, & Houghton, 1923; French carried; in his Collected Plays, Sidgwick, 1925, v. 2.

    Episodes built around Lee's personality and his momentous choice between command of the Northern or Southern forces. Brings out clearly the grounds on which the two sides rested their cause. Follows Lee's heroic campaigns through to his surrender and farewell to his soldiers.

    9 scenes; 18 men, 3 women; 4 interiors, 4 exteriors; some military costumes of the Civil War.

DRURY, Allen. Advise and Consent. See entry under Mandell, Loring.

DRYDEN, John. All for Love; or, The World Well Lost (1677). In various editions of his plays; BEL v. 13; BRI v. 2; DIB v. 1; DOB; GOSA; HARC v. 18; INCH v. 6; LIE; MAT; MCM; MIL; MOO; MOR; NET; SMN; STM; TAU; TUQ; TWE.

    A fine adaptation of Shakespeare's Anthony and Cleopatra. Centers on the emotions of the royal lovers and their personal reactions. Brings in the efforts of Ventidius, Octavia, and others to win Anthony from Cleopatra.

    5 acts; 8 men, 4 women; extras; 2 interiors; costumes of the period.

DUBERMAN, Martin B. In White America (1964). Samuel French.

    This is a series of enactments from the actual history of the United States. It traces the history of the Negro from slave times to Little Rock. The emotion filled scenes are as follows: The heart of a runaway slave is bared to his master in a letter answering a plea to come home; John Brown, the war and the Emancipation Proclamation; a heart rending account of a molested, widowed Negro woman and her crippled child and the Ku Klux Klan; a southern senator, in all his eloquence, delivers a moving speech justifying a lynching that is the height of emotionalism; Booker T. Washington, DuBoise, Father Divine, and the Scottsboro Case are all sufficient in themselves.

    3 Negroes (2 men, 1 woman); 3 white (2 men, 1 woman); platform stage. Royalty: $35-25.

DUERRENMATT, Friedrich. The Deadly Game. See entry under Yaffe, James.

_____. The Meteor (1964). Translated by James Kirkup. Dramatic Publishing Company.

A Nobel Prize winner named Wolfgang Schwitter has been declared dead twice by medical officials but has somehow come back to life. He ventures to Hugo Nyffenschwander's art studio, where he got his start, to die a real death--but he doesn't die there. Those around him who expect, count on, or look forward to his death begin to drop off like flies, and Schwitter is the cause of these spontaneous deaths. He sleeps with Hugo Nyffenschwander's wife Augusta, which causes Hugo to lunge at Schwitter, but The Great Muheim wants first crack at the author for the same reason, so Muheim throws Hugo down the stairs. Schwitter's third and present wife, Olga, who had been a prostitute before her vows, kills herself because of Schwitter's condition. Jochen, Schwitter's son, comes to Schwitter to collect his 1.5 million dollars, but Schwitter has burned it in the stove. He says he started with nothing and wants to die with nothing. "Hurl me down the steps of Hell!" he raves at the end, as a Salvation Army band plays and sings hymns.

3 acts; 11 men, 3 women; 1 interior. Royalty: $60-40.

_____. The Physicists (1961). Adapted by James Kirkup. BP 1964-65; Samuel French.

Three nuclear physicists in an asylum become pawns in a bizarre spy plot with the world as the stake. While they at first seem harmless lunatics, we soon realize that perhaps one is using the knowledge and disillusionment of the other two for his own selfish ends. In a final frightening episode the woman psychiatrist at the head of the asylum must enact a contrived scene which reveals the plotters.

16 men, 4 women; 1 interior. Royalty: $50-25.

_____. The Visit (1956). Adapted by Maurice Valency. BP 1957-58; Samuel French.

An incredibly wealthy woman returns to her home town and agrees to end its economic woes--for a price. She wants the life of a villager who had led to her expulsion from the town many years earlier. At first the burgomaster refuses. Then everyone in town gradually yields to the temptation of her money. The man is executed and the money passed over his coffin.

25 men, 5 women, 2 children; drop--and wings. Royalty: $50-25.

_____. Trapps. See James Yaffe's The Deadly Game.

DUKES, Ashley. The Man with a Load of Mischief (1924). Lond., Benn, 1925; in his Five Plays, Lond., Benn, 1931; French in revised edn, 1933; MAP.

To an English inn, called The Man with a Load of Mischief, in Georgian days, come a nobleman with his servant Charles and a lady with her maid. His lordship desires to humble the lady and asks his valet to make love to her. Charles had heard her sing years before and has adored her ever since. He woos and wins her,

and they find in each other the beauty of life together. The play satirizes aristocratic arrogance and champions the common man.
3 acts; 3 men, 3 women; 1 interior; costumes of the period.

_____. Ulenspiegel (1926). In his Five Plays of Other Times, Lond., Benn, 1931; in Theatre Arts Monthly, v. 10, 1926.
The son of Flemish parents is named Tyl Ulenspiegel, after the legendary German prankish trickster Tyll Eulenspiegel. He grows up to emulate his namesake by joyous heroic adventures with his fat pal, Lamme Goedzak. He displays his charlatanism with Lamme before a crowd in a market place; he is passed through the Spanish lines with his bride Nele, and culminates his exploits in a repulse of an attack by the soldiers of the Duke of Alva on a be-leaguered ship caught in the ice. The episodes of the play are based on a Flemish romance by Charles de Coster, published 1867.
7 scenes; 12 men, 5 women, extras; 3 interiors (one a ship's deck), 1 exterior; costumes of the period (ca. 1575).

DUMAS, Alexandre, fils. Camille (1852). Tr. anon, Page, 1906; tr. & adapted by Mildred Aldrich, Baker, 1907; tr. by Metcalf, French, 1931.
An intensely alive woman, Marguerite Gautier, is spending the summer happily with Armand Duval until his father comes to beg her to leave him. With a love that uplifts and redeems her, she lets Armand believe that she has jilted him to become the mistress of another. Not until she is dying does he learn the truth, when he comes to ask forgiveness; she dies in his arms.
11 men, 6 women, extras; 3 interiors; costumes of the period.
Royalty: $25-20.

_____. The Demi-Monde (1855). Tr. by Harper in CLF-2; tr. by Clark in MAU as The Outer Edge of Society; abridged in Pierce & Matthews v. 2.
Suzanne, calling herself a Baroness, seeks to forget the past and attain security through a respectable marriage. She is well on her way in her design through marriage with a younger soldier, Raymond de Nanjac, until her shady past is revealed to him by a friend, a former lover of Suzanne.
5 acts; 7 men, 5 women; 3 interiors; costumes of the period.

DUNCAN, Ronald. The Trojan Women. See entry under Euripides.

DUNLAP, William. André (1798). Ogilvy of London, 1799; Dunlap Society, Pubn #4, 1887; HAL; MOSS-1; QUIK; QUIL.
Major André has been arrested and various efforts are being made to save him: by Mrs. Bland, by young Bland, and by Honora, who came from England to see him. Through it all André is shown dignified and courageous.
5 acts; 9 men, 2 women, 2 children, extras; 3 interiors, 3 exteriors; civilian & military costumes of the period.

DUNLOP, Frank, with Jim Dale and Molière. Scapino (1975).
   Dramatic Publishing Company.
   A modern version of Molière's The Cheats of Scapin in which
two men get into trouble with their fathers by falling in love with
two girls of unknown family origin. Scapino comes to the rescue:
"The good Lord has blessed me with quite a genius for clever ideas
and inspired inventions which the less talented, in their jealousies,
call deceits and trickery."
   10 men, 4 women; 1 set. Royalty: $60-40.

DUNNING, Philip H. and George Abbott. Broadway (1926). Doran,
   1927; French, 1929; CARC; GASE; BP 1926-27.
   In a New York night club a hoofer, Roy, is in love with
Billie, a cute member of the chorus; he wants her to form a "team"
with him. Rival bootleggers are also present and their strife leads
to murder and its detection.
   3 acts; 11 men, 8 women; 1 interior.

DUNSANY, Edward Plunkett, Lord. The Gods of the Mountain
   (1914). In his Five Plays, Lond., Richards, & Kennerley, 1914;
   Little, 1917; separately, Lond., Putnam; MOSO.
   Some Oriental beggars contrive to be taken for gods disguised
as beggars, until the real gods leave their mountain thrones to
punish and turn the beggars into the idols they represented.
   3 acts (short); 10 men, 5 women, extras; 1 interior, 1 exterior; oriental costumes.

_____. If (1921). Samuel French.
   A prosaic London clerk misses the 8:10 train to work, and
for years he worries over what he may have missed. Looking into
a crystal globe he asks for another start, and finds himself in the
wilds of Persia, the country's swashbuckling ruler, where he has
adventure after adventure. His fortunes change and he returns to
London; he wakes from his dream, cured of regrets, and contented
to resume his placid humdrum existence.
   4 acts; 14 men, 4 women; 4 interiors, 2 exteriors; some
   costumes of the Orient. Royalty: $50.

DURANG, Christopher. Beyond Therapy (1983). Samuel French.
   Bruce and Prudence are insecure, neurotic people seeing
crazy, neurotic therapists. Stuart Framingham, Prudence's shrink,
thinks she should be more assertive with men. Charlotte Wallace
advises Bruce to meet someone of the opposite sex, not understanding that he has a male lover, Bob, who doesn't like that idea at all.
When Prudence answers Bruce's single ad in a paper, she gets
caught in the middle of Bruce and Bob's relationship and finds herself vigorously pursued by her psychiatrist, who sees himself as a
macho man. At the end of the play, Prudence and Bruce may have
a life "beyond therapy," may marry, and may let Bob live above
their garage.

2 acts; 4 men, 2 women; various interiors.   Royalty: $60-40.

_____. The Marriage of Bette and Boo (1985).   BP 1984-85; Dramatists Play Service.

In this black comedy Matt, as the only living child of Bette and Boo, narrates a history of his parents' marriage--not necessarily in the order in which events happened. Bette believes Boo drinks too much, which is true, just like his father, which is also true. (Boo's father calls Boo's mother "the dumbest white woman alive.") An Rh factor causes all but the first of Bette's babies to die, but the doctor always does the same thing when he brings them to her: he drops them on the floor and says they're dead. Bette's sister Emily wants to be blamed for everything that goes wrong with anybody and to apologize for it. Her father has had a stroke, and while no one can understand his speech, it doesn't keep people from asking for his advice (when he dies, they keep him around and just cover him with a sheet). Finally, Bette and Boo divorce, and by the end of the play she has died of cancer. Terminal illness, alcoholism, family hostilities, insanity, and the Roman Catholic Church are the objects of the humor and irony.

2 acts; 5 men, 5 women; unit set.   Royalty: $50-40.

d'USSEAU, Arnaud and James Gow. Deep Are the Roots (1945). BP 1945-46; Dramatists Play Service.

In a deeply moving human fashion presents striking aspects of the race question in the deep South. A Negro war hero, Brett, returns to the Langley family where he was raised with the white children, especially the daughter Genevra. After Brett has been accused of the theft of a watch and jailed, Genevra is willing to marry him, but he wants to help the Negro in the South and plans to do so. Senator Langley is still an unreconstructed Southerner and opposes his daughter Alice marrying a Northerner.

3 acts; 7 men, 4 women; 1 interior.   Royalty: $50-25.

_____. Tomorrow the World. See entry under Gow, James.

DYER, Charles. Rattle of a Simple Man (1963).   BP 1962-63; Samuel French.

A trollop, using the aristocratic background that she borrowed from novels she reads, picks up a lonely man who has come to London for a frolic. At her apartment the man's pretended worldliness quickly loses its genuiness, and he is totally incapable of the new situation. Neither is what he pretends; one by one they strip away the masks that cover their loneliness.

2 men, 1 woman; 1 interior.   Royalty: $50-25.

_____. Staircase (1966).   BP 1967-68; Samuel French.

A play about the tormented relationship between two aging homosexuals. The older one is awaiting the first visit of a daughter he fathered 20 years before. The younger one, a middle-aged former juvenile actor, has been caught in a transvestite situation and must go to court. As they wait for these events to take place the two barber/hair-stylists enjoy their Sunday off, and give one another trims, manicures, and the love of outcasts.

    2 men; 1 interior. Royalty: $50-25.

ECHEGARAY y EIZAGUIRRE, José. The Great Galeoto (1881). Tr. by Lynch, Lond., Lane, 1895; Doubleday, 1914; tr. by Fassett, Badger, 1914; tr. by Bontecou in CLDM; tr. & adapted by Nordlinger as The World and His Wife in MOSQ; abridged in Pierce & Matthews, v. 2.

    The false gossip of the neighbors links pure-minded Teodora with her husband's protegé, Don Julian, until her husband, Ernesto, comes to believe that she is unfaithful. Teodora, innocent up to now, decides she may as well live up to the accusations and takes Don Julian as her lover. Thus the tongue of gossip can do inestimable harm and ruin even the virtuous. The gossiping public tends to make real whatever it assumes, and, though unseen, is really the protagonist of the play.

    Prolog & 3 acts; 7 men, 2 women; 2 interiors.

_____. Madman or Saint (1877). Tr. by Lansing in Poet Lore, v. 24, 1913; tr. by Lynch as Folly and Saintliness, Lond., Lane, 1895.

    Lorenzo's old nurse, Jane, was put in prison for stealing a locket. She did so because it contained a letter from his mother saying she was not his mother; but Jane the nurse insists she was. Lorenzo believes the letter, and this in her mind would prevent the marriage of his daughter to a Duke. The generous-minded, even saintly Lorenzo is willing to give up name, wealth, and position because of this taint; and he will offer the letter as proof. But Jane has burned the letter and substituted a blank paper in order that he might not forego everything. Without any real proof, all are convinced that he is really mad.

    3 acts; 7 men, 4 women; 1 interior.

EDGAR, David. The Life & Adventures of Nicholas Nickleby (1982). Adapted from the novel by Charles Dickens. BP 1981-82; Dramatists Play Service.

    In the Royal Shakespeare Company's version, 42 actors take on 138 speaking roles, in two parts totaling 8-1/2 hours, staging virtually all of the episodes in Dicken's long novel and eliminating no subplots.

    2 parts; minimum of 40-45 players for full production; unit set. Royalty: $50 each part.

EDMONDS, Walter D. Rome Haul. See Frank B. Elser's Farmer Takes a Wife.

EHRMANN, Max. David and Bathsheba (1917). In Drama, v. 7, 1917.

Follows the Bible story closely. From his roof David sees Bathsheba bathing and summons her to visit him. She yields. David's counselor, Hushai, advises that her husband Uriah be summoned from the battlefield. He comes, but sleeps in the guardhouse. Then Hushai advises a letter to Joab, to have Uriah placed in the forefront of the battle--so that he might be killed. Nathan the prophet accuses David: "Thou are the man" and foretells that the child shall die.

3 acts; 4 men, 11 women (10 of them, wives of David); 1 exterior (the roof); Biblical costumes.

ELIOT, T. S.   The Cocktail Party (1949).   BP 1949-50; Samuel French.

Presents a group of urbane English people at a cocktail party given by a troubled husband, Edward, whose charming wife, Lavinia, seems to have left him to do the honors. They all have a neurotic sense of frustration, characteristic of contemporary society. The messiah-like doctor, with the aid of meddlesome Julia who gathers data for him, appears as an unorthodox psychiatrist--part mystic, part man-of-the-world. He treats his three patients according to their needs, telling them that illusions must be dropped and reality faced. He brings Edward and Lavinia together, relieving their feeling of loneliness. He gives Celia, the sensitive idealist, a release by which her selfishness turns into selflessness.

3 acts; 5 men, 4 women; 2 interiors.   Royalty: $50-25.

_____.   The Confidential Clerk (1953).   BP 1953-54; Samuel French.

Sir Claude Mulhammer, a British financier, believes himself to be the father of an illegitimate son and daughter. (His wife, Lady Elizabeth, thinks she has a son somewhere, too.) Both are partly right. Sir Claude's daughter is actually his, and the one he suspects as his illegitimate son--his new clerk, Colby, a frustrated organist--is really the child of his former love's sister. But other surprises follow.

4 men, 3 women; 2 interiors.   Royalty: $50-25.

_____.   The Elder Statesman (1958).   Samuel French.

A retired elder statesman goes to a retreat to rest from his labors and honors. Then his past begins to catch up with him. At the same retreat he meets a former show girl, bought off long ago by his father, and a rich South American, corrupted by the statesman. The lives of both acquaintances are stained with dishonor, and they go to work on the statesman and his family.

5 men, 3 women; 1 interior.   Royalty: $50-25.

_____.   The Family Reunion (1939).   Samuel French.

A family gathers for a supposedly happy reunion in this morality play, but one son is haunted by the impression that he has killed his wife. The New York Times calls this "... the finest verse play since the Elizabethans."

7 men, 4 women; 1 inteior. Royalty: $35-25.

_____. Murder in the Cathedral (1935). Samuel French.
After a quarrel with Henry II and a six-year exile in France,
Thomas à Becket returns to England and his cathedral in Canterbury, is partially reconciled to Henry, but infuriates him by his
utter devotion to the church. He is murdered on the steps of the
cathedral by Henry's order--martyred with grace and spiritual satisfaction. He is mourned by his flock, for his simple faith triumphs
over himself as well as his enemies, and gains for him martyrdom
and immortality.
10 men, 9 women; 3 interiors. Royalty: $50-25.

ELSER, Frank B., with Marc Connelly. The Farmer Takes a Wife
(1934). Adapted from the novel Rome Haul by Walter D. Edmonds. BP 1934-35; LEV.
Set in and around a hotel in Rome, New York, 1853, where
people who work boats on the Erie Canal hang out. Mostly, the
play revolves around Molly Larkins, a canal boat cook, and two
drivers she is interested in: Jotham Klore (hard drinking and a
bit uncouth) and Dan Harrow (a gentleman, who is trying to save
enough money to buy a farm). Though Molly's whole life is filled
with canal people and given texture by canal lore, by the end of
the play she is willing to try living on land as "the farmer takes a
wife."
3 acts; 18 men, 6 women; 2 interiors, 1 exterior.

_____. Low Bridge. See The Farmer Takes a Wife.

EMERSON, Eric E. Tracers. See entry under DiFusco, John.

EMERY, Gilbert. The Hero (1921). QUI; TUCD; BP 1921-22.
Two brothers are compared as types of moral and physical
courage. Andrew sacrifices himself to cover his brother's defalca-
tions; Oswald returns from the war in 1919 with a heroic record but
unchanged in his moral stamina. He steals again, but has the physical heroism to save his brother's child.
3 acts; 3 men, 3 women; 2 interiors.

_____. Tarnish (1923). Brentano, 1924; BP 1923-24.
Pictures the plight of Letitia, a girl of good social background,
when no longer sheltered but forced to work in an office and earn her
living in business. Nettie the vamp gets Emmett to call, though he
has broken relations with her and asked Letitia to marry him. When
Letitia finds him at Nettie's house, she thinks he has doublecrossed
her. The shrewd Irish landlady tells Tishy to take him: "the men
are a poor lot ... but the thing is, darlin', to get one that cleans
easy." So Letitia takes him for the love she has.
3 acts; 2 men, 6 women; 2 interiors.

ENGLAND, Barry. Conduct Unbecoming (1971). BP 1970-71; Samuel

French.
Two new lieutenants arrive at a British regiment stationed in 19th-century India. One of them is accused of assaulting the widow of a war hero, and the other serves as his defense counsel. In an unofficial trial, the "honor" of the regiment begins to unravel, and the investigation gets turned toward one of the senior officers, who is sick in a kinky sort of way.
14 men, 4 women, extras; 1 interior. Royalty: $50-35.

ERVINE, St. John G. The First Mrs. Fraser (1928). Macmillan, 1930; Baker carried; BP 1929-30.
After twenty years of marriage Janet Fraser lets her infatuated husband James get a divorce to marry Elsie, a hard-boiled self-seeking gold-digger. After a few years Elsie is seeking greener fields with Lord Larne who is wealthier. So James gets another divorce after Elsie has eloped with Lord Larne; and again courts the first Mrs. Fraser, who rather likes the idea.
3 acts; 4 men, 4 women; 1 interior.

_____. Jane Clegg (1913). Lond., Sidgwick, 1914; imported first by Holt and later by Macmillan; PLAP, v. 1; BP 1919-20.
In a sincere and engrossing way depicts the long-suffering wife, who remains the captain of her soul, the contemptible husband, who tries to steal her money and elope with another woman, and the way she finally dismisses him from her life. A credible transcript from life in London.
3 acts; 3 men, 2 women, 2 children; 1 interior.

_____. John Ferguson (1915). Lond., Allen & Unwin, 1915; Macmillan, 1928 & 1935; CHAR; THF; TUCD; TUCM; DUR; BP 1909-1919.
The old farmer, John Ferguson, remains triumphant in the midst of adversity. When his daughter Hannah is seduced by his enemy, Witherow, Jim Caesar rushes out to kill him. Next morning he confesses he didn't have the nerve to do it; but Witherow is found shot to death, and Caesar is arrested. Andrew, Ferguson's son, confesses he shot him and that he can't allow Caesar to die for a crime he didn't commit. As Andrew and Hannah go to confess, Ferguson laments like David of old "Oh, Absalom, my son, my son."
4 acts; 7 men, 2 women; 1 interior.

_____. The Lady of Belmont (1923). Lond., Allen, 1923.
Depicts the household of Portia exactly 10 years after Antonio's trial in the Merchant of Venice. Married life has not proved easy going for the three couples: Bassanio is a philanderer, this time intriguing with Jessica, and is despised by Portia; Lorenzo and his wife Jessica deceive each other; Gratiano is the drunken and faithless husband of Nerissa. To this disrupted household come others; Antonio in his dotage, grieved that no one recalls his trial; Dr. Bellario, Portia's lawyer cousin who deplores the way Portia conducted the trial; and Shylock, who wants to see his grandchildren,

though no one wants to have him around. Portia alone is gracious
to him.

    5 acts; 10 men, 1 boy, 3 women, extras; 3 interiors, 1 ex-
terior; costumes of the period.

_____. Mary, Mary, Quite Contrary (1923). Lond., Allen &
Unwin, & Macmillan, 1923; Baker 1928.

    Mary Westlake, a popular temperamental London actress,
journeys to the vicarage of a country town to hear read a play by
the young poet son. While there she disturbs the regularity of the
quiet English household and causes considerable stir by fascinating
the boy and also his uncle, a confirmed bachelor. After which, she
laughingly exits to London.

    4 acts; 5 men, 5 women; 1 interior, 1 exterior (or can be
played with 1 interior).

_____. Private Enterprise (1947). Lond., Allen & Unwin, 1948;
Macmillan, 1948.

    Edmund Delaware, with his son Philip, owns a factory in
England and insists on managing it. The workmen likewise insist
on the rights of the Labour Union. This brings on a strike. Various angles of the question are presented by members of his family
and by the workmen's representatives. It appears that the Government will have to step in, though the play is a vigorous polemic
against nationalism and in favor of private enterprise.

    3 acts; 9 men 4 women; 1 interior

_____. The Ship (1922). Lond., Allen & Unwin, & Macmillan,
1922.

    Unfolds the eternal struggle between the old order and the
new, the conflicting ideals of father and son. The old man's heart
is in his shipyard, the son refuses to carry it on; to him it is the
epitome of modern materialism. Finally he does carry out his father's wishes by directing the initial voyage of a fast liner, which
meets a disaster similar to that of the Titanic.

    3 acts; 4 men, 4 women; 2 interiors, 1 exterior.

EURIPIDES. Alcestis (438 B.C.). Tr. by Way in Loeb Library;
    tr. by Woodhull in Everyman's; tr. by Buckley in Bohn's; tr.
    by Gilbert Murray, Oxford, & in CLS; tr. by Fitts & Fitzgerald,
    Harcourt, 1947, & in FIT; tr. by Hadas & McLean, Dial, 1936;
    tr. by Potter in CLF-1; OAT.

    Admetus, King of Thessaly, threatened with death, was told
that he might live if some one would die in his stead. He asks his
father, mother, and kinsmen; they all refuse; but his wife, Alcestis,
offers to go to Hades for him. She dies, but Heracles brings her
back from the shades because Admetus had been kind to him. As
the play opens, Alcestis is loyally facing her doom. Admetus
promises the usual things; faithful devotion to her memory, etc.
His father sarcastically advises him "to woo many women so that
more may die for you."

1 continuous act; 7 men, 3 women, chorus of women; 1 exterior.

_____. Hippolytus (429 B.C.). Tr. by Way in Loeb Library; tr. by Buckley in Bohn's; tr. by Woodhull in Everyman's; tr. by Gilbert Murray, Longmans; GREN; HARC-8; MIL; OAT; FIT.

Phaedra, wife of Theseus, pines for the love of her stepson, Hippolytus, and falsely accuses him of making love to her. As he is going into exile, he is killed when his horses run away. On hearing this Phaedra commits suicide. His father however is assured of his son's innocence by Artemis, who appears in a cloud and explains that he was the innocent victim of Aphrodite's jealousy, because he worshipped only Artemis.

1 continuous act; 4 men, 4 women, choruses of men and of women; 1 exterior.

_____. Iphigenia in Tauris (414 B.C.). Tr. by Way in Loeb Library; tr. by Buckley in Bohn's; tr. by Hades & McLean, Dial, 1936; tr. by Gilbert Murray, Oxford; OAT; TEN.

Iphigenia, dedicated as a priestess in the Temple of Diana, has sworn to slay the first Greek who comes to Tauris. When it proves to be her brother Orestes, in a tense scene of recognition, she breaks her vow, and by her influence and cunning saves him and Pylades, and escapes with them.

1 continuous act; 5 men, 2 women, chorus of women; 1 exterior.

_____. Medea (431 B.C.). Many translations, among them: Way in Loeb Library; Woodhull in Everyman's; Buckley in Bohn's; tr. by Gilbert Murray, Longmans; MAU; SMP; TEN; several since 1936; in OAT; & FIT; tr. by Jeffers, Random House, 1946, French, 1948, in Theatre Arts, Ag S, 1948; GAS-3.

Depicts an ill-mated pair: Jason, a self-seeking, self-deluding husband, accepting the results of crimes committed by his wife; Medea, the bloodiest of heroines. Her love turns to hate when Jason deserts her for Glaucé, the daughter of the King of Corinth. In revenge she sends poisonous gifts to the bride, kills her two sons by Jason, and flies away in her dragon chariot.

1 continuous act; 4 men, 2 women, 2 children, chorus of women; 1 exterior.

_____. Medea. See entry under Jeffers, Robinson.

_____. The Trojan Women (Troades, 415 B.C.). Tr. by Way in Loeb Library; tr. by Buckley in Bohn's; tr. by Potter in Everyman's; tr. by Gilbert Murray, Longman's, (also in CAR; TEN); tr. by Lattimore in FIT; HAM; OAT; STA; TREA-1.

Presents one long lament over the consequences of war by those who suffer most--the women. After the fall and sacking of Troy, they bemoan their fate: they are brought into bondage by lot. Cassandra falls to Agamemnon (and prophecies his death);

Andromache falls to Neoptolemus; her son, Astyanax, is cast from
the walls and his mangled body is brought to Hector's mother. Troy
is burned to the ground, its red flames lighting up the last of the
horrors.
> 1 continuous act; 3 men, 5 women, chorus of women; 1 ex-
> terior. (For a modern acting version: Ronald Duncan's
> English version of John-Paul Sartre's adaptation of Euripides'
> play. Samuel French: 4 men, 6 women, extras. Royalty:
> $50-25).

EVERYMAN, a Morality Play (15th century). Carried by French;
ADA; ASH; BAT v. 4; CLF v. 1; COJ; KRE; LEV; LIE; MOO;
PAR; RUB; SCW; SNL; STA; TAU; TRE-1, -2 (v. 2); TREA-1.
> Everyman (symbol of Humanity) is summoned by Death to ap-
pear before God and give an account of his life. All his worldly
friends desert him: Fellowship, Riches, Kindred; others go with
him: Strength, Beauty, Discretion: Five-wits, until they approach
the grave when they likewise leave. Even Knowledge remains outside. Only Good Deeds will accompany him.
> 1 act in a succession of scenes; 11 men, 6 women (or all
> male or female). No royalty.

EVREINOV, Nikolai N. The Chief Thing (1919). Tr. by Bernstein
& Randole. Doubleday, 1926.
> Mr. Paraclete, as helper, advocate, and comforter, secures
the services of three actors--a lover, a dancer, and a comedian--
who, as suitor, slavey, and doctor, bring a feeling of happiness to
an unfavored stenographer, a depressed student, and a morose
school teacher. The chief thing is to "act" a part in life so as to
encourage others, by giving them at least an illusion of happiness
in life.
> 3 acts; 13 men, 11 women, extras; 3 interiors.

FAGAN, James Bernard. "And So to Bed" (1926). Samuel French.
> Samuel Pepys calls on attractive Mistress Knight to receive
her thanks for rescuing her. He is forced to hide in a closet when
his visit is interrupted, first by King Charles II who makes love to
the fascinating lady, and later by the jealous Mrs. Pepys, to whom
he is still later at some pains to explain his presence.
> 3 acts; 8 men, 8 women; 2 interiors; costumes of the period.
> Royalty: $50.

FARQUHAR, George. The Beaux' Stratagem (1707). In his Best
Plays, Fisher Unwin, Lond.; in Mermaid ser., Scribner; BAT
v. 22; BEL v. 7; BRI v. 1; CLF v. 1; DIB v. 1; GOSA; HUD;
INCH v. 8; MAT; MCM; BLO; MOR; MOSE v. 2; NET; OXB v.
7; STM; TAY; TUQ; TWE; UHL.
> Aimwell and Archer, two London beaux, who have dissipated
their fortunes, go to the country as master and servant to win a
country heiress. Aimwell rescues Dorinda from three highwaymen
and later inherits from his brother. Archer protects Lady Bountiful

and wins her after her separation from her brutal husband Squire
Sullen. The names of Boniface, the inn-keeper, and Lady Bountiful
have entered the language.
    5 acts; 11 men, 5 women, extras; 6 interiors; costumes of
    the period.

FAULKNER, William. Requiem for a Nun (1952). Adapted for the
    stage by Ruth Ford. BP 1958-59; Samuel French.
    Temple Drake (from Faulkner's novel Sanctuary) has married
the college boy who first led her astray but wants to run away with
her latest "find." She even plans to take her six-month-old baby
with her. Her maid, Nancy, will not permit the baby to go, and
smothers the child to prevent it. We learn of this in Temple's
confession to the Governor, to whom she goes, unsuccessfully, to
plead clemency for Nancy.
    5 men, 2 women; unit set. Royalty: $50-25.

FEIFFER, Jules. Feiffer's People (1973). Dramatists Play Service.
    Social satire in the perceptive Feiffer manner, on the state
of America and modern existence. Instead of a completed script,
the play is made up of sketches, observations, and playlets which
can be arranged, formed, and organized as the producing group
wishes.
    Flexible cast; simple and flexible staging. Royalty: $35-30.

_____. Knock Knock (1976). BP 1975-76; Samuel French.
    Two fiftyish men, one overweight and one under, live together
in a cabin in the woods, where they quarrel all the time about their
notions of reality and fantasy. Then Joan of Arc shows up, her intention apparently being to stock a new kind of Noah's ark spaceship
for God. She is to bring two of everything, in this case two
Schlepps. The effect of the world of magic on old Abe and old Cohn
is hilarious.
    3 men, 1 woman; composite interior. Royalty: $50-35.

_____. Little Murders (1967). Samuel French.
    Deals with meaningless violence in American life. A Manhattan
family made up of a domineering mother, a spineless father, a "normal" daughter, and a latently homosexual son have a paranoid fear of
snipers, muggers, and other purveyors of violence. After daughter
is married (she and her young man find a radical priest who will
marry them without pronouncing the name of God) and after the
priest has blown everyone's cover on hidden dreams and desires, the
girl is killed by a sniper. Paranoia soon turns into aggression, and
the new son-in-law and the rest of the family begin to pick people
off the street with rifles from the security of their fortress/apart-
ment.
    6 men, 2 women; 1 interior. Royalty: $50-25.

_____. The White House Murder Case (1970). BP 1969-70;
    Samuel French.

A satire set in the future. The war this year is in Brazil, and the President is worried about what to tell the American people about the poison gas attack which backfired, or even how to explain the existence of the gas in the U.S.'s "peace arsenal"--especially since the truth will cost him the approaching election. While the cabinet is concocting the cover story, the First Lady is murdered-- making more nasty business to report. (The murderer, by the way, uses his deed as leverage to be appointed the next Secretary of State.)

9 men, 1 woman; 1 interior and an interior inset. Royalty: $50-25.

FENELON, Fania. Playing for Time. See entry under Miller, Arthur.

FERBER, Edna. Dinner at Eight. See entry under Kaufman, George S.

_____. The Land Is Bright. See entry under Kaufman, George S.

_____. Minick. See entry under Kaufman, George S.

_____. The Royal Family. See entry under Kaufman, George S.

_____. Stage Door. See entry under Kaufman, George S.

FERNAND, Roland. Dear and Glorious Physician (1963). Adapted from Taylor Caldwell's novel. Dramatic Publishing Company.

The story of the apostle Luke, who wanted above all to be a healer, to alleviate pain and fight back the powers of death. As a young man he is embittered when he fights for the life of Rubria, the girl he loves, but who dies in spite of his efforts. His faith shattered, he buries himself in his work. But Luke finally finds he must rediscover his faith which he lost.

10 men, 13 women, extras (doubling possible); bare stage. Royalty: $35-25.

FERRIS, Walter. Death Takes a Holiday. See entry under Casella, Alberto.

FEUCHTWANGER, Lion. Warren Hastings (1916). Tr. by Muir in his Two Anglo-Saxon Plays. Viking, 1928.

As Governor-General of India, Hastings struggles against local prejudice and three representatives of the East India Company who have come out to investigate his administration, led by Sir Philip Francis, who will later bring up his impeachment in London. Hastings has built a road through the jungle to combat famine; he secured the money from two wealthy women, rather than tax further the poor of India. He will not take a bribe and his skirts are clean, but Lady Marjory Hicks has accepted a rich jewel, which implicates him.

Chief Justice Impey justifies his execution of Rajah Nuncomar.
    3 acts; 12 men, 1 woman, extras; 3 interiors, 1 exterior;
costumes of Indian in 1775.

FIELD, Salisbury. Wedding Bells (1919). BP 1919-20; French,
    1923.
    The wedding bells are ringing for Reggie, when in pops a
lady to whom he was married briefly in Santa Barbara; after a dis-
pute she left, and he couldn't follow because he got the measles.
Now she appears, grabs Reggie from his bachelor dinner, tips off
the clergyman about Reggie's divorce, and finds a new groom for
the bride. It looks as if the bells would ring again for her and
Reggie.
    3 acts; 5 men, 4 women; 1 interior.

FIELDING, Henry. Tom Jones. Adapted by David Rogers (1964,
    Dramatic Publishing Company)
    Tom Jones is a foundling, the ward of Squire Allworthy.
Although he and Sophia Western are in love, Sophia's father has arranged for her to marry Blifil, Allworthy's underhanded nephew.
Tom is banished when his love is discovered, but Sophia sets out to
find him. She, in turn, is followed by her father, his sister,
Squire Allworthy and Blifil. They find madcap adventures and a
host of strange characters on the road to London. Tom, already in
London, narrowly escapes marriage to an unscrupulous lady of fortune and then is sentenced to hang for murder. In an amusing and
unexpected ending, however, Tom and Sophia are united and Blifil's
true parentage is revealed.
    10 to 13 men, 8 to 11 women; bare stage with props.
    Royalty: $50-35.

FIELDS, Joseph. Anniversary Waltz. See entry under Chodorov,
    Jerome.

_____. The Doughgirls (1942). BP 1942-43; Dramatists Play Ser-
    vice.
    An irreverent comedy about wartime Washington, designed to
reflect wartime conditions without bringing up wartime miseries.
Washington is so overcrowded with people who have come to help in
the war effort that four girls have to share a small hotel suite,
which they're lucky to get at all.
    10 men (several bits), 6 women (several bits); 1 interior.
    Royalty: $35-25.

_____. Junior-Miss. See entry under Chodorov, Jerome.

_____ and Jerome Chodorov. My Sister Eileen (1940). BP 1940-
    41; Dramatists Play Service.
    Ruth, the ambitious writer, and Eileen, the pretty actress,
invade New York from Columbus, Ohio, in search of careers. They
suffer many Greenwich Village experiences in their basement apart-

ment, fighting off a variety of pests, from the Greek landlord to the
six Brazilian navy officers, but emerge victorious over the many un-
believably hilarious incidents.
     3 acts; 15 men (with 6 or more extras), 6 women; 1 interior.
Royalty: $50-35.

     _____, with Jerome Chodorov. The Ponder Heart (1956).
     Adapted from Eudora Welty's story. BP 1955-56; Samuel French.
     This comedy tells the story of a daffy Southern gentleman so
naïve that he doesn't even realize he's been accused of murder.
Uncle Daniel Ponder, getting on in years, decided one day to get
married. He picked an ignorant child-like young girl, who during
their one-month-trial marriage did nothing but order expensive ap-
pliances and play jacks with the maid. Because he loved the girl
so dearly and is himself so totally guileless, Uncle Daniel doesn't
know that he's being accused of murdering her. He buys ice cream
cones and invites everybody out to see the big trial. But at the
climax of the trial, the prosecutor makes it clear who the defendant
is, and the amiable Uncle Daniel really gets his dander up. With
his spirited, zany defense the play comes to a close.
     20 men, 10 women, extras (some unessential children); 2 in-
teriors, 1 exterior. Royalty: $50-25.

FIERSTEIN, Harvey. Torch Song Trilogy (1981). BP 1981-82;
     Gay Presses of New York, 1981-82; Viking Books, 1983-84.
     Actually a firmly connected set of three one-act plays,
centered around the life of Arnold Beckoff, a homosexual who
works as a female impersonator. In "The International Stud,"
Arnold tires of promiscuity, but the meaningful relationship he hopes
to create with a new lover ends when he loses Ed to a woman. In
"Fugue in a Nursery," Arnold and Alan, his new friend, become
tangled up in the lives of Ed and Laurel, the woman Ed left Arnold
for. There is confusion over who is gay and who is bi, but Arnold
believes that four wrongs may make a right. At the end of "Fugue"
Ed and Laurel decide to marry. Five years later, in "Widows and
Children First!," Arnold is acting as both mother and father to a
gay teenager he has taken in and is trying to legally adopt, attempting to persuade his mother that his sense of loss over Alan (who
was beaten to death by a gang with baseball bats) helps him understand what the loss of his father meant to her, and perhaps taking
back Ed, who has left Laurel, so that his new family will be complete.
     3 one acts; 4 men, 2 women; area staging.

FINKLEHOFFE, Fred R. Brother Rat. See entry under Monks, John
     Jr.

FISHER, Bob and Arthur Marx. The Impossible Years (1964).
     Samuel French.
     The story centers around a psychiatrist who is writing a
book about teen-agers. Unfortunately, in the same household are
his two teen-age daughters. The seventeen year-old has a court of

weird boyfriends; a Greenwich Village beatnik, the boy next door
with an overdeveloped itch, and an anemic Peace Corps reject. One
of the boys, the psychiatrist learns, has just married his daughter,
though neither will say which one. The younger daughter, meanwhile, is reading Fanny Hill and finding it tame. Other weird
people are also present.

    9 men, 5 women; 1 interior. Royalty: $50-25.

FITCH, Clyde. Barbara Frietchie, the Frederick Girl (1899). Life
    pub. co., 1900; French 1900; in his Plays, Little, Brown, 1915,
    v. 2; BP 1899-1909.
    Barbara is a noble charming girl of Southern family in
Frederick, Md., during the Civil war. She falls in love with a
Northern Captain and protects him when wounded. The display of
the flag climaxes the drama.
    4 acts; 13 men, 6 women, extras; 3 interiors, 1 exterior;
costumes of 1863, some military.

_____. Beau Brummell (1890). Lane, 1908; French, 1908; in
    his Plays, Little, Brown, 1915, v. 1; COH.
    Portrays the personality of the Georgian dandy and the arti-
ficial life during the Regency. Brummell sacrifices himself to give
the girl he so hopelessly loves to the man of her choice.
    4 acts; 10 men, 7 women, extras; 2 interiors, 1 exterior;
18th century costumes.

_____. The City (1909). Little, Brown, 1915; also in his Plays,
    Little, Brown, 1915, v. 4; MOSJ; MOSL.
    Father Rand had made a financial success in a small town
through shady deals. After his death the family moves to a great
city, where they succumb to its life, for each tries to lie to it.
Young George in confessing the graft says: "The city brings out
what is strongest in us; it gives the man his opportunity; it's up to
him what he makes of it. To the city he can't lie."
    3 acts; 7 men, 5 women; 2 interiors.

_____. The Climbers (1901). Macmillan, 1906; French, 1906; in
    his Plays, Little, Brown, 1915, v. 2; COT; BP 1899-1909.
    Satire on the foibles of New York society. Each character
strives to attain his ambition, whether in love, happiness, finance,
or social recognition.
    4 acts; 12 men, 9 women; 3 interiors.

_____. The Girl with the Green Eyes (1902). Macmillan, 1905;
    in his Plays, Little, Brown, 1915, v. 3; QUIL. Acting ed.,
    Samuel French.
    Possessed with the demon of jealousy, a hereditary fault,
Jinny would have been as happy in her married life as she was as
a bride. But she is so suspicious when Ruth asks her husband's
help, that she tries to kill herself with gas. Her husband discovers
her in time to save her and wins again her love by his understanding

sympathy.
>   4 acts; 10 men, 14 women, extras; 3 interiors. Royalty: $25.

_____. Nathan Hale (1898). Russell, 1899; Baker, 1899; in his Plays, Little, Brown, 1915, v. 1.
>   Effectively presents stirring incidents in the life of the young patriot, culminating in the final scene in which he "regrets he has only one life to give for his country."
>   4 acts; 12 men, 4 women, extras (schoolboys, soldiers, and townsmen); 4 interiors, 2 exteriors; costumes of the period (1776).

_____. The Truth (1906). Macmillan, 1907; French, 1907; in his Plays, Little, Brown, 1915, v. 4; DIC; STA; abridged in Pierce & Matthews, v. 1.
>   Shows the hard lesson that Becky, who fibbed unnecessarily, had to learn in order to speak and live the truth. Her habitual falsehoods cause her husband to lose faith in her, and she almost loses him.
>   4 acts; 5 men, 4 women; 2 interiors.

FLANAGAN, Hallie. See entry under Davis, Hallie Flanagan.

FLAVIN, Martin. Broken Dishes (1929). Samuel French.
>   Henpecked husband Cyrus is constantly reminded by Jenny of the brilliant match she might have made with a perfect model. The wonderman turns up and turns out to be a crook and a penniless fugitive from justice. Elaine, the youngest daughter, rebels and in spite of her mother marries the man she loves, aided and abetted by her father.
>   3 acts; 6 men, 4 women; 1 interior. Royalty: $25.

_____. Children of the Moon (1923). Samuel French.
>   Moon-madness--the curse of dreaminess, a sort of insanity, affects the Atherton family; for the selfish mother wrecks the love affair of her daughter in order to keep her at home.
>   3 acts; 5 men, 3 women; 1 interior. Royalty: $25-20.

_____. The Criminal Code (1929). Liveright, 1929; French took over; BP 1929-30.
>   Robert Graham accidentally kills the son of the city's big shot; Brady, the District Attorney, gets him a ten-year sentence. Six years later Brady is appointed warden of the prison and has Graham as the warden's chauffeur. This brightens his attitude, especially since the warden's daughter falls in love with him and he with her. As chauffeur he is present and witnesses a murder in the warden's office, but he adheres to the prisoners' criminal code and refuses to divulge the murderer. He is put in the dungeon; there he attacks Gleason, a prison official who has mistreated him, with fatal results.

3 acts; 20 men, 3 women; 9 interiors; prison costumes.

FLETCHER, John. A King and No King. See entry under Beaumont, Francis.

_____. The Knight of the Burning Pestle. See Beaumont.

_____. The Maid's Tragedy. See Beaumont.

_____. Philaster; or, Love Lies Bleeding. See Beaumont.

_____, with William Shakespeare. The Two Noble Kinsmen (1612). Harper, 1883 & 1898 ed. by Rolfe; in Temple dramatists ser., Dutton; in PAR; THA.
    The story of Palamon and Arcite, based on The Knight's tale by Chaucer. The two friends are captured and imprisoned in Athens. From the prison they see Emilia and both fall in love with her. Arcite is pardoned but exiled to Thebes, yet he remains in disguise. Palamon is released by the gaoler's daughter. They meet in the woods, but their fight over Emilia is interrupted by Theseus who declares they must do it later. Arcite prays to Mars, Palamon to Venus, Emilia to Diana. Arcite wins, but his horse kills him, so Palamon is successful in winning Emilia.
    5 acts; 12 men, 7 women, extras; 5 interiors, 13 exteriors; Greek costumes of the period.

FLETCHER, Lucille. Night Watch (1972). Dramatists Play Service.
    A mystery thriller which begins with Elaine Wheeler pacing the floor one sleepless night. Her husband tries to comfort her, but when he steps away she sees a dead body in the window of an abandoned tenement across the way. She screams and calls the police, but instead of a dead man they find only an empty chair. Next she sees the body of a woman. The police are skeptical, the husband claims she is having a nervous breakdown, and a lady psychiatrist he calls agrees that Elaine should commit herself to a Swiss sanitarium for treatment. From this point on the plot thickens.
    5 men, 4 women; 1 interior. Royalty: $50-35.

FONTAINE, Robert. Happy Time. See entry under Taylor, Samuel.

FORBES, James. The Famous Mrs. Fair (J1919). French, 1920; in his Famous Mrs. Fair & other plays, Doran, 1920; MOSJ; MOSL; BP 1919-20.
    Discusses the role of the married woman; can she combine successfully the duties of wife and mother with a public career? Mrs. Fair returns from war work, only to launch forth on a lecture tour. The first absence is in the line of duty; but the second one breeds disaster. She returns just in time to win back her husband and her daughter.
    4 acts; 3 men, 10 women; 2 interiors.

_____. The Show Shop (1914). French, 1920; in his Famous Mrs. Fair & other plays, Doran, 1920.

Mrs. Dean, a stage mother, wants her daughter, Betty, to be an actress and star on Broadway. Jerry, who wants to marry Betty, is not so sure that she will succeed. Her first show "The Wallop" is a failure; perhaps she will give up her theatrical career if another fails. Rosenbaum guarantees to pick a failure; but, alas, "Dora's Dilemma" is a great success. Nevertheless Jerry and Betty steal away to be quietly married. Introduces several delightful characters: the stage manager, older actors, the harassed author, and the stage hands.

4 acts; 14 men, 7 women; 3 interiors.

FORD, Ruth. Requiem for a Nun. See entry under Faulkner, William.

FRANCE, Anatole. The Man Who Married a Dumb Wife (ca. 1900). Tr. by Page, Lane, 1915, now carried by French; LEV; tr. by Jackson, in SMR.

After his marriage, wishing to hear her speak, the man has a surgeon operate. Then the wife talks so volubly that her husband seeks deafness to be at peace.

2 acts; 7 men, 3 women, extras; 1 interior with exterior view; fanciful mediaeval costumes. (French royalty: $25.)

FRANK, Anne. Anne Frank: The Diary of a Young Girl. See Frances Goodrich's Diary of Anne Frank.

FRANKEN, Rose. Another Language (1932). BP 1931-32; Samuel French.

Mother Hallam rules her four married sons with an iron hand. They and their wives must spend each Tuesday evening with her. The wives mutter at an evening of chit-chat, but the sons obey. Stella, Victor's wife, alone rebels; she even encourages Jerry, Paul's son, to break away from the deadly Hallam uniformity and pursue his artistic ambitions.

6 men, 5 women; 2 interiors. Royalty: $35-25.

_____. Claudia (1941). BP 1940-41; Samuel French.

Though married to the promising young architect David, Claudia is still attached to her mother's apron strings. Suddenly in 24 hours she develops and achieves spiritual stature, because she discovers she is going to have a baby and she learns that her mother has only a short time to live.

3 acts; 3 men, 5 women; 1 interior. Royalty: $50-25.

_____. Outrageous Fortune (1944). BP 1943-44; Samuel French.

A wealthy Jewish family lives a protected and secure life outside of New York City, failing to see the personal problems at home. Madeline Harris, the wife, is bored to death and has taken on a "protégé" named Barry, with whom she is in love. Bert, the husband, is certifiably middle-class conventional. Julian, Bert's brother, is homosexual. While Bert shuts his eyes and tries to hold his world together, a weekend visitor, Crystal Grainger, is the catalyst who changes everything. Mostly it is her ability to get Bert to fall in love with her and to display the kind of man that Madeline can fall in love with all over again.

    3 acts; 4 men, 7 women; 1 interior. Royalty: $35.

_____. Soldier's Wife (1944). BP 1944-45; Samuel French.
    While John was in the war in the Pacific, his wife Kate wrote him such excellent letters that, on his return, slightly wounded, his pal's father insists that they be published. They are issued under the title "Soldier's Wife." This brings much publicity and even a Hollywood offer to the wife. She is interviewed, and asked to many meetings. But Kate is satisfied to recapture and keep John, even though she is receiving an income from royalties which would give her financial independence.

    3 acts; 3 men, 2 women; 1 interior. Royalty: $25-20.

FRAYN, Michael. Noises Off (1983). BP 1983-84; Samuel French.
    In Act I of this farce within a farce, director Lloyd Dallas has his hands full trying to stage a play called Nothing On, in which several characters believe they are the only occupants of a country house and are puzzled by the appearance and disappearance of their belongings. Timing is everything in such a play, but at dress rehearsal the leading lady can't remember to do the simple business of putting the phone receiver back but leaving the plate of sardines before making her exit, the stage doors won't open, one of the male leads needs motivation and explanation for the simplest directions, and one of the supporting actors is behaving unreliably. In Act II, we see the performance of the play Nothing On from backstage, where the actors are fighting, whining, crying, drinking, and generally making one another miserable when they are not distracted by the requirements of making their stage entrances. In Act III, we see the play again as the audience does, but it is a farce in shambles. Cues are missed, lines are improvised and business made up ("How odd to find a telephone in the garden!"), personal animosities among the actors create chaos, and the Burglar in the final act has his scene interrupted by another cast member playing his part, and the two of them are surprised by a third.

    3 acts; 5 men, 4 women; 2 interiors. Royalty: $60-40.

FRECHTMAN, Bernard. The Balcony. See entry under Genet, Jean.

_____. The Blacks. See entry under Genet, Jean.

_____. The Screens. See entry under Genet, Jean.

FREDRO, Aleksander. Ladies and Hussars (1826). Tr. by Noyes, French, 1925 (in World's best plays series).

With amusing characterization presents scenes of military life, intrigue, and love-making.
3 acts; 6 men, 7 women; 1 interior; costumes and uniforms of the period.

FREEMAN, David. Creeps (1972). Samuel French.
The setting is the men's toilet of a Canadian sheltered work-shop for cerebral palsy victims. The men's room, it turns out, is the only place that CP people can be themselves—where they can retreat from the simple jobs they are given to do and deal with one another as human beings. The five principals have CP, and by the end of the play at least one of them will give up the security of the sheltered workshop to face the world on his own, using his own skills.
5 men; 1 interior. Royalty: $50-35.

_____. Jesse and the Bandit Queen (1976). BP 1975-76; Samuel French.
A two-character play featuring the legendary Jesse James and Belle Starr, both of whose lives were exploited by the series of stories that Richard Fox wrote about them in The Police Gazette, and touching on America's love/fear relationship with folk heroes. In this fantasy version of their lives (1865 to the early 1880's), Jesse and Belle wrap their legends and emotions around each other until they look alike, sometimes even portraying one another. Only their deaths are acted out with historical accuracy.
2 acts, 1 man, 1 woman; platform stage with cyclorama. Royalty: $50-35.

FREYTAG, Gustav. The Journalists (1853). Tr. by Henderson in FRARA, v. 12; tr. by House in Drama, v. 3, 1913.
Depicts the part newspapers play in politics. Oldendorf, editor of the Union, is to run for election, and is engaged to Ida Berg, daughter of the retired Col. Berg. When Berg is persuaded by a rival paper to run also, this rather breaks up the friendship and threatens the engagement. Rich Adelaide Runeck buys up a paper and enters the contest, putting Bolz, a real journalistic char-acter, in charge. Bolz wins over the vote of Piepenbrink, a wine merchant, in an amusing scene at a rival fete.
4 acts; 18 men, 5 women, extras; 3 interiors; costumes of the period.

FRIEBUS, Florida. Alice in Wonderland. See entry under Le Gal-liene, Eva.

FRIEDMAN, Bruce Jay. Scuba Duba (1967). BP 1967-68; Dramatists Play Service.
Harold Wonder has rented a chateau in the south of France for him and the Mrs., but she has run off with a Negro skin-diver. The American girl next door, who always wears a bikini, is willing to help Harold and tell him pointless stories. He has a run-in with

a thief, but the French policeman takes the (French) thief's side
against him. Other visitors to the chateau include Harold's vacationing psychiatrist and his floozie, Cheyenne, whose problem is too
many sexual climaxes (the good doctor is trying to "train her down"
to five a night). The group of characters presented has been
likened to a modern "You Can't Take It With You."
        7 men, 4 women; 1 interior. Royalty: $50–25.

_____. Steambath (1971). BP 1970–71; Samuel French.
        The steambath in this play is a kind of waiting room between
this world and the next, run by a Puerto Rican attendant who is
God. God, we learn, sends out his instructions to the world through
a television monitor--mixing up the good stuff with the bad, the serious with the insignificant. God also talks dirty and drinks six-foot
whiskey sours. Most people who die go immediately to the next
world, but the steambath is for neurotics, freaks, and people with
interesting stories to tell before they walk into the steamy haze and
forever disappear.
        12 men, 2 women; 1 interior. Royalty: $50–25.

FRIEL, Brian. Lovers (1968). BP 1968–69; Dramatic Publishing
     Company.
        A full-length play in two parts. In the first part, "Winners,"
two commentators are seated on either side of the stage, speaking
with emotion about a seventeen-year-old couple, Joe and Mag. Mag
bubbles with life and is very intense. She talks, teases, sulks, and
gets angry while Joe, more serious, tries to study for an examination. While the love scene develops, the commentators tell us that
the couple will soon be involved in a fatal accident. What we see,
then, is the lovers not only at the moment but for all time. They
are, as the title suggests, "Winners." The second part is called
"Weepers." It deals with a couple trapped by an invalid mother.
The mother, before their marriage, demands their immediate presence any time they stop talking in the parlor. After their marriage,
they are to come to her when they start talking.
        3 men, 5 women; 1 set. Royalty: $60–40.

_____. The Loves of Cass McGuire (1966). Samuel French.
        Cass returns home to Ireland after working fifty-two years
in America as a waitress. Her brother and family, to whom she
returns, promptly ship her off to an old people's home, and return
to her the five dollars a month she had sent them regularly. No
one needs her, nor was her money ever needed. At the rest haven
she begins to live off past memories.
        6 men, 4 women; unit set. Royalty: $50–25.

_____. Philadelphia, Here I Come! (1966). BP 1965–66; Samuel
     French.
        An Irishman looks over his rather hum-drum world the night
before he is to depart for Philadelphia. He sees little that is exciting and little that he will miss--except for the girl who is so fond

of him. But the image of Philadelphis is strong in his mind. What
the young man doesn't know, however, is that the aunt and uncle
he will be staying with are as unstylish as any he left behind. All
through the play the youth is saddled with a devilish alter-ego who
keeps putting irreverent thoughts in his head.
9 men, 4 women; composite interior. Royalty: $50-25.

_____. Translations (1980). BP 1980-81; Samuel French.
An 1833 episode in English-Irish hostility, set in a barn-like
"hedge school," where Irish adults are taught mathematics and
foreign languages (including English) by Hugh, the schoolmaster
who is usually drunk. A British lieutenant named Yolland, working
on orders to change the poetic but primitive place names of this
parish in County Donegal ("Poll na gCaorach" will become "Sheeps-
rock"), falls in love with an Irish girl named Maire, and is apparently killed by Gaelic political radicals because of it. In typical British
fashion, the captain in charge of the army unit headquartered there
will kill all of the livestock the first day and burn all the houses the
second if the lieutenant is not found.
3 acts; 7 men, 3 women; 1 interior. Royalty: $50-35.

_____. Weepers. See Lovers.

_____. Winners. See Lovers.

FRINGS, Ketti. Look Homeward Angel (1957) Adapted from
Thomas Wolfe's novel. Samuel French.
Through the characters of the hero, young Eugene Gant,
and his family, the familiar theme of a boy growing to manhood is
portrayed. The mother, Eliza, seems remote to her son because of
her obsession with material things; W. O. Gant, the stonecutter
father, is imprisoned by his own failure; and Ben, the brother,
could never break away from the strangling grips of his family's
meaningless existence. Richard Watts of the New York Post, called
it "One of the finest plays in American dramatic literature."
10 men, 9 women; 2 exteriors and inset. Royalty: $50-35.

FRISCH, Max. Andorra (1961). Translated by Michael Bullock.
BP 1962-63; Samuel French.
Andorra is the name of a "model state" that holds the color
white in high esteem. Next to it live the Blacks, who kill Jews.
The schoolteacher in Andorra has a foster child he is raising as a
son, Andri, who is said to be a Jew. Actually, Andri is the schoolteacher's real son, and the mother is a Black woman from across the
border. It is easier to pass him off as a Jew than as half-Black.
This deception fools not only all the Andorrans but Andri as well,
and when the loyal subjects project on to the boy all that is narrow
and small and greedy in their own minds, he begins to believe they
are right. The final blow comes when the schoolteacher will not
permit him to marry Barblin, his daughter; according to Andri the
reason is his Jewishness. Then the feared Blacks invade the

country, institute a "Jew Inspection," and kill Andri. The school-teacher hangs himself in shame, and Barblin's hair is chopped off for being the Jew's girlfriend. In the last scene she is white-washing the city square, because she says even the priests have turned black.

 Continuous action; 8 men, 3 women, extras; area staging.
Royalty: $50-25.

FRY, Christopher. The Dark Is Light Enough (1954). BP 1954-
 55; Dramatists Play Service.

 A "winter comedy" set near the Austrian-Hungary border during the Hungarian Revolution of 1848-49. A group of intellec-tuals gather for their usual Thursday evening soirée at the home of Countess Rosmarin Ostenburg, but she is off risking her life to save Richard Gettner, who has deserted the Hungarian rebels but whom she will not surrender to the rebel forces under Col. Janik. In fact, she will not even swap him for her son, Stefan. Later, she protects Col. Janik in a similar fashion. At her death, with the soldiers pounding on her door, she causes Gettner, for once in his life, to do the most courageous and honorable thing. "Go to the door," he tells the servant, "and let them in."

 3 acts; 12 men, 3 women; various interiors. Royalty: $50-
25.

_____. Judith. See entry under Giraudoux, Jean.

_____. The Lady's Not for Burning (1949). Dramatists Play
 Service.

 A discharged soldier, Thomas Mendip, half swashbuckler and half cynical misanthrope, wanders into the English market town of Cool Clary to find it conducting a witch hunt. He announces that he has committed murder and insists on being hanged. But when he sees the alleged witch, a young and beguiling Jennet Jourdemayne, he is willing to be cleared of the murder charge and of his misan-tropy. His death wish is changed into a life urge. He does not wish the lady to be burned.

 8 men, 3 women; 1 interior. Royalty: $50-35.

_____. A Phoenix Too Frequent (1946). Dramatists Play Service.

 A satiric comedy which retells the story of the famous Matron of Ephesus--the pious widow, and her maid, mourning the death of her husband in front of his bier. The new widow has resolved to withdraw from the world--until she sees a handsome guard. In no time at all the widow is ready to return to a worldly and pleasant life.

 1 man, 2 women; 1 interior. Royalty: $35-25.

_____. Tiger at the Gates (1935). Adapted from a play by Jean
 Giraudoux. BP 1955-56; Samuel French.

 At the outset of the Trojan War, Hector comes to the Greek hero, Ulysses, and convinces him and the populace of the insanity

of war. They agree that the war should not take place. Many selfish, special interest groups had not been considered, however.
The poets need the war for their odes and elegies; the kings, because custom dictates, must lead their people in battle; and even the
lawyer needs the war for his own personal honor. So in an incisive
commentary on the futility of war, logic and good will are tossed
aside, and the tiger of war once more roams freely.
   15 men, 7 women; 1 exterior. Royalty: $50-25.

_____. Venus Observed (1950). BP 1951-52; Dramatists Play
   Service.
   The star-gazing Duke of Altair has in mind to marry again.
He asks his son Edgar to help him choose one of three friends who
have been asked to his observatory. Edgar awards the apple to
Rosabel; but just then Perpetua arrives, the lovely daughter of the
Duke's clever but dishonest agent. This shifts the Duke's interest
to her and he becomes a rival with his son for Perpetua's attention.
While he and Perpetua are spending the evening in his observatory,
the jealous Rosabel sets the mansion on fire. The two are saved;
but Edgar wins Perpetua and the Duke will take Rosabel.
   7 men, 4 women; 1 interior, 1 exterior. Royalty: $35-25.

FUGARD, Athol. Boesman and Lena (1971). BP 1970-71; Samuel
   French.
   The simultaneously awful and tender story of a black couple
living in South Africa. They travel with the makings of a shack,
which they erect temporarily until a white man can knock it down.
Boesman's cruelty and physical violence is directed at his woman,
Lena, merely because she is the only object he can abuse and stay
clear of the white man's law. Their relationship becomes complicated by the arrival of an old and dying black African, and when
they set off to "walk" again it is with new awareness of who they
are.
   2 men, 1 woman; exterior set. Royalty: $50-25.

_____. (with John Kani and Winston Ntshona). The Island
   (1973). BP 1974-75; Samuel French.
   A play in which the South African black actors collaborated
in the "devising" of the story about two political prisoners doing
hard duty on Robben Island, the South African maximum security
prison for African political offenders. John and Winston, the
prisoners doing long stretches of time for crimes such as burning a
passbook in public, are beaten and forced to do senseless work.
Though they love one another, their relationship is strained when
John learns that he is to be released in three months, while Winston
will die on The Island. Their brutal existence is given meaning by
the rehearsal of a two-man play they will present to the other
prisoners--Antigone, especially her speeches about God's laws being
above the law of the state.
   4 scenes; 2 men; 1 exterior. Royalty: $50-35.

_____. A Lesson from Aloes (1981). BP 1980-81; Samuel French.
It is 1963 in Port Elizabeth, South Africa. Piet and Gladys
Bezuidenhout, Afrikaners in their forties, prepare for a dinner
party that will not take place. Piet grows and collects species of
aloe, a plant which Gladys calls thorny and disagreeable, but which
Piet finds remarkable for its ability to flower in defiant glory in
such a land as this. We learn that Piet has been a political radical
but that his colleagues in the movement now believe he is a traitor,
and that Gladys has suffered a nervous breakdown since the police
invaded their home and read--page by page--the diaries she had
always kept for her eyes only. The expected guests, Steve and
Mavis and their children, are the first to be entertained since
Gladys returned from the hospital. As it turns out only Steve
shows up, and he is two hours late. As a "Coloured man" known
to the authorities as a political troublemaker, Steve has been jailed
and permanently prohibited from working. He has no alternative
but to leave for England on a visa that will never permit his return.
The reason Mavis did not accompany him to the dinner, he admits
under Gladys's prodding, is that she believes Piet turned him into
the authorities. Piet was willing to let Steve believe this lie to make
it easier for him to start his life over again in England. Gladys believes that she is becoming sick again, like the country she loves/
hates, and tells Piet she must return to the hospital the next
morning for further treatments.
2 acts; 2 men, 1 woman; 1 interior. Royalty: $60-40.

_____. "Master Harold"...and the Boys (1982). BP 1981-82;
Samuel French.
The time is 1950, the place a Tea Room in Port Elizabeth,
South Africa. Hally, a white boy of 17 whose mother owns the tea
room, fears that his alcoholic father will be released from the hospital and again make his home life miserable, perhaps even borrowing
more money that his mother has given to him to buy schoolbooks.
His only real, positive relationship with a man has been with Sam,
a black man who has been in the family's service for years, who has
helped him learn his school lessons and dream of a future beyond
his present torments. As the emotional tension builds, Hally's in-
bred racism spills out to attack Sam, his long-suffering father-
figure, whom he insists call him "Master Harold." Sam warns him
that if he calls him Master once he will never call him anything else
again, but at the end of the play he stops him with his name,
"Hally," and gives him additional room to grow.
1 act; 3 men (1 white, 2 black); 1 interior. Royalty: $60-
40.

_____. Zooman and the Sign (1981). BP 1980-81; Samuel French.
Young Jinny, the daughter of Rachel and Reuben Tate, has
been killed by a stray youth-gang bullet as she sits on the porch of
her building in her Philadelphia neighborhood. Zooman, a teenage
punk who was picked up by the police 21 times last year, fired the
bullet but blames the child: she was in the wrong place at the wrong

time; he didn't even know the little bitch, he says. Jinny's father
has to talk Uncle Emmett out of going off to find and kill Jinny's
killer, but Victor, Jinny's brother, finds out who is responsible.
Since no one in the neighborhood wants to get involved, Reuben
puts up a sign: THE KILLERS OF OUR DAUGHTER JINNY ARE
FREE ON THE STREETS BECAUSE OUR NEIGHBORS WILL NOT
IDENTIFY THEM. The sign has its own negative effect on the
people in the neighborhood, some of whom respond violently.
Rachel wants the sign down because it's making people hate them.
Reuben claims the trouble with the world is that there aren't enough
signs. And, indeed, it is the sign that brings a puzzled Zooman
out of hiding, and when he tries to tear it down he is killed by
Emmett. Reuben replaces the sign with: HERE, LESTER JOHNSON
WAS KILLED. HE WILL BE MISSED BY FAMILY AND FRIENDS.
HE WAS KNOWN AS ZOOMAN.
    2 acts; 6 men, 3 women; composite interior/exterior.
    Royalty: $50-35.

FULDA, Ludwig. The Blockhead (1907). Tr. by Bagdad in Poet
    Lore, v. 39, 1928.
        Grandfather Beck leaves his whole estate to the grandchild
to be voted the stupidest. Since none of the five gets a majority
vote, he gives all to Justus, a dreamer who thinks well of everyone.
Ashamed of being the blockhead, he seeks to turn it over to his
cousins; each turns him down, and they ask a mental institution
doctor to pass on his being mad. The doctor finds he is physically
and mentally fit but too trusting to make his way in the world.
Doris, an American heiress, sees through the wiles of the cousins
and offers to take care of Justus by marrying him.
    5 acts; 9 men, 5 women; 3 interiors.

_____. The Lost Paradise (1890). Tr. & adapted by H. C. De-
    mille, Goldman,, 1897; French, 1905.
        To take money for his daughter Margaret, Knowlton steals
an invention from Warner, who keeps silent because he loves Margaret. But the secret is discovered by her and all is rectified.
    3 acts; 10 men, 7 women; 2 interiors.

FULLER, Charles. A Soldier's Play (1981). BP 1981-82; Samuel
    French.
        Waters, a black sergeant in charge of the post baseball team,
has been murdered off base in a Southern World War II training
camp for black recruits. Richard Davenport, a black captain, is
assigned to the case by the adjutant general's office, over the
strong objection and prejudice of the camp's white officers, some of
whom have never seen a black officer. Though at first it appears
that Waters was a victim of white political oppression and hatred
and that either the Klan or white officers killed him, the case takes
on more personal complexities. The dead sergeant had a personal
hatred toward bowin' and scrapin' "Southern niggahs" and in his
career ruined several of them. One, a popular new recruit named

C.J., was tricked into hitting him and sent to the stockade, where he killed himself. Waters' death was punishment for this, and he was shot by one of his black enlisted men.
    2 acts; 13 men (10 black, 3 white); unit set. Royalty: $60-40.

FUNT, Julian. The Magic and the Loss (1954). BP 1953-54; Samuel French.
    Grace Wilson is divorced from George, a college professor in the West, and lives in the Village with her 14-year-old son Nicki. She works as an advertising executive, sleeps with a man above her at the office, and politics for a vice-presidency. Her life becomes complicated when George returns and wants to take Nicki back with him, when Nicki discovers that her colleague Larry sleeps over sometimes, and when it appears that she will not get the promotion she wants because she is a woman. George, Larry, Nicki, the agency boss all want different things from her, but they all want her to be conciliatory. By the end of the play she permits Nicki to leave with his father and is offered the job she wants--the man who was the first choice wanted too much money.
    3 acts; 4 men, 2 women; 1 interior. Royalty: $35.

GALANTIERE, Lewis. Antigone. See entry under Anouilh, Jean.

GALE, Zona. Miss Lulu Bett (1920). Appleton, 1921; CORF.
    Pulitzer Prize play 1921. A typical unmarried woman in a small town, Lulu sees no career ahead. Unexpectedly Ninian appears to make her starved life blossom. They marry and go on a month's wedding trip. Suddenly Ninian remembers he has had a wife somewhere, maybe in Seattle; perhaps he is a bigamist. Lulu returns home, definitely glad of her marital adventure. Her family exasperate her and she is about to leave them, when Ninian returns with proof of his first wife's death. Lulu is triumphant.
    3 acts; 4 men, 5 women; 2 interiors, 1 exterior.

_____. Mr. Pitt (1924). Appleton, 1925.
    Mr. Pitt's fine qualities of generosity and goodheartedness are concealed under a lack of self-confidence and in oddities of manners and speech. He settles in a small mid-western town and marries Barbara. A year later Barbara has become so ashamed of him that she goes her own way (with a Mr. Maxwell), leaving a baby boy with Mr. Pitt. He places the baby in good care and goes to the Klondike. Twenty years later he returns to find his wife dead and his son in college. Alas, his son is as ashamed of him for a father, as Barbara had been of him for a husband. Yet he has overcome some of his deficiencies and his good qualities shine forth.
    3 acts; 5 men, 13 women; 5 interiors, 1 exterior.

GALLAVAN, Rick. Tracers. See entry under DiFusco, John.

GALLEN, Eleanor. Spring Dance. See entry under Barry, Philip.

GALSWORTHY, John. Escape (1926). BP 1927-28; Samuel French.
Capt. Denant is conversing with a young woman in Hyde Park
when a policeman arrests her. Denant sides with the woman, and
in the argument, the policeman falls, strikes his head against an
iron rail, and dies. Denant is sentenced to five years in Dartmoor.
In his escape from the prison, some befriend, others want to turn
him in. He finally reaches a church where the parson hides him,
but Denant gives himself up to avoid incriminating the parson.
Prolog & 9 episodes; 17 men, 9 women; 3 interiors, 7 exteriors. Royalty: $25.

_____. Justice (1910). Samuel French.
William Falder commits forgery to rescue Ruth from cruel
treatment by her husband and suffers the penalties. Effectively and
forcefully arraigns the English penal system; certain important reforms can be traced to this play. Dispassionately shows the inability of the law to cope intelligently with human problems and its
failure to assist the morally weak, as well as the failure of prison
authorities to meet individual needs.
4 acts; 17 men, 1 woman, many extras; 5 interiors. Royalty: $25.

_____. Loyalties (1922). BP 1922-23; Samuel French.
A young society man, Capt. Dancy, is accused of stealing a
sum of money from a Jew at a country houseparty in England. Immediately the various loyalties align themselves: the Jew for the
honor of his race, Dancy for the honor of an English gentleman,
loyalty to class, to race, to profession, even of wife to husband
who has deceived her. The clan spirit is stronger than justice and
right.
3 acts (7 scenes); 17 men, 3 women; 5 interiors. Royalty:
$50.

_____. Old English (1924). In his Plays, Scribner, 1928.
Sylvanus Heythorp, "Old English" to his associates, is a
shrewd individualist, who though over 80, still wields power as
Chairman of the Island Navigation Co. To insure financial security
for his two grandchildren by an illegitimate son, he gets his company to buy four ships for them, receiving a ten percent commission,
which he settles on their mother until the two are of age. In order
to get the money, she wants to borrow on her expectations; if Heythorp refuses to cooperate, he will be exposed. He dies of apoplexy
just before the scandal is to break.
3 acts; 17 men, 5 women; 3 interiors.

_____. The Pigeon (1912). Lond., Duckworth, & Scribner, 1912;
French carried; in his Plays, Scribner, 1924 & 1928.
Though the sentimental artist, the dupe or "pigeon" of the
social misfits, can accomplish little with his irresponsible philanthro-
py, yet his sympathetic human kindness in welcoming these few social outcasts enables them to understand a little better the lives they

are forced to live. He seems to do more than the three specialists in professional charity with their scientific theories. It is the understanding spirit that counts; he is not discouraged by failures but remains a pigeon to be plucked.
3 acts; 12 men, 2 women, extras; 1 interior.

_____. The Silver Box (1906). Putnam, 1909; Lond., Duckworth, 1910; Scribner, 1916; in his Plays, Scribner, 1924 & 1928; CHAR; MOSO; CLS.
A rich idler, Jack Barthwick, who has committed a theft, is brought home drunk by Jones, the husband of a poor charwoman. While in the house, Jones takes a silver cigarette box. In the court, the gilded fool lies, is protected by the law, and his father pays the theft with a check; the poor laboring man tells the truth, cannot pay, and is sent to jail. Demonstrates the failure of the law to administer justice to the poor.
3 acts; 11 men, 5 women, 2 children, extras; 3 interiors.

_____. The Skin Game (1920). BP 1920-21; Samuel French.
Pictures the bitter and costly feud in an English town between the Hillcrists, of the old landed aristocracy, and the Hornblowers, a newly rich family of manufacturers. The Hornblowers plan to build a factory on Crescent hill which will decrease the value of the Hillcrist property; the Hillcrists threaten to expose the scandal of the wife of Hornblower's son. It is a deadlock; but the odds are in favor of the Hornblowers who are in the stream of industrial progress.
3 acts; 11 men, 4 women; 3 interiors. Royalty: $25.

_____. Strife (1909). Putnam, 1909; Lond., Duckworth, & Scribner, 1916, 1920; in his Plays, Scribner, 1916, 1924 & 1928; DIC; MAP; WHI; WHK; DUR.
The strike in the industrial plant in England is led by Roberts, who represents labor and believes workmen should have some voice in management; the capitalist employer Anthony thinks workmen are too stupid for that. In the course of the play, strikes are discussed fairly and justly, giving the motives, opinions, and points of view held by capital, labor, labor-unions, and the public. Laments the waste and even the futility of conflict; for when Roberts' wife dies and the men desert him, and Anthony is forced to resign by his company, the leaders are both in the same boat; and the strike is settled by mutual concessions and a compromise-- which is identical with the agreement originally proposed before the strike was called.
3 acts; 23 men, 7 women, extras; 3 interiors, 1 exterior.

GARCIA LORCA, Federico. Blood Wedding (1933). Tr. by Richard O'Connell and James Graham Leyan. Samuel French.
A final tragedy strikes a Mother who has already lost all her sons except one in this passionate allegorical tragedy. Except for her youngest son, the Bridegroom, Mother has lost all her menfolk

in a feud with the Felix family. Now a wedding is arranged between
Bridgegroom and the Bride, a girl loved by Leonardo, the son of the
Felix family. Immediately following the ceremony, the Bride runs
away with Leonardo. With the help of Death (a Beggar Woman)
Bridgegroom overtakes the fleeing pair. He and Leonardo fight and
kill each other. Now the Mother is left alone in her empty house.
    9 men, 9 women, extras; 5 interiors, 2 exteriors. Royalty:
$50-35.

        . The Shoemaker's Prodigious Wife (1930). Tr. by O'Con-
nell and Leyan. Samuel French.
    An elderly shoemaker, marrying late in life, finds he has a
shrew for a mate. She berates, he is not up to her ideal; she
creates a scandal by her constant revilings. Almost driven out, he
leaves; but returns disguised to find to his joy, that, whatever her
previous treatment she loves him truly.
    2 acts; 7 men, 9 women, extras; 1 interior. Royalty: $50-
35.

GARDNER, Dorothy. Eastward in Eden (1947). Longmans, 1949;
    BP 1947-48.
    Presents the love story of Emily Dickinson. She would not
marry her youthful suitors; she was waiting for some one whom she
would know as her true love when she met him. She found him in
the Rev. Dr. Charles Wadsworth of Philadelphia, whom she met on
a visit there. They carried on an intimate correspondence; and it
was only later that she learned he was already married. After his
removal to California, she secluded herself in her home and garden,
but poured out her soul in unpublished poems. Some of the phrases
in her poems and letters are incorporated in the play.
    3 acts; 6 men, 8 women; 3 interiors; costumes of the period.

GARDNER, Herb. A Thousand Clowns (1962). BP 1961-62; Samuel
    French.
    This is the story of a bachelor uncle who has been left a
nephew to rear. The uncle tires of writing cheap comedy and finds
himself unemployed. The unemployment, however, leaves him with
the time to roam the streets of New York and do all the things he
has always wanted to do. This is hardly the right upbringing for
a young boy, and a social service team soon comes to investigate.
Soon the uncle is solving problems for them. He is faced with the
problem of either going back to work or losing his nephew. Maybe
he could even marry the social worker and solve both problems.
What ever he does will be of a nonconforming nature.
    4 men, 1 woman, 1 12-year-old boy; 2 interiors. Royalty:
$50-25.

GARRICK, David. The Clandestine Marriage. See entry under Col-
    man, George.

GASSEL, Sylvia. $E=MC^2$. See entry under Davis, Hallie Flanagan.

GAY, John. The Beggar's Opera (1728). In his Plays, Lond.,
Chapman, 1928, v. 1; ASH; BEL v. 2; BRI v. 1; BIB v. 1;
HAN; INCH v. 12; MCM; MOR; MOSE v. 2; NET; OXB v. 2;
STM; TAY; TUG; TWE; UHL.
A musical satire on thieving politicians and high-placed
rogues, with thieves and bandits the principal characters. The
highwayman, Macheath, is secretly married to Polly Peachum who
remains stedfast. He gets arrested, is reprieved, and acknowledges
her as his wife.
3 acts; 14 men, 12 women; 5 interiors; costumes of the
period. (Performance Publishing offers a modern acting
edition in which the 18th century grammar is "unscrambled"
and the street slang of the thieves is "clarified" for modern
audiences. 16 men, 12 women, extras; several representational settings. Non-royalty.)

GAZZO, Michael V. A Hatful of Rain (1955). Samuel French.
In a New York apartment live a husband, his wife, and his
brother. After the husband comes home from the hospital he is
strangely different--he can't hold a job and he stays away nights
without explanation. To make matters worse, he is visited by
strange people, and his brother is sexually attracted to the young
wife. We discover that during the hospital stay the husband has
been addicted to drugs, and his visitors are pushers who come to
collect. Though he vows to cure himself of the habit, it is not
certain that he will be successful. His wife will, however, see him
through his withdrawal.
7 men, 2 women; 1 interior. Royalty: $50-25.

GELBART, Larry. Sly Fox (1977). Based on Ben Jonson's Volpone.
BP 1976-77; Samuel French.
In this version of Ben Jonson's 350-year-old play, the Volpone figure's name is Foxwell J. Sly, an American. Assisted by
Simon Able, the right-hand man Sly employs but does not pay (Simon
is working off gambling loss IOU's), he operates in late 19th-century
San Francisco, cheating greedy people who think they are heirs of a
dying Sly's fortunes out of gold, wives, and other valuables. After
a close call in court, Sly stages his death and pretends to have left
everything to Simon (actually, Sly only gives him the IOU's he's been
holding). The gold has been sent on ahead ("the only way to take
it with you") to his next address, where he will pursue a career as
"The Reverend Slywell J. Fox."
2 acts; 15 men, 3 women; 2 interiors and insets. Royalty:
$50-40.

GELBER, Jack. The Connection (1957). BP 1959-60; SEVD.
In the first act a group of heroin addicts wait for their connection to show up, and in the second they are high from their fix.
A producer and playwright intrude through the whole ordeal, along
with a film crew to make art out of this slice of life. The junkies
"solo" with prearranged verbal improvisations interspersed with

instrumental improvisations by a jazz trio. There is no hero, no message, no solution to the problems the junkies face.
2 acts; 10 men, 1 woman; 1 interior.

GENET, Jean. The Balcony (1956). Translated by Bernard Frechtman. Samuel French.
The setting is a brothel in a place where revolution has wiped out the entire power structure except for the Chief of Police. He enlists the regular customers of the brothel to play out fantasy roles. The man from the gas company becomes a bishop; a bank clerk violates the Virgin Mary; one customer becomes a flagellant judge; another is a victorious general. A mocking view of man and society.
9 men, 4 women; various scenes. Royalty: $35-25.

_____. The Blacks (1957). Translated by Bernard Frechtman.
Samuel French.
A symbolic drama. A group of Negro players enacts before a jury of white-masked Negroes (caricatures of a missionary, a governor, a queen, and her dwarf lackey) the ritualistic murder of a white; a murder they have been accused of. When they have played out their crime, they turn on the judges and condemn them to death.
9 men, 5 women; 1 interior. Royalty: $35-25.

_____. Deathwatch (1949). Samuel French.
Three young men wait in a prison cell: a murderer who will soon be executed, a petty criminal who will soon be released, and a younger criminal. In the prison world the most depraved criminals are the most glorified; therefore the murderer is in command. The petty thief tries to build up his importance by borrowing from the legends of other criminals, but he is jeered at by the third man and finally strangles him. The murderer is not impressed. The stigma of criminal glory is not something one chooses, he says, and thus the petty thief has achieved nothing.
4 men; 1 interior. Royalty: $30-25.

_____. The Maids (1947). Samuel French.
Two servants, who are sisters, take turns pretending to be the rich lady of the house. They put on her clothes and act out their own vicious charades. It is the pretending that keeps them alive and willing to endure the hardships they suffer. While they are acting at being rich, Madame has gone for a rendezvous with her lover, who is out of jail on bond.
3 women; 1 interior. Royalty: $35-25.

_____. The Screens (1962). English version by Bernard Frechtman. BP 1971-71; Samuel French.
Genet's vision of life and death set in Algeria at the time of the war between the Arabs and the French colonials. The three continuing characters are a young Arab thief named Said, his ugly

wife Leila, and his mother. Around these three the story of the
rebellion is told, and the relationships between the French military
and colonials and the natives. The screens of the title have to do
with the props used, which permit more than one scene to be
played at a time.
     88 characters (can be played by 7 men & 8 women); plat-
     forms and screens. Royalty: $50-35.

GEORGE, Grace. The Nest. See entry under Geraldy, Paul.

GERALDY, Paul. The Nest (1921). Based on the French Les
     Noces D'Argent (Silver Weddings). Translated by Grace George.
     BP 1921-22; in Passion Playlets, ed. by J. Jex, Boston, The
     Cornhill Co., 1918.
     M. and Mme. Hamelin's nest is beginning to depopulate. First
daughter Suzanne marries and goes off on her honeymoon and then
son Max, 20, trying to be a man, has an affair with Marraine,
Madame's best friend. The two ladies feud, the son finds an actress
to throw his affections on, and the bride comes back in town to appropriate items from her parents to furnish her new apartment.
Both of the children talk a good bit about loving their mother, but
soon M. Hamelin dies and Mme. is, in fact, alone. At the end of the
play she has tried to get someone to be with her on her 25th wedding anniversary, but Suzanne and her husband are entertaining
young couples and Max is in Paris on the sly, since he has an engagement himself.
     4 acts; 3 men, 7 women, 4 interiors.

_____. Noces D'Argent. See The Nest.

_____. Silver Weddings. See The Nest.

GERSHE, Leonard. Butterflies Are Free (1969). BP 1969-70;
     Samuel French.
     Don is a young bachelor living in a cold-water flat, trying to
make it on his own as a song writer. The pretty actress next door
suggests that they remove the door connecting their two flats. The
actress (and the audience) learns that Don is blind, and that he is
trying to escape from an overprotective mother. Mother and actress
do not hit it off well together, and Don's mother succeeds in breaking up the two. When mother decides that the girl was actually
good for her son, she helps them get together again.
     2 men, 2 women; 1 interior. Royalty: $50-35.

_____. Miss Pell Is Missing (1963). Suggested by a story by
     Saki. Samuel French.
     Miss Pell has been missing for six weeks, and the police
have given up on the case for lack of evidence of wrong-doing.
Miss Pell's brother and niece hire a detective to find out what happened to her. Because Miss Pell was a stingy tyrant over the rest
of the family, nobody is really interested in finding her, and the

detective hired is one who has had a string of failures. But he does, much to everyone's consternation, find Miss Pell and restore her memory--making her as unbearable as ever. Then her brother discovers a way to bring back her amnesia and turn her into a pleasant house servant.

4 men, 3 women; 1 interior. Royalty: $35-25.

GIACOSA, Giuseppe. As the Leaves (1900). Tr. anon in Drama, v. 1, 1911; tr. by Updegraff as Like Falling Leaves, Kennerley, 1913; same in his Three Plays, Little, 1913; MOSQ.

With sympathetic character development depicts how some go up and others go down under the stress of a reversal of family fortune; the weak as leaves drifting into the path of least resistance. Giovanni has many disappointments, as do his wife and children. Cousin Massimo is healthy and lifts up the daughter Nennele by telling her of his love for her.

4 acts; 8 men, 7 women, extras; 2 interiors.

_____. The Stronger (1904). Tr. anon in Drama, v. 3, 1913; tr. by Updegraff in his Three Plays, Kennerley, later Little, 1913.

Depicts opposing views of honesty as represented by the banker Cesare Nalli and his artist son, Silvio. The son feels his father gets his money by ruining others; he is skillful but ruthless, honest within the letter of the law but evading its spirit. Silvio therefore will not accept such money; he leaves home to earn his living by his art; he stands as the stronger of the two.

3 acts; 9 men, 6 women, extras; 1 interior.

_____. Unhappy Love (1888). Tr. by Twombly in Poet Lore, v. 27, 1916.

Emma has an intrigue with a rather worthless dishonest fellow, Fabrizio, her husband's law assistant. Emma is a weak drifter; she longs for affection, which her husband Giulio fails to satisfy. She is willing to leave her home with Fabrizio, but as she is going, she is so touched by the sight of her child's doll that she cannot. Her husband does not forgive her indiscretion but is willing to have her remain--decency is thus preserved.

3 acts; 4 men, 2 women, 1 child; 1 interior.

GIBBS, Wolcott. Season in the Sun (1950). BP 1950-51; Random House, 1951.

A caustic magazine writer, George Crane, with his wife Emily and their two children, seeks to get away from the city in order to write his great novel in the idyllic environment of Fire Island. But his front porch becomes a sort of rendezvous of screwballs, dipsomaniacs and others, among them: forgetful Mrs. Jermyn, proprietor of the local boarding house and bungalows; Molly Burden, the madame of a New York bordello; Deedy Barton, a predatory blonde; and finally his editor, Arthur Dodd (who can be none other than Harold Ross of the New Yorker). They give up in

despair and return to the city.
    3 acts; 9 men, 6 women; 1 exterior (the front porch).

GIBSON, William. The Miracle Worker (1959). Based on the life
    story of Helen Keller. Samuel French.
    This is a dramatization of the story of Helen Keller and her
relationship with her blind tutor Annie Sullivan. Little Helen, a
deaf mute, is bitter, violent, spoiled and at first, almost animal-
like. Annie, however, realizes that there is a good mind waiting
to be rescued from that dark tortured silence, and in some very
emotional scenes the process of drawing Helen out and teaching her
to speak and love is revealed to the audience.
    7 men, 7 women; unit set. Royalty: $50-25.

_____. Two for the Seesaw (1958). Samuel French.
    After escaping a life and career run by the well-to-do mid-
western family of his socialite wife, a lonesome lawyer comes to
New York. There he meets a plain Jewish girl from the Bronx.
He needs love, understanding, and commiseration, and she seems
to be a woman who lives to make others happy. Each fills the
other's needs until reality catches up with them. He is an educated,
prosperous gentile who can not forget his wife; she is a plain Jewish
girl, uncultured, with a heavy Bronx accent. The happiness they
have found together is not enough to make them compatible for society, and they each realize the affair must end.
    1 man, 1 woman; 1 interior. Royalty: $50-25.

GIDE, Andre. The Immoralist. See entry under Goetz, Ruth and
    Augustus.

GILBERT, Sir William S. The Gondoliers (1889). In his Original
    Plays, Chatto, 1903, ser. 3; in his Plays & Poems, Random,
    1932; in his Complete Plays, Modern Lib. Giant, 1936; in his
    Authentic Libretti, Crown, 1939.
    The romances of three couples. One of the gondoliers in
Venice is thought to be the son of the King of Barataria and married
in infancy to the daughter of the Duke of Plaza-Toro. But the
Spanish nurse reveals her humble drummer boy is the king's son,
whom the Duke's daughter has loved all along. So he becomes King,
and the gondoliers as commoners can retain their brides.
    2 acts; 9 men, 8 women, extras; 1 interior, 1 exterior;
costumes of about 1750.

_____. H.M.S. Pinafore (1878). In his Original Plays, Chatto,
    1902, ser. 2; in Modern Lib., 1925, Giants, 1936; in Modern
    readers ser., Macmillan, 1929; in his Plays & Poems, Random,
    1932; in his Authentic Libretti, Crown, 1939; MOSO. Samuel
    French (with band arrangements).
    Babies are changed in their cradles by Little Buttercup, so
that Ralph the patrician is an able seaman and Corcoran of common
birth is the Captain of the ship; Josephine, the Captain's daughter,

loves Ralph the sailor, but her father wishes her to marry Sir
Joseph Porter. Of course all is straightened out in the end.

    2 acts; 7 men, 3 women, extras; 1 exterior (quarterdeck);
naval costumes.

_____. The Mikado (1885). In his Original Plays, Chatto, 1903,
    ser. 3; in Modern Readers ser. Macmillan, 1929; in his Plays &
    Poems, Random, 1932; in Complete Plays, Modern Lib. Giant,
    1936; in his Authentic Libretti, Crown, 1939. Samuel French
    (with band arrangements).

    Nanki-Poo, son of the Mikado, disguised as a minstrel, runs
away from marrying elderly and rather ugly Katisha, falls in love
with Yum-Yum, ward of Ko-Ko, the Lord High Executioner, whom
he wishes to marry himself. An execution must take place within a
month; he will allow Nanki-Poo to marry Yum-Yum for a month, if
he consents to be beheaded then. But when it turns out that Nanki-
Poo is the Mikado's son, the beheading is indefinitely postponed.
Many well-known songs are featured in this operetta.

    2 acts; 5 men, 4 women, extras; 2 exteriors; Japanese cos-
tumes.

_____. Patience (1881). In his Original Plays, Chatto, 1903,
    ser. 3; in Modern Lib. 1925 & Giants, 1936; in his Plays &
    Poems, Random 1932; in his Authentic Libretti, Crown, 1939;
    SMR.

    A delightful take-off on the esthetic extravagances of Oscar
Wilde. The pale fleshy poet Reginald Bunthorne loves the milkmaid
Patience, but she returns the love of an idyllic poet Archibald Gros-
venor. Being too near perfection, Archibald decides to become a
"commonplace young man" so he and Patience can be married. The
20 love-sick maidens all marry manly dragoons, and Bunthorne remains without a bride.

    2 acts; 6 men, 5 women, many extras; 2 exteriors.

_____. The Pirates of Penzance (1880). In his Original Plays,
    Chatto, 1902, ser. 2; in Modern readers ser., Macmillan, 1929;
    in his Plays & Poems, Random, 1932; in his Complete Plays,
    Modern Lib. Giant, 1936; in his Authentic Libretti, Crown, 1939.
    Samuel French (band arrangements).

    Frederic is raised by the pirate king instead of a pilot, be-
cause of the deafness of nurse Ruth. He falls in love with Mabel,
the daughter of "the very model of a modern major-general." A
slave to duty, Frederic feels obliged to help the police liquidate his
pirate friends, but the pirates all marry the General's daughters.

    2 acts; 5 men, 5 women, extras; 2 exteriors; costumes.

_____. Pygmalion and Galatea (1871). French carried as sepa-
    rate; in his Original Plays, Chatto, & Scribner, 1902; ser. 1;
    MAP; MAT.

    Pygmalion prays that his statue of Galatea come to life, and
to his surprise, it does. By her want of worldly knowledge she

causes considerable misunderstandings, even causing Cynisca his
wife to think Pygmalion unfaithful. Galatea reconciles them and returns to being a statue.
     3 acts; 5 men, 4 women; 1 interior (studio); Greek costumes.

GILBERT, Willie. Catch Me If You Can. See entry under Weinstock,
    Jack.

GILBRETH, Frank Bunker. Cheaper by the Dozen. See entry un-
    der Sergel, Christopher.

GILLETTE, William H. Electricity (1910). In Drama v. 3, 1913;
    French, 1924.
     Emeline will have nothing to do with the money her father
gained through a corrupt corporation, nor will she look at Jim, who
loves her but has also inherited great wealth. So Jim swaps jobs
with Bill, the electrical repairman; and because Emeline thinks he
is Bill and an underdog and earning his way, she is won by Jim,
who now goes into the electrical business with Bill.
     3 acts; 7 men, 5 women; 2 interiors.

_____. Held by the Enemy (1886). Samuel French.
     Shows the old South occupied by the Northern army during
the Civil war, with thrilling episodes of love and war, and an effective trial scene.
     5 acts; 13 men, 3 women, extras; 4 interiors; military cos-
tumes. Royalty: $25.

_____. Secret Service (1895). French, 1898; QUAK; QUAL;
    abridged in Pierce & Matthews v. 1; BP 1894-1899.
     Vivid and intense military drama of the Civil War (1864).
Pictures the cool and resourceful men of action who are in the
Secret Service. Presents the heroic motives of both the North and
the South, showing patriotism, loyalty, and personal honor.
     4 acts; 14 men, 5 women, extras; 2 interiors; some military
costumes.

_____. Sherlock Holmes (1899). London, 1922; Doubleday, 1935;
    CARC.
     Skillfully plotted American melodrama; developed from Conan
Doyle's stories. Introduces the famous detective, his foil, Dr. Watson, and his enemy, Moriarty. He shrewdly excapes from seemingly overwhelming dangers, as in the Stepney gas chamber. Demonstrates his well-known methods of deduction.
     4 acts; 15 men, 5 women; 5 interiors.

GILROY, Frank D. The Subject Was Roses (1962). BP 1964-65;
    Samuel French.
     A pampered son comes back from the war his own man, and
the varying effects on the father and mother are disastrous. The
family tries to love each other and rebuild the past, but the links of

communication between the trio have collapsed. They have grown irreparably apart and cannot sustain the dream and reality too. The mother and son dance together and are thrown into fits of laughter, but this isn't the son she once knew. The father breaks an important business appointment to take the boy to the ball game. They have a marvelous time, but the next morning an argument between the husband and wife turns the father-son love sour. They all want to love each other, but they do not know how.

   2 men, 1 woman; 1 interior. Royalty: $50-25.

GILSENAN, Nancy. Ordinary People (1983). Based on Judith
   Guest's book. Dramatic Publishing Company.

   Eighteen-year-old Conrad Jarrett is trying to cope with his family and friends and himself after his older brother, Buck, drowns in a sailing accident. He attempts suicide by slashing his wrists, and he later has to deal with his guilt-ridden feelings of failure, which he most strongly receives from his mother, Beth. His father, Cal, tries hard to please his son, and even goes to Conrad's psychiatrist, Dr. Berger. Beth thinks Cal is directing too much attention toward Conrad and not enough toward her, while Cal thinks Beth is being insensitive to Conrad's attempt to hold on to his sanity.

   2 acts; 6 men, 3 women; 1 interior. Royalty: $50-35.

GIRAUDOUX, Jean. Amphitryon 38 (1929). Adapted by S. N.
   Behrman. BP 1937-38; Dramatists Play Service.

   Jupiter comes down from Olympus in search of unselfish love. His early dalliance this time brings him to Alcmena while her husband is away at war. He wins her as Amphitryon; Hercules is the result.

   6 men, 5 women; 1 interior, 3 exteriors. Royalty: $35-25.

_____. The Enchanted (1950). Adapted by Maurice Valency.
   Based on Giraudoux's Intermezzo. BP 1949-50; Samuel French.

   A charming young lady obsessed with a belief in the supernatural runs afoul of the law in this widely acclaimed comedy. The girl lives in a small town where the inhabitants know her and tolerate her obsession quite tranquilly. The government inspector, however, regards her mystic dabblings as a threat to the order, security, and safety of the state. With all the authority at his disposal he tries to change the girl's preoccupation with spirits. Nothing seems to work until she falls in love. Then she discovers the joys of the real world and accomplishes in a split second what the inspector could not do with all the forces of law and logic.

   9 men; 11 women; 1 interior, 1 exterior. Royalty: $50-25.

_____. Intermezzo. See The Enchanted.

_____. Judith (1931). Translated by Christopher Fry. Drama-
   tists Play Service.

   This play treats the story of Judith and Holofernes. The Judean city is about to surrender to Holofernes. Its army has defected and its people are resigned to defeat. The prophets of the

city convince the beautiful virginal Judith that God has chosen her
to save her people, that only she can get an audience with Holofernes
and divert him with her charms--then kill him. Judith resolves to
go, refusing the offer of a prostitute, Susannah, who resembles her,
to go in her place. Holofernes, Judith finds, is not a barbarian,
but rather a man she can surrender to without restraint. The next
morning she kills him, but when her leaders celebrate her Godly
act she admits that the slaying was an act of love and that she also
wishes to be executed. An angel appears and convinces Judith that
she must preserve the lie that she murdered out of patriotism and
religious commitment. She agrees to play the role of a saint.
26 men, 7 women (doubling possible in both); 2 interiors.
Royalty: $50-25.

_____. The Madwoman of Chaillot (1945). Translated by Maurice
Valency. BP 1948-49; Dramatists Play Service.
At the suggestion of a prospector big businessmen are in-
duced to get at oil that underlies Paris. The madwoman overhears
and with practical goodness plans to exterminate the greedy ones
who make life unhappy. They are tried at a mad tea-party and pronounced guilty; they are lured into a bottomless pit to see the oil.
After the wicked and selfish are thus disposed of, joy and justice
and love return to the world again, but "what a bore if humanity
had to be saved every afternoon."
2 acts; 17 men, 8 women, extras; 1 interior, 1 exterior.
Royalty: $50-35.

_____. Ondine (1954). Adapted by Maurice Valency. Samuel
French.
The disparity between things as they should be and the actual situation leads to tragedy in this fantasy drama. An ideal love
develops between a beautiful sea nymph and a handsome knight, and
they are married at court. The harsh realities of the world soon
intrude on their idyllic life, and their love is too ideal to survive
the shock. The handsome knight, his world crumbling around him,
dies from grief; the nymph, totally disillusioned, returns to the
calm, perpetual beauty of the sea.
17 men, 11 women; 3 sets. Royalty: $50-25.

_____. Tiger at the Gates. See entry under Fry, Christopher.

GLASPELL, Susan. Alison's House (1930). BP 1930-31; French,
1931; CORF; SIXD.
Pulitzer Prize play 1931. A famous American poet, Alison
Stanhope (supposedly Emily Dickinson) left, at her death eighteen
years before, self-revealing poems of love. Agatha, symbolizing
the older generation, has guarded them and kept their secret from
the public. Agatha passes the poems on to young Elsa of the newer
generation, who like Alison has had an affair with a married man.
Elsa believes the family of a dead poet has no right to withhold
such fine poems.

3 acts; 5 men, 6 women; 2 interiors.

GLEASON, James. Fall Guy. See entry under Abbott, George.

_____ and Richard Taber. Is Zat So? (1925). Samuel French.
A prize-fighter, Chick Cowan, and his trainer, Hap Hurley, go to work as footman and butler in a fashionable New York home, being brought in by Clint Blackburn to superintend his training as a boxer, so that he may whip his brother-in-law, suspected of being the family crook. When the fight comes off, Clint is knocked out, but the blow clears his mind and he knows his brother-in-law for the crook he is.
3 acts; 9 men, 5 women, extras; 2 interiors, 1 exterior.
Royalty: $25-20.

_____. The Shannons of Broadway (1927). Samuel French.
The owner of the hotel in a small New England town refuses to take in Emma and Mickey Shannon, small-time vaudevillers, even when they are stranded there and ask to get warm. They buy the inn and become landlords themselves, help settle many local minor problems, present all kinds of farcical stunts, and then go back to the show business.
3 acts; 18 men, 6 women; 1 interior. Royalty: $25.

GODFREY, Thomas. The Prince of Parthia (1767). Little, Brown, 1917; in MOSS-1; QUIK; QUIL.
First play written by an American to be produced in America by professional actors. Arsaces returns in triumph from the war, to be welcomed by Evanthe with whom he is in love. But envy and jealousy cause his imprisonment. He is freed by his brother Gotarzes, and together they fight the attacking Arabians. Arsaces is reported killed; Evanthe takes poison; the lovers meet to say good-bye; she dies and he kills himself; and Gotarzes reigns.
5 acts; 8 men, 4 women, extras; 3 interiors, 1 exterior; costumes.

GOETHE, Johann Wolfgang von. Faust (1806). Tr. by Taylor in his Dramatic Works, Bohn, 1892; Houghton, 1898; Macmillan, 1930; Oxford, 1932; Grosset, 1936; in FRA v. 1; in HARC v. 19; BAT v. 11; TRE-1, & 2, (v. 2); TREA-1; WOR; tr. by Latham, Dutton, 1907; tr. by Andrews, Princeton, 1929; tr. by Raphael, Cape & Smith, 1930; tr. by MacNeice abridged, Oxford, 1952.
Mephistopheles gains permission to try to ruin Faust's soul. The discontented Faust promises to forfeit his soul if the devil can give him one moment of perfect contentment. He gains the sensual pleasure of Margaret, but gains no contentment. In Part 2, he gains the world of public affairs; but he now desires to serve mankind and in it finds the only real satisfaction and gains contentment. Though he has lost his wager, his soul is taken to heaven.
Various scenes; 13 men, 3 women, extras; various interior

and exterior scenes; various costumes.

_____. Iphigenia in Tauris (1787). Tr. by Swanwick in his
Dramatic Works, Bohn, 1892; FRA v. 1; BAT v. 11; tr. by
Dowden, Dutton, 1906.
Iphigenia is priestess in the temple of Diana in Tauris where
Thoas, King of the Taurians, seeks her as his bride; therefore he
seeks to kill each stranger. Orestes and Pylades arrive. They are
threatened with death until Iphigenia recognizes Orestes as her brother. Though she is a priestess, she is a living soul and is willing
to leave with her brother and Pylades; they go with the blessing of
Thoas.
5 acts; 4 men, 1 woman; 1 exterior; costumes of the period.

GOETZ, Ruth and Augustus. The Heiress (1947). Suggested by
Henry James's Washington Square. BP 1947-48; Dramatists Play
Service.
A rather shy girl, Catherine Sloper, falls in love with a
young fortune-hunter, Morris Townsend. Her father sees through
the money-seeking young man and forbids the marriage. She thinks
Morris is in earnest in his love and proposes an elopement; but this
would lose him the fortune and he will not do it. Two years later
he again proposes, but she realizes he has grown greedier and locks
the door against him.
3 acts; 3 men, 6 women; 1 interior; costumes of 1850.
Royalty: $50-35.

_____. The Immoralist (1954). Based on the novel by Andre
Gide. BP 1953-54; Dramatists Play Service.
In turn of the century France Michel's father has just died,
having never forgiven Michel for a homosexual incident at boarding
school when he was eleven years old. Marcelline, who has loved
Michel practically all of her life and who has high respect for his
work as an archaeologist, practically begs him to marry her, even
though her brother, Doctor Robert, holds Michel in contempt. They
marry and travel to Biskra, where the failure to consummate their
marriage is blamed on Michel's hemorrhaging coughing fits. Later,
however, when he has taken up with a notorious Arab homosexual,
Michel feels compelled to make love to his wife, but a few months
later he sends her home, writing a letter to her brother explaining
the life he has chosen to lead. Marcelline complies, not telling her
husband she is pregnant. Six weeks later Michel returns to France,
haunted by his cruelty to his wife. They will make a go of it
together, living in dignity, in the only place (as Michel phrases it)
"where those who are like me will not seek me out."
3 acts; 7 men, 2 women; interior and combined interior/ex-
terior. Royalty: $50-25.

GOGOL, Nikolai V. The Inspector-General (1935). Tr. by Sykes,
Lond., Scott, 1892; adapted by Anderson, French, 1931 & 1943;
Tr. by Mandell, Yale Dram. Assn., 1908; tr. by Davies in BAT

v. 18; tr. by Seltzer, Knopf, 1916; tr. by Garnett as The Government Inspector, Chatto, 1926, Knopf, 1927; tr. & adapted by Dolman & Rothberg, Baker, 1937; NOY; tr. by Seymour & Noyes in TREA-1.

An impoverished clerk, Ivan Khlastakov, finds himself stranded in a small Russian village where all the officials are grafters. Mistaking Ivan for an Inspector-general whom they are expecting and thinking he is incognito and to cover their guilt, the officials fete him handsomely and feed him generously. Ivan has a thoroughly good time and escapes from town just before the real Inspector-general arrives.

    4 acts; 14 men, 9 women, extras; 2 interiors; costumes of the period.

GOLDBERG, Dick. Family Business (1978). BP 1977-78; Dramatist Play Service.

    Isaiah Stein has been fooled by some of his sons in his old age, but when he dies suddenly all of the secrets come out in the open. Phil, the big spending hot-shot psychiatrist, is deeply in debt and above nothing in getting money to support his lavish lifestyle. (He even pretends to call for emergency help as a way of seeing to it that his father dies before he can change his will.) Jerry, the youngest son with a reputation as a playboy, is in fact a homosexual. Bobby, a middle son who has successfully run the family's toy business for his father and watched the fruit of his labor being given over to older brother Phil's extravagances, is so homophobic that his first response to Jerry's secret is to beat him up. Only Norman, a mama's boy, cares for everybody, but he is determined to have the whole family living together in the house under his supervision and caring support. At the end, it is Phil, and Phil's wife and children, who will be living with Norman at home.

    3 acts; 6 men; 1 interior. Royalty: $50-35.

GOLDEN, Harry. Only in America. See entry under Lawrence, Jerome.

GOLDMAN, James. The Lion in Winter (1964). BP 1965-66; Samuel French.

    King Henry of England and his queen are quarreling over a matter of great significance: who will rule the kingdom after Henry's death. Of the three sons the royal pair have, Henry prefers the youngest son. The queen favors the eldest. The middle son hopes to play both ends against one another to finally win out. And Henry, who understands the consequences for his kingdom if he does not decide, gives up the idea of having another heir by his mistress as just one more contender for his throne.

    5 men, 2 women; cyclorama, arches, wagons. Royalty: $50-25.

GOLDINI, Carlo. The Beneficent Bear. Tr. by Clark. French, 1915.

Crabbed, old M. Géronte has a rough exterior but a kind heart, sentimentally sympathetic. He saves his nephew Delancour from financial ruin and his niece Angélique from an undesirable marriage.

    3 acts; 4 men, 3 women; 1 interior; costumes of 18th century France.

_____. The Coffee-House (1750). Tr. by Fuller. French, 1925.
    The intrigues developed at the coffee-house give rise to much infectious mirth. Among the characters reflecting contemporary manners is an aristocratic scandalmonger, Don Marzio.

    3 acts; 8 men, 2 women; 1 exterior; costumes of the period.

_____. A Curious Mishap (1757). Tr. by Zimmern, McClurg, 1892; Dramatic Pub. Co. carried; tr. by Hollister, Ann Arbor, G. Wahr, 1924.
    A French lieutenant, M. de la Coterie, a younger son with no prospects, has been hospitalized for wounds in the home of Philibert, a rich Dutch merchant. He falls in love with the merchant's only daughter, Giannina, who reciprocates; but both feel that her father will not approve because of his having no money. So she tells her father that Costanza, daughter of the broker Riccardo, is in love with the lieutenant and he with her, but Riccardo will not consent. Philibert gives the lieutenant 500 guinea and tells him to go ahead and marry without the father's consent--which de la Cotterie and Giannina proceed to do.

    3 acts; 4 men, 3 women; 1 interior; costumes in character.

_____. The Fan (1765). Tr. by Zimmern, McClurg, 1892; tr. by McKenzie, Yale Univ. Press, 1911; tr. by Lloyd in Literature of Italy, 1907, v. 8; tr. by Fuller, French, 1925; CLF-2.
    Signora Candida breaks her fan. Her lover, Evaristo, buys her another, but, too bashful to present it to her direct, gives it to Giannina to deliver. This causes misunderstandings. The inanimate fan passes from hand to hand; Giannina's two lovers get it, then a count, then a baron; but finally the fan reaches Candida and Evaristo wins.

    3 acts; 10 men, 4 women; 1 exterior; costumes of the period.

_____. The Mistress of the Inn (1753). Tr. by Pierson in MAU; tr. by Lady Gregory, Putnam, 1924; French, 1924; Longmans, 1927; tr. by Lohman in LEG.
    Lively Mirandolina is the mistress. She forces the misanthropic misogynist Cavaliere di Ripafratta to succumb to her charm, and she benefits from the attentions of two noble lovers, a marquis and a count. But in the end she marries Fabrizio, her humble faithful servant.

    3 acts (6 scenes); 6 men, 1 woman; 4 interiors; costumes of the period. (In Lady Gregory's adaptation, entitled "Mirandolina," 5 men, 1 woman; 3 interiors.)

_____. The Squabbles of Chioggia (1762). Tr. by Lemmi in
Drama, v. 4, 1914.
Weaves a light comedy out of the sturdy folk in a small
fishing village. They squabble, they gossip, but they take the
consequences for the common good when matters become serious.
3 acts; 10 men, 5 women, extras; 2 interiors, 3 exteriors;
costumes in character and of the period.

GOLDSMITH, Clifford. What a Life (1938). BP 1937-38; Dramatists
Play Service.
Henry Aldrich, the somewhat frustrated son of a Phi Beta
Kappa father, is in high school and is expected to make Princeton
as his father did; but he can't even make the Spring Dance. He
runs into manifold student and faculty problems of adjustment in
the lives of boys and girls. An understanding Assistant Principal
helps Henry to get straightened out.
3 acts; 8 men, 10 women, extras; 1 interior. Royalty: $35-
25.

GOLDSMITH, Oliver. She Stoops to Conquer (1773). Many good
editions; BEL v. 11; BRI v. 1; CLF v. 1; DIB v. 10; HARC v.
18; HUD; INCH v. 17; MAT; MCM; MOO; MOR; MOSE; v. 2;
NET; OXB v. 4; RUB; SMO; STA; STM; TAU; TAY; TUQ;
TWE; UHL.
Young Marlow, supposedly bashful and reserved, goes to
visit the Hardcastles because his father has proposed a match with
the daughter, Kate. Tony Lumpkin sends him to the house as an
inn, where Marlow treats Hardcastle as a landlord and makes violent love to Kate as a maid servant. Kate continues the deception
to win him. Excellent situations make for successful revivals of
this famous play.
5 acts; 7 men, 4 women, extras; 2 interiors, 1 exterior;
costumes of the period.

GOODHART, William. Generation (1966). BP 1965-66; Samuel
French.
A comedy about the generation gap. Jim Bolton, 47, an advertising executive, learns that his daughter Doris has just married
a system-hating young writer/photographer, Walter Owen, and is
expecting a baby any day. The couple had hoped to be married
after the baby was born, but they found they loved one another
too much to wait that long. Not only that, but they insist that the
baby be born in their bohemian loft apartment, with Walter and
Doris the only participants. The action of the play consists of the
older man trying to undermine the young people's wishes, to justify
his own compromises with the world of business, and to find a way
of attacking Walter's individualistic righteousness. Finally, Bolton's
back-up plan of having a gynecologist friend show up saves the
day when Walter discovers he is up against a difficult breech delivery and he "could use the help."
3 acts; 5 men, 1 woman; 1 interior. Royalty: $50-25.

GOODMAN, Arthur. If Booth Had Missed (1932). Samuel French.
What Lincoln might have faced in the Reconstruction era.
Thaddeus Stevens, Stanton, and Grant enter into a political conspiracy and impeach "that pious humbug" (Lincoln) who would receive the Secessionists back into the Union without punishment or
political advantage. They are infuriated at his humaneness. He
is tried in the Senate and acquitted, but is shot down by an embittered newspaper editor.
> 3 acts; 17 men, 2 women, extras; 4 interiors. Royalty:
> $25-20.

GOODMAN, George. The Wheeler Dealers. See entry under Leslie,
F. Andrew.

GOODRICH, Frances and Albert Hackett. The Diary of Anne Frank
(1956). Dramatized from Anne Frank: The Diary of a Young
Girl. BP 1955-56; Dramatists Play Service.
> Winner of the Pulitzer Prize for 1956 and the New York
Drama Critics' Circle Award. Popularized further by the screenplay. No summary is needed for this touching story of a young
Jewish girl and her family and friends living in an attic hideaway
to escape the wrath of the Nazis. Their luck runs out at the end
of the play.
> 5 men, 5 women; 1 interior. Royalty: $50-35.

GORDON, Ruth. Over Twenty-One (1944). BP 1943-44; Dramatists
Play Service.
> In a training camp for flyers in Florida during World War II,
are Max and his wife Polly, he a brilliant journalist and she a successful writer. Because he is a bit over age, Max is having dif-
ficulty with his army flying studies but Polly keeps encouraging him.
His boss in New York wants him back and urges him to keep on
writing--which Polly does for him. They long to get to a pleasant
camp, but Max is sent to the very worst one; Polly goes with him.
> 3 acts; 6 men, 5 women; 1 interior; some military costumes.
> Royalty: $35-25.

_____. Years Ago (1946). BP 1946-47; Dramatists Play Service.
> Ruth at 16 wants to be an actress; she even gets an inter-
view with John Craig at his stock company theatre in Boston, but
he tells her to wait. Father thinks she might be an athletic instructor and insists that she graduate from high school. Friend
Fred wants her to go with him to Harvard Class Day exercises, but
instead she sets out for New York to make her own way. Father
relents enough to send her off with his old spy-glass which will be
good for $100 if she needs money.
> 3 acts; 4 men, 5 women, 1 cat; 1 interior; costumes of
> 1913. Royalty: #35-25.

GORDON, Stuart and Carolyn Purdy-Gordon. The Little Sister
(1982). Based on the novel by Raymond Chandler. Dramatic

Publishing Company.

A private-eye thriller set in 1949 Hollywood, packed with violence, deceit, and cover-ups and starring hardboiled dick Phillip Marlowe, the suave, bold detective hired by Orfamay Quest to find her brother Orrin, until a murder occurs. Others involved are gangsters led by Steelgrave, Mavis Weld, a beautiful actress who turns out to be Orrin's other sister, and Dr. Vincent Lagardie, who is caught in the middle.

2 acts; 7 men, 4 women, voices and dead bodies; area staging. Royalty: $50-35.

GORDONE, Charles. No Place to Be Somebody (1969). BP 1968-69; Samuel French.

The owner of a black neighborhood bar has big plans for the time when his former mentor gets out of prison and rejoins him. He discovers, however, that his friend is now pacified and against carrying on the fight against white society. Next, in response to Mafia pressure over his bar operation, the owner picks up a white liberal girl whose father is a judge and former Mafia lawyer, begins to live with her, and gets her to steal information from her father's files so that he can blackmail the mob. His black girl-friend commits suicide over the humiliation of losing him to a white girl, and in the finale the Mafia men, the bar owner, and his former mentor are all killed.

11 men, 5 women; 1 interior. Royalty: $50-35.

GORE, Christopher. Fame. See entry under Sergel, Christopher.

GORE-BROWNE, R. Cynara. See entry under Harwood, H. M.

_____. An Imperfect Lover. See H. M. Harwood's Cynara.

GORKI, Maxim. The Lower Depths (1902). Tr. by Hopkins, Four Seas, 1920; same in DID; SMP; TUCG; WATI; WATL v. 3; tr. by Covan in CEW; DIK v. 2; HAV; MOS; TRE-1, 2, & 3; TREA-2; tr. by Chambers as In the Depths in BAT v. 18; tr. by Hopkins as A Night's Lodging in Poet Lore v. 16, 1905; tr. by Irving, Lond., Unwin, 1912; tr. & adapted by Laurence as At the Bottom (the literal translation), French, 1930; tr. by Bakshy & Nathan, Yale Univ. Pr., 1945.

The scene is a lodging house of outcasts, rather revolting in its setting, almost devoid of plot (it is more a series of pictures), with no humor or romance. The grim biographies of the waifs are hinted at, and some of the derelicts are characterized. Into the group of wretched creatures comes the pilgrim, Luka, who still has hope—that he who seeks will find.

4 acts; 12 men, 5 women, extras; 1 interior, 1 exterior.

GOULDING, Edmund. Dancing Mothers. See entry under Selwyn, Edgar.

GOW, James. <u>Deep Are the Roots</u>. See entry under d'Usseau, Arnaud.

_____ and Arnaud d'Usseau. <u>Tomorrow the World</u> (1943). BP 1942-43; Samuel French.
     Treats the post-war problem of the indoctrinated Nazi youth. During World War II Emil Bruckner, a twelve-year old Nazi, is smuggled out of Germany, after his father has been murdered in a concentration camp because of his liberal ideas (which were unknown to Emil), and is brought to his uncle's home in a midwestern town. Emil thinks himself a good spy in an enemy country, resists his Jewess teacher (whom his uncle is to marry), and even strikes down his cousin Patricia (10 years old) who tries to make his birthday pleasant. He breaks down when he realizes that he really wants to have and give love. There is hope for him.
     3 acts; 2 men, 4 boys, 3 women, 1 girl; 1 interior. Royalty: $25-20.

GRANVILLE-BARKER, Harley. <u>The Madras House</u> (1910). Lond., Sidgkick, 1910; Kennerley, 1911, later Little; DIC; MOSO.
     The drapery trade depends on women largely and the proprietors of the Madras house discuss woman's relation to society, showing many aspects: the woman in business, the emancipated woman, woman's dress and the lure of the manikin, the six anemic Huxtable daughters who have no hope of a husband (horrible examples of what our artificial civilization leads to), the woman who doesn't care to have a husband, the flirtatious wife of a good but neglectful male, and the nagging wife whose husband has such peculiar ideas that he turns to Mohammedanism and its harem as his sane solution of woman's place.
     4 acts; 8 men, 12 women, extras; 4 interiors.

_____. <u>Marrying of Ann Leete</u> (1901). French, 1901; in his <u>Three Plays</u>, Kennerley, 1911, later Little.
     George Leete, son of a decadent 18th century family, marries a farmer's daughter, much to the wrath of his relatives. His sister Ann follows his example, renounces marriage with Lord John Carp, and marries the gardener.
     4 acts; 14 men, 6 women; 1 interior.

_____. <u>Prunella</u>. See entry under Housman, Laurence.

_____. <u>The Voysey Inheritance</u> (1905). Lond., Sidgwick, & Brentano, 1909; in his <u>Three Plays</u>, Kennerley, 1911, later Little; DIG; PLAP v. 1; abridged in Pierce & Matthews, v. 1.
     Studies the effect of commercialism on a typical English middleclass family. Edward Voysey, entering business with his father, finds their wealth has come through speculations with funds entrusted by clients, the spoils of which have come to his family. This crooked business, his father says, his father did before him-- all for the good of the clients. Edward who inherits the business

will try to put it straight, yet he must still use the same tactics as his father in doing so. A problem in practical ethics.
5 acts; 10 men, 8 women; 2 interiors.

GRAY, Patricia. The Hobbit (1968). Based on J. R. R. Tolkien's fantasy novel. Dramatic Publishing Company.

Bilbo, one of the most conservative of all Hobbits (Middle Earth creatures) is prodded by the wise magician Gandalf to leave his home and set off as chief robber in an attempt to recover an important treasure. The Hobbit is the first story of Tolkien's Lord of the Ring tales, all of which deal with the world of imagination, magic, fairies, and elves.
Large, variable cast (about 26); several playing areas.
Royalty: $50-35.

GRAY, Simon. Butley (1971). BP 1972-73; Samuel French.

A play about a university professor named Ben Butley and his former prize student, Joey, now Ben's colleague. The two not only share an office together but a flat as well. Butley's cynicism and futility overpower everything in his life, and, in the day we see him operate, his former wife cuts off their relationship to marry "the most boring man in London" and Joey himself leaves Butley to live with a homosexual lover.
4 men, 3 women; 1 interior. Royalty: $50-35.

_____. Otherwise Engaged (1976) BP 1076 77, Samuel French.

Simon Hench, a successful London publisher, has brought home a new recording of "Parsifal" with intentions of losing himself in a listening experience, but he meets with a series of interruptions which cause him to be otherwise engaged. His upstairs tenant borrows money and kitchen things and then vents his resentment. His best friend's girlfriend offers herself to him. His brother accuses him of despising his academic ambitions, his wife admits to having an affair with a man who may be the father of her unborn baby, and a former schoolmate, distraught over Simon's infidelity with his girlfriend, commits suicide over the phone. Through it all Simon loses his cool only once, but quickly regains it. He is either without feeling and therefore incapable of human relationships, or his detachment is a defense against those who would draw him out of his own life and into theirs.
5 men, 2 women; 1 interior. Royalty: $50-35.

_____. Quartermaine's Terms (1982). BP 1982-83; Samuel French.

St. John Quartermaine is a teacher in the Cull-Loomis School of English for Foreigners in Cambridge, England. When we see him in his first "term" (a spring school term), he is disconnected from the world around him, not even resenting the fact that the night before a colleague cancelled a dinner party he was invited to and then gave the party without him. A year later, at the beginning of summer term, he is even more disconnected—this time from his students as well. He is having trouble distinguishing names and faces, and sometimes sits through a whole class without speaking. A year and a half later, at Christmas time, Quartermaine's job is terminated, detaching him from what little reality he still had hold on. "Oh, Lord!," he says, but he says that about everything.

2 acts; 5 men, 2 women; 1 interior. Royalty: $60-40.

GREDY, Jean P. and Pierre Barillet. The Cactus Flower. See entry under Burrows, Abe.

_____. Forty Carats. See entry under Allen, Jay.

GREEN, Paul. The House of Connelly (1931). BP 1931-32; Samuel French.

Subtitle: "A play of the old and new South." The once proud Southern family of Connelly is disintegrating on a plantation, while in vivid contrast the tenant farmers show vigor. Patsy, the daughter of the tenant, poor white trash but with brains, urges spineless Will to brace up and be an active landlord; she will help him. She loves the land, then she comes to love him; and they marry. The opposing members of the family leave, unwilling to accept Patsy as mistress of the house. Undaunted, Will and Patsy go ahead to bring prosperity back to the House of Connelly.

6 scenes in 2 acts; 4 men, 6 women, extras; 1 interior, 2 exteriors. Royalty: $25.

_____. In Abraham's Bosom (1926). BP 1926-27; Samuel French.

Pulitzer Prize play 1927. Pictures the struggles of Abe, the mulatto son of a white man in a Southern community, to attain some small share in a white man's world where Negroes are not allowed. Abe's passionate nature has an intellectual groping for higher things; he wants to teach himself and others; but he is handicapped by his marriage to Goldie. He is a brave soul but not a leader of men; he is defeated by his own limitations and by circumstances.

7 scenes; 7 men, 2 women, 3 children; 3 interiors, 2 exteriors. Royalty: $25.

_____, with Kurt Weill. Johnny Johnson (1936). BP 1936-37; Samuel French.

Persuaded by his girl and Woodrow Wilson's assurance, Johnny, a pacifist, enlists in the war to end all wars (World War I). Many disillusionments come to him in the army. After being wounded, he comes out of the hospital with a tank of laughing gas, with which he sprays the French High Command and gets them to decree the end of the war. Before this order can be made, Johnny is committed to an asylum, though he is the only sane man there and is only a common soldier seeking to reconcile the insanity of war with the sanity of man. When the war is over, he is forced to sell toys on the street.

49 men, 6 women; 13 scenes. Royalty on application.

_____ (with Richard Wright). Native Son (1941). Based on the novel by Richard Wright. BP 1940-41; Samuel French.

Ten scenes in the life of Bigger Thomas, beginning with the State's Attorney requesting the jury to return a death penalty verdict for "this miserable human fiend" and then flashing back to his life in Chicago's South Side ghetto, where he learned to hate and fear white people. We see him exploited by the rich daughter of a slumlord, and watch him accidentally kill her, dispose of her body, and suffer through a manhunt. In the last scene, he awaits his death by electrocution, where he refuses to feel sorry for what he's done--he feels like a man.

3 acts; 15 men, 14 women (doubling possible); various interiors and exteriors. Royalty: $50-35.

_____. Peer Gynt. See entry under Ibsen, Henrik.

GREENE, Graham. The Complaisant Lover (1959). BP 1961-62; Samuel French.

At a dinner party a guest is propositioned by the daughter of a visiting couple. He explains that he only has affairs with married women and politely declines the invitation. After she leaves, the hostess appears and we learn that she is the guest's mistress. When the husband enters, the pair is almost discovered as they plan for a meeting abroad. Finally the husband does find out about the alliance, and he meets with his wife's lover. Neither wishes to lose her, so they plan to share her, becoming complaisant lovers.

6 men, 3 women; 2 interiors. Royalty. $50-25.

_____. The Living Room (1952). BP 1954-55; Samuel French.

Upon the death of her parents, a young girl moves in with her two maiden aunts and her crippled uncle, a priest. She is in love with an older married man, but she does not see this love as sinful or indecent. There is a blistering scene when the love affair is found out, and finally the man's wife visits the girl. Although the girl struggles, she is overwhelmed by the descending tragedy.

2 men, 5 women; 1 interior. Royalty: $50-25.

_____. The Potting Shed (1957). BP 1956-57; Samuel French.

A young man did something in the potting shed when he was fourteen years old which makes him quite the pariah to his own family in this melodrama. Although his father is on his deathbed, the mother will not allow her son to see him. The boy's mind is a blank, and his mother refuses to tell him what he did. With the help of his uncle, a pastor, the son finally pieces together the truth about that dark event.

6 men, 5 women; 3 interiors. Royalty: $50-25.

GREENE, Patterson. Papa Is All (1942). Samuel French.

Among the Mennonites in Pennsylvania Papa is a tyrant in his home. He won't let Mama go to the movies or have a telephone in the house. He won't let Emma his daughter have a surveyor as a beau; but Emma steals away with him to a picture show and Papa goes after them with a gun. His car stalls on the railroad crossing. Jake his son whacks him on the head with a wrench, and leaving his body in an empty freight car, returns to report that Papa is all (i.e., dead). There is much happiness until Papa turns up again; but in the meantime the telephone is in and other innovations have begun, and Papa is going to be powerless to stop these introductions of the mechanical age.

    3 acts; 3 men, 3 women; 1 interior. Royalty: $35-25.

GREENE, Robert. Friar Bacon and Friar Bungay (1589). In Mermaid ser., Scribner; ASH; BAS; GAY; HOW; MCI; MIO v. 2; NEI; PAR; OLH; OLI v. 1; SCI; SCW; SPE.

    Two English friars are conjurers and rivals in magical powers. They make a head of brass which the devil promises will speak in a month. It does, but after their servant and pupil Miles is carried off by the Devil, the head falls and breaks. A sub-plot concerns the romance of Margaret, the game-keeper's daughter, who is wooed by Lacy for Prince Edward, but she falls in love with Lacy and marries him.

    5 acts; 25 men, 4 women, extras; simple or elaborate scenery; costumes of the period.

GRESSIEKER, Hermann. Royal Gambit (1956). Translated and adapted by George White. Samuel French.

    Deals with King Henry VIII of England and his relationships with the six women in his life. Beginning with the divorce of Katherine of Aragon, we see Henry's alliances with Anne Boleyn, Jane Seymour, Anna of Cleves, Kathryn Howard, and Kate Parr. The women progress in dress right up to modern times, showing the lasting effects of Henry's thoughts. And Henry's thoughts progress from those of a Renaissance man to a contemporary liberal, finally concluding that the 20th century is the dead-end of humanism.

    1 man, 6 women; platform set. Royalty: $50-25.

GRIBOIEDOV, Aleksander S. The Misfortune of Being Clever (1824). Tr. by Pring, Lond., Nutt, 1914; tr. by Pares as The Mischief of Being Clever, School of Slavonic Studies, Univ. of London, 1925; in NOY as Wit Works Woe.

    A young intellectual, Chatski, returns to Moscow after three years abroad, eager to see Sophie whom he loves and his fatherland again. He finds Sophie throwing herself at a worthless and sneaking sycophant (her father's secretary); he finds Moscow still with the same old prejudices. He tells people what he thinks of them, and they look on him as a dangerous dreamer, a crazy madman, who has read too many books. He rails against the follies of society and leaves in disgust, bereft of Sophie.

    4 acts; 11 men, 7 women, 6 girls, extras; 2 interiors; costumes of the period (early 19th century in Russia).

GRIEG, Nordahl. The Defeat; a Play about the Paris Commune of

1871 (1936). Tr. by Watkins in Scandinavian Plays of the 20th Century, ser. 2, Princeton Univ. Pr., 1944; tr. by Arkwright, Lond., Gollancz, 1944.

Depicts vivid scenes in the streets of Paris during the Commune of 1871. Introduces some historical characters, but emphasizes the faith of the masses that a society of love and justice for all will finally triumph.

4 acts; 30 men, 10 women, many extras; 4 interiors, 3 exteriors; costumes of the period.

GRIFFITHS, Trevor. Comedians (1976). BP 1976-77; Samuel French.

Eddie Waters, a former comedian, teaches a group of would-be comics in night school. He has arranged for the whole class to perform at a workingman's club and for an agent he knows to audition the group there and offer professional bookings for the most promising. Waters's philosophy of comedy is to work through laughter, not for it, but as the audition turns out, the silliest comedians get the bookings and the brilliant one, Gethin Price, fails by coming too close to truth in a skit based on hatred toward the well-to-do. Price, like Eddie Waters many years ago, will not be able to make professional headway by trying to change the way things really are.

13 men, 2 women; 1 interior. Royalty: $50-35.

GRILLPARZER, Franz. Medea (1819). Tr. by Miller in FRA v. 6.

Jason and Medea are banished from Iolcus and seek refuge with Creon in Corinth. She tries to become a Greek but in vain. Banished from Corinth, she kills Creusa and her own two children. Exiled, they flee separately. The curse of the Golden Fleece is over them.

5 acts; 4 men, 3 women, 2 children, extras; 1 interior, 2 exteriors; costumes of the period.

_____. Sappho (1818). Tr. by Frothingham, Roberts, 1876; SMN.

Returning to Lesbos after receiving the crown for poetry in Greece, Sappho is accompanied by Phaon, a young peasant, who deceives himself into believing that admiration is love. He is undeceived when a naive maiden, Melitta, awakens in him sentiments which mean love. The artistic temperament of Sappho is ill-suited to the demands of practical life; thus she unfits herself to be high priestess of poetry. She forfeits her life by casting herself from the cliff into the sea.

5 acts; 3 men, 3 women, extras; 1 exterior; Greek costumes.

GRIMM BROTHERS. See Paul Sills' Story Theatre.

GUARE, John. The House of Blue Leaves (1971). BP 1970-71; Samuel French.

On the day that the Pope is visiting New York, a frustrated song-writing middle-aged zoo attendant is persuaded by his mistress to call an old school chum (now a big-time Hollywood producer) for a job writing movie scores. Before the producer arrives the zoo attendant's son does--AWOL from the Army and carrying a bomb to blow up the Pope and all of Yankee Stadium. Then comes the producer's fiancée, who has broken her hearing aid. About the time that the would-be songwriter calls for the men in white coats to come and take away his wife (her name is Bananas), three sightseeing nuns drop in and the son's bomb goes off prematurely. Finally, the producer elopes to Australia with the songwriter's mistress, and the poor soul is left with his nutty wife--whom he strangles.

> 4 men, 6 women; 1 interior. Royalty: $50-35.

GUEST, Judith. Ordinary People. See entry under Gilsenan, Nancy.

GUIMERÁ, Angel. Daniela (1902). Tr. by Gillpatrick, Putnam, 1916 (Hispanic Society, Pubn #107); CLDM.

Daniela, an adopted daughter of Ramón and Antonia, left 14 years before as a young girl to go to Paris with a Frenchman. Now suffering from heart attacks, she returns to them. Ramón doesn't want her back, for his early love for her turned to hate when she left; but on her return he falls in love again. Excitement caused by Antonia's jealousy brings on a heart attack from which Daniela dies.

> 3 acts; 8 men, 7 women, 1 little girl; 1 interior.

_____. Marta of the Lowlands (1896). Tr. by Gillpatrick, Doubleday, 1914.

With much human sympathy depicts the helpless and unfortunate exposed by society to the blows of chance, with the peasant and laborer in conflict with the landlord. A wealthy farmer, Sebastian, foists his mistress, Marta, in marriage on his laborer, Mannelich; after which he seeks to resume his former intrigue with her. Mannelich takes vengeance on him.

> 3 acts; 8 men, 3 women, 1 child; 1 interior.

GUITRY, Sacha. Deburau (1918). Tr. by Granville-Barker. Lond., Heinemann, & Putnam, 1920; BP 1920-21.

Delightfully fables the life of the famous French pantomimist of the early 19th century, presenting his love affair with Camille, his successes and failures, and his final retirement in favor of his son.

> Prolog & 4 acts; 12 men, 9 women, extras; 3 interiors, 1 exterior; costumes of the period.

_____. Pasteur (1919). Tr. by Brown in DID.

Presents scenes in the life of the great savant, centering especially on his researches in bacteria and inoculation. Dramatizes the event of the boy bitten by a mad dog.

> 5 acts; 9 men, 1 boy, 0 women, extras as students; 5 interiors, costumes of the period.

GURNEY, A. R. The Dining Room (1981). BP 1981-82; Dramatists

Play Service.

The central idea of the play is that the formal dining room, once famous as a functional room expressing WASP values, has disappeared along with those values. Characters of all ages and periods blend and flow in and out of the dining room, providing a series of "crisis" vignettes---a grandfather worrying about sending a boy off to a high Episcopalian boarding school ("He'll come home talking with marbles in his mouth") at the beginning and leading at the end to a father learning why his daughter has left her husband and children and wants to come back home ("I've been involved with a woman, Dad, but it's not working, and I don't know who I am, and I've got to touch base, Daddy").

2 acts; 3 men, 3 women; 1 interior. Royalty: $50-40.

GUTZKOW, Karl Ferdinand. Sword and Queue (1944). Tr. by Colbron in FRA v. 7.

Princess Wilhelmine, daughter of Frederick William I of Prussia, is sought in marriage by the Prince of Bayreuth, as well as by the English Prince of Wales and an Archduke of Austria. The Prince wins as a proposed grenadier recruit with Queue and Sword. One scene depicts an evening at the "Tobacco Parliament" where the Prince feigns tipsiness and in a mocking funeral oration tells the pseudo-deceased king some bitter truths.

5 acts; 10 men, 5 women, extras; 5 interiors; costumes of the period (about 1710).

HACKETT, Albert. The Diary of Anne Frank. See entry under Goodrich, Frances.

HAGAN, James. One Sunday Afternoon (1932). BP 1932-33; Samuel French.

Biff Grimes, a middle-aged small-town dentist, is drinking with his boyhood friend Snappy and singing the old songs that were popular in the 90's. They talk about Virginia, the girl Snappy says Biff should have married, and about Hugo Barnstead, now a wealthy banker, who stole her away. Biff thinks about Virginia and complains about his wife Amy, who is old-fashioned. When he has the opportunity to see Virginia and Hugo that day, he vows to change his life, "a change of everything," and he flashes back to the days in Avery's Park when his crush on Virginia was doomed to fail and his relationship with Amy destined to grow. We see Amy stick by him even when he has to serve two years in jail. At the end, back to present time, Hugo is so awful and Virginia so coarse and pretentious, that Biff falls in love with Amy all over again.

2 acts; 12 men, 7 women, extras; various interiors and exteriors; Gay 90's costumes. Royalty: $35-25.

HAIGHT, George. Good-Bye Again. See entry under Scott, Allan.

HAINES, William W. Command Decision (1946). BP 1947-48; Dramatists Play Service.

General Dennis is in charge of an airplane division in England during World War II. He must meet agonizing problems in deciding to bomb certain European areas in order to get the most effective results. Some government officials object, placing politics above practical issues. After their interference Dennis is delighted to be shifted to a B-29 command in the Pacific area.

3 acts; 18 men, 0 women; 1 interior. Royalty: $50-25.

HALBE, Max. Mother Earth (1897). Tr. by Grummann in FRA v. 20.

Having quarrelled with his father, Paul went to Berlin 10 years before and married Hella; with her he edited for the intellectuals a feminist magazine about the New Woman. When his father dies, he returns to bury him. After the funeral he meets again his old sweetheart, Antoinette, who had married rather out of spite; Paul realizes how they have loved each other and that he has forfeited real happiness for a vague ideal. Two days later Antoinette comes to him and they agree to die together at her old estate.

5 acts; 14 men, 7 women; 2 interiors.

_____. Youth (1893). Tr. by Barrows. Doubleday, 1916.

In wronging Annaschka, Stephen pleads that youth calls to youth in the spring when there is a sudden awakening. Her brother, the imbecile Amandus, shoots at Stephen to kill him but hits his sister instead, and the girl dies.

3 acts; 4 men, 2 women; 1 interior.

HAMILTON, Patrick. Angel Street (Gaslight) (1938). BP 1941-42; Samuel French.

The suave but sinister Mr. Manningham, under the guise of kindliness, is torturing his gentle wife into insanity. Enter Rough, amiable and paternal, from Scotland Yard, on the track of a murderer who committed the crime in this very house. Together he and his wife build up the evidence to convict.

3 men, 2 women, 2 extras as policemen; 1 interior. Royalty: $50-25.

_____. Rope (Rope's End) (1929). Samuel French.

Two rather degenerate undergraduates at Oxford, seeking a thrill just for the fun of it, murder a classmate, crowd his body into a chest in their room, and then serve tea from the top of it to the victim's father and aunt. Watched relentlessly by the suspecting lame poet Rupert Cadell, the two murderers break down under the strain and confess their guilt.

6 men, 2 women; 1 interior. Royalty: $50-25.

HAMLIN, Mary P. and George Arliss. Hamilton (1917). Baker, 1918.

Seizing on the moral courage of Hamilton as the central theme, when he would not be intimidated by fear of personal scandal in the Reynolds affair nor sacrifice his bill for the assumption of State debts, vitalizes him and other builders of the Republic.

4 acts; 11 men, 5 women, extras; 3 interiors; costumes of
the period (1790).

_____. The Rock (1921). Samuel French.
Develops the character of Simon Peter from his self-assertion
and overweening confidence, through his desertion and utter abase-
ment, to his forgiveness and realization that he has finally succeeded
where he seemed to fail.
3 acts; 5 men, 3 women, extras; 2 exteriors. Royalty: $10.

HAMPTON, Christopher. Doll's House. See entry under Ibsen,
Henrik.

_____. Ghosts. See entry under Ibsen, Henrik.

_____. Hedda Gabler. See entry under Ibsen, Henrik.

_____. The Philanthropist (1971). RP 1970-71; Samuel French.
A professor of philology, Philip, listens with another faculty
member to a student reading a play. Philip likes it. The other
finds it incredible--especially the suicide in it. The student playwright reenacts the scene for credibility's sake, and actually kills
himself. Later, at a party at Philip's house, the professor plays
"philanthropist" again: he lets a cynical novelist take his fiancée
home, while he sleeps with the hooker.
4 men, 3 women; 1 interior. Royalty: $50-35.

_____. Wild Duck. See entry under Ibsen, Henrik.

HANKIN, St. John E. C. The Cassilis Engagement (1906). In his
Three Plays with Happy Endings, Lond., French, 1907; also
separately, French; in his Dramatic Works, Secker, 1912, v.
2; in his Plays, Secker, 1923, v. 2; MOSO; DIG.
A wise mother maneuvers the breaking of a mistaken engagement of her son to a pretty girl much his inferior by showing what
his fiancée is really like when she visits his home.
4 acts; 6 men, 8 women; 2 interiors, 1 exterior.

_____. The Charity That Began at Home (1907). In his Three
Plays with Happy Endings, French, 1907; also separately,
French; in his Dramatic Works, Secker, 1912, v. 2; in his
Plays, Secker, 1923, v. 1.
An idealistic enthusiast, Margery, invites a miscellaneous
collection of outcasts to a houseparty. However, when Margery
goes so far in charity as to become engaged to the unworthy Hugh
Verreker, the liberal preacher Hylton and the cause of her enthusiasm, being in love with her himself, recants his principles and
contrives to have the engagement broken.
4 acts; 6 men, 6 women; 2 interiors.

_____. The Last of the DeMullins (1907). Lond., Fifield, 1909;

in his <u>Dramatic Works</u>, Secker, 1912, v. 3; in his <u>Plays</u>, Secker, 1923, v. 2; CHA; CHAR.

Hugo DeMullins is conventional, genteel, and proud of his ancestry. He wants his name carried on. Janet, his daughter, emancipated and exiled because she ran away without marrying, returns to her sick father with her eight year old son. She turns the merciless light of her experiences and reason on the absurdities and perils of an obsolete feudalism; also challenges conventional morality and demands as an individualist to live her own life.

3 acts; 5 men, 7 women, a boy of 8; 1 interior, 1 exterior.

_____. The Return of the Prodigal (1905). In his <u>Three Plays</u> with Happy Endings, French, 1907; also separately, French; in his <u>Dramatic Works</u>, Secker, 1912, v. 1; in his <u>Plays</u>, Secker, 1923, v. 1; MAP.

After various failures at home, Eustace has been sent to Australia with £1000. He loses that in the far country and works his way back to England. He fakes a faint on his father's front lawn and is taken care of. When he "recovers," the problem again arises, what to do with him. He is given an allowance to go to London and live, without any scandal in his home town, where his brother Henry is so successful, having become a partner in his father's manufacturing firm.

4 acts; 7 men, 5 women; 2 interiors, 1 exterior.

_____. The Two Mr. Wetherbys (1903). French, 1907; Kennerley, 1913; in his <u>Dramatic Works</u>, Secker, 1912, v. 1; in his <u>Plays</u>, Secker, 1923 v. 1.

The good and bad brothers Wetherby are married to sisters, both conventional and rather narrow-minded. One brother, Richard, has emancipated himself by telling the truth and letting others imagine the worst; the other brother, James, is still in bondage to his wife's apron-strings, though continually deceiving her by consistent lying. Aided and abetted by his "bad" brother Richard, James tries to free himself and it looks as if he would secure a better domestic life without Aunt Clara and Cousin Robert.

3 acts; 3 men, 4 women; 2 interiors (1 interior possible).

HANLEY, William. Slow Dance on the Killing Ground (1964). BP 1964-65; Dramatists Play Service.

The play takes place in a dusty stationery store near the Brooklyn Bridge. The owner of the store, an old man named Glas, is a non-Jewish refugee from Nazi Germany who deserted his Jewish wife and son during the bad times. In Act I Glas "dances" with a black street dude named Randall who is being hunted by the police for killing his mother. In Act II both "dance" with a black girl named Rosie, who is lost in this section of town while searching for the apartment of a doctor who will perform an abortion on her. The "Killing Ground" is Randall's name for the outside world, the world beyond the dirty windows of the store. The richness of the play comes from the way in which these three characters come to relate

to, and care for, one another.
   2 men, 1 woman; 1 interior. Royalty: $50-25.

HANSBERRY, Lorraine. A Raisin in the Sun (1959). BP 1958-59;
   Samuel French.
   A Negro family (a widow, her son, his wife, his sister, and
his son) live in a cramped flat in south side Chicago. The widow
is expecting a $10,000 insurance check on her late husband's life,
and the son, a chauffeur, begs her to give him the money to invest
in a liquor store. The widow, instead, puts a down payment on a
home for the family, one where there is sunlight and no roaches.
Reluctantly she gives her son the remaining $6,500, which he gives
to his liquor store partner who leaves town. Though that dream is
dead, the family will move to the new neighborhood--in spite of the
white representative who warns them against moving and offers to
reimburse them for the down payment.
   7 men, 3 women, 1 boy; 1 interior. Royalty: $50-25.

_____. The Sign in Sidney Brustein's Widow (1964). Samuel
   French.
   Sidney Brustein is a Jewish intellectual and editor, living in
Greenwich Village. His wife Iris is a striving actress. Their circle
of friends and relatives include crooked politicians, homosexuals, and
prostitutes. The plot revolves around idealistic Sidney's attempts to
get a reform politician elected, and to do so he must fight the establishment. The issues the play deals with are the fragility of love,
morality, drugs, interracial relationships, conformity, and withdrawal
from society.
   6 men, 3 women; 1 interior. Royalty: $50-25.

_____. To Be Young, Gifted, and Black (1969). Samuel French.
   A play based on the life and works of Lorraine Hansberry,
in her own words, adapted by her husband, Robert Nemiroff. Part
I deals with her childhood in Chicago. Part II draws on material
from her own plays, her novel, and other writings.
   3 men, 5 women; platform stage. Royalty: $50-25.

HARDT, Ernst. Tristram the Jester (1907). Tr. by Heard. Bost.,
   Wagner, 1913; FRA v. 20; same in Poet Lore v. 43, 1937.
   Tristram is denied access to King Mark's court because of
his attachment for Isolt, the King's wife. She is condemned to the
lepers, whence she is saved by Tristram. He returns a second time,
disguised as a jester. Isolt does not recognize him but his hound
does, and then she knows.
   5 acts; 11 men, 3 women, extras; 2 interiors, 1 exterior;
   medieval costumes.

HARDY, Thomas. The Dynast (1904-1908). Macmillan, 1904-1908,
   3 v.; in his Works, Macmillan, 1912-1913, v. 2-3; Macmillan,
   1 v., 1920 & 1931.
   Centers around the figure of Napoleon who represents Force

and Will that move the world. An episodic epic of the Napoleonic wars, with impressive scenes, rich in historic lore and literary fancy. Though written in dramatic form, it is hardly a stage play, but some scenes are powerfully dramatic and could be produced.
In 3 parts, with 19 acts & 130 scenes.

HARE, David. <u>Plenty</u> (1978). BP 1982-83; Samuel French.
Susan Traherne's World War II experience as a young English-woman in France, suffering for a righteous cause, becoming intimate with people she had never seen before nor would again, witnessing bravery and heroism as a regular part of life--this experience has mostly meant that her future was behind her. Though she marries a British diplomat and attempts to become respectable, about the only thing she succeeds in doing is making him as miserable as she believes post-war England has become. The scenes in the play span the period of 1943 to 1962 in flashbacks of her life in England, France, and Brussels. Her mental and emotional disintegration, some-times tied to events as real as the Suez Canal crisis of 1956, seem not only personal but national as well.
2 acts; 10 men, 4 women; various simple interiors and exteriors. Royalty: $60-40.

HART, Moss. <u>Christopher Blake</u> (1946). BP 1946-47; Dramatists Play Service.
Presents the problem of the divorce orphan--to which parent shall he go? Christopher is twelve years old; his parents have their divorce complete, except as to the boy. He dreams fantasies which might bring them together: he is a national hero, he is a famous playwright, he is an abandoned school-boy at Christmas, his parents are in the poor-house and he is a South American who spurns them. In the court the parents present their sides; the boy chooses his father.
12 men, 2 women; various interiors and exteriors. Royalty: $50-25.

_____. <u>The Climate of Eden</u> (1953). Based on the novel <u>Shadows Move Among Them</u> by Edgar Mittelholzer. BP 1952-53; Dramatists Play Service.
The Reverend Gerald Harmston runs a church in the jungle of British Guiana, where his family, a wife and four children, live a life somewhere between civilized and primitive. When Gregory, a nephew, comes to stay with them (he has been "ill with nerves" since his wife drowned), this strange world with "the climate of Eden" seems first to push him off the edge (he almost stabs Olivia, age 14) and then cure him of his guilt (he has been blaming his in-fidelity for his wife's suicide). He falls in love with Mabel, age 18, but when he hears from Mrs. Harmston that Mabel has had a native lover since she was 16, he snaps again and packs to return to civ-ilization.
2 acts; 6 men, 5 women; unit set; Royalty: $50-25.

_____. George Washington Slept Here. See entry under Kaufman, George S.

_____. Lady in the Dark (1941). BP 1940-41; Random House, 1941; World Pub. Co., 1944; Dramatists Play Service carried.

The successful editor of a fashion magazine, Liza, feels lost and seeks help from a psychoanalyst. There she sees (and acts) her dreams and memories, and through their analyses she comes out of the dark and back to her belief in herself and her sanity. The dreams are musical fantasy interludes.

2 acts; 9 men, 11 women; 2 interiors.

_____. Light Up the Sky (1948). BP 1948-49; Dramatists Play Service.

An experimental play by Peter Sloan is to be tried out in Boston. The tearful director, the temperamental leading lady, the dynamic backer and his sardonic wife--all have great hopes for its success. When they meet after the opening, they all believe they have a flop; they blame everyone in sight, but especially the author, who plans to escape by plane. The morning reviews however turn out to be favorable, and all are happy again--all except the author who now says he has graduated--and he lays down the law.

3 acts; 9 men, 4 women; 1 interior. Royalty: $50-35.

_____. The Man Who Came to Dinner. See entry under Kaufman, George S.

_____. Merrily We Roll Along. See entry under Kaufman, George S.

_____, and George S. Kaufman. Once in a Lifetime (1930). BP 1930-31; Samuel French.

Three down-and-out troupers go West to try their luck with the talkies, especially to teach them how to speak correctly. The most stupid of the three, George, blunders to the top of the industry because Glogauer, the big producer, mistakes his errors for marks of genius.

3 acts; 24 men, 14 women; 5 interiors. Royalty: $50-25.

_____. Winged Victory (1943). BP 1943-44; Random House, 1944.

A patriotic salute to the Air Corps, written during WWII in three weeks and produced in seventeen days with a cast of 300 soldiers, 41 soldiers' wives, and 9 professional actresses. Allan, Frankie, and Pinky (from Mapleton, Ohio) are ecstatic when their orders arrive to report to the Air Corps. During training, Pinky washes out and goes to turret gunner school and Frankie dies during his first solo night flight. Allan, together with his wife Dorothy, is the continuity in the play, which finds him in the South Pacific in the last scene, reading a letter from home announcing the birth of a son, and vowing to make the world a better place after the war.

2 acts; large flexible cast; various interiors and exteriors.

_____, with George S. Kaufman. <u>You Can't Take It With You</u>. (1936). BP 1936-37; Dramatists Play Service.

The slightly mad Sycamore family, headed by Grandpa Vanderhof, follows each his hobby: fireworks being manufactured in the basement, printing press running in the living room, artists at work, dancing, typing—wealth for them does not compare with the joy of human affection and doing what really interests them. In contrast, the rich Kirbys are basically unhappy. Tony, their son, is in love with Alice, and gets his parents to the crazy household on the wrong night. They act very snobbishly, but are finally converted, especially after Mr. Kirby's interview with an ex-Grand Duchess who is earning her living as a waitress.

3 acts; 9 men, 7 women, 3 extras; 1 interior. Royalty: $35.

HARTLEBEN, Otto Erich. <u>Hanna Jagert</u> (1893). Tr. by Holmes in <u>Poet Lore</u> v. 24, 1913.

Depicts the rise of a poor working girl to be a baroness. Hanna is intelligent and self-reliant. She advances beyond her fiancé Conrad, through her teacher Alexander. She experiments with socialism and individualism; and marries Baron Bernhard as a means of securing greater freedom.

3 acts; 6 men, 3 women, extras; 3 interiors; costumes of the period.

HARTOG, Jan de. <u>The Fourposter</u> (1951). BP 1951-52; Samuel French.

Presents Agnes and Michael in a series of rather uneventful incidents in their married life, from their arrival as a bridal couple, through the birth and marriage of their children, to their departure to another residence.

6 scenes in 3 acts; 1 man, 1 woman; 1 interior with furniture and costume changes, 1890 to 1925. Royalty: $50-25.

_____. <u>Skipper Next to God</u> (1949). BP 1947-48; Dramatists Play Service.

Pious and idealistic Captain Kuiper has brought 156 Jewish refugees from Europe during World War II, but he is not allowed to land at any port in South or North America. He arrives with them off Sandy Hook. He is unwilling to return them to Europe and feels he must do with them as if he were God. He schemes to blow up the boat and have the Jews rescued by the Yachts in a regatta there; this will give his passengers a decent chance for a safe home, for he feels the humans will be cared for through public opinion.

3 acts; 15 men, 0 women, extras; 1 interior (the cabin). Royalty: $50-25.

HARWOOD, H. M., with R. Gore-Browne. <u>Cynara</u> (1930). Based on the novel <u>An Imperfect Lover</u> by R. Gore-Browne. BP 1931-32; French, 1931.

Jim and Clemency Warlock's conversation one August night is

strained for a married couple, as he makes plans to leave for Africa. The trouble between them began three months before, when Clemency left Jim alone in London for six weeks while she accompanied her sister abroad. While she is gone, Jim falls in with an old friend of his father's, John Tring, who takes him places he's never been and encourages and even arranges a relationship with a young, working-class girl named Doris. One thing leads to another, and though it is really Jim who is seduced, it is Doris who cannot stand to live without him when Clemency returns from her trip. Jim tries to let her down gently, but finally has to write her a letter and tell her that he can't see her anymore. Doris, who has been fired from her job because she spends the days mooning over Jim, poisons herself. Jim's letter is discovered by the police, and at the coroner's inquest her death is ruled a suicide, but a rider to the verdict expresses the jury's "disgust at the conduct of Mr. Warlock." Jim's career in law is thereby destroyed, along with his long-range goal of running for public office. His friend Tring has offered him a position in Tanganyika to escape from his present situation. In the epilogue, we discover that Clemency is going to stick with him and make the move to Africa too.

Prologue, 3 acts, epilogue; 13 men, 18 women; 4 interiors, 4 exteriors.

HARWOOD, Ronald. The Dresser (1980). BP 1981-82; Samuel French.

An aging actor known only to us as Sir, touring the provinces with a second-rate Shakespearean company during the Nazi bombings of 1942, is taken to a hospital after making a spectacle of himself in public. He is worn out, exhausted, senile. Her Ladyship, the actress he has lived with for many years (he never divorced his wife because he feared it would jeopardize the knighthood he never got), believes the evening's performance should be cancelled, as does the stage manager. But Norman, long-time dresser to the actor, insists that the curtain go up on schedule. Even Sir believes that after 100,000 performances he deserves a one-night reprieve, but Norman, who reminds the actor that this night will be his 227th King Lear, keeps pumping him up, fussing with him, preparing him for the performance, though the old man can't even remember his first line. Norman pushes him through the whole play, after the first act reporting that Her Ladyship called his acting tonight "mighty." She denies it to Sir, carrying on a long-time argument that he must retire before it is too late. In his dressing room after the play Sir dies, taking away the whole reason for Norman's existence. Worse yet, in reading the dedication to the memoirs Sir had started working on, Norman finds, among credits to carpenters, electricians, and property men, not one word about himself and the 16 years of loyal and dedicated service as Sir's dresser.

2 acts; 10 men, 3 women; composite interior. Royalty: $60-40.

HAUPTMANN, Gerhart. The Assumption of Hannele (1893). Tr. by

Archer, Heinemann, 1894; in BAT v. 12; in Drama v. 12, 1922;
tr. by Meltzer, Doubleday, 1908; in his Dramatic Works,
Huebsch, v. 4, 1912; HAV; HUD; tr. by Bryan in Poet Lore
v. 20, 1909.

A young girl, Hannele, ill-treated by her drunken step-father,
tries to follow her mother by drowning herself. In the sordid hospital she dreams glorious fantastic pictures based on the Bible. She
thinks she is in heaven, where she sees the nurse as her mother,
the school-ma'am who reprimands her step-father becomes the Saviour
Jesus. As the doctor hovers over her, we realize she has died.
   2 acts; 7 men, 4 women; 1 interior.

_____. The Sunken Bell (1896). Tr. by Meltzer, Russell, 1896;
Doubleday, 1899 & 1914; Heinemann, 1900 & 1907; in his Dramatic Works, Huebsch, & Lond., Secker, 1914, v. 4; FRA v.
18; MOSQ; WHK; tr. by Harned in Poet Lore v. 10, 1898.

A pious bell-founder, Heinrich, is surprised by a goblin who
throws into the lake a bell meant for a chapel; he lures Heinrich
away to an amiable water nymph, an elf-maiden Rautendelein. He
sets about to construct a complete set of chimes, but becomes exhausted, and stricken with remorse, he returns home to die, as the
sunken bell tolls. Blends the natural with the supernatural, the
physical with the spiritual, presenting the creative soul of the
idealistic artist in his struggles to reconcile his highest aspirations
with every day duties.
   5 acts; 7 men, 2 women, 2 children, extras; 1 interior, 2 exteriors; some fanciful costumes.

_____. The Weavers (1892). Tr. by Morison, Heinemann, 1899,
in his Dramatic Works, Huebsch, & Secker, 1912, v. 1; FRA
v. 18; CEW; DIC; DIK v. 1; SMP; TRE-1, 2, & 3; TREA-2;
WHI; abridged in Pierce & Matthews, v. 2.

Presents the suffering of the oppressed weavers during the
labor riots in Silesia in 1844: a sociological study of the conflict
between capital and labor. Moritz Jaeger, back from the army,
shows righteous indignation at the treatment of the weavers. When
an old weaver is killed by accident, the maddened weavers sack the
home of the capitalist Dreisigger. In the end the mill owners accede
to their demands.
   5 acts; 27 men, 13 women, extras; 5 interiors; costumes of
the period.

_____. The White Saviour (1920). Tr. by Muir in KRE; in his
Dramatic Works, Huebsch, v. 8.

In the conquest of Mexico Catholic Cortez overcomes the mystic Montezuma who worships the white men as gods.
   11 scenes; 26 men, 4 women, extras; 6 interiors, 2 exteriors;
costumes of the period.

HAWTHORNE, Ruth. Mrs. Partridge Presents. See entry under
   Kennedy, Mary.

HAYDEN, John. Lost Horizons (1934). Based on the play by Harry
    Segall. BP 1934-35.
    Young Janet Evans has given up her aspirations to be an ac-
tress. All she wants to do in life is marry Ralph Bondley. When
he jilts her to make his reputation in New York, she kills herself.
The next scene finds her in the Hall of Records, which looks pretty
much like the reading room of a public library. She is told by her
Guide that she must read several books--of her own life and thin
volumes of people she has never heard of. Since she took her own
life, the Guide explains, she interrupted not only her own destiny,
but she ruined people's lives she was destined to save by knowing
them (like playwright-producer Adam Thayer, who committed suicide
over his failure to get his play on Broadway) or by accidentally con-
fronting people important to them (like David Prescott, who is executed for a crime he did not commit). In subsequent scenes we see
her do just that, as the play resumes as if she had lived, pursuing
her acting career, becoming a star on Broadway, and falling in love
with Adam Thayer. In the last scene we return to the Hall of
Records, where Janet is sobbing over the record of her life she has
been reading. Then Adam Thayer is brought in to pay the same
reading penance. She runs to him but discovers he doesn't know
who she is. Since she killed herself, she never showed up in his
life, so he killed himself.
    3 acts; 33 men, 15 women; 15 interiors, 1 exterior.

HAYES, Alfred. The Girl on the Via Flaminia (1954). BP 1953-54;
    Samuel French.
    The setting is liberated, cold, hungry, and bitter Rome of
1944. Lisa has been fixed up with Robert, an American sergeant,
who will pose as her husband so that they can share a room in an
apartment on the Via Flaminia. In the apartment is a young Italian
former officer who hates all the liberators for what they are doing to
his country, and whose bitterness at the disgrace of his countrymen's military record is only matched by what to him is the present
despicable behavior of Italian women. When Robert and Lisa are unable to produce their marraige papers one night, the police summon
Lisa to report to the Questura, where her civilian identity card is
taken up in exchange for the yellow card of a professional prostitute.
Robert, who doesn't understand, tears the card up, explaining that
he loves her. Lisa runs out, and is last seen running down the Via
Flaminia.
    3 acts; 7 men, 4 women; composite interior. Royalty: $50-
    25.

HAYES, Joseph. The Desperate Hours (1955). Adapted from his
    novel. BP 1954-55; Samuel French.
    This polished melodrama portrays a helpless suburban family
held prisoner in their home by three escaped criminals. One morning the Hilliard family is preparing for the day's activities when
three armed and desperate criminals invade the home. Mr. Hilliard
and 19-year old Cindy are allowed to go to work, while Mrs. Hilliard

and 10-year old Ralphie are held hostages. While the terror mounts within the home the police search is closing in on the Hilliard house.
    11 men, 3 women; unit set. Royalty: $50-25.

HAZELTON, George C., Jr. Mistress Nell (1900). Pub. in Phila.,
    1900; in v. 16 of America's Lost Plays, Princeton Univ. Pr.,
    1941.
    An orange-girl, Nell Gwyn, is made an actress by Jack Hart who loves her; the Duke of Buckingham courts her, and he in turn must yield to the King. She goes to a ball masked and disguised as the lad Beau Adair, where she is given papers signed by the King to be delivered to France. She is chased back to her rooms, where all follow to seek Adair. There she discloses what the King has signed--and also herself as Adair.
    4 acts; 11 men, 4 women, extras; 4 interiors; 1 exterior;
    costumes of the time of Charles II.

_____ and J. H. Benrimo. The Yellow Jacket (1912). Bobbs-
    Merrill, 1913; French, 1939; in DID.
    With delicate touches which reach the emotions and with whimsical and subtle art the story of Wu Hoo Git is unfolded, from his birth until he attains the Yellow Jacket of Emperor. Tests and develops the imagination of reader or listener. Furniture changes are made in full view of the audience by a supposedly invisible property man.
    3 acts; 17 men, 12 women; 1 set: interior or stage of a
    Chinese theatre; Chinese costumes. Royalty: $25-20.

HEBBEL, Friedrich. Agnes Bernauer (1855). Tr. by Pattee in
    Poet Lore v. 20, 1909; in SMK.
    Prince Albrecht, son of Ernest, Duke of Bavaria, marries a barber's daughter, the beautiful Agnes Bernauer. He is disowned by his father. After a few years of happy marriage, Agnes is condemned to death by a court, because she could not be recognized by the nobility and is also thought of as a witch. Asked to give up Albrecht, she refuses and drowns herself, the victim of social convention. Albrecht's father upholds the State at the expense of his own happiness and that of his son, who finally comes to recognize his responsibility.
    5 acts; 16 men, 3 women, extras; 7 interiors, 3 exteriors;
    costumes of the period (about 1425).

_____. Judith (1841). Tr. by Van Doren in Poet Lore v. 25,
    1914.
    Bethulia in the mountains of Palestine is besieged by the Assyrian general, Holofernes, sent by Nebuchadnezzar to subdue all that land. Judith a beautiful Jewish widow, offers to go to Holofernes. There he insults her dignity. After he has disgraced her and lies drunk, she cuts off his head and returns it to the people. When they see the head they rush out after the fleeing invaders.
    5 acts; 13 men, 3 women, extras; 2 interiors; costumes of

the period.

_____. Maria Magdalena (1944). Tr. by Thomas in FRA v. 9;
SMI; tr. by Green in Poet Lore v. 25, 1914; in Clark, W. S.;
tr. by Fairley in his Three Plays, Dutton, 1914; TRE-2 (v. 2);
TREA-1.
   When Karl, the son of the family, is accused of theft, his
stern father, Anton, does not defend him.   Later he is proved innocent.   Meantime Leonhard deserts Clara, the daughter of the
family, when Karl is arrested.   Through it all Clara is blamed by
her father; his strait-laced morality drives her to suicide; she jumps
down the well.
   3 acts; 8 men, 3 women; 2 interiors; costumes of the period.

HECHT, Ben, with Charles MacArthur.   The Front Page (1928).
   BP 1928-29; Samuel French.
   Authentically depicts the rushing atmosphere of a newspaper
office.   Hildy Johnson, an old school reporter, on his way to be
married, reaches the newspaper office as the news comes that Earl
Williams, about to be executed for killing a policeman, has made a
jail break, just as the Governor has sent a reprieve.   Williams drops
in through a window and is hidden in a desk.   The reprieve arrives
and Hildy has saved an innocent man; he leaves for New York with
his bride, but his boss finds a way to get him back on the job--as
a single man.
   17 men, 5 women; 1 interior.   Royalty: $50-25.

HEDBERG, Tor.   Johan Ulfstjerna (1907).   Tr. by Colquist in Poet
   Lore, v. 32, 1921.
   Scene is laid in Finland, formerly a Swedish province.   Johan's son Helge is pledged to kill the Governor of Finland, but the
father does it, so that his son may live and marry Agda.   Johan
meets a martyr's death as a patriotic champion of an oppressed
people, offering himself for the benefit of his fellowmen.
   5 acts; 5 men, 3 women; 2 interiors; costumes of the period.

HEGGEN, Thomas, with Joshua Logan.   Mister Roberts (1948).
   BP 1947-48; Dramatists Play Service.
   On board a drab Navy cargo ship in the Pacific during the
war with Japan, the martinet of a captain is hated by all.   Lt. (j.g.)
Douglas Roberts is popular and shares the crew's dislike of their
captain.   He secures shore leave for the entire crew from the captain by his own sacrifice.   He finally gets his transfer to a combat
zone, whereupon the crew award him the "Order of the Palm for
action above and beyond the call of duty"--for casting overboard the
captain's pet palm tree.
   2 acts (with fade-outs); 19 men, 1 woman, extras; 1 set
   (deck with 3 interiors).   Royalty: $50-35.

HEIBERG, Gunner.   The Balcony (1894).   Tr. by Vickner & Hughes
   in Poet Lore, v. 33, 1922.

Presents different aspects of the nature of love: the conflict between erotic passion and intellectual culture. Julie tires of her sensuous husband Ressman and takes on two lovers: idealistic Abel and healthy Antonio. She rejoices when her husband is killed by the fall off the balcony, by which her lovers have entered. She then marries Abel, but deceives him in turn, and when deserted by him, she is left with Antonio.

3 acts; 3 men, 1 woman, 1 servant; 1 interior.

_____. The Tragedy of Love (1904). Tr. by Björkman in DID.
Presents the difference between masculine and feminine love. Erling and Karen both experience the passion, but to her it is everything, to him it is subordinate to his work. When she finds existence meaningless, she ends her life.

4 acts; 3 men, 4 women, 2 children, extras; 3 interiors.

HEIJERMANS, Herman, Jr. The Ghetto (1899). Tr. & adapted by
    Fernald. Lond., Heinemann, 1899 & 1910.
In a sordid home in the Jewish quarter of Amsterdam old Sachel, a rich but blind merchant, wishes to marry his son Rafael to Rebecca, daughter of his neighbor Aaron, in order to secure a rich dowry and annex the two houses. But Rafael, a musician who is composing a symphony, has already married by civil ceremony Rosa, a Christian servant whom Sachel and his sister Esther have reared. Hounded by them and persuaded that Rafael has deserted her (he having gone to London about his symphony and his letters having been withheld), Rosa throws herself into the river. Just then Rafael returns; Rosa is carried in and revives. Rafael denounces his father and bears Rosa away to a happier world.

4 acts; 7 men, 3 women, extras; 1 interior, 2 exteriors; costumes of time and place.

_____. The "Good Hope" (1900). Tr. by Higgins in Drama,
    v. 2, 1912; tr. by Saunders & Heijermans-Houwink; abridged
    in Pierce & Matthews, v. 2. Acting edition: Samuel French.
A callous shipowner, Clemens Bos, allows a rotten schooner "The Good Hope" to sail again, though he knows that all the crew may be sacrificed. Chronicles the departure of the sailors, and reveals the agony of those left without a husband when the ship is lost. The sea is victor in man's struggle to gain a living from it; man is cruel to man in the eternal struggle for gold.

4 acts; 11 men, 7 women; 2 interiors; Dutch costumes.
Royalty: $25-20.

HELLMAN, Lillian. Another Part of the Forest (1946). BP 1946-47;
    Dramatists Play Service.
Going back twenty years, shows how the Hubbards (see Little Foxes, below) cut their eye teeth, the beginning of their dirty doings in the deep South. Father Marcus Hubbard is a self-made egomaniac and has a vicious influence over his children: Ben, a Machiavellian son; Oscar, a whining ninny who joins up with the KKK;

Regina, diamond hard and already talking of going to Chicago where she can get fine clothes. Ben is ordered out of the house, but he discovers a way to blackmail his father and become the new family tyrant.

    8 men, 5 women; 1 interior. Royalty: $50-25.

_____. The Autumn Garden (1951). BP 1950-51; Dramatists Play Service.

    Most of the guests at Constance Tuckerman's hotel are unhappy. Sophie, Constance's niece, is engaged to a man whose mother will never permit the marriage to take place. General Grigg's wife will not divorce him; she uses her heart condition to hold him. Edward Crossman blames his alcoholism on Constance for marrying another man. But when she, long since a widow, asks him to marry her, he realizes he never loved her. Nicholas Denery and his wife are miserable together. All of the characters come to realize that they cannot revolt from their own past.

    5 men, 7 women; 1 interior. Royalty: $50-25.

_____. The Children's Hour (1934). BP 1934-35; Dramatists Play Service.

    Demonstrates the havoc a lie can create. Two intelligent high-principled women, Karen and Martha, run a girls' school. A malicious lying youngster of 14, a rather intolerable child, starts a scandal to defend herself which wrecks the school. The girl claims that Karen and Martha have an "abnormal" relationship. Later is is proved that the gossip was entirely wrong, but the damage had been done, and Martha has killed herself.

    2 men, 12 women; 2 interiors. Royalty: $50-35.

_____, The Lark. See entry under Anouilh, Jean.

_____. The Little Foxes (1939). BP 1938-39; Dramatists Play Service.

    Sordid selfishness rules the Hubbard family in the deep South (see Another Part of the Forest, above). Scheming Ben is arranging to build a bigger cotton mill but needs $75,000 more. Leo, Oscar's son, "borrows" the bonds from Horace's safe deposit box. Horace, with a bad heart, discovers this but before he can carry out his will, dies on the stairs, going up after his medicine and unaided by his wife Regina. Now she demands of her brothers 75 percent in the mill instead of her third. But Ben rather suspects her, and her daughter Alexandra's love for her mother turns to hate.

    6 men, 4 women; 1 interior. Royalty: $50-35.

_____. Montserrat. See entry under Robles, Emmanuel.

_____. My Mother, My Father and Me (1963). Dramatists Play Service.

    An ironic study of a "modern" family, depicting its greed, stupidity, and lack of values. Though the Halpern family lives at a fancy Manhattan address, the various members are losers. Herman, the husband, is on the verge of bankruptcy; Bernie, the son, dabbles in everything in an effort to find himself; Rona, the mother, spends all of her time buying useless and expensive "bargains." Also present is Rona's mother, whom the family keeps in a broom closet before sending her off to a chamber-of-horrors rest home. Herman gets deeper in debt, Bernie turns to painting, and Rona continues to buy until the bankruptcy is complete. At the end the husband and wife have moved to Cleveland to begin the cycle again; and Bernie, now an "Indian" living in the Far West, is selling a huge order of hand-made jewelry to his mother.

14 men, 14 women (doubling possible in both roles); multiple sets. Royalty: $50-25.

_____. The Searching Wind (1944). BP 1943-44; Dramatists Play Service.

A probe into the people and events that brought on World War II, set in 1944 with flashbacks to Rome of 1922 (Mussolini taking over), Berlin of 1923 (bread costs 140 billion francs and well-financed and organized pogroms are going on), and Paris of 1938 (the French and Germans will appease Hitler and give him the Sudetenland). Through these events we experience the lives of an American family made up of a former liberal journalist grandfather who stands aside and mocks; a father, who works for the State Department and com- promises; a mother, who hobnobs with the European socially elite who play every end against the middle; and a son, whose leg is being amputated following combat in Italy. It is the son who exposes the appeasers and politicians who have messed up his world.

2 acts; 11 men, 3 women; 1 interior. Royalty: $50-25.

_____. Toys in the Attic (1960). BP 1959-60; Dramatists Play Service.

Two sisters live together in a southern town. Though they dream of going to Europe someday, they continue to spend their money bailing their brother out of trouble. This time brother re- turns rich. He pays off the home mortgage, buys them new clothes and fur coats, sends letters of resignation to his sisters' employers, and has $150,000 in cash left. Instead of being pleased, the sisters are disappointed that their assistance is no longer needed, and the younger one makes sure the secret deal the brother is pulling off does not succeed.

4 men, 4 women, 3 extras; interior-exterior. Royalty: $50- 25.

_____. Watch on the Rhine (1941). BP 1940-41; Dramatists Play Service.

An idealistic anti-Nazi German, Kurt, comes to America with his American wife and children, hoping for respite from his danger- ous work in the underground in World War II. What he finds is Teck, a Nazi agent who blackmails him for the large amount of money Kurt has--money to be used to free captured anti-Nazis. Kurt kills Teck, then leaves his family and returns to Germany, to what may

be his death.
>6 men (2 of them boys), 5 women (1 a girl); 1 interior.
>Royalty: $50-25.

HENLEY, Beth. Crimes of the Heart (1981). BP 1980-81; Dramatists
Play Service.
>The MaGrath sisters are having something of a reunion five
years after Hurricane Camille's devastation of their small Mississippi
town. Old Grandaddy is on his deathbed in the hospital, and youngest sister Babe is out of jail on bond for trying to kill her husband.
She has a good lawyer (though the best lawyer in town is the man
she shot), but her case is complicated because photographs exist of
her entertaining the 15-year-old son of one of her domestics--in the
garage. Meg, who left town in a scandal during the hurricane, has
failed as a singer in Los Angeles but probably not as "cheap Christmas trash" with the men. Sister Lenny, whose 30th birthday is now
the focus for celebration, let the only man who ever paid her any attention slip away because of her bad left ovary. What the sisters
refuse to do is to follow their mother's example--she hanged herself
in the basement along with her cat, making the national news.
Babe's attempted murder probably wouldn't even be getting state-
wide, she says, if her husband wasn't a senator from Copiah County. At the end of the play the girls get their wish of experiencing
just one moment when they were all together smiling and laughing.
>3 acts; 2 men, 4 women; 1 interior. Royalty: $50.

_____. The Miss Firecracker Contest (1984). BP 1983-84;
Dramatists Play Service.
>Carnelle Scott, 24 years old and suffering from a "Miss Hot
Tamale" reputation in her small Mississippi town, vows to change her
life by winning the annual July 4th Miss Firecracker Contest.
Popeye Jackson, a glowing down-to-earth young lady, will make
Carnelle's special talent costume. Her cousins Elain (she has left
her "perfect" home and fawning husband) and Delmount (he is just
out of a mental institution for having smashed a man in the face with
a bottle in a "duel") are drawn into the activity, too. The plan is
to sell the family home and let Carnelle leave town with a blaze of
glory as a Miss Firecracker. Elain, as a former winner, is asked to
speak at this year's festivities on the topic "My Life as a Beauty."
As it turns out, Carnelle is only appreciated by men from her
promiscuous past, and her performance is only good for a miserable
fifth place. Elain, who is good at running everything but her own
life, will return to her family, perhaps carrying home a special
present for her husband. Delmount and Popeye seem to have found
something special together, and as they sit on the roof of the big
tent watching the fireworks, Carnelle is invited to join them and to
enjoy life, not needing to have the vaguest idea of "what the main
thing is."
>2 acts; 2 men, 4 women; unit set. Royalty: $50.

HERBERT, Frederick Hugh. For Love or Money (1947). Dramatists

Play Service.

An unsophisticated girl is driven by an auto breakdown and a storm into the home of an aging matinee idol. He is pursued by women of his own age, but her innocence and enthusiasm conquer him. They decide to get married.

3 acts; 4 men, 4 women; 1 interior. Royalty: $50-25.

_____. Kiss and Tell (1943). BP 1942-43; Dramatists Play Service.

Corliss Archer at 16 wants to be grown up and acts the young lady when Private Earhart is entertained. She also must not reveal the secret that Mildred Pringle, her neighbor, and her brother Lennie are married, and even more--that Mildred is to have a baby. Because Corliss goes with Mildred to the doctor's, the parents think Corliss is to have the baby. Being sworn to secrecy, Corliss can say nothing and does not until the end, when all is cleared up.

3 acts; 9 men and boys, 6 women & girls; 1 interior. Royalty: $35-25.

_____. The Moon Is Blue (1951). Dramatists Play Service.

Patty O'Neill and Donald Gresham meet on the observation tower of the Empire State building. They agree to dine together, but the rain houses them in his apartment, where she prepares dinner. While he is getting the groceries, David Slater, father of Cynthia (Donald's fiancée), drops in and mixes things up. But once in a blue moon affairs straighten themselves out on short notice.

3 acts; 3 men, 1 woman; 1 interior, 1 exterior. Royalty: $50-25.

HERNE, James A. Hearts of Oak (1879). In his Shore Acres & Other Plays, French, 1928.

Terry and Ned are pals; both love Crystal. Terry marries Crystal who loves Ned. He finds this out and leaves for the Arctic. He returns blind, blesses them, and dies.

6 acts; 7 men, 4 women, extras; 3 interiors, 3 exteriors.

_____. Margaret Fleming (1890). QUIL.

Amid scenes of domestic happiness, Margaret's sister Lena has a child. Lena dies in childbirth, revealing to Margaret that her husband Philip was her lover. She entrusts the child to Margaret. At first she is horrified, but as she takes care of the illegitimate baby she develops the maternal instinct. The shock of the revelation however has increased her blindness, and Philip attempts suicide; but they find they need each other.

4 acts; 7 men, 5 women; 3 interiors.

_____. Shore Acres (1892). In his Shore Acres & Other Plays, French, 1928.

The scene is laid at the Berry farm, Shore Acres, near Bar Harbor, Me. The love of Helen for Dr. Sam is opposed by her father; they flee in a sail boat with Captain Ben to the lighthouse.

Uncle Nat brings about her freedom, her marriage, and her reconciliation with her father.
    4 acts; 19 men, 11 women; 2 interiors, 2 exteriors; costumes
of 1890's.

HERSEY, John. A Bell for Adano. See entry under Osborn, Paul.

_____. The Child Buyer. See entry under Shyre, Paul.

HERVIEU, Paul E. In Chains (1895). Tr. by Asckenasy in Poet
    Lore, v. 20, 1909; also by him in Dramatist, v. 1, 1910, as
    Enchained; also spoken of as The Nippers.
    Divorce is refused, first by the husband when the wife asks
it, later by the wife when the husband wants it; so both are riveted
to the same ball and chain. She refuses because the child they now
have is an obligation; they can no longer think of themselves only.
    3 acts; 4 men, 3 women; 2 interiors.

_____. Know Thyself (1909). Tr. by Cerf in DIC.
    Two triangles are precisely balanced: The General, his wife,
and his ward; his guest, his guest's wife, and his own son. The
General revises his advice as to honor when it concerns his wife
and his son. A thesis play, declaring against hasty judgments and
divorce, a theme which controls the action though it never obtrudes.
    3 acts; 5 men, 2 women; 1 interior.

_____. The Trail of the Torch (1901). Tr. by Haughton, Dou-
    bleday, 1915; abridged in Pierce & Matthews, v. 2, as The Torch
    Race.
    Depicts almost too perfectly maternal and filial love: The
instinctive self-sacrifice made by parents for their children who accept it as their right. Pictures the motives and actions of three
generations: Savine, the mother, steals money from her mother to
save her daughter, Marie-Jeanne; later she allows her mother to
die that Marie-Jeanne may be happy. A thesis play, demonstrating
one generation handing on to the next the torch of the joy of life.
    4 acts; 7 men, 8 women; 2 interiors, 1 exterior.

HEYWARD, Dorothy and DuBose Heyward. Porgy (1927). Double-
    day, 1927; Theatre Guild, 1928; GASE, THF; BP 1927-28.
    Crippled Porgy has super-luck at shooting dice and has super-
power in his arms. He chokes to death gigantic stevedore Crown
when he returns seeking Bess. Porgy has freed Bess from Crown,
but she has left for the North with Sportin' Life. (Made into an
opera, 1935, as Porgy and Bess; music by George Gershwin.)
    4 acts; 18 men, 6 women, extras; 2 exteriors.

HEYWARD, DuBose. Porgy. See entry under Heyward, Dorothy.

HEYWOOD, Thomas. A Woman Killed with Kindness (1603). In his
    Works; in Mermaid ser., 1888; in many collections.

When her husband Frankford discovers the guilty love of his wife Anne for his friend Wendoll, he sends her to his lovely manor seven miles away, with every comfort but never to see him nor her children. Loneliness and remorse break her spirit; at her deathbed there is a touching scene of forgiveness.

5 acts; 17 men, 3 women, extras; 11 interiors, 5 exteriors; costumes of the period.

HIGGINS, Colin, with Denis Cannan. The Ik (1984). Based on Colin Turnbull's The Mountain People. Dramatic Publishing Company.

Anthropologist Colin Turnbull receives permission to observe the Iks, once nomadic hunters in Northern Uganda, now forced to farm in a barren mountainous territory where the total annual rainfall is only four inches. Turnbull is guided by an Ik named Atum, who lies and steals to get food, cigarettes, and pills. The Ik, always living near starvation, feed only themselves, not their children or their elders. The only pleasure they get, according to Atum, is when they eat and defecate. Only a few tribesmen live like the Iks lived when they were hunters. One woman, Losike, feeds her sick husband and an old man who speaks to the spirits that the Ik tribe once needed and respected. The rest will do anything to put food in their bellies.

Flexible cast; area staging. Royalty: $60-40.

HILL, Lucienne. See entries under Anouilh, Jean.

HOCHHUTH, Rolf. The Deputy (1963). Adapted by Jerome Rothenberg. BP 1963-64; Samuel French.

The horrors of the World War II Nazi genocide are recalled in this historical drama about the Pope's refusal to speak out against the annihilation of the Jews. Sickened by his job, a German death camp officer goes to the Papal legate in Berlin with positive evidence that the Nazis are practicing genocide. His message is carried to Pope Pius XII himself, but he continues to vacillate, and with specious reasoning defends his refusal to get involved. In several documented scenes the bravery of the lower ranking church officials is shown as they hide as many Jews as possible in monasteries. One young priest is so intensely concerned that he pins the Star of David upon himself and joins the Jews in their march to the gas chambers.

22 men, 2 women, extras; several X-ray sets. Royalty: $50-25.

HODGE, Merton. The Wind and the Rain (1933). Gollancz, 1934; French, 1934 & 1938; FAME.

Charles Tritton arrives in Edinburgh to study for five years for his medical degree. He left Jill, his finacée, in London; he is homesick for her and for his mother. In Edinburgh he meets Anne Hargreaves, who comes to stand in the place of his fiancée and his mother. At the end of the five years he finds he can't go on without Anne and he goes to London to tell Jill, and returns to Edin-

burgh.
3 acts; 6 men, 3 women; 1 interior.

HODSON, J. L. Return to the Wood. See John Wilson's Hamp.

HOFFMAN, William M. As Is (1985). BP 1984-85; Dramatists Play
Service.
Rich, partner in a catering business and most recently an
author, tells his circle of friends and relatives that he has been
diagnosed as a victim of Acquired Immune Deficiency Syndrome
(AIDS). His partner eases him out of the business, his new homosexual lover leaves him, his brother's wife won't permit him to visit
their home for the sake of the children, and his other friends disappear. Only his former lover, Saul, will accept him "as is." Saul
helps him through the stages of the physical deterioration and
through the emotional upheavals of fear, anger, denial, and acceptance of his condition. By the end of the play, Rich is confined to
a hospice, with Saul beside his bed and sometimes in it.
1 act; 10 men, 3 women; unit set. Royalty: $50.

HOLBERG, Ludvig. Erasmus Montanus; or, Rasmus Berg (1731).
Tr. by Campbell & Schenck in MAU; also, American Scandinavian
Foundation, 1914 (Comedies of Holberg).
Rasmus Berg, son of a poor peasant, returns from the university as Erasmus Montanus, with all his newly acquired manners
and information. He proves his mother as a stone, the deacon a
cock; he argues with the bailiff, quarrels with his family and his
prospective father-in-law; he is finally subdued by a lieutenant who
threatens to draft him for the army. An effective satire on the
Latin-crammed pedantry of the Danish students of the 18th century.
5 acts; 8 men, 3 women; 1 interior, 1 exterior; costumes of
the period.

_____. Jeppe of the Hill (1722). Tr. by Campbell & Schenck,
(Comedies of Holberg) Amer. Scandinavian Foundation, 1914;
tr. by Jagendorf in CLF-2.
A laughter-loving baron plays a joke on Jeppe. He takes him
while drunk to his castle; the next morning he makes Jeppe think he
is a lord and that his memories of poverty are but illusions. Later
Jeppe reverts to being a peasant and remains the same drunkard.
(Compare Calderon's Life Is a Dream, and Shakespeare's Christopher
Sly in the Taming of the Shrew.)
5 acts; 13 men, 2 women, extras; 2 interiors, 1 exterior;
costumes of the period.

_____. The Political Tinker (1722). Tr. by Campbell & Schenck,
American Scandinavian Foundation (Comedies of Holberg), 1914.
Satirizes Herman the tinker and a group of other artisans who
sit and criticize the management of the city. It would appear that
they know everything; in reality they know nothing. When two practical jokers declare Herman burgomaster, he is quite set up, being

bitten by a desire to shine in politics. But when he has to make
some difficult decisions, he decides to remain a tinker without political aspirations.

     5 acts; 12 men, 6 women, extras; 1 interior, 1 exterior;
costumes of the period.

HOLM, John Cecil. Best Foot Forward (1941). Dramatic Publishing
     Company.

     High School Theater Classics, 1945-49, about the boys at
Winsocki Prep preparing for the arrival of girls to take to the annual
prom. Everyone is happy except Bud Hooper. Bud saw a movie the
month before starring Gale Joy, the wham girl. He got so carried
away that he wrote her an invitation to the dance and she needed
publicity so badly that she accepted. Now Bud must write his regular date Helen that he will be ill until after the dance. Then he
tries to pass Gale Joy off as his regular girl Helen. When Helen arrives, Bud gets into deeper and deeper trouble.

     10 men, 7 women; 1 set. Royalty: $35.

_____, with George Abbott. Three Men on a Horse (1935). Dra-
     matists Play Service.

     As he rides to town on the bus, a timid greeting-card poet,
Erwin, dopes out the probable winners at the race track. He gives
a trio his tips and they win. They shanghai Erwin and set him
picking winners. All goes well until he makes a bet of his own--and
the charm is gone. He goes back to his greeting-card job.

     3 acts; 11 men, 4 women; 3 interiors. Royalty: $35-30.

HOLMES, John Haynes and Reginald Lawrence. If This Be Treason
     (1935). Macmillan, 1935; French carried.

     Peace-minded John Gordon faces the problem of declaring war
on the very day of his inauguration as President of the United
States. He believes incitement to peace should be made as exciting
as incitement to war. The Japanese have attacked Manila. Congress
is certain to declare war; but he tells the Congressmen that as Com-
mander-in-Chief he will refuse to order the Army and Navy into action. His opponents call it treason and make plans to impeach him.
He goes on a mission of peace to Japan, where his proffers are refused. But the Japanese people have heard of his offer of peace;
they free their leader Koyé, and the soldiers will not shoot down the
populace. He feels he has proved his conviction that the masses do
not want war.

     3 acts (7 scenes); 23 men, 3 women, extras; 5 interiors.

HOLTZMAN, Jonathan. Foxfire. See entry under Cooper, Susan.

HOME, John. Douglas (1756). BAT; BEL v. 3; BRI v. 1; DIB v.
     4; INCH v. 16; MCM; MOR; MOSE; NET; OXB v. 12; STM.

     Shortly after the Lady's secret marriage with Douglas, one
of the family's bitterest enemies, a son is born, who is lost to her
when Douglas goes to war and is killed. Years later, that son,

Norval, now grown, saves Lord Randolph, now her husband, and is promised protection. By jewels she discovers that Norval is her son. At a secret meeting-place, Glenalvin, the villain of the play and in love with the Lady, stabs Norval, who however kills him before he dies. Lady Randolph in despair leaps off a cliff and Lord Randolph goes to the wars.

   5 acts; 4 men, 2 women, extras; 2 exteriors; costumes of the 12th century in Scotland.

HOPKINS, Arthur. Burlesque. See entry under Watters, George Manker.

HOPKINS, John. Find Your Way Home (1971). BP 1973-74; Samuel French.

   A homosexual play about Julian Weston (called Julie) and his lovers. Most of the action concerns a former lover who comes back to Julie--Alan Harrison, who is pursued (this is Act Two) by his wife. Julie and Mrs. Harrison attack and insult one another, as do Alan and his wife, in an indictment against modern heterosexual marriage and child-raising. In the end it is not exactly clear what will happen to Julie and Alan, who will attempt to make a go of it as a couple, nor how long their relationship is apt to last. Julie, we learn, has considerable experience as a male hustler; Alan is experienced at running away.

   3 men, 1 woman; 1 interior. Royalty: $50-35.

HOPWOOD, Avery. The Bat. See entry under Rinehart, Mary Roberts.

HOUGHTON, W. Stanley. Hindle Wakes (1912). Sidgwick, 1912; Luce, 1913; French carried; in his Works, Constable, 1914, v. 2; DIG; PLAP v. 1; TUCD.

   From their various viewpoints both families argue that the boy should be forced to marry the girl as a cure for sick honor, after their holiday lark at the Hindle Wakes. But Fanny doesn't respect him and declares she won't marry him; she insists on equal freedom with the man, thus upsetting all their calculations and giving a new turn to the familiar situation.

   3 acts; 4 men, 5 women; 2 interiors.

_____. Independent Means (1909). French, 1911; in his Works, Constable, 1914, v. 1.

   After his father, ruined financially, dies, his son Edgar, a rather hopeless weakling, can't get or hold any position--he was educated as a gentleman. His wife Sidney has independent ideas, takes the reins, and gets a position as a stenographer with their friend Ritchie, a motor car dealer. Later Edgar is engaged as a salesman there and develops out of his weakness, so that he and his wife are reunited.

   4 acts; 3 men, 3 women; 2 interiors.

_____. The Younger Generation (1910). French, 1910; in his
Works, Constable, 1914, v. 1.
Develops the idea that parents should alter their attitude and
realize that the younger generation has ideas and rights of its own.
The father and grandmother have been very strict with his three
children. Their Uncle Tom helps them to gain release. He takes
Arthur back with him to Hamburg, insists that Grace become engaged
to Clifford (on a year's trial basis), and maybe Reggie can get to
Canada, or Australia, or New Zealand.
   3 acts; 7 men, 4 women; 1 interior.

HOUSE, Ron, with Diz White, John Neville-Andrews, Alan Shearman,
and Derek Cunningham. Bullshot Crummond (1974). Samuel
French.
The play is a parody of a 1930's low-budget "B" detective
movie, with part of the fun coming from impossible attempts to trans-
pose film effects (a plane crash, a car chase) to the stage. On top
of that, the hero Bullshot Crummond is a bumbling British officer
who believes he is more clever and suave than he is, though he finally succeeds in saving Professor Fenton and his formula for syn-
thetic diamonds from an evil German adversary, Otto Von Brunno.
Through it all, Captain Drummond is hotly pursued by Rosemary
Fenton, the professor's daughter he is helping, and by Lenya Von
Brunno, Otto's evil mistress.
   2 acts; 3 men, 2 women; unit set. Royalty: $50-35.

HOUSMAN, Laurence. The Chinese Lantern (1908). Sidgwick,
1908; French carried in revised edition.
Depicts Chinese art student life. It is filled with the color,
movement, joy, humor, and poetic atmosphere of China.
   3 acts; 12 men, 2 women, extras; 1 interior; Chinese costumes. Can be produced with all-girl cast.

_____ and Harley Granville-Barker. Prunella (1906). Brentano,
1906; Lond., Bullen, 1907; Sidgwick & Jackson, 1914; Little,
Brown, 1916; PLAP v. 2. Samuel French.
Sub-title: Love in a Dutch garden. Tells of the awakening
of love in the heart of a young girl who lives in a little house
guarded by her three aged aunts. As a fantastic allegory in felici-
tous style, gently satirizes false restraints in secluding a girl from
life instead of preparing her for it.
   3 acts; 11 men, 10 women; 1 exterior (a garden); fanciful
   costumes. Can be produced with all-girl cast. Royalty:
   $50.

_____. Victoria Regina (1934). BP 1935-36; Scribner, 1935;
French, 1936; CEU.
Presents selected scenes in the life of the beloved Royal La-
dy "Her Gracious Majesty" from her accession in 1837 to the Diamond
Jubilee in 1897. Shows her selection of Albert as her Prince Con-
sort, her marriage, and a bit of their loving if a bit tempestuous

life together. A studied interpretation of her personality, vignettes
of an astute yet bigoted woman. All based on the recorded word.
    10 episodes in 3 acts; 20 men, 11 women, extras; 8 interiors.
    Costumes of the period. (May be produced as one-acts.)

HOWARD, Bronson. The Henrietta (1887). French, 1901; HAL.
    A satire on financial and social life with its rush and heart-
lessness. A grasping capitalist, Nicholas Van Alstyne, is opposed
by his elder son, Nick Jr., a thorough rogue, who tries to ruin his
father and get all the family wealth. The younger son, Bertie, the
Lamb, good-natured and unfitted for the ruthlessness of Wall Street,
has quiet and complete contempt for the feverish life of his father
and brother. Yet by a stroke of luck he achieves a financial coup
which gives his father everything and leaves Nick Jr. with nothing.
The deal is made in The Henrietta, the name of the mine in whose
stock they speculate. (Revised as The New Henrietta by Winchell
Smith & Victor Mapes & produced in 1913, pub. by French, 1913.)
    4 acts; 9 men, 4 women; 3 interiors.

_____. Shenandoah (1888). MOSS-v. 3; QUIK; QUIL; abridged
    in Pierce & Matthews, v. 1.
    Two West Point graduates are in Charleston when Fort Sum-
ter is fired on. Kerchival West from the North is in love with a
Southern girl, Gertrude Ellingham; her brother Robert, also from
the south, is in love with Kerchival's sister, Madeline West. These
lovers suffer, for they must take opposite sides in this struggle between the States. All meet again at a farm house in the Shenandoah
Valley, the day when Sheridan's Ride is featured.
    4 acts; 15 men, 7 women; 2 interiors, 1 exterior; military
    & civilian costumes of the 1860's.

_____. Young Mrs. Wintrhop (1882). French, 1899.
    When they lose their child Winthrop and wife drift apart, he
absorbed in his professional affairs, she taking refuge in the social
whirl. They think of divorce, but are brought together by the sentimental family lawyer who reminds them of their happy past. A
Mrs. Chetwyn demonstrates the power of rumor and provides much
comedy.
    4 acts; 5 men, 4 women; 1 interior.

HOWARD, Ed. Greater Tuna. See entry under Williams, Jaston.

HOWARD, Sidney. Alien Corn (1933). Scribner, 1933; French,
    1934; FAMD; BP 1932-33.
    Hemmed in by the depressing surroundings of a woman's col-
lege in a small mid-Western town, Elsa Brandt, a piano teacher and
talented daughter of a German musician, feels frustrated because she
is denied the greater opportunities which have come to several less
talented persons. Her concert was cancelled, but she gave it anyway. A tragic love affair nearly wrecks her career.
    3 acts; 11 men, 3 women; 1 interior.

_____. Dodsworth (1934). Based on the novel by Sinclair Lewis. BP 1933-34; Dramatists Play Service.

A typical American industrialist, Sam Dodsworth, retires from his auto company and goes to Europe with his wife Fran. She becomes interested in Kurt von Obersdorf and wants a divorce so as to marry him, but his mother points out the obstacles to that. During his wife's defection, he has come to appreciate the understanding Mrs. Cortright, so he leaves his selfish and cheating wife on the liner to go her own way.

22 men, 14 women, doubling possible; 9 interiors (unit set possible). Royalty: $35-25.

_____. The Late Christopher Bean (1932). BP 1932-33; Samuel French.

Satirically presents the Haggett family in a small New England town who had given refuge to the painter, Christopher Bean, but had deemed his paintings worthless. Abby, the housemaid, was the only one to appreciate him, so she kept what he had painted. Bean becomes famous after his death and his paintings are being sought by art dealers. The badgered Haggett family is shown up as hard, selfish, and ill-tempered; but they can't sell the paintings as they belong to Abby, who had also been Mrs. Christopher Bean.

5 men, 4 women; 1 interior. Royalty: $35-25.

_____. Ned McCobb's Daughter (1926). Samuel French.

Shrewd, honest, courageous Carrie proves her worth in preserving the tavern, in fighting for her children's future, in foiling the flashy bootlegger Babe Callahan, and in forgiving her worthless husband until he proves unfaithful. Her father, Captain McCobb, preserves his self-respect in raising the money stolen by Carrie's husband.

3 acts; 8 men, 2 women; 2 interiors. Royalty: $25.

_____. The Silver Cord (1926). BP 1926-27; Samuel French.

The Victorian-type mother loves her two sons too much; she is selfishly possessive, but with an air of preserving them from disaster. The young scientist, Christina, is more secure in her love and wins David her husband away; but Hester, Robert's fiancée, loses out--he remains tied to his mother's apron strings.

3 acts; 2 men, 4 women; 2 interiors. Royalty: $50-25.

_____. They Knew What They Wanted (1924). BP 1924-25; Samuel French.

Tony, a winegrower in California, gets a wife by mail by sending a picture of Joe, his hired hand. Amy is shocked to find out the fraud but marries Tony anyway. She needs the security of a home (and besides, Tony is in bed with two broken legs). On the wedding night Amy gives herself to Joe and becomes pregnant. By the time Tony finds out, Amy has begun to love Tony as a husband. After a very conventional reaction to the news of the pregnancy, Tony decides that what he wanted all along was children, what Amy wanted was a home, what Joe wanted was his freedom. They all got what they wanted.

> 9 men, 4 women, extras; 1 interior. Royalty: $35-25.

_____, with Paul DeKruif. Yellow Jack (1934). Dramatists Play Service.

> Vivid dramatization of the fight against yellow fever. Walter Reed heads a commission in Cuba in 1900, trying to discover how yellow fever is caused. Dr. Carlos Finlay suggests his belief that it is a mosquito bearing the germs. The heroic members of the Commission and four brave volunteer soldiers are inoculated and prove this is true. Having learned how the disease is contracted, it became possible to prevent it. This is a bright page in the records of the medical profession and of the U.S. Army Medical corps.
>
> 1 continuous act; 26 men, 1 woman, extras; 1 unit set, varied by lighting. Royalty: $35-25.

HOWE, Tina. Painting Churches (1984). BP 1983-84; Samuel French.

> Gardner Church is an elite New England poet in his seventies who is in the process of moving out of the family home in Beacon Hill, Boston, to a more affordable house on Cape Cod. His last Pulitzer didn't even cover the real estate tax, and he is so "doddery" now that he can't supplement his income with readings. His wife, Fanny, a Bostonian from a fine family and only ten years younger, believes that her husband is mad as a hatter now, writing gibberish criticism when he is not busy teaching his pet parakeet to recite parts of Gray's "Elegy." Meanwhile, she makes do with what she can: holding on to her grandmother's Paul Revere silver while she shops thrift stores for 85 cent Lily Dache hats. Into all of this turmoil comes their daughter, Mags, a portrait painter of some reputation (she's so out she's in) who will paint the Churches for her one-woman show in a prestigious New York gallery that has shown "ALL THE HEAVIES." Mags first insists that her father is in full control of his senses, then that her mother's humor is a kind of cruelty and humiliation. She comes to understand, however, that her mother is the full-time caring one, that she is merely attempting to put some life and fun into a deteriorating situation, and that it hurts a good bit more to see her parents than to paint them.
>
> 2 acts; 1 man, 2 women; 1 interior. Royalty: $60-40.

HOYT, Charles H. A Texas Steer (1894). MOSL.

> See entry of revised version (1940) above under Randolph Carter.
>
> 4 acts; 19 men, 4 women, extras; 3 interiors, 1 exterior; some Western costumes.

HSIUNG, S. I. See Lady Precious Stream.

HUGHES, Hatcher. Hell-Bent Fer Heaven (1924). BP 1923-24; Samuel French.

Pulitzer Prize play 1924. A half-crazed jealous fanatic who
has "got religion," Rufe Pryor, a pious rogue, hypocritically tries
to put his rival out of the way by reviving a slumbering feud; but
he himself suffers the consequences. Scenes are effective and the
native wit is skillfully introduced.

3 acts; 5 men, 2 women; 1 interior. Royalty: $25.

HUGHES, Richard. A High Wind in Jamaica. See Paul Osborn's
Innocent Voyage.

HUGO, Victor. Hernani (1830). Tr. by Crosland in CAR; CLF-2;
MAU.

Donna Sol de Silva is betrothed to her guardian, the aged
Don Ruy; she is also besought by King Charles of Spain, but she
is in love with the outlaw Hernani. Her plan to elope with Hernani
is overheard by the King, who seizes her. Don Ruy and Hernani
plan to rescue her. After King Charles is made Emperor of Germany,
he pardons Hernani, who proves to be the noble Don Juan of Aragon.
Now again Hernani and Donna Sol can plan to marry, but on his wedding night Hernani hears the blast of Don Ruy's horn and, according
to his vow, he drinks the poison. His bride joins him in death.

5 acts; 23 men, 2 women, extras; 3 interiors, 2 exteriors;
costumes of the period.

HUME, Cyril and Richard Maibaum. Ransom (1963). Samuel French.

The father of a kidnapped boy makes a startling plea to the
kidnappers in this exciting mystery drama. He's supposed to signal
the kidnappers that the half-million dollar ransom will be paid through
a TV program his firm sponsors. Instead he appears on the show
himself, shows the money, and then announces that the ransom will
not be paid. If the kidnappers do not return the boy unharmed, he
will offer it as a reward for their capture. The father receives universal condemnation; even his wife collapses in hysterics. Then the
tension ends in a shattering, harrowing climax.

11 men, 4 women, extras; 1 interior. Royalty: $25-20.

HURLBUT, William. Bride of the Lamb (1926). BP 1925-26; Boni &
Liveright, 1926.

Ina Bowman hopes her husband Roy, a dentist, is not about
to disrupt their drab life again by going on another drinking binge
when tent evangelist Rev. Sanderson T. Albaugh comes to town on a
crusade and stays at the Bowman house. Ina tries to keep her feelings under control, but the night before Albaugh is to leave town
they both give in to passion. The next morning she loathes her
husband ("I'd die if I had to touch him again!"), and takes all the
money she can find from her daughter's bank and Roy's pockets to
buy the minister a $90 watch. She wants to run away with him, but
he can't let her, having the Lord's work to do. As he goes to his
last revival alone, a woman enters--Albaugh's wife whom he thinks
is dead. Ina becomes hysterical. When Albaugh returns he sends
the Bowman daughter to get Roy, but Ina has poisoned him. In the

last scene she is completely psychotic, wearing a mosquito netting
for a wedding veil, introducing everyone to her imaginary bridegroom, "Mr. Christ," and humming the wedding march as the sheriff
takes her away.
3 acts; 6 men, 5 women; 1 interior.

HUSSON, Albert. My Three Angels. See entry under Spewack,
Samuel.

HUSTON, John. In Time to Come. See entry under Koch, Howard.

HYMAN, Mac. No Time for Sergeants. See entry under Levin, Ira.

HYMER, John B. East Is West. See entry under Shipman, Samuel.

IBSEN, Henrik. A Doll's House (1879). Tr. by Archer in his Prose
Dramas, v. 1, Lovell, 1890; in his Collected Works, v. 7, Scribner, & Heinemann, 1906-07; Baker, 1900; MAU; CLF-2; COJ; tr.
by Sharp, Dutton, 1910; tr. by Stratton, Ginn, 1931; tr. not
given, Macmillan (Mod. rdrs ser.) 1927; Nelson, 1941; in his
Eleven Plays, Modern Library giants, 1935; in his Works in 1
vol., Blue Ribbon, 1932 & 1941; abridged in Pierce & Matthews,
v. 2. Act. eds. tr. by Ginsbury, French; adapted by Christopher Hampton, French; tr. by Meyer, Dramatists Play Service.
Presents the right of a woman to self-development in a world
planned by and for men, and the falseness of marriage which does
not rest on true comradeship. Nora wants to help her husband,
Helmer, but in doing so by forging a check is brought face to face
with her position: her husband treats her like a doll and an orna-
ment to his house rather than as a thinking helpmeet. The slam of
the door as she leaves echoed around the world. (A valuable play
to study, with its unities of time, place, and action; with its un-
forced exposition; with scarcely a superfluous word, all tending
towards the final scene.)
4 acts; 4 men, 4 women, 3 children; 1 interior. Royalties:
Ginsbury, $15; Hampton, $50-25; Meyer, $35-25.

_____. An Enemy of the People (1882). Tr. by Aveling as An
Enemy of Society in his The Pillars of Society, Lond., Scott,
1888; same in his Collected Works, v. 8, Scribner, & Heinemann, 1907; tr. by Archer in his Prose Dramas, v. 2, Lovell,
1891; same Baker, 1900; tr. by Sharp in his Ghosts, Dutton,
1911; tr. by Stratton, Ginn, 1931; tr. not given, Grosset,
1931; in his 11 Plays, Modern Library Giants, 1935; in his
Works in 1 v., Blue Ribbon, 1932 & 1941; DUR; adapted by
Dramatists Play Service, 1952; tr. by Meyer, Dramatists Play
Service.
Everywhere Dr. Stockmann, in his desire to remedy a shameful condition of the water supply, is met by the opposition of the
vested interests. No one will listen to him, and he is voted an enemy of the people. A scathing stinging satire on the shortcomings of

society.

     5 acts; 7 men, 2 women, 2 boys, extras; 3 interiors. Royalties: Miller, $35-25; Meyer, $35-25.

     _____. Ghosts (1881). Tr. by Archer in BAT; MIL, & Baker, 1900; tr. by Sharp, Dutton, 1911; tr. & adapted by Leverton, French, 1937; tr. by Ginsbury, Baker, 1938, & Lond., French. 1938; tr. not given, Blue Ribbon, 1932 & 1941; in his 11 Plays, Mod. Liby Giants, 1935; Nelson, 1941; tr. by LeGallienne in BEN; TRE-3; TREA-2. Tr. by Koefoed, French; tr. by Arthur Kopit, French; adap. by Christopher Hampton, French; tr. by Meyer, Dramatists Play Service.

     Oswald Alving has inherited syphilis from his degenerate father. He returns home from his studies in Paris to be on hand for the dedication of an orphanage, built in honor of his deceased father. The orphanage, uninsured, is destroyed by fire. Oswald learns that the maid, with whom he desires an affair, is his half-sister. When he suffers a final attack from his dreadful disease, he begs his mother to kill him. Ibsen argues that Mrs. Alving should have left her husband, before Oswald's birth, when she discovered that the Captain was dissolute. Some critics feel that the play is an answer to the critics who objected to the ending of A Doll's House (above).

     3 men, 2 women; 1 interior. Royalties: Koefoed, $35-25; Kopit, $50-25; Hampton, $50-35; Meyer, $35-25.

     _____. Hedda Gabler (1890). Tr. by Gosse, U.S. Book Co., 1891; Baker, 1900; tr. by Archer in his Prose Dramas, v. 3, Lovell, 1891; tr. by Gosse & Archer in his Collected Works, v. 10, Scribner, & Heinemann, 1907; CLS; tr. by LeGallienne & Leyssac in LEG; tr. not given, Macmillan, 1927 (Mod. Reader Ser.); 4 Plays, Grosset, 1931; Works in 1 v., Blue Ribbon, 1932 & 1941; 11 Plays, Modern Lib. Giants, 1935; abridged in Pierce & Matthews, v. 2; BLO; HATS; TRE-1, 2, & 3; TREA-2; Act. ed. Christopher Hampton, French; tr. by Meyer, Dramatists Play Service.

     Realistic study of a woman who is out of harmony with her surroundings but cannot rise above them, who, with selfish individualism, wishes to test her will and influence, but fears to face the consequences; who is ever a compromiser. Like the pistols she makes use of, she attracts and fascinates, but is cold, unscrupulous, relentless, and passionless.

     4 acts; 3 men, 4 women, 1 interior. Royalties: Hampton, $50-25; Meyer, $35-25.

     _____. John Gabriel Borkman (1894). Tr. by Archer in his Collected Works, v. 9, Scribner, & Heinemann, 1907; tr. not given, in 11 Plays, Modern Lib. Giants, 1935. Tr. by Meyer, Dramatists Play Service.

     Borkman dreamed of the power which money could bring, for it he sacrificed love, the love of Ella, marrying her hard sister Gunhild because she could bring him more money. Even after his imprisonment for embezzlement he still tries for gain, but it is too late. All three have lost the power of real living; only the old clerk Foldal had really lived.

4 acts; 3 men, 5 women; 2 interiors, 1 exterior. Royalty: $35-25.

_____. The Master Builder (1892). Tr. by Gosse & Archer in his Collected Works, v. 10, Scribner, & Heinemann, 1907; Baker, 1900; in World's Great Plays, 1944; tr. by Stratton, Ginn, 1931; tr. not given, Macmillan, 1927 (Mod. Readers ser.); Works in 1 vol., Blue Ribbon, 1932 & 1941; 11 Plays, Mod. Liby Giants, 1935; 4 Plays, Nelson, 1941; in WOR; tr. by Meyer, Dramatists Play Service.

Solness had won success as an architect at the expense of his wife and associates, but his conscience still bothers him. A fascinating girl, Hilda Wangel, encourages him to do great things still. He climbs to the top of a tower, becomes dizzy, and falls to his death.

3 acts; 4 men, 3 women; 2 interiors, 1 exterior. Royalty: $35-25.

_____. Peer Gynt (1867). Tr. by Archer, Lond., Scott, 1902; in his Collected Works, v. 4, Scribner, & Heinemann, 1907; acting version, Baker, 1900; tr. by Roberts, Lond., Secker, & Kennerley, 1913; tr. by Sharp, Dutton, 1922; tr. by Stratton, Ginn, 1931; tr. not given, Blue Ribbon, 1932 & 1941; Mod. Lib. Giants, 1935; Lippincott, 1936; Oxford, 1940 (World's classics). Tr. by Fjelde, French; adap. by Paul Green, French; tr. by Meyer, Dramatists Play Service.

Effective satire on human nature, developing the failure of one who is a compromiser by heredity, and who trims so many times that there is little distinctive left of him. He steals a bride at a wedding, he forsakes Solveig, the young girl who remains true to him to the end, he has many adventures but is always the selfish egoist, ever looking out for himself.

5 acts in 12 scenes; 31 men, 14 women, many extras; 2 interiors, several exteriors; variety of costumes. Royalties: Fjelde, $50-35; Green, $35-25; Meyer, $35-25.

_____. The Pillars of Society (1877). Tr. by Aveling, Lond., Scott, 1888; tr. by Archer in his Prose Dramas, v. 2, Lovell, 1891; in his Collected Works, v. 6, Scribner, & Heinemann, 1907; tr. not given, Works, Blue Ribbon, 1932 & 1941; 11 Plays, Mod. Lib. Giants, 1935; abridged in Pierce & Matthews, v. 2; tr. Meyer, Dramatists Play Service; tr. by Leverton, French.

Bernick, the genial philanthropist and supposed model for the community, is in reality dishonest in thought, hypocrytical in action, murderous in will. His deeper nature is so stirred by the discovery that his son would have been lost at sea if the unseaworthy vessel had sailed, that he confesses his sins. The only pillars of society are truth and freedom.

4 acts; 10 men, 9 women, extras; 1 interior. Royalties:
Leverton, none; Meyer, $35-25.

_____. The Pretenders (1863). Tr. by Archer in his Collected
Works, v. 2, Scribner, & Heinemann, 1907; SMK; tr. by Sharp,
Dutton, 1913.
Out of the early Norse sagas the play develops the difference
between Haakon, who believes in himself and his ideals, and Skule,
who is cursed with self-doubt, a capable but not forceful regent.
The fortunate Haakon becomes king of united Norway in 1247.
5 acts; 15 men, 5 women, extras; 6 interiors, 4 exteriors;
costumes of the period (13th century, Norway).

_____. The Wild Duck (1884). Tr. by Archer, Baker, 1900; in
his Collected Works, Scribner, & Heinemann, 1907; LEV; MOSQ;
WHI; tr. not given in CEW; Plays, Macmillan, 1927 (Mod.
Readers ser.); Grosset, 1931; Blue Ribbon, 1932 & 1941; Mod.
Lib. Giants, 1935; Nelson, 1941. Tr. by Meyer, Dramatists
Play Service; adap. by Hampton, French.
The Ekdal family is living happily, their dreamy illusions
symbolized by the crippled wild duck in the attic, adapting itself to
its environment. A young idealist, Gregers Werle, believing that
the truth should always be told and at all costs, brings tragedy to
the once-happy family. He talks to Hedvig, the young daughter,
about the joy of sacrifice, tells her she must kill her cherished pet,
the wild duck; instead she shoots herself.
5 acts; 9 men, 3 women, extras; 2 interiors. Royalties:
Meyer, $35-25; Hampton, $50-35.

INGE, William. Bus Stop (1955). BP 1954-55; Dramatists Play
Service.
Several people are gathered at a bus stop restaurant in a
small Kansas town, but the main characters are a young cowboy,
Bo Decker, and a night club singer, Cherie. Bo has kidnapped
Cherie and insists she marry him and move to his Montana ranch.
She resists his blundering courtship procedures until it looks as if
Bo will have to sling her over his shoulder and carry a kicking
reluctant bride all the way to Montana. But Bo learns something
about tenderness, and by the end of the play Cherie, too, desires
the marriage.
5 men, 3 women; 1 interior. Royalty: $50-35.

_____. Come Back, Little Sheba (1950). BP 1949-50; Samuel
French.
Depicts two ordinary people, Doc and Lola his wife, living
rather drab lives because ambition is gone and dreams replace effective living. When their baby died, Doc took to drink, but for a
year has been a member of Alcoholics Anonymous. Lola still dreams
of a good life and the return of her pet dog Sheba. Doc goes off
the deep end until two A.A.'s take him away to recover. When he
returns a week later, he and Lola are ready to begin anew. Lola

has a new contentment and new dreams, but little Sheba is gone for
good.
>8 men, 3 women; 1 interior. Royalty: $50-25.

_____. The Dark at the Top of the Stairs (1957). BP 1957-58;
Dramatists Play Service.

It is dark at the top of everyone's stairs, especially for those
in the Flood family. Ruben, the father, sells harnesses on the road,
and is insecure over his job which is becoming rapidly obsolete.
Sonny, the ten-year-old son, is bullied by his schoolmaster and feels
secure only while playing with his movie star pictures. Reenie, the
teen-age daughter, is shy and introverted. The climax of the play
comes over a Country Club dance. Ruben quarrels with his wife
over a dress purchased for Reenie. When he is accused of being
unfaithful he strikes his wife and storms out. Reenie's date, a
Jewish boy, is insulted at the dance and commits suicide, while she
hides in the restroom. At the end, both children break out of their
shells, and Ruben returns home as a machinery salesman with great
hope for the future.
>13 men, 2 women, 3 boys, 2 girls; 1 interior. Royalty:
$50-35.

_____. A Loss of Roses (1959). Dramatists Play Service.

The widow Miss Field and her twenty-one-year-old son live
in a small town near Kansas City. The time is 1933, but both have
jobs: she as a nurse and he as a gas station attendant. The
mother wishes her son was the kind of man his father was. Into
the house moves an old friend, an actress, and soon the son is having an affair with her. He proposes marriage, changes his mind the
following day, and sets out on his own.
>4 men, 4 women; 1 interior. Royalty: $50-25.

_____. Natural Affection (1963). Dramatists Play Service.

Sue Barker has had a hard life. Her husband deserted her
before their son Donnie was born, and Donnie grew up in orphan
homes and penal farms. Presently Sue has a good job, a nice apartment, and a lover, Bernie Slovenk, who is not interested in marrying
her. Sue is satisfied with this arrangement, but finds it threatened
when her son arrives for a Christmas visit and announces that he
will not have to return to the penal farm if his mother will provide
a home for him. The showdown comes on Christmas Eve with a drinking party attended by the couple next door. The husband soon
passes out, and the wife throws herself at Bernie (who turns out to
be accustomed to it) and Donnie. The husband regains consciousness
and goes out on the town. Sue and Bernie quarrel, and he storms
out to spend the night next door. The next morning Donnie begs
his mother to let him make up for the loss of her lover, but she runs
off after Bernie. Donnie, who must now return to the penal farm,
takes out his anger by savagely attacking a woman in the building.
>7 men, 5 women; 1 interior. Royalty: $50-25.

_____. Picnic (1953). BP 1952-53; Dramatists Play Service.
Deals with the effect that Hal Carter, young man of great
animal vitality, has on the lives of a feminine household in a small
Kansas town. The Owens' house includes a woman who has been
deserted by her husband, two maturing daughters, and a spinster
school teacher who is a boarder. Hal seriously upsets all of their
lives. Madge Owens, the oldest daughter, is willing to give up her
chance for a wealthy marriage to spend the annual picnic evening
making love to Hal. Millie, the younger daughter, sees herself as
something other than a tomboy because of Hal's charm. And the
school teacher feels compelled to beg her boyfriend of long standing
to marry her. At the end of the play Hal must flee from the town
to escape a car stealing charge.
     4 men, 7 women; unit set. Royalty: $50-25.

_____. Splendor in the Grass (1966). Adapted from Inge's
    screenplay by F. Andrew Leslie. Dramatists Play Service.
The play is set in the midwest of the 1920's. Bud Stamper,
son of the town's richest man, is the star athlete at the local high
school; Deanie Loomis is his girl friend. The two young people have
powerful feelings about one another, but are restrained by the bad
example set by Bud's older sister. Though Bud wants to marry
Deanie and go on to agricultural school, his father insists that he
attend Yale and prepare to join the family oil business. The father
wins, and Bud convinces Deanie they should see less of one another
in preparation for his traveling East. Deanie reacts with an emotional crack-up which leads her to a mental institution. By the time
she is released, the stock market crash has forced Bud to leave
school and to take up farming with his wife, a former waitress.
Deanie is engaged to a fellow patient, a former doctor. A brief
meeting enables the former sweethearts to break the old ties.
     10 men, 9 women; unit set. Royalty: $35-25.

IONESCO, Eugene. The Killer (1959). Translated by Donald Wat-
    son. Samuel French.
This macabre morality comedy presents the author's observation on planned society, the welfare state, and regimentation.
Hiram Sherman is an average young man who leaves his dingy apartment one day and, after taking a wrong bus, ends up at a futuristic
housing development. Here everything is always perfect. As the
architect explains, "Nothing is left to chance." At first Hiram is
eager to buy a house; then, however, he notices how totally artificial, how dehumanized the development is. And the terrible truth,
as Hiram discovers, is that every day a killer disposes of 2 or 3
people in the beautiful lake which the development surrounds. Hiram
finds the killer's timetable and list of victims but can interest no
one, not even the police, in the bizarre situation. Then, at the end
of the play, Hiram meets the killer, alone.
     10 men, 2 women; cyclorama, collage, inset. Royalty: $35-
    25.

_____. Rhinoceros (1960). Translated by Derek Prouse. BP
1960-61; Samuel French.
Man's hypocrisy and self delusion receive a savagely satiric
treatment in this play. One normal Sunday morning a roaring rhinoceros appears in a small town, precipitating a pointless argument
over whether it is an Asian or an African rhino. Then one by one
all the citizens change to rhinoceroses; they have no integrity, no
identity as true humans. Finally only Berenger, the publishing
clerk, is left as a human, unable to join the others because he refuses to compromise his integrity.
11 men, 6 women, extras; 1 exterior, 2 interiors. Royalty:
$50-25.

IRVING, Washington. Charles the Second. See entry under Payne,
John Howard.

_____. Rip Van Winkle. In his Sketch-Book, 1819.
Rip escapes a shrewish wife, wanders up the mountain, meets
the Henry Hudson crew, and after drinking their liquor, sleeps twenty years. Returning to his village he identifies himself with difficul-
ty. In 1950 Charles Burke dramatized the tale in 2 acts; 11 men,
3 women, 1 child, simple scenery, costumes of the period. It was
published by French, 1857, in Bates, The Drama, v. 19; in MOSS-3.
In 1865 and thereafter Joseph Jefferson made the play famous in a
version by Dion Boucicault. It is in 4 acts; 7 men, 3 women, extras; 3 interiors, 3 exteriors; costumes of the period. It was published by Dodd, 1903; carried by Baker; LAW; CERC; QUIK; QUIL.
In 1937 G. H. Leverton revised an early dramatization by Walter
Kerr, pub. by French, 1937; has 3 acts; 25 men, 6 women; 3 exteriors; costumes of the period.

IRWIN, James. See Moore, Edward J.

ISHERWOOD, Christopher. The Ascent of F.6. See entry under
Auden, Wystan Hugh.

JACKSON, N. H. The Two Orphans. See entry under d'Ennery,
Adolphe P.

JACKSON, Shirley. The Haunting of Hill House. See entry under
Leslie, F. Andrew.

JAMES, Dan. Winter Soldiers (1943). BP 1942-43.
The time is November 1941. The Germans need to move all
available troops to the Eastern Front for the attack on Moscow, but
the "little people," or Winter Soldiers, of occupied Eastern Europe
collaborate in slowing down the troop trains through sabotage, union
strikes, missed signals, even military engagements so that the Nazis
do not get to the right place at the right time, and are therefore
repulsed and their lines broken and the battle lost. The Germans
may be a well organized war machine, but their efficiency and

planning can never override the will of the little people who can hold them up for a day, or an hour, in the cause of freedom.
2 acts; 38 men, 4 women; various interiors and exteriors.

JAMES, Henry. The Aspern Papers. See entry under Redgrave, Michael.

_____. "The Turn of the Screw." See William Archibald's The Innocents.

_____. Washington Square. See Ruth and Augustus Goetz's The Heiress.

JEFFERS, Robinson. Medea (1946). Freely adapted from Euripides' Medea. Samuel French.
    In this version, the ambitious Jason gives up Medea, his foreign wife, to take a new bride more politically helpful. Medea, living in a strange land, thinks of possible ways of revenge. On the day she is to be banished she brings death to the new bride and horror to Jason.
    5 men, 5 women, extras; 1 exterior. Royalty: $50-25.

JEROME, Helen B. Charlotte Corday (1936). Lond., H. Hamilton, 1937; FIP.
    Charlotte has made up her mind to kill Marat to rid France of him. She goes to Paris, on an excuse to help her friend recover her estates. She gets an appointment with Marat for 7:30, gets in, and stabs him in his bath. She is arraigned and tried. The final scene is in her cell.
    3 acts; 17 men, 7 women, extras; 5 interiors; costumes.

_____. Jane Eyre. See entry under Brontë, Charlotte.

_____. Pride and Prejudice. See entry under Austen, Jane.

JEROME, Jerome K. The Passing of the Third Floor Back (1908). Lond., Hurst, 1910, Dodd, 1908 & 1921; Samuel French.
    The failures and foibles of the boarders are presented with humor: the landlady who cheats her lodgers, the little slavey, the major who drinks and bullies his wife, a retired book-maker, and others. The mysterious passer-by who takes the Third Floor Back awakens in each by the right sympathetic touch and desire to develop a "better self." A parable which emphasizes the spirit of brotherly love.
    3 acts; 6 men, 6 women; 1 interior. Royalty: $25-20.

JIRÁSEK, Alois. The Lantern (Lucerna, 1905). Tr. by Buben & Noyes in Poet Lore, v. 36, 1925.
    The miller Libor has Hanicka, a waif, as a ward. He refuses to greet the Princess or allow Hanicka to go as a maid, though summoned by the bailiff and magistrate. But he has the duty of bearing

the lantern before the nobility. This makes the Princess curious
and she gets the miller to bear the lantern to the old castle from
the ancestral linden tree. Then she gives him rights, and he may
marry his ward.

4 acts; 17 men, 5 women, extras; 2 interiors, 3 exteriors;
costumes of the period.

JOB, Thomas. Thérèse (1947). Based on Emile Zola's novel.
Samuel French.

Thérèse Raquin is married to Camille, a dull, complaining
milliner who is not nearly as interesting as their boarder, an artist. So Thérèse and the artist take Camille out on a Sunday and
drown him. His mother accepts the story of an accident, and after
a year is pleased when Thérèse and the artist marry. But the
death of Camille comes between the two murderers, and they quarrel
continually. The mother overhears a conversation and is shocked
into paralysis. She is able, however, to communicate the incriminating information to the Inspector of Police--through the medium of
dominoes.

4 men, 4 women; 1 interior. Royalty: $50-25.

_____. Uncle Harry (1942). BP 1941-42; Samuel French.

Kindly, lovable Uncle Harry manages to do away with two
very unpleasant sisters, but ironically can not convince anyone that
he's guilty. Constantly bullied by the possessive spinsters, Harry
can stand it no longer. He murders one and frames the second for
the crime. Then his conscience begins to torment him and he decides to confess. However, no one can believe that such a likeable
fellow could commit murder. He loses all his friends and his
sweetheart; people avoid the brother of a condemned prisoner. Finally he begs his imprisoned sister for help. Strangely enough, she
refuses, realizing that for Harry the torture of his conscience and
being shunned by his former friends is the worst punishment he
could possibly face.

9 men, 6 women; 3 interiors. Royalty: $50-25.

JOHNSON, Bill. Dirty Work at the Crossroads (1942). Samuel
French.

Innocent Nellie Lovelace faces a series of evil assaults on her
virtue in this Gay Nineties melodrama. Nellie's mother has been
poisoned, and she is torn from the arms of the dying lady by the
very man who poisoned her, the villainous Munro. He is already
married to Ida Rhinegold, the belle of the New Haven Music Hall,
but that does not prevent his pursuing poor Nellie. In spite of
his many evil deeds--which include blackmail and bewithment--love
and virtue triumph in the end, and Munro receives his just punishment.

3 men, 7 women; 1 interior. Royalty: $15.

JOHNSON, Pamela H. The Rehearsal. See entry under Anouilh,
Jean.

JONES, Henry Arthur. The Case of Rebellious Susan (1894). Macmillan, 1894; French, 1901; in his Representative Plays, Little,
Brown, 1925, v. 2; BP 1894-1899.
Trying to retaliate on her disloyal husband, Lady Susan attempts a romance which is checked by her wise uncle. Socially,
sauce for the gander is not for the goose.
3 acts; 10 men, 4 women; 3 interiors.

_____. Dolly Reforming Herself (1908). French, 1910; in his
Representative Plays, Little, 1925, v. 4; CHA.
Making New Year's resolutions, extravagant Dolly decides to
economize and shake off her bad habits, her husband promises to
stop using profanity, and her friend Renie determines to end her
flirtation with Dolly's cousin. At the end, all three have failed to
live up to their New Year resolutions.
4 acts; 6 men, 3 women; 1 interior.

_____. The Liars (1897). Macmillan, 1901; French, 1909; in
his Representative Plays, Little, 1925, v. 3; DUR; MAP; MAT;
abridged in Pierce & Matthews, v. 1.
Lady Jessica, flirting with Edward Falkner and making her
husband furiously jealous, has a dinner engagement with Falkner.
Around this is fashioned a whole tissue of lies. With clever technique the follies and foibles of English society are satirized, em-
phasizing honesty as the best policy. A masterly climax at the end
of the 3d act.
4 acts; 10 men, 6 women; 3 interiors, 1 exterior.

_____. The Lie (1914). Doran, 1915.
Self-sacrificing Elinor gives up to her selfish younger sister
Lucy, helps her when she has a baby by a deceased lover, and by
wrong information (the lie) loses Gerald to Lucy with a Judas kiss.
Noll Dibdin offers a chance which Elinor will probably take.
4 acts; 4 men, 5 women, 1 boy of 5; 2 interiors.

_____. Mary Goes First (1913). Doubleday, 1914; taken over by
French; in his Representative Plays, Little, 1925, v. 4.
Amusingly pictures social rivalry between two ambitious ladies in a small community in England. Their social climbing is
complicated with a political campaign by their husbands. In the end
the deposed social queen regains her place.
3 acts & epilog; 8 men, 4 women; 1 interior.

_____. Michael and His Lost Angel (1895). Macmillan, 1895; in
his Representative Plays, Little, 1925, v. 3; DIC; abridged in
Pierce & Matthews, v. 1.
The clergyman Michael, living under a vow of celibacy, makes
a young girl Rose confess her sin before the congregation. Later
he commits a similar sin when left on an island with the insincere,
frivolous fascinator Mrs. Lesden. He publicly confesses as he made
Rose do. Feelingly pictures the struggle between religion and love,

code morality and nature.
    5 acts; 6 men, 4 women, many extras; 4 interiors.

_____. Mrs. Dane's Defence (1900). Macmillan, 1905; French,
1909; in his Representative Plays, Little, 1925, v. 3; COT.
    Mrs. Dane hopes to make amends for her past sins by mar-
rying Lionel, a generous youth who loves her devotedly and who is
only too willing to believe her innocent. But his step-father, Sir
Daniel, in his effective cross-examination, crumbles her defences
and assures Lionel he would always mistrust her. They give each
other up, and the moralities of society are upheld.
    4 acts; 8 men, 4 women; 2 interiors.

_____. The Silver King (1882). French, 1907; in his Represent-
ative Plays, Little, 1925, v. 1.
    Following Geoffrey Ware to his house, Will Denver is chloro-
formed by a group of thieves who shoot Ware with Denver's revolver.
He is accused of the crime but escapes to Nevada, where he strikes
it rich and becomes the Silver King. Returning to England, his old
servant Jaikes restores the old house for his wife Nelly and the
children; his name is cleared, for Spider Skinner, the real murderer
is arrested.
    5 acts; 21 men, 5 women, 2 children, extras; 11 interiors,
4 exteriors; costumes of the period.

_____. Whitewashing Julia (1903). Macmillan, 1905, French,
1909.
    When Mrs. Julia Wren returns to the English village she is
snubbed by her family and friends because of stories about her conduct, her puff-box, and her reported morganatic marriage with a
titled continental. She comes to the rescue of Eddie Pinkney and
helps Lady Pinkney in many ways, so that when Lady Pinkney's
brother, William Stillingfleet, proposes and burns some incriminating
confession, she is finally accepted socially and her reputation is
whitewashed.
    3 acts & epilog; 8 men, 10 women; 2 interiors, 1 exterior (a
tent).

JONES, LeRoi. Dutchman (1964). Samuel French.
    A sexy white blonde, riding in a subway car, tries every way
she can think of to seduce a young Negro youth sitting beside her.
When even vulgarity does not work, she humiliates him until he de-
scends to her level to exchange insults. When he shouts that the
murder of whites by blacks would make everyone sane, she stabs
him. The other whites dispose of his body while she primps for her
next Negro victim.
    2 men, 1 woman, extras; 1 interior. Royalty: $35-30.

_____. The Slave (1964). Samuel French.
    Negroes have revolted and are burning and bombing the civi-
lization of white America. One Negro bursts into the home of a

professor, married to his former wife. His intention is to kill the professor and his wife and take the children, two mulatto girls of which he is the father, with him. He only partly succeeds. The wife and children die in the collapsing house.

2 men, 1 woman; 1 interior. Royalty: $35-30.

_____. The Toilet (1963). BP 1964-65; ALLK; GARV.
The setting is a school toilet, which is ugly and foul-smelling. A group of black boys (and one white) wait for another white boy to be brought in to be beaten up by the leader of the group. The white boy, Jimmy Karolis, has sent the black leader, Ray Foots, a love letter telling him that he's beautiful. He must pay for this. He is brought into the toilet already beaten by the others, and when the fight finally does occur, Karolis appears to be winning when he is pulled off of Ray and is punched and kicked senseless by the gang. They drape him with wet toilet paper, throw toilet water in his face, and leave laughing and cursing, half-dragging Foots out with them. Back into the toilet comes Foots, who cradles the white boy's head in his arms, wipes the blood from his face, and weeps.

1 act; 11 men (9 black, 2 white); 1 interior.

JONES, Preston. The Last Meeting of the Knights of the White Magnolia (1973). BP 1976-77; Dramatists Play Service.
Part of A Texas Trilogy (see below). The Bradleyville, Texas chapter of the Knights of the White Magnolia (a splinter group of the Ku Klux Klan founded in 1902) is the last chapter left, and everyone knows that when Col. J. C. Kincaid dies (he is 75 and owns the ramshackle hotel where they meet) they will in fact be defunct. At this last meeting of the lodge (the Colonel will have a seizure and be taken home under oxygen) the members go through an initiation ceremony for Lonny Roy McNeil, a simple soul from nearby Silver City who could not resist joining a group for white men only which featured domino games. As it turns out, what has really held the group together is the dedication of an old black custodian named Ramsy-Eyes Blankenship, who knows how to light up the cross in the meeting room and who is the keeper of the only copy of the ritual book.

2 acts; 9 men; 1 interior. Royalty: $50-40.

_____. Lu Ann Hampton Laverty Oberlander (1976). Dramatists Play Service.
Part of A Texas Trilogy (see below). Claudine Hampton, a widow, is the mother of Skip and Lu Ann. Skip is the town drunkard who once tried to commit suicide. Later in life he ends up living with his sister, Lu Ann, who is reluctant to give him even a dollar for fear he will spend it on booze. Lu Ann was a popular girl in high school who had a child by a Dale Laverty, one of Skip's war friends. When he leaves her, she marries Corky Oberlander, who soon dies in an accident. Lu Ann ends up as a beautician caring for her mother, who has been in a coma for a long time with no

sign of improvement, her alcoholic brother Skip, and her spoiled
daughter Charmaine.
3 acts; 8 men, 3 women; 2 interiors. Royalty: $50-40.

_____. The Oldest Living Graduate (1974). BP 1976-77; Drama-
tists Play Service.
Part of A Texas Trilogy (see below). Colonel J. C. Kincaid
is a crotchety old man of 75, confined to a wheelchair and senile
when he wants to be, whose claim to fame is that General Black Jack
Pershing once told him to shut up. The Colonel lives and breathes
World War I. His son Floyd wants to go into business with "that
dumb-butted Clarence Sickenger" and to turn a farm the family owns
into a subdivision of exclusive summer homes. The Colonel won't
permit anything to be done with the property. He fell in love there
once and needs "havin' places that stay the same for rememberin' on."
He also won't permit himself to be used in a publicity stunt (benefit-
ting the proposed land development) where he is to be honored as
the oldest living graduate of Mirabeau B. Lamar Military Academy.
The only thing he wants to do is to go to his lodge meeting. (Note:
in "Bradleytime" this is the occasion dramatized as The Last Meeting
of the Knights of the White Magnolia.) While he is gone, Floyd admits to his wife Maureen that he has already made the property deal
in spite of his father's objection. She insists he tell the old man the
truth. Meanwhile, the Colonel has suffered a seizure at the lodge
meeting and is brought home unconscious. When he awakes, he tells
Floyd to do with the land whatever he wants.
2 acts; 6 men, 3 women; 1 interior. Royalty: $50-40.

_____. A Texas Trilogy.
Three full-length plays (Lu Ann Hampton Laverty Oberlander,
The Oldest Living Graduate, and The Last Meeting of the Knights of
the White Magnolia) all set in Bradleyville, Texas (6,000 people)--"a
small, dead West Texas town in the middle of a big, dead West
Texas prairie between Abilene and San Angelo. The new highway
has bypassed it and now the world is trying to." Some of the
characters make appearances in two of the plays.

JONSON, Ben. The Alchemist (1610). In his Collected editions;
ASH; BAS; BEL v. 4; GAY v. 2; HOW; LIE; NEI v. 2; OLH;
OLI v. 2; SPE; TAU; THA; new ed. by Bentley, Crofts, 1947.
Lovewit leaves his London house in charge of Face, his housekeeper. Subtle, the quack alchemist, with Face and Dol, his con-
sort, use it as a place to cheat people, for they expect all men to be
rascally and avaricious, all women to be vain and libertine. All who
come are duped through avarice in the hope of getting gold from
metal through the pseudo-science of alchemy. The scheme is ended
when Lovewit returns unexpectedly.
5 acts; 11 men, 1 woman, extras; 1 interior; costumes of the
period.

_____. Epicene; or, The Silent Woman (1609). In his Collected editions; CLS; GAY v. 2; STA.

Morose, a miserly bachelor, with an aversion to noise, would disinherit his nephew, Sir Dauphine, to marry a Silent Woman—if he can find one. Sir Dauphine brings in Epicene who does not speak and the marriage takes place. Immediately after the ceremony she recovers the use of her tongue. This is intolerable, and he accepts Sir Dauphine's offer to rid him of her for one-third of his income, whereupon Sir Dauphine pulls off Epicene's disguise and reveals that "she" is a boy trained for the part.

5 acts; 11 men, 5 women, 1 boy, extras; 5 interiors, 1 exterior; costumes of the period.

_____. Every Man in his Humour (1598). In his Collected works; BAS; BAT; BEL v. 8; BRI v. 2; CLF v. 1; GAY v. 2; INCH v. 5; MAT; NEI; OXB v. 16; PAR; SCI; SCW; SPE.

Each character represents a peculiarity of temperament, caricaturing their follies and foibles: Kitely, jealous of his wife; Dame Kitely, jealous of her husband (they are brought together where each thinks the other is frequenting for an immoral purpose); their servant Brainworm who devises tricks to cure them; Capt. Bobadil, a cowardly braggart, thrashed by Downright; stupid Stephen, suspicious Kno'well; kindly Justice Clement; and many others.

5 acts; 14 men, 3 women, extras; 8 interiors, 4 exteriors; costumes of the period.

_____. Sly Fox. See entry under Gelbart, Larry.

_____. Volpone; or The Fox (1605). In his Collected works; BAS; DUN; HUD; KRE; NEI; PAR; OLH; OLI v. 1; SCH; SCI; SPE; TRE-1, & -2 (v. 3); TREA-1.

Volpone, a rich Venetian nobleman but a miserly money-lender, gives out that he is at the point of death in order to draw gifts from his would-be heirs. They flock to him like birds of prey. Mosca, his knavish parasite, persuades each that he is named as heir and thus extracts a costly gift. Hailed into court, Volpone is betrayed by Mosca, his property is forfeited, and his sentence is to lie in the worst hospital in all Venice. The rest all receive just punishment.

5 acts; 14 men, 2 women, extras; 4 interiors, 2 exteriors; Venetian costumes of the period.

JORY, Jon. University (1983). Dramatic Publishing Company.

A play made up of 10 mini-plays about young university students. In one, for example, Magna and Delbert play with the minds of new freshmen on campus. In another, three girls discuss a plot to get money out of a dorky millionaire whose father invented frozen orange juice. Others are about love and romance, relationships that turns hostile, and, at the end of the play, seniors at graduation leave the university for entry into the "real world."

Variable cast of 5-18 men, 5-26 women; area staging.

Royalty: $60-40.

KAISER, Georg. From Morn to Midnight (1916). Tr. by Dukes in
Poet Lore, v. 31, 1920; Brentano, 1922; in DIE; in MOSH.
A petty bank clerk steals 60,000 marks, and to break his
deadly routine goes on a prolonged debauch, ending up in a Salvation
Army meeting. After testing humanity in a series of symbolical
groups, thoroughly disillusioned, he shoots himself.
7 scenes; 15 men, 11 women, extras; 5 interiors, 2 exteriors.

KALISADA. Sakuntala (ca. 500 A.D.). Tr. by Monier-Williams,
Dodd, 1885; also in CLF-1; & TRE-1, -2 (v. 2); TREA-1; tr.
by Ryder in Everyman's, 1913; tr. by Edgren, Holt, 1894; in
Eliot, Little Theatre Classics, Little, 1922, v. 4.
King Dushyanta marries the maiden Sakuntala and gives her
a royal ring. She loses the ring in a pond, and without it the king
does not recognize her. A fisherman finds the ring in a fish; it is
brought to the king, who now remembers and claims Sakuntala again
as his wife.
7 acts; 15 men, 13 women, extras; 1 interior, 1 exterior;
oriental costumes.

KANI, John. The Island. See entry under Fugard, John.

KANIN, Fay. Goodbye, My Fancy (1948). BP 1948-49; Samuel
French.
Twenty years after she hastily left Good Hope College, Agatha
Reed, now a Congresswoman, returns for Commencement and to receive an honorary degree. She thinks she may be still in love with
Jim Merrill, now its President; but she finds he is an irresolute
compromiser whom she cannot trust. She turns back to Matt Cole,
a Life photographer, who has filed a standing offer with her for six
years. She meets many characteristic campus folk: the students,
some of her old professors, and the prominent trustee whose gifts
cause her opinions to carry weight.
3 acts; 8 men, 12 women; 1 interior. Royalty: $50-25.

_____ and Michael Kanin. Rashomon (1959). Adapted from the
stories of Akutagawa. Samuel French.
The basic story is this: a Samurai warrior has been killed
and his wife assaulted by a bandit. The bandit is brought to trial,
where three versions (which have little in common) are told: by the
bandit, the wife, and (through the use of a medium) the warrior.
Then a fourth version is told by a peasant, who witnessed the
crimes.
6 men, 3 women; 1 exterior. Royalty: $50-25.

KANIN, Garson. Born Yesterday (1946). BP 1945-46; Dramatists
Play Service.
A domineering but ignorant egocentric, Harry Brock, who has
made a fortune by buying up junk, goes to Washington to get permission from Congress to secure post-war junk. With him is Billie,
a beautiful but uneducated chorus girl with good instincts, who has
signed for many years as silent partner to Harry's grafting schemes.

A newspaper man, Paul, is asked to instruct Billie, which he does
so successfully, that Harry and his gang (including Senator Hedges)
are in danger of indictment.
   12 men, 4 women; 1 interior. Royalty: $50-35.

KANIN, Michael. Rashomon. See entry under Kanin, Fay.

KATAEV, Valentine P. Squaring the Circle (1928). Samuel French.
   Two couples must share a single room in Communist Russia.
The wife of one is an earnest Communist, and her side of the room
is Spartan-like, hard and bare; the wife of the other is bourgeoise,
and she has pictures, cushions, and comforts. The husbands
hanker after the atmosphere of the other half. After discussion of
Soviet notions, etc., they exchange wives.
   3 acts; 7 men, 5 women; 1 interior. Royalty: $25-20.

KAUFMAN, Bel. Up the Down Staircase (1969). Adapted by Christopher Sergel. Dramatic Publishing Company.
   Sylvia Barrett's first day of teaching is a disaster. The
high school students are rude and difficult, the school administration
uncaring and impossible. Sylvia becomes involved in the problems of
her students, in a battle with the administration, in the start of a
romance, and in the defense of a hostile student named Joe Ferone
who is about to drop out of school.
   12 men, 18 women (doubling possible); 1 interior. Royalty:
   $50-35.

KAUFMAN, George S. The American Way (1939). BP 1938-39;
   Dramatists Play Service.
   The saga of a German immigrant to America, Martin Gunther,
who welcomes his wife in 1896. By his honesty and skill he attains
peace and happiness in their family group. He loses a son in the
First World War, lives through the depression of 1933 when he sacrifices all for his benefactor. In 1939 when his grandson is about to
join a fascist group, Martin interferes and is killed by the mob,
fighting still for freedom.
   2 acts; 27 men, 7 boys, 17 women, 3 girls, extras; 4 interiors, 13 exteriors (pageant effect possible with curtains).
   Royalty: $35-25.

_____, with Marc Connelly. Beggar on Horseback (1924). BP
   1923-24; Samuel French.
   A cheerfully distorted fantasy of modern materialism, big
business, and life among the idle rich. A young composer, Neil
McRae, is about to sell himself to a rich wife, which would enable
him to take a rest and study music. He falls asleep and dreams
what the marriage would mean: bride's bouquet consists of bank
notes; his life spent in manufacturing widgets; shut in a cell and
ordered to produce masterpieces. Aroused by the awfulness of his
dream, he gladly turns back to Cynthia across the hall.
   2 acts; 16 men, 5 women, with 6 men, 2 women in the

pantomime; 1 interior and an interior inset. Royalty: $50-25.

_____. The Butter-and-Egg Man (1925). BP 1925-26; Samuel French.
A seemingly simple country boy comes to New York and is inveigled into the play-producing game. He is instrumental in turning a "flop" into a "wow" after a highly satirical scene with the cast and the backers.
8 men, 5 women; 2 interiors. Royalty: $50-25.

_____. The Dark Tower. See entry under Woollcott, Alexander.

_____, with Edna Ferber. Dinner at Eight (1932). BP 1932-33; Samuel French.
A social climber, Millicent Jordan, invites various people to dine "a week from Friday" and meet the Ferncliffes of the British nobility. This event is more important to her than the fatal illness of her husband or her daughter's infatuation with an actor at his rope's end. Those invited are shown as they prepare to go to dinner, depicting love, jealousy, greed, ruin. In the culminating episode, the Ferncliffes couldn't come.
3 acts; 14 men, 11 women; 6 interiors. Royalty: $50-25.

_____, with Marc Connelly. Dulcy (1921). BP 1921-22; Samuel French.
Dulcy, the original blundering wife, invites a curiously assorted group for the weekend: a scenario writer (an escaped lunatic), a businessman and his wife and daughter, a rich young man, and an ex-convict. Dulcy nearly ruins her husband's business merger, but a final blunder brings success.
8 men, 3 women; 1 interior. Royalty: $35-25.

_____. First Lady. See entry under Dayton, Katherine.

_____, with Moss Hart. George Washington Slept Here (1940). BP 1940-41; Dramatists Play Service.
Newton Fuller wants a little place in the country. He comes with his wife and daughter, and they run into various troubles in making the place habitable. First the search for water, then a quarrelsome neighbor; his daughter tries to elope, and the usual week-end guests arrive. In the end their dream house isn't a failure.
3 acts; 9 men, 8 women; 1 interior. Royalty: $35.

_____. I'd Rather Be Right (1937). Random House, 1937.
Phil Barker can't get a raise nor get married until the President of the U.S.A. balances the budget. In trying to do this, the President gets into difficulties with the Supreme Court and a variety of other fantastic complications. Finally he decides to balance the budget and it becomes his platform for re-election.

2 acts; 22 men, 4 women, extras; 1 exterior (Central Park).

_____. June Moon. See entry under Lardner, Ring W.

_____, with Edna Ferber. The Land Is Bright (1941). Dramatists
Play Service.
    Gives a panoramic view of a rich family, showing outstanding
episodes in its social history. Lacy Kincaid amassed a fortune as a
robber baron and moved to New York in the '90s, one of the gilded
age dynasties. Three generations are depicted; the second ran with
the hounds and hunted with the rats; but the third generation,
sobered by the events leading up to the Second World War, were on
their way to demonstrate American idealism and love of democracy.
    3 acts; 19 men, 12 women; 1 interior. Royalty: $35-25.

_____. The Late George Apley. See entry under Marquand,
John P.

_____, with Moss Hart. The Man Who Came to Dinner (1939).
BP 1939-40; Dramatists Play Service.
    An irascible individualist, Sheridan Whiteside, falls on the
ice and breaks his hip as he is leaving after dinner and is marooned
for six weeks with the Stanleys, a conventional middle-class family.
From his wheel chair he plots wondrous events for all who come.
He doesn't want to lose his secretary, Maggie, who wants to marry
the local editor Bert Jefferson, so he brings glamorous Lorraine into
the picture to lure Bert away from Maggie. He receives marvelous
gifts, penguins and such. His plots culminate in shipping off Lorraine in a mummy case. As he finally takes his leave, he slips on
the ice and breaks his hip again.
    3 acts; 15 men, 9 women, extras; 1 interior. Royalty: $35.

_____, with Moss Hart. Merrily We Roll Along (1934). BP 1934-
35; Samuel French.
    It is 1934, and the party at the rented Long Island house of
playwright Richard Niles has turned sour. His friend Julia is drunk
and insulting and his wife, the actress Althea Royce, accuses him of
sleeping with the young starlet in his new play. He doesn't deny
it, nor does he deny that he has "sold out" for fame and success.
To get even with him, Althea throws a bottle of iodine in the starlet's face. In the next scene the time is seven years before, and
then progressively one year earlier until Richard, full of hope,
promise, and idealism, speaks of being true to oneself to his 1916
college graduation class. Meanwhile, we have observed him casting
off his old relationships every time it could advance his career, and
giving up serious playmaking for the fluff and glitter of trendy light
comedy.
    3 acts; 35 men, 22 women; 8 interiors, 1 exterior. Royalty:
$50.

_____, with Marc Connelly. Merton of the Movies (1922). Based on Harry Leon Wilson's novel. BP 1922-23; Samuel French.

A green country boy, Merton, comes to Hollywood to elevate the movies. He thinks of himself as a sincere emotional actor, but his crudeness makes a comedy of his performance. His ideals are shattered, but he decides to carry on as a comedian.

4 acts; 7 men, 5 women, extras; 3 interiors, 2 exteriors (all simple). Royalty: $50-25.

_____, with Edna Ferber. Minick (1924). BP 1924-25; Samuel French.

Old man Minick comes to live with his son and daughter-in-law. After comic and pathetic complications ensue, he concludes that contentment can be found only among his friends in an Old Man's Home.

3 acts; 6 men, 9 women; 1 interior. Royalty: $25-20.

_____, with Morrie Ryskind. Of Thee I Sing (1931). BP 1931-32; Samuel French.

Pulitzer Prize play 1932. "Put love in the White House" is the slogan of Wintergreen's campaign. He shall marry the winner of the beauty contest, who turns out to be Diana of Louisiana. Meantime he falls in love with Mary Turner "who bakes the best corn muffins." This brings on complications with France; and the buffoonery shrewdly satirizes the non-recognition of Throttlebottom the Vice-president, the nine old men of the Supreme Court, and other political material.

2 acts in 11 scenes; 14 men, 5 women, extras; 6 interiors, 4 exteriors (all simple). Royalty on application.

_____. Once in a Lifetime. See entry under Hart, Moss.

_____, with Edna Ferber. The Royal Family (1927). BP 1927-28; Samuel French.

Demonstrates the lure of the theatre for the Cavendish family through three generations (supposedly reflecting the Barrymores). Fanny in her 70's still rules; Julie, at the height of her career, tirades against the theatre but always returns to it; Tony, the movie idol, is wild and uncontrolled; Gwen, in her 20's, is a promising ingenue, but forsakes the stage and marries Perry Stewart; but a year later presents a 4th generation Cavendish to the theatre.

3 acts; 11 men, 6 women; 1 interior. Royalty: $50-35.

_____. The Solid Gold Cadillac. See entry under Teichmann, Howard.

_____, with Edna Ferber. Stage Door (1936). BP 1936-37; Dramatists Play Service.

A capable young actress, Terry Randall, determines to stick to the legitimate stage and not be lured into the easier and more profitable career in motion pictures. Many fellow aspirants are depicted: one gives up in despair; another marries; one goes to

Hollywood before she has learned to act; all are struggling debutantes of the theatre--eager, earnest, and brave. Terry is helped to overcome hardships and discouragements by idealistic David Kingsley.

    3 acts; 11 men, 21 women; 2 interiors (1 set possible).
    Royalty: $50-35.

_____, with Marc Connelly. <u>To the Ladies!</u> (1922). French, 1924; QUI, TUCD.

    As many wives are responsible for the success of their husbands (without their knowing it--"as every woman knows!"), so the clever young wife, Elsie, from down in Mobile, saves the day for Leonard, her rather conceited and not very able husband, when she makes his after dinner speech for him--after the previous speaker had rather stolen it from him.

    3 acts; 11 men, 3 women; 3 interiors.

_____. <u>You Can't Take It With You</u>. See entry under Hart, Moss.

KEEFE, Barrie. <u>Gimme Shelter</u> (1977). BP 1978-79; Methuen, 1977-78.

    An up-to-date <u>Look Back in Anger</u> in three related one-act plays: "Gem," "Gotcha," and "Getaway," dealing with youthful disillusionment about the hopeless British welfare state. In the first, a group of politically conscious working-class background employees of a large insurance firm attempt to submarine the company's annual holiday and cricket match. In the second, a schoolboy (the Kid) going nowhere bluffs his way into tormenting a headmaster and two teachers in a school that doesn't even know his name. Finally, we see the same radicals from "Gem" try to make a hero out of the Kid's notoriety, even though they have made compromises to rise in the prevailing system and the Kid is only interested in performing his job as groundsman for the cricket pitch.

    3 one acts; 6 men, 2 women; 1 interior, 1 exterior.

KELLER, Helen. See William Gibson's <u>The Miracle Worker</u>.

KELLY, George. <u>Behold the Bridegroom</u> (1927). BP 1927-28; Samuel French.

    Antoinette Lyle is a spoiled little rich girl with no regard or value for any person or any relationship. Then she meets Spencer Train, who does not approve of her and is not impressed with her life of leisure. The meeting changes her life. Believing that she has never accomplished anything and understanding how ruthlessly she has treated all of the men in her life, she breaks off with the one man who wants to marry her (he kills himself over the rejection) and chooses to remain secluded in her father's house, where she becomes ill. Finally, with the help of professional people, Spencer Train returns, but only to learn that while "behold the bridegroom" once meant him, it now refers to the early death she so desperately seeks.

    3 acts; 6 men, 6 women; 2 interiors. Royalty: $50.

_____. Craig's Wife (1925). BP 1925-26; Samuel French.
Pulitzer Prize play 1926. Incisive full-length portrait of a
woman who attempts to dominate her entire household--her husband,
his friends, and her relatives. Foiled by her selfishness, they
leave her to an empty future life. She wanted a house, but she
couldn't make a home.
3 acts; 5 men, 6 women; 1 interior. Royalty: $50-25.

_____. Daisy Mayme (1926). BP 1926-27; Samuel French.
A forty-year-old spinster teaches a bachelor of about the
same age how to handle his self-seeking relatives in the comedy.
In addition, she proves to him that there is a lot of fun to be got
out of life, and then marries him.
3 men, 5 women; 1 interior. Royalty: $50-25.

_____. The Fatal Weakness (1946). BP 1946-47; Samuel French.
Romantic Olivia simply can't resist a wedding. She learns
of her husband's infidelity, tracking it down with another feminine
detective, and gives him his freedom. Of course she has some injured pride, but curiosity takes her to witness her ex-husband's
marriage to another woman.
3 acts; 2 men, 4 women; 1 interior. Royalty: $50-25.

_____. The Show-Off (1924). BP 1923-24; Samuel French.
Veracious character study of a braggart, Aubrey Piper, with
a million-dollar imagination and an irritating personality. He nevertheless secures our sympathy despite his obnoxious traits through a
subconscious appeal to our own desire to reach the unattainable.
Presents also the serious problem of marriage for a young couple on
a meager salary.
3 acts; 6 men, 3 women; 1 interior. Royalty: $50-25.

_____. The Torch-Bearers (1922). Samuel French.
The leader in local amateur theatricals, Mrs. Pampinelli,
calls on Mrs. Fred Ritter to take a part in a play. Rehearsals
follow, and the final production is seen backstage, with the many
trials of amateur production. Fred is so greatly irritated that he
insists that his wife stop this nonsense and take care of her home.
3 acts; 6 men, 6 women; 2 interiors. Royalty: $50-25.

KELLY, Tim. M*A*S*H (1973). Based on the book by Richard
Hooker. Dramatic Publishing Company.
Hawkeye and Duke, two of the best chest surgeons in South
Korea, decide to wage a campaign to send a Korean boy to school
in the United States. Other characters include a woman psychiatrist,
Radar Reilly, a rip-off sergeant, and the baby-talking Bonwit sis-
ters (the worst tap-dancing act in the U.S.O. circuit).
15 men, 15 women (doubling possible); 2 interiors. Royalty:
$60-40.

KENDALL, Jane. Jane Eyre. See entry under Brontë, Charlotte.

KENNEDY, Charles Rann. The Servant in the House (1907). Harper, 1908; French carries; in his Repertory of Plays ... for 7 Players, Chicago, 1930; in Golden Book, v. 2, p. 795.

As the new butler, Manson comes into the troubled household of his clergyman brother and applies the teaching of Jesus Christ to the life of today. He teaches the spirit of service and brotherhood, indicating that brotherly love is greater than wealth or social position; that forms are nothing, humanity is everything.

5 acts (but playable in 3); 5 men, 2 women; 1 interior. (Continuous action, embodying the 3 unities of time, place, and action.) French royalty: $25-20.

KENNEDY, Mary and Ruth Hawthorne. Mrs. Partridge Presents (1925). BP 1924-25; Samuel French.

With great success Mrs. Partridge manages her business, her husband, her daughter, and her son. She has tremendous energy and wants to give her children the chances she missed. But the children revolt against her well-meant management: she wanted Philip to be an artist, he chooses to be an engineer; she wanted Delight to be an actress, she prefers to be married.

3 acts; 6 men, 6 women; 2 interiors. Royalty: $25.

KENYON, Charles. Kindling (1911). Doubleday, 1914; taken over by French; DIG.

Strongly indicts conditions in New York tenements. For the sake of her baby the young wife is driven to steal, hoping to provide an escape from the squalid surroundings by going to Wyoming. A tense moving story relieved by the humor of the Irish washerwoman.

3 acts; 6 men, 4 women; 1 interior.

KERR, Jean. Finishing Touches (1973). BP 1972-73; Dramatists Play Service.

The Cooper family lives in a comfortable suburban home with two sons (the third son is a Harvard senior, living away). Husband Jeff is in line for a full professorship in English, but since the passion has gone out of his marriage a good bit of his energy is going into an attractive student who has captured his attention. Wife Katy, for similar reasons, is attracted to a bachelor professor who rents the Cooper's garage apartment. Then the college son comes home with a young actress who is his mistress, and the parents, who are after all pretty conventional people, are shocked and put through a series of resolved crises.

3 men, 2 boys, 3 women; 1 interior. Royalty: $50-35.

_____. Jenny Kissed Me (1948). Dramatists Play Service.

Amiable Father Moynihan takes into his rectory an ugly duckling in Jenny, the 18-year old niece of his housekeeper. He tries to improve the mousy pathetic orphan with clothes and a hair-do, seeking such information from the beauty columns of a woman's magazine. He wants to make her attractive to the boys, and he tries to pick a husband for her in Owen, a neighborhood boy; but she picks her own--the harried but noble inspector of parochial schools, Michael Saunders.

3 acts; 4 men, 10 women; 1 interior. Royalty: $35-25.

_____. Lunch Hour (1981). BP 1980-81; Samuel French.

Oliver DeVreck is a psychiatrist, specializing in marriage counseling and writing books about his work. His wife, Nora, is paranoid about all of the beautiful, unhappy women he sees in his line of business, mostly because she has projected her own infidelity on to him. Their marriage is threatened by the uninvited appearance of Carrie, who has read Oliver's last book and who brings with her the news that her husband Peter is having an affair with Nora. When she confronts Nora with this knowledge, she goes on to report falsely that she and Oliver are having their own affair. Nora won't believe the story, which angers Oliver enough to lie about it himself. The remainder of the play deals with Oliver's sophistication about wife-swapping on one hand and Carrie's naiveté on the other, with their spouses stuck and manipulated in the middle. After all the wit and humor, conventionality triumphs.

2 acts; 3 men, 2 women; 1 interior. Royalty: $60-40.

_____. Mary, Mary (1961). BP 1960-61; Dramatists Play Service.

Mary is witty and clever, a condition which caused her marriage with Bob to fail. When she returns to Bob's apartment at the request of his attorney, to help her former husband with his income tax problems, her sense of humor has not waned. Bob is on the verge of marrying Tiffany Richards, a rich, beautiful health fiend. When Dirk Winston, a movie idol, offers Mary love, passion, and a weekend together in Florida, Bob realizes his need for Mary and locks her in the bathroom so that she can't make the Florida trip. After a disgruntled Dirk Winston leaves alone, we discover that Mary had her bathroom key all along. She attempts to stifle her sense of humor long enough for another wedding with Bob.

3 men, 2 women; 1 interior. Royalty: $50-35.

_____. Our Hearts Were Young and Gay (1946). Based on the book of Cornelia Otis Skinner and Emily Kimbrough. Dramatic Publishing Company.

The escapades of two young girls determined to prove how mature and cosmopolitan they are as they take a trip to Europe make this an entertaining comedy. Cornelia and Emily are in a frenzy of excitement as they prepare to sail for Europe. But they try hard to appear bored and casual. Then Cornelia's mother calls her "Baby" as Cornelia prepares to leave and embarrasses her in front of everyone. After the ship has sailed the two girls have a series of adventures, including Emily's stocking all the lifeboats with cookies, and Cornelia's bout with the measles. In Paris the girls encounter an exploding gas meter, sleep in a bed Cardinal Richelieu once used, and try to convince a great French actor to give them acting lessons. The girls experience other entertaining adventures.

8 men, 9 women; unit set. Royalty: $50-35.

_____. Poor Richard (1964). Samuel French.
A belligerent but gifted poet on the order of Dylan Thomas or Brendan Behan comes to America to see his publisher and to attend the dedication of a hospital to the memory of his late wife. He is loaned a secretary from his publisher, a girl who has been secretly in love with him since she was fifteen. Soon she announces plans to marry the poet. The publisher also loves the girl, but he is destined to lose both. Beneath all the poet's charm, however, he is terribly unsure of himself. His public image is of one who wrote beautiful haunting verses on the death of his wife and then turned to drink for comfort. What really troubles him is that he did not love his wife at all and that he is a complete fraud. The biggest trial comes when he refuses to go to the dedication. This brings truth, and from reading his wife's diary comes peace.
3 men, 2 women; 1 interior. Royalty: $50-25.

KERR, Walter. Rip Van Winkle. See entry under Irving, Washington.

KESEY, Ken. One Flew Over the Cuckoo's Nest. See entry under Wasserman, Dale.

KESSELRING, Joseph. Arsenic and Old Lace (1931). BP 1940-41; Dramatists Play Service.
Two mentally unbalanced old ladies with the aid of their grandfather's arsenic and elderberry wine help lonely old men escape from life and populate their cellar with 12 acceptable roomers. Their brother Teddy, who thinks he is Teddy Roosevelt, inters them in the "Panama Canal." Their brother Jonathan, equally unbalanced, wants to equal his sisters' record and plans to do so with his brother Mortimer. He is fortunately prevented. It turns out that Mortimer is only a step-brother and not affected with the family taint and can safely marry Elaine.
3 acts; 11 men, 3 women; 1 interior. Royalty: $35.

KEYES, Daniel. Flowers for Algernon. See entry under Rogers, David.

KIELLAND, Alexander L. Three Couples (Tre par, 1886). Tr. by Lindanger in Drama, v. 7, 1917.
Two married couples, the Sandbergs and the Friedmans, plus a bachelor, Mr. Waage, and a secretary, Miss Svendsen, get interested in each other. Mr. Sandberg is almost willing to divorce his wife for Miss Svendsen; Mr. Friedman enjoys talking to Mrs. Sandberg; Mr. Waage exchanges pleasantries with Mrs. Friedman. The discussion ends when Mr. Waage becomes engaged to Miss Svendsen.
3 acts; 3 men, 4 women; 1 interior, 1 exterior.

KIMBROUGH, Emily. Our Hearts Were Young and Gay. See entry

under Kerr, Jean.

KINGSLEY, Sidney. Darkness at Noon (1951). Adapted from Arthur Koestler's novel. BP 1950-51; Samuel French.

Rubashov, an old-guard Russian revolutionary, is imprisoned by younger sadistic Soviets, such as Gletkin. His former associate, Ivanoff, now head of the prison, can help him if he will "confess" to treason. Rubashov realizes his great dream, his whole philosophy of life, has been a delusion; he is the victim of misguided and false idealism: the destructive means used by him and the leaders have become an end in themselves. He remembers his past activities and especially his romance with his secretary Luba. A brilliant indictment of Communism.

18 men, 3 women; 1 interior. Royalty: $50-25.

_____. Dead End (1935). BP 1935-36; Dramatists Play Service.

On one side of a dead end street on Manhattan's East Side is a tenement. On the other side, a sharp contrast, is a posh apartment building. The young residents of the tenement belong to a street gang, joining together to protect themselves and to learn the tricks of the trade which permitted Baby Face Martin (from the neighborhood) to achieve success. Grimpty, an architecture student whose legs have been deformed by rickets, tries to dissuade them from a life of crime but realizes that the slum environment works against him. When Baby Face Martin returns to his old neighborhood, he finds that his former girl friend is now a prostitute and that his mother hates him for what he is. Grimpty reports Martin to the F.B.I., who kill the notorious criminal. Grimpty cannot persuade the girl he loves to leave her rich lover, so he will use the reward money to get a good lawyer for the leader of the street gang, arrested for knifing a wealthy resident of the posh apartment building. A harsh indictment of slum environment.

22 men (several bits), 6 women, extras; 1 exterior. Royalty: $35-25.

_____. Detective Story (1949). BP 1948-49; Dramatists Play Service.

Into the squad-room and office of a New York police station come all types of people in all sorts of trouble. One case stands out, however. A young man has been arrested for stealing money from his boss. Though the woman who loves him comes to his aid and his boss recovers all of the money, McLeod, a hard-working detective, refuses to let the young man off easily. McLeod has been hardened by his years on the force, and only severe punishment of law breakers ever satisfies him. He is about to complete his case against an abortioner when the man's attorney forces McLeod's wife to admit she once made use of the abortioner's services. The detective's whole world of good-guys-and-bad-guys collapses, and he seeks death in stopping a prisoner from escaping from the station.

24 men (doubling possible), 8 women, several nonspeaking extras; 1 interior. Royalty: $50-25.

_____. Men in White (1933). BP 1933-34; Samuel French.
    Pulitzer Prize play 1934. As an intern in a great hospital
Dr. George Ferguson is encouraged by Dr. Hochberg when he is
forced to choose between marriage to Laura with a comfortable practice and five years of further study abroad as a surgeon. The death
of a young nurse who has comforted him brings him closer to humanity. He leaves for Vienna without Laura.
    18 men, 9 women; 7 interiors. Royalty: $25.

_____. Night Life (1962). Dramatist sPlay Service.
    The play is set in the early morning hours at a New York
night club. Gathered there are a corrupt labor leader, a girl singer
in love with the union boss, an idealistic young attorney tortured by
the memory of the man he bayoneted in the war, a movie sex queen
with lesbian tendencies, and a tired old liberal and his wife--both
alcoholic. In the climax of the play the old liberal sacrifices his
life by saving the young attorney from the labor leader's knife.
    17 men, 7 women, extras; 1 interior. Royalty: $50-25.

_____. The Patriots (1943). BP 1942-43; Dramatists Play Ser-
    vice.
    Deals with Thomas Jefferson in the early days of the Repub-
lic. There are two main struggles in the play: Jefferson's personal
one to retire to private life, and the historical one between Jefferson
and Alexander Hamilton. These two statesmen have a falling out
when Jefferson learns that the economy measure he helped through
the Congress had worked only for the benefit of Hamilton and his
friends. At the end of the play, Jefferson's election to the presidency is being held up by Congress. Hamilton wants to make a
deal but Jefferson refuses. The two men understand that their goals
for America are similar, and Hamilton persuades Congress to elect
his rival.
    18 men, 5 women, extras; 1 exterior, 6 interiors. Royalty:
    $35-25.

_____. The World We Make (1939). Based on Miller Brand's
    novel The Outward Room. BP 1939-40; Dramatists Play Service.
    Virginia McKay blames her wealthy parents for the death of
her brother and refuses to leave Greendale Sanitarium, where she
has been a mental patient, to return to their care. Instead, she escapes, changes her name to Harriet Hope, and finds a life with John,
a steam laundry employee who lives in a tenement house. Soon she
is loved and respected by her neighbors and John's brother's family,
though occasionally her grief over her brother's death returns and
she withdraws into herself, trying to keep the world out. When
John's brother Jim dies and John tries to shut her out of his grief,
she is able to help him, help herself, and look forward to all the
things they have to live for and to fight for.
    Prologue & 3 acts; 10 men, 7 women; 3 interiors. Royalty:
    $35-25.

KIPPHARDT, Heinar. In the Matter of J. Robert Oppenheimer
(1968). BP 1968-69; Samuel French.
A documentary drama based on the actual transcripts of the
government security clearance trial of Dr. Robert Oppenheimer, the
prime mover in getting the atomic bomb for the United States and
the one who hesitated over proceeding with the hydrogen bomb. A
government search reveals an affiliation with communists (the scientist's wife and brother-in-law) and other unsavory people. The
trial, in which other scientists like Dr. Albert Teller testify, also
reveals the dangers in invasions of privacy and the stagnation of
creativity inherent in governmental conformity.
14 men; 1 interior. Royalty: $50-35.

KIRKLAND, Jack. The Man With the Golden Arm (1956). Based
on the novel by Nelson Algren. Dramatists Play Service.
Because of painful wounds suffered in the war, Frankie Machine, a dealer in a Chicago gambling joint, becomes a dope addict.
The play treats his unsuccessful attempts to shake the habit and
finally his own destruction.
16 men, 5 women; unit set.

_____. Tobacco Road. See entry under Caldwell, Erskine.

_____. The Music Master (1904). Samuel French.
The piano-player in a dime museum in New York, Herr von
Barwig, demonstrates his fine character in a number of ways.
When asked uptown to teach music to a girl of 18, he becomes assured that she must be his daughter whom his wife took with her
when she ran away from Germany with a rich American. In the
house he confronts the man and is made sure; but he goes away
with his secret still kept. He sees her happily married--but she
learns from her false father that the music teacher is her real father, and she carries him off to happiness.
3 acts; 14 men, 6 women; 3 interiors. Royalty: $25.

KLEIST, Heinrich von. The Prince of Homburg (written 1811, prod.
1821). Tr. by Hagedorn in FRA v. 4; SMK.
The Prince, a lover and a dreamer, doesn't realize the military order is not to advance against the Swedes, but he does advance and wins a great victory. However, for disobedience the
Elector and the Court condemn him to death; he begs for his life
and even will forego his loved Natalie. Told he must judge himself,
if the verdict is unjust, he admits his guilt--and is pardoned.
5 acts; 8 men, 2 women, extras; 6 interiors, 3 exteriors;
costumes of the period (1675).

KLIGMAN, Paul. It All Ends Up in a Shopping Bag (1982).
Dramatic Publishing Company.
The play begins with the death of Moishele Kay, a Jewish
immigrant to Winnipeg, and leads into flashbacks of his life as a
grocer and how he started and ran his business. Paul, his son,

recites the Kaddish and is the one who recalls all of the memories (with the help of a sister, an aunt, and friends) because Paul has never been as close to his father as he wanted to be. His father, known as Pa, was a hard-driving but fair businessman who put his whole life into his work. Arguments and quarrels with his wife were plenty and intense at times.

2 acts; 14 men, 6 women, extras (doubling possible); series of platforms. Royalty: $50-35.

KNOBLOCK, Edward. Miletones. See entry under Bennett, E. Arnold.

KNOTT, Frederick. Dial "M" for Murder (1952). BP 1952-53; Dramatists Play Service.

A mercenary man who tries to have his wife killed for her money has his plans confounded by his wife's courage in this melodrama. After arranging a perfect alibi for himself, the husband blackmails a scoundrel into strangling his wife. However, the murderer gets murdered and the victim survives. Then the husband tries to have his wife convicted for the hireling's death. But through the efforts of a Scotland Yard inspector and a young man who loves his wife, the truth is revealed. In a suspense-filled climax they trap the husband into revealing his guilt, thus freeing the wife.

5 men, 1 woman; 1 interior. Royalty: $50-35.

_____. Wait Until Dark (1965). Dramatists Play Service.

Three underworld figures attempt to recover a heroin-filled doll, innocently brought across the Canadian border by a young commercial photographer. When the photographer goes off on assignment, the three thugs descend upon his blind wife who, alone in their Greenwich Village apartment, is terrorized by men who will murder to achieve their goals. There are frightening moments and shocks in the final acts. An example of "the school of chilling menace," as Richard Watts, Jr. observed.

6 men, 1 woman, 1 girl; 1 interior. Royalty: $50-35.

KNOWLES, James Sheridan. The Hunchback (1832). In his Dramatic Works, Routledge, 1841, v. 1; in New York Drama, v. 4, #47, 1878.

Master Walter, the hunchback, has raised Julia in the country; he has posed as representing her father and carrying out his wishes. He plans to have her marry Sir Thomas Clifford, but he loses his money, so Julia goes to the city with Cousin Helen. There Julia is dazzled by the wealth of crude Master Wilford who becomes Earl of Rochdale, but Walter manages to expose his falseness. He brings about the marriage of Julia to Clifford and of Helen to Modus; and acknowledges that he is Julia's father.

5 acts; 14 men, 2 women, extras; 7 interiors, 3 exteriors; costumes of the period.

_____. The Love-Chase (1837). In his Dramatic Works, Rout-
ledge, 1841, v. 2.

Three ladies are courted: Lydia the maid is wooed by Waller; the vivacious Constance quarrels with Wildrake, until both find
they love each other; the widow Green sets her cap for Waller but
takes Sir William.

5 acts; 10 men, 7 women; 7 interiors; costumes of the period
(Charles II).

_____. Virginius (1820). In his Dramatic Works, Routledge,
1841, v. 1; in Brown, C. S.; Later English Drama, Barnes,
1898; MOSO.

A famous Roman story is dramatically unfolded. The father
Virginius slays his daughter Virginia to save her from the lust and
tyranny of Appius, whom he later also kills.

5 acts; 18 men, 3 women, extras; 5 interiors, 4 exteriors;
Roman costumes.

KOBER, Arthur. "Having Wonderful Time" (1937). Dramatists
Play Service.

Up in a summer camp for two weeks, Teddy a stenographer
meets Chick, a young lawyer waiting on table to cover expenses.
They are attracted to each other but must overcome some obstacles
before marriage--which they do; she will support him until he gets
a position as a lawyer.

3 acts; 17 men, 14 women (some doubling possible); 3 interiors, 2 exteriors (possible in 2 sets). Royalty: $35-25.

KOCH, Howard, with John Huston. In Time to Come (1942). BP
1941-42; Dramatists Play Service, 1942.

The story of Woodrow Wilson's inability to sell the idea of a
lasting peace for the world after WWI, to be guaranteed by a League
of Nations. Brooks Atkinson called the play "a record of the
greatest of the world's lost causes without rhetoric or recrimina-
tion." We see Wilson go to Europe himself against all counsel, have
his noble ideas for a peace treaty compromised by traditional European nationalism, and watch his political foes led by Sen. Lodge
win the minds of the American people, who after all they have been
through want merely the kind of "return to normalcy" that Harding
has promised them.

Prologue and 7 scenes; 20 men, 1 woman; 5 interiors.

KOESTLER, Arthur. Darkness at Noon. See entry under Kingsley,
Sidney.

KOPIT, Arthur. Ghosts. See entry under Ibsen, Henrik.

_____. Indians (1969). BP 1969-70; Samuel French.

This apology for the treatment and exploitation of the American Indian is set in the form of Buffalo Bill's Wild West Show. The
hero is Buffalo Bill himself, the man whose love of Indian culture is

always undermined by his greater love for money. He is instrumental in destroying the buffalo herds on which the Indians depend, and later he helps destroy the Indians themselves--and himself. (A special effects music tape is available for producing this play.)
22 men; special effects tape available. Royalty: $50-35.

_____. Oh, Dad, Poor Dad, Mama's Hung You in the Closet and I'm Feeling So Sad (1961). BP 1961-62; Samuel French.
A widow and her young son arrive at a hotel with enough baggage for an army of bellhops. The luggage includes the valuable stamp collection of the son; some tall, wild plants; a fish bowl containing a flesh eating piranha; and a coffin. Even though the widow has decided to replace all the bellhops the next day, they are still tipped with priceless coins worth thousands of dollars. Living at the hotel is a babysitter who sits for children whose parents never come home. The mother returns, however, accuses the sitter of harlotry, and kicks her out. A yachtsman with a tremendous yacht throws himself at the widow's feet, offering himself and his fortune to her. She accepts the money but refuses him. Similar incidents continue to happen until the sitter attempts to seduce the son. At this point poor Dad falls out of the closet.
4 men, 2 women; 2 interiors. Royalty: $50-25.

_____. Wings (1978). BP 1978-79; Samuel French.
Emily Stinson, in her seventies, has a stroke as the play opens, and for a period of two years we are in her mind as she tries to sort out the jumbled images of her past and her present in an attempt to reintegrate herself into reality. The predominant experience that emerges is that she was once a wing-walker on early airplanes, and that the memorable time she was lost in the dark--flying a Curtiss Jenny and looking for Omaha--may have been a kind of warm-up for the death she is about to experience.
1 act; 4 men, 5 women; unit set. Royalty: $50-40.

KRAMM, Joseph. The Shrike (1952). Random House, 1952; BP 1951-52; Dramatists Play Service.
Pulitzer prize play 1952. Ann Downs wants to control her husband Jim, even if he has left her and is interested in another. In his belief that he is a failure as a theatre director and as a husband, he attempts suicide. Acting as a shrike (a predatory bird), Ann gets Jim into a mental hospital. There she continues to persecute him subtly by keeping him a tormented prisoner in a psychopathic ward, where he is led by the psychiatrists to think he is an imbecile. Realizing that he is trapped, he becomes a hypocritical liar, and feigns sanity and goodwill, but is released only through Ann's consent and into her custody.
10 scenes in 2 acts; 17 men, 5 women; 1 interior with furniture changes. Royalty: $50-25.

KRASNA, Norman. Dear Ruth (1944). BP 1944-45; Dramatists Play Service.

Romantic 16-year-old Miriam has been writing letters filled with poetry to Bill Seawright, who had received the first in "Bundles to Britain" and had responded. But Miriam had been signing the letters with the name of her sister Ruth. Bill returns from the war unexpectedly. Ruth, though already engaged to staid Albert, is willing to give him two days of enjoyment. She ends up by marrying him.

2 acts; 5 men, 5 women; 1 interior. Royalty: $35-25.

_____. John Loves Mary (1947). BP 1946-47; Dramatists Play Service.

John brings Lily from England for Fred as his wife, but in the meantime Fred has married and a baby is expected. To clear the matrimonial tangle, since John wants to marry Mary, he plans to go to Reno for 6 weeks to get a divorce from Lily. But Mary's father, Senator McKinley, insists on a marriage at once. When Lt. O'Leary is brought in to order John to Nevada, Lily reveals she has been married to O'Leary in England and thought he was dead.

3 acts; 7 men, 3 women; 1 interior. Royalty: $35-25.

_____. Who Was That Lady I Saw You With? (1958). Dramatists Play Service.

A chemistry professor gets involved with innocent pastimes, like making liquor. His wife threatens to leave him, however, when she discovers him engaged in another harmless pastime, kissing a pretty co-ed. A friend convinces the professor to tell his wife that he is an F.B.I. agent and the girl a foreign spy, and that he had to kiss her to get some vital information for the United States. The comic episodes multiply when a real secret agent becomes involved followed by a group of genuine F.B.I. agents. Finally it's all straightened out in a fast and hilarious finish, and the professor finds that he's a hero to his government, but, more importantly, a hero to his wife.

15 men, 6 women; interiors, exteriors. Royalty: $50-25.

KRONENBERGER, Louis. Mademoiselle Colombe See entry under Anouilh, Jean.

KUMMER, Clare. Good Gracious Annabelle (1916). French, 1922; BP 1909-1919.

Always using the expression "Good gracious," Annabelle engineers herself and four temporarily impecunious friends as servants at the Wimbledon country estate. Then John Rawson arrives, a Montana mining millionaire, who has rented it while Wimbledon is supposedly away--and to be near Annabelle. Considerable complications ensue, until Rawson reveals himself as the Hermit (with beard) Annabelle had married out West six years before.

3 acts; 10 men, 4 women; 2 interiors, 1 exterior.

_____. Her Master's Voice (1933). BP 1933-34; Samuel French.

When Ned loses his job, rich Aunt Min, who has never seen

him, comes to their little home in New Jersey and takes Queenie, Nat's wife, away so she can forget her worthless husband. In doing so, Aunt Min mistakes Ned for the house servant and employs him on her estate. Here he does well and she grows fond of him; so, when she finds he is the husband of her niece, she still thinks him pretty good, especially as he now has a place on a radio program.
  3 men, 4 women; 1 interior, 1 exterior. Royalty: $25.

KURNITZ, Harry. A Shot in the Dark. See entry under Achard, Marcel.

KYD, Thomas. The Spanish Tragedy (1592). In his Works, Oxford; & Temple Dramatists, Dutton; BAS; HOW; MAT; MCJ; MIO v. 1; NEI; OLH; OLI v. 1; PAR; RUB; SCI; SCW; SPE.
  A famous drama of revenge, rather reveling in stage massacres (10 of them). Horatio, son of Hieronimo, is beloved by Bel-Imperia of Spain. Found together, he is caught and hanged. His father vows vengeance: he gets Balthazar her suitor and Lorenzo her brother to act in a play, during the action of which they are both killed. Later both he and Bel-Imperia kill themselves.
  4 acts; 25 men (12 of them important), 3 women, extras; 14 scenes (interior and exterior); costumes of the period.

LABICHE, Eugene H. and Michel Marc. A Leghorn Hat (1851). Tr. by Chesley in Poet Lore, v. 28, 1917; also separately, Badger, 1917.
  Fadinard's horse has eaten a hat that hung on a tree which must be replaced by him before he can be married to Anais. He can't find one like it at Clara's (an old flame), but she says she sold one to the Baroness de Champigney. There he finds that the hat has been given to her goddaughter Anais--which is the very hat eaten by the horse. But a hat has been brought from Florence which finally reaches Anais.
  5 acts; 9 men, 5 women, extras; 4 interiors, 1 exterior; costumes of the period.

LADY PRECIOUS STREAM (Wang Pao Chuan, produced 1934 in NYC). Tr. and adapted by S. I. Hsiung. Samuel French.
  A naive fantasy of love and fidelity, introducing charming Chinese conventions. Depicts the devotion of a wife, Lady Precious Stream, to her adventurous husband. Presents his prowess as a warrior, and his ultimate return after 18 years as King of the Western Regions.
  5 men, 5 women, extras; 1 Chinese set. Royalty: $35-25.

LAGERKVIST, Pär Fabian. The Man Without a Soul (1936). Tr. by Kökeritz in Scandinavian Plays of the 20th Century, ser. 1, Princeton Univ. Press, 1944.
  "The man" has committed a political murder and comes by accident to fall in love with "the woman" who bears a child of the murdered man. He develops from a callous instrument of political

doctrine to see the humanitarianism of brotherly love and sacrifice. His longing for peace symbolizes man's search for truth through the ages.

5 acts; 6 men, 6 women, extras; 4 interiors, 1 exterior.

LANGER, Frantisek. Camel Through the Needle's Eye (1929). Tr. & adapted by Moeller, Brentano, 1929; French, 1932.

Susi, illegitimate daughter of a Prague beggar meets Alik, the not-too-bright son of a rich father, and goes to live with him and makes a man of him. His father tries to buy her off, but together they open a model dairy lunch. It is a success; he marries her and acknowledges her child.

3 acts; 6 men, 4 women, extras; 3 interiors.

LANGLEY, Noel. Edward, My Son. See entry under Morley, Robert.

LAPINE, James. Table Settings (1980). BP 1979-80; Samuel French.

Three generations of a Jewish family's frictions and celebrations are depicted around a center stage table, mostly at home but occasionally at a restaurant. Mother, sixtyish, disapproves of modern social customs and longs for the old times in Minsk. Older Son's alcoholism is getting on Wife's nerves (she is tired of being stereotyped as a wasp, even though she always believed Jewish men were good catches because they ate before they drank). Younger Son is deep into drugs and aimlessness, and has a blunt-speaking shiksa Girlfriend of his own. Granddaughter goes off on her first date, worried and confused about sex, and Grandson hides under the table, seeing things he shouldn't see and telling on his sister.

1 act; 3 men, 3 women; unit set. Royalty: $50-40.

LARDNER, Ring W. and G. S. Kaufman. June Moon (1929). BP 1929-30; Samuel French.

A young would-be songwriter, Fred, comes to New York. From the song hit "June Moon" he spends all he makes on industrious little gold-digger, Eileen, but he finds his love in faithful little Edna. A devastating satire on tune factories.

7 men, 5 women; 3 interiors. Royalty: $50-25.

LAURENTS, Arthur. A Clearing in the Woods (1957). BP 1956-57; Dramatists Play Service.

Virginia, a mature woman, seeks a clearing in the woods—some peace in her life. She is tormented by her past, by her inability to find perfection, and by her belief that no one has ever really loved her. But phantoms from the past appear on stage, including Virginia at three stages of life and the men she has been involved with: father, first love, ex-husband, and a former fiance whom she dumped. At the end she arrives at an acceptance of her own nature.

5 men, 4 women, 1 small girl; unit set. Royalty: $50-25.

_____. Home of the Brave (1945). BP 1945-46; Dramatists Play
Service.
Among U.S. soldiers on a Pacific island in World War II,
Coney, a Jew, feels he failed in his duty toward a dying buddy.
His guilt complex is overcome by a sympathetic doctor through whom
he regains courage and confidence.
6 men, 2 interiors, 2 exteriors. Royalty: $35-25.

_____. Time of the Cuckoo (1952). BP 1952-53; Samuel French.
A middleaged, unmarried American secretary is vacationing
in Europe, where she falls in love with a middleaged shopkeeper
from Venice. The newly discovered love completely fulfills her until she finds that the man has a wife and children. The shopkeeper
freely admits these facts and finds nothing especially wrong about
their relationship. The American learns something of the difference
between European and American morality, and must choose between
having a short-term love-affair or none at all.
5 men, 5 women; 1 exterior. Royalty: $50-25.

LAVEDAN, Henri. The Prince d'Aurec (1892). Tr. by Clark, in
Three Modern Plays from the French, ed. by Clark, Holt, 1914;
abridged in Pierce & Matthews, v. 2.
The Prince, a suave but impoverished aristocrat, borrows
money from the bourgeoise banker, the Jew DeHorn, to pay his
gambling debts, but he feels no obligation to pay it back. His
mother saves him and secures a promise of amendment from her
volatile son.
3 acts; 15 men, 8 women; 2 interiors.

LAVERY, Emmet G. The Gentleman from Athens (1947). Samuel
French.
A West Coast roughneck gets into Congress. His secretary
tries to smooth out some of his rough edges. To attract attention,
he introduces a bill calling for World Government, which will stave
off atomic warfare. Using his gangster methods he gets it passed,
and he even comes to believe in it himself. It finishes him as a
Congressman, but makes a man of him.
3 acts; 10 men, 3 women; 1 interior. Royalty: $35-25.

_____. The Magnificent Yankee (1946). BP 1945-46; Samuel
French.
Episodes in the life of Justice Oliver Wendell Holmes, giving
snapshots of his family life with an understanding wife, and introducing some of the young men from the Harvard Law School who
each served a year as his secretary.
3 acts; 15 men, 2 women; 1 interior. Royalty: $50-25.

LAWLER, Ray. Summer of the Seventeenth Doll (1957). BP
1957-58; Samuel French.
Every year for the past sixteen years, Barney and Roo, two

itinerant cane-cutters, have been spending the summer with two bar
maids in a small southern Australian city. And every summer Roo
has presented Olive with a doll, a symbol of their unusual but
tender relationship. This seventeenth summer is different, however.
Change has taken place, and the characters must face for the first
time some unpleasant truths about themselves.
  3 men, 4 women; 1 interior. Royalty: $50-25.

LAWRENCE, Jerome and Robert E. Lee. Auntie Mame (1956).
  Adapted from the novel by Patrick Dennis. Dramatists Play
  Service.
  A hilarious play about Auntie Mame, a scatterbrained, energetic, warm lady who is completely devoted to her young nephew.
Her fortunes and marriages rise and fall. The scrapes she gets
herself into mostly rise.
  25 men, 12 women, 3 boys (doubling possible); interiors and
  exteriors. Royalty: $50-35.

_____. First Monday in October (1978). BP 1978-79; Samuel
  French.
  The time is properly called the Imaginary Now (1978, specu-
lating on the near future). The place is the backstage office area
of the U.S. Supreme Court. The President of the United States
has filled a vacancy to the most prestigious court in the world with
Judge Ruth Hagadorn Loomis, a tough, conservative, white woman
with a reputation as a hanging judge ("The Lysol Lady of Orange
County"). Justice Daniel Snow, a tough, liberal, white man in the
all-male, almost all-white court, resolves never to retire, lest he be
replaced by Shirley Temple. He is delighted with the appointment
of a woman but enraged at the political stance of this particular
one who seems to represent mindless moral-majority sentiments. The
two come into conflict immediately over a porno film called "The
Naked Nymphomaniac." Ruth, who finally has to watch the movie
by herself, believes it is disgusting filth which needs to be suppressed. Daniel, who refuses to see the film, does not doubt that
the film is disgusting, but believes that censorship of any kind is
an even greater outrage. They begin to spar with one another,
leading to respect for each other's professionalism ("the fierceness
of their disagreement is a bond"). When Ruth offers to resign her
position over a possible conflict of interest charge (her husband par-
ticipated in a cover-up that will be part of an upcoming case) Daniel
won't permit it. He makes a promise not to die of old age if she will
promise not to resign until they can argue a juicy community
standards-religious freedom case called "The First Atheist Church vs.
the City of Waco, Texas."
  2 acts; 14 men, 2 women; composite interior/exterior. Royalty: $50-35.

_____. The Gang's All Here (1959). Samuel French.
  A compromise candidate allows, even encourages, political
corruption after his election as president. Griffith P. Hastings is

a likeable sort of fellow, and when his party's nominating convention cannot agree between the two more deserving candidates, it nominates him. After his victory he brings all his poker-loving cronies along with him to the White House where they promptly begin arranging scandalous deals. The corruption spreads quickly until a senator finds convincing evidence of the shady dealings. When he confronts Hastings with this material, the President finds a new source of inner courage and exposes and fires all his crooked friends. Then he himself dies, a disillusioned man. The New York Times describes this play as "Effective drama with a conscience...."
     15 men, 4 women; 4 interiors. Royalty: $50-25.

_____. Inherit the Wind (1955). BP 1954-55. Dramatists Play Service.
     The play is based on the famous Scopes "Monkey Trial" in Dayton, Tennessee, 1925. Bertram Cates, the Scopes figure, has been arrested for teaching the theory of evolution in the public school, and is being defended by an important ACLU lawyer, Henry Drummond, who is against not religion but ignorance. The prosecution will be led by fundamentalist and nationally known politician Matthew Brady, who is a narrow-minded bigot. Through the course of the trial the cynical Yankee newspaperman Hornbeck mocks everybody. Though the figures represent the famous real players in the drama (Clarence Darrow, William Jennings Bryan, and H. L. Mencken), the play takes on significance beyond that specific battle, representing the struggle for the kind of truth that always sets an individual against the larger group.
     21 men, 6 women, 1 girl, 2 boys (doubling possible); unit set. Royalty: $50-35.

_____. The Night Thoreau Spent in Jail (1970). Samuel French.
     The play begins with Henry David Thoreau in jail and ends with his release. In between we see the famous visit from Ralph Waldo Emerson, Thoreau's refusal to pay taxes to a government conducting an unjust war against Mexico, his transcendental school which was too revolutionary for the student's parents, his friendship with an illiterate cellmate, his job as a handyman around the Emerson household.
     11 men, 5 women, extras; platform stage. Royalty: $50-35.

_____. Only in America (1959). Adapted from Harry Golden's book. Samuel French.
     This comedy is an account of an eastside New York Jew who sets up a humorous journal in North Carolina, "The Carolina Israelite." His publication, filled with witty aphorisms and homespun humor, soon becomes a success, and Harry becomes an accepted member of the community. Then Harry is asked to serve on the local school board, and in declining, is forced to explain that a short Depression prison term bars him from any political office. But the city's love for him does not lessen. Even when an anonymous letter to a New York paper reopens the old case, the people rally to his

support. One telegram summed up the people's attitude. "Harry,
we need you in Charlotte. You may be the best Christian we got."
17 men, 5 women, 3 extras; 1 interior-exterior, inset.
Royalty: $50-25.

LAWRENCE, Reginald. If This Be Treason. See entry under
Holmes, John Haynes.

LEARNING, Walter. The Incredible Murder of Cardinal Tosca.
See entry under Nowlan, Alden.

LEE, Harper. To Kill a Mockingbird (1970). Adapted by Christopher Sergel. Dramatic Publishing Company.
A young girl named Scout lives in a small southern town.
The time is 1935, and she doesn't understand why the black community has such a special feeling about her father, Atticus, a lawyer.
She also doesn't understand why some of her white friends are hostile. Her father explains that he is defending a black man wrongfully accused of a serious crime and that even though he is fighting
their friends they are still "friends." There are good roles for
black actors in this racially mixed cast.
12 men, 17 women, extras; 2 sets. Royalty: $50-35.

LEE, Robert E. See entries under Lawrence, Jerome.

LEGOUVE, Ernest. The Ladies' Battle. See entry under Scribe,
A. Eugene.

LEONARD, Hugh. "Da" (1975). BP 1977-78; Samuel French.
Charlie has returned to his boyhood Irish home to bury Da,
his adopted father who represented the only family he had. His
memory of Da is so clear and powerful--and the old man so strong
and colorful--that he can't shake him or the events from his past
involving his father. Da appears as a character, sometimes arguing
with Charlie (called Charlie Now) and sometimes with the boy he
once was, Young Charlie. Occasionally, in fact, it is Charlie Now
and Young Charlie who do the interacting. The memories are bitter-
sweet, involving Da's politics (he was for the Nazis and against the
British) and his attempts to set Charlie up in a way of life superior
to the way he makes his own living as a gardener to a wealthy
family. Charlie does everything he can to shake the memory of Da,
but it appears that his father will remain a presence with him wher-
ever he goes.
2 acts; 5 men, 3 women; interior/exterior, platforms. Royalty: $50-40.

_____. A Life (1980). BP 1980-81; Samuel French.
A closer look at a minor character introduced in the author's
previous play, Da. Irish civil servant Drumm's failing health
is overshadowed by his approaching retirement (he'll receive a lump
sum) and his wasted life. He is too intellectual for his place and

station, too dominant and bullying to his wife, and too willing to
substitute standards for friends. In many ways his wife Dolly is
his humanity, though she was not his first choice for a lifelong partner. He might have married his first love, Mary, if she could have
memorized a Chesterton poem, instead of dancing and partying with
his best friend Lars Kearns, who could hardly write his name.
Throughout the play, these four characters interact with one another in present time, blending in and out with four other actors
portraying the two couples forty years before.
    2 acts; 4 men, 4 women; unit set with combination interior.
Royalty: $60-40.

Le MAÎTRE, Jules. The Pardon (1895). Tr. by Clark, in Three
    Modern Plays from the French, ed. by Clark, Holt, 1914; tr.
    by Fay, in Poet Lore, v. 24, 1913, as Forgiveness.
    Suzanne has been unfaithful to her husband Georges and is
told by him to leave. When Therese brings them together again
after a few months' separation, Georges thinks he is in love with
Therese; now Suzanne is ready to leave, but he asks her to stay;
it was his vanity that erred. They are both equally guilty; accounts
are balanced. They forgive each other's unfaithfulness and will
start to live all over again.
    3 acts; 1 man, 2 women; 1 interior.

LENORMAND, Henri-René. The Dream Doctor (1922). Tr. by
    Orna, in his Three Plays, Lond., Gollancz, 1928; MOSH.
    Freudian Dr. Luke interprets the dreams of Fearon (she's a
happy thief) and Jeannine (she believes she killed her mother).
When she finds that she practically did, she kills herself, urged on
by jealousy of Fearon, who now claims Dr. Luke.
    Prolog & 9 scenes; 4 men, 5 women; 6 interiors, 2 exteriors.

_____. Time Is a Dream (1919). Tr. by Katzin, Knopf, 1923;
    DIE; HAV.
    A young man broods over his complex and torturing desire
and the unreality of time and space. His fiancée tells him of her
dream of a young man drowning. This gives him the idea, and he
does it.
    6 scenes; 3 men, 2 women; 1 interior.

LEONARD, Jim, Jr. The Diviners (1980). Samuel French.
    Buddy Layman, a teenage boy, has developed physical and
emotional problems concerning water (his mother drowned as she
saved Buddy from drowning). His father and his sister are very
tolerant of Buddy, but have not reached him the way a backsliding
preacher named C. C. Showers has. Buddy's fear of any kind of
water has resulted in a severe case of ringworm from not washing
and sleeplessness from itching. But C. C. Showers makes contact
with Buddy and eventually overcomes his fear to get him in the lake.
When Norma Henshaw, a true-believer in the Lord, hears this she
thinks a baptism is taking place, and she gathers up a bunch of

women who journey down to the lake singing religious songs. C.C. grows angry at the women and yells at them to go away. In the midst of the commotion, Buddy slips in the lake and drowns.

6 men, 5 women; unit set with platforms. Royalty: $50-35.

LESLIE, Aleen. A Date with Judy (1946). Dramatic Pub. Co., 1946.

High School Theater Classic, 1945-49, about teen-age Judy and her schemes to get ahead of Tootsie. She enters many contests, writes true confessions, and tries with Mitzi to get a job as an actress. Oogie turns her down and asks Tootsie to the Prom; but Judy gets there with Oogie and is crowned queen.

3 acts; 5 men, 9 women; 1 interior.

LESLIE, F. Andrew. The Haunting of Hill House (1964). Adapted from Shirley Jackson's novel. Dramatists Play Service.

This is a chilling suspense drama about four people who gather for a study of supernatural phenomena in a sinister mid-Victorian mansion. Hill House, the old mansion, allegedly has mysterious powers, and none of the local inhabitants will approach it except for its caretaker, Mrs. Dudley, and she refuses to stay after nightfall. The organizer of the investigating team, Dr. Montague, enlists three others, all unacquainted, to join him in his venture: Eleanor Vance and Theodora, two girls in their twenties; and Luke Sanderson, nephew of the present owner of Hill House. The terror begins the first night when some powerful but unseen force races through the house, trying to break into the girls' room. As their fears mount so does the anger of the spirits, leading to the death of one of the party before Dr. Montague and the rest of his group decide to leave.

3 men, 4 women; 1 interior. Royalty: $50-35.

_____. Lilies of the Field (1967). Adapted from William E. Barrett's novel. Dramatists Play Service.

Popularly known by the movie version starring Sidney Poitier. Homer Smith, an ex-G.I., is bumming around the country on his way West, stopping to do odd jobs to finance his trip. When he stops to repair a leaky roof for a group of German nuns, the Mother Superior believes that Homer has been sent to her by God. Despite his strong Baptist background and his urge to move on, Homer is drawn into the life of the nuns until he too shares their dream of building a chapel. Overcoming seemingly impossible obstacles, Homer and the local farmers build an adobe chapel. The play is a touching testimony of human goodness and the power of faith. (Note: in this version Homer Smith may be played either by a Negro or white actor.)

4 men, 5 women; open stage with movable props. Royalty: $35-30.

_____. Mr. Hobbs' Vacation (1963). Adapted from Edward Streeter's novel. Dramatists Play Service.

Mr. Hobbs comes to Rock Harbor for "rest and relaxation" over his objections. His wife, daughter, and aunt have all joined forces to pressure him to travel from Cleveland to an island off the coast of New England. Mr. Hobbs' objections are sustained. Their vacation house is a monstrosity, complete with a temperamental hot water tank. One comic crisis follows another until the exhausted Mr. Hobbs heads back home. In the rush, however, he has forgotten his boat tickets and will undoubtedly be back for more wild vacation adventures.

8 men (4 can be doubled), 7 women; 1 interior. Royalty: $35-25.

_____. The Spiral Staircase (1962). Adapted from the story by Mel Dinelli. Dramatists Play Service.

A series of apparently insoluble murders of young girls with some noticeable deformity has produced terror in the household of Helen, a girl who has lost her voice. Helen is the companion of the bed-ridden Mrs. Warren and lives there with Mrs. Oates, the housekeeper, and Professor Warren, the invalid lady's stepson. One stormy night the Constable arrives with the news that another girl has been murdered. After warning the Warren household that the murderer is still at large, the Constable leaves. Then one by one the other members of the household apparently depart, leaving Helen alone, or so she thinks. Her terror intensifies and finally reaches a climax when Helen realizes that the murderer is in the house with her. She is saved, however, in a surprising and exciting finish to this suspense-filled play.

4 men, 4 women; 1 interior. Royalty: $35-30.

_____. Splendor in the Grass. See entry under Inge, William.

_____. The Wheeler Dealers (1966). Adapted from George Goodman's novel. Dramatists Play Service.

Henry Tyroon, the wheeler dealer, arrives in New York from Texas to find potential investors. Instead, he finds Molly Thatcher, a young Wall Street security analyst. She is pushing shares of Universal Widget, an obscure company she has been ordered to dispose of. In wheeling and dealing for Molly, Henry also provokes great interest in Universal Widget, and soon all of Wall Street is buying stock in the company. Finally the Justice Department investigates the mysterious corporation, Henry is revealed as a Bostonian, and Henry loses and then wins Molly.

9-16 men, 4-6 women; open stage with movable props. Royalty: $35-25.

LESSING, Gotthold Ephraim. Minna von Barnhelm (1765). Tr. by Bell, Bohn, 1900; BAT v. 10; HARC v. 26; MAU.

Tellheim, a discharged army officer, who loses his fortune through a false charge of embezzlement, refuses to marry Minna because now he is poor and she is wealthy. He recovers his fortune, and to punish him a bit for his pride, she tells him that she now is

penniless, and therefore she refuses to marry him. But she tells
him the truth and they are married.
    5 acts; 7 men, 3 women; 2 interiors; costumes of the period.

_____. Nathan the Wise (1779). Tr. by Taylor, Lpz, 1868; Bohn
    Lib.; in his Dramatic Works, Lond., 1900; tr. by Maxwell,
    Bloch, 1939.
    The scene is laid in Jerusalem during the third Crusade.
Recha, the supposed daughter of Nathan, a Jew, is a baptized
Christian. She is saved from a burning building by Knight Templar, and they fall in love. Because Nathan has concealed the facts
about Recha, he is brought before the Mohammedan Sultan Saladin.
The three faiths thus come into close contact as Recha pleads for
Nathan's life. This shames the Templar into a broader tolerance and
permits the joining of the lovers.
    2 acts (8 scenes); 7 men, 2 women; 3 interiors, 1 exterior;
costumes of the period.

LETTICH, Sheldon. Tracers. See entry under DiFusco, John.

LEVERTON, G. H. Rip Van Winkle. See entry under Irving,
    Washington.

LEVIN, Ira. Deathtrap (1978). BP 1977-78; Dramatists Play Ser-
    vice.
    Sidney Bruhl, a playwright suffering a long dry spell and
financial pressures, reads a script entitled "Deathtrap," sent to
him by Clifford Anderson, a former student from one of his college
seminars. Though he doesn't remember what the student looks like,
he claims that he would kill for a script like "Deathtrap." In Act I
of the play it appears that he does, making his wife Myra an ac-
complice, when he discovers that he has in his possession all of the
copies and even the working notes for the script and that Clifford
won't accept a co-author. The rest of the play finds the audience
falling through one false floor after another, in an attempt to find
the deathtrap in the playwright-student relationship.
    2 acts; 3 men, 2 women; 1 interior. Royalty: $50.

_____. No Time for Sergeants (1955). Adapted from Mac Hyman's
    novel. BP 1955-56; Dramatists Play Service.
    The story concerns a simple and lovable, innocent young lad
who enlists in the Air Force with all its pompous earnestness of
military discipline and bureaucracy. The youth, a husky and good-
natured hillbilly, wants to be in the infantry. His determined efforts create chaos among generals, as well as sergeants. One of the
comic highlights occurs when he goes on a flight in an airplane man-
ned by some weary, hungover flying officers who get lost and unknowingly fly straight for an atomic explosion in Yucca Flats.
    34 men (some parts can be doubled), 3 women; unit set.
    Royalty: $50-25.

LEVINSON, Richard. Rehearsal for Murder. See entry under
Brooke, D. D.

LEVITT, Saul. The Andersonville Trial (1959). BP 1959-60;
Dramatists Play Service.
　　A courtroom drama about the trial of Henry Wirz, commander of the notorious Civil War prison at Andersonville. Wirz, a
Swiss immigrant doctor who had been wounded in battle, insists he
was just acting under orders but admits that a hundred Union soldiers died a day in his camp. The play raises the question of when
individual responsibility transcends the power of authority.
　　28 men (doubling possible); 1 interior. Royalty: $50-25.

_____. The Trial of the Catonsville Nine. See entry under Ber-
rigan, Daniel.

LEVY, Benn W. Clutterbuck (1946). BP 1949-50; Dramatists Play
Service.
　　On a tropical cruise two couples meet. The ladies, Deborah
Pomfret and Jane Pugh, are old friends but haven't met for five
years. The men meet for the first time: Arthur Pomfret, an aci-
dulous rubber planter, and Julian Pugh, a pompous novelist. A
third couple are also on board, Mr. & Mrs. Clutterbuck, with each
of whom the other four have had experiences before being married:
the ladies with Clutterbuck in Venice, the men with Melissa in London. The light feathery comedy depicts the mild ups and downs of
married life as the past comes back to their memories.
　　3 acts; 4 men, 3 women; 1 interior (the deck), 1 exterior
(on shore). Royalty: $35-25.

_____. The Devil Passes (1930). BP 1931-32; London, Martin
Secker, 1930.
　　The Prince of Darkness, in this play, is passing as a young
priest named Nicholas Luce in a small English parish. He attempts
to get a minor author to assume authorship of an unknown Conrad
story. He tries to persuade an actress to break her current play
contract and sign on as Lady Macbeth in the important production
she yearns to be a part of. He wants the Rev. Mr. Messiter to
profit from a blasphemous hypocrisy that passed for a sermon heard
by the Bishop. He does succeed in getting a young lady to fall in
love with him and choose to leave her lover. Then, he throws her
over and blames it all on God.
　　Prologue & 3 acts; 5 men, 4 women; 2 interiors.

_____. Mrs. Moonlight (1929). Samuel French.
　　Mrs. Moonlight gets her magic wish never to grow older nor
less beautiful, so that at 28 she still looks 18. She runs away, to
return later unknown to her family as her own niece. She guides
their destinies, helps her daughter to avoid an unhappy marriage,
then disappears again, to return at 70. When her husband dies,
she follows him into the shadows.

3 acts; 4 men, 4 women; 1 interior. Royalty: $50-25.

_____. The Rape of the Belt (1957). Adapted from the legend
   of Hercules. Samuel French.
   Heracles, for his ninth labor, must take away the jeweled
belt worn by Antiope, queen of the Amazons. He sets out with
Theseus, his companion, knowing how to fight any enemy in battle
but uncertain as to how to attack two charming women like Antiope
and Hippolyte, her sister. Two spectators from heaven, Zeus and
Hera, comment on the action as Heracles wins the belt as a man
from a woman, not as a soldier from an enemy, and Theseus takes
a willing Hippolyte back to Greece as a trophy of war.
   3 men, 7 women; 1 exterior. Royalty: $50-25.

_____. Springtime for Henry (1931). Samuel French.
   A blundering Englishman, Henry Dewlip, a wealthy bachelor
even after having many secretaries, leads a life of ease until he is
taken in hand by his apparently innocent, prim, young secretary,
Miss Smith, who tries to persuade him to forego all his pleasant
vices. He is quite disillusioned when he learns the story of her
life: she has been married, has a small son, and shot her husband.
He turns her over to his best friend Jelliwell, receiving in exchange
Mrs. Jelliwell.
   3 acts; 2 men, 2 women; 1 interior. Royalty: $50-25.

LEWIS, Sinclair. Dodsworth. See entry under Davis, Owen.

LINDSAY, Howard, with Russel Crouse. Life With Father (1939).
   Based on the book by Clarence Day. BP 1939-40; Dramatists
   Play Service.
   Father Clare may have been the head of the family, but Vinnie, his wife, knew how to get her way. Depicts many laughable incidents, as family, relatives, and friends help Vinnie to get father
properly baptized.
   8 men (some boys), 8 women; 1 interior. Royalty: $50-35.

_____, with Russel Crouse. Life With Mother (1948). Based on
   the book by Clarence Day. BP 1948-49; Dramatists Play Service.
   The Day family is older and Mother wishes to provide an engagement ring for one of the boys. She never had one herself.
When she learns that Father had given one to Bessie Fuller, now
Mrs. Logan, who wouldn't give it back when the engagement was
broken, and who now comes to visit, she demands that Father get
it back. It takes some maneuvering but Bessie finally relents.
   3 acts; 8 men, 8 women; 2 interiors. Royalty: $50-25.

_____, with Russel Crouse. Remains to Be Seen (1951). BP
   1951-52; Dramatists Play Service.
   A comedy-melodrama set in the Park Avenue apartment of
Travis Revercombe, whose death by natural causes is complicated
by someone who stabs him in the chest after he is dead. An

estranged niece, Jody Revere, a regional band vocalist, is brought
to New York by the deceased's attorney, Benjamin Goodman, but
she doesn't want the old man's inheritance—she only made the trip
because she thought the lawyer was the Benny Goodman. The real
culprits, a doctor and mistress with access to the apartment through
a secret passage behind the fireplace, are finally apprehended, and
Jody takes off to rejoin her band in Kansas, taking Waldo, the building superintendent, with her to be the hot new drummer.
     3 acts; 16 men, 3 women; 1 interior. Royalty: $50-25.

     _____, with Russel Crouse. State of the Union (1945). BP
    1945-46; Dramatists Play Service.
     Pulitzer Prize play 1946. A party leader gets Grant Matthews
to consider running for the Presidency of the U.S. if his wife will
agree. So he makes a cross-country trip to inspect his plants and
make speeches en route. Some of his addresses are too radical for
the politicians so that at the final meeting at his house he gives up
the idea, and he and his wife are again agreed.
     3 acts; 11 men, 6 women, extras; 4 interiors (can be re-
    duced to 3). Royalty: $50-25.

     _____, with Russel Crouse. Tall Story (1959). Adapted from
    Howard Nemerov's The Homecoming Game. Dramatists Play Ser-
    vice.
     Small Custer College has suddenly gained national prominence
because of its basketball team. Not only does the college now make
the newspapers, but alumni contributions have tripled, buildings are
going up all around, and academic standards have risen. The cause
of it all is star center Ray Blent, a science major who has worked
out a formula for perfect basket shooting. In fact Ray can do about
everything except marry June Ryder, and he would do that if he
could afford it. Before the big game with Ashmore College, Ray receives a phone call asking him to throw the game. He does not accept, but he receives $1,500 and a promise of $2,500 after his team
is defeated. Ray solves his problem by deliberately flunking two
exams and becoming ineligible to play. The real fun comes when
professors, students, alumni, and administration becomes involved in
the resulting furor.
     21 men, 8 women, 1 boy; interiors; Royalty: $50-25.

LINK, William. Rehearsal for Murder. See entry under Brooke,
    D. D.

LOCKRIDGE, Frances and Richard. Mr. and Mrs. North. See entry
    under Davis, Owen.

LOGAN, Joshua. Mister Roberts. See entry under Heggen, Thomas.

     _____. The Wisteria Trees (1950). Dramatists Play Service.
     On a run-down plantation in Louisiana where the oak trees
have been killed by the wisteria vines, Lucy Andrée Ramsdall of the

dreamy, wasteful, ineffectual aristocrats is at last forced to realize
that her lovely old family estate must be sold. It is bought at auction by capable, farsighted Yancy Loper, who has risen from shop-
boy to business success. He offers to keep it in the family, but
she refuses. So the trees are being cut down to make way for
truck farms and strawberry beds.
    3 acts; 8 men, 6 women; 1 interior. Royalty: $50-25.

LONG, Arthur Summer. Never Too Late (1957). Samuel French.
    A married man in his fifties suddenly learns that he is to
become a father again. He is not exactly overjoyed, since his other
child, now 24, still lives at home with her husband, a man who plays
solitaire all the time. To make matters worse, the mother-to-be
asserts herself and demands a nursery, a new bathroom, and her
own checking account. A delightful farce.
    6 men, 3 women; 1 interior. Royalty: $50-25.

LONG, J. L. The Darling of the Gods. See entry under Belasco,
    David.

LONSDALE, Frederick. Aren't We All? (1923). Brentano, 1924;
    French, 1925.
    Margot returns from Egypt to surprise her husband Willie
kissing Kitty Lake. She is inclined to be astonished and to protest,
but her father-in-law confronts her with her affair with John Wil-
locks, the romantic element in her Egyptian trip, so she subsides.
A sympathetic presentation of the natural foibles of a very human
set of people.
    3 acts; 8 men, 4 women; 2 interiors.

_____. The High Road (1927). Lond., Collins, 1927; French,
    1928.
    The serenity of the home of Lord Carlyle is quite upset at
his son John's engagement to an actress, Elsie Hilary. They ask
her down for a month. She turns the house upside down, getting
staid members to do frivolous things. She proves herself worthy,
but then refuses to marry John, Lord Tylesmore, being more in
love with his cousin, the Duke of Worrington. In the end she returns to the stage, her first love.
    3 acts; 8 men, 4 women; 1 interior.

_____. The Last of Mrs. Cheyney (1925). Lond., Collins,
    1926; French, 1929; BP 1925-26.
    In order to secure luxury, Mrs. Cheyney joins an accomplice,
Charles, to rob Mrs. Ebley of her pearls, in a house where he is
acting as butler. Lord Dilling, falling in love with her at the
house-party, traps her. She rouses the house and tells the truth.
The other guests prove to be quite a disreputable set, rather worse
than she. She bargains to reveal nothing about them for £10,000.
Upon receiving the check, she destroys it, rehabilitates herself, and
agrees to marry Lord Dilling.

3 acts; 8 men, 4 women; 3 interiors, 1 exterior.

_____. On Approval (1926). Samuel French.

Mrs. Wislack, thinking about a second romance, this time with Richard Halton, proposes they try each other out for a month at her house in Scotland without marital intimacies. They are followed there by the impecunious Duke of Bristol who wishes to sell his title to Helen Hayle, the daughter of a pickle millionaire. Thrown daily into contact, life becomes increasingly unbearable. Richard and Helen discover they love each other and sneak away, leaving the irascible Duke and the catty Mrs. Wislake to hate each other and discover how disagreeable they really are.

3 acts; 2 men, 2 women; 2 interiors. Royalty: $25-20.

_____. Once Is Enough (1938). French, 1938.

Really in love with her husband, Nancy, Duchess of Hampshire, is threatened with the loss of him when he thinks he is desperately in love with the wily Liz Pleydell. Liz would like to be a Duchess, but she and the Duke are no match for Nancy, and she withdraws when she discovers that Nancy has no intention of divorcing the Duke; so there is no elopement.

3 acts; 9 men, 5 women; 1 interior.

_____. Spring Cleaning (1923). Lond., Gollancz, 1925; French carried.

Richard is distressed because his beautiful wife Margaret insists on running with a terrible set of social degenerates. As heroic treatment, he brings a painted lady off the streets to the dinner. When the guests resent the insult, he pretends great surprise that amateurs should feel so about a professional. The shock sends his wife into the arms of the man with whom she has been flirting--but it wasn't marriage he had in mind. Discovering her philanderer's true character, Margaret is thankful to be taken back by her husband.

3 acts; 6 men, 5 women; 2 interiors.

LOOS, Anita. Gentlemen Prefer Blondes (1926). Dramatic Publishing Company.

Lorelei and her friend Dorothy are going to spend the summer in Europe with Lorelei's father. He is unable to get away from work, but they convince him to let them go alone. Lorelei, a blonde, begins posing as a woman of the world. She plays the role so well that she loses the affection of a young man she meets and likes and has to use her brain to get him back.

7 men, 10 women, extras; 2 interiors. Royalty: $35-25.

_____. Gigi (1951). Adapted from the novel by Colette. BP 1951-52; Samuel French.

Gigi, a young French girl, has been brought up by her mother, grandmother and aunt to be a stylish cocotte. The dissipated man they have picked out for her visits the home often, bringing candy and letting Gigi cheat him at cards. When Gigi turns sixteen she is expected to become the man's mistress, but she doesn't think she'd like such an arrangement. So, much to the consternation of the ladies, she maneuvers the roué into a proposition of marriage.

2 men, 5 women; 2 interiors. Royalty: $50-25.

_____. Happy Birthday (1946). Samuel French.

Addie Bemis is a rather shy little librarian in Newark. She follows Paul, a young bank clerk, into a cocktail bar, ostensibly to discuss her savings account. She experiments with "pink ladies" and a double Scotch; then quite fantastic things begin to happen. In the end she wins Paul away from a contriving hussy, and learns a lot about life and alcohol.

3 acts; 11 men, 10 women; 1 interior. Royalty: $50-25.

LUCE, Clare Boothe. See entries under Boothe, Clare.

LUKE, Peter. Hadrian the Seventh (1968). BP 1968-69; Samuel
    French.

Based on the life and works of Frederick William Rolfe, the play depicts the failed life of Fr. Rolfe, who lives in a drab London flat and bemoans his expulsion from seminary many years before. In a kind of dream excursion, a delegation of contrite priests arrives, bestows Holy Orders on him, and the new priest accompanies his bishop to Rome to elect a new Pope. In desperation, the conclave elects this new, unattached priest (Fr. Rolfe), who chooses the name Hadrian VII. As Pope, Hadrian sells all the Vatican art treasures to feed the world's poor, smokes on the throne, and entertains old friends. Finally, he is killed by an Irish assassin. In the last scene we are back at Fr. Rolfe's drab London flat, where the only visitors are a delegation of bailiffs, who have come to take possession of Rolfe's property--including the manuscript of the book he is writing.

26 men, 2 women; drop and wing set, with wagons. Royalty: $50-35.

LYNDON, Barré. The Amazing Doctor Clitterhouse (1937). Random
    House, 1937; French, 1938; THH; FOUP.

As part of his laboratory research work, Dr. Clitterhouse takes up crime in order to study the reactions of criminals at the moment of committing crime and how their nerves respond to their misdeeds. He joins a gang and helps further their illegal doings in a huge fur robbery during which a murder occurs. When he leaves to write up his material, he is trailed by Benny Keller who tries to blackmail him; but the Doctor outwits him, for he is first of all a gentleman.

3 acts; 10 men, 2 women; 3 interiors, 1 exterior. Royalty: $25-20.

_____. The Man in Half-Moon Street (1939). Lond., H. Hamilton,
    1939; SIXL.

A chemist, John Thackeray, by experimenting on himself, has lengthened his life by the transfer of adrenal glands, so that, though 90 years old, he appears to be 40. He needs another transfusion, as the present glands are weakening; also he needs money. So he arranges a transfer from Catty Sims and a bank robbery with Mr. Budd. Both go wrong, so that he fades away at 90 as he is arrested, and Mr. Budd is dissolved in a chemist's bath.

3 acts; 13 men, 1 woman; 4 interiors, 1 exterior.

LYTTON, Edward Bulwer-Lytton. The Lady of Lyons (1838). Both Baker and French carried; STA; TAU.

A snobbish provincial society girl, Pauline in Lyons, falls in love with Claude Melnotte, a humble birth, but who has been set up as a prince by some Parisians. She marries him despite her father's objections, who secures a separation, after which Melnotte leaves. Pauline is about to marry a wealthy suitor when Claude returns from the wars, an officer and a rich man.

5 acts; 10 men, 5 women, extras; 2 interiors, 3 exteriors; costumes of the period of the French Revolution.

_____. Money (1840). DeWitt, 1874; French carried; in BAT v. 16.

Well-written, to show how money, or the lack of it, affects people. Alfred Evelyn, as indigent secretary to Sir John Vesey, is rejected as a suitor by Clara Douglas, because she can't face a life of struggling poverty. After Alfred has been left the estate of a rich uncle, he pretends to have lost it all in order to show up those who toady to money.

5 acts; 17 men, 3 women, extras; 5 interiors; costumes of the period.

_____. Richelieu; or The Conspiracy (1839). In his Complete Works, Little; in his Dramatic Works, Dutton; Baker carried in Wm. Warren edition; French & Dramatic Publishing Co. carried; in Brown, C. S., Later English Drama, Barnes, 1898; in Winter, Wm., ed., Plays of Edwin Booth, Penn, 1899, v. 3; DUR; MAT; MOSO.

The astute Cardinal is plotted against and is in danger of losing his position at the French court. But he outwits King Louis XIII (and his henchman Baradis), regains the King's favor, and reunited his ward with the man of her choice.

5 acts; 16 men, 2 women, extras; 3 interiors, 1 exterior; costumes of the period. (A shortened version in 4 acts as used by Walter Hampden was pub. by Appleton, 1929.)

MACARTHUR, Charles. The Front Page. See entry under Hecht, Ben.

McCARTHY, Justin H. If I Were King (1902). Russell, 1901; Heinemann, 1921; French, 1922, BP 1899-1909.

François Villon, poet, duellist, brawler, vagabond, and lover,

becomes marshall of France with kingly power on the appalling condition, stipulated by the spider-king, Louis XI, that he forfeit his
life at the end of the week. He wins the love of Katherine de Vau-
celles and leads the French troops to victory. They save his life
from the scaffold, and he and Katherine go into exile.
    4 acts; 18 men, 9 women, extras; 1 interior, 2 exteriors;
    costumes of the period.

McCULLERS, Carson. The Ballad of the Sad Cafe. See entry under
    Albee, Edward.

_____. The Member of the Wedding (1949). BP 1949-50; Drama-
    tists Play Service.
    A sensitive character sketch of Frankie, a lonely twelve-
year-old girl in Georgia. Her mother is dead, her father busy, and
the older children neglectful of her, she spends most of the time
bored with the cook and her younger cousin. When her brother
marries, Frankie sees a way out of her rut: she will accompany the
couple on their honeymoon. She is heartbroken when this plan does
not materialize. A few months later she is Frances, not Frankie, and
she is very interested in a boy next door.
    6 men, 7 women; unit set. Royalty: $50-35.

_____. The Square Root of Wonderful (1957). Samuel French.
    A charming southern lady has been married twice to the
same man--a tormented intellectual who has made her miserable.
She is trying to break away finally so that she can marry a young
architect who both understands her and loves her. But her former
husband and his domineering mother block the way. The play deals
with the resolution of her problem.
    2 men, 3 women, 1 boy; 1 interior. Royalty: $50-25.

MACDONALD, Betty. Onions in the Stew. See entry under Dalzell,
    William.

McENROE, Robert E. The Silver Whistle (1948). BP 1948-49;
    Dramatists Play Service.
    A romantically-minded tramp finds the birth certificate of
Oliver Erwenter, showing him to be 77. He decides to impersonate
Erwenter and as such enters a home for the aged. To help along
the happiness of the inmates he promotes a bazaar for the church
next door. He is exposed by his tramp companion, Emmett, but the
bazaar takes place, furbished with many items appropriated by the
two tramps. He persuades the bishop and the victims that the bazaar is worthwhile; they even make presents of the things the men
have stolen. The call of the road takes them away, but not before
the romance is achieved between the Rev. Mr. Watson and the attractive Miss Tripp.
    3 acts; 10 men, 5 women; 1 interior. Royalty: $50-25.

McGUIRE, William Anthony. Six-Cylinder Love (1921). BP 1921-22.

The Richard Burtons and the Gilbert Sterlings are next-door neighbors in a Long Island suburb. Burton has made the mistake of mortgaging his home to buy a used, six-cylinder touring car, and the "upkeep" (new friends, hangers-on, dinners out, parties every night) has caused him to go broke. Now he must sell his house and the car and move back to the city. Sterling is persuaded to take the car off his hands, and soon the same thing happens to him, except that he "borrows" some money temporarily from his employer and can't pay it back. Finally, Sterling's boss relents when he sees how well Gilbert and his wife have handled adversity, and gives him his old job back. The only car he plans to purchase, he promises, is the little kind used for pushing babies about.

3 acts; 8 men, 5 women; 2 interiors, 1 exterior.

McINTYRE, Dennis. Split Second (1985). BP 1984-85; Samuel French.

Val Johnson is a black policeman in Manhattan. When the play begins, he has arrested a white man in the act of stealing a car. Val searches him, takes away his knife, handcuffs his hands behind his back, and radios for transportation. When the thief finds that he can't talk his way out of the arrest and that Val won't accept a bribe, he begins to use racial insults; Val gets so angry in a split second that he shoots the man and kills him. In a panic, he takes the cuffs off the dead man and puts everything back on the body, including the knife which he places in his hand. The rest of the play is an argument with family and friends over what to do at the police hearing--whether to confess and take the penalty or to continue with the lie. Val's best friend Charlie, a black cop, doesn't think he should confess. Val's wife, Alea, doesn't want their lives ruined by a jail sentence. Only his father, a former cop, insists that he tell the truth. At the end of the play, at the hearing, Val makes another split-second decision: he goes with the lie.

2 acts; 5 men, 1 woman; unit set. Royalty: $60-40.

MACKAYE, Percy. The Canterbury Pilgrims (1903). Macmillan, 1903; in his Plays, Macmillan, 1916.

The many travelers are introduced; they talk and act in harmony with their characters as sketched by Chaucer, forming a brilliant spectacle. Depicts the rivalry between the shy gentle Prioress and the Wife of Bath for the attentions of Chaucer. The Wife wins by trickery, but King Richard rules she must marry the Miller.

4 acts; 45 men, 7 women; 2 interiors, 2 exteriors (but may be set simply); costumes of the period.

_____. Jeanne d'Arc (1906). Macmillan, 1906; in his Plays, Macmillan, 1916; French, 1916.

The simple peasant girl, Jeanne, becomes a leader; she is the symbol of the faith that could arm a people to a supreme effort. Given a fine representation of her character and career, her life and martyrdom.

5 acts; 40 men, 7 women, extras; 4 exteriors; costumes of

the period.

_____. Mater (1908). Macmillan, 1908; in his Plays, Macmillan, 1916.
The interest centers around the Mother who dominates the play, helping her son to win his election, and bringing her daughter's love affair to a satisfactory conclusion. Mater has unconquerable youth; her children are solemn with the grim responsibility of growing up.
3 acts; 3 men, 2 women; 1 interior.

_____. The Scarecrow (1908, produced 1910). Macmillan, 1908; in his Plays, Macmillan, 1916; DIC; MOSJ; MOSL; QUIK; QUIL; abridged in Pierce & Matthews, v. 1.
In the days of New England witchcraft, Goody Bess, with the help of Dickon (a Yankee Mephistopheles), makes a scarecrow which comes to life but is animated only when puffing a pipe. She sends it as Lord Ravensbane to court Justice Merton's niece, with some success, until he sees himself in the Mirror of Truth as he really is, with his heart a red beet.
4 acts; 10 men, 6 women; 2 interiors; colonial costumes.

_____. A Thousand Years Ago (1913). Doubleday, 1914; French, 1914.
Strolling Italian players come to China. Their leader, Capocomico, rules for a day and finds her lover for the Princess; then they wander on again.
4 acts; 9 men, 2 women, extras; 3 interiors, 1 exterior; Chinese and fantastic costumes.

MACKAYE, Steele. Hazel Kirke (1880). French, 1899; QUIL in revised form.
Hazel is driven from her home by her stubborn father who objects to her marriage to a young man whom she had rescued and nursed. She elopes with him. He turns out to be an English nobleman in disguise. When the marriage is thought to be illegal, Hazel returns to her home and attempts suicide in the mill-race. She is rescued by her husband, who proves that the marriage was legal after all.
4 acts; 9 men, 5 women; 2 interiors, 1 exterior.

_____. Paul Kauver; or Anarchy (1887). MOSS-3.
When accusations of noblemen were being sought, Paul Kauver, President of the revolutionary section, gives a blank to Gouroc, who fills in the name of the Duke de Beaumont, Diane's father. His plan is to save the Duke and thus gain Diane. He gets Kauver to take the Duke's place, but the priest helps Kauver to escape. They all meet again in the Vendee where Gouroc's villainy is unmasked, especially with the help of Jean Litais, a peasant and former servant of the Duke.
5 acts; 15 men, 4 women, extras; 3 interiors; costumes of

France, 1794.

MACLEISH, Archibald. J.B. (1958). BP 1958-59; Samuel French.
The necessity and efficacy of man's reconciling himself to
the apparent injustices of God are compellingly presented in this
Pulitzer Prize winning verse drama. Using two circus peddlers who
pretend they are God and Satan as a backdrop, the story of J.B.,
a wealthy, happy business man unfolds. One by one his blessings
are capriciously taken away. Even his beloved wife is reported
dead. In spite of these humbling tragedies J.B., like his Biblical
counterpart Job, refuses to curse God. Then J.B. is reunited
with his wife, and with an unswerving devotion to God they begin
life again.
12 men, 9 women; 1 interior. Royalty: $50-25.

_____. Scratch (1971). Suggested by Stephen Vincent Benet's
"The Devil and Daniel Webster." Dramatic Publishing Company.
Daniel Webster has voted for the Fugitive Slave Act in order
to preserve the union. A desperate, debt-ridden farmer, Jabez
Stone, appeals to Webster to save him from a disastrous deal with
"Scratch" (the devil) in which he sold his soul for seven years of
prosperity. Daniel Webster fights for the imperfect Jabez in an old
barn at night before a jury of American traitors and murderers
summoned by Scratch from Hell.
4 principal men, and 13 small parts; 1 interior, 2 exteriors.
Royalty: $60-40.

McLELLAN, C. M. S. Leah Kleschna (1904). Samuel French, 1920;
BP 1899-1909.
Brought up by her father, a famous thief in Vienna, to help
him in his robberies, Leah is also to help do it in Paris. She is
discovered at the safe by Paul Sylvaine, an amateur criminologist.
He believes she can be redeemed and succeeds in having her leave
her father and the evil life.
5 acts; 11 men, 6 women; 2 interiors, 1 exterior.

McMAHON, Frank. Borstal Boy. See entry under Behan, Brendan.

McNALLY, Terrence. Bad Habits (1974). BP 1973-74; Dramatists
Play Service.
Two one-act plays requiring the same number of actors. The
first, "Ravenswood," is about an expensive sanitarium for the unhappily married, run by Dr. Pepper--confined to an electric wheelchair with a built-in martini holder. Dr. Pepper's technique in
handling unsatisfactory marriages is to permit each partner unabashed
indulgence in the traditional bad habits of smoking, drinking, and
sexual promiscuity. The second play, "Dunelawn," is about a different kind of sanitarium, this one run by a Dr. Toynbee. Dr.
Toynbee's technique is to put his patients in straitjackets and to
shoot them up with tranquilizers so that they cannot indulge them-

selves in their bad habits: alcohol, transvestism, and sadomaso-
chism.
      6 men, 2 women; 2 simple exteriors.   Royalty: $50-35.

_____.   "Dunelawn."   See Bad Habits.

_____.   "Ravenswood."   See Bad Habits

_____.   Next.   See Elaine May's Adaptation/Next.

_____.   The Ritz (1975).   BP 1974-75; Samuel French.
      Proclo, who is fat, straight, square, and married to the
daughter of a Mafia boss, is on the run.   The mob is trying to kill
him, and in desperation he hides out in a gay bathhouse called The
Ritz.   Inside the Ritz it is bedlam.   Proclo is pursued by homosexual "chubby chasers," an awful Puerto Rican version of Bette
Midler who thinks he is a Broadway producer (he thinks she's in
drag), a private detective, hired by his Mafia brother-in-law to
track him down (who thinks Proclo is his brother-in-law), and Proclo's own wife, who saves the zany day.
      14 men, 3 women; composite interior and 2 drops.   Royalty:
$50-35.

_____.   Where Has Tommy Flowers Gone? (1972).   BP 1971-72;
      Dramatists Play Service.
      In a series of skits and incidents, the protagonist Tommy
Flowers is revealed to be a disillusioned rebel against society.
Along the way he acquires a destitute old actor, a sheep dog, and
a lovely girl music student--none of whom can compensate for Tommy's unsatisfactory home life.   His bright red shopping bag accumu-
lates many things he has not paid for, but in the end its main use
is to carry the bomb that Tommy uses to blow himself up as his
final gesture of alienation.
      Flexible cast with a minimum of 3 men, 3 women; unit set.
Royalty: $50-25.

MAETERLINCK, Maurice.   The Blue Bird (1908).   Tr. by Teixeira
de Mattos, Lond., Methuen, & Dodd, 1911.
      Two peasant children Tyltyl and Mytyl, search everywhere
for the blue bird of happiness.   Accompanied by their Cat and Dog,
Bread, Sugar, Milk, et al., they visit in vain the Land of Memory,
the Realm of Night, and even the Kingdom of the Future.   Finally
it is found right at home in an act of unselfishness.   No sooner is
it found than it flies away, and the search must begin again.
      6 acts in 12 scenes; 9 men, 13 women, 2 or more children,
many extras; 1 interior, 9 exteriors; fanciful costumes.

_____.   Monna Vanna (1902).   Tr. by Coleman, Harper, 1903;
      tr. by Porter, in Poet Lore, v. 15, 1904; tr. by Sutro, in his
      Joyzelle & Monna Vanna, Dodd, 1907; MOSQ; abridged in Pierce

& Matthews, v. 2.

To save the starving city of Pisa in the 15th century, Monna Vanna heroically persuades her husband, Guido Colonna, the commander of the Pisan forces, to let her meet the opposing general's demand that she go to his tent for the night. Prinzivalle, the head of the Florentine besieging army, who has adored her for years, gallantly refuses her harm and escorts her back to Pisa. Her husband, madly jealous, refuses to believe that she has not been seduced, and by his lack of faith drives her into her lover's arms, with whom she will escape.

3 acts; 7 men, 1 woman, many extras; 2 interiors; costumes of the period.

_____. Pelléas and Mélisande (1892). Tr. by Porter & Clark, in Poet Lore, v. 6, 1894; tr. by Hovey, in his Plays, ser. 2, Stone, 1896; Dodd, 1911; also in DIC; DIK, v. 1; HAV; SMN; TUCG; TUCM; WATI; WATL, v. 2; WATR; WHI; tr. by Alma-Tadema, Lond., Scott, later Allen, 1895; tr. by Winslow, Crowell, 1894 & 1908; abridged in Pierce & Matthews, v. 2.

Beautiful Mélisande is found in the forest by Golaud, who takes her to his castle and marries her. Her sadness and charm appeal to Golaud's younger brother Pelléas and they fall in love. She loses her wedding ring in the pool, which makes Golaud suspicious. Later when he comes upon them as they are bidding each other a last farewell, the jealous husband kills his brother. Mélisande dies in childbirth. Features the mystic and romantic in atmosphere and setting and the poetic in dialog.

5 acts in 19 scenes; 6 men, 2 women, extras; scenes laid in castle, garden, & forest; costumes of an undated period.

MAIBAUM, Richard. Ransom. See entry under Hume, Cyril.

MAMET, David. American Buffalo (1977). BP 1976-77; Samuel French.

Donny owns a junkshop (Don's Resale Shop) that is a kind of meeting place for small-time hoodlums like his friend Teach, who has strong opinions about professionalism, free enterprise, loyalty, and knowing what you're talking about. Teach is a talker whose street language is like a musical instrument. Mostly, in fact, the whole play is talk (shocking language to many) between Donny and Teach, sometimes including a young drug addict, Bobby, who does odd jobs at the junkstore. Finally it is apparent that the coin collection robbery that is the subject of everyone's attention will not take place. That plan, like everything else, is mostly talk.

2 acts; 3 men, 1 interior. Royalty: $50-35.

_____. Glengarry Glen Ross (1983). BP 1983-84; Samuel French.

Act I is comprised of a series of conversations at a Chicago Chinese restaurant between salesmen who work for the same real estate company. They are hustling Florida property, called the Glengarry Highlands, and are in the middle of a cutthroat contest conceived by their bosses: at the end of the month the salesman who has made the most in commissions gets a Cadillac; the two who have made the least get fired. Much of the talk among the salesmen has to do with the quality of the leads they are getting. The people doing best in the contest, like the slick Ricky Roma, are getting the best leads to work with. Those struggling to hang on to the bottom rung of the ladder, like oldtimer Shelly Levene, resort first to attempting to bribe the office manager and finally to robbing the office.

2 acts; 7 men, 2 interiors. Roaylty: $60-40.

_____. A Life in the Theater (1977). BP 1977-78; Samuel French.

Robert is a veteran actor; John is a newcomer. They work together in a regional theater, where we see them on stage, in the dressing room, and in various other spots around the theater. Robert has a habit of making grand pronouncements on art and theater, and John, at first, soaks them all up in an attempt to win the older man's approval, even giving into Robert's theater superstitions he does not believe in. Finally John's ambition overtakes Robert's poses, and by the end of the play it is the young actor assuring the older one he should not cry over the "smallness" he feels, and it is Robert who needs to win favor by loaning John cash until payday.

26 scenes; 3 men (1 non-speaking); bare stage. Royalty: $50-35.

MANDELL, Loring. Advise and Consent (1961). Adapted from Allen Drury's novel. Samuel French.

Deals with the pressures and intrigues of government decision making at its highest levels. The President has nominated an old friend and apparently capable man for Secretary of State. What was expected to be little more than a routine confirmation suddenly develops into a political donnybrook when a witness appears who testifies that the nominee was once a Communist. Then the credibility of the witness is attacked, but no one can be sure if he were lying previously or not. The nomination is withdrawn when an unscrupulous Senator attempts to blackmail the investigation committee's chairman into supporting the nomination, forcing the chairman to commit suicide to save his family from scandal. As the play ends the entire Senate resolves to restore dignity and honor to that body.

18 men, 4 women, 12 extras; cyclorama, wings, wagon insets. Royalty: $50-25.

MANHOFF, Bill. The Owl and the Pussycat (1965). Samuel French.

A curious author with a pair of binoculars gets into trouble when he spies a prostitute plying her trade in a distant apartment window. After he complains to her landlord, the prostitute is evicted, and the author finds he has more trouble than he can handle. Having been dispossessed, the lady reasons the writer owes her a place to stay. The resulting situation provides high comedy and eventually romance. She is practically illiterate and begins to increase her vocabulary only to have trouble finding sentences in which to use her increased word power. He finds himself becoming softer and more understanding about human nature. Eventually they fall in love, an impossible situation that can only be resolved one of two ways: suicide or drastic change for both of them. After failing in a bumbling attempt to end it all, he gets a job clerking in a book store and she becomes a receptionist.

    1 man, 1 woman; 1 interior. Royalty: $50-25.

MANN, R. J. <u>Our Miss Brooks</u>. See entry under Sergel, Christopher.

MANNERS, J. Hartley. <u>Peg O' My Heart</u> (1912). Samuel French.
    Peg O'Connell, a poor Irish girl in New York, becomes an heiress through the death of an uncle. She goes to England to be reared for her new role in the household of her aunt, who is excessively aristocratic, conservative, and stern, even to her own son and daughter. Peg feels like a duck out of water, but she wins her way by her wit and goodness of heart. She saves her snobbish cousin Ethel from scandal, and also wins the love of a promising young Englishman, Sir Gerald.
    3 acts; 5 men, 4 women; 1 interior. Royalty: $35-25.

MANOUSSI, J. <u>The Purple Mask</u>. See entry under Armont, Paul.

MAPES, Victor. <u>The Boomerang</u>. See entry under Smith, Winchell.

MARASCO, Robert. <u>Child's Play</u> (1970). BP 1969-70; Samuel French.
    A thriller which takes place at a Catholic boys boarding school, where the students are becoming surly, sinister, violent, and unmanageable. The boys begin to beat up one another in a savage manner and to torture members of the class. Someone sends obscene photographs to the dying mother of the classics teacher, who later jumps to his death. At the end of the play the boys surround the teacher who has always thought of the school as his and who has never been afraid of any "of his boys."
    6 men, 9 boys; composite interior, interior wagon. Royalty: $50-35.

MARC, Michel. <u>A Leghorn Hat</u>. See entry under Labiche, Eugene H.

MARCEAU, Felicien. <u>The Egg</u> (1960). Translated by Robert Schlitt. BP 1961-62; Samuel French.
    A young, good-natured Frenchman named Magis is bound and determined to figure life out. The first thing he learns is that everyone <u>doesn't</u> wake up in the morning fresh as a daisy (as they claim), and that the men he knows are <u>not</u> as successful at bedding

women as they say they are. He discovers next that it isn't true
that crime doesn't pay, leading to the realization that life makes
sense only if you don't try to figure out a system that makes no
sense. After marrying the daughter of a district tax collector, who
gets him a Civil Service job that provides a comfortable middle-class
existence, Magis first steals from, then exacts bribes from his wife's
lover. Finally, for no special reason he cares about, he kills his
wife, frames the lover, and watches a jury convict the man of murder. "That's the system," he says at the curtain, smiling innocently.

    2 acts; 19 men, 14 women; various settings. Royalty: $50-
25.

MARCH, William. The Bad Seed. See entry under Anderson, Max-
    well.

MARCUS, Frank. The Killing of Sister George (1965). BP 1966-67;
    Samuel French.
    Sister George is a character in a BBC soap opera, a nurse
who rides around on her cycle singing hymns, doing good deeds, and
making everyone happy. But the radio show is slipping in ratings,
partly because of rumors about Sister George's private life. BBC
decides to write her out of the series by having her be killed by a
truck. The woman who comes to break the news to Sister George
finds her smoking cigars, drinking gin, cursing, and living with a
female lover. The radio executive promptly steals the lover from
Sister George.
    4 women; 1 interior. Royalty: $50-25.

MARLOWE, Christopher. Dr. Faustus (1588). In his Best Plays,
    Mermaid ser., Scribner, 1903; in his Three Plays, Nelson's
    classics, 1940; Oxford, 1950; BAS; CLF v. 1; COF; COH; DUN;
    HARC v. 19; HOW; HUD; LIE; MIL; MOO; NEI; OLH; OLI v. 1;
    PAR; RUB; SCH; SCI; SCW; SML; SPE; STA; TREA-1.
    Selling his soul to the devil, Faust revels for 24 years in
luxury and splendor, but when the bond is due he regrets his forfeited life. Shows the tragical futile progress of a man attempting
to appropriate all beauty, power, and knowledge, to end only in
damnation.
    4 acts; 16 men, 2 women, 2 angels, 7 deadly sins, many
extras; 4 interiors, 5 exteriors; costumes.

————. Edward the Second (1592). In his Best Plays, Mermaid
    ser., Scribner, 1903; in his Three Plays, Nelson's classics,
    1940; ASH; BAS; BAT; CLS; HARC v. 19; MAT; NEI; OLH;
    OLI v. 1; PAR; RUB; SCH; SCI; SPE; TAU.
    Covers the years of Edward's reign, 1307-1327. Chronicles
his fatal infatuation for Gaveston as his favorite. Later, Mortimer,
acting as chief of the nobles with Isabella, deposed him and put him
to death.
    5 acts; 26 men, 2 women, extras; 9 interiors, 8 exteriors;

costumes of the period.

_____. Tamburlaine the Great (1587). In his Best Plays, Mermaid ser., Scribner, 1903; in his Three Plays, Nelson's classics, 1940; BAS; HOW; KRE; NEI; RYL; SCI; SCW; SPE.

Depicts the rise and fall of the Oriental conqueror—the ruthless advancement of a peasant lad to mighty power, conquering, slaying, and overriding the ordinary moral code to fulfill his ambition.

In 2 parts, 5 acts each. Part 1: 5 acts; 20 men, 4 women, extras; many scenes; costumes.

MARQUAND, John P. (with George S. Kaufman). The Late George Apley (1944). Based on the novel by John P. Marquand. BP 1944-45; Dramatists Play Service.

George Apley is a proper Beacon Street Bostonian of 1912, affiliated with all the right clubs and associated with all the right charitable enterprises. He does his duty to his family and class, much as his father did. His children, however, are falling in love beneath their class, using slang, and reading Freud. He tries to stop it, just as his father stopped him long ago, but is only half successful. His son, John, does not get to marry the girl from Worcester (foreigners!) whose house has iron animals in the front yard, but his daughter does break away to marry the lecturer in American literature she loves. In the epilogue, many years after George's death, we see John at the club that was his father's and his father's father's, sounding just like all the Apley men, living in as narrow a world as they did.

3 acts & epilogue; 8 men, 8 women; 2 interiors. Royalty: $50-25.

_____. Point of No Return. See entry under Osborn, Paul.

MARQUIS, Don. The Dark Hours (1924). Doubleday, 1924.

Presents events of the last hours of the life of Jesus, from Thursday evening to Friday afternoon. Jesus does not appear in person, but His voice from off-stage uses the words of the New Testament. First Caiaphas and Annas secure witnesses and get the services of mentally confused Judas. Then comes the arrest in Gethsemane, followed by the trial before the Sanhedrin and Peter's denials. Then Jesus is tried before Pilate, after Herod has sent Him back. Pilate orders the scourging and is not dissuaded by his wife from ordering the crucifixion. Finally the scene at Golgotha is presented.

5 scenes; 8 men, 2 women, extras, & a Voice from Beyond; 2 interiors, 2 exteriors; costumes of the period.

_____. The Old Soak (1922). Doubleday, 1922; French, 1926; BP 1922-23.

A genial alcoholic, "with a feelin' for liquor," a domestic derelict with a weakness but a good heart, quite redeems himself

when the crisis comes. His wife has put away some bonds, their
son steals them because of a chorus girl; the Old Soak then takes
the blame, but all is cleared up.
    3 acts; 5 men, 4 women; 2 interiors.

MARSTON, Merlin. Tracers. See entry under DiFusco, John.

MARTENS, Anne Coulter. Onions in the Stew. See entry under
    Dalzell, William.

_____. Pride and Prejudice. See entry under Austen, Jane.

MARTIN, Elliot. More Stately Mansions. See entry under O'Neill,
    Eugene.

MARTINEZ-SIERRA, Gregorio and Maria Martinez-Sierra. The Cradle
    Song (1911). Tr. by John Garrett Underhill, Dutton, 1923; in
    Poet Lore, v. 28, 1917; French carries; CEW; HAV; BP 1926-27.
    Teresa was left as a foundling at a convent of Dominican nuns
where she was reared by the gardener's wife, the nuns lavishing on
her all their tenderness. When 18, she falls in love with Antonio
and leaves to marry him mid fond farewells. A sensitive, devoutly
pious play, told with Spanish grace and tender touch.
    2 acts; 4 men, 10 women, extras; 2 interiors; nun's costumes.
    Royalty: $50-25.

_____. The Kingdom of God (1916). Tr. by Granville-Barker in
    his Plays, v. 2, Dutton, 1923; carried by French; BP 1928-29.
    Sister Gracia appears first as a young girl of 19 just taking
her vows and serving in an asylum for poor old men. Next she is
serving at 29 in a maternity house where she represses her very
human love for a young doctor. In the 3d act she is an elderly
woman of 70 serving in an orphanage where she stops a revolt, commanding by her wisdom unruly and half-starved orphans whom she
tells to work and pray for the Kingdom of God.
    3 acts; 14 men, 17 women, extras; 2 interiors, 1 exterior;
    nun's costumes.

_____. Madame Pepita (1912). Tr. by Underhill & May Broun
    in his Cradle Song & other plays, Dutton, 1923 & 1929.
    Depicts events in the life of Pepita, who was a dressmaker
and had been brought up in the house of Don Luis Condé; she had
married a Russian nobleman in Paris who deserted her, but by
whom she had a daughter, Catalina, who is now 16 years old. Don
Guillermo, a roomer above, looks on Catalina as a daughter and instructs her; he also persuades Pepita to marry him. Fortunately
she inherits some wealth from the Russian husband, so Catalina can
go to Rome with Alberto, a rising young artist who has won a prize.
Pepita and her husband remain to comfort each other.
    3 acts; 5 men, 6 women; 1 interior, 1 exterior.

_____ . The Romantic Young Lady (1918). Tr. by Granville-
Barker in Kingdom of God & other plays, Dutton, 1922; also
in his Plays, v. 2, Dutton, 1923; French carried.

A romantic girl, who regrets that she can't have adventures
like a man, becomes interested in a strange young man whose hat
blows into her room during a storm. Seeking his hat, he writes a
letter of recommendation to be presented the next day. She applies
for the job at the office of a famous popular novelist who turns out
to be the young man. She is a bit disappointed, but his romantic
self, like his novels, proves irresistible.

3 acts; 5 men, 6 women; 2 interiors.

_____ . The Two Shepherds (1913). Tr. by Granville-Barker in
his Kingdom of God & other plays, Dutton, 1922; also in his
Plays, v. 2, Dutton, 1923; LEV.

In a small Spanish village two men are forced to give up
their posts: a priest, Don Antonio, for having too much faith, and
Don Francisco, a doctor, for having too little. They cannot pass
the necessary examinations in theology and science, chiefly because
of age, but they are true shepherds who understand human nature
and can give proper guidance to the souls and bodies of the country
people of their rural area.

2 acts; 10 men, 9 women, extras; 1 exterior (a garden).

MARX, Arthur. The Impossible Years. See entry under Fisher,
Bob.

MASEFIELD, John. The Tragedy of Nan (1908). Lond., Richards,
1909; Kennerley, 1909; in his Poems & Plays, Macmillan, 1918;
separately, Macmillan, 1921; in his Prose Plays, Macmillan,
1925.

In the house of her uncle, Nan an orphan is a drudge; she
is outcast because her father was hanged. Her lover deserts her.
Tormented on every hand, she is driven to kill her jilting lover and
to drown herself in the rising tide. Grimly but beautifully presents
a vision of the heart of life.

3 acts; 8 men, 5 women; 1 interior; costumes of 1810 in
England.

_____ . The Trial of Jesus (1925). Macmillan, 1925.

Follows through the trial before Annas and Caiaphas who convicts Him of blasphemy. Introduces Peter's denial and Judas' return of the money. Then depicts the trial before Pilate, who would
only scourge Him, but on further accusation by Annas, sentences
Him to be crucified. That evening the cynical Herod visits Pilate
and his wife, Procula. Longinus the centurion testifies to his belief that "that was the Son of God, if one may say that."

Prolog & 3 acts; 18 men, 6 women, extras as a Chorus; 1
curtain set: 2 levels, with a balcony; costumes of the period.

MASSEY, Edward. Plots and Playwrights (1917). Little, 1917;

French, 1929; BAK.

A satire on pot-boiling writers. A playwright must complete a play in a month but says he has no material. A short-story writer says there is material right in their boarding house and proves it by writing three episodes from the lives of the tenants.

Prolog & 2 acts; 10 men, 6 women; 2 interiors, 1 exterior.

MASSINGER, Philip. A New Way to Pay Old Debts (1633). In Mermaid ser., Scribner; BAS; BAT v. 13; in BRI v. 1; HARC v. 47; HOW; INCH; v. 6; KRE; MAT; NEI; OLH; OLI v. 2; OXB v. 1; PAR; RUB; SCH; SCI; SMO; SPE; WHE.

The avaricious usurer, Sir Giles Overreach, takes over all the property of his nephew Frank Wellborn and, in order to get more money, plans to marry his daughter Margaret to Lord Lovell. Lady Allworth, a wealthy widow, has a stepson Tom, who is in love with Margaret. Aided by Lord Lovell, she deceives Sir Giles into thinking Frank will marry her and Lord Lovell will marry Margaret. Thus Frank gets his money from his uncle and can pay his debts, Tom marries Margaret, and Lord Lovell marries Lady Allworth. The greedy Sir Giles has overreached himself and becomes insane at the deceit.

5 acts; 12 men, 5 women, extras; 3 interiors, 3 exteriors; costumes of the period.

MASTERS, Edgar Lee. Spoon River Anthology. See entry under Aidman, Charles.

MASTROSIMONE, William. Extremities (1983). BP 1982-83; Samuel French.

Marjorie, Terry, and Patricia are fixing up a dilapidated farmhouse where the cornfield meets the highway between Trenton and Princeton, New Jersey. Marjorie is at home alone when she is surprised by an intruder, Raul, who seems to know her name, her schedule, her roommates, the men she corresponds with. He has been staking her out, reading her mail; he knows how long he has with her alone before the others get home. He plans to rape them all ("Today's gonna be a triple header"). During his attempt on her, however, Marjorie sprays him in the face with wasp poison and is able to tie him up and put him in a makeshift jail in the fireplace. He says she can't prove anything against him and that he will come back in the future and cut her up. She threatens to torture him (she does a little) and to kill him and bury him in the back yard. When her roommates get home there are arguments about the course of action to take, about the role of female provocation in rape, of the law's inability to punish such a crime, of the failure of the victim's friends to offer appropriate support, of the fear, shame, and degradation of being violently abused as a person. At the end Raul admits to being a serial rapist, and the girls agree to have him picked up by the police.

2 acts; 1 man, 3 women; 1 interior. Royalty: $60-40.

MAUGHAM, W. Somerset. The Breadwinner (1930). Doubleday,
    1931; in his Plays, Heinemann, 1932, v. 4; in his Six Comedies,
    Doubleday, 1937 & Star books, 1939; CHA; CHAR.
        Bored by his fatuous wife Margery and two unbearably bright
children, Judy and Pat (aged 18), Charles Battle decides to quit
working and let them fend for themselves with the £15,000 he will
leave them. He no longer will be the breadwinner for the family, thus
shaking off domestic chains and meaningless drudgery. A satire on
the annoying self-assurance of modern youth.
        3 acts; 4 men, 4 women; 1 interior.

————————. The Circle (1921). Heinemann, & Doran, 1921; Baker
    carried; in his Plays, Heinemann, 1932, v. 4; in his Six Com-
    edies, Doubleday, 1937, & Star books, 1939; CEU; COT; DIG;
    DUR; MAP; MCD; MOSH; MYD; TRE-3; TREA-3; TUCD; TUCM;
    WATF, v. 2; WATI; WATO; BP 1921-22.
        Cleverly insists that the young never profit by the experience
of the old. Thirty years ago Lady Kitty had run away from her
rather stuffy husband; she now returns and finds her son's wife
about to do the same thing. Example, warning, advice, even permission fail to stop the romantic Elizabeth.
        3 acts; 4 men, 3 women; 1 interior.

————————. The Constant Wife (1926). BP 1926-27; Samuel French.
        Constance knows her husband is having an affair with her
best friend. She takes a partnership in Barbara's shop and earns
enough to pay back her board and lodging; then she plans to go off
for six weeks with Bernard; after which she will return to home and
husband. She claims, if her husband is not faithful to her and if
she supports herself, she is entitled to lead her own life in her own
way. The play is a protest against a double standard of morality
in marriage: what is sauce for the gander should be sauce for the
goose.
        3 acts; 4 men, 5 women; 1 interior. Royalty: $50-25.

————————. Jane. See entry under Behrman, S. N.

————————. Lady Frederick (1907). Heinemann, 1912; in his Plays,
    Heinemann, 1931, v. 1.
        Young Charles Mereston is devoted to Lady Frederick, a
widow of uncertain years, so his mother calls in her brother Paradine to aid her in curing her son's infatuation. They reveal to him
Lady Frederick's shady past, but this only drives Charles to declare his love. When however Lady Frederick reveals her real age
to Charles, he is sufficiently shocked. She now also refuses the
hand of Captain Montgomerie, who has helped her when in financial
straits, but does accept her former suitor Paradine.
        3 acts; 8 men, 5 women; 2 interiors.

————————. Our Betters (1917). Heinemann, 1923; in his Plays,
    Heinemann, 1932, v. 3; in his Six Comedies, Doubleday, 1937,

& Star books, 1939; DID; MOSO; SMO; WHI.

An American girl marries a titled Englishman and becomes Lady Grayson; then she tries to get her sister Elizabeth an English husband. But the scandalous lives of her sister's set are too much for her, so Elizabeth goes back to New York to marry Fleming Harvey. The play is a cynical exposé of American title hunters in London.

3 acts; 7 men, 4 women; 2 interiors.

————. Rain. See entry under Colton, John R.

————. Smith (1909). Heinemann, 1913; Dramatic Pub. Co., 1913; in his Plays, Heinemann, 1931, v. 2.

Tom Freeman returns from his Rhodesia farm to visit his sister Rose in London and if possible to find a wife. A former flame, Emily, gets him to propose again but balks at the prospect in South Africa. All of his sister's friends are the idle rich of London high society; he finds them objectionable, but he finds the house-maid Smith the kind he wants for a wife.

4 acts; 4 men, 4 women; 2 interiors (can be played in 1).

MAY, Elaine, with Terrence McNally. Adaptation/Next (1969). BP 1968-69; Dramatists Play Service.

A long running off-Broadway show made up of two one-acts: May's "Adaptation" and McNally's "Next." In the first play life is a television game show, and a Narrator and his two assistants play all the other roles except that of Phil Benson, the contestant. Benson plays the game fully, searching futilely for the square on the gameboard labeled The Security Square. What he doesn't know, the Narrator tells us before the contestant is brought out, is that "he, himself, may label any space on the Board the Security Square and declare himself the winner any time it occurs to him to do so." Of course it never does. McNally's "Next" deals with a reluctant draftee reporting for his physical. (He is Marion Cheever, a fat, late 40's, twice divorced, assistant manager of a Fine Arts Theater who knows there's been some mistake.) The person in charge is a hefty WAC named Sergeant Thech who finally rejects Marion, as everyone else in his life has, and causes him to freak out.

"Adaptation": 3 men, 1 woman; open stage, with lectern. Royalty: $25. "Next": 1 man, 1 woman; simplified interior. Royalty: $25.

MAYER, Edwin J. The Firebrand (1924). BP 1924-25; Samuel French.

The eager, glamorous, impetuous youth, Cellini, is continually in hot water, from killing men to courting women. He contracts to secure Angela from her mother, only to lose her to the Duke when his eyes light upon her, while Cellini is being pursued by the Duchess.

3 acts; 8 men, 4 women, extras; 1 interior, 1 exterior; costumes of the period. Royalty: $25-20.

MEDCRAFT, Russell G. and Norma Mitchell. Cradle Snatchers
    (1925). Samuel French.
    Three wives grow tired of sitting at home while their hus-
bands are enjoying themselves elsewhere, perhaps with flappers, so
they hire college boys to make love to them. The husbands return
from their "duck-shooting" to find a hilarious party with the hired
cake-eaters. A compromise may be expected by which the husbands
will be only too glad to act as escorts and attentive admirers.
    3 acts; 8 men, 7 women; 2 interiors. Royalty: $25-20.

MEDOFF, Mark. Children of a Lesser God (1980). BP 1979-80;
    Dramatists Play Service.
    The play takes place in the mind of James Leeds, a speech
teacher at the state school for the deaf. He has a special student,
Sarah, who refuses to learn to read lips and speak out loud, believing that her communicative skills are already more refined than
those of the hearing world. He falls in love with Sarah, marries
her, and becomes for a time the middleman between those pushing
the politics of deaf rights and the state school's establishment bureaucracy. The original production directed James to say out loud
to himself Sarah's signed lines, and to speak and sign his own lines
simultaneously. The other deaf characters in the play read lips
and speak.
    2 acts; 3 men, 4 women; unit set. Royalty: $50.

_____. The Wager (1975). BP 1974-75; Dramatists Play Service.
    In this peculiar comedy a bright graduate student, Leeds, re-
luctantly bets his roommate, super-jock Ward, that he can't seduce
a faculty wife in the next 48 hours. Ward accomplishes it with
Honor Stevens and has 47 left to spare. Her husband Ron hangs
around the graduate students' apartment and whines, once coming
back with a machine gun to kill somebody, but he can't pull the
trigger. (He later decides to shoot up his car, but the gun doesn't
work so he washes the car.) Through all of this it is Leeds who is
pulling everyone's strings out of his fear of feeling anything for
anybody. At the end of the play Honor Stevens and Leeds are
alone, and it is certain that she will seduce him. But first they
make a wager.
    3 men, 1 woman; 1 interior. Royalty: $50-35.

_____. When You Comin' Back, Red Ryder? (1974). BP 1973-74;
    Dramatists Play Service.
    Stephen (Red) Ryder is about to turn over his night attend-
ant duties at the 24-hour diner in a small southwestern town to the
daytime attendant, Angel. Her friend Lyle, who runs the motel/
filling station across the road, comes in for breakfast, followed by
two couples. One pair is bound for New Orleans; the other is driving a carload of marijuana to California. The male with the dope
begins to taunt and bully all of the other diner occupants, tearing
away at them verbally and exposing their innermost secrets and
fears.

5 men, 3 women; 1 interior. Royalty: $50-35.

MELVILLE, Herman. Billy Budd. See entry under Coxe, Louis O.

_____. See Orson Welles's Moby Dick--Rehearsed.

MEYERS, Patrick. K2 (1983). BP 1982-83; Dramatists Play Service.
   Two mountain climbers are trapped on a ledge 27,000 feet in the air in the Himalayas--1,250 feet below the summit of K2, the world's second highest mountain, which they have already scaled, insuring their place in history. On the way down, however, there has been an accident, and Harold, a physicist, liberal humanist, husband and father has broken his leg. The team leader, Taylor, a hard-nosed district attorney whose world view is soured by the crime and criminals he experiences every day, has for his part neglected to pack a spare length of rope essential for lowering his injured partner to possible safety. He tries several times to climb back up the mountain to retrieve the discarded rope. Between times they carry on a running right-left, conservative-liberal argument. Finally, it is decided that Taylor will make a dangerous attempt to save himself with only one rope and one ice screw.
   1 act; 2 men; 1 exterior. Royalty: $50-40.

MICHAELS, Sidney. Dylan (1964). Based on the memoirs of Caitlin Thomas and John M. Brinnin BP 1003 04; Samuel French.
   The life of one of the great twentieth century poets is depicted in this biographical drama. Feelings for the Irish poet, Dylan Thomas, were as diverse and extreme as his life. The play begins as he says goodbye to his wife before leaving on a poetry reading tour of the United States and follows him through colleges, lecture halls, bars and bedrooms, and finally to the hold of the ship that carried his body back home to Ireland. He died at the age of thirty-nine, but in his life he had exemplified the lines of his most famous poem, "Do not go gentle into that good night."
   15 men, 13 women; various sets. Royalty: $50-25.

_____. Tchin-Tchin (1962). Based on the play by François Billetdoux. BP 1962-63; Samuel French.
   Rough, passionate, clownish Caesario Grimaldi and proper, uptight Pamela Pew-Pickett have something in common: their spouses have been having an affair ever since Dr. Pickett removed Margaret's appendix. Appendicitis is nothing these days, Caesario says, "it's in the aftereffects where the danger lies." His solution to the problem is to drink himself senseless; hers is to have tea and think of some plan of action. The rest of the play is devoted to getting these two together in a celebration of themselves, which finally happens after each has given up virtually everything from the past--including their money.
   2 acts; 3 men, 2 women; various sets. Royalty: $50-25.

MIDDLETON, George. Adam and Eva. See entry under Bolton, Guy.

MILLAY, Edna St. Vincent. The King's Henchman (1927). Harper, 1927; Baker carried; TUCD.

King Eadgar of 10th-century England sends his foster brother AEthelwold to woo AElfrida for him. She finds him asleep in the forest of Devon; they fall in love and marry. He sends back word that she is unworthy of the King's love. When the King comes, AEthelwold asks her to dress as a hag, but she appears in beautiful garments. Because of her self-love and his mistake AEthelwold kills himself; the King denounces her as indeed unworthy.

3 acts; 13 men, 8 women, extras; 2 interiors, 1 exterior; costumes of the period.

MILLER, Arthur. After the Fall (1964). BP 1963-64; Dramatists Play Service.

At the beginning of the play Quentin seats himself at the edge of the stage and starts to talk to the audience as one would to a friend. Behind him the key figures in his life move in and out of narrative, revealing and illuminating Quentin's past. Some of the characters and incidents suggest Mr. Miller's personal past--especially Maggie, the sexy, popular entertainer who destroys herself (Marilyn Monroe) and the preoccupation with naming names of Communists (Miller's troubles with Senator Joseph McCarthy). A brilliant play.

12 men, 11 women, several non-speaking roles; unit set. Royalty: $50-25.

_____. All My Sons (1947). BP 1946-47; Dramatists Play Service.

Exposes war-time cheaters. Joe, the father, wants his son Chris in the business with him, but Chris won't go in because he knows that cracked cylinders had been sent out of his father's factory and installed in a military aircraft. The other son, Larry, was killed by a dropping plane, in a suicidal gesture prompted by his awareness of his father's corruption. Joe even framed his partner to serve the sentence for the defective parts. Chris refuses to believe that Joe had the family's interest at heart and convinces his father that a man is responsible to the world, too, that all men are his sons. Rather than go to prison, Joe shoots himself.

6 men, 4 women; 1 exterior. Royalty: $50-35.

_____. The Creation of the World and Other Business (1972, 1973). BP 1972-73; Dramatists Play Service.

Deals with the struggle between God and Lucifer; with Adam, Eve, Cain, and Abel as their pawns. The three acts of the play cover the creation of Eve (from Adam's observation that everything seems to come in pairs) and the eating of the forbidden fruit and the subsequent expulsion from Paradise to the murder of Abel by Cain. Each act poses a question on the human dilemma: 1) Since God made everything and God is good--why did He make Lucifer? 2) Is there something in the way we are born which makes us want

the world to be good? 3) When every man wants justice, why does
He go on creating injustice?
    8 men, 1 woman; unit set. Royalty: $50-35.

_____. The Crucible (1953). BP 1952-53; Dramatists Play Ser-
    vice.
    Though the scene is Salem, Massachusetts in 1692 (the year
of the famous witch trials) there are a number of parallels with
America of the 1950's and the McCarthy "witch hunts." The play
deals with lies and how they cause mass hysteria in the community.
To keep from being punished severely, Abigail and her friends make
up a story of witchcraft. They even name individuals who are in
communion with the devil. One of those named is Elizabeth Proctor,
wife of John Proctor whom Abigail loves. When John persuades his
serving girl, Mary Warren, to admit the fraud in the charges, the
rest of the girls pretend to faint and become stricken with Mary's
evil spirit. She soon changes her story and accuses John of witchcraft. Both of the Proctors, and other townspeople, are imprisoned.
John is offered his life for a confession of witchcraft, but he finally
refuses and goes to his death.
    10 men, 10 women; unit set. Royalty: $50-35.

_____. Death of a Salesman (1949). BP 1948-49; Dramatists Play
    Service.
    Pulitzer prize play 1948/49. After 40 years as a travelling
salesman, Willy Loman finds the hollowness of just good-fellowship
as a means of selling. He is told he must work on a commission
basis instead of a salary. He comes to realize he has become a
failure as a salesman, and also an ineffectual father to his two sons
who have developed as good fellows but without good purpose. Willy
recalls some of his past experiences and successes which show how
he deceived himself with little lies which have led to gradual disintegration. He represents Everyman in a tragedy of mediocrity as
he comes to the end of his rope.
    8 men, 5 women; combination interior-exterior set. Royalty:
    $50-35.

_____. An Enemy of the People. See entry under Ibsen, Henrik.

_____. Incident at Vichy (1964). BP 1964-65; Dramatists Play
    Service.
    Eight men have been picked up by the Nazis and are waiting
in the detention room of a Vichy police station. The time is 1942.
The men hope that their identification papers are merely to be
checked, but we discover that all of them are real or suspected Jews.
They will all be examined to see if they have been circumcised; those
who have been will be shipped in freight cars to Polish death camps.
Of special interest to the playwright are three characters: a German
guard who hates his present job and ironically is himself circumcised;
a former French officer who wants to escape and aid in the underground movement; and an Austrian nobleman who hates the Nazis only

because they are crude, vulgar, and tasteless. Finally the nobleman, who would undoubtedly have been released, sacrifices his life
so that the French Jewish officer can escape.
    21 men; 1 interior. Royalty: $50-25.

_____. Playing for Time (1985). Adapted from the television
    film, based on the book by Fania Fenelon. Dramatic Publishing
    Company.
    A harsh play set during WWII in the Auschwitz/Binkenau
Concentration Camp where women play in an orchestra in exchange
for their lives. Tania Tenelon, a French singer, is sought after to
liven up a monotonous-sounding orchestra, along with her young
friend Marianne, who will do anything with the male officers for
food. They are at first glad to be saved, but humiliation and gross-
ness set in when they are called to play for Jews being sent to the
gas chamber. Alma Rose is the harsh orchestra director who tries
to break Tania from her emotional ties, but it is all too much for a
soul to bear.
    2 acts; 4 men, 18 women, extras; area staging. Royalty:
    $75-50.

_____. The Price (1968). BP 1967-68; Dramatists Play Service.
    Two brothers meet after a 16-year estrangement to dispose
of their deceased father's belongings. One brother is a policeman,
who sacrificed his education and dreams of becoming a scientist to
care for his invalid father. The other is an eminent surgeon, who
walked out on the family to concentrate on his medical education.
The background is filled in with a conversation between the policeman and his wife. The philosophy is articulated by a Jewish dealer
of furniture who will not immediately set a price for the father's
possessions. The conflict and drama are provided by the meeting
of the sons after a long and bitter separation.
    3 men, 1 woman; 1 interior. Royalty: $50.

_____. A View from the Bridge (1955). BP 1955-56; Dramatists
    Play Service.
    This long one-act play is told by a wise and sympathetic
neighborhood lawyer in the Italian section of Brooklyn. The story
concerns Eddie Carbone, a longshoreman, who helps two of his
wife's relatives enter the country illegally from Sicily. Eddie makes
room for Marco and Rodolpho in his home. He changes his attitude
about the men when Rodolopho (whom Eddie believes is homosexual)
falls in love with Catherine, Eddie's niece. Though Eddie believes
he thinks of Catherine as a daughter, it is obvious that his affection is more physical. To prevent the two young people from marrying, Eddie informs the Immigration Authorities, and the two are arrested. When they are released on bail, Marco kills Eddie.
    12 men, 3 women; 1 interior. Royalty: $50-35.

MILLER, J. P. Days of Wine and Roses (1973). Dramatists Play
    Service.

This story was first a television play and then a major motion picture. It deals with Joe Clay, an up-and-coming Madison Avenue type who has a drinking problem. So does the woman he marries, but both pretend that drinking is merely something they choose to do. The failure to recognize alcoholism leads the couple right down the drain: their marriage breaks up, Joe's career is in shambles, friends and family find them hopelessly lost, and their child is victimized by the effects of booze.

10-15 men, 5-10 women, 1 girl; unit set. Royalty: $50-25.

MILLER, Jason. That Championship Season (1971). BP 1971-72; Dramatists Play Service.

Five men meet for their annual reunion. Four of the men were members of a hot-shot basketball team which won the state high school championship twenty years ago. The other man is their coach, now retired. The reunion is light-hearted at first, but the desperation which characterizes everybody's present life begins to emerge. The former players are now inept mayors, high school principals, "successful" businessmen, despairing alcoholics; each suffers from moral bankruptcy. At the end they are brought together again by feelings of self-preservation by the unconscious cynicism and bigotry of their coach.

5 men; 1 interior. Royalty: $50-35.

MILLER, Jonathan. Beyond the Fringe. See entry under Bennett, Alan.

MILN, Louise J. The Purple Mask. See entry under Armont, Paul.

MILNE, A. A. Belinda (1918). Samuel French.

A supposed widow, presenting her daughter as her niece, keeps two suitors dangling; one a long-haired poet, the other a prosaic gentleman. After 19 years the husband returns, unrecognized without his beard, and she falls in love again, just because he is an attractive man and she a charming woman.

3 acts; 3 men, 3 women; 1 interior, 1 exterior (may be played with 1 exterior throughout). Royalty: $25-20.

_____. The Dover Road (1921). BP 1921-22; French, 1923; DIE; MOD.

As a delightful bit of polite farce it depicts the amiable if eccentric Mr. Latimer detaining by gentle force eloping couples who are taking the Dover road to France. A double pair are thus brought to see each other under the strain of a fresh cold at the breakfast table, and are given a chance to change their minds.

3 acts; 6 men, 4 women; 1 interior.

_____. The Ivory Door (1927). Samuel French.

On the point of marrying lovely Princess Lilia, King Pervale decides to walk through the ivory door, in spite of the tradition that no one who has walked through it has ever returned. He does so, but on his return no one knows him except the Princess, who also walks through it. Since no one recognizes either, another King is chosen, while the real King and his Princess have discovered truth and happiness.

Prolog & 3 acts; 11 men, 4 women; 1 interior, 1 exterior; fantastic costumes. Royalty: $50-25.

_____. Michael and Mary (1929). Lond., Chatto, 1930; French, 1932; BP 1929-30.

Though knowing that despondent Mary has been deserted by her husband, Michael marries her, despite no divorce. This adds spice and even danger to their venture. Fourteen happy years later, the first husband appears and proceeds to blackmail them, but in a scuffle he drops dead of heart failure. They fabricate an explanation which satisfies the police, though there is still a possibility of danger and adventure.

3 acts; 10 men, 6 women; 3 interiors.

_____. Mr. Pim Passes By (1919). Samuel French.

Mr. Pim, an absent-minded old gentleman, nearly wrecks the hapiness of a charming couple on whom he chances to call by announcing that the lady's former husband, though dead, is alive. All is due to Mr. Pim's trouble with names, and he remembers the right name in time to avoid disaster.

3 men, 4 women; 1 interior. Royalty: $50-25.

_____. The Perfect Alibi (1928). Samuel French.

Two of his guests murder Judge Arthur Ludgrove (in full view of the audience) and plant evidence of suicide. His niece, Susan, a young sleuth-hound, becomes suspicious and brings about the apprehension of the two; they were vindictive because the Judge had sentenced them years before as diamond thieves in South Africa.

7 men, 3 women; 1 interior. Royalty: $50.

_____. The Romantic Age (1920). Samuel French.

Romantic Melisande, meeting a medieval knight in the woods, thinks he is her knight coming to rescue her; but he is only a stockbroker en route to a fancy-dress ball. She dreams of her knight, to meet him again the next morning. He comes for her that afternoon and she is quite disillusioned; she suffers agonies, but he succeeds in reconciling her. Romance can exist even on the Exchange.

5 men, 4 women; 1 interior, 1 exterior. Royalty: $50.

_____. The Truth about Blayds (1921). Samuel French.

The famous poet Blayds, who has dominated literature and his household, confesses on his death-bed that his whole career has been a lie--that he appropriated the poems of another and had published them as his own. What shall the family do about it? Isobel won't touch the royalty money and insists that the truth be told. The rest do not agree. Why does it seem best to keep silent? They

do, but Marian's husband may mention the scandal in his memoirs.
4 men, 4 women; 1 interior. Royalty: $25.

MILTON, John. Comus, a Masque (1634). In editions of his Works
or Poems; HARC; OLI v. 2; PAR; adapted by Lucy Chater, pub.
by Baker.
Comus, as the son of Bacchus and Circe, tempts travelers
to drink a magic liquor which would change their faces into those of
wild beasts. A lacy is left in the woods by her two brothers who go
to find a cooling fruit for her. She falls into the hands of Comus,
and just as the god is offering her his magic potion, the brothers
come to her rescue.
3 scenes; 6 men, 3 women, extras; 1 interior, 2 exteriors
(can be produced with 1 exterior); fanciful costumes.

MITCHELL, Adrian. Marat/Sade. See entry under Weiss, Peter.

MITCHELL, Langdon. The New York Idea (1906). Baker, 1908;
MOSS-3; QUIL; WATC-1; HAL; abridged in Pierce & Matthews, v.1.
An incisive satire on social conditions caused by easy divorce. The Englishman, Sir Wilfred, is much confused by meeting
so many divorcees, but he catches Vida Phillimore on the rebound.
Cynthia balks at Philip and takes up again with her first husband,
who reports that the divorce was invalid anyway.
4 acts; 9 men, 6 women; 3 interiors.

MITCHELL, Norma. Cradle Snatchers. See entry under Medcraft,
Russell G.

MITCHELL, Thomas. Little Accident. See entry under Dell, Floyd.

MITTELHOLZER, Edgar. Shadows Move Among Them. See Moss
Hart's Climate of Eden.

MOELLER, Philip. Madame Sand (1917). Knopf, 1917; HAL; TUCD.
Vitalizes the many friends of George Sand, even her husband
Baron Dudevant. She is the central figure in each act, first with
Alfred de Musset, then with Pietro Pagello, and finally with Frédé-
ric Chopin. Pictures her as a writer who turns out just so many
pages a day, as she records clever ideas and scenes for future use.
3 acts; 8 men, 7 women, extras; 3 interiors; costumes of
the period.

_____. Molière (1919). Knopf, 1919.
Gives a charming picture of the great French playwright in
the last year of his life, as he continues to act and also to write
(his last play: The Imaginary Invalid). Shows his break with
Louis XIV and Mme. de Montespan. In the final death scene, his
wife Armande returns in time, but the king is too late.
3 acts; 13 men, 7 women, extras; 2 interiors; costumes of 1673.

_____. Sophie (1919). Knopf, 1919.

Presents an evening in the life of the capricious temperamental opera singer Sophie Arnauld in the Paris of Louis XV. She
secures from Gluck the role of Iphigenia in Aulis, rids herself of
the aged Austrian Ambassador in order that her lover Dorval may
come at midnight, and avoids arrest by sponsoring the marriage of
Vivienne, the daughter of the Chief of Police.

    3 acts; 9 men, 5 women, extras; 1 interior; costumes of the
period.

MOLIÈRE. Le Bourgeois Gentilhomme (1670). In all complete editions of his translated works (for list see note under his Tartuffe); Van Laun translates title as The Citizen Who Apes the
Nobleman; Page as The Tradesman Turned Gentleman; Baker &
Miller as The Citizen Turned Gentleman; also in CLF-2; tr. by
Margaret Baker as The Merchant Gentleman, French, 1915; tr.
and adapted by Fernand as The Would-be Gentleman, in 3 acts
(4 men, 4 women, extras), Lond., Secker, & Dramatic Pub.
Co., 1926.

    A retired middle-class shop-keeper who has made a fortune,
M. Jourdain, resolves to be a gentleman and cut a figure in Society.
He studies dancing, fencing, music, and philosophy, and tries to
have an affair with a marquise. He is hoodwinked by all, especially
when made a mamamouchi. He unknowingly marries his daughter
Lucile to a commoner, Cleonte, who poses as the Grand Turk's son.

    5 acts; 9 to 12 men, 5 women, extras; 1 interior; costumes
of the period.

_____. The Cheats of Scapin. See Frank Dunlop's Scapino.

_____. The Doctor in Spite of Himself (1666). In all complete
editions of his translated works (for list see note under his main
entry for Tartuffe); the Wall translation also in SMR; tr. by
Baker & Miller as The Mock Doctor; tr. by Clark, Modern Lib.,
1924; same, French, 1925; LEV; tr. and adapted (with 2m, 3w)
by Hewitt, pub. by Row, Peterson, 1941. Acting ed.: Samuel
French, tr. by Albert Bermel.

    Sganarelle, a poor wood-cutter, is forced to act as a physi-
cian. Once in, he rather likes the trade and works miraculous
cures. He is called in by Géronte to cure Lucinde, who pretends
she is dumb because her father will not allow her to marry her lover,
Leandre. A sharp satire on the medical profession.

    3 acts; 6 men, 3 women; 1 interior, 1 exterior; costumes of
the period. French version: 7-8 men, 3-4 women. Royalty:
$50-25.

_____. The Imaginary Invalid (1673). In all complete editions
of his translated works (for list see note under his main entry
for Tartuffe); tr. by Baker & Miller as The Hypochondriak; tr.
by Clark, French, 1925; tr. by Stone, French, 1939; tr. and
adapted by Turner, Dramatic Pub. Co., 1939; tr. by Malleson,
French.

A hopeless hypochondriac, Argan, who imagines he has every complaint, wishes his daughter Angélique to marry a dull physician so as to have a doctor handy. However she loves handsome Cléante, and is saved by her maid Toinette, who disguised as a physician works a permanent cure and also shows up Beline, Argan's shrewish wife, who wishes Angélique to become a nun so she may inherit. Argan plays dead to discover his wife's devotion. She says, "Good riddance," but Angélique is sincerely grieved. Argan springs to life to be the head of the house and to permit his daughter to marry Cléante. A satire on the medical profession.

3 acts (or 5 in the original); 8 men, 5 women; 1 interior; costumes of the period. Royalties: Stone, $0-10; Turner, $25-20; Malleson, $35-25.

_____. The Learned Ladies (1672). In all complete editions of his translated works (for list, see note under his main entry for Tartuffe).

Philaminte, wife of Chrysale, her sister Belise (who sides with her sister), and her daughter Armande (who advocates free or platonic love) affect pretentious learning—a vogue popular at court. The younger daughter, Henriette, with more common sense, has little sympathy with these lofty flights and finds a sweetheart in Clitandre instead of Trissotin, whom her mother wishes her to marry. When Chrysale's brother announces that their money is all lost, Trissotin backs out, and old Chrysale finally musters up his courage to brave his wife's anger and to champion Henriette's marriage. Thus they escape from affectation.

5 acts; 8 men, 5 women; 1 interior.

_____. The Misanthrope (1666). In all complete editions of his translated works (for list, see note below under Tartuffe); Van Laun translation in CAR & TRE-1, -2 (v. 2); TREA-1; Page in KRE; Baker & Miller translate as The Man Hater; tr. by Clark, Modern Lib., 1924; tr. by Giese, Houghton, 1928; tr. by Bentley in MIL; tr. Richard Wilbur, Dramatists Play Service; tr. by Tony Harrison, French.

The hypochondriac Alceste is depicted as hating all mankind, for all are dishonest, flatterers, cheats, and thieves. Contrasted with him is Philinte, a sensible fellow, who believes in moderation and is prepared to accept the world as it is. When the posturing poet Oronte reads a very bad sonnet, Alceste frankly declares it terrible; Philinte is more kindly. Alceste perversely falls in love with a gay, frivolous coquette, Célimène—just the wrong kind of person for him. Becoming disgusted, he prepares to retire from the world. Philinte tries to persuade him to reconsider.

5 acts; 8 men, 3 women; 1 interior; costumes of the period. Royalty: Wilbur, $50-25; Harrison, $50-35.

_____. The Miser (1668). In all complete editions of his translated works (for list see note under his main entry for Tartuffe); Wall translation in CLS; tr. by Clark in Modern Lib.,

1924; tr. & adapted by Kerr, Dramatic Pub. Co., 1942; tr.
anon. in STA & THO; tr. by Parks in BEN and French; tr.
Malleson, French; tr. by Albert Bermel, French.

An old miser, Harpagon, and his son, Cléante, both wish to
marry Mariane. When Cléante gets hold of his father's casket of
gold, he gives him the choice between the girl and the treasure, as
the miser prefers the money, Cléante marries the lady. Next, Harpagon proposes to give his daughter Elise in marriage to an old
man because no dowry will be required. In the end the miser is
left with only his cash box.

 5 acts; 10 men, 4 women, extras; 1 interior; costumes of
the period. Royalties: Kerr, $35-25; Malleson, $35-25;
Bermel, $50-25.

   . The School for Wives (1662). Adapted by Miles Malleson. Samuel French; tr. Richard Wilbur, Dramatists Play Service.

 Arnolphe is a rich man, a bachelor of 50 years, who has
never married for fear of being cuckolded. He has, however, carefully educated his ward in convents, and now he plans to marry her.
But Agnes is so innocent that she curtsies to men who tip their
hats to her, and soon she falls in love with Horace. Horace tells
Arnolphe how he has pulled the wool over the eyes of Agnes' guardian, and Arnolphe tries to stop the romance. At the end Agnes'
father, thought dead, returns and awards his daughter's hand to
Horace. He thanks Arnolphe for his care in educating Agnes.

  6 men, 2 women; 1 interior-exterior. Royalties: Malleson,
$35-25; Wilbur: $50-25.

   . Tartuffe (1664). In all complete editions of his trans-
lated works (see note below); Page translation in HARC, v. 26;
HUD; MAU; tr. by Clark, Modern Lib., 1924; tr. by Andley,
Oxford, 1933; tr. anon., in SMO; tr. Malleson, French; tr.
Wilbur, Dramatists Play Service; tr. C. Hampton, French.

 Credulous Orgon is thoroughly deceived by the hypocritical
cant of the self-seeking imposter, Tartuffe, who uses his religion
as a means of getting money and position. Orgon gives Tartuffe
the run of the house, promises his daughter to him in marriage,
and even signs over the estate to him. When finally convinced of
Tartuffe's dishonesty, through the innate honesty of his wife, he is
reminded that Tartuffe now owns the house. In court, Tartuffe is
unmasked and recognized as a criminal. Orgon's house is restored
to him, and his daughter is free to marry the man she loves.

  5 acts; 7 men, 5 women; 1 interior; costumes of the period.
Royalties: Malleson, $35-25; Wilbur, $50-35; Hampton, $50-
35.

   , pseud. of Jean Baptiste Poquelin. Various complete editions of his translated works: Tr. by Wall, Bohn edition, 1875-
76, 3v. reprinted 1897-1900. Tr. by Van Laun, Peterson,
Edinburgh, 1875-76, 6v. Tr. by Wormley, Roberts, 1894-97,

6v.; later by Little, Brown, 1912, 6v. Tr. by Waller, Grant, Edinburgh, 1907. Tr. by Page, in verse, Putnam, 1908, 2v. Tr. by Baker & Miller, Everyman's Lib., Dent, & Dutton, 1929, 2v.

MOLNÁR, FERENC. The Devil (1907). Tr. & adapted by Herford. Kennerley, 1908.
    As a glib bland man of the world the devil brings about a love affair between an artist, Karl, and a married woman, Olga. Neither of them knows that he is destroying them for his own amusement.
    3 acts; 7 men, 7 women; 2 interiors.

_____. Fashions for Men (1915). Tr. by Glazer, Boni, 1922; also in his Plays, Vanguard, 1929, & Garden City, 1937.
    Depicts how a simple noble hero, Peter Juhasz, by his very naiveté and generosity wins out over his more scheming rivals. Paula, a poor pure-hearted girl, is menaced by a man of wealth who is somewhat of a rake. Her problem is that she wants to quit poverty but is in love with Peter. When he gets his job back he gets his girl.
    3 acts; 13 men, 8 women; 2 interiors.

_____. The Guardsman (1910). Samuel French.
    Growing suspicious of his actress-wife's fidelity, and to test her, an actor-husband writes her mash notes and sends her flowers in the name of a Russian guardsman. When she appoints a rendezvous, he impersonates the guardsman, and when she seems about to yield, he reveals himself. She insists that she knw him all the time--but did she?
    3 acts; 4 men, 3 women; 1 interior; costume of the guardsman. Royalty: $35-25.

_____. Liliom (1909). Tr. by Glazer, Boni, 1921; in his Plays, Vanguard, 1929, & Garden City, 1937; French, 1944; CEW; DIE; HAV; LEV; MOSH; STE; THF; TRE-1, 2 & 3; TREA-2; TUCG; TUCM; WHI; BP 1920-21; acting ed. Samuel French.
    Depicts the young and graceless tough, a rough-neck carnival barker, Liliom, as moving through a world compounded of nature and imagination, with love and mistreatment for Julie, with mock heroics on his own tragic death. In heaven he attains a soul, and is given a chance to return to Julie for one day and to do a good deed. His "good deed" is to steal a star from heaven and present it to his daughter. The play runs through a gamut of emotions: pert humor, wistful devotion, masculine harshness, and feminine tenderness.
    17 men, 5 women, extras; 1 interior, 4 exteriors. Royalty: $50-25.

_____. The Play's the Thing (1925). Samuel French.
    Albert is engaged to the actress Ilona. He with his playwright

friend Turai arrives earlier than expected at her castle, and having
adjoining rooms they overhear a very compromising conversation
between Ilona and her ex-lover, an actor named Almady. While Albert is shattered by it, Turai writes a one-act play incorporating
the lines they overheard. When Albert hears the rehearsal, he
feels relieved, Turai feels philanthrophic. Almady is grateful, and
Ilona is more affectionate than ever.
> 3 acts; 8 men, 1 woman; 1 interior. Royalty: $50-25.

_____. The Swan (1914). Tr. by Glazer in his Fashions for
Men & The Swan, Boni, 1922; in his Plays, Vanguard, 1929, &
Garden City, 1937; in CHA; arranged by Swartout, Longmans,
1929; BP 1923-24. Acting ed. tr. by Baker, David McKay.
With subtle satire on the ways of royalty, divertingly ana-
lyzes the varied emotions aroused when the haughtily-reserved
swan-like princess in sympathy kisses the tutor to the alarm of all.
The aristocratic patrician would lose her dignity if she married out
of her rank, so she sacrifices herself for the exaltation of her house.
> 3 acts; 9 men, 8 women, extras; 3 interiors; court costumes.

_____. The Tale of the Wolf (1912). Tr. by Baker in his Plays,
Vanguard, 1929, & Garden City, 1937.
Vilma dreams of Georg, a sweetheart of seven years ago, who
swore to return, famous and distinguished, and asked her to wait.
But she married Dr. Eugen and has a son, to whom her husband is
telling the tale of the wolf; and while he is telling it, she dreams of
the return of Georg. On awaking and recognizing him, he turns out
to be a failure; so the "wolf" goes away.
> 3 acts; 15 men, 8 women, extras; 3 interiors.

MONKHOUSE, Allan N. The Education of Mr. Surrage (1912).
Lond., Sidgwick, 1913; French, 1913.
At the age of 50 Mr. Surrage has retired, rich enough to
live on his income. His son and two daughters, holding rather advanced social views, invite for the weekend some questionable persons in the artistic and theatrical world. How will their conventional
father receive them? They find him very adaptable, and he takes to
the new social environment so readily that he remains master of the
situation.
> 4 acts; 6 men, 3 women; 2 interiors.

_____. Mary Broome (1911). Lond., Sidgwick, 1912; PLAP
v. 2.
The maid, Mary Broome, in an English household is seduced
by the son, Leonard, but marries him. The play depicts how she
is treated by his family and her own; reveals why she sticks to him
then, but later leaves him.
> 4 acts; 5 men, 8 women; 2 interiors.

MONKS, John, Jr. and Fred R. Finklehoffe. Brother Rat (1936).
Dramatists Play Service.

Pictures life at VMI where a cadet in good standing is Brother Rat. Bing, the star pitcher, is no student but hopes to win out as best athlete. But he has secretly married Kate, and the day before the crucial game she tells him he is to be a father. This and the fear of expulsion so unnerve him that he loses the game. He finally gets his diploma, and $300 for the first baby in the graduating class.
3 acts; 14 men (mostly boys), 5 women & extra girls; 1 interior, 2 exteriors; military uniforms. Royalty: $35-25.

MONTGOMERY, James. Nothing But the Truth (1916). Samuel French.
Bob bets it can be done--to tell the truth, the absolute truth, for 24 hours. He accomplishes the feat, winning over difficulties with his partner, his friends, and his fiancée.
3 acts; 5 men, 6 women; 2 interiors. Royalty: $35-25.

MOODY, William Vaughan. The Faith Healer (1909). Houghton, 1909; Macmillan, 1910; in his Plays (Works v. 2), Houghton, 1912; QUIK, QUIL.
In moving and effective fashion shows the effects of faith and disillusion. When discouraged, the power of Michaelis the faith healer ebbs away, but Rhoda's faith brings back the self-doubter's strength and exalts it. The potency of love makes love potent to regenerate faith.
3 acts; 6 men, 5 women, extras; 1 interior.

_____. The Great Divide (1906). Macmillan, 1909; in his Plays (Works v. 2), Houghton, 1912; French, 1938; DIC; BP 1899-1909; abridged in Pierce & Matthews v. 1.
Left alone in her brother's cabin in Arizona, Ruth Jordan from New England is attacked by three vagrants; she gets protection from Steve Ghent by promising to marry him, after he buys the others off. She is not content and returns to Massachusetts with her brother. Steve follows, and they are reconciled, despite the conflict between the rigid morality of Puritanic New England and the freer more human standards of the West.
3 acts; 11 men, 3 women; 2 interiors, 1 exterior.

MOORE, Dudley. Beyond the Fringe. See entry under Bennett, Alan.

MOORE, Edward J. The Sea Horse (1969). BP 1973-74; Samuel French.
Harry Bales arrives at The Sea Horse Bar, run by 200-pound Gertrude Blum, just as he always does when he gets shore leave from his job as a seaman. She is unsentimental and tough; he has returned from this voyage with a dream of getting married, having a baby, and buying his own boat. Gertrude, who makes part of her living upstairs after she closes the bar, will first have nothing to do with Harry's scheme. She can't even have children, she claims. But he has brought back a lace wedding dress as a present for her,

and after fighting and making up several times it appears that the two will get together permanently and compromise by running the Sea Horse as a team.
1 man, 1 woman; 1 interior. Royalty: $50-35.

MORATIN, José. Fanny's Consent (ca. 1925). Tr. by Bagstad in Poet Lore, v. 40, 1929.
Don Diego, aged 60, is in love with and plans to marry Donna Francisca (Fanny), a young girl who has been in a convent but who has met and loved Don Carlos, nephew of Don Diego. The wedding is planned, but through a note which comes into the hands of Don Diego, the love of Fanny and Don Carlos is uncovered and blessed.
3 acts; 3 men, 4 women; 1 interior.

MOREAU, Emile. Madame Sans-Gene. See entry under Sardou, Victorien.

MORLEY, Robert and Noel Langley. Edward, My Son (1947). BP 1948-49; Dramatists Play Service.
An ambitious but unscrupulous man, Arnold Holt, rises spectacularly, motivated by his devotion to his only son, Edward. The play depicts episodes in the life of Edward: a problem child of 12, kept in the school through his father; a playboy in his teens, dishonest and drinking, but defended by his father; a war hero, killed as a plane pilot; leaving a son by Phyllis his wife, who is not willing that the grandson be brought up under the influence of Edward's father. Arnold goes alone to Palm Beach.
3 acts; 10 men, 4 women; 6 interiors; costumes of the various periods. Royalty: $35-25.

MORRIS, Leslie. The Damask Cheek. See entry under van Druten, John.

MOSEL, Tad. All the Way Home (1960). Adapted from James Agee's A Death in the Family. BP 1960-61; Samuel French.
The inspiration for this drama is a typical family's encounter with death. The family consists of a husband, expectant wife, and young son. The husband also has a brother, an undertaker, who fears that he carries the smell of formaldehyde with him constantly. The husband's father is very ill, and he goes alone to visit the old man. He never returns from his trip. Somewhere along the way he was killed. The news of his death stuns and shocks his family. The young wife had always depended greatly on her husband, and while the son is still quite young, he has reached an age in which he most needs a father. Their reactions and their necessary adjustment makes this an interesting play.
6 men, 7 women, 1 child, extras; composite interior, exterior. Royalty: $50-25.

MOWATT, Anna C. (Ogden). Fashion (1845). Lond., 1850; Bost.,

1855; French; Baker, 1935; in Halline; MOSS-2; QUIK; QUIL.
Acting ed., Samuel French.

Socially ambitious Mrs. Tiffany tries to be a New York lady
of fashion, being coached by her French maid. She is anxious for
her daughter Seraphina to marry a French count, but the match is
broken off by the governess Gertrude; also the maid discloses that
the Count is really a continental crook whom she knew in France.
In the shallow world of fashion Gertrude stands out as the one upright person; she is found by Adam Trueman to be his long-lost
granddaughter and an heiress.

5 acts; 8 men, 5 women; 5 interiors; costumes of the period.
No royalty.

MUNK, Kaj. Niels Ebbesen (1942). Tr. by Larsen in Scandinavian
Plays of the 20th Century, ser. 2, Princeton Univ. Pr., 1944;
SCA-2.

Presents a 14th century German oppressor of the Danish
peasantry in Holstein, a brutal officer, Vitighofen, representing
Count Gerhard. Niels won't resist until he finds that he must meet
violence with violence; so he slays the Count as an absolute necessity. The play is a thinly veiled attack on the Nazi oppressors in
World War II and expresses Munk's scorn for German aggression and
all it stood for.

5 acts; 12 men, 2 women; 2 interiors, 3 exteriors; costumes
of the period.

MUNRO, C. K. At Mrs. Beam's (1921). Knopf, 1936; French
carried; MAP; MOSO; PLAP v. 3.

When Mr. Dermott and Laura Pasquale register as guests at
Mrs. Beam's boarding house, they are supposed by Miss Shore (who
has a vivid imagination) of being the notorious French Bluebeard and
his next victim. But they turn out to be a pair of thieves temporarily in hiding, and when they leave, they strip the place of everything that attracts them; they are an unscrupulous and romping pair
of crooks.

3 acts; 3 men, 7 women; 2 interiors.

MURDOCH, Iris and J. B. Priestley. A Severed Head (1964).
Samuel French.

Described as "fun with Freud," this comedy portrays a married man, with a mistress, who thinks he is fooling everybody. Then
he learns that his wife has taken her psychiatrist as her lover and
that his brother is the one who has the real good thing going. A
satire on upper class sexuality.

3 men, 4 women; composite interior. Royalty: $50-25.

MURRAY, John and Allen Boretz. Room Service (1937). Dramatists
Play Service.

A nimble-witted producer, Gordon Miller, desperately needs
a play. While staving off eviction from a hotel, he finds an angel
with $15,000, and he has the author in the room. The angel wishes

to withdraw, but they play hide-and-seek with him and with their creditors. Meantime the author plays sick to hold the room; then they have him fake a suicide, are obliged to announce his death and hold services over him. Finally the play is produced, but over many unexpected obstacles.

3 acts; 12 men, 2 women; 1 interior. Royalty: $35-30.

MURRAY, Thomas C. Autumn Fire (1924). Lond., Allen & Unwin, 1924; Houghton, 1926.

A widower at 55, Owen Keegan is still passionate and marries a young wife, Nance. His son Michael also loves her; the situation makes his daughter Ellen very bitter. Owen becomes enfeebled after being thrown from a horse; his brother Morgan hints at "youth to youth" which quite embitters Owen so that he sends his son away. There will be no solution of the situation until he dies.

3 acts; 4 men, 4 women; 2 interiors.

NASH, N. Richard. The Rainmaker (1954). Samuel French.

During a severe drought, one family has two serious problems: how to keep their cattle from dying and how to marry off their plain daughter/sister. Her father and brothers try every possible scheme to find a husband for her without success. Nor is there any relief in sight for the drought. Then a character arrives who will take care of both problems. He is, he says, a rainmaker, and promises to bring rain for $100. He also convinces the daughter that she is beautiful. Everyone believes in him, and rain and love follow.

6 men, 1 woman; composite interior. Royalty: $50-25.

_____. The Young and the Fair (1948). Dramatists Play Service.

Frances Merritt returns after ten years as teacher and personnel director at a girls' finishing school. Her younger sister, a student there, is falsely accused of stealing. The spoiled daughters of prominent trustees are involved but protected. Frances and her sister are glad to leave.

3 acts; 0 men, 21 women; 1 set in 3 sections. Royalty: $35-25.

NEIHARDT, John G. Black Elk Speaks. See entry under Sergel, Christopher.

NEMEROV, Howard. The Homecoming Game. See Howard Lindsay's Tall Story.

NEVILLE-ANDREWS, John. Bullshot Crummond. See entry under House, Ron.

NICHOLS, Anne. Abie's Irish Rose (1922). Samuel French.

Struck a note of universal appeal with 2,327 consecutive performances, representing every form of love: boy-girl; parents-

children; etc. Abraham Levy brings home as his bride Rosemary
Murphy, to the resentment of both families. To appease them, they
are married three times: by the Methodist minister, by the Jewish
rabbi, and by the Catholic priest.
>   3 acts; 6 men, 2 women; 2 interiors. Royalty: $35-25.

NICHOLS, Peter. A Day in the Death of Joe Egg (1967). BP
>   1967-68; Samuel French.
>   A teacher and his wife have a child named Josephine, who is
10 years old, spastic, and dependent upon her parents for everything. The wife believes that Josephine is a punishment to them
from God for their premarital indiscretions. The husband sees it as
black comedy. The two are visited one night by another couple who
seem to have solutions to their problem. The woman visitor, who
hates lameness in people, doesn't exactly believe in gas chambers
but thinks the state ought to do something in these situations. The
man visitor has a more direct plan for dealing with Josephine. The
teacher plays along with the game of murder, but then discovers he
can't laugh off his affliction, nor live with it either, so he runs
away.
>   2 men, 3 women, 1 child; 1 interior. Royalty: $50-25.

_____. The National Health (1970). BP 1974-75; Samuel French.
>   A kind of documentary of a men's ward in a British hospital.
People come and go, live and die, hold up to the reality of their
lives or don't. Through it all are discussions about socialism, about
old values lost, about the quality of medical care. While we are
watching the men on the ward, they are often watching a television
program, in which the hospital staff become the romanticized characters of a TV hospital drama (where white Dr. Neil Boyd longs to
marry black staff nurse Norton in spite of his family's objection).
>   16 men, 7 women; 1 interior. Royalty: $50-35.

NICHOLS, Robert, with Maurice Browne. Wings Over Europe (1928).
>   BP 1928-29; Samuel French.
>   To the English cabinet at #10 Downing Street Francis Light-
foot, a scientist, offers his secret--the control of the atom bomb.
But through pettiness and cowardice they vote to destroy the information. He refuses and gives them a limited time in which to reconsider or suffer the consequences with a timed bomb. But he is
killed before it goes off; he leaves behind him a powerful plea for
peace on earth. His main thought was to release energy from the
atom and thereby free man from labor.
>   3 acts; 20 men, 0 women; 1 interior. Royalty: $25-20.

NIMOY, Leonard. Vincent (1984). Based on the play Van Gogh
>   by Phillip Stephens. Dramatic Publishing Comapny.
>   The struggling life of Vincent Van Gogh, as narrated by his
brother Theodore. Vincent forfeits all personal pleasures to serve
mankind. He marries a whore, works night and day on his paintings, but refuses to sell any. His family rejects him except for

Theo, who supplies Vincent with money to support himself and his
wife. Vincent doesn't understand why people don't accept him for
the works he paints rather than his social manners and standards.
He is very insecure and wants to be loved, but can't love himself.
All of this is shown by letters to and from Theo and through his
paintings.

    2 acts; 1 man; bare stage with props and slides. Royalty
on application.

NIZER, Louis. My Life in Court. See Henry Denker's A Case of
    Libel.

NORMAN, Marsha W. Getting Out (1979). BP 1978-79; Dramatists
    Play Service.

    Arlene Holsclaw, a former prostitute, murderess, and sexually
abused child (by her father), has moved into a cheap room in Louis-
ville to begin her parole. The straight life she wants to lead is
constantly disturbed and interrupted by people from the past. Her
mother tells her bluntly that no one in the family wanted her son
Joie, so he lives in a foster home. A former pimp (and Joie's
father) insists she go with him to New York and let him peddle her.
Even Bennie, a prison guard who has befriended her, tries to rape
her. Worst of all, however, is the memory of her personal past as
an incorrigible girl named "Arlie" (she appears throughout the play,
sometimes outside and sometime part of the cheap room set). Arlie
is so strong a personality that while Arlene was in prison she almost
killed herself in an attempt to murder the child Arlie inside her. By
the end of the play she is secure enough as "Arlene," confident
enough in her ability to start all over again, that she can even smile
when she thinks of the time that the girl she once was, in response
to being locked in her mother's closet, urinated on the shoes for
revenge.

    2 acts; 7 men, 5 women; unit set. Royalty: $50-40.

_____. 'night, Mother (1983). BP 1982-83; Dramatists Play Ser-
    vice.

    Jessie Cates ("It is not possible to tell why she distrusts her
body, but she does.") has led an unremarkable life and now, in her
late 30's or early 40's, lives with her widowed mother, Thelma, in a
new house built way out on a country road. It is Saturday night,
and Thelma's weekly manicure is on Jessie's written To Do schedule,
but so is finding her father's pistol in the attic. Jessie has the
bullets and, as she so carefully explains to her mother, is trying
to tie some loose ends together so that she can kill herself. Thelma
tries, but fails, to dissuade her. It isn't just Jessie's epilepsy,
which is now under control, or her former husband, who ran off
with another woman, or her delinquent son, who will be in trouble
all of his life, or her socially outcast position. It is just that she
has no hope, that even her most modest dreams were unrealized,
and that her future is behind her. There is simply no way of convincing her that she is not correct in being, for once, master of her

fate and making an efficient exit. Her mother is to say only that
as she went to her bedroom before pulling the trigger she said,
"'night, Mother."
    1 act; 2 women; 1 interior. Royalty: $50.

NOWLAN, Alden, with Walter Learning. The Incredible Murder of
    Cardinal Tosca (1981). Dramatic Publishing Company.
    Set in London in 1895; Sherlock Holmes and his friend Watson
are investigating the satanic murder of Father Tichborne. Behind
the murder is Professor Moriarty, an evil and powerful man who has
tried to kill Holmes seven times, whose real motive is to assassinate
Archduke Franz Ferdinand of Austria-Hungary and blame it on a
Serb, thereby leading all of Europe into world war. Holmes stops
the war this time, though he knows it will eventually come in 5 or
10 or 20 years.
    2 acts; 8-14 men; 2-3 women; 4 interiors. Royalty: $60-40.

NOYES, Alfred. Sherwood (1911). Stokes, 1911, also acting edition
    1921; in his Collected Poems, Stokes, 1913.
    Subtitle: "Robinhood and the Three Kings." A fine poetic
interpretation of the ballads and legends about the famous outlaw.
Fanciful in thought and feeling, with good dramatic situations.
    5 acts; 16 men, 6 women, many extras; 3 interiors, 4 ex-
    teriors (all can be played as exteriors); costumes of the
    period (12th century in England).

NTSHONA, Winston. The Island. See entry under Fugard, John.

NUGENT, Elliott. Kempy. See entry under Nugent, J. C.

_____. The Male Animal. See entry under Thurber, James.

NUGENT, J. C., with Elliott Nugent. Kempy (1922). Samuel
    French.
    Kempy, a young architect-plumber, is called to fix a pipe at
a house in a small Jersey town, just as Katharine quarrels with her
fiancé. Kempy has read her books, thinks he understands her, and
has sworn to marry her. She drags him to a Justice of the Peace.
That night he sleeps on the sofa with the dog. Next morning they
find they have acted hastily; a way out is found, as he discovers it
was the other sister who loved him.
    4 men, 4 women; 1 interior. Royalty: $25-20.

_____. The Poor Nut (1925). Samuel French.
    A shy freshman with an inferiority complex, John falls in love
with a charming co-ed, rises above himself, wins a track meet, and
becomes a leader on the campus.
    3 acts; 11 men, 5 women, 3 interiors, 1 exterior. Royalty:
    $25-20.

OBEY, André. Lucrece (1931). Adapted by Thornton Wilder.

Houghton, 1933.
    Lucrece, the wife of Collatine, proves herself to be a vir-
tuous Roman matron. Tarquin gains hospitality but commits rape.
She sends for her husband, tells him how Tarquin has violated her,
and stabs herself. Then follows an edict of banishment for all
Tarquins.
    4 acts; 5 men, 6 women, extras; 2 interiors, 2 exteriors;
    Roman costumes.

_____. Noah (1931). Tr. & adapted by Arthur Wilmurt. Samuel
    French.
    The voyage of the ark starts well, with Noah, his wife,
three sons and their wives, in the hope of a brave new world.
When the rain is over, they dance on the deck with joy; but the
canker of the old world has crept on board. Ham is the sore spot;
he doubts, he taunts, he asks his father skeptical questions. Noah
grows lonely; he is a simple old man with doubts; he is deserted
by the young folks; he asks: "God, are you satisfied?" The answer
is the rainbow.
    3 acts; 5 men, 4 women, extras; 3 exteriors; Biblical cos-
    tumes. Royalty: $35-25.

O'BRIEN, Justin. Caligula. See entry under Camus, Albert.

_____. The Condemned of Altona. See entry under Sartre, Jean-
    Paul.

O'CASEY, Sean. Juno and the Paycock (1924). Samuel French.
    Juno's husband, Capt. Jack Boyle, struts but never does
anything; she calls him a "paycock." When he believes he has
inherited a fortune, he plunges the family into debt by buying
things; but there is no fortune. He goes back to his pal Joxer
and his liquor; his son is shot as an informer in the Irish Civil
War; and Juno, the magnificent mother, takes the daughter Mary
away to build a new life on the ashes of the old. An unforgettable
tale with quick shifts, from uproarious laughter to bitter despair
and anguish.
    14 men, 5 women; 1 interior. Royalty: $50-25.

_____. Pictures in the Hallway. See entry under Shyre, Paul.

_____. The Plough and the Stars (1926). BP 1927-28; Samuel
    French.
    A vivid picture of people in Dublin tenements during the
Easter riots of 1916 and the abortive revolution. Jack Clitheroe is
killed in the attack. Nora his wife is driven insane.
    10 men, 5 women; 3 interiors, 1 exterior. Royalty: $35-
    25.

_____. Red Roses for Me (1942). Dramatists Play Service.
    Ayamonn Breydon sees hope for a new world in the shilling

per week the railwaymen are striking for--the strike that led to the bloody Easter Week Rising of 1916. But the emphasis is on man's love, devotion, and hope in the future.

21 men, 9 women; 1 interior, exteriors. Royalty: $35-25.

_____. The Shadow of a Gunman (1923). Samuel French.

Donald Davoren and Seumas Shields are roommates in a Dublin tenement. Although he is merely a dreaming poet, the other residents consider Donald a gunman in the service of the Irish Republican Party. Donald, in fact, rather enjoys their speculation and says nothing to correct their mistaken impression. Then one of the Republicans visits the supposed sympathizers and leaves a bag of bombs with the young men. They are in danger of arrest when the house is raided by the authorities, but a friend, Minnie Powell, takes the bombs to her room, assuming that she would not be investigated. The bombs are discovered, however, and Minnie, vainly trying to escape, is killed by the authorities for resisting arrest.

8 men, 3 women; 1 interior. Royalty: $35-25.

ODETS, Clifford. Awake and Sing (1935). Covici, 1935; also in his Three Plays, Covici, 1935; in his Six Plays, Random House, 1939; CER; HAT; MOSL; TRE-2; FAMI; BP 1934-35.

The saga of the Berger family, a lower middle-class Jewish group in the Bronx, convincingly characterized, with their many frustrations and thwartings. Not until grandfather Jacob has jumped off the roof does son Ralph follow his advice to awake and sing.

3 acts; 7 men, 2 women; 1 interior.

_____. The Country Girl (1950). BP 1950-51; Dramatists Play Service.

Georgie Elgin is a lovable, faithful, and forgiving wife to her husband Frank, an alcoholic, has-been actor. Through the years she has bolstered up his morale, reassured him of his talent, and tried to help him leave the bottle alone. When director Bernie Dodd picks Frank for the lead in his new play, Frank questions whether he can get himself ready for the role. He tells Bernie that Georgie is responsible for his career troubles, and the director subsequently comes to hate Frank's wife. Later Bernie finds out just what she is--a magnificent person--and loves her himself. But Georgie will stick with her husband.

6 men, 2 women; 5 simple interiors. Royalty: $50-25.

_____. The Flowering Peach (1954). BP 1954-55; Dramatists Play Service.

When God tells Noah about His plan for the flood and Noah's role in the future, the first thing the old man does is to take to drink. The next thing is to fight with his family, especially two of his sons, one of whom is a go-getter with a deep love for worldly goods. It is only by being a despot that Noah can get the ark built on time, though when he physically tires God helps out by making him 20 years younger. On board the ark during the flood, Noah continues to be something of a tyrant, arguing always for the old laws when it suits him, or for God's private communication of His wants and desires. He refuses, for example, to remarry his sons and their women in the way everyone prefers, even though it is his dying wife's last request. When the ark hits shore, Noah refuses to leave unless God promises him that He won't destroy the world again and He gives Noah a sign. Turning, Noah sees a rainbow, and he walks off with a humility he learned on the ark.

8 scenes & epilogue; 7 men, 4 women, 4 animals (men or women); 1 interior, various exteriors. Royalty: $50-25.

_____. Golden Boy (1937). BP 1937-38; Dramatists Play Service.

A young Italian boy, Joe Bonaparte, cannot avoid compromise. He might have been a great violinist, but to gain money he becomes a prizefighter; he is torn between love for his art and gain. He becomes more brutish, breaks his hands, and can never play again. His spirit breaks after he has killed an opponent. He drives his auto madly through the night, ending in an accident which kills himself and Lorna, his girl.

3 acts; 17 men, 2 women; 4 interiors, 2 exteriors. Royalty: $35-25.

_____. Rocket to the Moon (1938). BP 1938-39; Dramatists Play Service.

"There are two types of marriages," Dr. Ben Stark's father-in-law tells him, "where the husband quotes the wife, or where the wife quotes the husband." Ben has the first type; his wife Belle runs his life like a credit manager. In his boredom and misery he falls into an affair with Cleo, his secretarial assistant, though when it comes down to it he cannot leave his wife for her. Nor will Cleo accept the father-in-law's offer to marry him. Though he can provide everything she ever wanted, he is too old, and she doesn't love him. What she is looking for, she tells the two men, is "a whole full world, with all the trimmings."

6 men, 2 women; 1 interior. Royalty: $35-25.

_____. Waiting for Lefty (1935). In his Three Plays, Covici, 1935; in his Six Plays, Random House, 1940; CET; DUR; HIL; in Kozlenko, Best Short Plays of the Social Theatre, Random House, 1939.

The leader of the taxi drivers in New York, Lefty, is expected at a meeting called to decide whether to strike or not. In flashbacks, the poverty and exploitation of the drivers is revealed. When word comes that Lefty has been killed by the strong-arm men of the company, the drivers decide to strike.

6 episodes; 14 men, 3 women, extras; black-out sets.

OEHLENSCHLÄGER, Adam G. Hakon Jarl (1807). Tr. anon., Lond., Hookham, 1840; tr. by Chapman, Lond., 1857; tr. by Lindberg, Univ. of Nebraska Studies, v. 5, 1905.

A mighty man in Norway for 18 years in the 10th century, Hakon, an Earl, wishes to be king and proposes to kill Olaf by treachery and thus void his kingly descent. Because he wishes to seize Gudrun, bride of a peasant, the peasants rise up against him and he loses his battle with Olaf. Though protected in a cave by his mistress Thora, his thrall Karker kills him. Olaf became King of Norway in 995.

    5 acts; 16 men, 4 women, extras; 4 interiors, 5 exteriors, costumes of the period.

O'NEILL, Eugene. Ah, Wilderness! (1933). BP 1933-34; Samuel
    French.

    Set in a small Connecticut town in 1906, this comedy portrays an average American family faced with average problems. Soon, however, one of their average problems becomes somewhat extraordinary, at least in the eyes of the mother and father. That problem is their rebellious teenage son, Richard, an incipient, capital hating anarchist who reads Swinburne, Shaw, and Wilde, and has a passionate love for the girl next door. Trouble really starts brewing when Richard begins to send her scraps of Swinburne love poetry. Her father intervenes and forces the girl to break with Richard. To spite her, Richard gets drunk with a strange woman. Now his parents are sure that the world has come to an end. But the neighbor's daughter proves her devotion to Richard at a moonlight beach rendezvous, and Richard forgets his wild, rebellious ways.

    9 men, 6 women; 3 interiors, 1 exterior. Royalty: $50-25.

_____. Anna Christie (1921). BP 1921-22; Dramatists Play Ser-
    vice.

    Pulitzer prize play, 1922. With intense emotion and inspired realism unfolds the tragic story of the poor bewildered Swedish waif Anna, who, in the clutch of relentless fate, is dragged by circumstances through a sordid life as a prostitute, but is redeemed by the very sea her father Chris hates and by the love of the Irish sailor lad Matt. Presents a veritable slice of waterside life.

    8 men, 2 women, 3 extras; 2 interiors, 1 exterior. Royalty: $35-25.

_____. Beyond the Horizon (1920). BP 1919-20; Dramatists Play
    Service.

    The Mayo brothers are as different in temperament as brothers can be. Robert is sensitive and a poet; he yearns for the adventure and romance of the sea. Andrew wishes only to run the family farm. But both brothers are in love with Ruth, and when she chooses to marry the poet, Robert, the brother interested in farming goes off to sea. After three years, Ruth is convinced that she married the wrong man; Robert has failed to make a go of the farm. Andrew returns from his adventurous exploits, bored with his life. Happiness is impossible for any of the characters.

    6 men, 4 women; 1 interior, 2 exteriors. Royalty: $35-25.

_____. Desire under the Elms (1924). BP 1924-25; Dramatists
Play Service.
   The New England Farmer Ephraim Cabot, at 70, marries
Abbie, age 35. His 32-year-old son Eben is jealous of his step-
mother, for he feels the farm should be his. Abbie seduces Eben
and has a child by him. Eben believes that he has been tricked
and that he is now completely disinherited. But Abbie strangles
the baby to prove her love is greater than her greed for the farm.
   3 acts; 4 men, 1 woman, extras; 1 interior: a cross-section,
showing 4 rooms and an exterior. Royalty: $35-25.

_____. The Emperor Jones (1920). BP 1920-21; Dramatists Play
Service.
   Haunted by the ghosts and voodooism of his Congo fore-
bearers, an ex-Pullman porter, risen to be Emperor on a West Indian
island, is conquered by the very superstition he has flouted. Depicts his struggle against fear and fate, as he relives his personal
and racial past.
   3 men, 1 woman, extras; 1 interior, 5 exteriors. Royalty:
$35-25.

_____. The Great God Brown (1926). BP 1925-26; Dramatists
Play Service.
   The various characters wear masks which represent the faces
they present to the world. Their true faces are presented only to
those who understand them or when they are soliloquizing. A subtle
play of character, its symbolism carried over into their names (as,
Margaret is Marguerite of Faust--the eternal girl-woman). Shows the
conflicts in the soul of man. Brown represents the success of materialism which is doomed to frustration.
   9 men, 5 women; 5 interiors, 1 exterior. Royalty: $35-25.

_____. The Hairy Ape (1922). Dramatists Play Service.
   Yank Smith, who is as elemental as a human being can be,
works in the stokehole of a steam ship. He thinks that he "belongs"
to steel, that it is he who makes everything move. When Mildred
Douglas, a rich social do-gooder, faints at the sight of this ape of
a man in his natural habitat, Yank's sense of belonging vanishes.
On shore he is rejected by all levels of society, from the radical
Wobblies to the wealthy people of Fifth Avenue. Finally he goes to
the zoo and steps inside the cage of an ape, where he is crushed
to death.
   6 men, 2 women; extras; 5 interiors, 2 exteriors. Royalty:
$35-25.

_____. The Iceman Cometh (1946). BP 1946-47; Dramatists Play
Service.
   Ten down-and-out drunks await the arrival of Hickey, who
always sets them up. Hickey comes; but he has sworn off drink
and wants each to stop and do the things he always intended to do,
but always put off. The next day they all start out, but drift back

to the old routine. Hickey confesses he has killed his wife, and gives himself up to the police.
4 acts; 16 men, 3 women; 1 interior. Royalty: $50-25.

_____. Long Day's Journey Into Night (1940). BP 1956-57; Dramatists Play Service.
The play is set in the living room of the Tyrone family's summer house, in 1912. We learn that the father, James, is a wealthy matinee idol who is somewhat of a miser. The mother, Mary, is a drug addict. The elder son, Jamie, is a drunk. Edmund, the younger son just home from sea, has tuberculosis. Then we learn the reasons. James has never gotten over his impoverished youth to spend money reasonably; Mary's drug addition has its roots in medicine prescribed by a second-rate physician attending Edmund's birth; Jamie's alcoholism is a result of disillusionment in following his father into the theater; Edmund's consumption is being treated by the cheapest local doctor, and his father plans to send him to the state sanatorium. All of this is almost embarrassingly biographical of the famous O'Neill family.
3 men, 2 women; 1 interior. Royalty: $50.

_____. A Moon for the Misbegotten (1943). BP 1956-57; Samuel French.
The last of O'Neill's plays to deal with one of the "four haunted Tyrones"; it follows his earlier play Long Day's Journey into Night. This play concerns only James Tyrone, Jr. (the O'Neill older brother figure). Tyrone is a hard-drinking, self-destructive Broadway playboy attempting, unsuccessfully, to blot out a haunting memory. Tyrone, staying at the home of his tenant farmer, Mike Hogan, encounters once again Hogan's daughter, Josie, a wonder-woman able to do the work of three men. The climax comes when James Jr. passes out on the farm porch and Josie is able to hold Tyrone and claim him for her own. But when dawn comes James is gone, and Josie is left with the challenge of bringing him back.
3 men, 1 woman; 1 exterior. Royalty: $50-25.

_____. More Stately Mansions (1964). An unfinished play edited and abridged by Elliot Martin. Dramatic Publishing Company.
O'Neill's last play--a contest between idealism and the drive for material success. The central conflict is between two women, Sara Harford and her mother-in-law, who alternately hate, love, and misunderstand each other in their battle to dominate Simon, the husband and son. He desires to be dominated by them, but is cruel to the two women--even suggesting that they murder one another. While seeking domination by the women, Simon also seeks to dominate as a businessman. He can never reconcile the poet in himself with the industrialist.
7 men, 3 women; 1 set. Royalty: $60-40.

_____. Mourning Becomes Electra (1931). Liveright, 1931; in his Plays, Wilderness edn, Scribner, v. 2; in his Plays, Random house, 1940, v. 2; BP 1931-32; Samuel French.

Reinterprets the Greek tragedy in terms of modern life in New England; the characters are hounded by their consciences instead of the Greek Fates. Lavinia loves her father as immoderately as she hates her mother; she brings tragedy to all and determines to live alone with the dead in the family's house, a prey to the ghosts which will haunt her. She has guarded the family honor through a mistaken but lofty sense of duty.

Trilogy in 13 acts; 13 men, 7 women; 4 interiors, 2 exteriors. Royalty: $75.

_____. Strange Interlude (1928). BP 1927-28; Dramatists Play Service.

Pulitzer prize play, 1928. A rather selfish woman, Nina Leeds, seeks to overcome her love frustration and searches for fulfillment with three men: Sam Evans, whom she marries; Dr. Darnell, by whom she has a son; and finally dear old Charley (who has had a mother complex) but with whom she finds peace after various interludes.

9 acts; 5 men, 3 women; 5 interiors, 1 exterior. Royalty: $35-25.

_____. A Touch of the Poet (1947). BP 1958-59; Dramatists Play Service.

Con Melody, a proud and profane Irishman, owns a tavern near Boston. He is forever boasting of his wealthy background, of his commission in the Duke of Wellington's army, and his contributions to the Duke's victory at Talavera--the date of which he always celebrates, in uniform, riding about on his blooded mare. His arrogance gets to the Yankees who surround him, and they beat him up. Finally he realizes who and where he is, and he shoots his mare--a symbol of the past and his pretensions.

7 men, 3 women; 1 interior. Royalty: $50-25.

ORTON, Joe. What the Butler Saw (1969). BP 1969-70; Samuel French.

First of all, there is no butler in this zany farce. There are, however, the Prentices. Dr. Prentice seduces his employees (he is a psychiatrist with his own hospital); Mrs. Prentice is a nymphomaniac. He has a young thing he is trying to hide from her, while she has a hotel bellhop she is trying to hide from him. At the same time, the state inspector is visiting the hospital, making it necessary for disguises, disappearances, and discoveries.

4 men, 2 women; 1 interior. Royalty: $50-25.

OSBORN, Paul. A Bell for Adano (1944). Based on the novel by John Hersey. BP 1944-45; Dramatists Play Service.

Major Joppolo, an Italian from New York, comes to the little town in Sicily just after its liberation in World War II, restores order, and inspires the natives with a feeling of confidence and affection. Most of all they want a bell, and he secures one from the

Navy. He is sent back by the General, but not before he hears the bell ring.

22 men (doubling possible), 5 women; 1 interior. Royalty: $35-25.

_____. The Innocent Voyage (1943). Based on the novel A High Wind in Jamaica by Richard Hughes. BP 1943-44; Dramatists Play Service, 1946.

The year is 1860, and Mr. and Mrs. Thornton are sending their five children, ages 3 to 10, back to England to escape the hurricanes that have frightened them in Jamaica. The children will only be alone on board the Clorinda for two or three days until it reaches Havana, where their aunt will board and accompany them the rest of the way. Unfortunately, they are accidentally kidnapped by pirates and held for months on a pirate ship, where they develop strong loyalties toward their captors and even assist them in boarding other ships. The oldest Thornton child, Emily, in the midst of one of the escapades, panics and kills a captured Swedish captain who is bound to a chair. Later, when both the children and the pirates are taken into custody, the Dutch captain of the pirate ship will take the blame for the murder in order to save Emily's future.

3 acts; 10 men, 5 women; various boat decks.

_____. Morning's At Seven (1939). BP 1939-40. Samuel French.

All the Gibbs family live near each other and are content to live on past middle age. To Ida's house comes Myrtle, for almost 15 years engaged to son Homer, who can't break away from home. Myrtle finally gets him to agree to marry and move into the house prepared five years before.

4 men, 5 women; 1 exterior. Royalty: $50-40.

_____. On Borrowed Time (1938). Based on the novel by Lawrence Edward Watkin. BP 1937-38; Dramatists Play Service.

Gramps is idolized by Pud, his grandson, who models his speech, behavior, and actions on the old man. Aunt Demetria, strait-laced and Puritan, does not approve. The action of the play consists of two conflicts: Aunt Demetria tries to take Pud away, and Gramps fights her. Death, in the person of Mr. Brink, tries to take Gramps away, and Gramps fights him, knowing that if he submits Pud will go to Demetria automatically. Finally Gramps gets Death to climb the apple tree, where he holds him with some strange power. Only when Pud dies accidentally does the old man let Death down from the tree so that he can die and rejoin his grandson.

11 men, 3 women; 1 set. Royalty: $35-25.

_____. Point of No Return (1951). Adapted from John P. Marquand's novel. BP 1951-52; Samuel French.

While bank executive Charles Grey wants an available promotion, he refuses to engage in the back-slapping apple-polishing tactics of his rival. To find out how he got in this business world to begin with, Charlie recalls his life, trying to decide at which point he made a decision which irretrievably committed him to his present occupation. As he engages in this reminiscing, a witty portrait of modern life unfolds. Through a series of humorous characterizations, Charlie recaptures his past, until he can finally come to a satisfactory conclusion about his present situation.

    14 men, 7 women, 2 children; 3 interiors, 1 interior inset. Royalty: $50-25.

_____. The Vinegar Tree (1930). Samuel French.
    Laura is restless because she realizes she is 40 with a husband still older. She relives an imaginative past when she spent an afternoon with a handsome young artist, Max Lawrence, who is coming to spend a weekend with the family. She maps out her strategy, but is distressed when her daughter seems to take Max away from her, but becomes reasonably content when she discovers it was Lawrence Mack, a pianist, and not Max Lawrence, the painter, with whom she spent the romantic afternoon.

    4 men, 3 women; 1 interior. Royalty: $50-25.

OSBORNE, John. The Entertainer (1956). BP 1957-58; Dramatic Publishing Company.
    Archie Rice is part of a family of English music-hall entertainers. He is glib, cheap, vulgar, and quarrelsome. He is insulting to his grandfather, Billy, and to his second wife, Phoebe. He plans to dump Phoebe soon and marry a girl the age of his daughter, Jean. He even reveals his plans to his daughter. His plot is slowed down when his son is killed overseas. After the funeral Archie tries to go on as before, but Billy informs the parents of the new bride-to-be of Archie's status as a husband and father. The old man dies, but Archie goes on singing.

    5 men, 2 women; exterior and interior sets. Royalty: $60-40.

_____, and Anthony Creighton. Epitaph for George Dillon (1958). BP 1958-59; Dramatic Publishing Company.
    George Dillon recites his own epitaph, and it is filled with self-contempt. He has sold whatever artistic talent he may have had in exchange for material and commercial success. He has lived off, and despised, his middle-class family, and his comments about his life are agonizing and bitterly ironic.

    5 men, 4 women; 1 set. Royalty: $60-40.

_____. Inadmissible Evidence (1965). BP 1965-66; Dramatic Publishing Company.
    The play opens in a courtroom which could be the conscience of Bill Maitland-English, an attorney, and a man tortured by a sense of failure and guilt. Then we see Bill at his office, where during the next two days he permanently alienates his wife, his mistress, his clerks, the staff, his daughter, and himself. He performs the role of inquisitor, confessor, torturer, executioner, and finally beholder.

3 men, 5 women; 1 interior. Royalty: $60-40.

_____. Look Back in Anger (1956). BP 1957-58; Dramatic Publishing Company.

Jimmy Porter is an "angry young man" who cannot find himself in a British society that is heavily stratified socially. His boiling resentment emerges by making life impossible for those he loves most. He is hardest on his wife, Allison, whose father is from the older, imperialistic Britain. Cliff Lewis also lives with Porters in their one-room flat, and Jimmy abuses Cliff too. An actress, Helena Charles, comes to live with them while she is in town and starts a quarrel between Jimmy and Allison which results in the wife leaving, apparently for good. Several months later Helena is playing the wife, and being treated exactly like Jimmy treated Allison. When Allison returns after a miscarriage, Helena leaves, and Jimmy and Allison, who need one another, are reunited. A powerful and often brutal play.

3 men, 2 women; 1 interior. Royalty: $60-40.

_____. Luther (1961). Dramatic Publishing Company.

Deals with the reformation hero Martin Luther--his self-doubts, his bodily ailments, and his brilliant intellectual achievements. The play opens as Luther takes his final vows as a monk and leads up to the trial at which Luther cannot recant for his "heresies."

13 men, 1 woman, extras; 8 sets. Royalty: $60-40.

OSTROVSKII, Aleksandr N. Easy Money (1870). Tr. by Magarshack in his Easy Money & other plays, Lond., Allen, 1944; tr. by Daniels & Noyes as Fairy Gold in Poet Lore, v. 40, 1929.

Several men promise money to Lydia, who needs instruction in the spending of it, for she looks on it as fairy gold. Telyatev is a man-about-town, who owes much and therefore can never lend; he nearly gets engaged to Lydia; Kuchumov promises much but never delivers; Glumov always has hopes; he also views money as fairy gold, but realizes to be real it must be earned. Vasilkov earns money and marries Lydia; she leaves him but asks to come back. He will take her back if she will learn to be a good housekeeper.

5 acts; 9 men, 3 women, extras; 3 interiors, 1 exterior; Russian costumes.

_____. Even a Wise Man Stumbles (1868). Tr. by Magarshack in Easy Money & other plays, Lond., Allen & Unwin, 1944; tr. as Enough Silliness in Every Wise Man in MOSA.

A trickster, George Glumov, aims to advance himself and wishes to marry the daughter of a rich widow, but he plays around with the wife of Mamayev, a distant relative. He keeps a diary in which he writes his real opinions of acquaintances; the jealous Mamayeva steals it and confronts him with the evidence in it. He loses their friendship, but they agree that after due punishment he must

be restored to favor, for they need such a "man of parts."
5 acts; 9 men, 7 women; 4 interiors, 1 exterior; Russian
costumes of the period.

_____. The Forest (1871). Tr. by Winlow and Noyes, French,
1926.
Two actors, Neschastlivtsev the luckless one and Arkushka
the lucky one, meet in the dark forest and go out to the former's
aunt, Raisa Pavlovna, who is a hard miserly country gentlewoman.
Neschastlivtsev saves a maiden, Aksyusha, the ward of his aunt,
from drowning herself and gives her a dowry, forced from his aunt,
to marry "play-actors" but they answer proudly that they have done
a good deed, and go off back to the forest, prefering that to life
with his relations.
5 acts; 9 men, 3 women; 1 interior, 3 exteriors; Russian
costumes of 1870.

_____. Poverty Is No Crime (1854). Tr. by Noyes in his Plays
Scribner, 1917.
Gordey Tortsov, a rich merchant, has a brother, Lyubim,
who is a sad rogue, a drunkard, albeit lovable. He reveals the
pettiness and meaness of his merchant-brother's household and serves
to bring about the marriage of Lyubov, daughter of Gordey, and
the poor but honest clerk, Mitya, instead of her marrying an older
man as her father wishes.
3 acts; 6 men, 1 boy, 6 women, extras; 3 interiors.

_____. The Storm (1860). Tr. by Garnett, Lond., Duckworth,
1898; same, Sergel (Dramatic Pub. Co.) 1899; same, Luce,
1907; tr. by Whyte and Noyes as The Thunderstorm, French,
1927; CLF-2.
A dreamy young girl, Katia, finds her husband is still dominated by his mother who makes life miserable for her and causes
her husband to neglect her. He is glad to go away for a couple of
weeks to escape from his domineering mother. Katia meets a dashing
young man, Boris, by whom she is seduced during her husband's
absence. When this is discovered by the husband and because Boris
has to leave for three years, Katia jumps into the Volga. Her husband is left to face his mother.
5 acts; 7 men, 5 women; 1 interior, 4 exteriors; Russian
costumes of the period (16th century).

_____. Wolves and Sheep (1875). Tr. by Colby and Noyes in
Poet Lore, v. 37, 1926; tr. by Magarshack in his Easy Money
& 2 other plays, Lond., Allen & Unwin, 1944.
Meropia wants to manage everything, and through her lawyer
plans to entrap a rich widow, Evlampia, for her nephew, Apollonius,
a sporting man. These predatory wolves are outwitted by Berkulov,
who comes to Moscow and succeeds in saving Evlampia from their
clutches, and wins her.
5 acts; 13 men, 4 women, extras; 3 interiors, 1 exterior.

OTWAY, Thomas. Venice Preserved; or, A Plot Discovered (1682).
In all editions of his Collected works; in several series, as
Mermaid, Temple; BEL v. 2; BRI v. 1; DOB; GOSA; INCH v.
12; MAT; MCM; MOR; MOSE v. 1; NET; OXB v. 4; RUB; STM;
TAU; TUQ; TWE.
A conspiracy against Venice is betrayed by Jaffeir who is
in love with Belvidera, daughter of Priuli, a senator. The plot is
varied and intense.
5 acts; 8 men, 2 women, many extras; 4 interiors, 4 exteriors; costumes of the period.

PAILLERON, Édouard. The Art of Being Bored (1881). Tr. by
Clark, French, 1914; abridged in Pierce & Matthews, v. 2, as
The Cult of Boredom.
At a houseparty the guests affect the bored mien of the
pseudo-intellectual, which is the accepted manners of society. But
when they escape to the conservatory, they behave more naturally.
The old Duchess de Reville overhears some of their talk and rights
the wrongs of this artificial society; she unites the well-suited and
gets political advancement for the deserving.
3 acts; 11 men, 9 women; 2 interiors.

PARKER, Louis N. The Aristocrat (1917). Lane, 1917.
During the Reign of Terror, Duke Louis of Carcassone refuses to recognize the Republic. He invites some old aristocratic
friends to celebrate mass on New Year's eve, excluding however
Gautier Lalance, beloved of his daughter Louise. An agent of the
Republic arrests them all; they are tried and condemned to the guillotine, but it is the night of Robespierre's death, and Louise, her
father, and some others are saved. Ten years later the old Duke
is reconciled to Louise and Gautier, though this time he despises
Napoleon.
3 acts; 13 men, 5 women, extras; 3 interiors; costumes of
the period.

_____. Disraeli (1911). Lane, 1911; Dodd, 1932; Baker car-
ried; abridged in Pierce & Matthews, v. 1; BP 1899-1909.
Deals ingeniously with an episode in the career of the Prime
Minister when he is negotiating for the purchase of the Suez Canal.
He is shown fighting racial, social, and political prejudice. The wit
and epigram seem natural; the character sketching is subtle.
4 acts; 14 men, 6 women, many extras; 4 interiors; costumes
of the period (1876 in England).

_____. Joseph and His Brethren (1913). Lane, 1913.
Joseph the dreamer is sold to Zuleika, who in Egypt becomes
Potiphar's wife. Resisting her blandishments, Joseph is put in prison with the Chief Butler and Chief Baker. Brought out, he interprets Pharaoh's dream and is promoted. His brothers come, and
his dreams come true. Follows the Biblical narrative in events and
language.

4 acts; in Canaan: 17 men, 5 women; in Egypt: 20 men, 12 women, extras; 5 interiors, 6 exteriors; costumes of the period.

_____. Pomander Walk (1910). Lane, 1911; French, 1915.
A delightful, graceful, old-fashioned romance, embroidered with clever lines, pathos, and sentiment, based on wholesome situations. A young and an elderly pair of lovers are united after a series of mishaps.
3 acts; 10 men, 8 women; 1 exterior (a street facing a house with practical doors and windows); costumes of the period (1805) in England.

_____ and Murray Carson. Rosemary (1896). French, 1924 (as revised by Parker).
Noble and gentle Sir Jasper at 40 falls in love with Dorothy, a young and excitable girl, who writes enthusiastically in her diary about Sir Jasper, much to the annoyance of her devoted admirer, William. Sir Jasper helps William secure Dorothy from her stern parent, and is persuaded by his friend Prof. Jogram to forego his belated love. Dorothy gives him rosemary--that's for remembrance.
4 acts; 6 men, 4 women; 2 interiors, 1 exterior.

PARTRIDGE, Bellamy. January Thaw. See entry under Roos, William.

[PATHELIN]. The Farce of Master Pierre Patélin (1469). Tr. by Holbrook, Houghton, 1905; Baker, 1914; THO; tr. & adapted by Brueys as Master Patelin, Solicitor, French, 1915; tr. by Relonde as Pierre Pathelin the Lawyer, in Poet Lore, v. 28, 1917, also separately, Badger, 1917; tr. by Jagendorf, Appleton, 1925; CAR; CLF-1; tr. & adapted into 1 act by Stone, French, 1939.
Pathelin gets cloth from a draper on credit and by acting crazy gets out of paying. He later instructs a thieving shepherd how to avoid paying his debts. His seemingly stupid pupil learns the trick so well that he refuses to pay him his lawyer's fee.
3 acts; 7 men, 3 women, extras; 1 interior, 1 exterior; costumes of the period.

PATRICK, John. The Curious Savage (1950). Dramatists Play Service.
The efforts of an old lady to use her inheritance for a good cause and the attempts of her greedy stepchildren to get the money for themselves provide this comedy with many humorous episodes. Hoping to force Mrs. Savage to give up her inheritance, the scheming stepchildren commit her to a sanatorium. In the sanatorium she meets many social misfits who cannot adjust themselves to life. In getting to know them she realizes that she can find happiness in helping these people and decides not to return to the harsh, outside world where people will do anything for money. The stepchildren

are driven to distraction by their vain attempts to get her money.
Mrs. Savage, however, remains calm and leads them on a merry
chase with all sorts of ridiculous mishaps for the completely frustrated relatives. After outwitting the stepchildren, Mrs. Savage is
persuaded to leave the sanatorium and manage her inheritance as a
trust fund for such unfortunates as she met there.
5 men, 6 women; 1 interior. Royalty: $35.

_____. Everybody Loves Opal (1961). Dramatists Play Service.
The bumbling attempts of three would-be assassins to murder
a kindly, scatterbrained lady provide many humorous episodes for
this comedy. Opal Kronkie, a middle-aged recluse, lives in a tum-
bledown mansion at the edge of the city dump. Her house, like her
life, is totally disorganized since she has filled it with stacks of junk
collected while meandering through the dump. No matter how she is
treated by others, Opal always responds with kindness. Into this
rather bizarre existence come three equally bizarre characters:
Gloria, Bradford, and Solomon, con artists on the run from the law.
They decide what Opal needs is plenty of life insurance, a rapid de-
mise, and three beneficiaries named Gloria, Bradford, and Solomon.
No matter how sinister their schemes, however, they all go away
when faced with the disorganized jumble of Opal's life. Through it
all Opal radiates kindness, and one by one the plotters are won over,
realizing that friends are worth more than money. Then to their
shame and consternation they find that there was plenty of money
around all the time--bags full of it. In fact, any friend of Opal's is
welcome to as much as he wants.
4 men, 2 women; 1 interior. Royalty: $50-35.

_____. The Hasty Heart (1945). BP 1944-45; Dramatists Play
Service.
A wounded Scotch soldier in a convalescent ward of a hospital
in the Orient is very independent and suspicious, and this nearly
wrecks the good intentions of those who want to make him happy.
He learns (after falling in love with the nurse) the great lesson of
love for one's neighbor and not to be indignant at offers of friendship.
3 acts; 8 men, 1 woman; 1 interior. Royalty: $50-35.

_____. The Story of Mary Surratt (1947). BP 1946-47; Drama-
tists Play Service.
The boarders at Mary Surratt's are shown, with Mary innocent of the plot to kill Lincoln, although her son was in it with
money from Booth. Later that evening, after the shooting of Lincoln, officers come for her son John and arrest Mary. Reverdy
Johnson, an old sweetheart, now in Congress, offers to be her attorney. The conviction at the trial was on slim evidence.
35 men, 2 women; 3 interiors. Royalty: $35-25.

_____. Teahouse of the August Moon (1953). Based on the novel
by Vern Sneider. BP 1953-54; Dramatists Play Service.

The efforts of an Army of occupation officers to teach democracy to natives on Okinawa result in many humorous situations in this familiar comedy. To complicate his job, the young officer's commander is a Colonel who demands the strictest enforcement of the Manual of Occupation. The charms of the village people, however, take all sterness out of the young officer's attitude. Within a few days he owns a Geisha girl, has built a Teahouse with materials sent for a school, and has begun selling the village's principal product, potato brandy, to all the surrounding Officer's Clubs. Then the Colonel arrives and threatens a court martial. Just as things seem the worst word arrives that Congress considers this the most progressive village on the island and sends its congratulations to all involved.

18 men, 8 women, 3 children; 1 goat; interiors and exteriors. Royalty: $50-35.

PAYNE, John Howard. Brutus; or, The Fall of Tarquin (1818). In O'Connor's Great Plays, Appleton, 1904; in Winter's Plays of Edwin Booth, Penn Pub. Co., 1899, v. 3; MOSS-2.

Episodes in the life of Brutus, a great Roman patriot who fought against the lust and tyranny of the Tarquins. Includes the rape of Lucrece by Sextus and the vengeance taken by Brutus and Collatinus, her husband. Pictures the establishment of the Republic about 510 B.C. and the election of Brutus and Valerius as consuls. His son, Titus, commits treason through love for Tarquina and is condemned to death by his own father.

5 acts; 15 men, 6 women, extras; 5 interiors, 6 exteriors; costumes of the period.

_____ and Washington Irving. Charles the Second (1824). QUIK; QUIL.

Disguised as sailors, the merry monarch, Charles II, and the Earl of Rochester visit Copp's tavern at night; the King is left to pay the bill, and leaves his watch as earnest. After various intrigues the King rather improbably promises to reform.

3 acts; 4 men, 2 women, extras; 2 interiors, 1 exterior.

PEABODY, Josephine P. The Piper (1910). Houghton, 1909; in her Collected Plays, Houghton, 1927; French carried; DID; MOSJ; MOSL.

Emphasizes love as a compelling force--love in the home, in the city, in religion. The Piper brings back crippled Jan to Veronica, his mother, because of Christ's love for little children. Has imaginative quality and literary distinction.

4 acts; 13 men, 6 women, 5 children, many extras; 3 exteriors; medieval costumes.

PECK, Richard E. The Cubs Are in Fourth Place and Fading (1978). REPertory, Swarthmore, PA.

Harry Poulsen, recently retired, now has more time for his two great passions: the Cubs on television and sex with his wife

Marie. These freedoms are inhibited when analytic daughter Joyce divorces her husband Phil and moves back home. Then, when son Bob and his wife decide on a "trial separation," Harry feels compelled to fight back and make the world right. He browbeats Marie into helping him shock some sense into the kids by announcing their own divorce. While the plan does appear to keep the kids together, Marie finds that she likes life without a pushy husband, and soon she is dating a younger man and going dancing for the first time in 20 years, which causes Harry to change some of his ways. On the couple's 40th anniversary, they make an agreement to live together after their divorce is final, picking up extra social security benefits at the same time. The plan is approved by their lawyer, former son-in-law Phil, who is accused of having flexible morals. "I don't have any morals," he explains. "I'm an attorney."

    3 acts; 4 men, 3 women; 1 interior. Royalty: $50-25.

PELLICO, Silvio. Francesca da Rimini (1818). Tr. by Bingham,
    Lond., Francis, 1856; Unwin, 1915; Frowde, 1905; Cambridge,
    Mass., Seaver, 1897.

    Francesca had met Paolo some years before and loved him, but because he had killed her brother and to conceal her real feeling toward him from her husband, she pretends to hate him. The husband however suspects the mutual passion, quickly changes to a revengeful spouse, and kills them both.

    5 acts; 4 men, 1 woman, extras; 1 interior.

PÉREZ GALDÓS, Benito. The Duchess of San Quentin (1894). Tr.
    by Hayden in CLDM.

    Rosario, the Duchess of San Quentin, a young widow, comes to visit Don José. His son, Don César, a rather conventional nobleman, pays suit to her, but she becomes interested in his apparently illegitimate son, Victor, who has been educated well and has ideals. When it turns out that Victor is not his son but is of unknown parentage, Victor is to be turned out of the house. Then it is, to the surprise and horror of all the family, that Rosario declares she will go with him to America.

    3 acts; 5 men, 4 women, extras; 1 interior, 1 exterior (1
    interior possible).

_____. Electra (1900). Tr. anon. in Drama, v. 1 # 2, 1911; tr.
    by Turrell in TUR; TUCG.

    A young girl of 18, Electra, full of life and spirits, has an affection for Maximo Yuste, an electrical engineer. Don Pantoja, a religious fanatic, wishes to educate her for the convent. He plants the idea that she and Maximo are brother and sister. He learns in time from her mother's spirit that this is not so; so she joins Maximo, having discovered in time that she was not suited for convent life. The play was interpreted as symbolic of the conflict in Spain between the Church and the modern scientific spirit.

    5 acts; 10 men, 6 women; 4 interiors, 1 exterior.

_____. The Grandfather (1904). Tr. by Wallace in Poet Lore, v. 21, 1910.

An aging nobleman is informed that one of his two grand-daughters is not the child of his son. Henceforth his ruling passion is to ascertain which is the legitimate grandchild and to disown the other, thus wiping out the blot on the family name. The problem drives him almost insane until he realizes that honor is rather "pure living, neighborly love, and wishing no evil." At last he understands that love, and not honor is supreme. He finds perfect love in the illegitimate child and great affection in the other, and gains peace of spirit.

5 acts; 7 men, 4 women; 1 interior, 2 exteriors.

PERL, Arnold. Tevya and His Daughter (1958). Based on the stories of Sholom Aleichem. Dramatists Play Service.

The desires of a Jewish couple to see their daughters happily married are presented in this amusing and warm-hearted play. Tevya is a poor drayman with seven daughters. He and his wife, Golde, are attempting to arrange advantageous matches for the two eldest girls, but in each instance their well-intentioned plans are foiled when the girls fall in love with someone else. Tzeitl has attracted the interest of a prosperous butcher, Lazar Wolf, which pleases Golde immensely. The girl, however, falls in love with and marries a poor tailor. Then Hodel falls in love with a poor student. To compound their already difficult situation the new groom is exiled to Siberia. Tevya, however, finds consolation in the fact that the five remaining daughters are "too young to be problems; but they'll grow into it."

6 men, 6 women; bare stage with some furniture. Royalty: $35-25.

PERRY, Eleanor. David and Lisa. See entry under Reach, James.

PETERSON, Louis. Take a Giant Step (1954). BP 1953-54; Samuel French.

Spence Scott is middle-class black, growing up in a white neighborhood in New England. Now that he is seventeen and the rest of the gang is interested in girls, he finds himself more and more isolated from his white friends. At school one day, the history teacher deals with Southern blacks during the civil war as if they were morons, and Spence stalks out of class, smokes a cigar in the boy's room, and gets kicked out of school. At home, only his grandmother, with her tough sensibilities, seems to understand him. When she dies, he goes into a long mourning, which is ended by a sexual experience with a woman who has been hired to nurse him back to health. In the last scene, the giant step he takes is to have one last meeting with "the gang" and to ask them to leave him alone so that he can practice more piano and study harder for college. "I just said it to them before they said it to me," he tells his mother. And he begins a way of dealing with his color that his Uncle Tom parents do not understand.

6 scenes; 9 men, 7 women; 4 interiors. Royalty: $50-25.

PHILLIPS, Stephen. Herod (1900). Lane, 1901; later, Dodd;
abridged in Pierce & Matthews v. 1.
In stately and beautiful blank verse develops the conflict between Herod's love for his queen and his self-love, his lust for
power, and his overmastering ambition. He puts to death the younger brother of his queen, for fear a new king will supplant him; and
when the queen spurns him, he thinks she will poison him and so
sanctions her death.
3 acts; 12 men, 6 women; 1 interior; oriental costumes.

_____. Paolo and Francesca (1899). Lane, 1900; later, Dodd;
DIG; SMN.
Unfolds the story of a jealous husband. Though married to
the older brother, Francesca cannot control her love for Paolo nor
his for her. Youth goes toward youth, and unhappiness and death
come apace, caused by love which cannot be returned. Fine verse
with a touch of pageantry.
4 acts; 7 men, 7 women, extras; 4 interiors, 3 exteriors;
costumes of the period in Italy.

_____. Ulysses (1902). Macmillan, 1902; in his Collected Plays,
Macmillan, 1921; in Cohen, H. L. ed., Junior Play Book, Harcourt, 1923.
Gives pictures of his adventures from his departure from
Calypso's Isle and his descent into Hades to the vigorous combat
with the suitors in his palace in Ithaca. The verse flows freely;
real drama emerges in the final act.
Prolog & 3 acts; 21 men, 8 women, many extras; 1 interior,
6 exteriors; Greek costumes.

PIELMEIER, John. Agnes of God (1982). BP 1981-82; Samuel
French.
Dr. Martha Livingstone is the psychiatrist appointed by the
court to determine whether or not Sister Agnes was legally sane
when she killed her newborn infant and placed it in a convent waste-
basket. Sister Miriam Ruth, the mother superior of the small con-
templative order to which Agnes came four years before, tells Dr.
Livingstone that Agnes has completely blocked it out and forgotten
it. Agnes, we learn through scenes flashing through the doctor's
mind, is an innocent who sings like an angel, who loves everyone,
but believes she is bad. It may be that she is possessed and tormented by the memory of her wicked mother--she does have the
ability to bleed hysterically through the palms. Dr. Livingstone's
objectivity is threatened by her hostility toward the church in general and convents in particular: her sister, a nun, died of unat-
tended appendicitis. The mother superior's personal stake is that
Agnes is her niece. Finally, the doctor removes herself from the
case but can't explain a God who would send such a "wonder one"
as Agnes through this world.

2 acts; 3 women; bare stage.   Royalty: $60-40.

PINERO, Arthur Wing.   The Amazons (1893).   Lond., Heinemann,
   & Baker, 1895.
    The young daughters wear boys' clothes at home, but when
lovers appear--the eternal feminine reappears.   Whimsical farce
comedy on the tendency to educate girls in masculine pursuits.
    3 acts; 7 men, 5 women; 1 interior, 1 exterior.

_____.   Dandy Dick (1887).   U.S. Book Co., 1893; French car-
   ried; Baker, 1912.
    Dandy Dick is a horse, owned by Georgianna, sporty sister
of the Rev. Augustus Judd, who places a bet on him.   He adminis-
ters a stimulating bolus to help him win, but Blore, his butler, who
has a bet against the nag, secretly inserts a poisonous dose.   The
Dean is caught and is in a mess.
    3 acts; 7 men, 5 women; 2 interiors.

_____.   The Enchanted Cottage (1922).   Heinemann, & Baker,
   1922; French carried.
    A war invalid, Oliver, and a plain girl, Laura, marry and
move into a country cottage.   They come to think they have changed,
Oliver becoming strong and Laura lovely, for the enchanted cottage
through love makes them see each other differently, as handsome
and beautiful.
    3 acts; 5 men, 4 women, extras; 1 interior, 1 exterior.

_____.   The Gay Lord Quex (1899).   Heinemann, & Baker, 1901;
   Russell, 1900; in his Social Plays, Dutton, 1918, v. 2; MOSO;
   SMO.
    Lord Quex resolves to reform and settle down in order to
marry the charming Muriel, but he must first lay several ghosts of
his gay past.   He does succeed however in convincing the sisters
that he is sincere.   The play is a triumph of technique, a play for
playwrights, in which Pinero essayed a hard task and fulfilled it.
The third act is an accomplished orgy of dexterity with climax and
suspense and surprise and surprise again.
    4 acts; 4 men, 10 women, extras; 2 interiors, 1 exterior.

_____.   The Magistrate (1885).   Lond., Heinemann; U.S. Book
   Co., 1892; Baker, 1912; French, 1936; SMR.
    A police court magistrate, Mr. Posket, marries a widow
with a precocious son, who persuades his step-father to visit a
sporty restaurant.   Mrs. Posket also goes there, in search of her
boy's godfather just returned from India.   When the place is raided
by the police, all the family must appear as criminals in her husband's own court.
    3 acts; 12 men, 4 women; 3 interiors.

_____.   Mid-Channel (1909).   Lond., Heinemann, & Bost., Baker,
   1910; French carried; in his Social Plays, Dutton, 1922, v. 4;

HAU; SMI; WATF-1; WATI; WHI.

Married life is compared to crossing the English channel with its shoal halfway over. Theodore and Zoe, after 13 years, fail to weather the perils of mid-channel through selfishness, especially in not encumbering themselves with children. They seek to find amusement elsewhere and both have outside liaisons. Weary of sowing wild oats, they are ready to be reconciled, but it is too late.

4 acts; 8 men, 5 women; 3 interiors.

_____. The Second Mrs. Tanqueray (1893). Lond., Heinemann, & Bost., Baker, 1894; French carried; in his Social Plays, Dutton, 1917, v. 1; DUR; FULT; COF; CEU; DIC; HUD; MAT; STE; TAU.

Study of a woman with a past, Paula, marrying a bit out of her station so that she is not cordially accepted by her husband's friends nor by her 19-year-old daughter Ellean. When Ellean becomes engaged to Captain Ardale, to whom Paula had been mistress, she feels she must advise Ellean against the match, after which she lacks the courage to face further consequences. An epoch-making play, with the climax seized and the story built out of results rather than causes.

4 acts; 7 men, 4 women; 2 interiors.

_____. Sweet Lavender (1888). Hurst, 1893, Baker, 1893; French carried.

The banker Wedderburn is rather upset when his adopted son Clement falls in love with Lavender, the daughter of his housekeeper Ruth Holt. He becomes reconciled however when Lavender proves to be his own daughter through an early association with Ruth. The play idealizes sordid human nature.

3 acts; 7 men, 4 women; 1 interior.

_____. The Thunderbolt (1908). Lond., Heinemann, & Baker, 1909; in his Social Plays, Dutton, 1922, v. 4; CHAR; TUCD; TUCM; abridged in Pierce & Matthews, v. 1.

On the death of Edward Mortimer, a bachelor brewer, his brothers expect to inherit his money, although they have had nothing to do with him for years. Since no will is found, they begin to plan on spending the inheritance, showing the hypocritical conduct to which this craving for money will lead professedly respectable and pious persons. They become much discomfitted when they find that Phyllis, the wife of Thaddeus (a poor professor), destroyed the will when she found that all was left to Helen Thornhill, Edward's daughter by a secret marriage.

4 acts; 9 men, 5 women, 2 children (14 & 15 years old), extras; 3 interiors.

_____. Trelawney of the "Wells" (1898). DeWitt, & Dramatic Pub. Co., 1898; Russell, 1899; French, 1936; MAP. BP 1894-1899.

Rose Trelawney, a beautiful actress from the Wells Theatre, becomes engaged to aristocratic Arthur Gower. His uncle and aunt oppose the match; ultimately their disapproval is overcome, and so they are married. But she is a born trouper; she can't go to bed at reasonable hours, she can't conform to his family's life; she returns to the theatre, her first love.

4 acts; 14 men, 9 women; 3 interiors; costumes of 1860.

PINERO, Miguel. Short Eyes (1972). BP 1973-74; Samuel French.

"Short Eyes" is prison slang for a child molester and the name given to Clark Davis, a white man just brought into the dayroom of this house of detention where most of the inmates are black or Puerto Rican. Everyone hates a Short Eyes, from the straights to the homosexuals to the prison guards. First the new prisoner is beaten up, then brought to consciousness by being soaked in a toilet filled with urine; finally he is murdered by having his throat slit. At the end of the play the prisoners learn that Clark Davis has been the victim of mistaken identity, that he was not, in fact, a Short Eyes. An investigation into the killing reveals that he committed suicide.

14 men; 1 interior. Royalty: $50-35.

PINSKI, David. The Treasure (1906). Tr. by Lewisohn, Huebsch, 1915.

As Judka buries his dog, he finds ten gold imperials. His sister Tille gets half and dresses herself to catch a husband. When word gets out about the treasure, many want a share in it. They even dig up the graves of their ancestors in the hope of finding supposed treasure. Search for money makes men sordid, hard, and ugly.

4 acts; 12 men, 2 women, extras; 1 interior, 1 exterior.

PINTER, Harold. Betrayal (1978). BP 1979-80; Dramatists Play Service.

The play begins with Jerry, a literary agent, and Emma, the wife of Robert, a book publisher and his best friend, winding down their love affair of nine years. Emma complains that she has recently learned that Robert has "betrayed" her for years and that he knows of her relationship with Jerry. Jerry is further disappointed when he discovers that Emma herself told Robert about their affair some four years before. What happens next is the story in reverse chronology--we see the couple giving up the flat they so carefully furnished for their trysts, dealing with Emma's pregnancy (by Robert, of course), and finally we observe the moment, at a party nine years earlier, when Jerry, who is drunk, makes the first sexual move on his best friend's wife.

2 acts; 2 men, 1 woman; unit set. Royalty: $50-40.

_____. The Caretaker (1960). BP 1961-62; Dramatists Play Service.

Aston, a gentle man who has been forced to submit to electro-

shock therapy, plays good samaritan by intervening in the life of
Mac Davies, who is down on his luck. He sets the old man up in
the cluttered room of an abandoned house Aston is supposed to be
"decorating" for his brother, Mick, who is extroverted and pushes
for confrontations at every turn. Far from appreciating the kindness of his benefactor, the old man whines, complains, makes
feeble excuses, and finally tries to play the brothers against one
another for any advantage he can get. By the end of the play
there is no way to salvage any pride at all, and he is forced to
leave by the kind one who brought him in.
     3 acts; 3 men; 1 interior. Royalty: $50-25.

_____. The Collection. See The Dumb Waiter and the Collection.

_____. The Dumb Waiter and The Collection (1962). BP 1962-
    63; Dramatists Play Service.
     An off-Broadway long-running show made up of two Pinter
short plays. In "The Dumb Waiter," two professional killers, Ben
and Gus, wait, argue, and worry in the windowless basement of an
abandoned restaurant for their next assignment. In "The Collection,"
the set is divided in two. On one side an older man named Harry
and a young dress designer named Bill live together. On the other,
a husband and wife, James and Stella, own a flat. Stella, a model,
confesses that she had a one-night affair with Bill. James wants to
see what this other man looks like, so he visits Bill (they are attracted and repulsed by each other). Harry casts doubt as to
whether the Bill-Stella affair ever took place.
     "Dumb Waiter": 2 men; 1 interior. Royalty: $25-15.
     "Collection": 3 men, 1 woman; divided interior. Royalty:
$25-15.

_____. The Homecoming (1965). BP 1966-67; Samuel French.
     Four men live alone in a London home: a widower, who is a
retired butcher; his brother, who is a chauffeur; and two sons, one
a boxer and the other a pimp. The third son arrives home from
America, where hs is a philosophy professor. He brings with him
his wife, a woman he was ashamed of in the past but now is the
mother of his three sons. The four Englishmen feel they need someone like her around the house, and as her husband is leaving soon
for the states, she agrees to stay in London and serve as cook, mistress, and part-time prostitute to earn her keep.
     5 men, 1 woman; 1 interior. Royalty: $50-25.

_____. Old Times (1971). BP 1971-72; Dramatists Play Service.
     In a converted farmhouse near the English coast a movie-
maker named Deeley and his wife, Kate, prepare to entertain a
former friend and roommate of Kate's whom she hasn't seen in 20
years. The friend, Anna, is on stage when the curtain opens (she
is present in space but not in time), and the husband and wife talk
about her as if she isn't there. Later, the time frame shifts from
present to past, and we are never quite sure what people did, or

did not do, years before. Finally, Deeley and Anna enter into some kind of struggle for Kate's soul, often acting as if she is not, in fact, in the same room with the two of them.
    1 man, 2 women; 1 interior. Royalty: $50-35.

PIRANDELLO, Luigi. As You Desire Me (1930). Samuel French.
    Bruno Pieri thinks he has found his long-lost wife Lucia who has been missing for ten years, captured by the enemy in World War I; she is suffering from amnesia so that she cannot recover her past. Now she must be as they desire her to be, though the audience is not quite sure that she is the lost wife. When another woman appears who may be Bruno's wife, Lucia loses her newfound security and leaves them for the open road, still the Unknown One. By the time she departs, the audience is more convinced than ever that she is the one Bruno seeks.
    9 men, 7 women; 2 interiors. Royalty: $50-25.

_____. Each in His Own Way (1918). Tr. by Livingston, Dutton, 1923; CHA; in Naked Masks, Everyman's Lib., Dutton, 1952.
    For the sake of Rocca, a young woman, Delia, deceives a man and he commits suicide. Two men, Doro and Francesco, discuss the event, the former indulgently, the latter slanderously. They quarrel, change their opinions, quarrel again and plan a duel. Delia, ignorant of their change of sides, thanks Doro, who now returns to his indulgent position. The spectators of the play meet in the story, connecting it with a real scandal in the supposed audience. When Rocca reappears, he and Delia decide to run away together.
    2 acts & 2 interludes; 8 men, 2 women, many extras; 2 interiors in one set.

_____. Henry IV (1922). Tr. by Storer in his Three Plays, Dutton, 1922; WATI; WATL-4.
    A young Italian marquis is injured by a fall from a horse while portraying Henry IV in a pageant. Henceforth he believes himself to be the real Henry, has a throne room built and courtiers in costumes of the 11th century. Matilda, his old sweetheart, likewise appropriately disguises herself. After becoming apparently sane, he must maintain the role of madness and continue in his world of illusion to secure his self protection. When the madness returns he stabs Baron Belcredi who caused his accident.
    3 acts; 11 men, 2 women; 2 interiors; costumes of the periods.

_____. Naked (1922). Tr. by Livingston in his Plays, Dutton, 1923; CLS; DIE.
    In the drab life of Ersilia, a governess, had occurred a passing flirtation by Franco, a young naval officer who had deserted her, and an affair with the consul. Because of the death of the consul's child by falling off a roof (for which her negligence was blamed), in a fit of despair she takes poison, from which she recovers. Deprived of creating a new life for herself, she takes poison a second time, for death seemed the only solution for her

muddled existence. All her life she had felt naked--unable to obtain a respectable position.
3 acts; 4 men, 3 women; 1 interior.

_____. No One Knows How (1935). Translated by Marta Abba.
Samuel French.
Conscience and guilt, will and impulse are pondered in this morality play. Tormented by his conscience, Romeo goes mad.
He has committed two impulsive crimes, murder and the seduction of his best friend's wife. Then the cuckold husband yields to impulse and kills Romeo.
3 men, 2 women; 2 interiors. Royalty: $50-25.

_____. Right You Are! (If You Think So) (1916). Tr. by Livingston in his Three Plays, Dutton, 1922; MOSH; in Naked Masks, Everyman's Lib., Dutton, 1952.
Ponza's wife died four years ago; he marries again. Signora Frola, mother of the first wife, believes the second wife to be her lost daughter, all evidence being lost in an earthquake. They refuse to disillusion the mother. She thinks he is crazy; he thinks she is.
He keeps his second wife and the mother apart. He laughs at his neighbors who try to learn the truth.
3 acts; 7 men, 7 women, extras; 2 interiors (1 possible).

_____. Six Characters in Search of an Author (1921). Tr. by Storer in his Three Plays, Dutton, 1922; DIK-?; CEW; TRD 1, 2, 3; TREA-2; WHI; in his Naked Masks, Everyman's Lib., Dutton, 1952.
Six characters are abandoned by Piradello because they won't behave as he has planned; they insist on acting a play he doesn't wish to write. So they drift into a theatre and demand that the director let them act. They put on a play in which the husband permits his wife to elope with his secretary; then he lives to behold the outcome 20 years later, when his wife's offspring suffers disgrace and death. The director finds their play is terrible and shoos them out of the theatre; "Bring on," he says, "'The Bride's Revenge'-- that's what the people want."
2 acts; 10 men, 10 women; 1 interior.

_____. Tonight We Improvise (1930). Translated by Marta Abba.
Samuel French.
This play encompasses many of the dramatic techniques originated by Pirandello: direct address, improvisations, and in-and-out-of-character speeches. The play within the improvisation concerns the wooing of a wife by a man who finds her bizarre family quite a revelation. The players actually live their parts, as the drama, which includes narration, interludes, mime, film, and song unfolds.
Approximately 50 characters; 1 interior, 1 exterior. Royalty: $50-25.

PLAUTUS, Titus Maccius. The Braggart Soldier (205 B.C.). Translated by Erich Segal. Samuel French.
A vain braggart of a soldier receives a fitting punishment in
this comedy. He has kidnapped a beautiful girl, but her lover
manages a rescue. Then they bamboozle the lecherous braggart into thinking that the girl next door is madly in love with him. The
girl, a prostitute hired for the job, instead rejects him completely.
6 men, 3 women; 1 interior. Royalty: $25-20.

_____. The Captives (ca. 190 B.C.). Tr. by Nixon in Loeb Li-
brary; tr. by Riley in Bohn's; tr. by Sugden, Sonnenschein,
1873; CIF-1; MAU; DUC.
Hegio had two sons. The elder, Tyndarus, was stolen when
4 years old by a slave, Stalagmus, sold in Elis, where he grew up
as a slave to Philocrates. During a war, both were captured. The
younger son, Philopolemus, during the same war, was captured by
the Eleans and held by the father of Philocrates. Hegio buys the
two war captives in the hope of ransoming his son. Philocrates and
Tyndarus exchange places in the hope that the slave might escape.
Hegio ransoms his son and sends the supposed slave (really Philocrates) to negotiate the exchange, meantime in anger sending Tyndarus to the quarries. Philocrates returns with Stalagmus who identifies the real Tyndarus, who is now welcomed as Hegio's long-lost
son.
1 continuous act; 8 men, 1 boy, 0 women; 1 exterior.

_____. The Pot of Gold (ca. 200 B.C.). Tr. by Nixon in Loeb
Library; tr. by Riley in Bohn's; tr. by Rogers as The Crock of
Gold in his Three Plays, Routledge, & Dutton, 1925; tr. by
Sugden, Sonnenschein, 1873; tr. by Bennett in CLS; DUC; STA.
An aged miser, Euclio, finds a pot of gold buried by his
grandfather. He becomes so fearful lest he be robbed of it that he
re-buries it deeper and keeps a worried watch over it. His elderly
neighbor is promised to his daughter Phaedra and a wedding feast
is under way. But Phaedra is in love with young Lyconides, whose
slave Strobilus finds the pot of gold. With this in hand, he forces
Euclio to give both his daughter and the gold to him, much to
Euclio's relief.
5 acts; 8 men, 3 women, extras; 1 exterior.

_____. The Twins (ca. 200 B.C.). Tr. by Nixon in Loeb Li-
brary; HUD; tr. by Riley in Bohn's; tr. by Clark, French; tr.
by Thornton & Warner in SMR; tr. anon. in TRE-2 (v. 2);
TREA-1; DUC.
One of twin boys, Menaechmus (I), had been stolen as a lad.
The other, originally Sosicles, had been given his name (Menaechmus
(II) and lives with his wife in Epidamnus. When Menaechmus I arrives, he is mistaken for Menaechmus II, offered hospitality by his
brother's mistress, reprimanded by his brother's wife, and chided
by his brother's parasite. He feigns madness to get rid of them, a
doctor intervenes, but the brothers finally meet and find they are

the long-separated twins.
    1 continuous act, or in 5 scenes; 7 men, 2 women; 1 exterior
(a street).

PLAYFAIR, Nigel. R.U.R. See entry under Capek, Karel.

POLLOCK, Channing. The Enemy (1925). Brentano, 1926; Long-
    mans, 1927; BP 1925-26.
    Carl Behrend, the son of a war profiteer, is drafted into the
Austrian army in World War I, leaving his bride of a month, Pauli,
with her father, a pacifist university professor. On the eve of his
homecoming Carl is killed. Hate is the real enemy of man; banish
hatred, and greed and wars would cease.
    4 acts; 7 men, 3 women; 1 interior.

_____. The Fool (1922). BP 1922-23; Samuel French.
    Daniel Gilchrist, a young idealistic minister in a wealthy
parish, attempts to answer the question: What would happen if anybody really tried to live like Christ? He forfeits his church, his
friends, and the girl he loves; even the poor he tries to serve betray and desert him, but he finds happiness and contentment in service. Presents many striking evils in the world today in sincere and
dramatic situations, and depicts a fine ideal of living.
    4 acts; 13 men, 8 women, extras; 2 interiors. Royalty:
$25-20.

POMERANCE, Bernard. The Elephant Man (1979). BP 1978-79;
    Samuel French.
    The Elephant Man, a hideously deformed freak-show exhibit,
loses his appeal as a show business attraction and is set loose in
Victorian England to make his own way. He finds refuge in a London hospital under the supervision and care of Dr. Frederick Treves,
an up-and-coming physician and lecturer in anatomy, where he soon
is known by his real name, John Merrick, and where his charm and
poetic imagination cause him to be courted and lionized by the best
and brightest of British society. Only the famous actress Mrs.
Kendal sees the universal humanity in John Merrick, while the rest
of the visitors, and the doctor himself, engage in the kind of cruel
and mindless hypocrisy that the period is famous for. (Note: the
physical distortions of John Merrick must be imagined by the
audience, suggested only by the actor's ability to twist his body into
the appropriate malformations. Merrick is a whole human being
spiritually, if not physically.)
    21 scenes; 6 men, 2 women (with doubling); unit set.
    Royalty: $50-40.

PORTO-RICHE, Georges de. A Loving Wife (1891). Tr. by Craw-
    ford in DID.
    A middle-aged writer, Etienne, wearies of the passionate dis-
plays of affection by his younger wife, Germaine. He rather throws
her into the arms of his artist friend, Pascal, Even though he knows

of her infidelity, he cannot resist her physical attraction and asks
that she stay with him. They must endure each other, though unhappy.
    3 acts; 2 men, 5 women; 1 interior.

PRIDEAUX, James. The Last of Mrs. Lincoln (1972). Dramatists
    Play Service.
    Deals with the unhappy life of Mary Todd Lincoln following
her husband's assassination. Rumors persist that as a southerner
she hampered the Union cause. She is unable to obtain a pension
from Congress to meet her financial needs. Her favorite son (Tad)
dies, and for a time she is institutionalized by her sole surviving
son (Robert). Nevertheless, she is courageous, understanding and
compassionate.
    9 men, 2 boys, 5 women; unit set. Royalty: $50-35.

PRIESTLEY, J. B. Dangerous Corner (1932). Samuel French.
    After a dinner party, one of the guests chances to remark
that she had seen the musical cigarette box in the home of Martin
Chatfield, Mrs. Chatfield's brother-in-law, who had been murdered.
That was impossible, says Mrs. Chatfield; and out of this chance
remark most of the group are exposed as the rotters they are. If
this chance remark had passed unnoticed, the dangerous corner
would have been passed. So, by returning to the first scene in the
play, it is shown that, had these sleeping dogs of suspicion been
permitted to lie, there would have been no unpleasantness--nor any
play!
    3 acts; 3 men, 4 women; 1 interior. Royalty: $50-25.

_____. An Inspector Calls (1947). BP 1947-48; Dramatists Play
    Service.
    In an English city the Birling family is celebrating the en-
gagement of the daughter, Sheila, to Gerald Croft when an inspector
calls. Gradually by pointed questions he relates each member of the
comfortable group to the suicide of Eva Smith, though it had appeared
they had nothing to do with it. But the father had fired the girl,
Sheila was responsible for her dismissal from a store, Gerald had
toyed with her as Daisy Renton, Eric had gone home with her and
stolen money on account of an expected baby, and the mother
wouldn't let a Board help her. Just as they think they have been
fooled by a fake inspector, they learn that Eva Smith has really died
on her way to a hospital and a real inspector is on the way.
    4 men, 3 women; 1 interior. Royalty: $50-25.

_____. Laburnum Grove (1933). Samuel French.
    Living among the lower middleclass English suburbanites,
George Ladfern frightens off prospective borrowers by admitting that
he was making his money by counterfeiting. Though they think he
is spoofing, he really was providing the paper for the banknotes, and
he deceives for a time even the Inspector from Scotland Yard.
    6 men, 3 women; 1 interior. Royalty: $35-25.

_____. The Linden Tree (1947). Samuel French.
When a college professor reaches retirement age, everyone
urges him to leave his gloomy academic surroundings and go off to
live comfortably. Not only do his wife and children want him to
leave; so does the university administration, which dislikes his edu-
cational views. He fights all of them; and even when most of his
work is taken away, he plans to stay on and teach those students
who continue to come to him.
4 men, 6 women; 1 interior. Royalty: $50-25.

_____. A Severed Head. See entry under Murdoch, Iris.

_____. Time and the Conways (1937). Samuel French.
During a family party to celebrate her 21st birthday and
while charades are being acted, Kay Conway dreams what will happen to the other five members of her family. In Act 2 she sees
them 20 years hence, each a failure: petty, mean, with unfulfilled
ambitions and a bitter outlook. This vision depresses her, but her
calm brother Alan assures her that time is purely relative and that
there is something fine and worthwhile beyond.
3 acts; 4 men, 6 women; 1 interior. Royalty: $35-25.

_____. When We Are Married (1938). Samuel French.
A young church organist, faced with a father's objections to
the attention he is paying his daughter, reverses the situation with
a surprising revelation in this comedy Gerald, the organist, is
courting Nancy, Alderman Helliwell's daughter, and the Alderman
doesn't think much of Gerald's mixing romance and music. When he
comes to tell Gerald to stick to the organ, however, Gerald shocks
the Alderman with the news that the parson is not qualified to perform marriages. This means that three of the most respected
families in the village are not really married. With this information
Gerald forces the villagers out of their smug, condescending attitude
and gains permission to marry Nancy.
7 men, 7 women; 1 interior. Royalty: $35-25.

PURDY, James. Malcolm. See entry under Albee, Edward.

PUSHKIN, Alexandr S. Boris Godunov (1825). Tr. by Hayes,
    Lond., Kegan Paul, & Dutton, 1918.
After Godunov became Czar (1598-1605) he lived in terror
that some usurper would take it from him. The grim Boris treats
his children with kindness but the common people in quite a different
key. He is suspected of having murdered Czarevitch Dimitri, son
of Ivan the Terrible. A young monk, Gregory, pretends he is Dimitri, heads up an uprising, is acclaimed by the people, and leads
an attack on Boris. Before the contest is decided, Godunov dies,
half insane.
24 scenes (acts not indicated); 24 men, 5 women, extras;
interior & exterior scenes; costumes of the period.

RABE, David. Hurlyburly (1985). BP 1984-85; Samuel French.
Eddie and Mickey, in business together as casting directors,
share a house in Hollywood Hills that is a refuge for other down-
and-out, fringe show business drug abusers. The worst of all is
Phil, whose hostility is always present and whose violent behavior
is easily provoked, especially by women. All the characters are
self-destructive and egocentric, and though their interrelationships
are complex and compelling, it is difficult to care for any of them,
desperate as they may be for companionship and meaning in their
lives.
3 acts; 4 men, 3 women; 1 interior. Royalty: $60-40.

_____. Sticks and Bones (1969, 1972). BP 1971-72; Samuel
French.
The setting is an American middleclass home in 1968. Ozzie,
the father, is a hypocrite and a failure. Harriet, the mother, is
religious, racist, and willing to push anyone into her image of how
she wants people to be. The sons are coincidentally named Rick
and David--the latter home from the Viet Nam War, newly blind, but
perceptive to middleclass ways and values. Finally, Ozzie, Harriet,
and Rick get together to help David commit suicide.
5 men, 2 women; 1 interior. Royalty: $50-35.

_____. Streamers (1976). BP 1975-76; Samuel French.
Three soldiers share a barracks room on a Virginia military
base: Billy, a straight middle American; Roger, a black; and
Richie, a homosexual. The three suffer from personal stresses, but
can get along peacefully together. With the addition of an angry
black street dude named Carlyle, everything falls apart. Carlyle is
strung so tight that when he turns loose in the final scene he kills
Billy and a sergeant with his knife.
11 men (2 blacks); 1 interior. Royalty: $50-35.

RACINE, Jean. Andromaque (1667). Tr. by Boswell in his Dramatic Works, Bell (Bohn edn.), 1889, v. 1; also in Clark, W.
S.; tr. by Henderson in Six Plays by Corneille & Racine,
Modern Lib., 1931; tr. by Lockert, Princeton, 1936.
Pyrrhus (also named Neoptolemus), the son of Achilles, falls
in love with Andromache, who is now his captive after the fall of
Troy. Andromache is still devoted to her dead Hector and her living son Astyanax. Pyrrhus neglects Hermione, his affianced bride,
and threatens to kill Astyanax if Andromache does not marry him;
so she promises, intending to kill herself after the ceremony.
Orestes comes to love Hermione; and she, tortured by love and hate,
says she will marry him if he kills the faithless Pyrrhus. After he
does so, Hermione kills herself on Pyrrhus' dead body, and Orestes
goes insane.
5 acts; 4 men, 4 women, extras; 1 interior (hall in Pyrrhus'
palace); Greek costumes.

_____. Athalie (1691). Tr. by Boswell in his Dramatic Works,

Bell (Bohn edn.), 1890, v. 2; KRE; tr. by Henderson & Landis, Modern Lib., 1931; tr. by Lockert, Princeton, 1936.

Athaliah, daughter of Jezebel and like her, and a follower of Baal, dreams she will be killed by a child, whom she later identifies as Joash. She believes she has killed all the sons of her son Ahaziah. But Jehosheba, the wife of the High Priest Jehoiada, has saved and guarded Joash for six years. At the age of seven he is crowned King of Judah. Athalia tries to get him out of the way or to kill him, but he is protected by the Levites, and Athaliah is killed as she leaves the temple.

5 acts; 11 men, 4 women, extras; 1 exterior (court of the temple); costumes of the period.

_____. Bérénice (1670). Tr. by Boswell in his Dramatic Works, Bell (Bohn edn.), 1889; CLF-2; STA; adapted by Masefield in Esther and Bérénice. Lond., Heinemann, & Macmillan, 1922.

The beautiful but sensuous daughter of Agrippa has become the mistress of the Emperor Titus, but the people of Rome demand that he renounce his passion for her. In the conflict of love and honor, duty to the State triumphs. He sends Antiochus to command her to leave the city; he also comes under her spell. She leaves them both.

5 acts; 5 men, 2 women; 1 interior; costumes of the period.

_____. Esther (1689). Tr. by Boswell in his Dramatic Works, Bell (Bohn edn.) 1890, v. 2; adapted by Masefield in Esther and Bérénice, Lond., Heinemann, & Macmillan, 1922.

King Ahasuerus, urged on by Haman, orders the slaughter of all the Jews, not knowing that his queen Esther is a Jewess. Esther saves her people and discloses the treachery of Haman. Mordecai, her uncle, is put in Haman's place. Brings in the episode of honoring Mordecai with Haman leading him through the city.

3 acts; 5 men, 4 women, extras; 2 interiors, 1 exterior; costumes of the period. (An all-girl cast is possible.)

_____. Iphigénia (1674). Tr. by Boswell in his Dramatic Works, Bell (Bohn edn.), 1890, v. 2.

Iphigenia, the frail lovely daughter of Agamemnon, affianced to Achilles, must be sacrificed at Aulis so that the Greek forces may sail. Her father tries to avoid the sacrifice by warning her not to come, but it is too late. She arrives at the camp with Eriphyle, who also wishes to have Achilles. Instead of a wedding, the sacrifice is to be offered. When Eriphyle kills herself, she is accepted by the seer, Calchas, as the victim demanded by the gods, because her name is also Iphigenia.

5 acts; 5 men, 5 women, extras; scenes in and before the tent; costumes of the period.

_____. Mithridate (1673). Tr. by Boswell in his Dramatic Works, Bell (Bohn edn.), 1890, v. 2; tr. by Spoerl, Tufts College, 1926.

When Mithridates, King of Pontus, sworn enemy of Rome, has not returned from an expedition, his two sons, untrustworthy Pharnaces and gallant Xiphares, aim to seize the throne. Both become attached to Monima, the King's betrothed. After his return, Mithridates plans to march against Rome; Pharnaces opposes the plan, Xiphares favors it. Mithridates is defeated and fatally wounded; before his death he sanctions the union of Xiphares to Monima.

　　　　5 acts; 5 men, 2 women, extras; various scenes in the palace; costumes of the period.

_____. Phèdre (1677). Tr. by Boswell in his Dramatic Works, Bell (Bohn edn.), 1890, v. 2; CAR; HARC-26; MAU; MIL; SMP; tr. by Henderson in Six Plays by Corneille & Racine, Modern Lib., 1931; same in TRE-1, & 2 (v. 2); TREA-1; tr. by Lockert, Princeton, 1936. Acting edition: Samuel French. Tr. in alexandrine couplets by William Packard.

　　　　Phaedra, wife of Theseus, confesses to her old nurse, Oenone, her love for her stepson, Hippolytus, which he does not return, since he is in love with Aricia. Theseus, falsely reported dead, returning, is told by the nurse that Hippolytus has made advances to Phaedra. Hippolytus decides to flee into exile with Aricia, but is dragged to death by his horses. Oenone drowns herself, and Phaedra takes poison after exonerating Hippolytus.

　　　　5 acts; 3 men, 5 women, extras; 1 interior; costumes of the Greeks. (S. French Royalty: $35-25.)

RAND, Ayn. Night of January Sixteenth (1935). Longmans, 1936; David McKay carried.

　　　　Karen Andre is being tried for the murder of Bjorn Faulkner, for whom she was secretary before his marriage to Nancy Lee Whitfield. A body of a man, after being shot, has fallen or been pushed from a penthouse parapet. The prosecution calls it murder, the defense claims it was suicide; but Larry Regan testifies the body was not Faulkner's, that he escaped but later crashed in an airplane, that Karen was party to this escape and was to join him in South America. The jury in the play is impanelled from the audience and is asked to bring in a verdict: if guilty, she will get a new trial; is not guilty, she goes free.

　　　　3 acts; 11 men, 10 women; 1 interior (the courtroom).

RANDALL, Bob. 6 Rms Riv Vu (1970). BP 1972-73; Samuel French.

　　　　A middle-aged man and woman accidentally get locked in a vacant apartment when the superintendent takes off the doorknob. Anne Miller and Paul Friedman are happily married, but they find one another interesting. They become better acquainted a few hours later when they get out of the apartment and meet again later that night for dinner. Paul wants to have an affair, but Anne can't bring herself to that. It is a battle of urges. They eventually meet each others' spouses when they go back the next day to look at the apartment at the same time. Though Anne and Paul feel they some-

how haven't "lived" yet, they are happy with their present lives.
4 men, 4 women; 1 interior. Royalty: $50-35.

RANDAZZO, Angela. Zara, or Who Killed the Queen of the Silent
  Screen? (1985). Dramatic Publishing Company.
    Zara St. Cyrias, a beautiful silent screen star, gave every-
one she knew a reason to kill her. Sixty years later writer Martin
James and his wife Susan, with the help of a gypsy, go back in
time to 1925 in order to solve the mystery. Immediately they become
part of the past, Zara insisting that Martin is a movie director. In
fact, Martin gets so caught up in the intrigue that he becomes a murder suspect himself, along with Zara's past and present lovers, their
nephews, her chauffeur whom she calls a "lounge lizard," and
Zara's aunts, who are her housekeeper and cook. It all gets tricky
and intricate as the ending nears.
    2 acts; 6 men, 4 women; 1 interior. Royalty: $50-35.

RANDOLPH, Clemence. Rain. See entry under Colton, John R.

RAPHAELSON, Samson. Accent on Youth (1934). BP 1934-35;
  Samuel French.
    A middle-aged playwright, Stephen, works harmoniously with
his young secretary, Linda. He stands aside for Dickie and even
helps him with his courting. But Linda wearies of the strenuous
youth; she returns to Stephen and marries him.
    3 acts; 6 men, 3 women; 1 interior. Royalty: $35.

_____. Jason (1942). BP 1941-42; Dramatists Play Service.
    A conservative dramatic critic, Jason is upset when Mike
Ambler comes into his life to make him enjoy it more. Mike is also
attracted to Jason's wife, but she comes to realize Jason's worth.
Called on to review Mike's new play, shall Jason praise it, or damn
it? He finds he can realize what is good and detect what is immature,
and thus his spiritual education is complete.
    3 acts; 7 men, 4 women; 1 interior. Royalty: $35-25.

_____. The Jazz-Singer (1925). Samuel French.
    Rather than follow his father as cantor, Jakie Rabinowitz
runs away at 15 to sing jazz. As Jack Robin he returns to New
York to make his successful debut in a big revue, greeted by his
mother with love, by his father with suspicion. During the dress
rehearsal he learns that his father is too ill to sing at the Day of
Atonement--a date not missed in five generations. Torn by conflicting emotions, he finally hearkens to the call of race and quits
the show to sing as cantor.
    3 acts; 14 men, 3 women, extras; 2 interiors. Royalty on
application.

_____. Skylark (1939). BP 1939-40. Dramatists Play Service.
    Too absorbed in his advertising business, Tony even puts it
ahead of a proper celebration of his tenth wedding anniversary. His

wife Lydia, the skylark, rebels and walks out on him, threatening divorce. His friends advise meeting the situation by starting all over again, giving up his job, and selling the house. A wonderful week of enjoyment follows. Then Tony is offered a splendid position, which he now pretends he doesn't want. Lydia realizes how he has worked to deceive her and joins him as he goes to accept the new position.

3 acts; 6 men, 4 women; 1 interior. Royalty: $35-25.

RASPANTI, Celeste. I Never Saw Another Butterfly (1971). Dramatic Publishing Company.

This play deals with a real place: Terezin, a castle outside of Prague which was used by the Nazis as a concentration camp for Jewish children of Prague before they were shipped to the gas chambers of Auschwitz. Of the 15,000 Jewish children who passed through Terezin, only about a hundred were still alive when the castle was liberated by the allies. One of the survivors, Raja, is the central character. She taught the children of Terezin when there was nothing to teach with, gave them hope at a time when there was little reason to hope, created a world for them of laughter, flowers, and butterflies--their symbol of life and defiance.

4 men, 7 women; simple set. Royalty: $50-35.

RATTIGAN, Terence. Deep Blue Sea (1952). French carried; FAOS.

Described by the Herald-Tribune as "Probing, literate, and meticulously written," this drama tells the story of a woman determined to face up to what she has done. She had left her upright husband and nice home to live with her charming, but incorrigible lover. When the lover leaves her, she tries to escape by committing suicide. A neighbor saves her, however. Then her husband entreats her to come home, but she must face up to decisions, so she rejects his offer and goes to find her lover.

5 men, 3 women; 1 interior.

_____. French Without Tears (J1936). Samuel French.

Several young Englishmen are studying French in the south of France. A fellow-student is frivolous Diana Lake, sexy and flirtatious, who plays with each in turn only to turn the last one over to any newcomer. The victims conspire to teach Diana a lesson by individually ditching her. She is hurt, but immediately lays plans to subjugate Lord Heybook who is on his way. On his arrival he is discovered to be a sturdy lad of 11 years.

7 men, 3 women; 1 interior. Royalty: $25-20.

_____. Man and Boy (1963). Samuel French.

An international financier finds that his empire is crumbling around him. His big merger with an American oil company has hit a snag following a financial investigation. At the time his indictment is announced he is arranging a meeting with the president of the other company, and he plans to sacrifice his son's reputation to

save himself. His scheme backfires, however, and when his colleague and wife desert him he decides to kill himself.
     5 men, 2 women; 1 interior. Royalty: $50-25.

_____. O Mistress Mine (1946). BP 1945-46; Samuel French.
     Michael's mother, Olivia, is living in a house donated by Sir John Fletcher, a cabinet minister, who waits to be divorced from his wife until the war is over to avoid any embarrassment to the government. Michael is a young radical who objects to the arrangement and wants to save his mother. So he gets her to return to her own apartment; but he becomes reconciled when they propose going to a fancy restaurant so as to impress his snobbish flame, Sylvia.
     2 men, 5 women; 2 interiors. Royalty: $35-25.

_____. Separate Tables (1954). BP 1956-57; Samuel French.
     Except for the two leading roles, the characters are the same in this successful combination of two plays, "Tables by the Window," and "Table Number Seven." Each play is set in the lounge and dining area of a shabbily genteel hotel, and each tells the story of a couple whose love is threatened. In each case, however, Miss Cooper, the hotel Manageress, comes to the rescue and leads the couples in regaining their love.
     3 men, 8 women; 2 sets. Royalty: $50-25.

_____. The Winslow Boy (1046). DP 1947-48; Dramatists Play Service.
     Innocent Ronnie Winslow is expelled from an English school for an alleged theft. His father challenges the right of the Royal Naval College to do this without a trial; and the case is carried up to the House of Lords. Sir Robert Morton defends Ronnie; the Admiralty withdraws the case and Ronnie is exonerated. Right is done, but during the process the family is faced with social ostracism and economic ruin.
     2 acts; 7 men, 4 women; 1 interior. Royalty: $50-25.

RAYFIEL, David. P.S. 193 (1963). BP 1962-63; Samuel French.
     A university philosophy seminar turns to more than talk when Prof. Jonathan Kobitz is blamed for the death of a former student briefly under the military command of one of his present students, Mario Saccone, a veteran studying under the G.I. Bill. Mario blames Kobitz for all of his talk, that it is talk that starts wars and kills, though the talkers stay home to do more talk and the young ones go off to die. He says he wants the professor to learn about terrorism first hand, so he begins to stalk him, leading Kobitz to want to leave university teaching and get a job at P.S. 193, the elementary school he attended as a child. Finally, Mario beats up and holds overnight Kobitz's alcoholic wife, bringing her to class the next day and watching Kobitz still in control of his passions. It is only when the wife, in her rage, hits Kobitz in the face for being so civilized that Mario finally sees something real:

the prof has been surprised by his wife's action. With that, he leaves the class to the talkers.
3 men, 1 woman; 1 interior. Royalty: $35-25.

REACH, James. David and Lisa (1967). Adapted from the book by Theodore Isaac Rubin and the screenplay by Eleanor Perry. Samuel French.
Tells the story of David and Lisa, two mentally disturbed teen-agers. David, the only son of wealthy parents, has a mania against being touched. Lisa, who has never known parental love, has a split personality: one Lisa only speaks in childish rhymes and insists upon being spoken to in the same manner. The play follows them, and others, through their progress with psychiatrists at Berkley School, and through their retrogressions.
11 men, 11 women; drapes and representational props. Royalty: $35-25.

_____. For the Defense (1967). Samuel French.
In this courtroom drama, the audience as a whole becomes the jury at the end of the play and determines the guilt or innocence of the defendant. The defendant in this case is Lucky Sam Luckey, boss racketeer, who has been accused of shooting Marvin Stump. The prosecuting attorney has only skimpy evidence to work with, but he is confident of obtaining a conviction on the basis of Luckey's shady reputation. The defense attorney, flamboyant Russell Holloway, does his best to keep the trial focused on the present charge. A final witness turns the case topsy-turvy.
8 men, 7 women; 1 interior. Royalty: $25-20.

REDGRAVE, Michael. The Aspern Papers (1959). Adapted from Henry James' story. Samuel French.
This intellectual mystery begins with a 90-year-old woman and her niece living in seclusion in a once-palatial home in Venice. Because they are poor, an American publisher convinces them to lease some rooms to him. His apparent purpose is to write in their garden, but his real purpose is to dig out the mystery of a brilliant writer who once loved the aunt but who has been dead for years. The renter is convinced that the writer will one day rise from obscurity to fame, and he is in search of more of his letters, writings and biography. The old aunt, however, rejects all inquiries into the past. One night the young writer finds a trunk and is pilfering in it when the old woman discovers him. She throws herself upon the trunk, suffers a stroke and dies. After the funeral the young writer returns to find the niece all alone. Pathetically she proposes to him. He asks for the papers, but she says she has burned them. He rejects her. Then, truly alone, she locks the house and burns the papers in the trunk one by one.
2 men, 1 woman; 1 interior. Royalty: $50-25.

REED, Mark. Petticoat Fever (1935). Samuel French.
A wireless operator in Labrador, Dascome Dinsmore, has had

no contact with people for months, and he is bored. Down drops
Sir James and his fiancee Ethel, en route to Montreal but forced to
land. While awaiting rescue, Dascome tries to entertain and makes
feverish advances to Ethel. Then his discarded sweetheart arrives,
and in the end Dascome wins Ethel and Sir James gets Clara.
    6 men, 4 women; 1 interior. Royalty: $35-25.

_____. Yes, My Darling Daughter (1937). BP 1936-37; Samuel
    French.
    Ellen's mother had campaigned for women's rights twenty-five
years before in Greenwich Village. Now Ellen, just out of college,
quotes her mother's writings to justify a farewell weekend trip with
Douglas, who is leaving for two years. After a farewell fling she
agrees to marry the young man.
    3 men, 4 women; 2 interiors (1 possible). Royalty: $35-25.

REGAN, Sylvia. The Fifth Season (1953). Samuel French.
    The plush office of partners in the clothing business is all
show. There are beautiful models, beautiful furnishings, but no
business. Bankruptcy is always just around the corner, but the two
will hock anything to put up a good front for a buyer. Finally it is
the models, and not the clothes, that pull the partners out of the
hole, and the fast life that comes with being successful nearly wrecks
the younger of the two.
    6 men, 7 women; 1 interior. Royalty: $50-25.

REINER, Carl. Enter Laughing. See entry under Stein, Joseph.

RESNIK, Muriel. Any Wednesday (1964). Dramatists Play Service.
    A young businessman is looking for the millionaire corporation
president that he sold his factory to (the millionaire has ordered the
factory closed to take advantage of a tax benefit for himself). A
new secretary directs the young man to the executive suite, but all
he finds there is the wealthy man's mistress (this is Wednesday, and
she's waiting for her sugar-daddy). Next comes the president's
wife, looking for her husband and believing merely that the young
man and woman are a married couple. Then the millionaire arrives,
who doesn't know what's going on.
    2 men, 2 women; 1 interior. Royalty: $50-35.

RICE, Elmer. The Adding Machine (1923). Samuel French.
    A powerful satire on the modern mechanistic world. Mr.
Zero, an overworked, underpaid bookkeeper, kills his boss in a
rage because he is being fired after 25 years to be replaced by an
adding machine. After his trial and execution he goes to the Elysian
Fields, where he is joined by his co-worker Dorthea, who committed
suicide after Zero's death. Zero vows to leave the Fields when he
discovers that he and Dorthea, who are in love, could live together
without being married. He remains hopelessly insignificant even in
heaven, and his servile soul is sent back to earth to become an even
greater mechanical slave.

14 men, 9 women; 5 interiors. 2 exteriors. Royalty: $50-25.

_____, with Philip Barry. Cock Robin (1928). French, 1929.
      During rehearsals at the local Little Theatre, Hancock Robin-
son becomes disliked; in the duel scene at the performance he is
shot with the stage pistol which actually kills him. At the same moment he is stabbed in the back. The murder is solved and justified
because of Robinson's insulting treatment of a young lady in the cast.
      3 acts; 8 men, 4 women; 2 interiors (1 possible).

_____. Counsellor-At-Law (1931). French, 1931; in his Plays,
      Gollancz, 1933; in his Seven plays, Viking, 1950; FAMC.
      An East-side New York Jewish boy, George Simon, rises to
a commanding position as a criminal lawyer. A breach of ethics
during his climb catches up with him, and he is on the verge of dis-
barment. He is ready to commit suicide, but is thwarted by his ever
faithful Jewish secretary, in whom he finds real love and understanding in contrast to his Gentile wife.
      3 acts; 19 men, 9 women; 2 interiors.

_____. Cue for Passion (1958). Dramatists Play Service.
      Transposes the Hamlet legend to contemporary California.
A wealthy widow has recently remarried. Her new husband is the
only witness to the fatal accident which took the life of her former
husband. Her son, a college senior, returns home from a trip to
the Far East, and is determined to investigate closely his father's
death and his mother's hasty marriage. Like Hamlet, he disturbs
his mother's household and brings despair to his sweetheart and best
friend. His wild convictions are reported to those nearest him, but
their full implications are not revealed until the end of the play.
      4 men, 3 women; 1 interior. Royalty: $50-25.

_____. Dream Girl (1945). BP 1945-46; Dramatists Play Service.
      The imaginative Georgina, who runs a bookstore, has romantic
daydreams involving a series of men and women: a doctor, a book
reviewer, her sister, and others.
      25 men (some doubling possible), 7 women; 3 interiors, 1 ex-
      terior (all suggestive rather than realistic). Royalty: $50-
      25.

_____. Flight to the West (1940). BP 1940-41; Dramatists Play
      Service.
      On a plane flight from Lisbon to Bermuda during World War
II the passengers present a cross-section of the warring elements in
Europe and America, showing the antagonisms and convictions, the
problems of spying, appeasement, and persecution, and ending with
the discovery and detainment of a Nazi spy.
      3 acts; 16 men, 5 women; 1 interior. Royalty: $35-25.

_____. The Grand Tour (1951). Dramatists Play Service.
      Nell Valentine, a middle-aged schoolteacher, for the first

time in her life falls desperately in love during the course of a summer tour through Europe. Then the man she is in love with tells
her he is already married and that he is a fugitive from justice.
Nell is still willing to marry him, but his wife appears on the scene.
In parting, the schoolteacher offers to help both of them in any way
she can. In the last scene Nell is showing slides of her trip to her
students. Her superficial comments on her travels have undertones
of pathetic personal experiences. She is not bitter, however; rather
she is more mature and understanding.
      6 men, 3 women; various interiors and exteriors suggested by
backdrops. Royalty: $50-25.

_____. The Iron Cross (1915). Dramatists Play Service.
      One of the earliest plays about World War I, dealing with the
brutality and stupidity of war. The Dreiers, William and Margaret,
have a small farm in East Prussia. Brother Paul has already died
a hero, and now William and his friend Karl are called into the army. Soon Karl returns, blind, and Margaret carries on valiantly by
caring for the sick, the injured, and those dispossessed by war.
By the time her husband returns, wounded and ragged, Margaret has
become the unwilling mother of a Cossack officer's child. William
leaves to seek restitution from his government but returns, empty
handed, realizing that Margaret struggled to preserve life while he
attempted to destroy it.
      6 men, 1 boy, 5 women, 1 girl; 1 interior. Royalty: $25.

_____. The Left Bank (1930). BP 1931-32; Samuel French.
      John and Claire Shelby live in a third-rate hotel in bohemian
Paris. They are part of a radical set of expatriate Americans who
find that France is "spiritual home," believing they could never again
live in "a spiritual vacuum, a cultural desert" like America. John, a
writer, believes he has been "ruined" by growing up in America, so
he makes sure that his teenage son is brought up differently by
sending him off to a British progressive school. When the couple
entertains Waldo and Susie Lynde, American friends who are tourists,
John takes Susie away on business, leaving Waldo and Claire to fall
in with one another. When the two return, Susie announces she is
divorcing Waldo, Claire announces that she is leaving John, picking
up her son in England, and going "home to America" to live, and
Waldo decides to go with her. "Ah, ces Américains!," mutters a
French servant.
      3 acts; 8 men, 7 women; 1 interior. Royalty: $50.

_____. Not for Children (1935). Samuel French.
      The author's philosophy of the theater is explained by a
group described as expert lecturers in this comedy. They illustrate
their discussions with blackouts and vaudeville skits. In the process
they take tongue-in-cheek pokes at playwrights, producers, actors,
critics, backers and audiences.
      7 men, 5 women; bare stage. Royalty: $50.

_____. On Trial (1914). In his Seven Plays. Viking, 1950; CARC; BP 1909-1919.

As incidents are uncovered by the testimony at the trial, they are presented in acted form, similar to cut-backs in motion pictures. In this way the events work backward until the mystery is cleared up.

4 acts with 11 scenes; 15 men, 4 women, and a jury of 12 men; 5 interiors.

_____. Street Scene (1929). BP 1928-29; Samuel French.

Pulitzer prize play, 1929. A panorama of the comedy and tragedy of daily life in front of a New York tenement. The wife of a theatrical scene-shifter has a sordid affair with the milkman. Her husband returns and kills them both. This crystalizes the viewpoint and shows the very human reactions of the entire neighborhood, as it touches every tenant indirectly.

3 acts; 16 men, 11 women, extras; 1 exterior. Royalty: $50-25.

_____. Two on an Island (1940). Dramatists Play Service.

Two young people, John from Iowa, Mary from New Hampshire, arrive in New York on the same day and seek a place in the world of the great city. Their paths cross several times, and when John is about to depart, discouraged, they decide to stick it out together. Presents many vignettes of life in Manhattan--the Bagdad on Hudson of O. Henry.

11 scenes; 38 speaking parts, only a few long ones; several stylized scenes. Royalty: $35-25.

_____. We the People (1933). BP 1932-33; Coward, 1933.

The depression has had tragic effect on the Davis family: it loses its home; William, the father, a foreman, loses his job and is shot during a strike; the daughter, Helen, a school teacher, hasn't been paid for months and can't marry her fiancé; the son, Allan, who was to go to college, is arrested for stealing coal, becomes a radical pacifist, and is convicted on a trumped-up charge of murdering a policeman. By contrast, some capitalists are pictured: the wealthy banker, the pompous university president, the unctuous Senator--many who talk much about suppressing agitators and such.

21 scenes; 33 men, 11 women; 12 interiors, 3 exteriors.

RICHARDSON, Howard and William Berney. Dark of the Moon (1945). Samuel French.

A mountain witch-boy sees the beautiful Barbara Allen and promptly falls in love with her. However, he is allowed to assume human form and marry her only if she remains faithful. After the marriage Barbara gives birth to a witch child. In the frenzy of a religious revival Barbara is led to betray her husband, resulting in her death and his return to the world of the mountain witches.

28 roles; various scenes. Royalty: $50-35.

RICHMAN, Arthur. <u>Ambush</u> (1921). Duffield, 1922; BP 1921-22.
    A clerk, Walter, tries to live within his moderate income.
His daughter, Margaret, wants pretty clothes and accepts gifts from
richer men but deceives her father and mother about them. Walter
loses out on his investments and his job. He confesses himself
beaten and accepts money to pay the rent from his daughter's current lover. Circumstances of life lie in ambush to prevent him
from living an upright decent life.
    3 acts; 7 men, 3 women; 1 interior.

RIGGS, Lynn. <u>Green Grow the Lilacs</u> (1930). BP 1930-31; Samuel
    French.
    A Western pioneer play later developed into the musical
comedy "Oklahoma!" by Oscar Hammerstein II. Laurey loves Curley the cowhand and is afraid of the dark-minded ranch hand Jeeter,
with whom she goes to the dance. In the course of the shivaree
following her marriage with Curley, Jeeter is killed.
    6 scenes; 10 men, 4 women, extras; 6 exteriors; costumes of
    the Southwest. Royalty: $50-25.

_____. <u>Roadside</u> (1930). Samuel French.
    In the Indian Territory before it became Oklahoma, Hannie,
a strapping hearty girl and her father (a tumbleweed) stop in their
covered wagon and make camp by the side of the road. Along
comes Buzzie, her divorced husband, to plead with her to come
back. But Texas, a tall-talking big man, has fallen for Hannie;
meantime the Law wants Texas for disorderliness; he staves them
off--the road is between--and the covered wagon plunges away.
Pictures the conflict between free spirits and law and order.
    3 acts; 8 men, 2 women; 1 interior, 1 exterior; costumes of
    the period there (1905). Royalty: $25-20.

_____. <u>Russet Mantle</u> (1936). Samuel French.
    On a ranch near Santa Fé, Kay is restless, unhappy, and
headstrong. Along comes John Galt, a young poet on a tramp. He
is given work and they are attracted; they are disgusted with the
failures of the older generation and express their freedom with the
usual biological result. But John brings Kay around to reality, and
helps others in the family to readjust their disappointed lives.
    3 acts; 6 men, 5 women; 1 interior, 1 exterior. Royalty:
    $35.

_____. <u>Sump'n Like Wings</u> (1928). French, 1928.
    Rebelling against the too strict bringing-up by her mother,
Willie Baker runs away and into adventures as she struggles to find
the meaning of her own life. She returns home in disgrace; but is
inspired by her uncle to face life fighting.
    4 acts; 8 men, 6 women; 4 interiors.

RILEY, Lawrence. <u>Personal Appearance</u> (1934). Samuel French,
    1934.

The motion picture star, Carole Arden, with her manager, is making personal appearances to promote her play. She flirts with the good-looking youth at the filling station and guest house where they are stalled, and even suggests that he go with her to Hollywood. But the manager (who is with her to keep her out of mischief) nips this plan as they leave for her next appearance.

3 acts; 4 men, 6 women; 3 interiors. Royalty: $35-25.

RINEHART, Mary Roberts and Avery Hopwood. The Bat (1920). Samuel French.

Four people are after the money, missing from a dead banker's bank, which may be hidden in a secret chamber in his house. Cornelia Van Gorder, a determined lady of 60, has rented the house for the summer and despite threats and mysterious happenings refuses to move.

3 acts; 7 men, 3 women; 2 interiors. Royalty: $50-25.

ROBERTSON, Thomas W. Caste (1867). Roorbach, 1890; French #380; Baker, 1913; in Heath's Belles Lettres ser., 1905; in his Principal Dramatic Works, Lond., Low, 1889, v. 1; COD; COT; DUR; MAP; MAT; MOSO; TAU.

A ballet girl, Esther Eccles, marries the Hon. George D'Alroy, to the great annoyance of his rather arrogant mother, who will scarcely admit the existence of Esther's father and Sam Gerridge. George is reported killed in battle, but returns to rescue his wife and child from poverty and social snobbery.

3 acts; 4 men, 3 women; 2 interiors; costumes of 1860's.

_____. David Garrick (1864). Penn Pub. Co., 1903; French & Dramatic Pub. Co. carried; in his Principal Dramatic Works, Lond., Low, 1889, v. 1.

David Garrick has promised Ada's father to cure her of her infatuation for him, although he finds that she is the girl in his audience who has inspired him. He keeps his word by acting like a drunken boor at dinner in order to disgust her, but the scheme is disclosed and they are married with the father's blessing--hat in hand.

3 acts; 8 men, 3 women; 2 interiors; costumes of the period.

_____. Society (1865). Lond., Lacy, 18--; in his Principal Dramatic Works, Lond., Low, 1889, v. 2; BAT v. 16; RUB.

A poor but honest gentleman, Sidney Daryl, wins the love of Maud Hetherington and a seat in Parliament over his wealthy rival, John Chodd, Jr. whose father thinks money can buy anything, even a place in society. Before Sidney inherits his brother's estate he has a chance to compare his impecunious artistic friend with the men encountered at clubs and dinners.

3 acts; 16 men, 4 women; 4 interiors, 2 exteriors; costumes of the period.

ROBINSON, Barbara. The Best Christmas Pageant Ever (1982).

Samuel French.

The woman who usually handles the Christmas pageant has a broken leg, so Grace Bradley, Beth and Charlie's mother, takes over. The rehearsals begin in chaos because the Herdman kids-- Ralph, Imogene, Leroy, Claude, Ollie, and Gladys--volunteer their services. They are all badly behaved poor children on welfare whom no one likes. But Grace is determined to make a go of the pageant despite the town's negative reactions, with the Hardmans playing the parts of Mary, Joseph and the Wise Men. The church has a big turnout the night of the play, mainly because everyone wants to see the damage the bad kids would cause. But with the Herdmans' awkward but well-behaved actions, the play turns out to be one of the best ever.

4 men, 6 women, 8 boys, 9 girls; 2 interiors. Royalty: $35-25.

ROBINSON, Lennox. The Far-Off Hills (1928). Samuel French.

Sober-minded Marian plans to become a nun after she gets her blind father settled and her two sisters educated and matched off. A melancholy man, Harold, with an insane wife, persistently woos her. When at last she is free, she loses her interest in the convent and in Harold, and marries another.

3 acts; 5 men, 5 women; 2 interiors. Royalty: $35-25.

_____. Is Life Worth Living? (1933). Samuel French.

A certain type of modern drama is amusingly satirized in this play described by its author as an "exaggeration." Modern, introspective drama often seems to present a rather hopeless view of man's existence. The reactions of an unsophisticated audience who takes plays of that type in all seriousness provide an interesting and amusing commentary.

8 men, 5 women; 1 interior. Royalty: $25-20.

_____. The White-Headed Boy (1916). Putnam & French, 1921; PLAP ser. 3; MYB.

A doting mother and family have tried to make a genius out of Denis, the youngest boy, their pet, but the hope of the family turns out not to be "so different" after all. He fails in his medical examination, he squanders his brother's money, he is self-satisfied and irresponsible; they seem to have sacrificed themselves needlessly. Then Duffy demands payment for Denis' trifling with his daughter's affections, but when he finds that she is already married to Denis, he gives them the money as a wedding present.

3 acts; 5 men, 7 women; 1 interior.

ROBLES, Emmanuel. Montserrat (1949). Adapted by Lillian Hellman. Dramatists Play Service, 1950.

During the revolution in Venezuela in 1812 led by the great patriot Bolivar, the Spanish commander Izquiardo arrests Montserrat, a young Spanish officer who knows where Bolivar is hiding. He tortures him mentally and spiritually by ordering six passersby

to be shot if he doesn't reveal the hiding place. They plead in vain
for their lives, but one of them realizes the ideals of freedom from
tyranny that Bolivar and Montserrat have. As word comes that
Bolivar has escaped, Montserrat goes willingly to his death.
  2 acts; 15 men, 2 women; 1 interior.

ROGERS, David. Flowers for Algernon (1969). Based on the novel
    by Daniel Keyes. Dramatic Publishing Company.
  Experimental surgery on Algernon the mouse has increased
the creature's intelligence fourfold, so the technique is tried on
Charlie, a mentally retarded adult who rapidly changes from a
moron to a genius. At the peak of his brilliance Charlie is far
more intelligent than his teacher, with whom he is in love, and a
good deal smarter than the doctors who created the operating technique. Then Algernon shows signs of regression, and Charlie begins racing with time.
  10 men, 17 women (8m and 9w with doubling); drapes with
  set pieces. Royalty: $60-40.

_____. "The Sting" (1984). Based on the screenplay by David
    Ward. Dramatic Publishing Company.
  The story of a big con called "The Wire" is framed in present
time by a version Mrs. Vanderkieft is telling to writer Cynthia
Hastings, who will attempt to write a best seller. A grifter named
Johnny Hooker makes the mistake of conning a runner who works
for a big-time crook named Doyle Lonnegan, who retaliates by having
one of Hooker's friends killed. When Lonnegan fails in his attempt
to knock off Hooker, Johnny goes to work for a master con man,
Henry Gondorff, in an attempt to nail Lonnegan for good. Gondorff
and Hooker work together with Kid Twist, Ivy Niles, and J. J.
Singleton to set up "The Wire" to sting Lonnegan.
  2 acts; large flexible cast; area staging. Royalty: $50-35.

_____. Tom Jones. See entry under Fielding, Henry.

ROLLAND, Romain. Danton (1900). Fourteenth of July (1902).
    Tr. by Clark in his Fourteenth of July, & Danton, Holt, 1918.
    Two French Revolution plays.
    Danton: 3 acts; 13 men, 3 women, extras; 3 interiors; period
    costumes.
    14th of July: 3 acts; 10 men, 4 women, extras; 3 exteriors;
    period costumes.

_____. The Game of Love and Death (1925). Tr. by Brooks,
    Holt, 1926.
  A level-headed Girondist, Jerome, discovers that his young
wife Sophie is harboring Claude Vallee, a fugitive, with whom she
seems to be in love. Jerome secures passports for them, which
he turns over to his wife and lover, and prepares to meet death.
Sophie, inspired, sends Claude to freedom and remains to share
her husband's fate.

3 acts; 8 men, 2 women, extras; 1 interior; costumes of the period.

_____. The Wolves (1898). Tr. by Clark, in Drama, v. 8, 1918; same, Random Huse, 1937.

Like a pack of wolves, the officers in the French Revolutionary army in Mayence are beset by personal quarrels, hates, jealousies, and suspicions. D'Oyron, an aristocrat, is accused by a spy's letter of being in the service of the enemy. He alleges a conspiracy, is defended by Teulier, but the generals refuse to listen and send him to the guillotine.

3 acts; 13 men, 0 women, extras; 1 interior; costumes of the period.

ROMAINS, Jules. Doctor Knock (1923). Tr. by Granville-Barker, Lond., 1925; French carried.

Depicts how an unlicensed doctor takes the place of old Doctor Parpalaid. The quack Dr. Knock builds up a lucrative practice by persuading the people that they are ill. Thus by creating unanimity of feeling that every healthy man is a potential patient, he bluffs his way.

3 acts; 8 men, 6 women; 2 interiors, 1 exterior.

ROMAN, Lawrence. Under the Yum Yum Tree (1961). Dramatists Play Service.

Hogan is ostensibly a good-hearted landlord. He rents one of his apartments at very reasonable rates to beautiful women. There are advantages to the arrangement: it gives Hogan the opportunity to lie, eavesdrop, peek through keyholes, use his passkey, and invent a mirror device with which to look in windows from a position on top of the roof. He becomes more than usually frustrated, however, when a beautiful Berkeley student moves in, and he discovers that she has invited her boyfriend to live with her (platonically, of course) in a kind of trial marriage. Though complications ensue, everything remains above board.

3 men, 2 women; 1 interior. Royalty: $50–35.

ROOS, William. January Thaw (1946). Adapted from the novel of Bellamy Partridge. Dramatic Publishing Company.

High School Theater Classic, 1945-1949, about the Gage family moving to an old farmhouse so that Mr. Gage can have the peace he needs to write a "best seller." The peace is short lived. Jonathan Rockwood and his family, who according to an old deed have the right to live in the house, move in too. Neither family is able to turn the other out, and finally a blizzard isolates them, all together, in the old house. The electric lines fail, the oil-burner and range refuse to work, and the Gages breakfast on old cereal and olives. From the old-fashioned Rockwoods' rooms come the smell of coffee and ham and the warmth of an old woodburner. When the aroma of fresh biscuits reaches the Gages, everyone deserts Mr. Gage. It even looks like Barbara Gage has eloped with the Rockwood

boy. But finally everything is happily ended.
7 men, 6 women; 1 interior. Royalty: $35-25.

ROSE, Reginald. Dino (1956). Adapted by Kristin Sergel. Dramatic Publishing Company.
High School Theater Classic, 1950-59, about a boy named
Dino, 17, who has already spent four years behind bars. He has
just returned home from Reform School, and his parents are totally
inadequate to deal with him. Dino's parole officer, though, compe-
tent, but kind, takes the young man to a psychotherapist for treatment. Dino rejects the help, and his father tells him not to go back
because there aren't any "crazy people" in the family. Finally a
sixteen-year-old girl is able to help him, but when she discovers
his background it appears she may reject him too, and he almost
joins a new gang. A serious play about the very real problem of
rehabilitating juvenile delinquents.
7 men, 11 women, extras; 1 set. Royalty: $50-35.

_____. The Remarkable Incident at Carson Corners (1955).
Adapted by Kristin Sergel. Dramatic Publishing Company.
High School Theater Classic, 1950-59, about a group of students holding a mock trial to determine who is responsible for a
student's death. In this play the actors come up from the audience
to hold what looks to be a humorous mock trial. But it isn't. The
purpose of the hearing is to fix responsibility for the death of the
boy who fell from the school fire escape. One revelation forces the
next until the whole town is implicated: the druggist who should
have known better than to move the boy and thereby aggravate the
injury, the doctor who didn't think the emergency call serious, and
the politician who thought the school appropriations could wait.
Several attempts are made to stop the trial, but it goes on, and the
tension builds.
13 men, 13 women; bare stage (chairs). Royalty: $50-35.

_____. Twelve Angry Men (or Twelve Angry Women or Twelve
Angry Jurors) (1955). Adapted by Sherman L. Sergel. Dramatic Publishing Company.
One foreign-born juror reminds his fellow jurors about some
basic truths in the American judicial system in this drama about
the deliberations of a jury in a murder trial. A nineteen-year-old
boy has just stood trial for the fatal stabbing of his father. Apparently the jury plans to return a verdict of guilty. As each juror
begins to speak, however, one juror reminds them that they must
be sure "beyond a reasonable doubt." As they continue to discuss
the testimonies, tempers get short, arguments grow heated, and the
jurors become twelve angry men. Before they reach the verdict a
new murder threat develops among their own number, giving an unexpected ending to this absorbing drama.
Cast can be all men, all women, or any combination giving
a total of 15; 1 interior. Royalty: $50-35.

ROSENBERG, James L. The Death and Life of Sneaky Fitch (1968).
Dramatists Play Service.
A Western spoof about a no-good, drunken, brawling nuisance
named Sneaky Fitch, whom everyone in Gopher Gulch hates. The
town is relieved when Sneaky dies, but then he rises from the coffin and takes over--without opposition--the positions of sheriff, mayor, and banker. He even faces down the man who is the fastest
gun in the West. When Doc Burch returns to town (it was his medicine that "killed" Sneaky in the first place) the truth comes out and
Sneaky is done for good.
10 men, 3 women, extras; 1 exterior. Royalty: $35-25.

ROSTAND, Edmond. L'Aiglon (1900). Tr. by Parker, Russell,
1900; tr. by Norman as The Eaglet in his Plays, Macmillan, &
Lond., Palmer, 1921, v. 2; tr. by Davenport, Yale, 1927.
Recounts the tragic story of Napoleon's son, the little King
of Rome, called The Eaglet by Victor Hugo, who has neither the
strength of will nor of body to recapture his father's empire. He
is held captive in Vienna among his enemies who are determined to
tame his spirit. Covers the years 1830-32.
6 acts; 33 men, 7 women, 2 boys, 1 girl, many extras;
3 interiors, 2 exteriors; costumes of the period.

_____. Chanticleer (1910). Tr. by Hall, Duffield, 1910; tr. by
Newberry, Duffield, 1911; tr. by Norman, in his Plays, Macmillan, & Lond., Palmer, 1921, v. 2.
Dressed out in the garb of the barn-yard animals, men and
women are laughed at, especially the egotist in the rooster who
believes his crowing evokes the sunrise.
4 acts; 32 men, 14 women, many extras; 4 exteriors; fanciful costumes.

_____. Cyrano de Bergerac (1897). Tr. by Kingsbury, Bost.,
Lamson, 1898; LEV; same adapted by Kruckemeyer, French,
1934; tr. by Hall, Doubleday, 1898; DID; MOSQ; tr. by Dole,
Crowell, 1899; same carried by Baker; & World Book Co.,
1942; tr. by Norman in his Plays, Macmillan & Lond., Palmer,
1921, v. 1; tr. by Hooker, Holt, 1923; same Modern Lib.,
1929; abridged in Pierce & Matthews, v. 2; tr. by Wolfe in BEN;
BLO; TRE-1, 2, 3; tr. by Whitehall in WOR; tr. by Hooker,
Dramatists Play Service; tr. by Forsyth, Dramatic Publishing
Company.
Cyrano is courageous and witty, but his proud spirit is hampered by his ridiculous nose. In love with Roxane, he nevertheless
aids young Christian to win her. She doesn't realize his devotion
until he is dying. Has high literary value and dramatic power,
realizing perfectly the spirit of romance.
5 acts; 12 leading men, 3 leading women, many extras; 2 interiors, 3 exteriors; costumes of the period. (Kruckmeyer:
30 men, 16 women. No royalty. Hooker: 10 men, 5 women
extras. Royalty: $35-25. Forsyth: 5 men, 2 women,

extras. Royalty: $50-35.)

_____. The Last Night of Don Juan (1921). Tr. by Riggs,
    Yellow Springs, O., Kahoe, 1929; KRE.
    The immortal lover, Don Juan, reviews his past just before
his death and discovers that, though he may have conquered, he
still possesses nothing. Stripped of pride and vanity, he is
turned into a squeaking doll in the devil's puppet show.
    Prolog & 2 acts; 5 men, many women as ghosts; 1 interior;
fanciful costumes and puppet dresses.

_____. The Princess Far-Away (1895). Tr. by Renault, Stokes,
    1899; tr. by Bagstad, Badger, 1921; tr. by Norman in his
    Plays, Macmillan, & Lond., Palmer, 1921, v. 1; tr. by Heard
    as The Far Princess, Holt, 1925.
    The troubadour Rudel is dominated by his hopeless quest for
his distant princess, Melissinde. He finally comes to her court
only as he is dying in the ecstasy of his bliss. She in reality is a
very human woman, and though weak and selfish, she becomes strong
through his idealization.
    4 acts; 21 men, 2 women; 2 interiors; costumes of the medie-
val period.

_____. The Romancers (Les Romanesques, 1894). Tr. by Hen-
    dee, Doubleday, 1899; same, Baker, 1906; tr. by Fleming as
    The Fantasticks, Lond., Heinemann, & Russell, 1900; tr. by
    Clark, French, 1915; tr. by Bagstad in Poet Lore, v. 32, 1921;
    tr. by Norman in his Plays, Macmillan, & Lond., Palmer,
    1921, v. 1.
    An amusing, dainty, and charming piece in which the lovers
carry on their romance over a wall between their gardens to the
pretended disapproval but secret delight of their fathers.
    3 acts; 5 men, 1 woman, extras; 1 exterior (an excellent
out-of-doors play). No royalty.

ROSTEN, Norman. Come Slowly, Eden (1966). Dramatists Play
    Service.
    Treats the story of Emily Dickinson. The play opens shortly
after the poetess' death with Lavinia Dickinson's discovery of her
sister's poems and letters. With the help of T. W. Higginson, the
literary critic, an attempt is made to discover which Emily Dickinson is the real one--the proper, protected Emily whom everyone
knew, or the passionate, love-starved woman who wrote the poems.
Tension develops in what Lavinia voluntarily offers about her sister
and what she attempts to hide.
    5 men, 2 women. Royalty: $35-25.

ROTHENBERG, Jerome. The Deputy. See entry under Hochhuth,
    Rolf.

ROTTER, Fritz and Allen Vincent. Letters to Lucerne (1941). BP

1941-42; Samuel French.

The girls in a boarding school in Lucerne, Switzerland, read aloud the letters from their families. Erna, a sensitive German girl, suffers because of the anti-German feeling. Her brother is in the German air force and is beloved by a Polish girl in the school, who has heard that Warsaw has been bombed and her parents killed; Erna too has a letter from her family, telling of her brother's death: he chose to destroy himself and his plane rather than to drop bombs on Warsaw.

3 acts; 4 men, 9 women; 2 interiors (1 possible). Royalty: $35-25.

ROWE, Nicholas. Jane Shore, A Tragedy (1714). In his Works, Lond., 1728, v. 3; Belles Lettres ser., Heath, 1907; BEL v. 8; BRI v. 1; DIB v. 6; HAN; INCH v. 10; MOSE-2; NET; OXB v. 8; STM; TUQ (1934 edn.).

Jane Shore left her husband to become the mistress of Edward IV. After his death, Richard III drives her into the streets where she drifts, half-starved for several days, deeply penitent. Her husband tries to rescue her but in vain; he is caught by Richard's men and Jane dies.

5 acts; 7 men, 2 women, extras; 3 interiors, 1 exterior; costumes of the period.

ROYLE, Edwin M. The Squaw Man (1905, pub. 1906). BP 1899-1909.

Jim leaves England for the American West to protect Diana's husband, assuming the blame for his embezzlement. In the West Jim becomes Carston and has a loyal group of cowboys. When Cash Hawkins is shot in a saloon, an Indian woman, Nat-u-ritch, saves Jim's life. He marries her and is called a Squaw man; they have a son, Hal. Jim inherits an English estate and is to send Hal abroad. His mother can't stand the separation and shoots herself, thus leaving Jim free to go to England with Hal and Diana.

4 acts; 23 men, 7 women; 1 interior, 2 exteriors; costumes.

RUBIN, Theodore Isaac. David and Lisa. See entry under Reach, James.

RUDKIN, David. Ashes (1974). BP 1976-77; Samuel French.

A parable of the political tragedy in Northern Ireland, set in current England and featuring a British couple (he is Northern Irish) who will pay any cost and go through any indignity to preserve their heritage. After two years of trying to have children, Colin and Anne Harding initiate the routine lab tests to check for fertility, follow directions and advice about increasing the likelihood of conception, try strange sexual positions, keep charts and set alarm clocks, and finally succeed with a pregnancy but lose out to miscarriage and hysterectomy. They even endure the humiliation accompanying application to serve as adopted parents to a child, but even here the bureaucracy coldly rules them out. Their dreams of

preserving their heritage are ashes.
    3 acts; 2 men, 2 women (with doubling); bare stage. Royalty: $50-35.

RYER, George W. The Old Homestead. See entry under Thompson, Denman.

RYERSON, Florence. See entries under Clements, Florence Ryerson.

RYSKIND, Morrie. Of Thee I Sing. See entry under Kaufman, George S.

SACKLER, Howard. The Great White Hope (1968). BP 1968-69; Samuel French.
    Based on the life and career of Jack Johnson, the first black heavyweight boxing champion of the world. Johnson, the symbol of black aspiration, wins the championship from Frank Brady in a Reno, Nevada fight (white man's country where large numbers of Negroes will not be spectators) but loses it to another "Great White Hope" a few years later.
    8 men, 3 women, many extras; representational sets. Royalty: $50-35.

SAKI. See Leonard Gershe's Miss Pell Is Missing.

SANDEAU, Jules. The Son-in-Law of M. Poirner. See entry under Augier, Emile.

SARDOU, Victorien. The Black Pearl (1862). Tr. by Clark. French, 1915.
    During a thunderstorm a pearl in a cabinet in a house has disappeared. Christine is accused of the theft. All doubt her except her betrothed, Cornelius, who tracks down the real thief--a bolt of lightning which has melted the medallion.
    3 acts; 7 men, 3 women; 1 interior; Dutch costumes of 1825 may be used, or modern costumes.

_____ and Émile Moreau. Madame Sans-Gêne (1893). Tr. by Reed, Street, & Smith, 1900; French, 1901.
    Catherine Hubscher, a spirited French washerwoman, called Madame Sans-Gêne, became the Duchess of Danzig in Napoleon's court when she married Marshall Lefebvre. She retains her blunt crudities which amuse the court, until she is ordered by Napoleon to retire. She reminds him of his days of struggle 19 years before, in which she shared, and also of his unpaid laundry bill of that time. The Emperor relents and reinstates her.
    Prolog & 3 acts; 21 men, 13 women; 3 interiors; costumes of the period.

_____. Patrie! (1860). Tr. by Clark. Doubleday, 1915; LEV.
    The fatherland is the Netherlands in the time of the Duke of

Alva (1568). The Count de Rysor has three loves: his country, his wife, and his friend Karloo. He plots to capture Brussels and kill Alva and the Spaniards. The plot is betrayed by his wife Dolores, who is also carrying on a liaison with Karloo. To avoid revealing the plot under torture, the Count stabs himself. Karloo discovers it was Dolores who betrayed them; he stabs her and gives himself up to die with the others.

    5 acts; 31 men, 6 women, extras; 4 interiors, 3 exteriors; costumes of the period.

_____. A Scrap of Paper (1860). Tr. & adapted by Simpson. Carried by Baker, Dramatic Pub. Co., & French; abridged in Pierce & Matthews, v. 2.

    Centers around an insignificant but mischievous bit of paper until it is destroyed. It was written by Louise prior to her marriage, and now she fears her husband will find it. Her cousin Suzanne helps her hunt; they find it only to lose it. The excitement continues until the paper is again found and this time done away with.

    3 acts; 6 men, 6 women; 3 interiors.

SAROYAN, William. The Beautiful People (1941). Samuel French.

    The belief that love is the only thing of consequence in the world comes through in this comedy peopled with innocent characters who engage in some of the most impractical activities possible. One, a fifteen-year-old boy writes one-word novels, while the father supports his family by cashing the pension checks of a complete stranger, dead for seven years.

    7 men, 2 women; 1 interior. Royalty: $35-25.

_____. The Cave Dwellers (1957). Samuel French.

    An abandoned theater provides a temporary home for a group of penniless nomads in this comedy about performers who have seen much better times. Although the building is cold and the food is scarce, the main problem these people face is that the theater is soon to be torn down for a housing project. Their difficulties hardly dampen their spirits, however, and they spend their time amusing themselves, as well as the audience, with memories of former days of glory. Among the characters is the Queen, a former actress; the King, who used to be a famous clown; and the Duke, a former prizefight champion. Their adventures together and the stories they tell of earlier adventures results in an innocently humorous comic improvisation.

    9 men, 5 women; bare stage. Royalty: $50-25.

_____. A Decent Birth, A Happy Funeral (1949). Samuel French.

    Death is predicted by the cards of the gypsy girl for Ernest as he goes to war; August is to have a child by the burlesque woman he married. Word comes of Ernest's death and August occupies the coffin for a happy funeral as his wife gives birth to his son.

    3 acts; 11 men, 5 women; 3 interiors. Royalty: $35-25.

_____. Get Away Old Man (1943). Samuel French.

An infinitely wealthy and somewhat degenerate Hollywood producer finds that his money cannot corrupt a young pure-in-heart
writer in this comedy about young love and movie making. Although
the producer can usually buy and despoil any youthful movie aspirant
he wants, he runs into firm resistance from the writer who refuses
to compromise his talents for the promise of wealth. The young
writer's strength bolsters his girlfriend's will to resist, for she too
was the object of the producer's talent-grabbing quest. In the end
the bullheaded producer persists in thinking one can buy the talents
and loyalties of others and exploit them. The writer and his beloved,
however, disavow this carnivorous Hollywood existence and find real
happiness with each other.

8 men, 3 women; 1 interior. Royalty: $35-25.

_____. Love's Old Sweet Song (1940). Samuel French.

Out in California Ann Hamilton, unmarried at 44, receives a
fake telegram from Barnaby Gaul, so that when Jim Doherty, a
pitchman for a patent medicine, appears whistling "Love's old sweet
song" she claims him and he pretends he is Barnaby. The Yearling
family (Pa, Ma, and 14 children) appear from Oklahoma and take
possession of her house, even burn it to the ground, but Georgie
Americanos, the telegraph messenger, and his father rescue her
and reunite Ann and Jim.

20 men, 10 women; 1 interior, 1 exterior. Royalty: $25-20.

_____. My Heart's In the Highlands (1939). Samuel French.

To the family of a fantastically improvident poet comes old
Jasper McGregor, playing so sweetly on his bugle that the neighbors
bring food as a tribute. But Jasper is a runaway from an Old
People's Home, and the guards take him back. Some months later
he returns, just as the family is being evicted for non-payment of
rent. His bugle reverberates the Scottish song as he dies. The
young son of the family is wistful, ingenious, and inquiring, asking
about the meaning of life.

No act divisions; 13 men, 2 women, extras; 1 interior,
divided to show 2 rooms. Royalty: $35-25.

_____. Sam Ego's House (1949). Samuel French.

Sam Ego is America's dream, and his house is the American
nation. He is successful and builds a fine house, but many events
spoil the dream and almost shatter the house. It is moved from its
fine location to a junk yard in the slums. Ironic fun is made of
many things, from Boy Scouts to church pastors.

3 acts (in 7 scenes); 20 men, 4 women, extras; 4 exteriors.
Royalty: $35.

_____. The Time of Your Life (1939). BP 1939-40; Samuel
French.

Pulitzer prize play, 1940. Kindly Joe, drinking and dreaming,
searches for happiness and the answers to the enigma of life in

Nick's waterfront saloon in San Francisco. Many characters pass
in and out. His errand boy Tom, huge and simple, falls in love
with Kitty, a fragile prostitute. Joe almost shoots a vice raider who
threatens Kitty, but Kit Carson, a character out of the Old West,
takes care of that. The play seems a hymn to the joy of life and
is suffused with nostalgic melancholy.
    3 acts; 18 men, 7 women; 2 interiors. Royalty: $50-25.

SARTRE, Jean-Paul. The Condemned of Altona (1959). English
    version of Justin O'Brien. Samuel French carried; Knopf, 1964.
    The head of a German family dynasty, before he dies, forces
his second son, his daughter-in-law, and his daughter to swear that
they will carry on the family tradition. The son and his wife resent their promise because it places them in the bondage of guilt of
the elder son, certified dead, but actually living in the attic. This
son struts about in his Nazi uniform, mumbles into a tape recorder,
and relives his inhuman acts of World War II. The two women convince him that what he thought of as a demolished Germany has now
been resurrected, and he drives off into the night to die.
    7 men, 2 women; 2 interiors.

_____. Dirty Hands (Red Gloves) (1948). Tr. by Abel in his
    Three Plays, Knopf, 1949; adapted & produced in 1948 by Tara-
dash as Red Gloves.
    A young intellectual and political fanatic, Hugo, joins the
communist revolution in Illyria in 1940 and is commissioned to kill
the party leader, Hoederer. He becomes his secretary, but cannot
bring himself to kill him until he sees his wife Jessica kissing
Hoederer's hand. Then he shoots. Hoederer exonerates him by
saying it was only a "crime passionel." When Hugo is released from
prison after two years, he is bitter and disillusioned, for he finds
the Party is following the very program he sought to prevent.
    Prolog, 3 acts, & epilog; 9 men, 2 women; 3 interiors.

_____. The Flies (1943). Samuel French.
    The flies represent the little avenging Furies (Eumenides)
which afflict all in Argos with a sense of guilt and self-condemnation
because of the murder of Agamemnon fifteen years before, and for
which they seek to be condoned. Orestes returns, and, to secure
freedom, plots with Electra to kill Aegisthus and Clytemnestra in
revenge for killing Agamemnon. Introduces Zeus as the supreme
god in which all have some belief and as much allegiance as faith
justifies.
    3 acts; 8 men, 6 women, extras; 2 interiors, 2 exteriors.
Royalty: $25-20.

_____. No Exit (1946). Samuel French.
    Two women and one man are locked up together for an eter-
nity in one horrible room in hell. The windows are sealed, there
are no mirrors, no exit, and the lights can never be turned off.
This is not a hell of fire but of the humiliation of a soul stripped

of all pretenses. Even the blackest deeds are mercilessly exposed
to the fierce light of hell, an eternal hell. And the various sexual
preferences of the trio make physical love impossible.
2 men, 2 women; 1 interior. Royalty: $35-25.

_____. The Trojan Women. See entry under Euripides.

SAUNDERS, James. Next Time I'll Sing to You (1963). BP 1963-
64; Dramatists Play Service.
Five actors grudgingly go through their nightly ritual of
acting a series of philosophical meanderings they don't understand,
which center on Jimmy Mason, the Hermit of Great Canfield, Essex,
who lived in his own loneliness between the years of 1857 and 1942.
Or, as one of the actors puts it, "we are discussing not so much
the man nor even the reason for the man but the reason for the discussion of the reason for the man." Through it all, the miracle of
man's role in the universe is emphasized.
2 acts; 4 men, 1 woman; open stage. Royalty: $35-25.

SCHARY, Dore. The Devil's Advocate (1961). Based on the novel
by Morris L. West. BP 1960-61; Samuel French.
Monsignor Meredith, who has terminal cancer, is sent from
Rome to the Italian countryside to act as Devil's Advocate in the
Cause for Beatification of Giacomo Nerone, who was murdered by
the Communists in 1945 in circumstances which may warrant martyrdom. In his investigation, Meredith meets up with the proposed
saint's illegitimate son and the mother of the boy, a Jewish doctor
who collaborated with the Communists, a countess with a voracious
sexual appetite, and a homosexual painter, who jumps off a mountain-
side wall in front of the priest. Meredith, after giving the painter
Absolution, dies himself of his illness, recommending the investigation of the proposed saint to continue, begging for a Christian burial
for the painter, and requesting that he be buried here among the
people he has recently met. "Here for the first time," he says, "I
have found myself as a priest and as a man."
3 acts; 9 men, 2 women, extras; 5 interiors. Royalty:
$50-25.

_____. Sunrise at Campobello (1958). BP 1957-58; Dramatists
Play Service.
A personal, rather than political, portrait of the pre-White
House days of Franklin D. Roosevelt. The play covers Roosevelt
from 1921, when he was stricken with infantile paralysis at his
Canadian summer home, to 1924, when he was able to stand up at
Madison Square Garden and nominate Al Smith for President.
19 men, 5 women (a few parts can be doubled); interiors.
Royalty: $50-25.

SCHAUFFLER, Mrs. Elsie T. Parnell (1935). French, 1936; FAMJ.
The leader of the Irish party, Charles S. Parnell, falls desperately in love with Mrs. Katharine O'Shea, whose husband is

rather a blackguard, as he uses her merely as a source of money. She promotes Parnell politically and lives with him for nine years. At the peak of Parnell's success in forcing Gladstone's support of Home Rule for Ireland, Capt. O'Shea brings suit for divorce, naming him as co-respondent, thus raising such a scandal that Gladstone withdraws his support. Parnell is driven from the Irish party; he dies shortly after.

3 acts; 13 men, 5 women; 3 interiors; costumes of the period.

SCHILLER, Johann Christoph Friedrich von. The Death of Wallenstein (1800). Tr. by Coleridge in his Works, Bohn, 1903; FRA v. 3; KRE.

Wallenstein was capable but a bit unscrupulous; he commanded the armies of Germany in the 30 Years' War and repelled the invasion of the Swedes under Gustavus Adolphus. To protect himself from enemies in the Emperor's Court who were jealous of him he opened negotiations with the Swedes. When discovered, he was relieved of his command, which was transferred to Octavio Piccolomini. His assassination was arranged and executed by an Irish commander named Butler.

5 acts; 21 men, 4 women, extras; 8 interiors; costumes of the period.

_____. Maria Stuart (1800). Tr. by Mellish in his Works, Bohn, 1901; & in the Weimar ed.; separately, Baker.

Imprisoned by an English court and pronounced guilty, Mary awaits Queen Elizabeth's death sentence. They meet in the park; Elizabeth fears her too much to free her. Mortimer plans an escape, but when the plan is frustrated, he commits suicide. Double-dealing Leicester fails to win either lady as his wife. Mary goes with dignity to her death, having abased Elizabeth in an outburst.

5 acts; 13 men, 4 women, extras; 4 interiors, 1 exterior; costumes of the period.

_____. Wilhelm Tell (1804). Tr. by Martin in his Dramatic Works, Bohn, 1903; CLF-2; FRA v. 3; HARC v. 26; MAU; STA.

The famous Swiss archer, Tell, is ordered by the cold-blooded tyrant Gessler to shoot an apple off his son's head. He does so, remarking that the next arrow was meant for Gessler. Tell is imprisoned but escapes and kills Gessler. This was a signal for revolt; the Austrian tyranny was destroyed, and the Swiss became independent. Wilhelm Tell is the strong self-reliant man who rises and frees himself from oppressors.

5 acts; 20 men, 7 women, 2 boys, extras; 4 interiors, 10 exteriors; costumes of the period (1307).

SCHISGAL, Murray. All Over Town (1975). BP 1974-75; Dramatists Play Service.

In this zany comedy, Dr. Lionel Morris, a psychiatrist who is contemplating becoming a Buddhist, takes on as a special patient in his home a man named Louie Lucas, who has fathered nine

children by different welfare mothers. The trouble is that everyone
believes that a black delivery man named Lewis is Louie. Lewis
plays along, since all he is after is front money which will let him
establish a tapdancing school in the ghetto. Finally this mad house
is filled with this threesome plus the doctor's wife and the military
colonel she's having an affair with, the colonel's wheel-chaired
wife, the doctor's daughter and her social worker boyfriend, servants, hard-of-seeing burglars, and gay business managers.
     12 men, 6 women; 1 interior. Royalty: $50-35.

_____. Luv (1963). BP 1964-65; Dramatists Play Service.
     As Howard Taubman points out, the fun in this play "is lar-
gely in misery." The play opens as Harry Berlin, looking like
something the cat wouldn't drag in, prepares to jump off a bridge
and end his ruined life. Milt Manville, an old friend who is the
picture of prosperity, intervenes. But Milt has his own problems--
his wife won't divorce him so that he can marry the woman he
loves. Ellen, Milt's wife, isn't the happiest of women either.
Milt's plan for ending everybody's frustration is to spruce Ellen up,
palm her off on Harry, and marry the girl of his dreams. Problems
ensue, the more the funnier.
     2 men, 1 woman; 1 interior. Royalty: $50-35.

SCHLITT, Robert. The Egg. See entry under Marceau, Félicien.

SCHNITZLER, Arthur. Anatol (1893). Boni, 1917; Modern Lib.,
   1933; CEW; French carried.
     A series of seven different scenes, centering on a melancholy
philanderer, Anatol, who has a different woman in each scene. He
thinks to find happiness by flying from one to another, but he remains unhappy; his experiences puzzle and worry him.
     7 scenes; 4 men, 7 women; 7 interiors.

_____. Light O'Love (1896). Tr. by Morgan in Drama v. 2,
   1912; DIK-1; TUCG; TUCM; WATI; WATL-1; tr. by Shand,
   Lond., Gey & Hancock, 1914.
     A girl of the people learns her lover, a young man of the
upper classes, has fought a duel for another woman. Realizing she
was but a plaything to him, she kills herself at his grave. Treats
a commonplace theme so artistically as to make a play full of delicate charm and soft melancholy atmosphere.
     3 acts; 4 men, 3 women, 1 girl; 2 interiors.

_____. The Lonely Way (1904). Tr. by Björkman, Kennerley,
   1915; Little, 1922; MOSQ; tr. by Leigh in WHI.
     Julian is spurned by Gabrielle and his son by her because
he thought only of himself. His sister, Johanna, is in love with
von Sala, who is likewise selfish. She drowns herself and he commits suicide. The lonely way is the way of the selfish.
     5 acts; 7 men, 4 women; 2 interiors, 2 exteriors.

_____. La Ronde (1900). English version by Eric Bentley.
Samuel French.
A rondelay of love in ten interlocking scenes, each scene
consisting of two characters. In the first, a soldier and a prostitute; then the soldier and a parlor maid; next the parlor maid and
her wealthy employer. The scenes which follow are: the wealthy
man and his mistress, a married woman; the married woman and
her husband; the husband and a girl of the streets; the girl and her
poet; the poet and an actress; the actress and the count; and, finally the count and the prostitute of scene one.
5 men, 5 women; several scenes. Royalty: $35-25.

SCHULBERG, Budd, with Harvey Breit. The Disenchanted (1958).
Based on the novel by Budd Schulberg. BP 1958-59; Samuel
French.
Depicts the decline of a famous novelist's (F. Scott Fitzgerald's) powers and marriage. Manley Halliday, the novelist, and
his beautiful wife, Jere, find their gay, whirlwind existence disintegrating. Once the most famous writer of his generation, Manley is
so beset by problems that his productivity has practically ceased.
He drinks constantly and tries to write while his wife is in New York
under psychiatric care. Since his financial situation is so bad, Manley agrees to write for a very commercial motion picture which he
considers contemptible. Subjected to unceasing pressures from his
wife and his producer, Manley begins to realize that men delude
themselves when they think they have a second chance. "A first
chance, that's all we have," but by then the realization can do him
no good.
10 men, 4 women, extras; 3 interiors. Royalty: $50-25.

SCOTT, Allan and George Haight. Good-Bye Again (1932). Samuel
French.
A popular novelist and lecturer, Kenneth Bixby, with his
secretary, Anne Rogers, arrives in a Midwestern city where he is
greeted by Mrs. Julia Wilson. She claims undying love though now
married to Mr. Wilson. Kenneth gets into a mess in trying to say
good-bye again to Julia. It might result in his losing Anne, but
the lecture tour goes on.
3 acts; 8 men, 4 women; 1 interior. Royalty: $25.

_____. Joy to the World (1948). Samuel French.
An executive in the production of Hollywood films, Alexander
Soren, broadcasts such a liberal speech that he is fired. The
speech had been prepared for him by Ann in the research department, and it attacked censorship and Hollywood's concern with
matters of little moment. He is at once hired by an independent
idealistic producer and wins Ann. They believe that films should
not only purvey joy, but also present serious matters to the world.
3 acts; 15 men, 5 women, extras; 1 interior. Royalty: $50.

SCRIBE, A. Eugène and Ernest Legouvé. The Ladies' Battle (1851).

Tr. by Coale, DeWitt, 1883, carried later by Dramatic Pub.
Co.; also carried by French.

Two ladies, the Countess and Leonie, fall in love with Henri,
a spy whom they have saved from capture and are employing as a
domestic servant disguised as Charles. As they fight this duel of
love, the Baron comes to arrest him. Gustav de Grignon appears
in Henri's place, but honorably returns to clear the man who has
been arrested in his place. An amnesty saves Henri, the Baron is
defeated, and Henri wins Leonie.

3 acts; 7 men, 2 women, extras; 1 interior; costumes of
the period.

SEARS, Joe. Greater Tuna. See entry under Williams, Jaston.

SEGALL, Harry. Lost Horizons. See entry under Hayden, John.

SELVER, Paul. R.U.R.. See entry under Capek, Karel.

SELWYN, Edgar, with Edmund Goulding. Dancing Mothers (1924).
BP 1924-25.

Ethel Westcourt, known as "Buddy" to her family, gave up an
acting career 20 years ago to raise a family. Now her daughter
Kittens is 19, drinking too many cocktails and visiting bachelors in
their rooms. Her husband, Hugh, spends too many nights on
business in the city, or "in Philadelphia," and has in his manner
toward her not the "tiniest element of sex." All of this turns the
staid and proper mother into a "dancing mother," and soon it is she
who is running in the fast lane, stealing the heart of Gerald
Naughton, the man both her daughter and her husband's mistress
are hotly pursuing. She finally gets the homefront straightened
out, and husband and daughter beg for her to return as their old
"Buddy." But she won't. As Ethel leaves on a trip to Europe, it
doesn't appear that she will ever be back.

4 acts; 13 men, 9 women; 3 interiors.

SERGEL, Christopher. Black Elk Speaks (1976). Based on the
book by John G. Neihardt. Dramatic Publishing Company.

Black Elk has lived the Indian experience from a time before
the white man to the massacre of Wounded Knee. He fought in the
battle against Custer at Little Big Horn. He is the key source for
information on his second cousin, Crazy Horse. The story that is
acted out is the American Indian's plea for justice. It is full of
grief, fear, death and destruction of the original Americans.

2 acts; flexible cast (16, with doubling); area staging.
Royalty: $60-40.

_____. Cheaper by the Dozen (1950). Adapted from the novel by
Frank Bunker Gilbreth and Ernestine G. Carey. Dramatic Publishing Company.

This is an amusing play about a father's attempts to turn his
family of teenage daughters into an efficient, smoothly functioning

organization. Despite his daughters' interest in boys and dates, Dad pushes ahead with better organization for his family. He puts up a chart for the young people to initial after completing each household task, instructs them in taking an "efficient" bath, and levies fines on wasters of electricity. Although the girls don't understand his emphasis on running things smoothly Dad has an imperative reason for it. He has a terminal heart condition and wants them to be able to care for themselves. The play has many humorous as well as some rather moving scenes as the girls and their father move toward a new understanding.

9 men, 7 women; 1 interior. Royalty: $50-35.

_____. Fame (1985). Based on the screenplay by Christopher Gore. Conceived by David De Silva. Dramatic Publishing Company.

New York City's School of the Performing Arts is having auditions for a new freshmen class at the beginning of the play, and putting on a senior class show at the end. In between a variety of kids are changed in some way, including insecure Doris (who changes her name to Dominique), Ralph, Coco, Bruno, Montgomery, and Michael. Even Leroy, who has badgered and been badgered by Mrs. Sherwood, the English teacher, realizes how important this teacher has been in helping him land the job with the top dance company.

2 acts; 9 men, 15 women, extras; bare stage with platforms. Royalty: $60-40.

_____. Meet Me In St. Louis (1948). Based on Sally Benson's novel. Dramatic Publishing Company.

High School Theater Classic, 1945-49 concerning the efforts of five children to force their father to remain in St. Louis instead of moving to New York to accept a better job. Four of the children are attractive girls, and they are afraid they will lose their boyfriends if they move to New York. Also the World's Fair is to open in St. Louis in a few days and the girls, along with their only brother, hate to think of missing that. Father refuses to yield to their pleas, forcing the girls to unite for action. Their schemes, however, almost land the entire family in jail. But as the fireworks signalling the start of the World's Fair go off, they win through to a solution which gets Father that better job there in St. Louis and also straightens out their romantic complications.

7 men, 9 women; 1 interior. Royalty: $35-25.

_____. Our Miss Brooks (1950). Adapted from the original material of R. J. Mann. Dramatic Publishing Company.

High School Theater Classic, 1950-59 about high school English teacher Miss Brooks, with so many troubles that she dreams about her vacation coming up. She has collected travel folders which she discusses with the basketball coach, a sailing enthusiast, who seems to her to be "the man" for her. But then the directorship of the school play is thrust upon her, and she and the coach argue over who gets to practice in the gym. Then his star athlete quits the team to take the male lead in the play. And to top things off, the daughter of the school board president is so bad as the girl lead that Miss Brooks replaces her with a talented nobody. Because of this change the principal becomes involved, and soon Miss Brooks' personal and professional problems are hopelessly inter-tangled until the final curtain. (A musical version is also available.)

     5 men, 12 women; 1 interior. Royalty: $35-25.

————. To Kill a Mockingbird. See entry under Lee, Harper.

————. Up the Down Staircase. See entry under Kaufman, Bel.

————. Welcome to the Monkey House. See entry under Vonnegut, Kurt.

————. Winesburg, Ohio (1960). Based on the novel by Sherwood Anderson. Dramatic Publishing Company.

    Elizabeth Willard, the seriously ill mother of 18-year-old George, is desperately trying to recapture the hopes and dreams of her youth to pass on to her son. She always felt trapped living in a town that was boring and enduring a way of life that was tedious. She grew up in a run-down hotel owned by her father, and married the hotel clerk after her father's death. The money her father left her she has saved as an escape for her son. Due to her illness, George would not leave her, so she makes his leaving possible by recklessly going out into a rainstorm to hasten her death.

    3 acts; 12 men, 4 women; divided interior. Royalty: $50-35.

SERGEL, Kristin. Dino. See entry under Rose, Reginald.

————. The Remarkable Incident at Carson Corners. See entry under Rose, Reginald.

SERGEL, Sherman L. Twelve Angry Men. See entry under Rose, Reginald.

SHAFFER, Anthony. Sleuth (1970). BP 1970-71; Samuel French.

    The five roles in this suspense thriller are played by the two male principals. The setting is the English country home of a famous mystery writer, Andrew Wyke. The play begins with a conversation between the writer and Milo Tindle, who is in love with Andrew's wife. The two engage in a phony robbery at the writer's house, where Milo is killed. But Milo returns in the second act pretending he is a police inspector investigating his own death. By the end of the play he has been murdered all over again.

    2 men; 1 interior. Royalty: $50-35.

SHAFFER, Peter. Amadeus (1981). BP 1980-81; Samuel French.

Old Antonio Salieri, former musical mentor and court composer to the Emperor of Austria, tells a story of passion and intrigue that took place thirty years before, when he claims to have personally destroyed the brilliant Wolfgang Amadeus Mozart, whom he used as a battlefield in waging his war against God. Salieri's vows of virtue and promises of giving glory to God through his musical compositions were mocked, he tells, when God chose instead to be heard through the notes and harmonies created by a boorish, arrogant, amoral, filthy-mouthed former prodigy. In the long dramatic monologue we learn how devastating the sense of mediocrity was on Salieri's life, and how bitterly he accepted his public accomplishments knowing the genius of Mozart's virtually unheard compositions. Salieri sets out to ruin Mozart at court, drive him to the poorhouse, seduce his wife, and cut him off permanently from the wealthy Free Masons who can offer living subsistence. He is successful, and after Mozart's early death Salieri becomes the most famous musician in Europe. Unfortunately, he outlives his fame. By the time he is an old man not only is his music never played but it has been forgotten, while Mozart's compositions resound throughout the world. Old Salieri tries to kill himself and even fails at that.
    2 acts; 12 men, 3 women, extras; unit set with insets.
Royalty: $60-40.

_____. Black Comedy (1965). BP 1966-67; Samuel French.
    An uproarious farce which begins in total darkness (light to the characters). Then a fuse blows and the stage lights come on (darkness to the characters) and the fun begins. What we see is a young sculptor preparing to entertain a wealthy art patron and a prospective father-in-law. To impress both, he moves the expensive furniture from his neighbor's apartment into his own. But when the neighbor returns unexpectedly, he tries to move the furniture back under the cover of darkness and much to the dismay of the gathered guests. During all of this, he must endure the escapades of a former girl friend, hiding in the bedroom.
    5 men, 3 women; 1 interior. Royalty: $50-25.

_____. Equus (1974). BP 1974-75; Samuel French.
    A psychiatrist in a psychiatric hospital is urged to take on one more case: that of a 17-year-old boy who has just blinded six horses with a metal spike. Dr. Martin Dysart begins to work on Alan Strang, to try to unravel the mysterious connection between horses and religion and the boy's sudden violent outburst against creatures he obviously loves. This puzzle is more than the doctor bargained for, and pretty soon Alan's problem is all mixed up in the lack of meaning the doctor finds in his own life. This is a powerful play. The setting is a simple wooden one in which all the characters are present throughout the play.
    5 men, 4 women, 6 actors as horses; basic setting. Royalty: $50-35.

_____. Five Finger Exercise (1958). BP 1959-60; Samuel French.

A German orphan comes to England to tutor the daughter of
a nouveau riche family. He comes hoping to be adopted by both the
new country and the new family. The family, however, is not capable of love, but only of selfish passions. The immigrant sets them
free from restraint. The audience is able to watch, knowingly, as
the innocent tutor slowly comes to know that the pretended family
love is a farce.
      3 men, 2 women; 1 interior. Royalty: $50-25.

_____. The Private Ear and the Public Eye (1962). Samuel
      French.
      A pair of comedies presented together. The first is a ro-
mance in which a boy makes a date with a girl he meets at a concert
and receives coaching for the occasion from a worldly friend. Neither
the coaching nor the girl meets the boy's expectations. The second
features a snappy, eccentric private detective who dresses garishly
and maintains a diet of yogurt and grapefruit. He has been hired to
tail an accountant's wife, but he gives himself away at every turn.
      Each play: 2 men, 1 woman; 1 interior. Royalty for both
      together: $50-25.

_____. The Royal Hunt of the Sun (1966). BP 1965-66; Samuel
      French.
      Deals with the Spanish expedition under Pizzaro to the land
of the Incas. The play shows the crossing of the sea, the climbing
of the mountains, and the meeting of the Inca god. The Inca god
wants to meet the Spanish God and is confused when that God cannot
be seen. There is a slaughter of 3,000 unarmed natives and finally
the murder of the Inca god.
      22 men, 2 women; extras; cyclorama, drops, inset. Royalty:
      $50-25.

_____. White Lies (1967). Samuel French.
      A young man comes to a fortune teller, dragging along his
friend. He doesn't want his fortune told, but he wants to bribe the
fortune teller to frighten his friend so that he will give up his girl
friend to him. The friend sees through the scheme, and both he
and the fortune teller make a discovery about love.
      2 men, 1 woman; 1 interior. Royalty: $50-25.

SHAIRP, Mordaunt. The Green Bay Tree (1932). BP 1933-34;
      Baker, 1933; CEU.
      A revealing drama of social decadence, depicting degenerate
exquisites, spiritually bankrupt dilettantes, flourishing like a green
bay tree. Julian at 8 is adopted by Mr. Dulcimer, rich but utterly
selfish. They live in exquisite luxury. When Julian falls in love
with Leonora, his allowance is cut off. His father kills Mr. Dulcimer, but his influence extends after his death, for Julian returns
to live as Mr. Dulcimer did, without Leonora.
      3 acts; 4 men, 1 woman; 2 interiors.

SHAKESPEARE, William. Anthony and Cleopatra; adapted as All for Love by John Dryden.

_____. As You Like It (ca. 1600). Acting editions readily available; many reading editions, OLI; OXB v. 6; INCH v. 3.

In the lovely Forest of Arden Rosalind's father, the rightful duke, deposed by Celia's father, Frederick, lives in contentment with his followers, among them the melancholy Jaques. There Rosalind goes, when banished from the court, disguised as the boy Ganymede, accompanied by Celia as a rustic maiden and by the witty clown Touchstone. There Orlando has also fled from his cruel brother Oliver, and meeting with the girls, talks ceaselessly to Ganymede about his love for Rosalind, until she finally discloses her identity. Meantime Oliver has had a change of heart toward his brother, falls in love with Celia, and a double wedding takes place, with word also coming that Duke Frederick has restored the kingdom to the rightful duke.

5 acts; 17 men, 4 women, extras; simple exterior scenes; costumes of the period.

_____. A Comedy of Errors; based on The Twins by Plautus.

_____. Hamlet (1602). Acting versions readily available; many reading editions; HARC v. 46; OLI; STA; INCH v. 1; in OXB v. 3; TRE-1, 2 (v. 2); TREA-1.

After he learns that his uncle Claudius has killed his father to become king and marry his mother Gertrude, Hamlet broods and wonders what to do. He hesitates to take action; his calculating consideration exhausts his power of action. Although in love with Ophelia, he pretends madness until she too gets worried, goes mad, and drowns herself. Her brother, Laertes, blames Hamlet and challenges him to a duel. The King has poisoned the tip of one of the foils and also a cup of wine. Both the young men die of the poisoned tip, the mother takes the poisoned cup (intended for Hamlet), and just before he dies, Hamlet stabs and kills the usurping King.

5 acts; 20 men, 2 women, extras; simple interior & exterior scenes; costumes of the period.

_____. Henry the Fifth (1599). Acting editions readily available; many reading editions; INCH v. 2; OXB v. 18.

When Prince Hal becomes king as Henry V, he lays aside the riotous tavern life and the wildness of his youth with Falstaff and his pals (as developed in Henry the Fourth, parts 1 and 2). He proves his virtues, winning the brilliant victory over the French at Agincourt.

5 acts; about 30 men, 4 women, extras; simple interior and exterior settings; costumes of the period.

_____. Julius Caesar (ca. 1601). Acting editions readily available; many reading editions; INCH v. 4; OLI v. 1; in OXB

v. 16.

Cassius persuades Brutus to join the conspirators in the plot against his friend Casesar. This culminates in Caesar's assassination in the Senate on the Ides of March. Mark Antony's funeral oration discredits the assassins, who are defeated at the battle of Philippi by Caesar's friends.

    5 acts; 31 men, 2 women, extras; simple interior and exterior settings; costumes of the period.

_____. King Lear (1605). Acting editions readily available; many reading editions; HARC v. 46; INCH v. 4; OLI v. 1; OXB v. 10.

At the age of 80, Lear, King of Britain, turns his realm over to his two flattering daughters, Goneril and Regan, disinheriting the youngest, Cordelia, since she says she loves him only as becomes a daughter to love her father. Cordelia goes to France, where she marries the King. Meanwhile Lear is being so ill-treated by his two ungrateful daughters that he goes out into the stormy night, attended only by his faithful fool and the Earl of Kent. Cordelia returns from France to try to solace her father, but he has gone mad and dies of grief. Cordelia is defeated and dies in prison; Goneril poisons her sister Regan and takes her own life. Her husband, the Duke of Albany, who has never approved her actions, becomes King.

    5 acts; 17 men, 3 women, extras; simple interior and exterior scenes; costumes of the period.

_____. Macbeth (1606). Acting editions readily available; many reading editions; HARC v. 46; INCH v. 4; OLI v. 2; OXB v. 14.

Macbeth is hailed by three witches as a future King of Scotland, though he is only a thane. Urged on by his unscrupulous wife, he murders King Duncan, and the prophecy is fulfilled. More violence follows as the new King attempts to clear the field of all who might supplant him. The murders torment the conscience of Lady Macbeth until she commits suicide. Macbeth is killed by Macduff in further fulfillment of the witches' prophecy.

    5 acts; 20 men, 6 women, extras; simple interiors and exteriors; costumes of the period.

_____. The Merchant of Venice (ca. 1595). Acting versions readily available; many reading editions; INCH v. 2; OLI v. 1; OXB v. 10.

In order to aid his friend Bassanio to woo Portia at Belmont, the merchant Antonio borrows 3,000 ducats from Shylock and pledges a pound of his flesh. Bassanio is successful at Belmont through his choice of a leaden casket, but Antonio's ships fail to return as expected and his bond is forfeited. On hearing this, Portia, disguised as a young doctor of law, conducts his defense and saves Antonio's life by insisting on the exact terms of the bond—only flesh, but no blood, and neither more nor less than an exact pound.

    5 acts; 17 men, 3 women, extras; simple interior and exterior

scenes; costumes of the period.

_____. A Midsummer Night's Dream (ca. 1595). Acting versions
 readily available; many reading editions; OLI v. 1.
 Written doubtless to celebrate a wedding, strange mixups occur in a forest near Athens during a midsummer night. Puck, the
spritely servant of the fairy king, Oberon, secures a love juice
which shifts the loves of two pairs of Athenians and causes Titania
to fall in love with Bottom the weaver while he wears an ass' head.
Later at the Duke's wedding feast, three weddings are celebrated,
during which the tradesmen present as an interlude a burlesque
version of the play Pyramus and Thisbe.
 5 acts; 13 men, 8 women, extras; simple scenes, mostly exterior; costumes of the period.

_____. Much Ado about Nothing (1599). Acting versions readily
 available; many reading editions; INCH v. 2; OXB v. 18.
 The best remembered plot of the two in this play concerns
Beatrice and Benedick who carry on with each other a merry war of
words and wit, both having foresworn love and matrimony. Their
friends cleverly trick them into becoming lovers, each being told
that the other is pining away of unrequited affection. The other
plot involves Hero, engaged to Claudio, who rejects her at the altar
because of a false impression of her unfaithfulness. Hero faints,
and it is given out that she is dead. Through the local constabula-
ry, Dogberry and Verges, the ruse is discovered, and Claudio
agrees to marry Hero's cousin to atone for Hero's death. At the
altar this time the "cousin" turns out to be Hero herself.
 5 acts; 14 men, 4 women, extras; simple scenes, mostly exterior; costumes of the period.

_____. Othello (1604). Acting editions readily available; many
 reading editions; SMP; in OLI; in OXB v. 5; INCH v. 5; BEB;
 BLO.
 The Moor of Venice, Othello, wins Desdemona as his wife,
and as Commander after a signal victory promotes Cassio as his
chief lieutenant. This arouses the jealousy of Iago who plots revenge. He fosters suspicion in Othello to disgrace Cassio, involving
Desdemona through a handkerchief which his wife Emilia steals and
which he places in Cassio's room. The tortured Othello, believing
her false to him, strangles Desdemona, but when he learns how he
has been duped, he kills himself. When Emilia reveals the villainy
of Iago, he stabs her and is led away to torture and to death.
 5 acts; 10 men, 3 women, extras; simple interior and exterior scenes; costumes of the period.

_____. Richard the Third (1592). Acting editions available; many
 reading editions; INCH v. 1; OXB v. 3.
 The hero and villain of this tragedy, Richard, marches on to
be king. He murders Henry VI and his brother the Duke of

Clarence, and after the death of Edward IV, he has the two young princes (one, Edward V) killed in the Tower, thus gaining the throne as Richard III. Ambitious and ruthless, he executes those who oppose him but he is defeated and slain by the Earl of Richmond at the battle of Bosworth Field.

     5 acts; 30 men, 3 boys, 4 women, 1 girl, extras; simple interior and exterior settings; costumes of the period.

_____. Romeo and Juliet (1591). Acting editions readily available; many reading editions; OLI; SMN; THO; OXB v. 6; INCH v. 1.

A Montague, Romeo, goes to a ball at the Capulets and there sees Juliet. They fall in love. Because of the feud between the two houses, they are secretly married by Friar Lawrence. Returning from the ceremony, Romeo against his will mixes in a street brawl and kills Tybalt, who had previously slain Romeo's great friend Mercutio. For this Romeo is banished from Verona. To avoid a marriage with Paris, which is being forced on her, Juliet takes a sleeping potion given her by Friar Lawrence, which brings on a semblance of death, and she is placed in the Capulet tomb. Romeo, not having received the word about the magic potion, arrives at the tomb and there takes poison and dies. Juliet awakens, finds Romeo dead, and stabs herself. The double tragedy reconciles the two houses.

     5 acts; 16 men, 4 women, extras; simple interior and exterior scenes; costumes of the period.

_____. The Taming of the Shrew (1596). Acting versions readily available; many reading editions; SMR.

Baptista of Padua says his younger daughter, the lovable Bianca, cannot marry until her older sister, the shrewish Katherina, is married. Petruchio of Verona becomes a willing suitor of the willful temperamental young woman. He appears for the wedding in uncouth garments, behaves outrageously, and carries Katherine off to Verona. There he refuses to let her eat, sleep, or dress respectably (all done in reverent care of her), until he has "tamed" her. His high-handedness makes her a more submissive wife, wining a bet with two other men on a test of their wives' obedience. Bianca is won by Lucentio by becoming her tutor in disguise.

     5 acts; 11 men, 3 women, extras; simple interior & exterior scenes; costumes of the period.

_____. The Tempest (1611). Acting versions readily available; many reading editions; HARC v. 46; INCH v. 5; OXB v. 17.

Prospero, the rightful Duke of Milan, lives with his daughter Miranda on a desert isle, where he has drifted, and where through his books he has developed magical powers. He is served by Ariel, a spirit of the air, and by Caliban, a misshapen monster, son of Sycorax, who had been an enchantress there. Prospero by his magic arts raises a tempest which wrecks on the island a ship bearing his usurping brother and others. Ferdinand, son of the King

of Naples, falls in love with Miranda, and after hard trials is accepted as son-in-law by Prospero. He and Ariel foil plots, after
teasing the conspirators with visionary banquets. Antonio asks his
brother's forgiveness, Prospero is restored to his dukedom, and all
sail with favoring winds under Ariel's guidance back to Italy.
     5 acts; 13 men, 1 woman, 1 youth as Ariel, extras; exterior
scenes; costumes of the period.

_____. Twelfth Night (1600). Acting versions readily available;
     many reading editions; MIL; OLI v. 1; INCH v. 5; OXB v. 12;
     BEN.
     The twin sister of Sebastian, Viola, is shipwrecked, dis-
guises herself as a boy, and becomes page to Duke Orsino, with
whom she falls in love. But Orsino is wooing the Countess Olivia
and sends his page (Viola) to convey his love; Olivia, however, is
attracted to the page. When Sebastian arrives, Viola's identity is
revealed, Olivia transfers her affections to Sebastian, and the Duke
transfers his to Viola, so both couples are married. The subplot
attracts as much interest through the famous comic characters;
boisterous Sir Toby Belch, brainless Sir Andrew Aguecheek,
and joyous Maria, who arrange a duel between Sir Andrew and
the supposed page Viola, which neither of them desire. They also
plan the humiliation of the self-important steward Malvolio by making
him think Olivia is deeply in love with him and who ask him to dress
in an outlandish fashion.
     5 acts, 11 men, 3 women, extras; simple interior and exterior
scenes; costumes of the period.

_____. The Two Noble Kinsmen. See entry under Fletcher, John.

SHARKEY, Jack. The Murder Room (1977). Samuel French.
     A mystery-comedy involving the disappearance of Edgar
Hollister, newly married and rich. His bride of one day, Mavis
Templeton Hollister, is already having an affair, and when Edgar
inquires of her whereabouts on their wedding night, she believes
things have gone too far, so she shoots him and hides his body.
Inspector Crandall and Constable Abel conduct the search for his
body, while Lottie the housekeeper, Susan Hollister, Edgar's
daughter who has just come back home after graduating from college, and her fiancé Barry Draper provide a funny interchange of
communication since they too are involved in finding some answers.
Things turn insane when Abel turns out to be Edgar in disguise,
and Inspector Crandall the man Mavis has been plotting and having
an affair with.
     3 acts; 3 men, 3 women; 1 interior. Royalty: $50-25.

SHAW, George Bernard. Androcles and the Lion (1912). Lond.,
     Constable, & Brentano, 1916; in his Nine Plays, Dodd, 1935;
     in his Complete Plays, Constable, 1931. Acting ed., French
     or Baker.
     In the Roman arena the lion remembers the friend who re-
moved the thorn from his foot. Androcles wins the respect of

Caesar, who pardons all the martyrs.
        Prolog & 2 acts; 10 men, 5 women; 1 interior, 2 exteriors;
Roman costumes. Royalty: $50-25.

_____. The Apple Cart (1929). Samuel French.
      In a future time the King of England does almost upset the
proverbial apple cart. The King, tired of being simply a yes man
for the Cabinet decisions, attempts to gain some real authority.
Faced with the antagonism of his Prime Minister, the King threatens
to abdicate and run for a seat in the House of Commons. Then
comes the news that the United States desires to forget its Declaration of Independence and rejoin the British Empire. Such a move
could only increase his problems, so the King, to prevent its occur-
rence, forgets his demands and resumes his position.
        10 men, 5 women; 2 interiors, 1 exterior. Royalty: $50-25.

_____. Arms and the Man (1894). In his Plays, Pleasant,
   Brentano, 1913; in his Complete Plays, Constable, 1931; in his
   Nine Plays, Dodd, 1935. Acting ed., French or Baker.
      With whimsical satire shows the romantic Sergius and "the
chocolate soldier" Bruntschi as without illusions concerning the nature of war. Bruntschi wins Raina; Sergius finds consolation in
marrying the maid.
        3 acts; 4 men, 3 women; 2 interiors, 1 exterior; some mili-
tary costumes. Royalty: $20-15.

_____. Back to Methuselah (1922). Condensed version by Arnold
   Moss. Samuel French.
      The play begins in the Garden of Eden and ranges through
time up to the future of 30,000 years from now. Mr. Moss com-
pressed the original five play cycle into one of conventional length.
        17 characters; various sets. Royalty: $50-25.

_____. Caesar and Cleopatra (Pub. 1899). Brentano, 1899 &
   1913; in his Three Plays for Puritans, Brentano, 1906; in his
   Complete Plays, Constable, 1931; in his Nine Plays, Dodd, 1935;
   abridged in Pierce & Matthews, v. 1; in Theatre Arts for Sep.,
   1950. Act. ed., French or Baker.
      Caesar, weary of war, finds Cleopatra in Egypt. She is a
petulant charmer. He undertakes to establish her on the throne of
Egypt. Her brother's adherents attack, he fights them off, scolds
Cleopatra, and in leaving promises to send Mark Anthony. Shaw
has endeavored to make Caesar more human than history has recorded him.
        5 acts; 18 men, 4 women, extras; 2 interiors, 3 exteriors;
costumes of the period. Royalty: $20-15.

_____. Candida (1898). In his Plays, Pleasant, Lond., Richards,
   & Stone, Chicago, 1898 (later Brentano); Lond., Constable, &
   Brentano, 1905; 1919; Brentano, 1913; in his Complete Plays,
   Constable, 1931; in his Nine Plays, Dodd, 1935; TRE-1, 2, 3;

TREA-3.   Act. ed., French or Baker.

A satire on marriage, offering a sane solution of the eternal triangle.   Candida with tact and intelligence will help her ministerial husband, the Rev. James Morell, to success--for he is the one who needs her love more than the visionary young poet Marchbanks.

3 acts; 4 men, 2 women; 1 interior.   Royalty: $20-15.

_____.   Captain Brassbound's Conversion (1900).   In his Three Plays for Puritans, Brentano, 1906; in his Complete Plays, Constable, 1931; in his Six Plays, Dodd, 1941.   Act. ed., Samuel French.

Captain Brassbound, a sort of freebooter in Morocco, is asked by Lady Cicely and her brother-in-law, Judge Hallam, to escort them through Algeria.   Brassbound is glad to get a chance for revenge on the judge, who is his uncle, and plans to sell him into captivity.   But he falls victim to Lady Cicely's charm and graciousness and seems completely converted from his piratical ways when she secures his acquittal.   He is saved from proposing marriage to her by being summoned back to his ship.   She murmurs: "What an escape."

3 acts; 12 men, 1 woman, extras; 2 interiors, 1 exterior. Royalty: $20-15.

_____.   The Devil's Disciple (1899).   Brentano, 1899 & 1913; in his Three Plays for Puritans, Brentano, 1906; in his Complete Plays, Constable, 1931; in his Nine Plays, Dodd, 1935.   Act. ed., French or Baker.

During the American Revolution the British have captured a New Hampshire town and decide to hang the most prominent citizen, the Rev. Mr. Anderson, as a lesson to the rebels.   They mistake for the parson a godless scamp, Dick Dudgeon, who calls himself the devil's disciple as a protest against the bogus piety of his Puritan mother.   Dick insists on carrying out the imposture but, with the noose around his neck, expecting to die nobly, is delivered by the parson.   Shaw writes calculated insults to Americans and heavy potshots at Puritanism.

3 acts; 10 men, 3 women, extras; 4 interiors, 1 exterior; costumes of the period.   Royalty: $20-15.

_____.   Fanny's First Play (1911).   In his Misalliance, etc., Brentano, 1914; Lond., Constable, 1915; Brentano, 1917; in his Complete Plays, Constable, 1931; in his Nine Plays, Dodd, 1935. Act. ed., Samuel French.

A play within a play.   Unknown Fanny has written a play to the production of which all the well-known (English) critics are invited.   After the performance, the critics all agree they can't say whether it is good or not until they know who wrote it--thus Shaw ridicules his critics.   The plot of Fanny's play concerns the son of the Lilley family who is thrown into jail after a brawl.   Margaret, his fiancée, is also there for hitting a policeman.   While the families feel disgraced, the young people are drawn together still further.

Prolog & 3 acts & epilog; 12 men, 5 women; 3 interiors.
Royalty: $50-25.

_____. Heartbreak House (written 1914; produced 1919). Bren-
tano, 1919; in his Complete Plays, Constable, 1931; in his Six
Plays, Dodd, 1941. Act. ed., Samuel French.
     At Heartbreak House a group of social parasites are assem-
bled, among them Boss Mangan, a business executive. They discuss social and political affairs which might lead to war, as they
did in 1914. A burglar intrudes and passes the hat. Bombs fall;
Mangan and the burglar are the only ones killed.
     3 acts; 6 men, 4 women; 1 interior, 1 exterior; costumes of
the period. Royalty: $50-35.

_____. Major Barbara (1907). In his John Bull's Other Island,
Brentano, 1907; in his Complete Plays, Constable, 1931; in his
Six Plays, Dodd, 1941. Act. ed., French or Baker.
     Barbara Undershaft, daughter of a munitions maker, re-
nounces high society to become a Salvation Army major. To her
dismay she learns that the Army and other charitable organizations
accept money even from the capitalists--income from any source is
desirable, even if tainted. Finally she is ready to accept her
father's dictum that poverty alone is shameful; she marries a man
in the munitions factory.
     3 acts; 9 men, 6 women; 1 interior, 2 exteriors. Royalty:
$50-25.

_____. Man and Superman (1905). Lond., Constable, & Bren-
tano, 1905; Brentano, 1913; in his Complete Plays, Constable,
1931; in his Nine Plays, Dodd, 1935. Act. ed., French or
Baker.
     Jack Tanner, appointed Ann Whitefield's guardian, discovers
she is interested in him romantically; in fact, she has decided to
marry him. He objects to the idea, and warned by his chauffeur,
he flies from her in his motor car. But she aggressively pursues
him and captures him in the mountains of Spain, for she is Every-
woman, the Life Force, which cannot be denied.
     4 acts (but Act 3 is usually omitted in production, showing
Don Juan in hell): 12 men, 5 women, extras; 1 interior, 3
exteriors. Royalty: $20-15.

_____. Pygmalion (1913). In Everybody's 31:577, Nov. 1914; in
Androcles, Overrules, & Pygmalion, Constable, & Brentano,
1916; Constable, Sep. 1920; in his Complete Plays, Constable,
1931; in his Six Plays, Dodd, 1941; Penguin books, 1942. Act.
ed., French or Baker.
     A guttersnipe cockney flowergirl, Eliza Doolittle, is made
over in her speech into a duchess by a Professor of Phonetics, Henry Higgins. She has the sensitivity of the respectable poor; he is
fanatically absorbed in his work and is insensitive to the feelings of
others. He does not face the question: What are you going to do

with me now? The satire on middle-class morality, lifting the un-deserving poor into respectability, as developed by Eliza's father, the dustman, is highly amusing.

    5 acts; 4 men, 7 women, extras; 2 interiors, 1 exterior. Royalty: $50-35.

_____. Saint Joan (1923). Brentano & Macmillan, 1924; in his Nine Plays, Dodd, 1935; Penguin books, 1942; THF. Act. ed., French or Baker.

    Pictures the Maid of Orleans in successive episodes of her life of faith and disillusionment: before Baudrecourt, at the Dauphin's court, her victory of Orleans, the crowning at Rheims, her trial before judges who have fanatic faith in their system. Twenty-five years later her sentence is reversed by Charles VII. The epilog takes place in 1920 when she is canonized.

    6 acts & epilog; 22 men, 2 women, extras; 6 interiors, 1 ex-terior; costumes of the period. Royalty: $50-35.

_____. You Never Can Tell (1898). In his Plays, Pleasant, Lond., Richards, & Stone, Chicago, 1898 (later Brentano); Lond., Constable, & Brentano, 1905, & 1919; sep. Brentano, 1913; in his Complete Plays, Constable, 1931; abridged in Pierce & Matthews, v. 1. Act. ed., Samuel French.

    Satirizes many social conventions, making heroes of wise William the waiter with a pompous lawyer-son and of a struggling young dentist, Mr. Valentine, who falls impetuously in love with Gloria. Unmasks the woman's rights' advocate, Mrs. Clandon, who has failed to make her daughter Gloria impervious to the advances of men, or to control the twins, Dolly and Phil. Mrs. Clandon has brought up her three children in Madeira, away from their father and has taken her maiden name; so they demand to know who their father is. He turns out to be Valentine's landlord, Fergus Crampton.

    4 acts; 6 men, 5 women; 2 interiors, 1 exterior. Royalty: $20-15.

SHAW, Irwin. Children from Their Games (1963). Samuel French.

    A modern misanthrope has a thousand grievances with the world, and he takes great pleasure in playing back to it, on his re-corder, the awful sounds of the city. He wants to end it all but has theological reasons against suicide. He tries to persuade an army buddy to kill him, but the friend has married money and doesn't wish to throw it all away on a murder rap. And people keep getting in the way of his hoped-for death: a quack doctor, a daughter-in-law, a pro football player, and a widow who bribes him with 1,000 phonograph records and the knowledge of a bar that sells sixty-five cent martinis. For every step toward destruction he takes he meets frustration.

    5 men, 2 women; 1 interior. Royalty: $50-25.

_____. The Gentle People (1939). Dramatists Play Service.

A Brooklyn fairy tale in which the meek seem justly to triumph. Two old pals, Jonah and Philip fish off Steeplechase pier; they are saving up for a boat to travel South to the Gulf. Harold Goff, a Brooklyn racketeer gangster, makes them pay $5 a week for protection; makes passes at Stella, Jonah's daughter; and learning they have saved up $190 toward the boat, he takes that too. Though they appeal to the law, a crooked judge dismisses the case. Outraged, the pair plan a way to be rid of Goff. They take him for a boatride, knock him off, and toss him overboard. They recover their savings and a bit more, and dream again of their cruise to the tropics. Their crime is never discovered.

10 men, 3 women; 3 interiors, 2 exteriors. Royalty: $35-25.

_____. The Survivors. See entry under Viertel, Peter.

SHAW, Robert. The Man in the Glass Booth (1968). BP 1968-69; Samuel French.

A rich New York real estate operator boasts of his German Jewishness and carries a handgun for his protection. But when Israeli agents track him down to take him home to stand trial for war crimes as a Nazi killer of Jews he surrenders meekly to them. In his glass booth he confesses to being a Nazi killer and guilty of all counts, but this mask is ripped off him by a Jewish woman who remembers him--not as a Nazi, but as a Jew like herself.

18 men, 3 women; 3 interiors. Royalty: $50-35.

SHEARMAN, Alan. Bullshot Crummond. See entry under House, Ron.

SHELDON, Edward. The Boss (1911). QUIK; QUIL.

Courageous boss Regan, devoted to his standards, attracts Emily, his wife, through his strength of character, getting first pity, then sympathy, and finally love.

4 acts; 13 men, 4 women; 3 interiors.

_____. The Jest. See entry under Benelli, Sem.

_____. The Nigger (1909). Macmillan, 1910.

One of the first plays to deal with the social problem of the Negro. Portrays the tragic discovery by a Southern Governor that he is the grandson of a Negress. Introduces as issues connected with the Negro question: lynch law, prohibition, and political disfranchisement.

3 acts; 11 men, 3 women, extras; 2 interiors, 1 exterior.

_____. Romance (1913). French, 1914; Macmillan, 1924; BAK; Baker carried; BP 1909-1919.

Pictures the love of a young rector in New York for an Italian opera singer and its purifying effect upon her. Unites realism harmoniously with romantic passion.

Prolog, 3 acts, & epilog; 12 men, 9 women, 4 interiors;
costumes of 1860. Royalty: $25.

SHELLEY, Elsa. Pick-Up Girl (1944). BP 1943-44; Dramatists Play
Service, 1946.
A sociological study of sex delinquency among New York
teenage girls during WW II. Elizabeth Collins, 15, has been arrested in her family's apartment along with a middle-aged man she
had been "entertaining." She has already had an abortion, and
she now has syphilis. There are many reasons suggested for her
behavior: her father has had to move to California to find work;
her mother's job requires her absence from the home until late at
night; the other children in the family cause a heavier workload for
a teenage girl than is reasonable; with no one at home to look out
for her she has fallen in with a fast and wild group. At the end of
the play Elizabeth prooves how adult and conscientious she can be
when she makes a personal sacrifice for a neighbor boy, Paul, who
loves her.
3 acts; 10 men, 9 women; 1 courtroom interior.

SHEPARD, Sam. Buried Child (1979). Dramatists Play Service.
An absurdist view of the American family, set in a squalid
farm in rural Illinois. Dodge, 70, sits on the couch and drinks.
Hallie, his wife, goes on overnight drinking bouts with a local
minister. Tilden, a middle-aged son who was once an All-American
fullback, is now a semi-idiot. Bradley, the other living son, wears
a wooden leg for the one he lost to a chain saw. A third son,
Ansel, a soldier, died mysteriously in a motel room. Into this madness Tilden's son Vince appears with his girlfriend Shelly, and the
reason for the family's misery and suppressed violence is revealed:
years ago Dodge took a baby born to his promiscuous wife, drowned
it like a puppy, and buried it in the backyard. At the end of the
play Tilden digs the body up, Dodge dies willing the farm to Vince,
and the young grandson sends Shelly away so that he can take his
rightful place in the family. His first act is to torment Bradley,
who is crawling on the floor trying to get possession of his wooden
leg.
3 acts; 5 men, 2 women; 1 interior. Royalty: $50-40.

_____. Fool for Love (1983). BP 1983-84; Dramatists Play Ser-
vice.
In a drab motel room at the edge of the Mojave Desert, Eddie
and May argue and abuse one another, alternately throwing one another out and physically restraining one another from leaving. They
have done this before; they always find themselves doing this; they
are, Eddie claims, connected: "We'll always be connected. That
was decided a long time ago." The violence of the relationship is
witnessed by an Old Man, whom no one but Eddie sees and hears,
who frequently comments on the action, sometimes correcting the
stories that are told, or doubting that events actually occurred. He
may be the father of both Eddie and May, who were originally

brought together when May's mother tracked down the "other" family headed by her bigamous husband. Eddie's mother may have killed herself to keep her son and his half-sister apart. At the end of the play Eddie disappears, as he apparently always does, leaving May once again to her own devices. The Old Man is victorious in his desire to keep the couple from coming together.

    1 act; 3 men, 1 woman; 1 interior. Royalty: $50-40.

SHERIDAN, Richard Brinsley. The Rivals (1775). Acting editions readily available; BRI v. 1; DIB v. 9; INCH v. 19; MOR; NET; OXB v. 1; STM; TUQ; TWE; UHL.

    A country squire, Bob Acres, is a willing rival to Capt. Jack Absolute for the hand of a romantic young lady, Lydia Languish. She wants to elope with Ensign Beverley, the lower rank which Capt. Jack assumes to win her. A duel is arranged, but when Acres finds that Beverley is his friend Capt. Jack, he calls the match off and relinquishes all claims to Lydia. Her aunt, Mrs. Malaprop, has become famous for her blunders in the use of words.

    5 acts; 9 men, 5 women; 5 interiors, 4 exteriors (reducible to 2 interiors, 2 exteriors); costumes of the period.

        . The School for Scandal (1777). Acting editions readily available; BRI v. 2; CLA; CLF v. 1; COF; COH; HARC v. 18; HUD; LIE; MAT; MOO; MOSE v. 2; NET; RUB; SMO; STA; STM; TAU; THO; TREA-1; TUQ; TWE; UHL.

    Young Lady Teazle, married to older Sir Peter but quarreling with him, joins the scandal-mongers: Sir Benjamon Backbite, Lady Sneerwell, and Mrs. Candour in their discussions of London high society. The two brothers, Joseph and Charles Surface, are contrasted: Joseph is hypocritical and making advances to Lady Teazle; Charles is goodnatured but extravagant. When their uncle Sir Oliver returns from India and poses as needing help, Joseph refuses, alleging the stinginess of his rich uncle; Charles is willing to help by selling the family portraits--all save the one of his uncle. In the famous screen scene, Joseph is completely exposed as a villain, and Sir Peter and Lady Teazle are reconciled.

    5 acts; 13 men, 4 women, extras; 7 interiors; costumes of the period.

SHERMAN, Martin. Bent (1979). BP 1979-80; Samuel French.

    Max is a homosexual German living in the 1930's during the Third Reich. His appetite for variety and violence has caused one of his pickups to be murdered in his apartment, and the authorities arrest him and his longtime lover, Rudy. On the train to Dachau, Max not only claims not to know Rudy, but helps to kill him. Later, he has intercourse with a murdered 13-year-old girl to prove his heterosexuality (though at first it appeared he was going to be "bent,") and wins a yellow star ("Jew") on his prison uniform rather than a pink triangle ("Queer"). At the prison, he uses sexual favors to bribe the guards into assigning him Horst, a homosexual inmate, with whom he has daily "sexual encounters" during their three-minute work breaks without actually touching. When Horst is given the "hat treatment" (his hat is thrown into the high-voltage electric fence where he must either electrocute himself in retrieving it or be shot), Max takes off his yellow star jacket, puts on Horst's pink triangle one, and deliberately walks into the fence.

    2 acts; 11 men; various simple interiors and exteriors. Royalty: $50-40.

SHERRIFF, R. C. Home at Seven (1950). Samuel French.

    The Prestons are happily, respectably, and dully married. The husband, David, works in the city but always returns from the office at 7 o'clock. Mrs. Preston always has his tea ready at that time. But one day David stays away for twenty-four hours. His wife fears an "interest" somewhere, but it turns out that David lost his memory momentarily. He does, however, try to hide the fact that he stopped for some sherry at a hotel on his way home. But complications arise: the club's money is missing, the club steward murdered, and the crimes committed during David's lapse and disappearance.

    5 men, 2 women; 1 interior. Royalty: $35-25.

_____. Journey's End (1928). BP 1928-29; Samuel French.

    Pictures the effect of war on a group of young English officers in a dug-out in World War I. Young Raleigh is bewildered by the metamorphosis of Capt. Stanhope, his school hero, into a hardened drinker and ruthless soldier. Stanhope's pose is abandoned when Raleigh is wounded, for it was his way of enduring the war. Stanhope comforts Raleigh before he dies.

    10 men; 1 interior. Royalty: $50-25.

_____. A Shred of Evidence (1960). Samuel French.

    A hit-and-run accident threatens to destroy Richard Medway's recently won business success in this mystery. Although he can recall no accidents, Richard's car is dented and a man attempts to blackmail him, claiming he can prove Richard was the driver. Finally Richard confesses and faces imprisonment, but a last minute discovery of a shred of evidence changes the course of the play.

    6 men, 3 women; 1 interior. Royalty: $35-25.

_____. St. Helena (1936). Lond., Gollancz, 1934; Stokes, 1935; BP 1936-37; FAMI.

    Covering the last seven years of Napoleon's exile, depicts various episodes as revealing the character of the military genius, now an aged warrior. He insists on being addressed as Emperor, he sees pitiful quarreling among his friends, and he suffers minor persecutions by the British government.

    3 acts; 20 men, 4 women; 4 interiors, 2 exteriors; costumes of the period.

SHERWOOD, Robert E. Abe Lincoln in Illinois (1938). BP 1938-39; Dramatists Play Service.

Pulitzer prize play, 1939. Episodes in his life from New Salem days up to his departure for Washington in 1861. Shows a maturing and apprehensive young man slowly realizing the great destiny before him. Presents Mary Todd's persistent pursuit and capture of a coming great man; his anti-slavery debates with Douglas; his desperate hope that he would not be elected; his dejected departure for Washington; his growing conviction that the ideals of liberty and equality are not decadent nor doomed.

12 scenes; 25 men, 7 women; 7 interiors, 3 exteriors; costumes of 1830 through 1861. Royalty: $35-25. (Almost any scene can be done as a one-act with a fee of $10.)

_____. Idiot's Delight (1936). BP 1935-36; Dramatists Play Service.

Pulitzer Prize play, 1936. A group of guests--an English couple, a German scientist, a French Communist, a munitions magnate, vulgar but lovable Harry Van and his troupe of chorus girls--are at a small winter resort in the Alps, where an air raid threatens and finally comes. Exposes the idiocy of war; an ironic picture of man who brings about wholesale destruction by war and can make only a futile gesture against the forces he has set in motion.

3 acts; 17 men, 10 women, extras; 1 interior. Royalty: $35-25.

_____. The Petrified Forest (1935). BP 1934-35; Dramatists Play Service.

On his way to the Petrified Forest, where he anticipates death and burial in a defunct world, Alan Squire, a disillusioned intellectual, stops at a lunch room in Arizona where Gabby is the waitress. Duke Mantee and his gangsters come to hide out there. Alan finds Gabby a worthwhile dreamer and signs over his life insurance to her before he welcomes being shot by Mantee.

2 acts; 18 men (several bit parts), 3 women; 1 interior. Royalty: $35-25.

_____. The Queen's Husband (1928). Scribner, 1928; Longmans, 1929; French, 1932.

A courageous king is ruler of all the people of the land except one--his wife--in this romantic comedy. Princess Anne loves her father's secretary, Granton, but her mother insists she marry a strange prince. But her father, King Eric VIII, helps her elope with Granton, and then goes bravely to face his wife's displeasure.

11 men, 4 women; extras optional; 1 interior.

_____. Reunion in Vienna (1931). BP 1931-32; Dramatists Play Service.

Reassembles, after ten years, a group of exiled Austrian royalists. Former mistress Elena of the wild Hapsburgian crown prince Rudolph, now the wife of an eminent psychiatrist Dr. Krug, is advised by her husband to cure her old infatuation with Rudolf by renewing contact with its inspiration. She succumbs, but only

for one night. Morning brings reality; she returns to her husband;
Rudolf returns to his taxicab in Nice.
     3 acts; 23 men, 7 women; 2 interiors. Royalty: $35-25.

_____. The Road to Rome (1927). BP 1926-27; Samuel French.
     Amytis, the flighty, beautiful wife of Fabius the Dictator,
decides to see Hannibal, whose troops have surrounded Rome, rather
than to flee to her mother in Ostia. He falls for her instead of killing her. Amusing satire on the stolid Roman senators, giving as
good a reason as any why Hannibal failed to capture the city.
     3 acts; 22 men, 3 women; 1 interior, 1 exterior. Royalty:
$35-25.

_____. The Rugged Path (1946). BP 1945-46. Charles Scrib-
ner's Sons, 1946.
     Morey Vinion, the editor of an urban newspaper, has had
enough experience as a correspondent in Europe to believe his
paper must editorialize in favor of lend-lease for Russia in
1941. As a result of his stand and the local business community's
reaction, he quits the paper and joins the Navy, where he serves
as a cook on a destroyer that is sunk in the Pacific by the Japanese.
His raft carries him to the Philippines, where he volunteers to serve
with Task Force Zero, a small group of Americans and Filipinos
working toward the eventual return of U.S. forces. It is here,
and on his lost destroyer, that his faith in the American people is
restored. Morey dies in action, and his wife, Harriott, on whom
the President confers his Medal of Honor, presents it to the
Philippine people.
     2 acts; 21 men, 3 women, extras; 6 interiors, 1 exterior.

_____. Second Threshold. See entry under Barry, Philip.

_____. Small War on Murray Hill (1959). Dramatists Play Ser-
vice.
     A comedy about the American Revolution. Sherwood hypothe-
sizes on why British General Sir William Howe tarried at the home
of Mrs. Robert Murray instead of driving a wedge between the armies of Generals Isaac Putnam and George Washington, and thereby
defeating the American patriots. Sherwood suggests that the de-
laying tactics of Mrs. Murray consisted of unique cocktails, an excellent creole lunch, bright conversation, good brandy, a steamed
clam dinner, and her own beauty.
     10 men, 3 women, 8 non-speaking men, 5 non-speaking
women; unit set. Royalty: $50-25.

_____. There Shall Be No Night (1940). BP 1939-40; Drama-
tists Play Service.
     Deals with the Nazi invasion of Finland. Pulitzer Prize, 1941.
Eric, the son of a patriotic Finnish scientist with an American wife,
marries Kaatri. He is killed in the Russian invasion of Finland.
Kaatri goes to America to carry on. Uncle Waldemar philosophizes

on the struggle of man for freedom versus war with its ignorance
and bestiality; he emphasizes faith and courage of free men everywhere and the essential soundness of democracy. Rich in wisdom
and pity, fired with the flame of indignation.
>   13 men (2 bits), 4 women (2 bits); 3 interiors. Royalty:
> $35-25.

————. Tovarich. See entry under Deval, Jacques.

SHIPMAN, Samuel and John B. Hymer. East Is West (1918).
>   French, 1924.
>   Billy Benson persuades a Chinese merchant from San Francis-
co at the auction in China, to buy Ming Toy instead of letting her
go to Charlie Yong, a trafficker in maids. So she is taken to San
Francisco and becomes a maid in the Benson household. Billy declares his love for Ming Toy, but the family objects. When Charlie
Yong comes with three tong men, Hop Toy, her supposed father,
reveals that Ming is not his daughter but was stolen as a babe from
some American people in China.
>   Prolog & 3 acts; 13 men, 5 women, extras; 2 interiors, 1
>   exterior; some Chinese costumes.

SHUE, Larry. The Foreigner (1985). BP 1984-85; Dramatists Play
>   Service.
>   A situation farce in which a Britisher named Charlie is left
for a few days at a rundown fishing lodge resort in Georgia. He
is so shy that his friend Froggy establishes a cover story that
Charlie is a "foreigner" who understands no English and is distressed when anyone tries to speak to him. Charlie, therefore,
hears about all of the mischief going on around him--how the Rev.
David Marshall Lee has got his fiancée, Catherine, pregnant, is
pursuing her only for her inheritance, is determined to cheat her
somewhat slow-witted brother out of his share of the family fortune,
and is trying to drive the woman who owns the lodge out of the
business so that he can set up headquarters for the Georgia Ku
Klux Klan. By the end of the play Charlie has saved the good
people, chased off the bad, destroyed the plans of the evil minister,
and is beloved by everyone (especially Catherine, who will give
him "all the time in the world" to learn to speak English).
>   2 acts; 5 men, 2 women; 1 interior. Royalty: $50-40.

SHYRE, Paul. The Child Buyer (1962). Adapted from John Her-
>   sey's novel. Samuel French.
>   How a joint government and giant corporation scheme to "buy"
child prodigies and give them special training is analyzed in this
science fiction drama. The corporation has a fifty-year defense contract and needs some super-intelligent specially educated children.
Their plan is to buy young prodigies, wipe out their memories, and
retrain them electronically, teaching nothing but science. The process, however, atrophies their senses, making them nothing but
human-like computers. At first citizens are horrified, but the child

buyer has unlimited amounts of purchase money and teachers. Finally one boy does submit, but only because he believes he can beat the system.

10 men, 4 women, 1 child; 1 interior. Royalty: $35-25.

_____. Pictures in the Hallway (Dramatic Reading) (1956). Adapted from the autobiography of Sean O'Casey. Samuel French.

In this section of O'Casey's early autobiography we find him in his first confrontation with women; in the episodes and skirmishes of the Irish Rebellion; in his first disastrous job at a book store; and in his first acquaintance with a family death. O'Casey makes a momentous decision here to move into the thick of life and mold his own impression on history.

4 men, 2 women; no scenery. Royalty: $50-25.

_____. U.S.A. See entry under Don Passo, John.

_____. A Whitman Portrait (Stage Reading) (1967). Dramatists Play Service.

A sketch of Walt Whitman, the poet and the man, from his early days in Brooklyn, through the Civil War, to his death. Both prose and poetry are included which emphasize Whitman's faith in man, his great humanitarianism, and his buoyant optimism. Brooks Atkinson wrote: "It is a portrait of not only a stirring American poet but of an exultant American nation."

3 men, 1 woman; unit set; incidental music included. Royalty: $35-25.

SIGURJÓNSSON, Jóhann. Eyvind of the Hills (1911). Tr. by Schanche in Modern Icelandic Plays, American-Scandinavian Foundation, 1916.

Halla loves the real character of the heroic Eyvind and elects to share with him the enforced outlaw life and hardships of a bleak wilderness. An intense inner life is revealed with poetic vision which creates actual flesh and blood, exalted with noble passion.

4 acts; 7 men, 5 women, 2 children, extras; 2 interiors, 2 exteriors, old Icelandic costumes.

_____. The Hraun Farm (1908). Tr. by Schanche in Modern Icelandic Plays, American-Scandinavian Foundation, 1916; in Smith, Short Plays.

Sveinung, a patriarch, the owner of the farm with a lava field on it, is torn between his love for the homestead and his daughter. He wants her to marry his neighbor's son who would keep up the estate. The tearful pleading of his wife wins his consent to the daughter's marriage to the man she loves, Sølvi, a geologist.

3 acts; 6 men, 6 women, 2 children; 3 exteriors.

_____. Loft's Wish (1915). Tr. by Johnson in Poet Lore, v. 46,

1940.

As an Icelandic Faust, Loft sells his soul to the Devil. He employs black magic to destroy Steinunn in order to marry Disa. Steinunn commits suicide, which drives Loft mad and on to his death. He fails because of his selfishness.

2 acts; 5 men, 4 women, 1 girl, extras; 1 interior; costumes of early 18th century in Iceland.

SILLS, Paul. Story Theatre (1970). Based on fables from Aesop and the Brothers Grimm. Samuel French.

Adult theater which dramatizes the stories of Henny Penny, The Golden Goose, Venus and the Cat, the Fisherman and his Wife, the Robber Baron, the Bremen Town Musicians, and others.

5 men, 3 women; stage projections. Royalty: $50-35.

SIMON, Neil. Barefoot in the Park (1963). BP 1963-64; Samuel French.

After a six-day honeymoon, a new lawyer, who has just won his first case (six cents in damages), and his young wife, who is as pretty and befuddled as can be, move into a new high-rent apartment that she has chosen. They find as many problems, however, for in order to get to the apartment one has to climb six steep flights of stairs. Once in the apartment there are more troubles: the paint job is atrocious, there is no furniture, the skylight leaks snow, and there is no room for a double bed. There is also an un-believeable gourmet who lives in a loft on the roof and uses the window ledge and the apartment as his only access to his perch. The situation breaks the heart of the young lawyer. His wife kicks him out when he refuses to walk barefoot in the snow in the park. He returns, not for reconciliation, but because he thinks that since he pays the rent she should be the one to go.

4 men, 2 women; 1 interior. Royalty: $50-35.

_____. Biloxi Blues (1985). BP 1984-85; Samuel French.

Part two of the author's autobiographical memory play dealing with Eugene Morris Jerome, a young and innocent Brooklyn boy, who is drafted into the WW II army and sent to Biloxi, Mississippi for basic training. He vows to use this new opportunity to (1) lose his virginity, (2) stay alive, and (3) become a successful writer. In one scene he accomplishes the first goal, and in another he gets into trouble with the other recruits when his journal (highly sensi-tive entries on everyone in the platoon) is discovered and read out loud, including such insights as who Eugene believes to be merely an animal and therefore a prime candidate for a Medal of Honor, and who is complex and fascinating but probably a homosexual. By the end of the play the ruthless discipline of Sergeant Toomey has forced everyone to drop a little of their personalities, but the train-ing has little effect on their essential characters. (Note: The first play in this sequence is Brighton Beach Memoirs.)

2 acts; 6 men, 2 women; various sets. Royalty: $60-40.

_____. Brighton Beach Memoirs (1984). Samuel French.

Part one of the author's autobiographical memory play, dealing with the life of young Eugene Morris Jerome growing up in a
working class Jewish home in Brighton Beach, Brooklyn in the late
1930's. The Jeromes have taken in widowed Aunt Blanche and her
two daughters, and what the family lives on is mostly love, when
what they need is money. At the end, the good news (besides
Eugene's acquisition of a porno postcard) is that a cousin with a
wife, mother, and four children has escaped from Poland and will
be joining the household. (Eugene goes off to World War II basic
training in the second play, Biloxi Blues.)

 2 acts; 3 men, 4 women; combined interiors/exterior set.
Royalty: $60-40.

_____. California Suite (1977). BP 1976-77; Samuel French.

Four playlets set in the same suite in a Beverly Hills hotel.
In "Visitor from New York," a divorced couple, Hannah and Billy
Warren, argue in witty one-liners over who their teenage daughter
will live with for the coming year. The daughter wants to stay
with her father in California. Hannah wants her in the East with
her, though she reluctantly gives up her claim. In "Visitor from
Philadelphia," Marvin Michaels is caught by his wife with a hooker
in his room (a gift from his brother). Millie, the wife, will forgive,
forget, understand, never mention it again, but will go immediately
into Beverly Hills and spend every cent Michael has. In "Visitors
from London," an aging British actress, accompanied by her bi-
sexual husband, fails to receive the Academy Award she was nominated for. In "Visitors from Chicago," two couples who started off
as best friends have destroyed their relationship and parts of their
bodies in what appears to be the most horrible vacation anybody has
ever experienced.

 2 acts; 2 men, 2 women; 1 interior. Royalty: $50-40.

_____. Chapter Two (1978). BP 1977-78; Samuel French.

George Schneider, a novelist in his 40's, is trying to fit
together the pieces of his life since his wife Barbara died. He has
already collapsed, sought therapy, and toured Europe alone. He is
ready for Chapter Two, which his brother Leo is helping out with,
making sure that George keeps meeting eligible women. Jennie
Malone, an actress getting over a divorce, receives the same kind of
support from her friend Faye. Leo and Faye get George and Jennie
together, and though both believe it is too early to become involved
in a serious relationship, they fall in love and marry within two
weeks. It was, however, too early. George's guilt won't let him
alone, and Jennie's personality won't permit her to be like Barbara.
They part, then come back together for a new beginning. They will
find an "Our" place to live, and George will work on his new novel,
"Chapter One."

 2 acts; 2 men, 2 women; composite interior. Royalty: $50-
40.

_____. Come Blow Your Horn (1961). Samuel French.

Harry Baker, owner of a large artificial fruit business, has two sons. Alan, a thirty-three year old playboy, works two days and plays five--usually accompanied by beautiful girls. Buddy, twenty-one, has been up to now an obedient son. But he asserts himself too, leaving a rebellious letter for his father and moving into his older brother's bachelor pad. Comic complications follow.

3 men, 4 women; 1 interior. Royalty: $50-25.

_____. The Gingerbread Lady (1971). BP 1970-71; Samuel French.

Evy Meara is a pop singer, gone to pot from too much alcohol and sex. When the play opens, she is nearing the end of a ten-week "drying out" period. A lady friend, a homosexual actor, a daughter, and a former lover all try to help her adjust to her new sober life, but they leave her worse off than before, and by the end of the play Evy Meara is definitely off the wagon.

3 men, 3 women; 1 interior. Royalty: $50-35.

_____. The Good Doctor (1974). BP 1973-74; Samuel French.

A play made up of vignettes from the short stories of Anton Chekhov: a scolding woman who berates a bank manager for his gout and lack of money, a father who takes his son to a place where he can be initiated into the mysteries of sex but then loses his nerve and abandons his son there, a man who offers to drown himself for three rubles. The principal role is that of Writer--a composite of Chekhov and Neil Simon himself.

2 men, 3 women; various settings. Royalty: $50-35.

_____. I Ought to Be in Pictures (1980). BP 1979-80; Samuel French.

Herb Tucker is a rather down and out Hollywood script writer, married three times and not anxious to commit to Steffy, who spends every Tuesday night with him. He is surprised by a visit from his 19-year-old daughter, Libby, whom he has not seen since she was three. Libby has hitchhiked from New York to touch base with her father and to break into movies as an actress. Herb's one-liners, which seem to be his way of keeping the world at bay, don't work on Libby, who claims to get her ideas from her deceased grandmother, who was both mother and father to her. Finally Libby breaks through to Herb in a way that no person apparently ever has. She improves his life, gets him on the right track again, and leaves for home on foot with a backpack just the way she arrived.

2 acts; 1 man, 2 women; 1 interior or wagon. Royalty: $50-40.

_____. Last of the Red Hot Lovers (1970). BP 1969-70; Smauel French.

Barney Cashman is forty-seven years old and has been faithful to his wife for 23 years. He decides to join the Sexual Revolution before it's too late for him, but it turns out that he is just too

gentle, or too inexperienced, to pull it off. His first attempt at
adultery (with a sex-pot) fails when he takes her to his mother's
apartment. His second (with an actress) and third (with his wife's
best friend) are also unsuccessful.
        1 man, 3 women; 1 interior. Royalty: $50-35.

_____. The Odd Couple (1965). BP 1964-65; Samuel French.
        The boys are gathered in the messy apartment of one of the
group, recently divorced. They are waiting for another member
who is late. When they discover that his wife has just left him,
they fear he might commit suicide, and so they lock all of the windows and take other precautions. When he does arrive, he decides
to stay and live with the resident of the messy apartment. Then
the patterns of their former marriages begin to reappear. One man
is too meticulous--the other too much a slob. They even quarrel
over the necessity to telephone if one will be late for dinner. A
hilarious comedy.
        5 men, 2 women; 1 interior. Royalty: $50-35.

_____. Plaza Suite (1968). Samuel French.
        Three playlets about marraige, all taking place in the same
suite at the Plaza Hotel. In the first, a couple discovers that the
suite they have taken while their house is being painted is the same
one they honeymooned in 23 or 24 years ago. Their anniversary is
today, according to one, and yesterday according to the other. In
the second play a thrice-married Hollywood producer arranges a
meeting with a childhood sweetheart (now a suburban housewife) for
a little sexual diversion. She turns out to be more than he bar-
gained for. In the last play a mother and father try to get their
daughter out of the locked bathroom and down to the ballroom for
her wedding.
        7 men, 5 women; 1 interior. Royalty: $50-35.

_____. The Prisoner of Second Avenue (1972). BP 1971-72;
    Samuel French.
        Sympathetic humor over the plight of a well-paid executive
named Mel. He loses his job in a company rift. His wife takes a
job to tide them over, but she loses hers too. Pollution is killing
everything that grows outside on the terrace, the paper-thin walls
of the high-rise they live in reveal everything they never wanted to
know about the lives of the German stewardesses next door, burglars hit their apartment, and Mel's psychiatrist dies with $23,000
of his money. Mel does the only thing left to do--he has a nervous
breakdown. Then he recovers from it, getting stronger and surviving in spite of his troubles.
        2 men, 4 women; 1 interior. Royalty: $50-35.

_____. The Star-Spangled Girl (1966). Dramatists Play Service.
        Andy Hobart and Norman Cornell struggle to put out a pro-
test magazine in their combination office-apartment in San Francisco.
The two endure near-starvation, threatening calls from their unpaid

printer, and (to keep Mrs. Mackininee, the landlady, from asking for the rent) dates with a middle-age woman who wants to go motor-cycling, surfing, and sky-diving. Into the lives of the two young radicals comes Sophie Rauschmeyer, a Deep South Olympic swimmer and all-American girl, who moves into the apartment next door. Sophie becomes convinced that the pair are editing a dangerously subversive magazine, but when the right member of the pair becomes romantically interested in her, she finds that some political accom-modation is possible.

2 men, 1 woman; 1 interior. Royalty: $50-35.

_____. The Sunshine Boys (1973). BP 1972-73; Samuel French.
Willie Clark used to be half of a dynamite vaudeville team with Al Lewis. Now in their seventies, the two haven't seen one another for 11 years and haven't spoken for 12. Willie's nephew Ben arranges for the two to get together once more for a CBS tele-vision salute to comedy (they'll earn $10,000). Willie doesn't want to, because Al is always sticking his finger into his chest and ac-cidentally spitting in his face. He finally relents, however, only to walk off the rehearsal stage when Al pokes him in the chest and ac-cidentally spits in his face. At the end of the play, while Willie recovers from a heart attack, the two old friends/foes look forward to spending the rest of their lives together at a New Jersey old actors' home--insulting one another.

5 men, 2 women; 2 interiors. Royalty: $50-35.

_____. Visitor from New York. See California Suite.

_____. Visitor from Philadelphia. See California Suite.

_____. Visitors from Chicago. See California Suite.

_____. Visitors from London. See California Suite.

SIMPSON, N. F. One Way Pendulum (1960). Samuel French.
Based on a rather unique premise of a man's dedicated at-tempts to make penny scales sing the chorus of Handel's "Messiah," this farcical comedy presents a host of bizarre and zany characters. The man who wants the scales to sing "Messiah" also has a cash register, which he bought in case he should ever want a typewriter and need a trade-in. Then his aunt arrives, after getting on the wrong train, and constantly harrasses him to buy her a tricycle. In a desperate attempt to establish some sort of order in his life, the man reconstructs the Old Bailey courthouse right in his own living room and begins dispensing "justice" to all the characters who appear until the man finally resolves his problems.

10 men, 4 women; composite interior. Royalty: $35-25.

SKELTON, Geoffrey. Marat/Sade. See entry under Weiss, Peter.

SKINNER, Cornelia Otis. Our Hearts Were Young and Gay. See

entry under Kerr, Jean.

SKLAR, George. <u>Laura</u>. See entry under Caspary, Vera.

SLADE, Bernard. <u>Same Time, Next Year</u> (1975). BP 1974-75;
Samuel French.
George is a C.P.A. and Doris a housewife. Each is happily
married with three children, but the two strangers get together one
night in February of 1951. George has flown to northern California
to do somebody's books; Doris is there on a religious retreat. They
carry on their affair by meeting at the same country inn every February. We track them as they meet all the way up to 1975, during
which time George has been neurotic and uptight, stuffy and rich,
into analysis, a with-it encounter groupie, a late blooming hippie,
and finally back into the establishment. Doris, meanwhile, has
moved from awkward young wife to restless, to back to college, to
overaged flower child, to successful businesswoman, to what is finally a mature woman. The transitions of the two are always revealing, but never are they in synch with one another.
1 man, 1 woman; 1 interior. Royalty: $50-35.

_____. Tribute (1978). BP 1977-78; Samuel French.
Scottie Templeton, who has just learned he has leukemia, is
trying to get to know his son Jud, 20, whom he left with his
former wife years ago. He insists on teaching Jud "the art of having fun" before he dies. There are many false starts in the development of their relationship. Scottie is superficial and social; Jud is
serious and private. At first the father refuses to participate in
the chemotherapy that will extend his life, but he is persuaded by
the boy, who argues that the two of them need more time together
in order to learn what his father has to transfer to him. At the end,
Jud organizes a "Tribute" to his father, attended by his hundreds
of friends who celebrate his temporary victory over leukemia and
listen as the joking father plays straight man to a serious son who
now delivers the punch lines.
2 acts; 3 men, 4 women; 1 interior and a stage. Royalty:
$50-35.

SMITH, Dodie (pseud. of C. L. Anthony). <u>Autumn Crocus</u> (1932).
French, 1933; FAMA; PLAD.
Two English school ma'ams are on holiday at an inn in the
Austrian Tyrol, Edith and Fanny. Fanny yearns for romance and
thinks she finds it with André, the young and handsome innkeeper,
amid the mountains and fields of autumn crocus. She wants to stay
on, even when she discovers he is married and has a little girl; but
Edith persuades her with hints of what might happen. She takes
the bus with Edith and goes back home to drudgery; but she has a
memory.
3 acts; 4 men, 8 women; 1 interior, 2 exteriors.

_____. Call It a Day (1936). BP 1935-36; Samuel French.

Crowds into the 16 hours of the first day of Spring the ups
and downs of the Hilton family: Roger, in and out with an actress;
Dorothy, touched by the loneliness of a rubber planter; Cathy,
falling for a philandering painter with a watchful wife; Ann, achiev-
ing a Rossetti drawing; Martin, experiencing love at first sight;
while below stairs, the cook and Vera and the daily help are living
with equal zest.
    3 acts; 5 men, 11 women; 2 interiors, 1 exterior. Royalty:
    $25-20.

_____. Dear Octopus (1938). Samuel French.
    Four generations of the Randolph family assemble for the
golden wedding of Charles and Dora--the family is the octopus which
holds them together, and from which none wishes to escape. Each
member of the family is distinctively sketched. A love plot revolves
around bachelor Nicholas (35) and Fenny (29), Dora's companion for
ten years.
    3 acts; 4 men, 10 women, 1 boy of 10, 2 girls of 9 & 12; 3
    interiors. Royalty: $25-20.

SMITH, Harry James. Mrs. Bumpstead-Leigh (1910). French 1917;
    MOSJ; MOSL; BP 1909-1919.
    Richly characterizes the social climber who endeavors to land
herself and family as from England where hyphenated names are
popular. Her advance becomes complicated when she is recognized
by a unique fellow townsman from Ohio who is now agent for tomb-
stones--a monumentalist, as he calls himself.
    3 acts; 6 men, 6 women; 1 interior.

SMITH, Winchell and Victor Mapes. The Boomerang (1915). French,
    1915.
    The young doctor is so anxious to have a case that he under-
takes to cure Bud of the disease of love. However he develops the
same symptoms himself and succumbs to the nurse, Virginia.
    3 acts; 6 men, 5 women; 2 interiors.

_____ and Frank Bacon. Lightnin' (1918). French, 1918; CERC.
    Lovable ne'er-do-well Lightnin' Bill Jones has a hotel on the
Nevada-California border, so that the Nevada sheriff can't arrest
the men who step over into California. Lightnin' refuses to sell the
hotel to two fake promoters who are trying to swindle his wife. He
pleads his own case in court with striking success.
    Prolog & 3 acts; 12 men, 12 women; 3 interiors.

SNEIDER, Vern. Teahouse of the August Moon. See entry under
    Patrick, John.

SOPHOCLES. Antigone (441 B.C.). Many translations, among them:
    Storr in Loeb Library; Young in Everyman's; Campbell in
    World's Classics; Coleridge in Bohn's; tr. by Jebb, Macmillan;
    HUD; TRE-1, -2, (v. 2); THO; tr. by Gilbert Murray, Oxford;

tr. by Way, Macmillan; adapted & carried by Baker; BLO; tr. by Plumptre, Heath; tr. by Fitts & Fitzgerald, Harcourt; FIT; OAT; TEN; tr. by Wildman, adapted by Cocteau in BEN; see also Anouilh's Antigone.

Antigone rebels against Creon's edict that the body of her brother Polynices remain unburied. She covers his body with dirt. Brought before Creon, she is punished by being buried alive. Creon rescinds the decree too late, for not only has she died, but his son, Haemon, her betrothed, has stabbed himself beside her, and his wife Eurydice has also killed herself. The shattered Creon is left alone to long for death.

1 continuous act; 6 men, 3 women, chorus of Elders; 1 exterior.

_____. Electra (ca. 420 B.C.). Many translations, among them: Storr in Loeb Library; Young in Everyman's; Campbell in World's Classics; Coleridge in Bohn's; other recommended translations: by Way, Macmillan; by Jebb, Macmillan; by Plumptre, Heath; by Ferguson, W. R. Scott; FIT; by Percy, French; OAT; Plumptre tr. in CLS. Compare treatment by Euripides, tr. by Murray in TRE-1 & 2 (v. 2).

After the murder of her father, Agamemnon, Electra has remained in the household, enduring insult and humiliation for many years. She had sent her young brother Orestes away for safe keeping. Grown to manhood, Orestes returns with his friend Pylades. He reveals himself to Electra, and, spurred on by her, murders both Clytemnestra and Aegisthus. She marries Pylades.

1 continuous act; 4 men, 3 women, extras, chorus of women; 1 exterior.

_____. Oedipus Tyrannus (ca. 431 B.C.). Many translations, among them: Storr in Loeb Library; Young in Everyman's; Campbell in World's Classics; Coleridge in Bohn's; other recommended translations: Jebb, Macmillan; MAU; by Gilbert Murray, Oxford; CAR; COJ; MIL; by Way, Macmillan; Plumptre, Heath; (also in SMP); Fitts & Fitzgerald, Harcourt, as Oedipus Rex; Yeats as Oedipus the King, Macmillan; FIT; GREN; HARC-8; OAT; TEN; TREA-1.

The citizens of Thebes appeal for relief from the plague which the oracle has said was caused by the presence of the murderer of King Laius. Oedipus the King vows he will find out who he is. Tiresias the seer accuses him of being the man. Slowly he realizes that it is indeed himself who has fulfilled the prophecy, having killed his father and married his mother. In this hopeless struggle against fate, he blinds himself, to live out his life in misery.

1 continuous act; 7 men, 1 woman, 2 girls, extras; chorus of Theban men; 1 exterior.

_____. Philoctetes (409 B.C.). Tr. by Storr in Loeb Library; by Young in Everyman's; by Campbell in World's Classics; by

Coleridge in Bohn's; by Plumptre, Heath; by Way, Macmillan; by Jebb, Macmillan; in OAT.

On the way to the Trojan war, Philoctetes, a renowned archer, is left on the desolate isle of Lemnos because of a wound. He has become naturally embittered by 9 years' neglect, but his nature has been chastened by suffering. Because of a prediction that the Trojan war could be won only through the bow of Heracles (entrusted to Philoctetes), Odysseus the unscrupulous and the young Neoptolemus, the generous-hearted son of Achilles, undertake to secure it. Odysseus plans to get it by consciencless intrigue. Neoptolemus wants no part in the deception. Philoctetes defies Odysseus, when Heracles appears in divine effulgence and promises renown and healing of his wound; whereupon he follows them to Troy.

1 continuous act; 5 men, chorus of sailors; 1 exterior.

SOWERBY, Githa. Rutherford & Son (1912). Lond., Sidgwick, & Doran, 1912; DIG; PLAP v. 2.

Old John Rutherford is masterful and obstinate; he regards his work as his religion and he sacrifices all for business. He tries to get a trade secret from his son, John Jr., who leaves because of this, and he turns his daughter Janet out of the house because she married Martin, a foreman in his glass factory. Industrialism is the villain of the play; old Rutherford is its victim.

3 acts; 4 men, 4 women; 1 interior.

SPARK, Muriel. The Prime of Miss Jean Brodie. See entry under Allen, Jay.

SPEWACK, Bella. See entries under Spewack, Samuel.

SPEWACK, Samuel, with Bella Spewack. Boy Meets Girl (1935). BP 1935-36; Dramatists Play Service.

An extravagant lampoon on Hollywood and the cinema industry. To develop a story for Larry Toms, the cowboy film hero, the energetic writing team, Law & Benson, devise the starring of Susie-the-waitress' baby, who shall be called Happy. He steals the scenes from Larry, much to the producer's distress; then he gets the measles! They pose Rodney as the father, and after Susie marries him, he turns out to be a lord's son. So they must find another baby to succeed Happy as a star.

3 acts; 14 men, 5 women; 2 interiors. Royalty: $35-25.

_____, with Bella Spewack. My Three Angels (1953). Based on Albert Husson's book. BP 1952-53; Dramatists Play Service.

Three convicts (two murderers and a swindler) play Robin Hood to a family besieged by conniving relatives. The convicts take on the intruders, and by their warm hearts, sunny natures, and expertise of crime they make possible a Merry Christmas where, Time pointed out, it is easier "to bump Scrooge off than convert him."

7 men, 3 women; 1 interior. Royalty: $50-35.

_____ . Two Blind Mice (1949). BP 1948-49; Dramatists Play
Service.

Two nice elderly ladies, Mrs. Letitia Turnbull and Crystal
Hower, still maintain the Office of Medical Herbs in Washington
though it was abolished four years before, since no steps have been
taken to close it out. A newspaper reporter, Tommy Thurston,
takes them over and staffs their hideaway with people from other
Departments, alleging security reasons. Thus he mystifies literal-
minded government employees. A caustic satire on governmental
bureaucracy, stupidity, and red tape.

3 acts; 14 men, 4 women; 1 interior. Royalty: $50-25.

_____ . Under the Sycamore Tree (1952). Dramatists Play Service.

The reaction of ants who can speak, love, and hate to the
present state of the world is presented in this farcical fable. The
ant colony which we see has just achieved superiority over their
enemies, the brown ants. In addition, they have radios and tele-
phones. Then a scientist discovers the secret ingredient that makes
man's world go around--love. He teaches it to a boy and girl ant
and the queen, bringing contentment and happiness to their world.
They even discover how to wage a nondeadly war, and being unselfish ants, try to pass this information on to the President of the
United States. Although the scientists' attempts to talk to the
President are unsuccessful, he and his queen are happy with their
discoveries, concluding that now, they have really lived.

5 men, 2 women, plus the nonspeaking roles for 3 men, 1
woman; 1 interior. Royalty: $50-25.

SPIGELGASS, Leonard. Dear Me, The Sky Is Falling (1963).
Adapted from a story by Gertrude Berg and James Yaffe.
Samuel French.

This comedy recounts the madcap escapades of a know-it-all,
yet lovable, mother. This stern lady has ruled her husband and
daughter completely and tries to take on the rest of the world, too.
Finally the husband and unmarried daughter make some decisions on
their own, decisions which are contrary to Mother's opinions.
Faced with this rebellion, Mother calls for her psychiatrist, and
after a humorous consultation with that Freudian expert, Mother
emerges again with all the right answers. And surprisingly enough,
the answers suit all the others as well.

5 men, 7 women; 1 interior and inset. Royalty: $50-25.

_____ . A Majority of One (1959). Samuel French.

A Jewish widow from Brooklyn establishes a warm friendship
with a Japanese gentleman and unwittingly almost wrecks some very
delicate commercial treaty negotiations. The widow's son-in-law is
a diplomat engaged in the negotiations which are of paramount importance to both the U.S. and Japan. He takes his wife and mother-
in-law along when he has to go to Japan, and en route the widow
meets a Japanese gentleman with whom she soon becomes close

friends. The son-in-law, making some mistaken assumptions about the relationship, demands that it be broken off. This insult to the Japanese almost causes negotiations to be halted, but with a display of wisdom and tolerance, the elderly couple rescue the deal and demonstrate that nations as well as individuals need understanding in dealing with each other.

6 men, 8 women; 4 interiors. Royalty: $50-25.

SQUIRE, J. C. Berkeley Square. See entry under Balderston, J. L.

STALLINGS, Laurence. What Price Glory? See entry under Anderson, Maxwell.

STEELE, Richard. The Conscious Lovers (1722). In his Plays, Mermaid edn., Scribner; BEL v. 9; INCH v. 12; MCM; MOR; MOSE v. 1; NET; STM; TAU; TAY; TUQ.

Young Bevil is to marry wealthy Lucinda Sealand, old Sealand's daughter by his second wife, but he really loves Indiana, a poor orphan. When Indiana turns out to be the long-lost daughter of Sealand by his first wife, Bevil can marry her, while Lucinda can be won by his friend Myrtle. In the course of the play, the young man avoids a duel but remains a fine gentleman.

5 acts; 8 men, 5 women; 4 interiors, 2 exteriors; costumes of the period.

STEIN, Joseph. Enter Laughing (1963). Adapted from Carl Reiner's novel. Samuel French.

The hilarious account of a delivery boy in a sewing machine factory who yearns to be an actor. Though his parents want the boy to be a druggist, as soon as he saves up enough money he buys his way into a semi-professional company, directed by a man who will put anybody on stage for the right price. The boy is a terrible actor, and we see him flub his way through romantic scenes with the director's daughter, with another man's date, and finally with an office girl who was meant for him.

7 men, 4 women; stage, wagons, insets. Royalty: $50-25.

STEINBECK, John. The Moon Is Down (1941). BP 1941-42; Dramatists Play Service.

Steinbeck's dramatization of his novel, depicting the military invasion of a fascist power over a small, neutral country with a long history of peaceful coexistence. Though the invaders do, by force, brutality, and violence keep the upper hand, their tactics merely cause the resolve and resistance of the occupied town to deepen and accelerate. Finally, "the flies have conquered the flypaper." Or, as civilian Mayor Orden explains to the invading army colonel who is about to have him executed, the free men of the village are a different breed than the "herd men" who blindly follow leaders. "And so it is always," he says, "that herd men win battles, but free men win wars."

2 parts; 17 men, 3 women; 2 interiors. Royalty: $35-25.

_____. Of Mice and Men (1937). BP 1937-38; Dramatists Play Service.

A character study of two roving farm hands. One of them, Lennie, is a powerful giant of a man who has the intelligence of a child. When he is teased by the young wife of the foreman, Lennie kills her, though that is not his intention. He in turn is killed by his friend, who cannot bear to see him arrested, tried, and imprisoned.

9 men, 1 woman; 2 interiors, 1 exterior. Royalty: $35.

STEPHENS, Harry. Tracers. See entry under DiFusco, John.

STEPHENS, Phillip. Van Gogh. See Leonard Nimoy's Vincent.

STERNHEIM, Karl. A Place in the World (1913). Tr. by Katzin in KAT.

Having advanced financially to the President of the Corporation, Christian Maske sacrifices his former sweetheart Sybil who has helped him develop social graces, also his father and mother, advising Count Palen that they are dead. He asks the Count for the hand of his daughter, Countess Marianne. He is accepted; and he even creates fictitious ancestry and implies that he is the bastard son of a Vicomte, hence with blue blood in his veins.

3 acts; 4 men, 4 women; 2 interiors.

STEVENSON, William. Gammer Gurton's Needle (1500). ADA; BA3; BOA; GAY-1; LEV; also in Manly, Pre-Shakespearean Drama, Ginn, 1897, v. 2.

While mending the breeches of her man, Hodge, Gammer Gurton loses her valuable needle. Complications in the small village society follow and the whole parish is set by the ears, from the curate down to the village ne'er-do-well, when Diccon tells her the needle has been stolen by her neighbor, Dame Chat. However the needle is discovered in Hodge's leg when he changes his breeches. (Long attributed to John Still.)

1 continuous act of about an hour; 6 men, 4 women; 1 exterior; costumes of the period.

STEWART, Donald Ogden. Rebound (1930). BP 1929-30; French carried.

Bill and Sara get married, after Bill has been given the air by Evie, and Johnnie has failed to propose to Sara. Although Evie is now married to Lyman, she still makes up to Bill. Disruption is threatened for Bill and Sara, but the situation is intelligently exposed and sanely adjusted.

3 acts; 7 men, 5 women; 2 interiors.

STITT, Milan. The Runner Stumbles (1976). BP 1975-76; Dramatists Play Service.

Father Rivard, priest of the remote Solon, Michigan parish, is in jail on charges of murdering a nun. The action of the play is

part interrogation, part courtroom, and part personal memory of
Father Rivard's relationship with Sister Rita--an extraordinary woman
who sees no conflict between the love of God and the love of life.
At the end it is revealed that Sister Rita was actually murdered by
Father Rivard's housekeeper, who saw the lively nun as a threat to
decency, the church, and the priest's reputation.
   5 men, 4 women; unit set. Royalty: $50-35.

STOKER, Bram. <u>Dracula</u>. See entry under Deane, Hamilton.

_____. <u>Count Dracula</u>. See entry under Tiller, Ted.

STOPPARD, Tom. <u>Jumpers</u> (1972). BP 1973-74; Samuel French.
   Professor George Moore is getting ready to debate with a
logician the existence of a moral absolute, of metaphysical reality,
of God (his field is moral philosophy), when the logician is killed
in George's living room while performing gymnastics (the close association between gymnastics and philosophy is unique to George's
university). Thumper, George's pet rabbit, is also killed, and
later eaten by George's wife Dotty (former musical comedy star)
and one of her boyfriends. A wild and absurd comedy.
   4 men, 2 women, 8 extras; basic set with three playing
   areas. Royalty: $50-35.

_____. <u>The Real Inspector Hound</u> (1972). Samuel French.
   A farce with a play-within-a-play framework. Two critics
show up to review a play. One critic is substituting for a missing
regular reviewer, and the other is a lustful man. They watch the
action on stage performed by the four principal characters: a
countess, a girlfriend guest, a roué the countess has met through
the girlfriend, and the crippled brother of the countess's dead
brother. The roué is shot, and Inspector Hound arrives (though
nobody ever called him) to inspect the body, which turns out to be
that of the missing first-string critic. The phone begins to ring on
stage and is finally answered by the lustful critic who leaves his
theater box just to shut it up. (The call is from his wife, whom he
berates for bothering him at work.) Then he begins to repeat the
lines of the roué shot in the beginning of the play, and the same
things start to happen all over. The substitute critic takes the
place of the Inspector this time, and the original roué and Inspector
take the places of the critics in the box. The former Inspector in
fact, turns out to be the countess's long-lost (but not dead) husband.
   6 men, 3 women; 1 interior. Royalty: $50-35.

_____. <u>The Real Thing</u> (1984). BP 1983-84; Samuel French.
   Henry is a playwright famous for his crisp, witty, and
flippant dialogue between husbands and wives as they torment one
another over sexual infidelities. His wife, Charlotte, who is starring in his new play, fears that people will think she got the part
because of her relationship to him and that their real at-home con-

versations are as brilliant as the stage ones. She believes that if
he ever caught her with a lover he wouldn't "sit around being witty
about place mats." He'd come apart, she thinks, and first his
"sentence structure would go to pot, closely followed by his sphinc-
ter." The truth is that Henry is working on the other side of the
issue: he is having an affair with Annie, the wife of the leading
man in his play, whom he leaves Charlotte to marry. Two years
later, when Annie is caught up in the passion of a revolutionary
play and the attentions of a young leading man, Henry cannot make
a game of her infidelity--his expertise is in literary form and clever
words.

> 2 acts; 4 men, 3 women; various settings. Royalty: $60-40.

_____. Rosencrantz and Guildenstern Are Dead (1967). BP 1967-
68; Samuel French.

An existential comedy featuring two student acquaintances of
Hamlet and what went on behind the scenes of Shakespeare's play.
Actually, the two don't know. They don't even know why they were
in Elsinore at the time (they were "sent for"). As it turns out they
have a hard time remembering which one is Rosencrantz and which
one Guildenstern. The Players come and go, Hamlet comes through
reading words, people are killed, and the two anti-agents find that
their only exit is death.

> 14 men, 2 women, 12 extras, 6 musicians; unit set. Royal-
> ty: $50-35.

_____. Travesties (1975). BP 1975-76; Samuel French.

Travesties is an intellectual literary fantasy, made partly out
of characters and techniques from Oscar Wilde and partly out of
an obscure historical fact: James Joyce, Lenin, and Dadaist artist
Tristan Tzara all lived in Zurich during World War I, as did minor
British consular official Henry Carr. Of course when the author
puts these things together he ends up letting Henry Carr be the
hero, appearing in the play as an old man in one scene and a contemporary of revolutionaries in the next. One interesting technique
in the play is the "time slip," when the story jumps off the track
and has to be started again at the point where it went wild.

> 5 men, 3 women; 2 interiors. Royalty: $50-35.

STOREY, David. The Changing Room (1972). BP 1972-73; Samuel
French.

Americans would call the changing room a lockerroom, which
is the setting of the play before, at halftime, and after a rugby
football game in the North of England. The players on the team are
working-class men who play this kind of blood-letting football to
earn a few dollars and put some glory in their lives. We see them
arrive, joke and banter, dress out, come in injured from a brutal
first half, and finally enter victorious after the game, clean up, and
leave.

> 22 men; 1 interior. Royalty: $50-35.

_____. The Contractor (1970). BP 1973-74; Samuel French.
    There is no dramatic incident in this play. In the first act
a tent is being assembled on Mr. Ewbank's lawn, in the second act
it is being decorated, in the third it is taken down. In between,
a wedding takes place (Ewbank's daughter), and we are introduced
to Ewbank's family, parents, and the men who work for him (he is
"the contractor" who owns the tent company). His workmen are
social outcasts whom no one else will hire, and though they may
quit him, he never fires anybody.
    9 men, 3 women; 1 interior. Royalty: $50-25.

_____. Home (1971). BP 1970-71; Samuel French.
    The setting is a bare terrace, peopled by mental patients
who think they are in a private hotel, or on an island, or who know
exactly where they are. There is no real plot, only dialogue--some
of which makes sense and some which doesn't. The events are confined to one day on the terrace, where we learn compassion, sympathy, and respect for the people institutionalized there.
    3 men, 2 women; exterior set. Royalty: $50-35.

_____. In Celebration (1973). Dramatic Publishing Company.
    Three sons, educated up the social ladder from the working
class existence of their British parents, return home to celebrate
their parents' wedding anniversary. One son is wild and cruel; one
is successful and smug; the youngest is self-pitying. Layers of
fears and hatreds, guilts and atonements are revealed within the
family setting.
    5 men, 2 women; 1 interior. Royalty: $60-40.

STOWE, Mrs. Harriet Beecher. Uncle Tom's Cabin (1853). Ver-
    sion by George L. Aiken, French in the 1850's; also in MOSS 2;
    Aiken version revised by A. E. Thomas, Appleton, 1934; CERC.
        Introduces Eliza crossing the ice, Topsy (who just growed),
and the faithful slave Uncle Tom with his loyalty to the St. Clare
family, his love for little Eva, and his death under Simon Legree.
    French editions: 6 acts; 15 men, 6 women; simple interiors
    and exteriors. Thomas' version: 26 men, 10 women, extras;
    23 scenes in 3 acts, with 9 interiors & 7 exteriors.
    Costumes of the period. No royalty.

STREETER, Edward. Mr. Hobbs' Vacation. See entry under Leslie,
    F. Andrew.

STRINDBERG, August. Comrades (1888). Tr. by Oland, Luce,
    1913; in TUCG, in TUCM; tr. by Samuel, Lond., Hendersons,
    1914.
        A gifted artist, Axel, prostitutes his art to earn money for
his wife Berta, also an artist. When both send pictures to a salon,
he attaches his number to hers to insure it a place. When this is
rejected, she humiliates him by having it returned during a party.
Learning it was her picture, she tries to propitiate him, but he

drives her out into the streets. The play rather shows Strindberg's anti-feministic attitude and cynicism toward women.

4 acts; 4 men, 8 women; 1 interior.

_____. The Father (1887). Tr. by Erichsen, Lond., Duckworth, & Luce, 1907; DIC; TRE-1, 2, & 3; in TREA-2; tr. by Oland in his Plays, v. 2, Luce, 1912; tr. by Locock, Lond., Cape, 1931; tr. by Locock & others in Lucky Peter's Travels, Anglo-Swedish Literary Foundation, 1931.

The wife definitely plots to drive her husband insane, and the mental struggle is so great that she succeeds. The situation and atmosphere are well developed and show strikingly his animus against women.

3 acts; 5 men, 3 women; 1 interior.

_____. Swanwhite (1902). Tr. by Bjorkman in his Plays, ser. 3, Scribner, & Lond., Duckworth, 1913; tr. by Oland in his Plays, v. 3, Luce, 1914.

A fantastic trifle about Swanwhite and her Prince, based on the magical power of love which breaks all spells and makes good triumph over evil. Has a poetic mystical atmosphere.

2 acts; 10 men, 7 women; 1 interior; fanciful costumes.

STRONG, Austin. Seventh Heaven (1922). French, 1922.

Chico, a sewer cleaner in Paris, is courageous because he has faith in himself. He is able to help all who come in contact with him. He rescues Diane, who is rather adrift in Paris, and proclaims her his wife just as he must leave for the First World War. Diane waits four years for his return, but on Armistice Day gets word that she believes he is dead. But he returns, and she is restored to her lover and her religion.

3 acts; 11 men, 4 women; 1 interior, 1 exterior; French and military costumes.

_____. Three Wise Fools (1918). Samuel French.

A splendid trio--doctor, judge, and financier--live in a self-made rut, when into their machine-like lives bursts Sidney Fairchild, a young girl, daughter of the woman they all three had loved in earlier years. At first they are annoyed, but they adopt her as a ward. Changes take place which quite upset their routine, but make them more human.

3 acts; 11 men, 2 women; 1 interior. Royalty: $25.

STURGES, Preston. Strictly Dishonorable (1929). BP 1929-30; Samuel French.

In the days of the speak-easy, Isabelle gets interested in an opera singer, Gus di Ravo. To escape arrest she must spend the night somewhere, and Gus takes her to his apartment, assuring her that his intentions are strictly dishonorable. But he retires to another room while she sleeps on the sofa. In the morning he is romantic again, announces his love for Isabelle and his intention to

marry her.
    3 acts; 7 men, 1 woman; 2 interiors. Royalty: $50-25.

SUDERMANN, Hermann. <u>Honor</u> (1889). Tr. by Baukhage.
    French, 1915.
    Presents situations in which various aspects of satisfying
honor are shown, from patching up sick honor with money to fighting
a duel. Robert Heinecke, of humble parents returns from India after
10 years, where he managed things for the Mühlingk firm, and so
successfully that he became a protégé of Count Trast, a coffee king.
Robert finds his proletariat home in sad condition and his sister Alma seduced by Kurt, the merchant's son. Mühlingk gives 40,000
marks to her father to satisfy her honor, expels them from their
home, and fires Robert. He makes his final report and pays back
the money (lent by his friend Trast), and as he leaves, the merchant's daughter, Leonore, who has loved him since childhood,
though forbidden by her father to show it, leaves her family to go
with him to a new position with Trast.
    4 acts; 11 men, 6 women; 2 interiors.

_____. John the Baptist (1893). Tr. by Marshall in FRA v. 17;
    in <u>Poet Lore</u>, v. 11, 1899; Lane, 1909; abridged in Pierce &
    Matthews, v. 2.
    Presents scenes in the life of John, the forerunner of Jesus.
John has believed in an eye for an eye but is impressed by the new
doctrine of love and forgiveness of enemies. He makes an enemy
of Herodias because of reproof for her evil doings. Salome, the
sensuous young girl would entice him. Herod would spare him.
    5 acts; 29 men, 8 women, 2 children, extras; 3 interiors,
    4 exteriors; costumes of the period.

_____. The Joy of Living (1902). Tr. by Wharton. Scribner,
    1902.
    Countess Beata, wife of Michael, has intrigued for 15 years
with Richard. When she finds that the two men have become
friends, she ends the love affair. After Richard has been elected
to the Reichstag his opponent Meixner brings up this affair as a
scandal. Richard sets his affairs in order to do away with himself
and makes a speech on the sanctity of the home. Meixner is so impressed he returns the compromising letters. Then Beata gives a
luncheon to the two men, asks who dares to live, and drinks to the
joy of living; she falls dead of the poison.
    5 acts; 14 men, 3 women; 2 interiors; costumes of the
    period (1899).

_____. Magda (1893). Tr. by Winslow. Bost., Lamson, 1895;
    French, 1895; in WATI; in WATL-2.
    As a young girl Magda has left home to avoid a marriage
which her father desired. She returns as a successful singer, but
her free attitude, which has resulted in an illegitimate child, continues to cause trouble. Her claim of a right to develop her own

individuality brings about a well-defined struggle between the old
and the new, the conservative and the radical, the conventional
idea of home, parental authority, moral standards and the modern
idea of the rights of children and personal freedom.
4 acts; 6 men, 8 women; 1 interior.

_____. The Vale of Content (1896). Tr. by Leonard in DIC.
Elizabeth has married the headmaster of the school; she meets
again a former lover, von Roecknitz, who urges her to go away with
him. She confides in her husband and goes back to happiness in
the corner. Treats the eternal triangle with good sense and subtle
psychology, showing that happiness and content come rather from
duties faithfully performed.
3 acts; 6 men, 6 women; 1 interior, 1 exterior.

SUTRO, Alfred. The Fascinating Mr. Vanderveldt (1906). French,
1906.
Clarice, a young widow, is told by her domineering mother
that she must marry again and some one with money. She is told
to choose between an elderly judge and a musician. Meantime she
is wooed by Mr. Vanderveldt, who has a bad reputation with women.
He plans an episode of a stranded car in an isolated community, but
she outwits him with a spark-plug and finds Col. Rayner more to
her liking.
4 acts; 8 men, 8 women, 1 lad of 15; 3 interiors, 1 exterior.

_____. The Two Virtues (1914). Lond., Duckworth, Brentano,
& French, 1914.
Deftly characterizes four women, two of whom, Isabel and
Lady Milligan, represent Chastity, while the other two, Freda and
Alice, represent Charity. The charity pair oppose the love of Freda
and Jeffrey and cause them to part, but cannot keep them separated.
4 acts; 3 men, 5 women; 2 interiors.

_____. The Walls of Jericho (1904). French, 1906; MAP.
Fighting Jack Frobisher, having made his pile in Queensland,
returns to England, and with his money is welcomed into the smart
set. He marries Alethea, daughter of the Marquis of Steventon, an
autocratic aristocrat, but is losing his grip in the fast London society. Urged on by Hankey Bannister, his old pal in Australia,
Jack resolves to assert his strength and raise his voice in protest
to make the walls come tumbling down. When he does, in tense
scenes with the Marquis and Alethea, he reestablishes himself as
Fighting Jack.
4 acts; 13 men, 8 women, extras; 4 interiors.

SYNGE, John Millington. Deirdre of the Sorrows (1910). N.Y., J.
Quinn, 1911; in his Works, Mansel, & Luce, 1912; in his Plays,
Lond., Allen, 1924 & 1932; in Theatre Arts for Aug. 1950.
Develops poetically the ancient Irish legend. Though pledged
to Conchubor, the elderly King of Ulster, Deirdre marries young

Naise and lives for seven idyllic years in the forest with him and
the sons of Uena. The king tricks them into returning and traitor-
ously slays the men. Deirdre kills herself in sorrow and remorse.
    3 acts; 6 men, 3 women, extras; 2 interiors, 1 exterior;
costumes of the period.

_____. The Playboy of the Western World (1907). Dublin,
    Maunsel, 1909; Luce, 1911; in his Works, Maunsel, 1910 &
    Luce 1912, v. 2; in his Plays Lond., Allen, 1924 & 1932; Ran-
    dom House, 1935; French carried; CEW; CLS; DUR; FIG; HAU.
    Act. ed., Samuel French.
    Develops a strange imaginative Irish character, Christy Ma-
hon, who deceives himself and others into thinking he is a hero because he has killed, as he thinks, his domineering old father. When
his resurrected father appears, and he tries to kill him again,
Christy loses his glamor as hero, even with Pegeen. He and his
father escape together. The lilt and cadence of the diction, of
which Synge was a master, are its supreme excellence.
    3 acts; 7 men, 5 women, extras; 1 interior. French royalty:
$25-20.

_____. The Well of the Saints (1905). Lond., Bullen, 1905; in
    his Works, Dublin, Maunsel, 1910 & Luce, 1912; in his Plays,
    Lond., Allen, 1924 & 1932.
    A blind old couple are beautifully happy because every one
has told them how beautiful they are. The Saint restores their
sight and they see their ugliness. In course of time they lose their
sight again, but when the Saint gives them the chance to restore it,
the husband dashes the holy water from the Saint's hands, and they
persist in their blindness.
    3 acts; 4 men, 3 women; 2 interiors.

SZOGYI, Alex. A Country Scandal. See entry under Chekhov, An-
    ton P.

TABER, Richard. Is Zat So? See entry under Gleason, James.

TABORI, George. Brecht on Brecht. See entry under Brecht,
    Bertolt.

_____. The Emperor's Clothes (1953). BP 1952-53; Samuel
    French.
    An idealistic young boy who worships his father creates ser-
ious problems for the man in this tragicomedy set in Budapest.
The father, an outspoken liberal, has been dismissed from his job
as a teacher because he refused to compromise his principles. To
support his family he takes a job as a proofreader of trashy fiction
but this pays so poorly he cannot afford to buy a Christmas tree
for his family. The son, thinking he can raise money, starts a
secret society and charges dues for membership. Although he gets
the money for the tree, the totalitarian regime learns of the society

and arrests the father as the head of the organization. Faced with inquisition and imprisonment the man compromises himself, but this destroys the idealistic respect of his son. So, in spite of the tortures he must face, the father retracts his earlier confession and redeems himself as a hero in the eyes of his son.

12 men, 3 women; 1 interior. Royalty: $50.

TAGGART, Tom. Deadwood Dick (or, A Game of Gold) (1953). Samuel French.

A blood-and-thunder western melodrama based on the most exciting situations, colorful characters, and amusing dialogue from Edward L. Wheeler's dime novels of Deadwood Dick, published in the 1870's. Daughters are long-lost, gold mines are stolen, heroines are kidnapped, and escapes are hairbreadthed.

7 men, 7 women, extras; 1 interior. Royalty: $35-25.

TAMAYO y BAUS, Manuel. A New Drama (1867). Tr. by Fitzgerald & Guild, Hispanic Society Pubn. #90, 1915.

Depicts Shakespeare and his company rehearsing and presenting a new play. In technique a well-nigh perfect example of a play within a play. The lines of the new drama fit the situation of jealousy and envy among the actors of the company, Yorick the comedian and Walton the tragedian with Edmund, Yorick's foster-son, contending for the affections of Yorick's wife Alice.

3 acts; 7 men, 1 woman, extras; 3 interiors; costumes of 1605 in England.

TARKINGTON, Booth. Clarence (1919). BP 1919-20; French, 1921; GARU.

Clarence, whose last name is uncertain, but who "has been in the army," enters the Wheeler household in a rather vague capacity, which develops into that of a solvent for the perplexities of the whole family.

4 acts; 5 men, 5 women; 2 interiors.

_____. The Intimate Strangers (1921). French, 1924; COH.

Pits the adult charm and humor of Aunt Isabel against the rambunctious youth of her niece Florence, to the perplexity of the male.

3 acts; 4 men, 4 women; 2 interiors.

_____ and H. L. Wilson. The Man from Home (1907). Harper, 1908; revised form. French, 1934; CERC; BP 1899-1909.

The shrewd Indiana lawyer, Daniel Pike, outwits the fortune hunters in the Italian resort who have victimized his wards by pseudo-aristocratic snobbishness.

4 acts; 11 men, 3 women, extras; 1 interior, 2 exteriors.

French royalty: $25-20.

_____. Seventeen (1918). Samuel French.

Willie Baxter woos Lolo the baby-talk lady, steals his father's

best suit, and has many difficulties, some caused by his little sister Jane, some by the Negro servant Genesis, and others by Lolo's worthy swains.
4 acts; 8 men, 6 women; 2 interiors; 1 exterior (can be played with 1 interior). Royalty: $35-25.

TAYLOR, C. P. And a Nightingale Sang... (1979). BP 1983-84; Dramatic Publishing Company.
This is a memory play, set in the years of World War II in England (Newcastle-on-Tyne). The narrator is Helen Stott, the elder daughter in a working-class home peopled by parents, an unwanted grandfather, and a pretty, but terribly indecisive sister ten years younger, soon to marry a soldier. Sister never seems to know what to do, mother is always at church either praying or fantasizing about the priest, father turns communist during the frequent air raids, and grandfather tries to find a place where somebody wants him and his cat. Through all of this Helen attempts to find something for herself, but Norman, the soldier she falls in love with--the first man, in fact, who ever gave her a sense of her attractiveness--not only is married with a child, but has been called home on a hardship discharge and can't promise ever to see her again. At the end of the play D-Day is celebrated, and Helen, who is about to explain to her brother-in-law that she can't dance because of her slight limp, remembers that Norman taught her how and that now she can.
2 acts; 4 men, 3 women; area staging. Royalty: $75-50.

_____. Good (1982). BP 1982-83; Dramatic Publishing Company.
Johnny Hadler's anxiety neurosis is tied up with music, so that music rising and falling in his mind keys moods and scenes from his life as a German university professor caught up in the Nazism of the middle and late 1930's. A book of the professor's, in which mercy killing is considered (a work prompted by his mother's pathetic and demanding senility), attracts the attention of Adolph Hitler, who sends Eichmann to recruit Hadler first for the Party and later for the S.S. He compromises his principles more and more, beginning with his withdrawal form his Jewish psychiatrist and best friend, leading to his participation in book burnings, violent demonstrations, and "humanitarian" solutions to the "sick," "diseased," and "unfit," and ending with his specialist role in assisting Eichmann with his logistical problems at Auschwitz.
2 acts; 6 men, 4 women, optional musicians; bare stage. Royalty: $75-60.

TAYLOR, Renee, with Joseph Bologna. Lovers and Other Strangers (1968). Samuel French.
A set of four comedies on the general subject of the superiority of women. In the first, a young man who sets out to seduce a young woman has the tables turned on him. In the second, a married couple can't figure out whose turn it is to initiate sex. Next comes a nervous fiancé to his girl's apartment at four in the morning,

trying to get out of the wedding. By the time he leaves she is
dealing with the important matters like renting his wedding suit.
In the last "playlet" a married couple of 30 years confess their
failures and their fights in order to save their son's marriage.
     5 men, 5 women; 4 interiors. Royalty: $50-25.

TAYLOR, Samuel. The Happy Time (1950). Based on Robert Fon-
     taine's book. BP 1949-50; Dramatists Play Service.
     Depicts the Bonnard family in their French-Canadian home.
Their uninhibited behavior has its effect on the adolescent Bibi.
The charming girl Mignonette is brought in to help and thrills Bibi
with young love. He steals her nightgowns; Uncle Desmonde is
accused of the theft though he had retained only her gloves. When
Uncle Desmonde and Mignonette become engaged, and Sally takes
the braces off her teeth, Bibi finds he is thrilled by her.
     3 acts; 8 men, 4 women; 2 interiors. Royalty: $50-25.

_____. The Pleasure of His Company (1958). Dramatists Play
     Service.
     This successful comedy has drawn much critical praise for
its wit as well as its sound philosophy. The story concerns an international playboy who returns to his wife's home to give away their
daughter in marriage. Since he hasn't seen her since she was a
little girl, he is surprised and pleased to find she has grown into a
beautiful young woman. He turns on all his playboy charms, and
despite the efforts of the mother and the fiancé, completely capti-
vates the girl. The impasse is finally resolved, however, when the
girl decides she still wants to marry. But first she wants to take
a trip abroad with her father, solving the problem happily for all
involved.
     5 men, 2 women; 1 interior. Royalty: $50-25.

_____. Sabrina Fair (1953). Dramatists Play Service.
     Interesting characters and a surprising finish make this an
entertaining romantic comedy. Sabrina is the daughter of the family
chauffeur for the Larabee family, who are very wealthy and impec-
cably genteel. After working in Paris for five years, Sabrina, an
extremely intelligent and attractive girl, returns home to see if she
still loves the oldest Larabee son, Linus, a cynical tycoon who has
taken over control of the family fortune. Sabrina discovers she
does love Linus, but his brother pays the most attention to her.
Mr. Larabee forgets his only passion--attending funerals--when Sabrina's father reveals that he too is a millionaire and consents to
Linus' marrying Sabrina. A rich Frenchman who is in love with
Sabrina, a wise-cracking magazine editor, and the exaggeratedly
narrow-minded Mrs. Larabee all add to the comic situations in the
play.
     7 men, 7 women; 1 exterior. Royalty: $50-25.

TEAGUE, Oran. Ludie (1984). Dramatic Publishing Company.
     Ludie Mae Inez is a young girl growing up in the 1930's in a

rural Southern community; her life is ruined by her parents' blind faith in their religion. Ludie's older sister is in the state home for the insane because she has sinned (she's in "a family way"). Her mother and father begin to think Ludie is also possessed by the devil because of her unconforming ideas and her negative attitude toward fundamentalist Preacher Lovett, who has just taken over the congregation. Ludie saw the preacher in a private place with her sister, and believes that he raped her. As it turns out, Lovett is wanted by his former congregation for passing bad checks, stealing church funds, and raping two girls.

2 acts; 4 men, 2 women; 1 interior. Royalty: $50-35.

TEICHMANN, Howard, with George S. Kaufman. The Solid Gold Cadillac (1953). Dramatists Play Service.

The President of General Products has accepted a governmental position, and his successor must be elected along with other new corporation officers. Things go smoothly at the annual stock holders' meeting until a little old lady who owns ten shares of stock begins asking questions--like what does the chairman of the board do to earn $170,000 a year. To shut her up, the corporation gives the lady a $150 a week job, which, the officers are frightened to learn, she takes seriously. She writes chatty letters to other minority stockholders and discovers that the corporation has forced into bankruptcy one of their own subsidiary firms. When she approaches the former president with the mess that the new board of directors has caused, the president quits his government job and tries to regain control of his company. A power fight results, and the bad guys are about to win. Then the proxies from the small shareholders start pouring in and the company is saved.

26 men (doubling possible); 10 women (extras); exterior and interior sets. Royalty: $50-35.

TENNYSON, Alfred Tennyson, 1st Baron. Becket (pub. 1884; prod. 1893). In his Poetical Works, Houghton; in his Works, Macmillan, 1893; MOSO; SMK; abridged in Pierce & Matthews, v. 1.

Becket irritates King Henry II before his appointment as Archbishop of Canterbury because he does not deem himself worthy of the honor. After his appointment he enrages the king by his utter devotion to the Church, refusing any compromise with the State, for while he signs the Customs, he will not seal. To rid himself of "this pestilent priest," the king causes his murder in his cathedral. A second theme concerns Henry's romantic and domestic life, pictured his morganatic wife Rosamund in her secret bower, but tracked there by his jealous neglected wife, Eleanor of Aquitaine. Becket arrives in time to save Rosamund from dagger and poison.

Prolog & 5 acts; 22 men, 1 boy, 3 women, extras; 8 interiors; costumes of the period.

_____. The Foresters, Robin Hood and Maid Marian (1892). Macmillan, 1892; in his Works, Macmillan, 1893, v. 6; also Macmillan, 1908, v. 9.

Maid Marian with her sick father takes refuge in Sherwood Forest where Robin Hood heads his band of outlaws. She is made their queen. There also comes King Richard Coeur de Lion, who settles matters with his brother John and the Sheriff.

4 acts; 12 men, 3 women, extras; 1 interior, 5 exteriors; costumes of the period.

TERENCE (Publius Terentius Afer). The Brothers (Adelphi, 160 B.C.). Tr. by Sergeaunt in Loeb Library; by Riley in Bohn's, tr. by Colman, Harper, 1859; tr. by Perry, Oxford, 1929; in DUC; TREA-1.

The two brothers represent two schools of thought as to the way to bring up boys. Demea, a married man with two sons, living in the country, is very strict with his son Ctesipho and believes he is a proper youth. Micio, a bachelor, living in the city, is mild and kind to the other son, Aeschinus, his nephew, whom he has adopted. Ctesipho, however, is a real profligate and hypocritical; he abducts a girl, for which the kindhearted Aeschinus takes the blame. When Demea learns of this, he seeks out Micio, and decides to become more kind and considerate. Micio is persuaded to marry his neighbor Sostrata.

5 acts; 10 men, 4 women; 1 exterior (a street before the 2 houses of Micio and Sostrata).

_____. Phormio (161 B.C.). Tr. by Sergeaunt in Loeb Library; tr. by Riley in Bohn's; tr. by Perry, Oxford, 1929; tr. by Clark, French; tr. by Morgan in CLF-1; CLS; DUC; MAU.

Old Chremes had secretly married the wealthy Nausistrata in Lemnos and is the father of a son, Phaedria, and a daughter, Phanium, who comes to Athens as a slave girl and of course without money. His brother Demipho has a son Antipho and they wish him to marry a music-girl, but he hasn't the money. Phormio, the benevolent intriguer, now steps in and schemes to get the money, and by his success, both Antipho and Phaedria can marry. When Chremes tries to get some money back from Phormio, a secret affair of his is brought to light. The scheming parasite, Phormio, is typical of the Roman comedies, providing much of the humor of the plays.

5 acts; 11 men, 2 women; 1 exterior (a street before 3 houses).

THOMA, Ludwig. Moral (1908). Tr. by Recht, Knopf, 1916; DID.

Some worthy dignitaries of a small town, leading citizens and officers in the Society for the suppression of vice, are aghast at realizing that all their names are recorded in the account books of a bawd lately arrested. They are in a panic for fear they will be exposed. The list is stolen by the president. The police official berates the zeal of his subordinates. The lady is paid off and the affair smoothed over.

3 acts; 9 men, 7 women, extras; 2 interiors.

THOMAS, A. E. No More Ladies (1934). BP 1933-34.

Before Marcia Townsend agrees to marry playboy Sherry Warren she makes sure he is aware of the risks of marriage and the hard work it will take to make it last. Seven months later he is back to his old ways, staying out all night with a night club performer. Out of revenge, after a boring evening of bridge Marcia goes off with one of the guests and does not return until the following noon. Sherry will not stand for this kind of behavior, and it appears that both will sue for divorce on grounds of adultery. By the end of the play, however, urged on by Marcia's grandmother, they will keep their marriage intact because they love one another, and Marcia will wait until their Golden Wedding Anniversary to confess what she did the night she spent away from home.

3 acts; 7 men, 6 women; 2 interiors.

_____. Uncle Tom's Cabin. See entry under Stowe, Harriet B.

THOMAS, Augustus. Arizona (1899). Russell, 1899; Dramatic Publishing Company, 1915.

Vivid scenes are enacted at the Canby ranch and Col. Bonham's army post, where the dashing villain, Capt. Hodgman, creates predicaments for honest Lt. Denton, who is accused of betraying the Colonel's wife Estrella, of the theft of the jewels, and later of shooting Hodgman.

4 acts; 11 men, 5 women; 2 interiors, 1 exterior; some military costumes of the period.

_____. As a Man Thinks (1911). Duffield, 1911; BAK; abridged in Pierce & Matthews, v. 1.

The Jewish physician, Dr. Seelig, advises the Christian editor Clayton that life's assurance depends on "as a man thinks." He may have a foolish wife, but he must have confidence that if he forgives it will be forgiven unto him.

4 acts; 9 men, 4 women; 3 interiors.

_____. The Copperhead (1917). French, 1922; COH.

Like Cooper's Spy, Milt Shanks heroically performs his misunderstood mission in the Civil war and endures revilings for 40 years, confessing only when his granddaughter would suffer. Then he is honored.

4 acts; 9 men, 6 women; 1 interior, 1 exterior (1 interior possible with a 40-year change).

_____. The Witching Hour (1907). French, 1916; DIC; MOSJ; MOSL; QUIK; QUIL; BP 1899-1909; abridged in Pierce & Matthews, v. 1.

Based on mental telepathy and thought transference, the hypnotic power attained by Jack Brookfield is doubtless false to reality, but can be believed in dramatically. The mellow second act gives a charming atmosphere. Has several exciting moments and good comedy.

4 acts; 11 men, 3 women; 2 interiors.

THOMAS, Brandon. Charley's Aunt (1892). Samuel French.
Two Oxford undergraduates, Jack Chesney and Charles Wykeham, must have a proper chaperone when entertaining their sweethearts, Kitty and Amy; so when Charley's aunt, Donna Lucia d'Alvadorez (from Brazil "where the nuts come from") cannot arrive for the luncheon and tête-à-tête in their room, they induce Lord Babberley to impersonate her. He has a merry time with the girls, and, as the very wealthy aunt, he is much sought after by Jack's father and the solicitor. The situation is further complicated when the real aunt shows up.
    3 acts; 6 men, 4 women; 2 interiors, 1 exterior. Royalty: $50-25.

THOMAS, Caitlin. Dylan. See entry under Michaels, Sidney.

THOMAS, Dylan. Dylan. See entry under Michaels, Sidney.

_____. Under Milk Wood (1953). BP 1957-58; Samuel French.
    The lives and souls of the inhabitants of a provincial Welsh fishing village are explored in this earthy drama. The conflicts and problems of a series of characters are revealed through the eyes of the dramatist (The Onlooker). There is a sea captain who dreams of the dead, a draper who makes promises of love to his wife, children playing kissing games, and a lunatic who eats out of his dog's dish while his 66 clocks tick away the time.
    17 men, 17 women; area staging. Royalty: $50-25.

THOMAS, Robert. Catch Me If You Can. See entry under Weinstock, Jack.

THOMPSON, Denman and George W. Ryer. The Old Homestead (1886). Baker, 1927 (revised from original text); CERC.
    Small-town lad goes to the big city. His father, the lovable old farmer, Joshua Whitcomb, worries about him there, but the boy makes good and returns in time to pay off the mortgage on the old homestead.
    4 acts; 9 men, 7 women (reduced by doubling from 19 men, 12 women), extras; 2 interiors, 2 exteriors.

THOMPSON, Ernest. On Golden Pond (1979). BP 1978-79; Dramatists Play Service.
    Norman Thayer, Jr., age 79, and his wife Ethel, ten years younger, are spending their 48th summer on Golden Pond in Maine. Ethel is exuberant and coddling; Norman is cynical and an "old poop." Their 42 year-old daughter Chelsea arrives for her father's 80th birthday, bringing with her a prospective second husband, Bill Ray, and a built-in family, 13-year-old Billy. Chelsea and Norman's relationship has always been strained, but a bond formed between the old man and the boy grows so strong that the past is forgiven and the future seems bright enough for even Norman to shrug off a seizure requiring a nitroglycerin pill and look forward,

uncharacteristically, to another summer on Golden Pond.
2 acts; 3 men, 1 boy, 2 women; 1 interior. Royalty: $50.

THURBER, James, with Elliott Nugent. The Male Animal (1940).
BP 1939-40; Samuel French.
Starts with the mild announcement by Tommy Turner, a young
teacher of English, that he will read Vanzetti's last letter to his
class as a model of prose. This inflames the editor of the college
paper and Tommy may be fired as a "Red." His life is further complicated by the return for the 10-year reunion of Joe Ferguson,
the great football hero and former suitor to Tommy's wife. He even
tells Ellen to go with Joe. But she finally realizes that Tommy is
a pretty good male animal and sticks to him.
3 acts; 8 men, 5 women; 1 interior. Royalty: $50-25.

_____. A Thurber Carnival (Revue) (1960). BP 1959-60; Samuel
French.
A delightful revue of Thurber sketches. Includes "The Night
the Bed Fell," the fable of the unicorn in the garden, "Gentlemen
Shoppers," "The Secret Life of Walter Mitty," "File and Forget,"
and many scenes out of Thurber cartoons. No musical talent needed
to produce this revue.
5 men, 4 women, extras (if desired). Periaktos and travel-
lers. Royalty: $50-25.

TILLER, Ted. Count Dracula (1972). Samuel French.
Mina is the latest victim of Count Dracula, who can trans-
form himself into a bat, materialize from fog, dissolve in mist.
The beautiful young woman is the ward of Dr. Seward, who runs
an insane asylum. Mina's fiancé arrives from London, worried over
her trance-like state and anxious for Professor Van Helsing
(specialist in rare diseases) to cure her. On the other side are
Dr. Seward's demented sister and a schizophrenic inmate in league
with the vampire.
7 men, 2 women; 1 interior (and one inset). Royalty: $50-
25.

TOBIN, John. The Honeymoon (1804). Dramatic Pub. Co., &
French, carried; in N.Y. Drama, v. 4 #40, 1878; in Inchbald,
v. 25; BAT v. 16.
Pretending that he is a peasant, the Duke Aranza conducts
his bride to a cottage in the country. Proud Juliana, after a struggle, submits to a month's trial, during which she is tamed less rough-
ly than Shakespeare's Katherina. On the other hand, the woman-
hating Rolando is won by Zamora, who has followed him as his page
Eugenio.
5 acts; 10 men, 4 women, extras; 5 interiors, 3 exteriors;
costumes of the period.

TOLKIEN, J. R. R. The Hobbit. See entry under Gray, Patricia.

TOLLER, Ernst. The Blind Goddess (1932). Tr. by Crankshaw,
Lond., Lane, 1934; in his Seven Plays, Lane, 1935; adapted by
Denis Johnston as Blind Man's Buff, Random House, 1939.
    A doctor is accused of poisoning his wife because of his love
for his secretary. In the trial scene he admits so much that he is
convicted. Later evidence is found which proves it was suicide.
He is released, but has no prospect ahead. Justice, which im-
prisons the innocent as well as the guilty, damages for life.
    5 acts; 22 men, 10 women, extras; 6 interiors, 1 exterior.
The Johnston adaptation has 3 acts; 11 men, 2 women, 1 girl,
extras; 4 interiors.

_____. The Machine-Wreckers (1922). Tr. by Dukes, Lond.,
Benn, & Knopf, 1923; in his Seven Plays, Lane, 1935; MOSH.
    Jimmy Corbett, leader of revolting weavers, is slain by the
thoughtless mob which refuses to see that nothing can be accomplished by the destruction of machinery. The play is based on the
revolt of the English Chartists in Nottingham in 1811; the prolog
includes Lord Byron's speech in defense of the rioters, 1812.
    Prolog & 5 acts; 20 men, 2 women, children & extras; 7 in-
teriors, 4 exteriors; costumes of the period.

_____. Man and the Masses (1921). Tr. by Untermeyer, Dou-
bleday, 1924; WATI; BATL-4; tr. by Mendel in his Seven Plays,
Lane, 1935.
    Sonia tries in vain to convert the raging masses to the prin-
ciple of peaceful humanitarianism. She wants to free the slaves in
coal mines and factories; her revolt is too successful, for they want
to war against the State. When the rebellion is crushed she is made
the scape-goat and sentenced to execution. The play is based on
the social revolution of 1873.
    7 scenes, 6 men, 3 women, extras; 5 interiors, 2 exteriors.

_____. No More Peace (1937). Tr. by Crankshaw, Farrar,
1937; CALM.
    On Mt. Olympus Napoleon and St. Francis are arguing
whether mankind really wants peace. They look down at the imaginary State of Dunkelstein where a peace festival is interrupted by
a telegram from Napoleon that war has been declared. The behavior
of the people is brilliantly satirized; even Socrates fails to restore
peace by reason. Peace comes only when they learn that the war
was a trick of the Olympians.
    2 acts; 14 men, 3 women, extras; 3 interiors.

_____. Pastor Hall (1938). Tr. by Spender & Hunt, Random
House, 1939.
    A German clergyman, Pastor Hall, defies the Nazi storm-
troopers, and because of letters found among his papers, he is sent
to a concentration camp. When threatened with 25 lashes, he escapes; he will return to his pulpit and will doubtless be re-arrested.
Shows how the Nazis got their way through family threatenings.

3 acts; 14 men, 3 women, extras; 2 interiors, 1 exterior.

TOLSTOI, Graf Lev N. The Fruits of Enlightenment (1891). Tr.
anon., Luce, 1911; tr. by Maude as Fruits of Culture, Constable, 1905; same in his Plays, Oxford, 1923; tr. by Dole in
his works, v. 16, Scribner, 1902; same in his Dramatic Works,
Crowell, 1923.
    In the midst of the idle rich, a group of starving peasants
asks for payment of land agreed to be sold. A peasant girl, pretending to have the powers of a medium, helps her fellows to purchase land from a proprietor who had hitherto refused to sell it.
Depicts the so-called cultured classes, who, despite pretended enlightenment and happiness, are underneath really unhappy and
gullible.
    4 acts; 22 men, 11 women; 3 interiors; Russian costumes.

_____. The Living Corpse (1900). Tr. by Evarts, Phila.,
    Brown Bros., 1912; tr. by Wright as The Man Who Was Dead,
    Dodd, 1912; tr. anon. as Redemption, N.Y., 1919; tr. by
    Maude in his Plays, Oxford, 1923; tr. by Dole in his Dramatic
    Works, Crowell, 1923; CHA.
    Fedya, unhappy at home, leaves Lisa his wife and is believed
to be drowned; Lisa marries again. Fedya sinks into social depths
but kills himself rather than to have Lisa arrested for bigamy.
    6 acts; 19 men, 8 women; 10 interiors.

_____. The Power of Darkness (1886). Tr. by Dole in his
    Works, v. 16, Scribner, 1902; same in his Dramatic Works,
    Crowell, 1923; tr. by Maude in his Plays, Constable, 1905;
    same Oxford, 1923; & in his Plays, v. 17, Oxford, 1937; DIK-
    1; NOY; TRE-3; TREA-2.
    A peasant farmhand, Nikita, has wronged an orphan girl,
Marina, has caused a wife to murder her husband so as to marry
him, and has taken his wife's young step-daughter as his mistress.
When she gives birth to a child, Nikita, urged on by his evil-
spirited mother, kills the baby by crushing it with a board in the
barn. Haunted by the baby's cries, he takes to drink and tries to
kill himself; an old soldier succeeds in giving Nikita courage to
give himself up to justice. His God-fearing father assures him that
God will forgive him.
    5 acts; 13 men, 7 women, 1 girl; 2 interiors, 3 exteriors.

TOPOR, Tom. Nuts (1980). BP 1979-80; Samuel French.
    Claudia Draper has been indicted for manslaughter, but a
psychiatric examination determined that she was not fit to stand
trial. Claudia is fighting the determination in a judicial proceeding
being held in the psychiatric wing of Bellevue Hospital. It turns
out that all of the bureaucrats and her mother and stepfather want
her to be "nuts," since they cannot handle the reality of a middle-
class, college educated, white girl from Mount Kisco consciously
choosing to make a living as a prostitute (it was a "john" she killed

in self-defense). Claudia is far from being the paranoid schizophrenic the system wants to label her, and though she refuses to
permit her lawyer to call a psychiatric witness in her behalf, she
cannot keep him from revealing that as a little girl she was sexually
abused by her stepfather and consequently alienated from her
mother. At the end she is judged sane, sent to trial, and acquitted
of the manslaughter charge. Her mother and stepfather, however,
file for legal separation.
     3 acts; 6 men, 3 women; 1 interior. Royalty: $50-40.

TOTHEROH, Dan. <u>Moor Born</u> (1934). Samuel French.
     Presents three years in the lives of the Brontë family at Ha-
worth parsonage in bleak Yorkshire. The three sisters discover
they have a common talent--to write; but their dissolute brother
Bramwell has none of their native genius. While sacrificing for
him, they proceed for each to write a novel. They are published
under their pseudonym of Bell: Anne, the gentle, wrote <u>Agnes
Gray</u>; Charlotte the practical, as Currer Bell, wrote <u>Jane Eyre</u>;
Emily, the passionate, wrote <u>Wuthering Heights</u>.
     5 scenes; 3 men, 5 women; 1 interior; costumes of 1840.
Royalty: $25-20.

_____. <u>Wild Birds</u> (1924). BP 1924-25; Samuel French.
     A stark tragedy set in a Middle West prairie farm owned by
John Slag, a brutish and slave-driving man. The marginal existence of the farm is due to the forced labor of a girl, Mazie (a
"wild bird"), that Slag "acquired" from an orphanage, and a boy,
Adam, who ran away from a reform school. When the two young
people fall in love, Slag refuses to permit them to marry, and when
they run off together, he catches them and forces them to continue to slave for him. Mazie, Slag discovers, is pregnant with
Adam's child, and he whips the boy so ruthlessly that he dies.
Mazie, in response, commits suicide by jumping into the well. Slag
will be accused of murdering both.
     3 acts; 7 men, 4 women; 1 interior, 4 exteriors. Royalty:
$25.

TOWNLEY, James. <u>High Life Below Stairs</u> (1759). BAT v. 16;
    BRI v. 2; MOR; OXB v. 15.
     Servants are feasting and making merry at his expense while
Lovel, the master, is away, on a pretended trip into the country.
He returns, armed with pistols, feigning to be drunk, calls forth
the ringleaders, and discharges them. He replaces them with honest
servants.
     2 acts; 5 men, 3 women, extras; 1 interior; costumes of the
period.

TRAVERS, Robert. <u>Anatomy of a Murder</u>. See entry under Winer,
    Elihu.

TREADWELL, Sophie. <u>Hope for a Harvest</u> (1941). French, 1942;

BP 1941-42.

Immigrants have taken most of the land of Elliott Martin, a peach-grower in California; he is making his living at a filling station. His cousin, Carlotta, returns from fallen France and rouses him to improve the once-fertile land. His daughter is matched with an Italian boy, Victor de Lucchi, and the future has hope.

3 acts; 5 men, 5 women; 2 interiors.

_____. Machinal (1928). BP 1928-29; GASB.

Inspired by the sensational Ruth Snyder-Judd Gray murder trial, this play deals with a mechanistic world which grinds down the life of Helen, known as Young Woman. At work, she is pursued by a man who makes her skin curl when he touches her, but she marries him to get away from the empty life she must endure to support her nagging mother. She has a child and is abused by the male doctors. Out of her loneliness she takes a lover, and finally kills her boring husband and confesses to it at her trial. In prison she learns from a priest the only thing she knows about religion (that she has committed a mortal sin), and she dies in the electric chair.

2 parts; 21 men, 7 women; 10 interiors.

TRZCINSKI, Edmund. Stalag 17. See entry under Bevan, Donald.

TULLY, R. W. The Rose of the Rancho. See entry under Belasco, David.

TURGENEV, Ivan S. A Month in the Country (1850). Tr. by Mandell in his Plays, Macmillan, 1924; tr. & adapted by Williams, Lond., Heinemann, 1943; NOY; FAMK; tr. by Noyes, TREA-1; tr. by Garnett in his Three Famous Plays, Scribner, 1952; adapted by Williams, French.

Natalia is bored in an isolated community. Mikhail, a friend of her husband, comes to visit but his platonic friendship does not suffice. Aleksei, a young tutor, is engaged to teach her son, and the lonely woman falls in love with him. Because of jealousy of her ward, Vera, she confesses her love to Aleksei, which frightens him away. Mikhail also leaves, and she is left to her routine existence.

5 acts; 7 men, 5 women, 1 boy; 2 interiors, 1 exterior; Russian costumes of the period. French royalty: $35-25.

TURNBULL, Colin. The Mountain People. See Colin Higgins's Ik.

TURNEY, Robert. Daughters of Atreus (1936). BP 1936-37; Dramatists Play Service.

A retelling of the tragedy of the House of Atreus. Agamemnon, to atone for his family's sins and enlist the help of the gods in the Trojan War, offers the life of his daughter Iphegenia as a sacrifice. His wife, Klytaimnestra, plots her revenge over her daughter's death for almost ten years of his absence, taking on his enemy Aegisthos as her lover, and killing Agamemnon herself the

night he returns from the war. The two other children of the marriage, Orestes and Elektra, plot the revenge of their father's death,
and ten years later kill both Aegisthos and Klytaimnestra, carrying
on the hatred that has plagued the House of Atreus for generations.
3 acts; 13 men, 14 women; 1 interior, 3 exteriors. Royalty:
$35-25.

TUTTLE, Day. $E=MC^2$. See entry under Davis, Hallie Flanagan.

TWEDT, Jerry L. Murder on Center Stage (1976). Dramatic Publishing Company.
A thriller about an old man obsessed with a career as an
actor. Mr. Stanley, the head janitor for the Fine Arts Building,
sets up a scene at an old theatre to murder Helen and Jessica, the
women who made fun of his Shakespeare reading over 20 years ago.
Helen Blestar is the head of the theatre department in charge of
student rehearsals of "Romeo and Juliet." The students, Mike,
Terry, Sharon, and David, get trapped in the theatre along with
Helen on a cold winter night. Jessica is the "crazy" janitor, whom
Mr. Stanley tries to frame for the murder(s).
3 acts; 3 men, 6 women; bare stage with props. Royalty:
$50-35.

TYLER, Royall. The Contrast (1787). Dunlap Society, 1887; HAL;
MOSS-1; QUIK; QUIL.
First play by an American on an American subject to be produced on the American stage. Introduces Jonathan, an agreeable
Yankee rustic of sturdy New England stock who unwittingly attends
a theatre. Maria, the unwilling fiancée of Dimple, a scheming
English fop, meets her ideal in Col. Manly, who has native worth
but is lacking a social grace. Her father discovers the true qualities of the two suitors and sees the wisdom of her choice.
5 acts; 5 men, 4 women, extras; 3 interiors, 1 exterior;
costumes of the period.

UDALL, Nicholas. Ralph Roister Doister (1553). ADA; BAS; BAT;
BOA; GAY; MAT; MIO v. 2; PAR; SCW.
Ralph is a confident braggart, and believes he can win the
lady by writing his love, but Merrygreek changes the punctuation
which alters the sense. Ralph is out of luck with Dame Custance,
who is won by Gawin Goodluck.
5 acts; 9 men, 4 women; simple scenery; costumes of the
period.

USTINOV, Peter. The Love of Four Colonels (1953). BP 1952-53;
Dramatists Play Service.
Four colonels, representing the United States, England,
France, and Russia, are arguing around the conference table in the
four-power zone of Germany following World War II. The conference
is getting nowhere, and when the four are invited to a nearby castle
by a man called Wicked Fairy, they decide to go. There they are

joined by The Good Fairy, and they meet The Sleeping Beauty. Each colonel sees Sleeping Beauty as his own national ideal, and each gets a chance (unsuccessful) to waken and claim her.
6 men, 2 women; stylized sets, interiors and exteriors. Royalty: $50-25.

_____. Photo Finish (1962). Dramatists Play Service.
Sam, a rather important author, is eighty years old. For sixty of these years he has been married to, and has fought with, his wife Stella. One night he receives a strange visitor who turns out to be Sam at age sixty. Next comes Sam at age forty and Sam at twenty. Old Sam tries to keep the others from making what he realizes were mistakes in his life: marrying Stella at twenty, not leaving her at forty, becoming involved with another woman at sixty. He is unsuccessful. Finally the Victorian version of Sam appears.
6 men, 5 women; 1 interior. Royalty: $50-25.

_____. Romanoff and Juliet (1956). Dramatists Play Service.
The president of a small country (it has a standing army of two soldiers) is being courted by both the communist and free world countries because it lies right between the East and the West. The Russians send an ambassador (Romanoff) who has a son. The United States sends a diplomat who has a daughter (Juliet). While the two governmental representatives alternately bribe and threaten the president of the strategic country, young Romanoff and Juliet quietly fall in love. National rivalries are forgotten in the midst of the excitement of a wedding.
9 men, 4 women; unit set. Royalty: $50-25.

VAJDA, Ernö. Fata Morgana (1915). Tr. by Burrell & Moeller, Doubleday, 1924; French, 1931.
A Budapest coquette, Mathilde, wife of Gabriel, arrives to spend the night and go to a ball with relatives. But the telegram not having been delivered, there is no one home except Georg, an 18-year-old student, who immediately falls in love with her. She leads him on and even goes to him for the night. Next morning all return, with them her husband. Georg protests that she is engaged to him; she appeals to him, and he gallantly tells Gabriel that he imagined things. His mirage has vanished, and, disillusioned, he goes back to his studies.
3 acts; 7 men, 8 women; 1 interior.

VALE, Martin. The Two Mrs. Carrolls (1935). Allen & Unwin, London, 1936.
The handsome painter, Geoffrey Carroll, is married happily to his second wife, Sally, until he meets Cecily. Then he thinks to get rid of Sally by slow poison, even as he had tried to get rid of Harriet, the first Mrs. Carroll. In the nick of time Harriet hears of the affair and warns Sally. Geoffrey tries to strangle Sally; failing in this he commits suicide.

3 acts; 3 men, 5 women; 2 interiors.

VALENCY, Maurice. The Enchanted. See entry under Giraudoux, Jean.

_____. The Madwoman of Chaillot. See entry under Giraudoux, Jean.

_____. Ondine. See entry under Giraudoux, Jean.

_____. The Visit. See entry under Duerrenmatt, Friedrich.

van DRUTEN, John. Bell, Book, and Candle (1950). BP 1950-51; Dramatists Play Service.
     Even in modern Manhattan we find a modern enchanting sorceress, Gillian Holroyd. Through her familiar, a cat named Pyewacket, she quickly but naturally brings things to pass, such as the arrival of the lodger upstairs, Shepherd Henderson, and the author, Sidney Redlich. She shares this witching power with her brother Nicky and her Aunt Queenie. She wins the love of Shep until he learns he was hexed. When she tries to lure him back, she finds she has lost her power, for witches can't fall in love. He finds her different, quite human in fact, and realizes he loves her. She gives up witchcraft for love.
     3 men, 2 women; 1 interior. Royalty: $50-35.

_____, with Leslie Morris. The Damask Cheek (1942). BP 1942-43; Samuel French.
     A demure English girl in her 30's, Rhoda, comes to visit her snobbish aunt in New York. She falls in love with Jimmie, who is already engaged to a superficially glamorous actress, Calla. She doesn't love Jimmie any too much; Rhoda buys her off, and Jimmie discovers the feminine graces and resources of Rhoda.
     3 men, 6 women; 1 interior. Royalty: $35-25.

_____. The Distaff Side (1933). BP 1934-35; Samuel French.
     Presents the problems of the women in an English middle-class family: the mother, querulous Mrs. Venables; her three daughters: Nellie, dully living her married life in the provinces; Liz, socially rebellious, divorced, and living on the continent; Evie, a womanly widow, who has had a happy life, doing for others; and Evie's daughter, Alex, unconventional, with present-day sex freedom, and wooed by two suitors who represent very different things.
     5 men, 8 women; 2 interiors. Royalty: $35-25.

_____. The Druid Circle (1947). Dramatists Play Service.
     The passionate young love of Tom Ellis and Megan, students in a small university near the border of Wales, is dangerously threatened by the coldness of old Professor White and his domineering elderly colleagues of the Druid Circle who sit in judgment. Their affairs are discussed also by the gossiping women of the small

community. The young people are defended by Maddox and his wife Brenda.

     5 men, 6 women; 3 interiors (can be played with 2). Royalty: $50-25.

_____. I Am a Camera (1951). BP 1951-52; Dramatists Play Service.

Drama Critics' Award, 1951/52. A character study of a giddy English girl in Berlin in 1930, a night-club singer who is quite amoral. Young Isherwood reports their devoted relationship as they drift along, acting as a camera which sees all. He also reports the love story of a young Jewish couple who are victims of savage Nazi persecution.

     7 scenes in 3 acts; 3 men, 4 women; 1 interior. Royalty: $50-35.

_____. I Remember Mama (1944). BP 1944-45; Dramatists Play Service.

(There are two versions of this play: one for high schools and another for college and community groups.) A heartwarming study of American family life with a Norwegian background. Presents several episodes showing Mama, with the help of her husband and Uncle Chris, bringing up children in a modest San Francisco home. Mama is a sweet and capable manager, gets her children educated, starts one of them as a writer.

     2 acts; 9 men (including boys), 13 women (including girls); 1 unit set, showing interior and exterior. Royalty: high school version, $35-25; college version, $50-35.

_____. Old Acquaintance (1940). Samuel French.

A serious novelist, Katharine, and a popular novelist, Mildred, are great friends. Katharine becomes interested in Rudd, 10 years younger, but he falls for Deirdre, Mildred's daughter. The two women discuss the situation in scintillating fashion, and to the astonishment of all it cements their friendship further; it strains but does not break it.

     3 acts; 2 men, 5 women; 2 interiors. Royalty: $35-25.

_____. There's Always Juliet (1931). Samuel French.

Leonora, an Englishwoman, and Dwight, an American, meet at a tea party in England and are attracted to each other. As she is trying to learn his identity, he calls. As they begin to understand each other, he is recalled to America. He proposes, she hesitates, and reluctantly they part. But he gets three more days of grace before he sails, during which she accepts him.

     3 acts; 2 men, 2 women; 1 interior. Royalty: $50-25.

_____. The Voice of the Turtle (1943). BP 1943-44; Dramatists Play Service.

Sally is living in Olive's apartment and is left to entertain Olive's attractive boy friend, Sgt. Bill Page, when Olive goes to

meet another flame. Sally and Bill get interested in each other during the three days of his leave; they fall in love, and agree to
marry. A gay, amoral play which seems to make immorality attractive, as each of the three is sophisticated and has had many past
affairs which have exceeded rigid social conventions.
>3 acts; 1 man, 2 women; 1 interior. Royalty: $50-25.

————. Young Woodley (1925). BP 1925-26; Samuel French.
>An upright and sensitive young student believes himself so
in love and so attracted to Laura, the wife of the school's headmaster, that he thinks he has done something dreadful and is
ashamed of it. Laura, with maturer understanding, helps him find
a proper perspective of true love.
>3 acts; 7 men, 2 women; 2 interiors. Royalty: $25.

VANE, Sutton. Outward Bound (1923). BP 1923-24; Samuel
>French.
>To the various passengers on a Stygian steamship, who have
been fearful at facing the unknown Examiner, it is implied that
death does not release from struggle nor punish for weakness but
starts them anew in their fight for ultimate contentment. They are
all allotted their proper places. The two suicides (called "half-
ways") are enabled to return to life again.
>3 acts; 6 men, 3 women; 1 interior. Royalty: $35-25.

van ITALLIE, Jean-Claude. America Hurrah (1967). BP 1966-67;
>Dramatists Play Service.
>A single bill comprised of three one-acts ("Interview," "TV,"
"Motel") comprising a satirical, stylized, comic, and absurdist view
of modern life. The first topic is an employment interview, where
the four masked interviewers try to destroy the self-respect of a
scrubwoman, a house painter, a banker, and a lady's maid. The
second topic is television, and we watch three normal workers moni-
toring a television program in progress. Last, three actors in doll
masks perform to an off-stage voice as a motel landlady mouths
platitudes and a tough couple wrecks everything in sight.
>4 men, 4 women to 8 men, 8 women, 3 either sex; stylized
interiors. Royalty: $50-25.

————. Interview. See America Hurrah.

————. Motel. See America Hurrah.

————. TV. See America Hurrah.

————. The Serpent (1969). BP 1969-70; Dramatists Play Ser-
>vice.
>This play, the author says, "is a ceremony reflecting the
minds and lives of the people performing it." Therefore the words
and movements in the text are a skeleton on which the actors will
"put their own flesh." Mostly the play is a celebration of love,

using the story of The Book of Genesis as it relates to modern experience.

Approximately 16 performers with a minimum of 7 men, 7 women; open stage. Royalty: $50-25.

VARESI, Gilda and Dolly Byrne. Enter Madame (1920). Putnam, 1921; Longmans, 1924; BP 1920-21.

Contrasts the artistic and the scientific minds in marriage. A temperamental prima-donna, spoiled, petted, stormy, alternating tantrums and tenderness, has differences with her more prosaic husband. He wearies of trotting from place to place with all her entourage (including the dog), but she wins him back.

3 acts; 5 men, 5 women; 1 interior possible.

VAUGHN, Stuart. The Royal Game (1974). Dramatic Publishing Company.

A historical drama set in King Henry VII's court in 15th-century England at odds with Shakespeare's Richard III. In this version, King Richard does not kill the Little Princes in the tower, and one of them, Richard of York, grows up to be enough of a threat to Henry so that he crushes Elizabeth's scheming ambitions by marrying her daughter Beth, crowning her queen, thus satisfying his critics and uniting the people.

2 acts; 16 men, 4 women, extras; unit set. Royalty: $50-35.

VEGA CARPIO, Lope Félix de. The Gardener's Dog (1618). Tr. by Underhill in his Four Plays, Scribner, 1936; tr. by Chambers as The Dog in the Manger in BAT v. 6.

Diana, Countess of Belflor, sought by many in marriage, falls in love with Teodoro, her secretary, but he has already pledged himself to Marcella. Diana will not marry him nor let him marry Marcella; she is a dog in the manger, the gardener's dog who will not eat himself nor let others eat. Two suitors, a Count and a Marquis, wish to do away with Teodoro and hire a lackey, Tristan, to kill him; but Tristan arranges for him to be found as the long-lost son of a Count Lodovico, and through this honor Teodoro gets Diana.

3 acts; 14 men, 4 women, extras; many scenes, interior and exterior; costumes of the period.

_____. The King, the Greatest Alcalde (1635). Tr. by Underhill in Poet Lore, v. 29, 1918; also in his Four Plays, Scribner, 1936; CLF-2.

Don Tello blesses the betrothal of his shepherd Sancho to Elvira, daughter of the farmer Nuño, but when he sees the beauty of the girl, he carries her off and tries to persuade her to become his mistress. Sancho appeals to the King, who comes in person, after Don Tello had disregarded his order. He has Don Tello acknowledge Elvira as wife, so she might inherit, then he has him beheaded and his property given to Sancho and Elvira.

3 acts; 11 men, 4 women, extras; 9 interiors, 5 exteriors;

costumes of the period.

_____. The Sheep Well (1619). Tr. by Underhill in his Four Plays, Scribner, 1936; KRE; TREA-1.

The peasants in the village of Fuente Ovejuna unite to resist oppression by the military. The local Commander has seized and aims to seduce Laurencia, married to a peasant Frondoso. No longer acting like sheep, the peasants attack the palace and the Commander is killed. They all agree that they will say the entire populace did it. The judge can find no one in the village of 300 who will confess otherwise than that Fuente Ovejuna did it, even under torture, though they know that Estaban gave the actual stroke.

3 acts; 20 men, 4 women, extras; various exterior scenes; costumes of the period (1476).

_____. The Star of Seville (ca. 1615). Tr. by Hayden in MAU; also in Clark, W. S.

The King orders a Spanish knight, Don Sancho, to kill his friend, the brother of Stella, his fiancée. He does as ordered, and the King tries to protect him; Don Sancho escapes the death penalty only when the King has made full confession, for even he must bow to justice. Even though they are betrothed with the King's blessing, Don Sancho and Stella mutually agree they must abandon their prospective marriage through chivalric sentiments of honor and gallantry, but especially because, though exonerated, he has killed her brother.

3 acts; 12 men, 3 women, extras; 4 interiors, 2 exteriors; costumes of the Middle Ages.

VEILLER, Bayard. The Thirteenth Chair (1916). Samuel French.

During a seance Edward Wales is stabbed to death but with no dagger in evidence. The medium's daughter is suspected but cleared when her mother uses her mindreading power to discover the real murderer.

3 acts; 10 men, 7 women; 1 interior. Royalty: $35-25.

_____. The Trial of Mary Dugan (1927). Samuel French.

Entire action takes place in the courtroom. With the evidence all against her, her younger brother, Jimmy, a fledgling lawyer, arrives from California, takes over the case, and defends her passionately. He also learns for the first time the sacrifices she has made to pay for his education. He proves the murderer was lefthanded and shows him up.

3 acts; 20 men, 7 women, extras; 1 interior. Royalty: $25-20.

_____. Within the Law (1912). French, 1917; CARC.

Mary Turner is sent to prison for three years for a theft in Gilder's Emporium which she did not commit. On her release she vows to get even; she operates a blackmailing scheme but always

within the law, being supervised by a clever lawyer. After trapping the merchant's son, Dick Gilder, into marriage, she feels her cup of vengeance is about full. Then she becomes involved in a murder at the Gilder house and finds she loves Dick.
  4 acts; 15 men, 5 women; 4 interiors.

VERNER, Gerals. Toward Zero. See entry under Christie, Agatha.

VERNEUIL, Louis. Affairs of State (1950). BP 1950-51; Samuel French.
  On a background of Washington political intrigue a love story is developed. A young Senator, George Henderson, is persuaded to take Irene Elliott as wife in name only, to offset his affection for Constance, wife of Philip Russell, a former Secretary of State. Irene, a mousy schoolteacher, in love with George from the start, blossoms into a charming hostess, as he falls in love with his hired wife, while Philip gets to keep Constance.
  3 acts; 4 men, 2 women; 1 interior. Royalty: $50-25.

VIDAL, Gore. The Best Man (1960). BP 1959-60; Dramatists Play Service.
  Deals with the fight for the presidential nomination. William Russell, ex-Secretary of State, is a scholar and a man of high principles. Joseph Cantwell is an intense, ruthless politician without moral scruples. Cantwell gets possession of some papers revealing that his rival once suffered a mental crackup. He threatens to release the information if Russell does not throw his support to him. Russell then uncovers evidence which suggests that Cantwell was once homosexual. Arthur Hockstrader, an ex-President who supports Russell, tries unsuccessfully to persuade his man to use the dirt he has uncovered. Finally, at the convention, Russell ruins Cantwell by withdrawing from the race and supporting another candidate.
  14 men, 6 women; interiors. Royalty: $50-25.

_____. Visit to a Small Planet (1957). BP 1956-57; Dramatists Play Service.
  A visitor from another planet decides to start a war for his own amusement in a very average town. The visitor has intended to arrive in time for the Civil War but arrives in 1957. He tries to make the best of it, though, and is quite impressed by such things as hydrogen bombs. In fact, he's enchanted by all the new playthings the 20th century has invented for war-making, and he sees no reason why they can't be put to use for his own amusement. It takes the combined efforts of the entire cast--an average general, an average boy and a girl in love, an average TV newscaster, and an above average Siamese cat--to persuade him to abandon his war.
  8 men, 2 women; 1 interior. Royalty: $50-25.

VIERTEL, Peter and Irwin Shaw. The Survivors (1948). Dramatists Play Service.
  Young Steve Decker, a Union soldier just out of four years in

a Confederate prison, returns to Missouri to take part in the feud
between the Deckers and the Camerons. His plan is to kill the hard-
bitten ranchman, Tom Cameron; but first he wants to know the
truth of the case against the Camerons. Thus arguments on both
sides are presented, concluding with the futility of killing as a means
of settlement.
> 3 acts; 13 men, 2 women, extras; 2 sets; costumes of 1865.
> Royalty: $35-25.

VILDRAC, Charles. Michel Auclair (1922). Tr. & adapted by
Sidney Howard in LEV 1932; carried by French.

Michel returns after a year and finds his old sweetheart Suzanne has married a stupid dishonest soldier, Blondeau. Michel
studies his rival's character and goes about to make him a husband
worthy of the girl.
> 3 acts; 5 men, 2 women; 1 interior, 1 exterior.

_____. The Steamship Tenacity (1920). Tr. by Newberry in
Poet Lore, v. 32, 1921; DIE; tr. by Sidney Howard in TUCG;
TUCM.

Two ex-soldiers, Bastien and Ségard, are on their way to
Canada but are delayed at the French seaport while the steamship
is being repaired. Both fall in love with Thérèse, the pretty waitress at the café, but Bastien the realist runs off with her, leaving
Ségard the dreamer to sail alone. Old Hidoux represents the voice
of experience.
> 3 acts; 5 men, 2 women, extras; 1 interior.

VINCENT, Allen. Letters to Lucerne. See entry under Rotter,
Fritz.

VOLLMER, Lula. The Hill Between (1939). Longmans, 1939.

A mountain boy, Brent, has become a successful doctor in
the city and married Anna, a society girl. They come back to visit
the mountain folk, among whom he realizes there is great need for
medical aid. Anna doesn't fit in with the mountain people and wants
to go back to the city at once; she also wishes to take with her his
sister Ellen, although she is in love with and engaged to Lars, a
wholesome mountain boy. When the time comes to leave, Brent decides his place is in the mountains, and he lets Anna go back to the
city.
> 3 acts; 4 men, 3 women, plus 6 men and 5 women at the
> dance, also extras; 1 interior; mountain costumes.

_____. Moonshine and Honeysuckle (1933). French, 1934.

Features a feud in the Kentucky mountains between the Be-
vinses and the Gaddises, the origin of which is forgotten. Clem
Betts strives to bring harmony by marrying off Annie Bevins to
Buck Gaddis. "Cracker" Gaddis, a little shrew, wants to keep the
feud alive, and Peg Leg (Paw) Gaddis rides his mule into the church
to break up the wedding. But after his trial for disturbing the

peace, the feud is finally ended.
  3 acts; 8 men, 5 women; 1 exterior; mountain costumes.

_____. Sun-Up (1923). Brentano, 1924; also Longmans; QUIL;
  TUCD; TUCM; BP 1923-24.
  The widow Cagle in the mountains of North Carolina has been
ever opposed to that dread abstraction--the law. She believes "the
law" killed her husband and took away her boy Rufe to fight that
feud war in France--about 40 miles east of Asheville! As she is
ready to shoot the son of the revenuer who killed her husband, the
spirit of Rufe whispers love and less hate; she has a change of
heart and resolves to live in peace.
  3 acts; 7 men, 2 women; 1 interior; mountain costumes.

VOLTAIRE. Mérope (1743). Tr. by Fleming in his Dramatic Works,
  Paris, Dumont, 1901.
  Mérope welcomes back to Messenia her son Aegytus. He returns unknown, but his identity is revealed by his father's armor
and is confirmed by old Narbas, who rescued him as an infant and
has brought him up for 15 years as father and son. Aegytus slays
Polyphontes who has usurped the crown after killing his father and
hoping to marry Mérope to confirm the accession. Written by Voltaire as a play from which the ordinary love interest is excluded;
emotion is created through Mérope's love for her son.
  5 acts; 5 men, 2 women, extras; exterior scenes; Greek
  costumes.

_____. Zaïre (1732). Tr. as Zara in Inchbald v. 7; tr. by
  Fleming in his Dramatic Works, Paris, Dumont, 1901-03.
  Zaïre, captive since birth in Palestine, wins the love of Osman, Sultan of Jerusalem, and though a Christian by birth, has
been brought up as a Moslem. Nérestan, a French gentleman, who
had escaped two years before from the Moslem prison to obtain ransom money, returns and is granted the release of all but Zaïre and
the aged Lusignan. At Zaïre's request Osman also releases him from
20 years' captivity. He proves to be the father of both Zaïre and
Nérestan, and begs her to become a Christian. She is torn between
her love for Osman and her desire to be baptized as a Christian.
In trying to leave the seraglio, she is wrongfully stabbed by Osman
who thinks she is going to a lover, but on learning the truth, stabs
himself.
  5 acts; 7 men, 2 women, extras; 1 interior; costumes of the
  period and place.

VONNEGUT, Kurt, Jr. Happy Birthday, Wanda June (1970). Samuel
  French.
  A woman with a little boy is about to be declared a widow
(her husband, a famous big game hunter and adventurer, disappeared
in the Amazon jungle years ago). She and her son and her two
suitors (a doctor and a vacuum cleaner salesman) are celebrating
her "late" husband's birthday with a cake decorated for a Wanda June

when her husband unexpectedly shows up after all this time with
his friend, a bush pilot. He is an awful person, it turns out, who
is unsuccessful in getting his son to shoot him and unsuccessful at
shooting himself. A wild and funny story in the Vonnegut manner.
    5 men, 2 women, 2 children; 1 interior, scrim. Royalty:
    $50-35.

_____. Welcome to the Monkey House (1970). Adapted by
    Christopher Sergel. Dramatic Publishing Company.
    Scenes from Vonnegut's collection of short stories, beginning
with a young man who searches for identity and companionship by
acting in amateur theatricals and ending with a high school music
teacher's attempt to salvage a rebellious male student.
    Variable cast of 10 to 24; bare stage with props. Royalty:
    $60-40.

WALKER, Joseph A. The River Niger (1973). BP 1972-73; Samuel
    French.
    John Williams, a mid-fifties poet/house painter, and his
family live in Harlem. John is proud of his son Jeff, who is sched-
uled to return from service as an Air Force lieutenant, even though
his best friend Dudley is unimpressed by any black man serving in
the "white man's air force." When Jeff gets home, it turns out that
he is too anti-establishment to suit his father and not enough to
suit his militant black friends. At the end of the play the hero is
John, whose hard drinking and poetic composition have left him tho
kind of strength to assume the penalties of a younger generation's
clash with the white man's law.
    Black cast of 9 men, 4 women; 1 interior. Royalty: $50-35.

WALLACH, Ira. The Absence of a Cello (1965). Dramatists Play
    Service.
    A physicist is so broke that he is willing to seek a job with
a big corporation at a salary of $60,000. When the scientist becomes
aware of corporation standards of conformity, he stores away the
rolled-up trousers he wears, hides the books on medieval history
his wife writes, and conceals the cello he plays with pick-up quar-
tets. Even friends and relatives are brought in to reinforce the conservative image. But the man from personnel sees through the pose,
and suggests that any man who alters himself to please a corporation
is in no position to blame a corporation for its demands on employees.
More fun follows.
    3 men, 4 women; 1 interior. Royalty: $50-25.

WALPOLE, Hugh. Kind Lady. See entry under Chodorov, Edward.

WALTER, Eugene. The Easiest Way (1908). Dillingham, 1911:
    Houghton, 1921; DID; MOSS-3; BP 1909-1919.
    An actress, Laura, after a life of struggle, meets a man she
really loves, a newspaper reporter. But she is the mistress of a
wealthy man who can give her ease; she hasn't the strength to take

the hard narrow path that would lead to happiness. In the end she loses both men.
4 acts; 3 men, 3 women; 2 interiors, 1 exterior.

WANG, David Henry. The Dance and the Railroad (1982). BP 1981-82; Dramatists Play Service.
It is the summer of 1867, on a mountaintop near the tracks being laid for the transcontinental railroad. Lone, a two year veteran of railway labor, practices the exacting, ballet-like art of traditional Chinese opera as a way of countering the dehumanizing effect of coolie labor. He is spied on by a newly arrived worker, Ma, who first chides him for not spending time with his fellow workers (they call him "Prince of the Mountain," he says), urges him to celebrate with the men on what first appears to be a strike victory over the white man, but comes to see Lone's position that "attitude is everything" and one must engage in personal beauty and discipline to keep from becoming "a dead man."
1 act; 2 men, 1 exterior. Royalty: $35-25.

WARD, David. "The Sting." See entry under Rogers, David.

WARD, Douglas Turner. Happy Ending and Day of Absence (1965). Dramatists Play Service.
Two short plays with an all black cast, part of a single bill which had a long run off-Broadway. In "Happy Ending," sisters Ellie and Vi sit in the kitchen of a Harlem tenement bemoaning the end of their jobs. One is maid and the other laundress for the wealthy (white) Harrisons, but since Mr. H. discovered his wife in adultery it appears that the marriage and home will break up, along with the black women's jobs. A nephew chides the two for caring, but Ellie explains to him all the fringe benefits (household graft) that go along with their employment. By the end of the play the Harrisons have got together again and have called Ellie to come baby-sit for them. In "Day of Absence," described by the author as "a Reverse Minstrel Show," the black cast makes up in whiteface and plays the residents of a Southern town in which all the blacks have strangely disappeared. A crisis is clearly at hand. White infants scream when they are cared for by their own parents, policemen have no one to club, the Klansmen no one to intimidate. The mayor of the town pleads with the Governor, the President, the NAACP to send him some black citizens.
"Happy Ending": 2 men, 2 women; 1 interior. Royalty: $25-15. "Day of Absence": 8 men, 6 women (many roles doubled); unit set. Royalty: $25-15.

WARREN, Robert Penn. All the King's Men (1948). Dramatists Play Service.
Mr. Warren's disclaimer notwithstanding, the play treats the story of Huey Long, Governor of Louisiana. Willie Stark is the name of the political figure in the play who rises from a simple country boy to absolute dictator of the state. Though his methods

are corrupt, Stark is able to accomplish things for the people which remain only unattainable ideals for more honest politicians.

14 men, 4 women; extras; open stage with minimum props. Royalty: $35-25.

WASSERMAN, Dale. One Flew Over the Cuckoo's Nest (1963). Based on Ken Kesey's novel. Samuel French.

A devil-may-care character makes the mistake of arranging to spend time in a mental institution instead of a prison. He runs into a head nurse who runs the hospital with an iron hand and who hates him for interfering with the way she handles her "boys." A power struggle develops, and the new inmate is given electro-shock treatments for his first offense, and finally a frontal lobotomy. To keep him from living the rest of his life as a vegetable, the other inmates smother him.

17 men, 5 women; 1 interior and inset. Royalty: $50-25.

WATKIN, Lawrence Edward. On Borrowed Time. See entry under Osborn, Paul.

WATKINS, Maurine. Chicago (1926). Knopf, 1927; BP 1926-27.

Roxie Hart shoots Casely and is of course arrested. Such a story is a set-up for Jake the reporter and Bill Flynn the lawyer. Coached by Flynn, Roxie so works on the jury that she is found "not guilty."

3 acts; 18 men, 8 women; 4 interiors.

WATTERS, George Manker, with Arthur Hopkins. Burlesque (1927). BP 1927-28; Samuel French.

Skid and Bonny Johnson are burlesque performers, playing with a troupe that tours the midwest. Skid is a hard drinker but he has plenty of talent. When he gets a shot at the big time, Bonny helps him get off, even though she knows she will lose him to booze and women. In New York Skid becomes a big star, though his drinking gets more and more in the way of his performances. After making a fool of himself in front of Bonny and the man who wants her hand in marriage, Skid goes way over the edge, even running out on a show, about to open, that showcases his talent. Bonny, who is waiting for her divorce from Skid to be final, is sent for, and she not only gives up her retirement from show business to join the show, but she immediately straightens Skid out and promises to remarry him.

3 acts; 11 men, 4 women; 3 interiors. Royalty: $25-20.

WEBSTER, John. The Duchess of Malfi (ca. 1617). In his Complete Works, v. 2, Houghton, 1928; (earlier edns., 1830, 1857); in Mermaid ser., Scribner, 1888; in Belles Lettres ser., Heath, 1904; in Ebony ser., Dodd, 1930; in Temple classics, Dutton, 1937; BAS; DUN; HARC v. 7; HOW; MAT; NEI; OLH; OLI v. 2; SCH; SCI; TAU; THA; TRE-1 & 2; TREA-1; WHE.

The widowed Duchess secretly marries her steward Antonio,

thus giving offense to her brothers. In revenge, the brothers kill her and her children; the betrayer, de Bosola, kills the brothers and Antonio. In the end, all are wiped out: a total of 10 slain, one poisoned, and one going mad.

    5 acts; 12 men, 3 women, extras; 7 interiors, 2 exteriors; costumes of the period.

WEDEKIND, Frank. Spring Awakening (1892). Translated by Edward Bond, 1979. Dramatic Publishing Company.

    A play about curious teenagers and their fascination with sex, in which an innocent search in an atmosphere of repression leads to abortion, suicide, and death. Melchior Gabor, an intelligent youngster, writes an essay on human reproduction, complete with details and illustrations, which society believes caused his friend Morizt Stiefl to rape young Wendla Bergman and then kill himself over guilt. Wendla, who thinks her situation could have been avoided had her mother been willing to answer her questions about babies, later dies from an abortion. At the end, Melchior is beckoned by a Masked Man into the realm of death.

    3 acts; large cast; multiple simple sets. Royalty: $60-40.

_____. Such Is Life (1903). Tr. by Ziegler, Phila., Brown, 1912 & 1916; in DIE; in TUCG.

    King Nicolo and his daughter, Alma, are thrust out of the kingdom of Perugia when the citizens revolt and place a Master Butcher on the throne. He becomes a tailor and Alma a stenographer. For lèse majesté he is arrested; after release they join a circus where he gives a take-off of a king before his supplanter who appoints him (unrecognized) as the Court Fool. He dies as such, trying to prove that Alma is a princess.

    5 acts; 24 men, 2 women, extras; 4 interiors, 4 exteriors; costumes.

WEILL, Kurt. Johnny Johnson. See entry under Green, Paul.

WEINSTOCK, Jack and Willie Gilbert. Catch Me If You Can (1965). Based on the play by Robert Thomas. Samuel French.

    A whodunit that takes place at a mountain lodge, where an advertising man has just brought his new bride for a honeymoon. Immediately she disappears. A young woman arrives who claims she's his new wife (though he denies it) and a priest who backs up her story. After a delicatessen owner arrives there are two murders at the isolated lodge. A mystery-comedy with some startling twists.

    5 men, 2 women; 1 interior. Royalty: $50-25.

WEISS, Peter. The Investigation (1966). Dramatic Publishing Company.

    Deals with the Frankfurt trial of the atrocities of Auschwitz. The house lights are kept on during the play, contributing to the sense of participation, and the stage is bare except for some chairs and tables. Through the course of the play testimony is heard from the accused and from the witnesses for the prosecution. A powerful and intense play.

28 men, 2 women; bare stage. Royalty: $60-40.

_____. The Persecution and Assassination of Jean Paul Marat as Performed by the Inmates of the Asylum of Charenton Under the Direction of the Marquis de Sade (Marat/Sade) (1965). English version by Geoffrey Skelton. Verse adaptation by Adrian Mitchell. BP 1965-66; Dramatic Publishing Company.

The basic action of the play is a play put on by the inmates of the Charenton Asylum for the benefit of the Director of the institution and his two lady friends. The Marquis de Sade (who actually was an inmate there and was known to have staged plays during his confinement) stages a wild drama dealing with events leading up to the slaying of Marat by Charlotte Corday. The inmate-actors, in grubby dress, have their own anguish to express besides that inherent in their play.

9 men, 3 women, bits and extras; 1 set. Royalty: $75-50.

WEITZENKORN, Louis. Five-Star Final (1930). French, 1931; BP 1930-31.

In this strong attack on yellow journalism, the tabloid paper plays up the Nancy Voorhees murder of 20 years ago in order to boost its circulation. When this is published, Nancy and her husband poison themselves, and Jenny, their daughter, accuses Hinchcliffe, the owner of the paper, of murder. Philip, her fiancé, stands by her. Randall, the managing editor, has to carry it through, but he denounces Hinchcliffe as he leaves the paper.

3 acts in 19 scenes; 16 men, 10 women; various interiors.

WELLER, Michael. Loose Ends (1979). BP 1979-80; Samuel French.

Paul and Susan, coming of age in the late sixties, truly are at loose ends as we watch them meet overseas in 1970 and subsequently marry and pursue independent, professional careers in Boston and New York. Though their careers in the photography and movie business flourish, their personal relationship does not, and the final straw for Paul is his discovery that Susan--a year ago--had aborted the child that he longs for but that she is not yet ready for. They divorce, only to end up meeting a couple of years later, both committed to other people and still with as many loose ends as ever.

8 scenes; 7 men, 4 women; various simple interiors and exteriors. Royalty: $50-40.

_____. Moonchildren (1971). BP 1971-72; Samuel French.

The setting is a student apartment in a university town inhabited by five college senior men and three coeds. What they have in common is the senselessness of their lives, their inability to commit to any purpose, and their mockery of the plastic up-tight establishment and straight world. They take on policemen, landladies,

and salesmen with the same kind of witty boredom that they bring
to the anti-war movement and other causes they think they feel
deeply about.
    12 men, 3 women; 1 interior. Royalty: $50-35.

WELLES, Orson. Moby Dick-Rehearsed (1965). Based on Herman
    Melville's novel. Samuel French.
    In this melodrama, Welles manages to accommodate the story
to the stage with an ingenious contrivance. First he presents a
Shakespearean company rehearsing King Lear. Then they decide to
try a new play entitled "Moby Dick." With rehearsal platforms as
the deck, and a ladder serving as mast, the company proceeds to
enact the epic saga of Captain Ahab and the Pequod.
    12 men, 2 women; stage props. Royalty: $35-25.

WELTY, Eudora. The Ponder Heart. See entry under Fields,
    Joseph.

WERFEL, Franz. Jacobowsky and the Colonel (1944). Adapted by
    S. N. Behrman. BP 1943-44; Dramatists Play Service.
    The little Jewish refugee, Jacobowsky, who has survived by
his wits, is contrasted with the Polish Colonel, who maintains his
feudalistic attitude. They want to escape from France ahead of the
invading Germans. Finally the Colonel realizes that Jacobowsky
has precisely those admirable qualities necessary for survival. Marianne is a symbol of the spirit of oppressed France; she will await
the Colonel's return.
    3 acts; 23 men (some as extras), 5 women; 2 interiors, 4
exteriors. Royalty: $50-25.

_____. Juarez and Maximillian (1924). Tr. by Langner, Simon
    & Schuster for Theatre Guild, 1926.
    Presents incidents in the Mexican career of Emperor Maxi-
millian. After he signed a decree that all revolutionaries be shot,
his popularity waned rapidly; his troops were defeated by the
troops of Juarez, led by Diaz; he was taken and shot. Maximillian
was the victim of his own blind idealism and failure to understand
the Mexicans. The influence of Juarez is felt throughout the play
though he never appears.
    3 acts & epilog in 13 scenes; 26 men, 1 boy of 3, 3 women,
extras; 8 interiors, 3 exteriors.

_____. Paul Among the Jews (1926). Tr. by Levertoff, Lond.,
    Diocesan House, 1928; Lond., Grey Walls Press, 1943.
    Paul returns to Jerusalem as a Christian and visits his old
teacher, Gamaliel, also Barnabas, Peter, and James. He believes
that orthodox Judaism has been transcended by the new faith and
gospel of love; that the Jews by their fanaticism have given the Romans a pretext for denying their liberties. Peter takes one attitude,
Paul another.
    6 scenes; 18 men, 1 woman, extras; 5 interiors, 1 exterior.

WESKER / 391

WESKER, Arnold. Chips with Everything (1962). BP 1963-64;
   Samuel French.
   A patrician youth with all the qualifications for officers
school has no desire for leadership in this drama about the training
of Air Force recruits. These military novices are first exposed to
drill-master Corporal Hill whose opening words are, "I am not a
happy man." Then the wing commander informs the group that they
are not really at peace. But the recruits survive the officers and
such adventures as a boisterous, rebellious Christmas party, and
finally arrive at their graduation as the play comes to a close.
   23 men; various settings. Royalty: $50-40.

WEST, Morris L. The Devil's Advocate. See entry under Schary,
   Dore.

WETZEL, Donald. All Summer Long. See entry under Anderson,
   Robert.

WEXLEY, John. The Last Mile (1930). BP 1929-30; French, 1930.
   A thrilling presentation of a jailbreak, depicting the actions
and psychology of several men in the death-cell in an Oklahoma
prison. Killer Mears engineers the break, but when he realizes he
is licked, he walks out into machine gun fire.
   3 acts; 16 men, 0 women; 1 interior.

_____. They Shall Not Die (1934). BP 1933-34; Samuel French.
   Negro boys and two white girls are taken off a freight train
and thrown into jail. The girls are bribed by the sheriff to charge
the colored boys with rape, and the boys are beaten into confessing.
Later Lucy admits she has given false testimony. In the final court
room scene, despite the excellent brief by the defense lawyer, it is
evident the trial is a complete frame-up motivated by race prejudice,
with little hope for the boys.
   52 men, 5 women; 5 interiors. Royalty: $25.

WHARTON, Edith. Ethan Frome. See entry under Davis, Owen.

_____. The Old Maid (1935). Adapted by Zoë Akins. BP 1934-
   35; Samuel French.
   Pulitzer prize play for 1935. Charlotte, the real mother,
never reveals her secret that the child who regards her as a hard-
hearted old maid is her illegitimate daughter. Her yearning mother-
love strikes a tragic note when her sister wins the girl's affection.
   5 men, 9 women; 3 interiors. Royalty: $25-20.

WHEELER, Edward L. Deadwood Dick. See entry under Taggart,
   Tom.

WHEELER, Hugh. Big Fish, Little Fish (1961). BP 1960-61;
   Dramatists Play Service.
   William Baker, a textbook editor, is the big fish in the small

pond he runs out of his Manhattan bachelor apartment. His circle of friends and hangers-on consists of misfits and has-beens in the fringes of the world of arts and letters who need him to keep themselves going. Even his two regular women are in that category (the plain one is married and stays over only when her husband is out of town; the other lives in Philadelphia). It is believed that William had a stroke of misfortune as a college professor 20 years before (a coed fell in love with him without cause and killed herself in his apartment) and has been doing penance in a job beneath his abilities every day since, and getting drunk every night. When he is offered the opportunity to go into big time editing he resists, since he would have to move to Switzerland and leave behind all of the people who count on him. He does decide to make the move, however, and immediately the oldest and most vulnerable of William's friends dies. At the end of the play, the attractive job offer is withdrawn, and William will only go to Europe for a visit and then return to be the big fish again.

    3 acts; 5 men, 2 women; 1 interior. Royalty: $50-25.

WHITE, Diz. <u>Bullshot Crummond</u>. See entry under House, Ron.

WHITE, George. <u>Royal Gambit</u>. See entry under Gressieker, Hermann.

WHITEMORE, Hugh. <u>Pack of Lies</u> (1985). BP 1984-85; Samuel French.

    Bob and Barbara Jackson live in a comfortable London suburb with their teenage daughter Julie--the time is the early sixties. Their best friends, Peter and Helen Kroger, formerly from Canada, live across the street. Most of the socializing is done at the Jackson home during the week since Peter, who deals in antiquarian books, works every weekend. The couples are so close that Julie calls Helen "Aunt Helen" and the Krogers even own a car exactly the model and color of the Jackson's car. The friendship is destroyed when a man named Stewart, from Scotland Yard, asks to use Julie's bedroom as an observation post. Little by little information comes out that implicates the Krogers in something illegal. Barbara, especially, despises the lies she must begin to tell Helen, and even to her daughter Julie. Finally, the Krogers (who are really Americans working for the Russians) are rounded up along with a major spy named Gordon Lonsdale and sentenced to 20 years in prison. Eight years later they are exchanged for a British spy held by the Russians and leave the country. Barbara, who has never recovered from her sense of being used by Helen and her guilt over having betrayed Helen to the authorities, dies a few weeks later of a heart attack.

    2 acts; 3 men, 5 women; combination interior set. Royalty: $60-40.

WHITMAN, Walt. See Paul Shyre's <u>A Whitman Portrait</u>.

WIBBERLEY, Leonard. The Mouse That Roared (1963). Dramatic
    Publishing Company.
    High School Theater Classic, 1960-69. Duchess Gloriana, the
pretty 22-year-old ruler of a tiny nation in the Alps, learns that
her country is near bankruptcy. To get funds she decides to declare war on the U.S., reasoning that though her country would
certainly lose, the U.S. would pour in aid, relief, and rehabilitation
on the vanquished. But the U.S. State Department considers
Gloriana's "Declaration" a prank, and she orders her army to invade
so that they can surrender and reap the rewards. In a completely
unexpected development, however, the invasion succeeds and her
army wins!
    20 or more characters; 1 interior. Royalty: $50-35.

WIED, Gustav Johannes. 2 × 2 = 5 (1906). Tr. by Boyd & Koppel
    in LEG.
    A liberal champion of truth and freedom accepts a position
with a good salary on a newspaper whose policy he had formerly
disapproved; he does so for the sake of his wife and children.
Others in the play change readily, as when a radical concedes to
convention. Thus all are inclined to adapt the truth to suit themselves.
    4 acts; 11 men, 7 women; 3 interiors.

WIERS JENSSEN, Hans. The Witch (1910). Tr. by Masefield,
    Little Brown, 1917; Brentano, 1926.
    Anne Petersdotter at 17 marries the palace chaplain, the el-
derly (55) Absolon. For love of Anne he had spared her mother,
accused of being a witch. Martin, his son, returns form study
abroad and falls in love with his young step-mother, and she with
him. She tries her hypnotic power which she believes she has inherited from her mother and succeeds in willing the death of Absolon. Accused of sorcery, she is asked to prove her innocence by
touching the corpse. In doing so she loses her reason and confesses she tried to bewitch both husband and stepson.
    4 acts; 9 men, 5 women; extras; 2 interiors, 1 exterior;
    costumes of 16th century, Norway.

WILBRANDT, Adolf. The Master of Palmyra (1889). Tr. by Stork
    in FRA v. 16; tr. by Olive in Poet Lore, v. 13, 1902.
    Apelles, the Master, returns as conqueror and is greeted by
Pausanius, the Care-releaser. Apelles asks to live forever. He
has four episodes with women in his long life: Zoe, Phoebe, Per-
sida, and Zenobia. At the end of each experience, Pausanius appears and asks if he still wishes to live forever. In the epilog,
Apelles sees in Zenobia, who is a humble benefactress of the poor,
a reincarnation of Zoe and Phoebe, and he is content to die.
    Prolog, 3 acts & epilog; 13 men, 6 women, extras; 1 inte-
    rior, 3 exteriors; costumes of the period (4th century A.D.).

WILDE, Oscar. An Ideal Husband (1895). In the various editions of his Works: French carried.

Robert Chilton, now an Under-Secretary and famous for his probity, sold a state secret 18 years before. This appears in an incriminating letter held by the adventurous Mrs. Cheveley. She forces him to favor a project which he had formerly opposed; but since his wife is so disappointed, he advises Mrs. Cheveley that he cannot keep his promise. Though his dishonesty in the matter is revealed, the affair is cleared up and he is offered a Cabinet post.

4 acts; 9 men, 6 women; 3 interiors.

_____. The Importance of Being Earnest (1895). In every edition of his Collected Works; acting editions carried by Baker & French; in ASH; CAR; CEU; MOSO; SMR; STE; TRE-1, 2, & 3; TREA-3; TUCD; TUCM; WHI; abridged in Pierce & Matthews v. 1.

As an alibi for week-end holidays Jack Worthing invents a younger brother Earnest who frequently demands attention. His friend Algy introduces himself as Earnest to Jack's ward, Cecily, but confusion reigns when Jack proposes to Gwendolyn (Algy's cousin) as Earnest, for she feels she is fated to marry an Earnest. Jack and Algy decide to be rechristened, since both girls seem to be engaged to Earnest. Jack turns out to be Algy's long lost brother, left as a baby in a handbag in Victoria station, and he is actually named Earnest.

3 acts; 5 men, 4 women; 2 interiors, 1 exterior. No royalty.

_____. Lady Windermere's Fan (1892). In every edition of his Collected Works; acting editions carried by Baker and French; DIC; HUD; LIE; MAT; MOO; RUB; SMO; TAU; abridged in Pierce & Matthews v. 1.

Young Lady Windermere quarrels with her husband for his attentions to a Mrs. Erlynne, unaware that she is her mother, whom she supposed deceased, and that he is only trying to help the lady. Leaving a note that she is leaving to elope with her lover, she goes to Lord Darlington's apartments. Mrs. Erlynne, finding the note follows her there and persuades her to escape unnoticed. When the men come and find Lady Windermere's fan, Mrs. Erlynne emerges as if from an assignation and takes the blame for having brought along the fan by mistake. She thus saves her daughter's reputation at the cost of her own.

4 acts; 7 men, 6 women; 3 interiors. No royalty.

_____. A Woman of No Importance (1893). In most of his Collected Works; COT.

When Gerald Arbuthnot, a clerk, is offered the position of secretary to Lord Illingworth, his mother is unwilling to reveal to him that Lord Illingworth is his father who never married her because she was a woman of no importance. But when Lord Illingworth insults Gerald's fiancée Hester and Gerald attempts to kill him, she confesses that he is his father. Illingworth now offers to marry her, but she dismisses him as a man of no importance.

4 acts; 8 men, 7 women; 3 interiors, 1 exterior.

WILDENBRUCH, Ernst von. <u>King Henry</u> (1896). Tr. by Wernaer
in <u>Drama</u> v. 5, 1915; FRA v. 17.
Henry is the conqueror of the Saxons and King of Germany,
but he wishes to be crowned Emperor by the Pope. The Pope refuses. When Henry writes a deposing letter, the Pope excommuni-
cates him. His wife Bertha persuades him to be a penitent, and he
is one for three days at Canossa. Later he wins over Pope Gregory
and is to be crowned Emperor by the succeeding Pope.
Prolog & 4 acts; many men, 3 women, some children, extras; 6 interiors, 1 exterior; costumes of the period (about
1075).

WILDER, Thornton. <u>Lucrece</u>. See entry under Obey, Andre.

_____. <u>The Matchmaker</u> (1954). BP 1955-56; Samuel French.
Set in 1880 New York, this farce humorously depicts the attempts of a rich old Yonkers merchant to find a suitable mate. To
this end he employs a matchmaker, a woman who involves him in a
series of madcap escapades resulting in chaos for his business and
the lives of all around him. The merchant soon finds he loves his
matchmaker and the two become engaged, but not before the wily
lady has forced him to give up his blustery, domineering ways.
9 men, 7 women; 4 interiors. Royalty: $50-25.

_____. <u>Our Town</u> (1938). BP 1937-38; Samuel French.
Pulitzer prize play 1938. Saga of a small New England town,
depicting life, love, and death. George Gibbs and Emily Webb fall
in love and marry. Emily, after her death, returns for her 12th
birthday, but finds the living are unseeing and troubled, not realizing their possibilities.
3 acts; 17 men, 7 women, extras; 1 bare stage. Royalty:
$50-25.

_____. <u>The Skin of Our Teeth</u> (1942). BP 1942-43; Samuel
French.
Pulitzer prize play 1943. Playful spoofing with a serious un-
dertone. Presents a satiric story of the extraordinary adventures
of the Antrobus family (i.e. Man) down through the ages from the
Ice Age. They have survived a thousand calamities by the skin of
their teeth and are practically indestructible while Man has his
family and his books. Introduces many outstanding events in the
history of man, such as the discovery of the wheel and the invention of the alphabet. Man has learned much and is still learning.
3 acts; 5 men, 5 women, many extras; 1 interior; 1 exterior. Royalty: $50-25.

WILLIAMS, Emlyn. <u>The Corn Is Green</u> (1938). BP 1940-41;
Dramatists Play Service.
A school-teacher, Miss Moffat, goes to a Welsh mining town,

starts a school for the underprivileged miners, and there discovers a genius in a young tough collier, Morgan Evans. She coaches him through to win a scholarship at Oxford.
    3 acts; 10 men, 5 women, extras; 1 interior. Royalty: $50-25.

_____. A Murder Has Been Arranged (1928). Samuel French.
    Sir Charles Jasper stands to inherit two million pounds on his fortieth birthday. When that day arrives he gives a party to celebrate his new wealth. The gaiety is momentarily interrupted by the arrival of Maurice, a nephew who will receive the fortune if Sir Charles dies. Maurice induces his uncle to drink poison and write a suicide note. In the climax to this melodrama, however, the remaining guests trap Maurice into confessing the murder.
    4 men, 5 women; 1 interior. Royalty: $35-25.

_____. Night Must Fall (1935). Samuel French.
    Danny is a bell-hop in a resort hotel, and yet a dashing young assassin. The murder of a guest in the hotel is traced to him by Olivia, who nevertheless is fascinated by him when her aunt, old Mrs. Bramson, adds him to the household servants. Danny is powerless in the grip of his homicidal instincts and plots to murder Mrs. Bramson for her money. The police take him away to be hanged, leaving Olivia relieved but desolate.
    3 acts; 4 men, 5 women; 1 interior. Royalty: $50-25.

_____. Someone Waiting (1953). Dramatists Play Service.
    A student has failed his law exams. Part of the reason is that he hates his adopted father, but mostly the boy is upset because his best friend has just been executed for murdering a servant girl in their apartment. The new tutor for the student turns out to be the father of the executed friend, and has taken the position to administer justice to the real murderer. After many misdirections, the murder is solved.
    4 men, 5 women; 1 interior. Royalty: $35-25.

WILLIAMS, Herschel. Janie. See entry under Bentham, Josephine.

WILLIAMS, Hugh and Margaret Williams. The Irregular Verb to Love (1961). Samuel French.
    Hedda Rankin returns home from prison to find that nothing has gone right during her absence. Her husband, a zoo official, has been unfaithful; her daughter will not marry the man she loves; and her son has just returned from abroad with a Greek girl who speaks no English. Hedda sets out to straighten out everyone's affairs, and takes credit for doing so. But it is her husband who makes things right again.
    4 men, 5 women; 1 interior. Royalty: $50-25.

WILLIAMS, Jaston, with Joe Sears and Ed Howard. Greater Tuna (1981). Samuel French.

Thurston Wheelis and Arles Struvie are co-anchors of the
Wheelis-Struvie Report on radio station OKKK, Tuna, Texas, serving
the Greater Tuna area with news, weather, gossip, funeral reports,
call-in programs, and live meetings. In the Off Broadway production
of the play, two male actors played all of the 20 parts, including
Aunt Pearl, who poisons every stray dog she sees, and Berta Bu-
miller, whose son Jody brings the rest of the strays home to live.
Only in Greater Tuna can one find judges like Roscoe Buckner (found
dead wearing a 1950 turquoise, Dale Evans, one-piece swimming suit
with lots of cow-gal fringe) and a Censorship of the Text Books
Committee attempting a nationwide ban of Roots (it only shows one
side of the slavery issue).
    2 acts; 2 men (cast expandable up to 14 men, 6 women);
various simply suggested locales. Royalty: $50-40.

WILLIAMS, Jesse Lynch. Why Marry? (1917). Scribner, 1918;
    CORF; QUI; BP 1909-1919.
    1st Pulitzer prize play, 1918. Skillfully depicts within the
circle of one family the various kinds of marriages, from the girl
brought up to be married to the one who doesn't want to be married. Centers around the problem of Helen and whether to go to
Paris with Dr. Ernest Hamilton with or without marriage. Deftly
defines the ancient and necessary institution. Originally pub. 1914
as "And so they were married."
    3 acts; 7 men, 3 women; 1 interior.

_____. Why Not? (1922). BP 1922-23; Boston, Baker, 1924.
    An attack on the absurdities of divorce laws in New York
State. Mary and Leonard are servants in the home of Bill and
Evadne. Both couples are miserable and know that they should
have married differently long ago, when Leonard loved Evadne and
Bill loved Mary. They decide to fix things by marrying correctly
now, but New York laws do not allow for this kind of fine tuning.
The girls could go to Reno and sue for divorce on grounds of desertion, but Mary is Episcopalian and can only remarry if her husband
commits adultery. Since Leonard will not "sin" for her, she turns
Presbyterian. A year later the new marriages are happy, but the
children complain about seeing their real fathers so infrequently.
They propose, and the adults agree, to live in opposite wings of
the same big house with the middle as a neutral zone.
    3 acts; 4 men, 4 women, 1 interior.

WILLIAMS, Samm-Art. Home (1978). BP 1979-80; Samuel French.
    Cephus Miles is black and beautiful, raised by God-fearing
people in rural North Carolina. Pattie Mae, the girl he loves, goes
off to college and develops greater expectations than a small farmer
like himself will ever be able to provide. When he gets his draft
notice during the Vietnam War he refuses to be inducted and is sent
to prison. By the time he gets out, his farm has been sold for back
taxes, and he tries to make a life for himself in the city but succeeds only with drugs and the "wino school of survival." When a

mysterious person from home buys back his farm and sends him the deed, Cephus returns Home, to the Deep South, where even Pattie Mae is now waiting for him.

1 act; 3 men, 2 women; 1 exterior. Royalty: $50-35.

WILLIAMS, Tennessee. Camino Real (1953). Dramatists Play Service.

A fantasy set in a walled community. The only character who has access to the outside is Don Quixote, the "victim of romantic folly." Other people shut in include Camille, Casanova, and Kilroy, a former boxer, always a patsy, whose heart has been corrupted. Finally Kilroy becomes fit to be the companion of Don Quixote, and they leave together.

26 men (doubling possible); 10 women; extras; exterior, interiors. Royalty: $50-25.

_____. Cat on a Hot Tin Roof (1955). BP 1954-55; Dramatists Play Service.

All of the characters in the play are as insecure and desperate as the proverbial "cat" of the title. Big Daddy is dying of cancer, and everyone is greedy for his wealth. Brick is tortured by the notion that he is a latent homosexual, and he refuses to sleep in the same bed with his wife, Maggie, who finds her own desires unfulfilled. Sins of the past, greed for the future, and an unwillingness to face the truths of the present motivate Big Daddy's family.

8 men, 5 women, 4 children; 1 interior. Royalty: $50-35.

_____. The Glass Menagerie (1945). BP 1944-45; Dramatists Play Service.

The fragile cripple, Laura, is so repressed that she has lost contact with reality and finds refuge in the enjoyment of her glass figures. To her mother's regret she has no "gentlemen callers." For Mother Amanda lives in the past, reminiscing of her youth. She is much excited when son Tom brings Jim home to dinner, until it turns out that Jim is already engaged to be married. Tom leaves home as his father did, but he can't lose the memory of Laura.

2 men, 2 women; 1 interior. Royalty: $50-35.

_____. The Milk Train Doesn't Stop Here Anymore (1962). BP 1962-63; Dramatists Play Service.

Mrs. Goforth has lived a full and lecherous life. Now, in one of her villas on the southern coast of Italy, she dictates her memoirs to secretaries and tape recorders with the absurd notion that they will provide an important social commentary. Chris Flanders, a young poet, arrives at the villa. His enemies call him "the angel of death" because of his presence at the deaths of so many elderly women. Mrs. Goforth sees in Chris the opportunity to have one last sexual fling before death, and she tries to buy him. Only near the end does she realize he is not for sale--he merely wishes to soothe her at the time of death.

5 men, 4 women; unit set. Royalty: $50-25.

_____. The Night of the Iguana (1959). BP 1961-62; Dramatists
Play Service.
     Maxine, a nymphomanical widow, runs a cheap resort hotel
in Mexico. For her comfort, she keeps two young native house-
boys. The chief visitors to the hotel are the Rev. T. Lawrence
Shannon, defrocked as a result of his sexual activities; Miss Hannah
Jelkes, a forty-year-old virgin who does quick portraits for a fee;
and her aged grandfather, who recites poems. The chief conflict
among the characters is between Shannon and Hannah, who clash immediately but who finally assist one another. Throughout the play
the message comes across that life must be endured, and that one
must find a way--any way--to survive.
     8 men, 6 women; 1 exterior. Royalty: $50-35.

_____. Orpheus Descending (1957). BP 1956-57; Dramatists Play
Service.
     Transfers the Orpheus legend to a small Southern town. Val
Xavier, a wandering guitar player, is given a job in the Tarrance
Mercantile Store. The storekeeper is an invalid, and soon Val becomes the lover of the storekeeper's wife, Lady. The townspeople
are outraged over the alliance, especially the sheriff, who orders
Val to leave town. Later he organizes a lynch mob to take care of
him. When Val embraces Lady in a goodbye scene, her husband
appears and shoots her. Val runs away but is killed by the townspeople.
     10 men, 9 women; 1 interior. Royalty: $50 25.

_____. Period of Adjustment (1960). BP 1960-61; Dramatists
Play Service.
     Tennessee Williams' only comedy, a delightful one involving
"periods of adjustment" for two married couples. One couple, Ralph
Bates and his wife, have just broken up after five years of marriage. Another couple, George Haverstick and his bride of a day,
turns up at Ralph's house on Christmas Eve. Ralph and George,
it seems, were war buddies. The problem with Ralph and his wife
is that they have in-law trouble. The problem with George, the
groom, is that he has the shakes and cannot go through with his
wedding night responsibilities. At the end, both couples are reconciled.
     4 men, 5 women; 1 interior. Royalty: $50-25.

_____. The Rose Tattoo (1951). BP 1950-51; Dramatists Play
Service.
     In a village on the Gulf Coast between New Orleans and
Mobile, populated mostly by Sicilians, Serafina delle Rose waits for
her husband Rosario to come home from his job of trucking (bananas
on top, drugs underneath). It is a special celebration, since his
rose tattoo has mysteriously appeared on Serafina's breast, leading
her to believe that she has conceived a son for her husband. This
is the day he is shot and killed, and in her grief she loses the baby.
Three years later Serafina continues to worship the ashes of her

husband as a kind of shrine. She does not get dressed anymore, nor leave the house. She has hidden her daughter Rosa's clothes to keep her from attending her high school graduation and seeing a sailor she is infatuated with. A teacher helps the girl get free, and neighbors tell Serafina that her husband had a mistress at the time of his death. Serafina goes to pieces at this news, and takes into her bed a clownish truckdriver with a rose tattoo on his chest and the smell of rosewater in his hair. When Rosa discovers this man in the house, she screams and runs off to give herself to her sailor. During a scuffle the urn holding Rosario's ashes breaks, and the wind blows the ashes away.

3 acts; 9 men, 14 women; unit set. Royalty: $50-25.

_____. Small Craft Warnings (1972). BP 1971-72; Dramatists Play Service.

The setting is "Monk's Place," a seedy bar on the coast of Southern California. A storm is approaching, and small craft warnings have been posted, leading the aging physician who has lost his license to practice to remark to bar owner Monk: "You're running a place of refuge for vulnerable human vessels." Which is true. Each of the social rejects tells his/her story of the emptiness of existence.

7 men, 2 women; 1 interior. Royalty: $50-25.

_____. A Streetcar Named Desire (1947). BP 1947-48; Dramatists Play Service.

Blanche DuBois comes to visit her sister Stella and her brother-in-law Stanley Kowalski, something of a brute. Blanche plays the southern lady, but Stanley discovers that she has driven to suicide her homosexual husband, has lost her teaching job for an affair with a teenage boy, and has been virtually thrown out of town for promiscuity. Her pretense enrages Stanley, and while Stella is having his child he rapes Blanche, who is committed to a mental institution.

6 men, 6 women; 1 interior-exterior set. Royalty: $50-35.

_____. Suddenly Last Summer (1958). Dramatists Play Service.

The long one-act play treats the sensual and corrupt life of poet Sebastian Venable, who does not appear on stage. We find out about Sebastian's shocking death from his cousin, Catherine Holly, who witnessed it. The rest of the old New Orleans family, especially Mrs. Venable, is anxious to have Catherine deny the death story. Sebastian's mother is so anxious, in fact, that she has had the girl placed in a mental institution and will even order a frontal lobotomy performed to silence her. Catherine's mother and brother, greedy for Mrs. Venable's wealth, beg and threaten Catherine to please their rich relation.

2 men, 5 women; 1 exterior. Royalty: $50-25.

_____. Summer and Smoke (1948). Dramatists Play Service.

A prim, restrained, somewhat puritanical Southern girl, Alma

Winemiller, falls in love with a lecherous unpuritanical young doctor next door, John Buchanan. They are drawn to each other, yet repelled by the truths of propriety, which however are as unsubstantial as smoke. The doctor has thrown away his talents in dalliance, but straightens up when he has to carry on his father's practice and finally realizes that her ideals are basically right. But now he has given his love to another, leaving Alma frustrated and disillusioned.

8 men, 6 women; 1 unit set. Royalty: $50-35.

_____. Sweet Bird of Youth (1958). BP 1958-59; Dramatists Play Service.

Chance Wayne, an actor, has become the kept man of Princess Kosmonopolis, a has-been movie actress who is addicted to liquor, drugs, and young men. Though she is using Chance, he is using her too--he lures her to his southern home town so that he can see the girl he loved and left behind, Heavenly Finley. Chance discovers that before he left town he transmitted a disease to Heavenly, which her father corrected by having her sterilized. He feels the guilt for having ruined her young life and does not resist when her brothers arrive to castrate him.

15 men, 7 women; interiors. Royalty: $50-25.

_____, with Donald Windham. You Touched Me! (1945). French, 1947.

As a lad of 12, Hadrian had been adopted by Capt. Cornelius Rockley. At 15 he left for Canada; at 20 he returns to find everything the same, only more unattractive. He is now a Flight Lieutenant in the Canadian Air Force. He was always in love with the timid and repressed Matilda, who has been domineered over by her prudish Aunt Emmie. The Captain drowns his sorrows in drink but assists Hadrian in overcoming the sensitiveness of Matilda and finally blesses their engagement.

4 men, 3 women; 1 interior.

WILMURT, Arthur. Noah. See entry under Obey, Andre.

WILSON, August. Ma Rainey's Black Bottom (1985). BP 1984-85; Samuel French.

In a dingy recording studio where this Chicago record company records its "race records" in 1927, everyone waits for the arrival of Ma Rainey, Mother of the Blues. The white man who runs the studio, Sturdyvant, warns the white man who is Ma's manager, Irvin, that he wants everything to go quickly and smoothly. Ma's band, all black, is waiting too, arguing about music and God and race relations. Everyone seems to take orders well except Ma, who knows perfectly well that the only time she can make demands on the white world is when it wants something from her. Thus she won't sing until the heat is turned up, or until she has a soft drink. She won't sing in a style that doesn't suit her, and she insists on her nephew doing a speaking voice intro to her song.

Finally, she gets everything her own way because she has not signed the release forms for the session, and she makes Sturdyvant put them in the mail to her. Her toughness, which borders on the tyrannical, stands in contrast to the vulnerability of the members of her band, who are at the mercy of the white music men. When the horn player is doublecrossed by Sturdyvant, he takes his rage out on the piano player, stabbing him to death for accidentally stepping on his new shoes.

    2 acts; 5 black men, 3 white men, 2 black women; unit set. Royalty: $60-40.

WILSON, H. L. The Man from Home. See entry under Tarkington, Booth.

_____. Merton of the Movies. See entry under Kaufman, George S.

WILSON, John. Hamp (1966). Based on an episode from the novel Return to the Wood by J. L. Hodson. BP 1966-67; London, Evans Plays, 1966.

    It is 1917 during the Battle of Passchendaele. An illiterate young soldier, Hamp, has been arrested as a deserter and is subsequently tried and executed. The story revolves around Lt. Hargreaves's unsuccessful attempts to focus on Hamp's character, situation, and mental/emotional state. Hamp left school at age 12, volunteered because his mother-in-law dared him to, watched practically all of his first battalion die around him, and received a letter from his wife telling him she had found another man. Not only is Hamp not made to be a soldier, but he doesn't even remember why he walked away that day--not from the front line but from a rest area in the back. Hamp isn't even smart enough to lie about himself. It is, however, wartime. Hamp is sentenced to die in front of a firing squad. They let him get drunk and pass out, shoot him up with morphine, and the next dawn carry him out and strap his unconcious body to a chair.

    3 acts; 12 men; 2 interiors.

WILSON, Lanford. Angels Fall (1983). BP 1982-83; Dramatists Play Service.

    A nuclear accident causes the Army to take emergency precautions in Northwest New Mexico: roads and bridges are closed to traffic, and helicopters warn travelers to seek shelter. This accounts for the strange group of people assembled at the Navaho mission run by Father William Doherty. Niles, a professor of art history has recently experienced a crisis of faith (he's made the mistake of rereading his own books) and is on the way to psychiatric help. Marion, the widow of a famous artist, travels around the country with a young tennis pro. Don Tahaba, a young Indian doctor, is trying to escape his destiny as an overworked physician to the poor by taking a prestigious position in medical research. All the characters are pushed and prodded by Fr. Doherty, whose faith

and commitment seems to improve everyone he comes in contact with.
2 acts; 4 men, 2 women; 1 interior. Royalty: $50.

_____. The 5th of July (1978). BP 1977-78; Dramatists Play
Service.
   It is the 4th of July, 1977, on the Talley place near Lebanon,
Mo. Several survivors of the 1960's Counter Culture are meeting for
a holiday weekend. The host, Ken Talley, is a war hero, a veteran
of Viet Nam who walks on two artificial legs and is watched over by
his lover, Jed, whose interest in life is gardening. Ken's sister
June is present, with her teenage (and fatherless) daughter Shirley;
John and Gwen, a couple from the old days with plenty of inherited
money and an expensive cocaine habit; Wes, a songwriter, and old
Aunt Sally, who has come to scatter the ashes of her deceased husband Matt on the family place and who turns out to be more hip than
any of the former hippies. At the end, Ken will not sell the Talley
place to a corporation owned by John and Gwen, but Aunt Sally will
sell her retirement home in Sun City and put some money into fixing
up this place, and Ken will accept a job as a teacher in the local
schools.
   2 acts; 4 men, 4 women; 1 interior, 1 exterior. Royalty:
$50.

_____. The Hot L Baltimore (1973). BP 1972-73; Dramatists Play
Service.
   The action takes place in the lobby of a rundown hotel with
an "e" missing from its marquee. The residents meet and interact
with one another during the course of a day--the young and the old,
the defiant and the resigned, each character emerging clearly
through the overlapping conversations which humorously go on.
   10 men, 7 women; 1 interior. Royalty: $50.

_____. The Rimers of Eldritch (1967). Dramatists Play Service.
   Eldritch is a Middle Western town that operates out of catch-
word morality and maintains a capability for the vicious. The citizens of the town are on stage throughout the play, speaking from
platforms. Framed around a mystery (a man has been murdered but
we don't know who it was, who killed him, or why), the play highlights individual townspeople and relationships--ugly and beautiful:
a middleaged woman who has fallen in love with a young man who
works for her, a coarse woman mistreating her senile mother, a
tender relationship between a young man and a crippled girl.
   7 men, 10 women; platform staging. Royalty: $50-35.

_____. Serenading Louie (1976). BP 1975-76; Dramatists Play
Service.
   A single setting represents the homes of two couples in this
play, "as though such residences are so alike and furnished so
similarly as to make scene changes redundant." Carl and Mary
are one couple (he is a businessman and former college quarter-
back; she is having an affair with his accountant). Gabby and Alex

are their longtime friends (she is always in control; he is infatuated with a 17-year-old flower child). What is going on in marriages mostly has to do with loneliness, which is communicated to the characters on stage and directly to the audience as well. The end of the play, a murder-suicide, is especially powerful.

2 men, 2 women; 1 interior. Royalty: $50-25.

_____. Talley's Folly (1979). BP 1979-80; Dramatists Play Service.

A 97-minute two-character waltz, set in an old boathouse on the Talley Place farm during World War II, in which Max Friedman duels with and finally wins the love of Sally Talley. Her family despises him for his Jewishness and radical politics; she has been cast aside earlier in life with a TB infection left her unable to bear children and made her an unwelcome prospective daughter-in-law to the wealthy family looking mostly for an heir. What is revealed, and finally believed by the couple, is that Max's resolve never to bring children into the world is what she always considered unfair to subject Sally to, and that her infertility is what held her back from marrying Max. They will go away this very night together, and return to the boathouse once a year so they don't forget.

1 act; 1 man, 1 woman; 1 exterior. Royalty: $50.

WILTSE, David. Doubles (1985). BP 1984-85.

All of the action in this comedy takes place in the men's locker room of an upscale Norwalk, Conn. tennis club, where Lennie (a grocer), Arnie (a lawyer), and George (a stockbroker) have to use a newcomer, Guy (a tennis reporter), to make up their regular weekly doubles match. Throughout the next few months Guy becomes a regular himself, though he finds it hard to fit into this community of friends who don't necessarily even like one another and whose interpersonal relations are abrasive, always searching for personal soft spots to probe and exploit. Always, though, they help one another out of a jam, and when Guy is suddenly fired from his job, it is Lennie, who likes him least of all, who bails him out.

2 acts; 6 men, 2 women; 1 interior.

WINCELBERG, Shimon. Kataki (1959). BP 1958-59; Samuel French.

Kataki (Japanese for "the enemy") takes place on a South Pacific island late in WW II. An 18-year-old American GI named Alvin has parachuted to safety on this island and has been captured by a Japanese soldier, Kimura, a mature man whose troopship was sunk by an American submarine. At first Alvin believes he is to be murdered, and for a long time he is sure he will be suddenly betrayed, but Kimura, whose wife has been killed in a bombing raid but who has three children surviving in his homeland, is far more sophisticated as a human being and teaches the young American by the purity of his actions. Though in the few weeks they live together they never learn one another's language, there is a solid bond between the two from having saved one another's lives. But when an American rescue boat comes to the island, Kimura must do

what he believes is the honorable thing: he commits hari-kiri.
　　2 acts; 2 men, 1 exterior.　Royalty:　$35-25.

WINDHAM, Donald.　You Touched Me!　See entry under Williams,
　　Tennessee.

WINER, Elihu.　Anatomy of a Murder (1964).　Adapted from Robert
　　Travers' novel.　Samuel French.
　　　　This play depicts the attempts of a former district attorney
to establish himself as a defense lawyer after his re-election bid
had failed.　Paul Biegler is the lawyer, and his first case is a
sensational one.　He takes on the defense of an Army lieutenant accused of murdering a bartender who had allegedly raped his wife.
Biegler soon finds that he has more than just legal problems.　He
develops an intense dislike for his client, but is constantly dis-
tracted by his client's seductive wife.　This becomes a case with
political overtones, too, as the State Attorney General's office gets
involved to try to insure that the newly elected district attorney
wins this case.　Using every legal device and dramatic courtroom
revelation possible, however, Biegler wins his case.
　　16 men, 2 women; 4 interiors, 2 insets.　Royalty:　$50-25.

WINTER, Keith.　The Shining Hour (1934).　BP 1933-34; Samuel
　　French.
　　　　This story, which runs the gamut of human emotions, centers
around the Linden family, who inhabit an English countryside estate.　Henry Linden, after being absent for several years, brings
Mariella, his bride, home to live.　She is different from Henry's
people in that she is only half English and cannot understand fully
the feelings of the true English.　She falls in love with David, her
brother-in-law, but complicates matters by thinking so highly of
David's wife that she has trouble betraying her.　A climax follows
that tends to wreck the whole household.
　　3 men, 3 women; 1 interior.　Royalty:　$25-20.

WISHENGRAD, Morton.　The Rope Dancers (1958).　BP 1957-58;
　　Samuel French.
　　　　It is in the turn of the century in a New York tenement.
Margaret Hyland is moving into two fifth-floor rooms with her 11-
year-old daughter Lizzie, who wears a mitten on one hand.　Soon
the two are found by James, the estranged father, and by the
school truancy officials who have been tracking little Lizzie all over
the city (she has never been to school).　We learn that the cause
of the mother's shame is that the girl has six fingers on one hand--
a manifestation of evil, brought on by God because James had
visited a prostitute before conceiving the child, and because Margaret had, in spite of all that, lusted after him.　Thus she has
thrown James out, convinced Lizzie that she is "unnatural," and
made her a loner, permitting her only to jump rope (be a rope dancer) for diversion.　Under the eyes of the school authorities, Lizzie
has an attack of St. Vitus Dance.　A physician is called who, after

giving the girl a sedative, surgically removes the sixth finger. She
dies anyway, though James will stay with Margaret and help her
deal with her pathology.

    3 acts; 5 men, 4 women; 1 interior; Royalty: $50-25.

WOLFE, Thomas. Look Homeward Angel. See entry under Frings,
    Ketti.

WOLFSON, Victor. Excursion (1937). BP 1936-37; Dramatists Play
    Service.

    After 30 years on the route from Manhattan to Coney Island,
Captain Obadiah Rich's excursion ship "Happiness" is to be turned
into a garbage scow. The Captain and his brother Jonathan plan
on the final return trip to head for a magic isle south of Trinidad
where his passengers may begin life anew. But the fog holds them
back and the Coast Guard makes them return, so they must go back
to their unromantic dull jobs.

    3 acts; 18 men, 10 women; 1 interior in 2 parts: the ship's
cabin and the ship's deck. Royalty: $35-25.

WOOD, Mrs. Henry. East Lynne (1861). In N.Y. Drama, v. 4 #46,
    1878; Penn Pub. Co., 1894; carried by French; CERC.

    Isabel is happy with her husband, Archibald Carlyle, until
Sir Francis Levison plants suspicion in her mind that he is untrue
to her while he is meeting Barbara Hare to help her brother. Isabel leaves with the villainous Sir Francis; they go to France where
he deserts her. Meantime Archibald thinks she is dead and marries
Barbara. He also proves her brother innocent of the murder, which
is fixed on Sir Francis. Isabel comes back to East Lynne, disguised
as an old governess, Madame Vine. On her death-bed she is recognized by Archibald and forgiven.

    5 acts; 7 men, 7 women, 1 boy; varied interior and exterior
sets; costumes of the period. Royalty: $0-10.

WOOLL, Edward. Libel! (1934). Samuel French.

    Sir Mark Loddon brings libel suit against a London news-
paper which says he is neither a baronet nor a Loddon. He resembles Frank Wembley, a Canadian. Both escaped from a German
prison camp; suffering shell-shock, Mark remembers nothing of
his life before the First World War. His wife comes to doubt him
too, believing he is Wembley. His trench coat is produced at the
trial; from the lining he produces her photograph and other docu-
ments; thus he is proved to be Sir Mark.

    3 acts; 20 men, 4 women; 1 interior (court room). Royalty:
$25-20.

WOOLLCOTT, Alexander and George S. Kaufman. The Dark Tower
    (1933). French, 1937.

    The leading actors, Jessica Wells and her brother Damon, are
ready to produce "The Dark Tower" when her supposedly dead husband, Stanley, appears. He has always had a vicious hypnotic

influence over her, and she again goes into a decline. Stanley is willing to be bought off, and proposes an arrangement with a Mr. Sarnoff. At the meeting Stanley is stabbed to death and Sarnoff disappears--but he reappears privately, for he is her brother Damon disguised, and he has saved his sister.

3 acts; 9 men, 5 women; 2 interiors.

WOUK, Herman. The Caine Mutiny Court-Martial (1954). BP 1953-54; Samuel French.

This World War II sea story was described by the New York Times as a version superior to the novel "in the artfulness of its craftsmanship." The court-martial arises from a young lieutenant's relieving his captain of command during a typhoon on the grounds that he was psychopathic. Naval tradition clearly forbids any such usurpation of power, but in the intriguing courtroom scenes the defenses of the captain finally collapse. With his disintegration of sanity evident to them, the court clears the lieutenant.

19 men (6 non-speaking); curtained set, desks and chairs. Royalty: $50-25.

_____. The Traitor (1949). Samuel French.

An idealistic young scientist, Allen Carr, believes that the safety of the world lies in all nations (especially U.S.A. & Russia) having the atom bomb. So he altruistically turns over bomb secrets to a Russian spy. Realizing his mistake in thus betraying his country, he redeems himself by leading the chief spy into a trap.

15 men, 3 women; 1 interior. Royalty: $50-25.

WRIGHT, Richard. Native Son. See entry under Green, Paul.

YAFFE, James. Dear Me, The Sky Is Falling. See entry under Spigelgass, Leonard.

_____. The Deadly Game (1960). Based on the novel Trapps, by Friedrich Duerrenmatt. BP 1959-60; Dramatists Play Service.

An American, Howard Trapp, is lost in a snowstorm and seeks refuge at an Alpine mountain house occupied by several old men who had been, before their retirements, a criminal court judge, a prosecuting attorney, a public defender, an official hangman, and a convicted murderer. After a gourmet dinner, Trapp agrees to play defendent in a parlor game simulating a court of law, designed merely to pass the evening, but he refuses the advice to plead guilty to any small crime he may have committed. Instead, after considerable probing by the prosecuting attorney, he reveals too much about his moral indiscretions and those of his wife in New York, and he is charged with murdering the European agent for his company in order to get his job. The court finds him guilty and sentences him to death by hanging. Trapp runs out the door in panic and falls to his death from the mountain. On another evening his widow comes to call, and agrees to participate in "a little parlor game" the old men wish to play.

2 acts; 6 men, 2 women; 1 interior.   Royalty: $50-25.

YORDAN, Philip.   Anna Lucasta (1944).   BP 1944-45; Dramatists
Play Service.

Anna has erred and is driven from her home in Pennsylvania
by her father; she goes to New York, where she associates with
Danny.   Meanwhile Papa Lucasta gets a letter from his old friend in
Alabama that he is sending his son Rudolf north with $800 to find a
wife, perhaps his daughter.   So Anna is brought back and finds
that Rudolf suits her; they are married.   But Danny follows her and
persuades her to go back to New York with him; she goes, but
Rudolf follows and wins her back again.

3 acts; 9 men, 5 women; 2 interiors.   Royalty: $50-25.

ZAMACOIS, Miguel.   The Jesters (1907).   Tr. by Raphael in rhymed
hexameters, Brentano, 1908.

Two wealthy noblemen, to decide a bet and win a wife, assume
the characters of jesters, René as Chicot, and Robert as Narcissus.
In this guise they woo Solange, the daughter of the impoverished
noble, Baron de Mautpré.   René gives the impecunious baron a chest
of gold which he says was dug up on his grounds, and by artful
talk, despite a false hump, is successful.

4 acts; 13 men, 2 women; 2 interiors, 2 exteriors; costumes
and settings of the 16th century.

ZANGWILL, Israel.   The Melting Pot (1908).   Macmillan, 1908; revised
edition, Macmillan, & Lond., Heinemann, 1914.

Represents America as the crucible in which immigrants from
all nations are to be fused into the perfect human type; America as-
similates the alien.   Bases the situations on the love of a Jew for a
Christian.   Strong in ideals and patriotism.

4 acts; 5 men, 4 women; 2 interiors, 1 exterior.

ZEYER, Julius.   Diarmuid and Grainne (ca. 1886).   Tr. by Noyes
& Mezirka in Poet Lore, v. 44, 1938.

The young daughter of the King of Erin, Grainne, is given in
marriage by her father to Finn, King of the Fennians.   He has power
of healing in his hand.   But Brainne loves Diarmuid, and together
they flee to Midac's castle.   Midac has sworn vengeance on the murderer of his father, who, he believes, is Finn; but Diarmuid confesses it was his father; whereupon Midac stabs him.   When Finn
comes he refuses to heal him and he dies.   When Grianne returns
she stabs herself.   Finn's son and grandson desert him and he is
left alone in his old age.   One of the legends of Erin.

4 acts; 7 men, 1 woman, extras; 2 interiors, 2 exteriors;
costumes of the period (3rd century in Ireland).

ZINDEL, Paul.   And Miss Reardon Drinks a Little (1971).   Dramatists
Play Service.

The three Reardon sisters have been brought up in a home

with a domineering mother and an absent father. The mother has died, one sister is married and on her own, one is drinking too much, and one is on the brink of madness. The married sister arrives for dinner to argue for committing her "sick" sister to an institution. Resentments which have been dormant for many years begin to crop up, and the unexpected arrival of a neighborhood couple only makes things worse.

2 men, 5 women; 1 interior. Royalty: $50-35.

_____. The Effect of Gamma Rays on Man-in-the-Moon Marigolds (1970). BP 1969-70; Dramatists Play Service.

Even a dung heap can occasionally produce a beautiful flower, which is what happens in this play. The flower is Tillie, who undertakes a gamma ray experiment for her school science project. The dung heap is her home, run with an iron hand and an acid tongue by her mother Beatrice, who can only hurt when she needs to love and ridicule when she needs to encourage and praise. She is even harder, in fact, on her daughter Ruth, who is prettier than Tillie but subject to convulsions as a way of coping.

No men, 5 women; 1 interior. Royalty: $50-35.

_____. The Secret Affairs of Mildred Wild (1972). Dramatists Play Service.

Mildred Wild lives in Greenwich Village in quarters behind the candy store which she operates with her husband. Her place is filled with movie magazines and memorabilia, a tribute to the 3000 movies she has seen and the fantasy life she has created to escape reality. When the outside world intrudes on her through her husband, her sister-in-law, landlord, butcher, or man in charge of tearing down her building she plays a movie scene on the world.

4 men, 5 women; 1 interior. Royalty: $50-35.

ZOLA, Emile. Thérèse. See entry under Job, Thomas.

ZWEIG, Stefan. Jeremiah (1917). Tr. by Paul, Seltzer, 1922; Viking Pr., 1939.

Depicts scenes in the life of the prophet, from his poignant realization that he has been chosen to interpret the Lord to his people, through his fruitless attempts during the siege and capture of Jerusalem.

9 scenes; 10 men, 2 women, extras; 3 interiors, 3 exteriors; costumes of the period.

CAST INDEX

1 Character

Krapp's Last Tape   40
Vincent   263

2 Characters

Dance and the Railroad   386
Dumb Waiter   287
Fourposter   162
Gin Game   77
Greater Tuna   396
Green Julia   2
Happy Days   40
I'm Herbert   15
Island   125
Jesse and the Bandit Queen
   121
K2   247
Kataki   404
Mass Appeal   92
Next   245
'night, Mother   264
Owl and the Pussycat   237
Same Time, Next Year   349
Sea Horse   259
Sleuth   324
Staircase   104
Talley's Folly   404
Two for the Seesaw   136
Zoo Story   6

3 Characters

Agnes of God   283
American Buffalo   236
Aspern Papers   300
Betrayal   286
Boesman and Lena   125
Caretaker   286

Dutchman   193
Greater Tuna   396
I Ought to Be in Pictures   346
I'll Be Home for Christmas   15
Lesson from Aloes   126
Life in the Theater   237
Luv   320
Maids   133
"Master Harold" ... and the
   Boys   126
Murder at the Howard Johnson's
   76
Old Times   287
Painting Churches   181
Pardon   220
Phoenix Too Frequent   124
Private Ear and the Public Eye
   326
Rattle of a Simple Man   104
Rivalry   82
Slow Dance on the Killing
   Ground   158
Star-Spangled Girl   347
Subject Was Roses   138
Voice of the Turtle   378
White Lies   326

4 Characters

Adaptation   245
Any Wednesday   301
Ashes   313
Butterflies Are Free   134
California Suite   345
Chapter Two   345
Collection   287
Deathwatch   133
Emperor Jones   270
Endgame   40
Extremities   243

411

7 Characters

8 Characters

9 Characters

12 Characters

13 Characters

14 Characters

15 Characters

18 Characters

23 Characters

22 Characters

*Cast size is given in parentheses

All Women

INDEX OF SELECTED SUBJECTS

431

THE BLACK EXPERIENCE

COURTROOM

FANTASY

SCHOOL AND COLLEGE LIFE

TEENAGER

PRIZE PLAYS

444

(1953-54)
That Championship Season (1971-72)
Tiger at the Gates (1955-56)
Time of Your Life (1939-40)
Toys in the Attic (1959-60)
Travesties (1975-76)
Venus Observed (1951-52)
Visit (1958-59)
Waltz of the Toreadors (1956-57)
Watch on the Rhine (1940-41)
White Steed (1938-39)
Who's Afraid of Virginia Woolf? (1962-63)
Winslow Boy (1947-48)
Winterset (1935-36)
Witness for the Prosecution (1954-55)

PULITZER PRIZE AWARD PLAYS

Abe Lincoln in Illinois (1938-39)
Alison's House (1030-31)
All the Way Home (1960-61)
Anna Christie (1921-22)
Beyond the Horizon (1919-20)
Both Your Houses (1932-33)
Buried Child (1978-79)
Cat on a Hot Tin Roof (1954-55)
Craig's Wife (1925-26)
Crimes of the Heart (1980-81)
Death of a Salesman (1948-49)
Delicate Balance (1966-67)
Diary of Anne Frank (1955-56)
Effect of Gamma Rays on Man-in-the-Moon Marigolds (1969-70)
Gin Game (1977-78)
Glengarry Glen Ross (1983-84)
Great White Hope (1968-69)
Green Pastures (1929-30)
Harvey (1944-45)
Hell-Bent fer Heaven (1923-24)
Icebound (1922-23)
Idiot's Delight (1935-36)
In Abraham's Bosom (1926-27)
J.B. (1958-59)
Long Day's Journey into Night (1956-57)
Look Homeward, Angel (1957-58)
Men in White (1933-34)

Miss Lulu Bett (1920-21)
'night, Mother (1982-83)
No Place to be Somebody (1969-70)
Of Thee I Sing (1931-32)
Old Maid (1934-35)
Our Town (1937-38)
Picnic (1952-53)
Seascape (1974-75)
Shadow Box (1976-77)
Shrike (1951-52)
Skin of Our Teeth (1942-43)
Soldier's Play (1981-82)
State of the Union (1945-46)
Strange Interlude (1927-28)
Street Scene (1928-29)
Streetcar Named Desire (1947-48)
Subject Was Roses (1964-65)
Talley's Folly (1979-80)
Teahouse of the August Moon (1953-54)
That Championship Season (1971-72)
There Shall Be No Night (1940-41)
They Knew What They Wanted (1924-25)
Time of Your Life (1939-40)
Why Marry? (1917-18)
You Can't Take It with You (1936-37)

ANTOINETTE PERRY (TONY) AWARD PLAYS

Amadeus (1981)
Becket (1961)
Biloxi Blues (1985)
Borstal Boy (1970)
Children of a Lesser God (1980)
Cocktail Party (1950)
Crucible (1953)
Da (1978)
Death of a Salesman (1949)
Desperate Hours (1955)
Diary of Anne Frank (1956)
Elephant Man (1979)
Equus (1975)
Fourposter (1952)
Great White Hope (1969)

Homecoming (1967)
J.B. (1959)
Life & Adventures of Nicholas
    Nickleby (1982)
Long Day's Journey into Night
    (1957)
Luther (1964)
Man for All Seasons (1962)
Miracle Worker (1960)
Mister Roberts (1948)
Persecution and Assassination
    of Jean Paul Marat as Per-
    formed by the Inmates of the
    Asylum of Charenton under
    the Direction of the Marquis
    De Sade (1966)
Real Thing (1984)
River Niger (1974)
Rose Tattoo (1951)
Rosencrantz and Guildenstern
    Are Dead (1968)
Shadow Box (1977)
Sleuth (1971)
Sticks and Bones (1972)
Subject Was Roses (1965)
Sunrise at Campobello (1958)
Teahouse of the August Moon
    (1954)
That Championship Season (1973)
Torch Song Trilogy (1983)
Travesties (1976)
Who's Afraid of Virginia Woolf?
    (1963)

POPULAR PLAYS FOR HIGH SCHOOL PRODUCTION,
1945-1984*

Postwar Top Twenty: 1945-1984
(New York Professional Production Date in parentheses)

1. You Can't Take It With You (1936)
2. Our Town (1938)
3. Arsenic and Old Lace (1941)
4. Harvey (1944)
5. The Curious Savage (1950)
6. Oklahoma (1943)
7. The Miracle Worker (1959)
7. The Diary of Anne Frank (1955)
9. The Music Man (1957)
9. Our Hearts Were Young and Gay (None)
9. The Night of January 16

12. Bye Bye Birdie (1960)
13. The Man Who Came to Dinner (1939)
14. Up the Down Staircase (None)
14. You're a Good Man, Charlie Brown (1967)
14. Sound of Music (1959)
17. Guys and Dolls (1950)
18. Godspell (1971)
19. Teahouse of the August Moon (1953)
20. The Crucible (1953)

Popular High School Productions by Decade

The Top Twenty: 1945-1949

1. A Date with Judy (None)
2. You Can't Take It with You (1936)
3. Our Hearts Were Young and Gay (None)
4. We Shook the Family Tree (None)
5. Junior Miss (1941)
6. January Thaw (1946)
7. Dear Ruth (1944)
8. Brother Goose (None)
9. Arsenic and Old Lace (1941)
10. Spring Green (None)
11. Don't Take My Penny (None)

---

*Each year since the 1930s, the International Thespian Society polls its member troupes (currently 2,300 high schools in the United States and abroad) to find out what plays they are producing, with the results published in the fall issue of Dramatics magazine. The following summary of the postwar period was compiled from these statistics by Patti P. Gillespie and is reprinted with the permission of Dramatics magazine.

12. The Fighting Littles (None)
13. Little Women (1931)
14. Our Town (1938)
15. The Night of January 16 (1935)
16. Nine Girls (1943)
17. The Divine Flora (None)
18. Snafu (1944)
19. Best Foot Forward (1941)
20. Meet Me in St. Louis (None)

The Top Twenty: 1950-1959

1. The Curious Savage (1950)
2. Our Town (1938)
3. You Can't Take It with You (1936)
4. Our Hearts Were Young and Gay (None)
5. Time Out for Ginger (1952)
6. The Night of January 16 (1935)
7. Arsenic and Old Lace (1941)
8. Our Miss Brooks (None)
9. Mother Is a Freshman (None)
10. Seventeenth Summer (None)
11. Cheaper by the Dozen (None)
12. Little Dog Laughed (None)
13. Dino (None)
14. The Man Who Came to Dinner (1939)
15. Onions in the Stew (None)
16. I Remember Mama (1944)
17. Men Are Like Streetcars (None)
18. The Remarkable Incident at Carson's Corners (None)
19. We Shook the Family Tree (None)
20. Mrs. McThing (1952)

The Top Twenty: 1960-1969

1. Our Town (1938)
2. You Can't Take It With You (1936)
3. The Mouse That Roared (None)
4. The Diary of Anne Frank (1955)
5. Arsenic and Old Lace (1941)
6. The Curious Savage (1950)
7. The Night of January 16 (1935)
8. Harvey (1944)
9. The Man Who Came to Dinner (1939)
10. The Miracle Worker (1959)
11. Oklahoma (1943)
12. Bye Bye Birdie (1960)
13. Our Hearts Were Young and Gay (None)
14. Teahouse of the August Moon (1953)
15. The Music Man (1957)
16. Brigadoon (1947)
17. Time Out for Ginger (1952)
18. Ask Any Girl (None)
19. Sound of Music (1959)
20. South Pacific (1940)

The Top Twenty: 1970-1979

1. Up the Down Staircase (None)
2. Our Town (1938)
3. You're a Good Man, Charlie Brown (1967)
4. You Can't Take It with You (1936)
5. Arsenic and Old Lace (1941)
6. Harvey (1944)
7. The Miracle Worker (1959)
8. The Crucible (1953)
9. The Music Man (1957)
10. Oklahoma (1943)
11. The Curious Savage (1950)
12. Fiddler on the Roof (1964)
13. The Diary of Anne Frank (1955)
14. Flowers for Algernon (None)
15. David and Lisa (None)
16. The Wizard of Oz (1968)
17. Bye Bye Birdie (1960)
18. Guys and Dolls (1950)
19. Godspell (1971)
20. Hello, Dolly (1964)

The Top Twenty: 1980-1984

1. Oklahoma (1943)
1. Guys and Dolls (1950)
1. The Music Man (1950)
1. Godspell (1971)
1. Bye Bye Birdie (1960)
1. You Can't Take It with You (1936)
1. Our Town (1938)
1. Harvey (1944)
1. Curious Savage (1950)
10. You're a Good Man, Charlie Brown (1967)
10. Hello, Dolly (1964)
10. The Miracle Worker (1959)
13. Sound of Music (1959)
13. Fiddler on the Roof (1964)
13. Arsenic and Old Lace (1941)
13. Up the Down Staircase (None)
13. Ten Little Indians (1944)
19. Annie Get Your Gun (1946)
19. Grease (1972)
19. L'il Abner (1956)
19. Once upon a Mattress (1060)
19. South Pacific (1940)
19. Barefoot in the Park (1963)
19. Dracula (1927)
19. Blithe Spirit (1941)

MOST POPULAR PLAYS FOR AMATEUR GROUPS

(Nominated by the major play publishers)

Agnes of God 283
All My Sons 248
And a Nightingale Sang 364
Antigone 17
Arsenic and Old Lace 206

Barefoot in the Park 344
Bell, Book and Candle 377
Best Christmas Pageant Ever
  306
Beyond Therapy 103
Bingo 53
Black Comedy 325
Black Elk Speaks 322
Blithe Spirit 82
Born Yesterday 197
Bullshot Crummond 178
Bus Stop 186

Cat on a Hot Tin Roof 398
Charley's Aunt 369
Cheaper by the Dozen 322
Children of a Lesser God 246
Children's Hour 169
Cloud Nine 75
Come Blow Your Horn 346
Crimes of the Heart 171
Crucible 249
Curious Savage 278

Dark of the Moon 304
David and Lisa 300
Deadwood Dick 363
Death of a Salesman 249
Deathtrap 223
Dial "M" for Murder 210
Diary of Anne Frank 146
Dining Room 154

Dirty Work at the Crossroads
  191
Diviners 220
Don't Drink the Water 7
Dracula 94

Effect of Gamma Rays on Man-in-
  the-Moon Marigolds 409
Entertainer 274

Fame 323
Fifth of July 403
Flowers for Algernon 308

Glass Menagerie 398
Good 364
Good Doctor 346
Greater Tuna 396

Harvey 68
Hobbit 149
Hot L Baltimore 403
House of Blue Leaves 153

I Never Saw Another Butterfly
  298
Ik 174
Incredible Murder of Cardinal
  Tosca 265
It All Ends Up in a Shopping
  Bag 209

Last Meeting of the Knights of
  the White Magnolia 194
Last of the Red Hot Lovers 346
Life with Father 225
Lion in Winter 143
Little Sister 146

450

ADDRESSES OF PLAY PUBLISHERS REPRESENTED

The Dramatic Publishing Company
311 Washington, P.O. Box 109
Woodstock, Illinois 60098

Dramatists Play Service, Inc.*
440 Park Avenue South
New York, New York 10016

Samuel French, Inc.
45 West 25th Street
New York, New York 10010

---

*Note: Dramatists Play Service offers a free pamphlet written by playwright Howard Lindsay called "HOW TO START A THEATRE," for encouragement to those who wish to organize a Community or Little Theatre.

ABBREVIATIONS USED FOR CITING COLLECTIONS

Note: Most of the following are Francis K. W. Drury's abbreviations
used in the original edition of <u>Guide to Best Plays</u>. I have retained
these citations, and added some others, for plays not handled by a
major play publisher, plays which represent most of the Classical and
Early National Drama entries included in this volume.   The reader is
advised, however, that these abbreviations to collections are not comprehensive.   For the latest information, see the current edition of
<u>Ottemiller's Index to Plays in Collections</u> (The Scarecrow Press).

ADA   Adams, J. Q., ed.   Chief pre-Shakespearean Dramas.
                Houghton, 1924.
ALLK   Allison, Alexander Ward, Arthur J. Carr and Arthur
                M. Eastman, eds.   Masterpieces of the drama, 3d ed.
                Macmillan, 1974.
AND   Anderson, G. K. & Walton, E. L., eds.   This genera-
                tion.   Scott, Foresman, 1939.
ASH   Ashton, J. W., ed.   Types of English drama.   Mac-
                millan, 1940.
BAK   Baker, G. P., ed.   Modern American plays.   Harcourt,
                1920.
BARR   Wilson, A. E.   The plays of J. M. Barrie.   London,
                Hodder & Stoughton, 1942.
BAS   Baskervil, Heltzel, & Nethercot, eds.   Elizabethan and
                Stuart plays.   Holt, 1934.
BAT   Bates, Alfred, ed.   The drama.   22v.   London, Athenian
                Society, 1903-04.
BEL   Bell, John.   British theatre.   36v.   Lond., 1791-1802.
BEN   Bentley, Eric, ed.   The play.   Prentice-Hall, 1951.
BLO   Bloomfield, M. W. & Elliot, R. C., eds.   Ten plays.
                Rinehart, 1951.
BOA   Boas, F. S., ed.   Five pre-Shakespearian comedies
                (Early Tudor period).   Oxford, 1934.
BP   Best Plays of (the year).   Begun by Burns Mantle,
                currently edited by Otis L. Guernsey, Jr. New York:
                Dodd, Mead, published annually.   Series begins
                1894-1899, 1909-1919, and theater seasons 1919-1920
                to the present.
BRI   British drama.   2v.   Lond., 1824-25; reprinted in
                Phila., T. Davis, 1850.

CALM	Campbell, Van Gundy, & Shrodes, eds. Patterns for living. Macmillan, 1940.
CAP	Canfield, Curtis, ed. Plays of the Irish renaissance, 1880-1930. N.Y., Washburn, 1929.
CAR	Carpenter, Bruce, comp. A book of dramas. Prentice-Hall, 1929.
CARC	Cartmell, Van H. & Cerf, B. A., eds. Famous plays of crime and detection. Blakiston, 1946.
CATH	Committee for the revision of English curricula ... American profile. (The Catholic high school literature series. Book III.) W. H. Sadlier, 1944.
CER	Cerf, B. A., ed. Pocket book of modern American plays. Pocket Books, 1942.
CERC	Cerf, B. A. & Cartmell, Van H., comps. S.R.O. (Standing Room Only); the most successful plays in the history of the American stage. Doubleday, 1944, 1946.
CET	Cerf, B. A. & Cartmell, Van H., eds. Sixteen famous American plays. Garden City, 1941; Modern Library, 1942.
CEU	Cerf, B. A. & Cartmell, Van H., comps. Sixteen famous British plays. Garden City, 1942; Modern Library, 1943.
CEW	Cerf, B. A. & Cartmell, Van H., eds. Sixteen famous European plays. Garden City, 1943.
CHA	Chandler, F. H. & Cordell, R. A., eds. Twentieth century plays. Nelson, 1934.
CHAP	Chandler, F. W. & Cordell, R. A., eds. Twentieth century plays, American. Revised Nelson, 1939.
CHAR	Chandler, F. W. & Cordell, R. A., eds. Twentieth century plays, British. Rev. & enl. Nelson, 1941.
CLA	Clark, B. H. & Davenport, W. H., eds. Nine modern American plays. Appleton, 1951.
CLDM	Clark, B. H., ed. Masterpieces of modern Spanish drama. Duffield, 1917; later Appleton-Century.
CLF	Clark, B. H., ed. World drama. 2v. Appleton, 1933.
CLS	Clark, Wm. Smith, II. Chief patterns of world drama, Aeschylus to Anderson. Houghton, 1946.
COD	Coffman, G. R., ed. A book of modern plays. Scott, Foresman, 1925.
COF	Coffman, G. R., ed. Five significant English plays. Nelson, 1930.
COH	Cohen, Helen L., ed. Longer plays by modern authors (American). Harcourt, 1922.
COJ	Cohen, Helen L., ed. Milestones of the drama. Harcourt, 1940.
CORF	Cordell, Kathryn Coe & W. H., eds. The Pulitzer prize plays. Various new eds. Random House, 1935- .
COT	Cordell, R. A., ed. Representative modern plays, British and American. Nelson, 1929.
CRI	(The) Critics' prize plays. World Pub. Co., 1945.

DAVI   David, Sister Mary Agnes. Modern American drama.
              Macmillan, 1961.
DIB   Dibdin, T. J. The London theatre. 12v. London,
              1814-25.
DIC   Dickinson, T. H., ed. Chief contemporary dramatists,
              [ser. 1]. Houghton, 1915.
DID   Dickinson, T. H., ed. Chief contemporary dramatists,
              ser. 2. Houghton, 1921.
DIE   Dickinson, T. H., ed. Chief contemporary dramatists,
              ser. 3. Houghton, 1930.
DIG   Dickinson, T. H. & Crawford, J. R., eds. Contempo-
              rary plays: England & America. Houghton, 1925.
DIK   Dickinson, T. H., ed. Continental plays. 2v. Hough-
              ton, 1935.
DOB   Dobrée, Bonamy, ed. Five restoration tragedies. Ox-
              ford, 1928.
DUC   Duckworth, G. E., ed. The complete Roman drama.
              2v. Random House, 1942.
DUN   Dunn, Esther C., ed. Eight famous Elizabethan plays.
              Modern Library, 1932.
DUR   Durham, W. H. & Dodds, J. W., eds. British and
              American plays, 1939-1945. Oxford, 1947.
FAMA   Famous plays of 1931. Lond., Gollancz, 1932.
FAMB   Famous plays of 1932. Lond., Gollancz, 1932.
FAMC   Famous plays of 1932-33. Lond., Gollancz, 1933.
FAMD   Famous plays of 1933. Lond., Gollancz, 1934.
FAME   Famous plays of 1933-34. Lond., Gollancz, 1934.
FAMF   Famous plays of 1934. Lond., Gollancz, 1934.
AMG   Famous plays of 1934-35. Lond., Gollancz, 1935.
FAMH   Famous plays of 1935. Lond., Gollancz, 1935.
FAMI   Famous plays of 1935-36. Lond., Gollancz, 1936
FAMJ   Famous plays of 1936. Lond., Gollancz, 1936.
FAMK   Famous plays of 1937. Lond., Gollancz, 1937.
FAML   Famous plays of 1938-39. Lond., Gollancz, 1939.
FAO   Famous plays of today. Lond., Gollancz, 1929.
FAOS   Famous Plays of today. London: Gollancz, 1953.
FIG   Five great modern Irish plays. Modern Library, 1941.
FIP   Five plays of 1937. Lond., Hamilton, 1937.
FIR   Five plays of 1940. Lond., Hamilton, 1940.
FIT   Fitts, Dudley, ed. Greek plays in modern translation.
              Dial Press, 1947.
FOUP   Four plays of 1936. Lond., Hamilton, 1936.
FRA   Francke, Kuno, ed. The German classics of the 19th
              and 20th centuries. 20v. German Pubn Society,
              1913-14.
FUL   Fullington, J. F-J. & others, ed. The new college
              omnibus. Harcourt, 1938.
FULT   Fulton, A. R., ed. Drama and theatre, illustrated by
              7 modern plays. Holt, 1946.
GARU   Gassner, John, ed. Best American plays; supplemen-
              tary vol. 1918-58. Crown, 1961.

GARV   Gassner, John and Olive Barnes, eds. Best American
            plays, 6th series, 1963-67. Crown, 1971.
GAS   Gassner, John, ed. Twenty best plays of the modern
            American theatre [ser. 1]. Crown Pubs., 1939.
GAS-2   Gassner, John, ed. Best plays of the modern American
            theatre, 2nd series. Crown Pubs., 1947.
GAS-3   Gassner, John, ed. Best American plays, 3rd ser.,
            1945-1951. Crown Pubs., 1952.
GASB   Gassner, John, ed. Twenty-five best plays of the
            modern American theatre: Early series. Crown,
            1949.
GASE   Gassner, John, ed. Twenty-five best plays of the
            modern American theatre; early series. Crown
            Pubs., 1949.
GAY   Gayley, C. M. & Thaler, Alwin, eds. Representative
            English comedies. 4v. Macmillan, 1903-36.
GOSA   Gosse, E. W., ed. Restoration plays from Dryden to
            Farquhar. (Everyman's Library) Dent, & Dutton,
            1932.
GOW   Gow, J. R. & Hanlon, Helen T., eds. Five Broadway
            plays. Harper, 1948.
GREN   Grene, David, tr. Three Greek tragedies in transla-
            tion. Univ. of Chicago Pr., 1942.
HAL   Halline, Allan G., ed. American plays. Amer. Book
            Co., 1935.
HAM   Hamilton, Edith, tr. Three Greek plays. Norton,
            1937.
HAN   Hampden, John, comp. Eighteenth century plays. (Ev-
            eryman's library) Dent, & Dutton, 1928.
HARC   Harvard classics. 50v. Collier, 1909-10.
HAT   Hatcher, H. H., ed. Modern American dramas. Har-
            court, 1941.
HATS   Hatcher, H. H., ed. Modern dramas, shorter edition.
            Harcourt, 1944.
HAU   Hatcher, H. H., ed. Modern British dramas. Har-
            court, 1941.
HAV   Hatcher, H. H., ed. Modern continental dramas. Har-
            court, 1941.
HIL   Hildreth, W. H. & Dumble, W. R., eds. Five contem-
            porary American plays. Harper, 1939.
HOW   Howard, Edwin J., ed. Ten Elizabethan plays. Nelson,
            1931.
HUD   Hubbell, J. B. & Beaty, J. C., eds. An introduction
            to drama. Macmillan, 1927; revised ed., 1932.
INCH   Inchbald, Mrs. Elizabeth S., ed. The British theatre.
            25v. London, 1808.
KAT   Katzin, Winifred, comp. Eight European plays. Bren-
            tano, 1927.
KRE   Kreymborg, Alfred, ed. Poetic drama. Modern Age
            Books, 1941.
LAW   Law, F. H., ed. Modern plays, short and long.

Century, 1924.

LEG LeGallienne, Eva, ed. Eva LeGallienne's Civic reper-
     tory plays. Norton, 1928.

LEV Leverton, Garrett, ed. Plays for the college theatre.
     French, 1932.

LIE Lieder, P. A. & others, eds. British drama. Hough-
     ton, 1929.

LOC Locke, A. L. & Montgomery, G., eds. Plays of Negro
     life. Harper, 1927.

     Mantle, Best plays. see BP

MAP Marriott, J. W., ed. Great modern British plays.
     Harrap, 1929.

MAT Matthews, Brander & Lieder, P. R., eds. Chief Brit-
     ish dramatists. Houghton, 1924.

MAU Matthews, Brander, ed. Chief European dramatists,
     500 B.C. to 1879 A.D. Houghton, 1916.

MCD McDermott, J. F., ed. Modern plays. Harcourt, 1932.

MCI McIlwraith, A. K., ed. Five Elizabethan comedies.
     Oxford, 1934.

MCJ McIlwraith, A. K., ed. Five Elizabethan tragedies.
     Oxford, 1938.

MCM MacMillan, W. D. & Jones, H. M., eds. Plays of
     the Restoration and 18th century. Holt, 1931, &
     1938.

MIL Millett, F. B, & Bentley, G. E., eds. The play's the
     thing. Appleton-Century, 1936.

MIO Minor Elizabethan drama. (Everyman's library) Dent,
     & Dutton, 2v. 1939.

MOD Modern plays. (Everyman's library) Dent, & Dutton,
     1937.

MOO Moore, J. R., ed. Representative English drama.
     Ginn, 1929.

MOR Morgan, A. E., comp. English plays, 1660-1820.
     Harper, 1935.

MOS Sayler, O. M., ed. Moscow art theatre series of Rus-
     sian plays [ser. 1]. Brentano, 1923.

MOSA Sayler, O. M., ed. Moscow art theatre series of Rus-
     sian plays [ser. 2]. Brentano, 1923.

MOSE Moses, M. J., ed. British plays from the Restoration
     to 1820. 2v. Little, Brown, 1929.

MOSH Moses, M. J., ed. Dramas of modernism and their
     forerunners. Little, Brown, 1931; rev. by O. J.
     Campbell, 1941.

MOSJ Moses, M. J., ed. Representative American dramas,
     national and local. Little, Brown, 1925.

MOSL Moses, M. J., ed. Representative American dramas,
     national and local. Revised by J. W. Krutch. Little,
     Brown, 1941.

MOSO Moses, M. J., ed. Representative British dramas, Vic-
     torian and modern. Little, Brown, 1918; rev. ed.,
     1931.

MOSQ   Moses, M. J., ed. Representative continental dramas,
            revolutionary and transitional. Little, Brown, 1924.
MOSS-1   Moses, M. J., ed. Representative plays by American
            dramatists; v. 1; 1767-1819. Dutton, 1918.
MOSS-2   Moses, M. J., ed. Representative plays by American
            dramatists; v. 2; 1815-1858. Dutton, 1925.
MOSS-3   Moses, M. J., ed. Representative plays by American
            dramatists; v. 3; 1856-1911. Dutton, 1921.
MYB   My best play; an anthology of plays chosen by their
            own authors. Lond., Faber & Faber, 1934.
NAG   Nagelberg, M. M., ed. Drama in our time. Harcourt,
            1948.
NEI   Neilson, W. A., ed. Chief Elizabethan dramatists.
            Houghton, 1911.
NET   Nettleton, G. H. & Case, A. E., eds. British drama-
            tists from Dryden to Sheridan. Houghton, 1939.
NOY   Noyes, G. R., ed. & tr. Masterpieces of the Russian
            drama. Appleton, 1933.
OAT   Oates, W. J. & O'Neill, E. G., Jr., eds. The com-
            plete Greek drama; all the extant tragedies. 2v.
            Random House, 1938.
OLH   Oliphant, E. H. C., ed. Elizabethan dramatists other
            than Shakespeare. Prentice-Hall, 1931.
OLI   Oliphant, E. H. C., ed. Shakespeare and his fellow
            dramatists. 2v. Prentice-Hall, 1929.
OXB   Oxberry, W., ed. The new English drama. 21v. Lon-
            don, 1818-25.
PAR   Parks, E. W. & Beatty, R. C., eds. The English dra-
            ma; an anthology, 900-1642. Norton, 1935.
PEN   Pence, R. V., ed. Dramas by present-day writers.
            Scribner, 1927.
Pierce &   Pierce, J. A. & Matthews, Brander, eds. Masterpieces
Matthews-1 of modern drama: English and American. [v.1].
            Doubleday, 1915.
Pierce &   Pierce, J. A. & Matthews, Brander, eds. Masterpieces
Matthews-2 of modern drama: Foreign [v.2]. Doubleday, 1915.
PLAD   Plays of a half-decade. Gollancz, 1933.
PLAP   Plays of to-day. 3v. London, Sidgwick & Jackson,
            1925-30.
POP   Popkin, Henry, ed. The new British drama. Grove
            Press, 1964.
QUI   Quinn, A. H., ed. Contemporary American plays.
            Scribner, 1923.
QUIK   Quinn, A. H., ed. Representative American plays.
            Century, rev. ed., 1921.
QUIL   Quinn, A. H., ed. Representative American plays,
            1767-1935. Century Co. Ed. 3, 1925; Ed. 5, 1930;
            Ed. 6, 1938.
RUB   Rubinstein, H. F., ed. Great English plays. Harper,
            1928.
RYL   Rylands, G. H. W., ed. Elizabethan tragedy; six

representative plays (excluding Shakespeare). London, Bell, 1933.

SCA-1, 2, 3 Scandinavian plays of the 20th century. (American-Scandinavian Foundation) Princeton Univ. Press, 1944.

SCH   Schelling, F. E., ed. Typical Elizabethan plays, by contemporaries and immediate successors of Shakespeare. Harper, 1926.

SCI   Schelling, F. E. & Black, W. W., eds. Typical Elizabethan plays. Rev. ed. Harper, 1931.

SCW   Schweikert, H. C., ed. Early English plays. Harcourt 1928.

SEVD   Seven plays of the modern theatre, introduction by Harold Clurman. Grove Press, 1962.

SIXD   Six plays. London, Gollancz, 1931.

SIXH   Six plays. London, Heinemann, 1934.

SIXL   Six plays of 1939. London, Heinemann, 1939.

SIXP   Six plays of today. London, Heinemann, 1939.

SMI   Smith, R. M., ed. Types of domestic tragedy. Prentice-Hall, 1928.

SMK   Smith, R. M., ed. Types of historical drama. Prentice-Hall, 1928.

SML   Smith, R. M., ed. Types of philosophic drama. Prentice-Hall, 1928.

SMN   Smith, R. M., ed. Types of romantic drama. Prentice-Hall, 1928.

SMO   Smith, R. M., ed. Types of social comedy. Prentice-Hall, 1928.

SMP   Smith, R. M., ed. Types of world tragedy. Prentice-Hall, 1928.

SMR   Smith, R. M., ed. Types of farce-comedy. Prentice-Hall, 1928.

SPE   Spencer, Hazelton, ed. Elizabethan plays. Little, Brown, 1933.

STA   Stauffer, Ruth M., comp. The progress of drama through the centuries. Macmillan, 1927.

STE   Steeves, H. R., ed. Plays from the modern theatre. Heath, 1931.

STM   Stevens, D. H., ed. Types of English drama, 1660-1780. Ginn, 1923.

TAU   Tatlock, J. S. P. & Martin, R. G., eds. Representative English plays, from the miracle plays to Pinero. Ed. 2 rev. & enl. Appleton-Century, 1938.

TAY   Taylor, W. D., ed. Eighteenth-century comedy. Oxford, 1929.

TEN   Cooper, Lane, ed. Ten Greek plays. Oxford, 1929.

THA   Thayer, W. R., ed. The best Elizabethan plays. Ginn, 1890.

THF   Theatre Guild anthology. Random House, 1936.

THH   Theatre omnibus: six outstanding recent successes. London, Hamilton, 1938.

THO	Thomas, Russell, ed. Plays and the theatre. Little, Brown, 1937.
THR	Clark, B. H., ed. Three modern plays from the French. Holt, 1914.
TRE	Mantle, Burns & Gassner, J., eds. A treasury of the theatre. 2v. Simon & Schuster, 1935.
TRE-2 (2v.)	Mantle, Burns & others, eds. A treasury of the theatre, rev...for colleges by Buck, Gassner, & Alberson. Simon & Schuster, 1940 2v. (v.1 from Ibsen to Odets; v.2 from Aeschylus to Hebbel)
TRE-3	Gassner, John, ed. A treasury of the theatre [ser. 3]. Dryden press, 1950. (From Ibsen's Ghosts to Miller's Death of a Salesman)
TREA-1	Gassner, John, ed. A treasury of the theatre [v.1]. Simon & Schuster, 1951. (From Aeschylus' Agamemnon to Turgenev's A Month in the Country)
TREA-2	Gassner, John, ed. A treasury of the theatre [v.2]. Simon & Schuster, 1951. (From Ibsen to Sartre)
TREA-3	Gassner, John, ed. A treasury of the theatre [v.3]. Simon & Schuster, 1951. (From Wilde to Miller)
TUCD	Tucker, S. M., ed. Modern American and British plays. Harper, 1931.
TUCG	Tucker, S. M., ed. Modern continental plays. Harper, 1929.
TUCJ	Tucker, S. M., ed. Modern plays. Macmillan, 1932.
TUCM	Tucker, S. M., ed. Twenty-five modern plays. Harper, 1931; revised ed., 1948.
TUQ	Tupper, F. & Tupper, J. W., eds. Representative English dramas from Dryden to Sheridan. Oxford 1914; rev. ed., 1934.
TUR	Turrell, C. A., ed. Contemporary Spanish dramatists. Badger, 1919.
TWE	Twelve famous plays of the Restoration and eighteenth century. Modern library, 1933.
UHL	Uhler, J. E., ed. The best eighteenth-century comedies. Crofts, 1930.
WATC	Watson, E. B., Pressey, W. B., comps. Contemporary drama: American plays. 2v. Scribner, 1931 (v.1), 1938 (v.2).
WATF	Watson, E. B. & Pressey, W. B., comps. Contemporary drama: English and Irish plays. 2v. Scribner, 1931.
WATI	Watson, E. B. & Pressey, W. B., comps. Contemporary drama: European, English, Irish and American plays. Scribner, 1941.
WATL	Watson, E. B. & Pressey, W. B., comps. Contemporary drama: European plays. 4v. Scribner, 1931-34.
WATO	Watson, E. B. & Pressey, W. B., comps. Contemporary drama: nine plays, American, English, European. Scribner, 1941.
WATR	Watson, E. B. & Pressey, W. B., eds. Five modern

	plays. Scribner, 1933.
WHE	Wheeler, C. B., ed. Six plays by contemporaries of Shakespeare. (World's classics) Oxford, 1928.
WHI	Whitman, C. H., ed. Representative modern dramas. Macmillan, 1936.
WHK	Whitman, C. H., ed. Seven contemporary plays. Houghton, 1931.
WOR	World's great plays; a collection of seven. World Pub. Co., 1944.

INDEX OF TITLES